James Comper Gray

The Biblical Museum

A collection of notes, explanatory, homiletic, and illustrative, on the Holy

Scriptures, especially designed for the use of ministers, Bible students, and

Sunday-school teachers (Volume 1)

James Comper Gray

The Biblical Museum
A collection of notes, explanatory, homiletic, and illustrative, on the Holy Scriptures, especially designed for the use of ministers, Bible students, and Sunday-school teachers (Volume 1)

ISBN/EAN: 9783744754897

Printed in Europe, USA, Canada, Australia, Japan

Cover: Foto ©Lupo / pixelio.de

More available books at **www.hansebooks.com**

THE
BIBLICAL MUSEUM:

A COLLECTION OF NOTES
EXPLANATORY, HOMILETIC, AND ILLUSTRATIVE,

ON THE

Holy Scriptures,

ESPECIALLY DESIGNED FOR THE USE OF MINISTERS, BIBLE-
STUDENTS, AND SUNDAY-SCHOOL TEACHERS.

BY

JAMES COMPER GRAY,

Author of "Topics for Teachers," "The Class and the Desk," &c., &c.

OLD TESTAMENT.

VOL. I.

Containing Genesis and Exodus.

LONDON:
ELLIOT STOCK, 62, PATERNOSTER ROW.
1899.

THE HOLY BIBLE.

I. THE PENTATEUCH

THE FIRST BOOK OF MOSES,

CALLED

GENESIS.

THE HOLY BIBLE.

I. Title: BIBLE, fr. Gk. βίβλος (= *book*) the name of inner bark of linden, or teil-tree: applied to this bk., bec. it is of all books "*The Book*"—par excellence. **II. Other names.** (1) SCRIPTURES, *i.e.* writings: or, in Gk. *Hagio-grapha* = Holy Writings. (2) WORD OF GOD, the most full and significant title. **III. Divisions.** 1. TWO CHIEF:—(1) *The Old Test.* The record of the *covenant* (see *N. Test.* Bibl. Mus. i. 1) of salvation through a Saviour who should come in the fulness of time. (2) *The New Test.* The record of the fulfilment of that cov. in our Lord Jesus Christ. 2. OTHER DIVISIONS. i. The Old Test. contains—(1) The *Pentateuch* (or 5 bks. of Moses). (2) *Historical* (Joshua to end of Chrons.). (3) *Poetical* (Job to end of Song of Sol.). (4) *Prophetical* (Isa. to Mal.). ii. The New Test. contains—(1) *Historical* (Mat. to Acts). (2) *Epistolary* (Roms. to Jude). (3) *Prophetical* (Rev.). 3. MINOR DIVISIONS. i. *Chapters.* As first projected, and still used, were arranged (*cir.* middle of 13th cent.) by Card. Hugo de Sancto Caro, to facilitate the use of his concordance to the Lat. Vulg. ii. *Verses.* By R. Stephen, who printed the first Gk. Test. with his vv. at Geneva (1551). The 1st Eng. Bib. so divided was print. at Geneva (1560). **IV. Genuineness.** The A. V. is the final result of a careful collating of many anc. MSS. i. HEB. MSS. For his crit. Heb. Bib. Kennicott coll. 630; De Rossi coll. 734 more. The oldest Heb. MS. (now at St. Petersburg) cannot be less than 1,300 years old. From these Heb. MSS., the Septuagint trans. (made ab. 300 B.C.) does not dif. in any important degree; and as that trans. was usually quoted by our Lord and the Apostles, it may be regarded as truly representing the old Heb. original. ii. GK. MSS. Of these there are many hundreds in existence, of wh. the chief are (1) *C. Vaticanus* (A.D. 300—400). (2) *C. Alexandrinus* (A.D. 400—500). (3) *C. Sinaiticus* (A.D. 300—400). No one doubts the genuineness of the present versions of the Gk. and Rom. classics, yet of only 15 MSS. of Herodotus, wh. have come down to us, the oldest is of the 10th cent. **V. Ancient Translations.** 1. The SEPTUAGINT, or trans. of the *seventy* (hence written LXX.) of the O. T. into Gk. Prob. begun at Alexandria in the reign of P. Lagus, at the instigation of Demetrius Philareus, and finished in the reign of P. Philadelphus (*cir.* B.C. 285). 2. The PESCHITO (or literal) SYRIAC. O. T. (*cir.* A.D. 100—200). 3. THE LATIN VULGATE, by Jerome, presbyter of Dalmatia, who (in 382) at wish of Damascus, Bp. of Ro., undertook revision of old Lat. ver. The present Lat. Vulg. is a transcript of the corrected edition of Jerome's pub. by Pope Clement VIII. (1593). **VI. Famous Eng. Vers.** 1. BEDE, trans. Bib. into Saxon (735). 2. WICLIFF'S (1380), not printed for many yrs. 3. TYNDALE'S (1525), the first printed Eng. Bib. 4. COVERDALE'S (1535), a revis. of No. 3. 5. MATTHEWS', or *J. Rogers'* (1537). This founded on Nos. 3 and 4. 6. TAVERNER'S (1539), revis. of No. 5. 7. CRANMER'S, or *the great Bible* (1539); this a reprint in large fol. of No. 4, revised. The first pub. "by authority." 8. GENEVA (1557—60), ed. by Coverdale and others: and also called "the Breeches Bib." (see on Ge. iii. 7). 9. THE BISHOPS' BIBLE (1568), revis. and ed. by Abp. Parker. 10. PARKER'S (1572), same as No. 9, with prefaces, etc. 11. THE AUTHORISED VERSION, *written A. V.* (1611). 54 learned men, forming 6 companies, of wh. 2 comps. sat at Westminster, 2 at Oxford, and 2 at Cambridge, began this ed. in 1607, and completed it in 4 yrs. (For names of translators, rules, etc., see *Bible Lore*, 87—91.) **VII. Hebrew Comments.** 1. TARGUMS, fr. Chaldee word = explanation. (1) The most anc. is the T. of Onkelos (*cir.* 1—200 A.D., on the Pentateuch. (2) Of Jonathan Ben Uzziel. (3) Pseudo-Jonathan. (4) Jerusalem T. 2. MISHNAH, the *second* or oral law of the Jews (A.D. 150), trads. explanatory of the law of Moses. 3. GEMARA, *i.e.* perfection (*cir.* A.D. 300—500). 4. TALMUD, doctrine or learning, composed of Mishnah and Gemara united. 5. MASORAH, *i.e.* tradition. Not known who compiled it. Consists of notes on letters, words, verses, etc. In course of time took the form of marg. notes to text. As applied to Eng. Bib., and including the N. Test., they are as follows :—*Books,* in O. T., 39 ; in N. T., 27 ; total, 66. *Chapters,* in O. T., 929 ; in N. T., 260 ; total, 1,189. *Verses,* in O. T., 23,214 ; in N. T., 7,959 ; total, 31,173. *Words,* in O. T., 592,493 ; in N. T., 181,253 ; total, 773,746. *Letters,* in O. T., 2,728,100 ; in N. T., 838,380 ; total, 3,566,480. Middle chap. (and least). Ps. cxvii. ; mid. ver., Ps. cxviii. 8. The word "*and*" in O. T., 35,535 ; in N. T., 10,684 ; total, 46,219. Word "*Jehovah,*" 6,855 times. Of the *Old Test.,* Prov. is middle bk. ; Job xxix., mid. cap. ; 2 Ch. xx. 18 the mid. ver. ; and 1 Ch. i. 1 the shortest ver. Of the *New Test.,* 2 Thess. is mid. bk. ; betw. Ro. xiii., xiv. the mid. cap. ; Ac. xvii. 17 mid. ver. : and Jo. xi. 13 is the shortest ver., both in the N. T. and in the whole Bible. All the letters in the alphabet are in Ezra vii. 21 ; 2 Kings xix. and Isa. xxxvii. are alike. Neither the word "God" nor "Lord" occurs in Esther. VIII. **English Comments.** 1. J. CALVIN (trans.) 52 vols. 8*vo.* (1845—56). 2. J. DIODATI, *fol.* (1651). 3. ASSEMBLY OF DIVINES, 2 vols. *fol.* (1657). 4. DR. J. MAYER, 6 vols. *fol.* (1653). 5. J. TRAPP, 5 vols. *fol.* (1654). 6. PATRICK, LOWTH, ETC., 6 vols. 4*to.* (1822). 7. M. POOLE, Annotations, 2 vols. *fol.* (1700). 8. S. CLARKE. *fol.* (1690). 9. M. HENRY. 10. DR. E. WELLS, 8 vols. 4*to.* (1724). 11. DR. W. WALL, 3 vols. 8*vo.* (1730—34). 12. DR. J. GILL, 9 vols. *fol.* (1763). 13. R. GOADBY, 3 vols. *fol.* (1759—70). 14. J. ALLEN, 2 vols. *fol.* (1763). 15. BP. T. WILSON, 3 vols. 4*to.* (1785). 16. J. BROWN, of Hadington. 17. J. WESLEY, M.A., 4 vols. 4*to.* (1764). 18. T. HAWEIS, 2 vols. *fol.* (1765—66). 19. DR. W. DODD, 3 vols. *fol.* (1770). 20. J. PRIESTLEY, LL.D., 4 vols. 8*vo.* (1803). 21. DR. J. FAWCETT, 2 vols. 4*to.* (1811). 22. J. HEWLETT, 3 vols. 4*to.* (1811). 23. DR. R. HAWKER, 10 vols. 12*mo.* (1816—22). 24. DR. BOOTHROYD, 3 vols. 4*to.* (1824). 25. T. SCOTT, 6 vols. 4*to.* (1841). 26. DR. A. CLARKE, 6 vols. 8*vo.* (1844). 27. DRS. D'OYLEY AND MANT, 8*vo.* (1845). 28. J. BENSON, 6 vols. 8*vo.* (1848). 29. INGRAM COBBIN, *Condensed* 8*vo.* (1839), *Portable* 12*mo.* (1846). 30. DR. KITTO, 4 vols. 8*vo.* (1855). 31. DR. WM. JENKS, 5 vols. 8*vo.* (1855). 32. BP. WORDSWORTH, 8 vols. 8*vo.* (1870). 33. BROWN AND FAUSSETT, *Port. Com.,* 2 vols. 8*vo.* (1863). 34. THE SPEAKER'S COMMENTARY, now (1875) in course of publication :—" We have long held that a *perfect* commentary on the *whole* Bible cannot be produced by any *one* author. The very unequal value of *parts,* where this has been attempted, warrants this belief. Even those that aim less at the critical than at the devotional and exposition of the sacred writings, are not of equal merit throughout. The various languages in which the books of Scripture were originally composed ; the purposes for which they were written : the subjects of which they treat ; and their other manifold characteristics, require for their apt elucidation specially constituted minds and appropriate mental tastes. Each book, too, has many sides : the historical, the scientific, the doctrinal, the devotional, the practical, often meet in one brief treatise. Hence not only may all the resources of *one* mind be laid under contribution by one short book, but a combination of minds peculiarly gifted is often needed for its full and perfect explanation. Some are skilful in clearing up verbal difficulties, others in identifying natural objects, or in tracing historical or scientific allusions, while the special forte of a third class is to deal with doctrinal matters. From all this it follows that so far from any one mind being fully competent to produce a perfect commentary on the entire Holy Scriptures, many minds are needed fully to expound each individual book."—*J. C. Gray.*

Introduction.

I. THE PENTATEUCH.

PENTATEUCH = five books, fr. Gk. πέντε, *five*, and τεύχος, wh. meant orig. a vessel, tool; and came in Alex. Gk. to sig. *book*. The Jews termed it "the law," or "the five-fifths of the law;" or, in brief, "the fifths," ea. bk. being called "a fifth." The names in the A. V. are fr. the Gk. Ver. (*i.e.* LXX.), and partially denote their subjects. The orig. Heb. name of ea. bk. was its first word or words. The Pentateuch forms the first chief div. of the O. T.: *see Intro. to ea. of the five Books respectively.*

THE FIRST BOOK OF MOSES, CALLED GENESIS.

I. **Title.** GENESIS, fr. Gk. γίνεσις, *a birth :* bec. it descr. the generation or production of all things. This is the LXX. title. The Hebs. called this bk. *Bereshith* = in the beginning: fr. the first word in the Heb. text. II. **Author**, MOSES; for, at least, 3,000 yrs. never doubted by Jews or Xtians. T. Hobbes (1650) objected that these bks. were so called not bec. *written by*, but *relating to* Moses. In proof of his authorship, we have—1. Unanimous test. of antiquity. 2. M. is declared to be the author. (Ex. xvii. 14; xxiv. 4—7; xxxiv. 27; Nu. xxxii. 2; De. xxxi. 9, 19—24.) 3. Confirmed by other O. T. writers (Jos. i. 7, 8; viii. 34, 35; Jud. iii. 4; 2 K. xxiii. 25; 2 Ch. xxx. 16; Ezr. viii. 3; Ne. i. 7, 8). 4. By Xt. and Aposs. (Ma. xix. 7; Lu. xvi. 29; xxiv. 27; Jo. i. 17; vii. 19; Ac. iii. 22; xxviii. 23; Ro. x. 5). 5. All the Hist. events of Hebrews rest upon authority of these Bks. 6. Objections can be, and oft. have been, easily refuted. III. **Time**, UNCERTAIN. Some (as *Eusebius, etc.*) think it was written in Midian while M. was keeping the flocks of Jethro; others (as *Theodoret, etc.*) that M. wrote it after the exodus and giving of the law, since prior to the call (Ex. iii.) he was a private person, unendowed with the spirit of prophecy. So also the time covered by the hist. is unsettled. Acc. to usual computation, 2,369 yrs.; but acc. to Dr. Hales, 3,619 yrs. IV. **Design**, twofold. 1. To solve the problems of the *creation*, and the *intro. of moral evil.* 2. To furnish the hist. of the patriarchal church, as showing the line of the predicted Saviour. "It is a purely historical work. It serves as the narrative preamble to the legislation of Moses. It is the first vol. of the hist. of man in relation with God" *(Murphy).* V. **Sources.** Since the latest events in Gen. occ. cents. bef. the death of M., it becomes a question what are the sources to wh. it is to be traced back. The chief hypotheses are—1. *Documentary, i.e.* That M. formed Gen. fr. an Elohim, and a Jehovah record, with the aid of 10 smaller memoirs. (This sugg. by *Astruc*, 1753, is, in part, adopted by *Eichhorn, Gramberg, Bohmer, etc.*) 2. *Fragmentary, i.e.* that Gen. was single, small, fragmentary pieces. Hence var. superscriptions, concluding formulas, repetitions, vars. of style. (This the view of *Michaelis, Jahn, Vater, Hartmann, Grunde, etc.*). 3. *Complementary, i.e.* that the Jehovist author of Pent. had bef. him an older document, that of the Elohist, wh. he remodelled and extended *(Ewald, de Wette, Bleek, etc.)* 4. *Crystallization* (so called by Delitzsch), sugg. by Ewald, who thought there might be 4 sources: 2 Elohistic, and 2 Jehovistic. 5. *The original unity of Gen.* (in com. with rest of Pentateuch). (This is the view of the Rabbins, and of nearly all the older theologians.) And that the use of the two dif. names of God is owing solely to the two dif. significations of those names *(Ranke, Hengstenberg, Drechsler, Havernick, etc.).* "The use of ea. of the two names—Jehovah and Elohim—is everywhere in Gen. adapted to the sense of the passages in wh. the writer has purposely inserted the one name or the other" *(Havernick).*

Synopsis.

(According to Bush.)

1. The Creation......................................i. ii.
2. Sabbath and Fall ....ii.–iii.
3. Adam and Posterity to the Flood.........iv.
4. Genealogy of Patriarchs ....v.
5. World bef. the Flood................vi.–vii. 1–5
6. The Flood ....vii. 5–viii. 1–13
7. Covenant with Noah..........viii. 13–ix. 1–18
8. Noah prophesies conc. his Sons...ix. 18–29
9. Confusion of Tongues and Dispersion x. xi. 10–27
10. Life of Abraham ....xi. 27–xxv. 1–11
11. Death of A. to Sale of Joseph ...xxv. 11–36
12. Joseph and Israel in Egypt xxxvii.–xlvii.–27
13. Death of Jacob and the Patriarchs xlvii. 27–1.

(According to Ayre.)

PART I. Early hist., etc., of Mankind.

1. Creation and Eden.......................i. ii.
2. Man's Fall and Expulsion ....iii.
3. Antediluvian World iv.–vi.–8
4. Flood and Restoration.........vi. 9–ix.–29
5. Call of Abram, etc...........................x.
6. Confusion of Tongues, and Descent of the Chosen Race...............xi.–1–26

PART II. Early hist. of Jews.

1. Abraham ....xi. 27–xxv. 18
2. Isaac ....xxv. 19–xxxviii. 9
3. Jacob ....xxxv. 28–xxxvi. 43
4. Israel in Egypt ....xxviii. 10–1.–26

(According to Murphy.)

	Sections.		Chapters.	Documents.	
I. CREATION		i. Creation	i., ii. 3	I.	1ST BIBLE
II. DEVELOPMENT.	Before.	ii. The Man	ii. 4–25	II.	
		iii. The Fall	iii.		2ND BIBLE
		iv. The Race	iv.		
		v. Line to Noah	v., vi. 8	III.	
	After the Deluge.	vi. The Deluge	vi. 9, viii.	IV.	
		vii. The Covenant	ix.		3RD BIBLE
		viii. The Nations	x., xi. 9	V.	
		ix. Line to Abram	x. 10–26	VI.	
		x. Abraham	x. 27, xxv. 11	VII.	
		xi. Isaac	xxv. 12–18	VIII.	
			xxxv. 19, xxv.	IX.	
		xii. Jacob	xxxvi.	X.	
			xxxvii. 1.	XI.	

PRACTICAL HINTS.—1. Read the Bible with prayer. 2. Go to it to learn, not to judge. 3. Read it methodically, regularly, day by day. 4. Compare Scripture with Scripture. "God is His own interpreter; and He will make it plain." 5. Apply as you read, and practise what you learn. 6. Read with a spirit of self-examination. 7. Judge of and interpret other books by this; not this by others. 8. Be men of one book, and that book the Bible. When Sir Walter Scott was dying, he said to the watcher, "Bring the Book." "What book?" asked Lockhart. The dying man replied, "There is but ONE Book."—*Topics for Teachers.*

CHAPTER THE FIRST.

B.C. 4004.

the creation
a Jo. i. 1—3, He. i. 10; Ps. cii. 25.
b Augustine.
c cf. McCaul, "Aids to Faith," 200—203.
d Murphy.
e He. xi. 3; Col. i. 16; Re. iv. 11.
f Pr. iii. 19; Ne. ix. 6; Ps. xcvi. 5; Je. xxxii. 17.
g Alford.
h Ps. civ. 30; Is. xl. 13.
"The order of the universe has a spiritual root; the purpose of love which changes is also the purpose of love which directs it. He who can bind and loose the forces of nature has thus revealed the eternal purpose in which they originate."—Westcott.
i L. D. Bevan, LL.B.
k Dr. Chalmers.
"Let us read both of God's books — Nature and Scripture—with reverence, humility, and prayer for the illumination of His Holy Spirit; and He will reveal Himself to us in both."—Wordsworth.
l Dr. Buckland.

1, 2. [vv. 1, 2 include the hist. of the world prior to the begin. of the six days.] (1) **beginning,**ᵃ absolutely: begin. of time: "no time bef. creation"ᵇ: this may ref. us back to an epoch, hundreds of thousands of yrs. fr. our age.ᶜ **God,** Heb. *Elohim,* (*plu*)= "eternal powers."ᵈ The Divine Name fr. this v. to ii. 3. **created,**ᵉ out of nothing: gave being to: **the** .. **earth,**ᶠ an idiomatic formula = the whole world, the universe.ᵍ (2) **earth,** wherein now we live, was then **without** .. **void,** *lit.* wasteness and emptiness; *i.e.* Chaotic. **deep,** "a raging deep of wild waters and storm." **moved,**ʰ lit. was hovering, or brooding.

The creation (on the whole chapter).—We learn that—I. There was a beginning, and this was the act of God. II. The disorder of primal creation is reduced to order by the power and intelligence of this Divine will. We might have had matter created by will, but all might have remained shapeless and inane. The life of God is imparted to the chaotic world. Light is approved by God. Power develops through will and intelligence into emotion. III. This progress of creation passes from order, through organization, into life, until it culminates in man. Plants and animals are *after their kind.* Man is *after the likeness of God.* He is subject to expressed law—a king, he is yet to obey. Moral law must be recognised by him.ⁱ

The beginning.—"Between the initial act and the details of Genesis, the world, for aught we know, might have been the theatre of many revolutions, the traces of which Geology may still investigate, and to which she, in fact, has confidently appealed as the vestiges of so many continents that have now passed away."ᵏ—"The first verse of Genesis seems explicitly to assure the creation of the universe and the heaven, including the sidereal system and the earth, more especially specifying our planet, as the subsequent scene of the operations of the six days about to be described. No information is given as to events which may have occurred upon this earth, unconnected with the history of man, between the creation of its component matter, recorded in the first verses, and the era at which its history is recorded in the second verse; nor is any limit fixed to the time during which these intermediate events may have been going on. Millions of years may have occupied the indefinite interval between the beginning in which God created the heaven and the earth, and the evening or commencement of the first day of the Mosaic narrative."ˡ

day one
a Ps. xxxiii. 9; cxlviii. 5.
b Job xxxviii. 19; Is. xlv. 7; Ps. lxxiv. 16; 2 Co. iv. 6.
c Wordsworth. "It is in vain to inquire scien-

3—5. (3) **said**ᵃ .. **light,**ᵇ it is not said that L. was now first made:ᶜ but that now at God's bidding it *was, i.e.* where the darkness had been (God Himself is light). (4) **good,**ᵈ fitting, suitable, beautiful, perfect. **divided .. darkness,**ᵉ separated, suffered not the light to blend with the darkness:ᶠ but to alternate with it. (5) **and .. day .. night,** *i.e.* the distinguishing mark of what we call day, and night. **evening .. day,** *lit.* "the evening was: and the morning was.—DAY ONE." We

[Cap. i. 6—8.] GENESIS. 11

know not how often the evening and the morning were repeated during the period here called *One Day*.

Light, and its laws.—I. The light God has made, and His mind concerning it: 1. Physical light—*good;* light, sweet; pleasant. Sun, the emblem of many things; cheerful revealing; 2. Mental light—*good*. Hence in some parts an idiot is called "dark." 3. Gospel light—*good;* the light of the story of God; light that shined out of darkness to enlighten Gentiles; Christ the Light of the world, the Sun of Righteousness; 4. Spiritual light—*good;* 5. Essential light—light of heaven from the Father of lights. II. The law by which it is governed: 1. Not mixed, but separated; 2. Sons of light must have no communion with darkness; 3. Churches should be lights in the world; 4. Truth not to be mixed with error. Learn—(1) Love the light; (2) Walk in it; (3) Enforce the law concerning it.

An ancient testimony to the sublimity of the first creative fiat.— "In the same way the Jewish lawgiver, a man of no ordinary genius, when he had conceived in his mind a just idea of the grandeur of the Supreme Being, has given expression to it in noble language, in the beginning of his work containing his laws:—'And God said,' what? 'Let there be light: and there was light. Let the earth be: and the earth was.'" *g*—*Days of Creation.* The correct translation, "evening was, and morning was, day one," makes it clear, that throughout the periods described as "day one," "a second day," etc., there were evenings and mornings, the natural result of the revolution of the earth on its axis; and that the period wh. is styled "a day" represents a series of days and nights.*h*

6—8. (6) **firmament,***a* expanse, that wh. is spread out: as by beating; as leaf-gold. (7) **made,** (not create as v. 1) formed out of what now existed. **the . . under,** ocean, seas, etc. **the . . above,** rain, etc. (8) **heaven,** here the region of cloud. **and . . evening,** *etc., lit.* "and evening was, and morning was. —DAY TWO"

The creation of the firmament.—Observe, concerning the firmament,—I. God's command—"let there be." II. Its creation— "and God made," etc. III. Its use and design—to divide the waters from the waters. IV. Its naming—"heaven." It is the visible heaven, the pavement of the holy city.*b*

Never-changing clouds.—With the movements, though silent, of the clouds, as, massively dark or softly brilliant, their swelling mountains change, unite, separate, and unite again, unveiling infinite depths of calm, sweet azure, or, if it be sunset, fields of clear burning brightness that seem to reach into heaven itself. Looking at the clouds merely as aqueducts, we miss the chief part of their beautiful ministry, which is to fill the sky with the idea of life. Rhymesters and parlour naturalists would have us believe that skies, to be perfectly beautiful, must be "cloudless." It is not only not true, but it would be contrary to the nature of things for it to be. The skies even of Italy are not cloudless, except, as in our own country, at certain periods, and derive their charm from their transparency, rather than from cloudlessness. Clouds are to the heavens what human beings are to the earth. They dwell in them and move about in them, various in their aspects and their missions, as men and women; and as of the latter

---

B.C. 4004.

tifically, as some have done, of what kind this first-created light was."—*Alford.* "It is now tolerably well understood, that the light is not conditioned by perfected luminous bodies, but, on the contrary, that light bodies are conditioned by a preceding luminous element." — *Lange.* "God's speaking is His willing, and His willing is His doing."— *Bp. Hall.*
d Ecc. xi. 7.
e 2 Co. vi. 14; Ps. lxxiv. 16; civ. 20.
f but *see* Bush *in lcc.*
"Light ethereal, first of things, quintessence pure."—*Milton.*
g Longinus, De Subl. ix.
h McCausland.

day two
a Job ix. 9; Ps. xix. 1; cxlviii. 4; cxlvii. 8; Is. xl. 22; Je. ll. 15; Job xxxvii. 16.

b M. Henry.

"The poets fabulously fancied that the giants scaled heaven by heaping mountain upon mountain. What was their fancy is the Gospel truth. If you would get to heaven you must climb thither by putting Mount Sion upon Mount Sinai." — *Bp. Hopkins.*

"Clouds that looked as though an angel in his upward flight had left his mantle floating in mid-air."—*J. Baillie.*

B.C. 4004.

c *Grindon.*

day three
a Je. v. 22; 2 Pe. iii. 5; Job xxvi. 10; Ps. xxx. 7; xcv. 5; cxxxvi. 6; Ecc. l. 7.
"1. The use of the sea in the economy of creation should lead us to admire the wisdom of God. It supplies water for rain, rivers, etc.; cools the air and wind; preserved fresh by currents, tides, salt, etc.; is a wonderful storehouse of provision. 2. Are our sins like a stone cast into the sea — forgiven and forgotten? 3. Have we that righteousness that abounds as the waves of the sea? 4. Avoid that wickedness which makes man as a troubled sea."—*Topics for Teachers.*
v. 9, 10. *W. Jones* (Nayland), Considerations on the Natural History of the Earth and its Minerals. *Wks.* vi. 58.
b Dr. *H. Bushnell.* "I cannot look upon the ocean and the mountains without loving them; and I am greater than they because I can do so."
c *Hartwig.*

a Ps. cxlvii. 8; He. vi. 7.
This div. is simple and nat. It proceeds upon two concur. marks, the structure and the seed. In the first the green leaf, or blade, is prominent; in the

come all the true dignity and grace of earth, so of the former comes every splendour that glorifies the sky.*c*

9, 10. (9) **gathered,***a* out of the watery desert. Hitherto land and water formed one mass. **and .. appear,** the upheaving of the land, etc. (10) **earth,** Heb. *Aretz* = land. earth-soil. **seas,** the ocean. The Heb. *yamin,* is fr. a word = tumultuous agitation.

Moral uses of the sea.—I. One great problem of God, in building a school for man, was, how to distribute the school. No one government could occupy the whole domain. But, since the world is distributed into nations, which are likely to be hostile to each other, they need to be separated by natural barriers. This is well effected by spreading the sea between them. II. It will be found that the sea has oftentimes contributed to the moral and social advancement of the race, by separating one part of the world even from the knowledge of another, and preserving it for discovery and occupation at an advanced period of history. III. While oceans have a disconnecting power, they have, at the same time, a connecting power, bringing all regions and climes into correspondence and commercial interchange. The good resulting from commerce is incalculable : 1. Its spirit is the spirit of peace ; 2. The nations engaged in it will, of course, be the most forward nations ; 3. Through it, these nations, most forward in art, are gradually civilizing barbarous tribes ; 4. It opens the way for the universal spread of Christianity. IV. The sea has yet another kind of moral use, more direct than the others, in the influences it has over the minds of men. How many have received lessons of patience and humility from the ocean !*b*

The benefits of the ocean.—How numberless are the blessings we owe to the ocean, the father and sustainer of all organic life ! He it is that feeds the streams, that fills the lake, that bubbles in the spring, that foams in the cataract, or rushes along in the mountain torrent. Should his eternal fountains be dried up, the blooming surface of the earth would be converted into a naked waste. To him we owe the magnificence of our forests, the verdure of our meadows, the beauty of our fields. It is his waters we enjoy in the luscious fruits of our orchards, or quaff in the juice of the exhilarating grape. They circulate in the veins of numberless animals,—of the bee, which offers us the sweet tribute of its honey ; of the bird, that charms us with its melodious song ; of the domestic quadruped, on whose flesh we feed, and whose services are indispensable to our welfare. Nay, our own blood is originally drawn from the wells of the ocean, and is constantly refreshed and replenished from its exhaustless sources.*c*

11—13. (11) **grass,***a* tender budding grass. **seed,** the striking feature of this second class. **fruit,** the distinguishing mark of the third class. (12) **seed .. kind,** answering to the nature of the herb, fr. wh. the same kind of herb would grow. **whose .. itself,** whose seed is in the fruit. **good,** answering to His purpose. (13) **and .. day,** Heb. AS BEFORE.—DAY THREE.

Creation of plants.—These verses show God's thoughtfulness and care with regard to—I. The present : 1. Man is about to be created : 2. At his creation, his wants will require to be satisfied ; 3. Therefore, to meet these wants at once the means for supplying them are created beforehand. II. The distant future. Each herb contained the seeds of future representatives of their kind. Thus, a second creation was avoided.[b]

The fruitfulness of plants.—The botanist Ray tells us that he counted 2,000 grains of maize on a single plant of maize sprung from one seed, 4,000 seeds on one plant of sunflower, 32,000 on a single poppy plant, and 36,000 seeds on one plant of tobacco. Pliny tells us that a Roman governor in Africa sent to the Emperor Augustus a single plant of corn with 340 stems, bearing 340 ears,—that is to say, at least 60,000 grains of corn had been produced from a single seed. In modern times 12,780 grains have been produced by a single grain of the famous corn of Smyrna. In *eight* years as much corn might spring from *one seed* as would supply all mankind with bread for *a year and a half.*[c]

14, 15. (14) **lights,** luminaries, repositories of light, centres of radiant light. **divide .. night,**[a] the purpose they were to serve in relation to the earth. **signs,** of time, and place. **seasons,**[b] the nat. seasons of the year. **and .. years,** marking off, by the earth's revolution, days and years. (15) **to .. earth,** to shine upon. **and .. so,** the result was as God willed.

The great time-keeper.—What are the benefits God intends to secure for us, by the arrangements here made? By this means, He—I. Compels men, as far as they can be compelled, to reckon their time, or number their days aright. II. Calls us often to a reckoning with ourselves under the most impressive influences. III. Invites us to new purposes of future life. IV. Teaches us, in the most impressive manner possible, the value of time. V. Impresses upon us, as a truth of practical moment, that everything must be done in its time. VI. Reminds us both of our rapid transit here and immortality hereafter. VII. Teaches us that there is a changeless empire of being, which the established round of seasons and years, and the mechanical order of heaven itself suggests and confirms.[c]

Sunset on the mountains.—First there comes a flood of rosy light, and then a deep bright crimson, like the ruby's flash or the sapphire's blaze, and then a circlet of flaming peaks studs the horizon. It looks as if a great conflagration were about to begin. But suddenly the light fades, and piles of cold pale white rise above you. You can scarce believe them to be the same mountains. But, quick as the lightning, the flash comes again. A flood of glory rolls once more along their summits. It is a last and mighty blaze. You feel as if it were a struggle for life—as if it were a war waged by spirits of darkness against these celestial forms. The struggle is over; the darkness has prevailed. These mighty mountain tombs are extinguished one after one; and cold ghastly piles of sepulchral hue, which you shiver to look up at, and which remind you of the dead, rise still and calm in the firmament above you. You feel relieved when darkness interposes its veil betwixt you and them. The night sets in deep and calm, and beautiful, with troops of stars overhead. The voice of streams, all night long, fills the silent hills with melodious echoes.[d]

16—19. (16) **two .. lights,**[a] sun and moon. **the .. day, the sun:** Dia. 853,000 ms.; Bulk, 1,400,000 times larger than

---

B.C. 4004.

second, the stalk; in the third, the woody texture. In the "rst, the seed is ot conspicuous; in the second, it is conspicuous; in the third, it is enclosed in a fruit, wh. is conspicuous."—*Murphy.* v. 11, 12. *D. Williams, S.S.,* t. 115.

b *L. Masters.*
c *Gaussen.*

day four

a Ps. lxxiv. 16, 17; civ. 19—23.
b Ge. viii. 22.

Light passes from the sun to the earth, a space of ninety-one millions of miles, in eight minutes, and the beams of the smallest taper are visible at sea, in a dark night, for at least three miles; so that the particles of light instantaneously fill a spherical space of six miles in diameter, or 1,130,976 cubical miles.

c *Dr. H. Bushnell.*

"The sun doth rise, and shuts the lids of all heaven's lesser eyes." — *Poole's "Parnassus."*

The sun, God's crest upon His azure shield the heavens."—*Bailey.*

v. 14. *J. Fawcett, S.S.,* ii. 419; *W. Sharpe,* 160; *Bp. Wilberforce,* 73.

d *Dr. Wylie.*

a Je. xxxi. 35; Ps. cxxxvi. 7—9; xix. 4—6.

GENESIS. [Cap. 1. 20—25.

B.C. 4004.

b Ps. cxlviii. 3; viii. 3, 4; Is. xl. 26.
Herschel calculated that in fifteen minutes, 16,000 stars crossed the field of his telescope when directed towds. one pt. of the Milky Way. "Biblical astronomy is derived fr. mere optical appearance; the eye alone is the judge; the moon is represented as the second of the great heavenly orbs, and as a luminous body; the stars are nothing else but her companions; and their only end is to shed their chaste lustre on our small planet."—*Kalisch.*
c Lange.

earth; Dist. ab. 91,000,000 ms. fr. earth; Rota. on axis 25 dys. 8 hrs. 9 min. **lesser .. night,** *moon:* Dia. 2,165 ms.; Bulk, one eighty-ninth part of earth; Dist. 239,000 ms. **He .. also,**[b] number incalculable, ab. 2,000 visible to naked eye on a clear night: nearest fixed star 19 billions of ms. fr. earth: and this S. is estimated to be more than half as large ag. as the Sun. (17) **give .. earth,** all light, whether physical or spiritual, the gift of God—the Father of lights. (18) **rule .. divide .. darkness,** the purpose they serve in rela. to the earth. (19) **and .. day,** Heb. as bef.—DAY FOUR.

The office of the stars for the earth.—They are—I. God's sign for faith. II. Sacred signs for the festive periods of the solemnization of the faith. III. Spiritual watchers, and guides for the spiritual life of man. IV. Homes of life for creature-life.[c]

The order of nature.—A clergyman asked an old negro his reasons for believing in the existence of a God. "Sir," said he, "I have been here going hard upon fifty years. Every day since I have been in this world, I see the sun rise in the east and set in the west. The north star stands where it did the first time I ever saw it; the seven stars and Job's coffin keep on the same path in the sky, and never turn out. It ain't so with man's works. He makes clocks and watches: they may run well for a while; but they get out of fix, and stand stock still. But the sun and moon and stars keep on the same way all the while. There is a power which makes one man die, and another get well; that sends the rain, and keeps everything in motion."

day five

a Ps. civ. 24, 25.

b Bush.

c Kalisch. "Monstrous crawlers that wriggle through the water, or scud along the banks."—*Murphy.* "Vast fishes, crocodiles, serpents."—*Wordsworth, cf.* Job vii. 12; Is. xxvii. 1; Ex. vii. 9. *Gesenius* 869. *r.* 20. *R. Theed, Sacred Biography,* 32.

20—23. (20) **let .. forth,**[a] let the waters *crawl, teem, swarm.* **the .. life,** breath, the vital principle. **and .. fly,** birds not formed fr. the water (*see* ii. 19): it may be trans. " and let the fowl fly, etc."[b] **above .. heaven,** *lit.* towards the face of the expanse. (21) **whales,** sea *monsters:* inclusive of mammifers and non-mammifers.[c] **moveth,** or creepeth. **kind,** variety, species, nature. (22) **blessed,** *i.e.* gave them power to propagate their several species. (23) **and .. day,** Heb. as bef.—DAY FIVE.

The sea teeming with life.—A correspondent of the newspaper press writes the following account from the Gulf of Siam: "We steamed forward at the rate of six or seven knots an hour, and a wonderful spectacle presented itself. Athwart the vessel long white waves of light were seen rushing towards it, ever brighter and in swifter motion, till they seemed to flow together, and at length nothing could be seen on the water but a whirling white light. Looking steadfastly at it, the water, the air, and the horizon seemed blended in one; thick streamers of mist seemed to float by both sides of the ship with frantic speed. The appearances of colour resembled those which arise when one turns a black and striped ball so quickly that the white stripes seem to run together. The spectacle lasted for five minutes, and was repeated once again for two minutes. No doubt it was caused by shoals of animalculæ in the water."

day six

"I have carefully examined the figures of animals and birds engraven on the

24, 25. (24) **cattle,** graminivorous, tamable. **and .. thing,** as reptiles. **and .. earth,** beast of prey. (25) **God .. earth,** Heb. for earth *aretz.* **creepeth .. earth,** Heb. for earth *Adamah. Aretz,* used hitherto = the earth as a whole. *Adamah,* now first used, cognate to Adam.

[Cap. 1. 26—31.] GENESIS. 15

The animals of the earth as the forerunners of man.—I. The first signs and pictures of human life. II. Its most intimate assistants. III. Its first conditions.[a]

The animal creation.—Agassiz and A. A. Gould estimate the number of *vertebrated animals* at 20,000. About 1,500 species of *mammals* are ascertained; probable number, 2,000. *Birds*, well known, 4,000 or 5,000 species; probable number 6,000. *Reptiles*, 1,500 described species; probable number, 2,000. *Fishes*, 5,000 to 6,000 in the museums of Europe; probable number, 8,000 or 10,000. *Mollusks* in collections, 8,000 or 10,000. *Marine shells*, bivalve and univalve, in collections, 5,000 or 6,000; and *land and fluviatile shells*, 2,000. Total number of mollusks probably exceeds 15,000 species. *Insects*, in collections, probably 60,000 or 70,000 species; probable number of *articulata*, 100,000; species, 200,000. Add to these 10,000 for *radiata* (echini, star-fishes, medusæ, and polypi), and we have about 250,000 species of living animals; and supposing the number of *fossil* species to equal them, we have, at a very moderate computation, half a million species. We quote this estimate from MM. Agassiz and Gould's *Principles of Zoology*, Part I. 1848. The numbers are considered to be mostly under the present mark; the birds, for example, are certainly more numerous, and probably amount to 8,000 species.[b]

26—31. (26) **and .. said,** now that the home had been prepared. **man,** Heb. *Adam* = red. **image .. likeness,** prob. synonymous terms = shadow, resemblance: ref. to man's spiritual nature. **dominion,**[a] rule, authority. **over,** *etc.*, relation of man to rest of creatures that of sovereignty: by force of reason he everywhere makes his power felt. (27) **so,** *etc.*,[b] having thus deliberated; He executed His resolve. (28) **blessed,** *etc.*,[c] see on v. 22. The chief element in this blessing being supremacy.

Man in God's image.—I. In what the image of God upon man consisted. In—1. The possession of moral powers and susceptibilities; 2. The pure and righteous state of his whole nature; 3. His relative position towards other terrestrial creatures. II. That great blessedness was involved in the possession of God's image. 1. What were its elements? The image of God in man was a mirror—(1) Of God; (2) Of God to other creatures; (3) In which God saw Himself. 2. What blessings resulted from it? (1) Supreme good to man himself; (2) High satisfaction and glory to God. Reflections—(1) How sadly changed is human nature! (2) How elevated is the Christian! (3) How blessed is God![d]

The sovereignty of man.—Among the pictures at Apsley House is "Van Amburgh in the Den with Lions and Tigers," painted by Sir E. Landseer, R.A., after the instructions of the Duke of Wellington, who, with the Bible in his hand, pointed out the passage (Gen. i. 26) in which dominion is given to Adam over the earth and animals. The Duke "caused the text to be inscribed on the frame as an authority which conferred on him a privilege of power, and gave to himself 'the great commission,' which he carried out on the fields of battle and chase."

29—31. (29) **said,** to man. **behold,** all this thoughtful consideration is indeed a matter for wonder. **given .. herb,** *etc.*,[a] the whole vegetable world. **meat,** food, sustenance. (30) **and .. earth,** *etc.*,[b] assignment of food to animals.

B.C. 4004.

numerous obelisks brought from Egypt to ancient Rome. In the general character, which is all that can have been preserved, these representations perfectly resemble the originals as we see them. M. Geoffrey St. Hilaire collected numerous mummies and skeletons of the present day."—*Cuvier.*

a *Lange.*
b *Timbs.*
v. 25. *W. Jones, Wks.* vi. 27.

creation of man

a Ge. ix. 2. Ps. viii. 6; Ja. iii. 7.
b Ec. vii. 29. Is. lxiv. 8; Ge. v. 1; Ja. iii. 9; Ps. c.
c Ps. cxxvii. 3; cxxviii. 3, 4; Is. xlv. 18.

"The new and brilliant science of geology attests that man was the last of created beings in this planet. If her data be consistent and true, and worthy of scientific consideration, she affords conclusive evidence that, as we are told in Scripture, he cannot have occupied the earth longer than six thousand years." — *Hutchcock.*

d S. *Martin.*

food for man
a Ps. xxiv. 1; cxv. 16; 1 Ti. vi. 17; Job xxxvi.

B.C. 4004.

31; Ge. ix. 3; Ps.
cxxxvi. 25; cxlvi.
7; Ac. xlv. 17.
b Ps. civ. 14, 15;
cxlv. 15, 16;
cxlvi. 9.
c Ps. civ. 24; 1
Ti. iv. 4; De.
xxxii. 4.
d Ex. xxxi. 17.
"God, we are told, looked upon the world after He had created it, and pronounced it good; but ascetic pietists, in their wisdom, cast their eyes over it, and substantially pronounce it a dead failure, a miserable production, a poor concern."—*Boree.*
e *Anon.*
"There is not the least flower but seems to hold up its head, and to look pleasantly, in the secret sense of the goodness of its heavenly Maker."—*South.*
f *D. Page.*

(31) **saw**, perfect knowledge in that omniscient glance. **and .. good,**^{e} ca. step was *good;* the whole, *very good.* **and .. day,**^{d} *lit.*—DAY SIX.

God's approbation of His works.—Let us consider—I. The natural truths asserted by our text. Among these are—1. The true origin of all things—"God saw everything that He had made;" 2. The original perfection of all things—"very good," "very good," as being—(1) Well adapted to answer their particular intention; (2) Conducive to the perfection of the whole; (3) Well calculated to promote the Creator's glory; 3. God's approbation of His work. He saw it very good. II. The moral truths suggested. 1. Gratitude; 2. Hatred of sin; 3. The discontinuing of all evil; 4. Reformation and return to virtue; 5. Humility; 6. A ground of hope and encouragement.^{e}

The creation of man.—The study of life, palæontologically regarded, necessarily involves the creation and first appearance of man on the globe; and on this subject much discussion has taken place, unprofitable alike to science and to the cause of Christian theology. So far as geological evidence goes, we have no trace of man or of his works till we arrive at the superficial accumulations—the coral conglomerates, the bone breccias, the cave deposits, and the peat mosses of the current epoch. It is true, that so far as the earlier formations are concerned, the evidence is purely negative; but taking into account all that palæontology has revealed touching the other families of animated nature, the fair assumption is that man was not called into being till the commencement of the current geological era, and about the time when in the northern hemisphere the sea and land received their present configuration, and were peopled by those genera and species which (with a few local removals, and still fewer extinctions) yet adorn their forests and inhabit their land and waters.^{f}

CHAPTER THE SECOND.

the Sabbath

a He. iv. 4.

"Such an hypothesis [that the day was twenty-four hrs. long] would be involved in the absurdity of limiting God's rest on the seventh day to a day of the same length, whereas we know that that rest is enduring."—*Alford.*

b Ex. xx. 8—11;
xxxi. 13—17; Is lvi. 2; He. iv. 9 —11; Jo. xx. 19, 26; Ac. xvi. 13; xx. 7; 1 Co. xvi. 2.

1—3. (1) **finished**, perfected. **host,** *Heb. sig.* a band duly disposed and marshalled: an army in battle array. Creation perfected, arranged, laws and relations fixed. (2) **ended,** had ended. **rested,**^{a} ceased fr. work: not involving idea of weariness. (3) **sanctified,**^{b} set it apart as holy. "Separated fr. other days, and gave it a higher significance."^{c}

The Divine Sabbath.—We see in God's Sabbath—I. The Divine completion of His creative work. Creation ended with the sixth day's work. The fact is in harmony with—1. The disclosures of science in its history of the world's crust; 2. The world's history as the record of moral and religious special acts on God's part; 3. The brief references in the other sacred writings to the physical activity of the Creator. II. The Divine contemplation of it. Learn here—1. Evil has no natural place in the universe; 2. Matter is not necessarily hostile to God; 3. The present condition of things, so changed from that which God first looked upon, must be the result of some catastrophe. III. The Divine rest after it. 1. It was a season of rest; 2. The rest was blessed by God; 3. There was an appointment of a similar blessed rest for His creatures. Learn—(1) There is a place and time for rest; (2) The condition on which rest may be claimed is that men work; (3) This rest should be a happy rest; (4) The rest under such sanction ought to be religious; (5) The rest for man which God's sabbath implies is not limited to any particular portion of the race.*d*

The first Sabbath.—Hugh Miller remarks, that while we find it recorded at the end of each of these "days" that "the evening and the morning were the first day," it is not said of the seventh day that "the evening," &c. What is the natural conclusion, but that the day is not yet ended? And hence Miller's sublime suggestion, that God, having made man, rested on the seventh day from His material creation; and this is now God's sabbath day, in which He is carrying on the redemption of man, the transformation of man, the salvation of man, and eventually the glorification of man.*e*

4—7. (4) **generations**, origin, order, purpose, etc. **day**, period, course of time. **Lord God**, *Jehovah Elohim* (hitherto the Divine Name is Elohim). The word Jehovah occurs ab. 6,000 times in Scripture. (5) **plant .. herb**, reversion to third day of creation (i. 11—13), when the earth was void of vegetable life. **rain .. man .. ground**,*a* both conditions of cultivation—rain and human care—being absent. (6) **mist**, fog-vapour. **earth**, *ha-aretz*. **ground**, *adamah*. (7) **formed**, fashioned, shaped. **dust .. ground**,*b* man a fragile "vessel in the potter's hand." **and .. life**,*c* of no other living creature do we read this. **man .. soul**,*d* " materialism will never explain these words."*e*

The primeval condition of the earth and of man (on v. 4—25).—In these verses the state of things on the earth at its first creation is briefly described. I. The economy of the kingdom of inanimate nature, or the vegetable world, was fitted at once to maintain the sovereignty of God, and to provide for the welfare of man, as a compound being having both body and soul (vs. 5—7). Three things are here implied as necessary to the growth of plants—1. Soil; 2. Climate; 3. Culture. II. The moral world also, the spiritual kingdom, was rightly adjusted. Man—1. As a sentient being, was placed in an earthly paradise (vs. 8—15); 2. As a rational and religious being, was subjected to a Divine law (vs. 16, 17); 3. As a social, or companionable being, was furnished with human fellowship (vs. 18—25).*f*

Man, a living soul.—He did not merely possess it; he *became* it. It was his proper being, his truest self, the man in the man. All organised beings have life in common, each after its kind. This, therefore, all animals possess, and man as an animal. But, in addition to this, God transferred into man a higher gift, and specially inbreathed even a living—that is, self-subsisting—soul; a soul having its life in itself.*g*

8, 9. (8) **and .. planted**, man's first home in the world divinely contrived: specially fruitful and beautiful. **garden**, or park, idea of inclosure. **eastward**, foreplace: this suggestive of its being in the best part of the district called **Eden**,*a delight*, this the name, not of the garden, but of the region wherein it was situated. It is quite undecided where E. was.*b* (9) **grow .. food**, realising the old Spartan prayer, " grant us the beautiful with the good." **the .. life**,*c* " the fruit whereof conferred immortality."*d* " A symbolical tree, a sign not only of a

B.C. 4004.

c Knobel, "This higher significance was not fully brought out till the giving of the Mosaic law; though there are traces of the recurrence of the day being observed in pre-Mosaic times; *cf.* iv. 3; viii. 10, 12."—*Alford.*
d L. D. Bevan, LL.B.
e Bibl. Treas.

man a living soul
"By the use of the name *Jehorah*, the narrative advances a very important step towards the peculiar theocratical character of the Pentateuch; but by combining it with *Elohim*, it reminds, also, of the omnipotent Creator. The God of the universe is the God of Israel; but the God of Israel is, at the same time, Governor of the whole world."—*Kalisch.*
a Ps. civ. 14; Job v. 10.
b 1 Co. xv. 47; Ge. iii. 19; Job iv. 19; Ps. ciii. 14; Ec. xii. 7; Is. lxiv. 8.
c Job xxvii. 3; xxxiii. 4; Ac. xvii. 25; Is. ii. 22.
d 1 Co. xv. 45; He. xii. 9.
e Coleridge.
f Dr. Candlish.
g Coleridge.

Eden
a Is. li. 3; Ez. xxviii. 13.
b "Eden comprised that tract of land where the Euphrates and Tigris separate; fr. that spot the 'Garden of Eden' cannot be

GENESIS. [Cap. II. 10—14.

B.C. 4004.

distant. Let it suffice that we know its general position; but we are not permitted to penetrate within, as if the angel with the flaming sword forbade the access."—*Kalisch.*
c Ge. iii. 22; Pr. iii. 18; Ro. ii. 7; xxii. 2, 14.
d *Alford.*
e *Ainsworth.* "The tree of life, it is prob., was designed to sustain and refresh the life infused into man at his creation."—*Wordsworth.*
f *Alford.*
g *Lange.*

blessed natural life in Paradise, for a time; but of a spiritual life after in heaven for ever, if he continued in obedience to his Creator."*c* **midst**, visible, accessible. **tree . . evil**, wh. "conferred knowledge of the difference betw. right and wrong."*f* To eat of this tree was wrong: he who did so would at once see and feel the dif. betw. that state and one of innocence.

Paradise.—Paradise, as—I. A fact in the earth. 1. The bloom of the earth; 2. The home of the first man. II. An emblem. An emblem of—1. The paradisaical disposition of the earth; 2. Its paradisaical power, namely, for children, and in festal contemplation; 3. Its paradisaical prefiguration; as of the new paradise in the other world and in this.*g*

Man and woman.—Man is strong; woman is beautiful. Man is daring and confident; woman is diffident and unassuming. Man is great in action; woman in suffering. Man shines abroad; woman at home. Man talks to convince; woman to persuade and please. Man has a rugged heart; woman a soft and tender one. Man prevents misery; woman relieves it. Man has science; woman taste. Man has judgment; woman sensibility. Man is a being of justice; woman of mercy. Each possesses peculiar gifts and a wide sphere of usefulness, and, by the wise use of these respective gifts, society is benefited and God is honoured.

the river of Eden

a Re. xxii. 1.

b Many critics, as Baumgarten, Kitto, etc., are of opinion that the position of the rivers has totally changed in the course of time, especially since and by the deluge.

c Ge. xxv. 18; 1 Sa. xv. 7; Ge. x. 7.

d Nu. xi. 7; Ex. xvii. 14.

e Da. x. 4.

f H. Scott, B.A.

"1. Rivers fertilise and beautify; lives should be useful. 2. The cold and rapid river of death will soon have to be passed. That it may not bear us away to eternal death, seek a present Saviour; so shall we, like Israel of old, find the passage safe and easy, and we shall be willing to advance at

10—14. (10) **river . . Eden**,*a* *one* great river, wh. may or may not have had its source in E. **parted**, divided, branched out. **heads**,*b* arms, streams. (11) **Pison** (*overflowing*), not identified. As all is conjecture, it is useless to enumerate the var. opinions. **Havilah**,*c* where, uncertain. (12) **bdellium**, Heb. *bedolah,* of wh. we know little, but that it was like manna,*d* and as that resembled coriander-seed, some (as *Kimchi*) think pearls are meant. But most think it was a kind of gum. **onyx**, Heb. *shoham* = pale. (13) **Gihon**, prob. the Nile. **Ethiopia**, Heb. "land of Cush." (14) **Hiddekel**,*e* Heb. *Dijlah*. rapid : prob. the Tigris. **Euphrates**, Heb. *Frat.,* the sweet or broad stream.

The four rivers of Eden.—Here we have—I. Treasure—the Pison. 1. Here were gold and precious stones; 2. Moreover, that gold was good. II. Ignorance—the Gihon. Ethiopia was in darkness. The true light was lost there. III. Power and wickedness—Hiddekel and Euphrates, on which were Nineveh and Babylon. IV. Righteousness and peace—the river of Eden, the fountain-head of the four.*f*

The act of creation.—Long lay the type of creation in His searchless bosom. From eternity it had there been resolved. It now emanates in the perfection of beauty. It now beams out with the self-furnished evidences of wisdom and love. Chaos hears and obeys! The work is begun and swiftly hastens to its consummation. The waters fall back to appointed channels; the solid masses are fixed to sustain and bind a framework of a thousand orders and kinds; the distorted twinklings of light are embodied and find " their tabernacle in the sun ;" the rugged shapes and swells into lovely forms, and melts away into enchanting landscapes; the repulsive differences of attraction, instead of agitating the globe to its centre, gird and balance it; the latent seeds of each fair flower and luscious fruit break out along the river which flowed in Eden to water the garden; and the wild war of discords hushed into soft sunrise, and fragrant breath, and holy calm of a Sabbath dawn, in which God rested from His work and "was refreshed," in which man was "made upright," stretched forth his hands to his Father-Creator, with songs of praise comely for one so upright, and with the effectual fervent prayer of one so righteous; in which higher intelligences took a holy sympathy, and performed a benevolent part,—while hanging with wondering delight over the teeming scene, the sons of God pressed into view and shouted for joy !*g*

15—17. (15) **dress,**^a till, cultivate. **keep,** guard. (16) **Of .. eat,**^b of every tree of the garden, eat, eat mayest thou, *i.e.* eat without stint or fear. (17) **But .. evil,** see v. 9. **thou .. it,** the only prohibition by wh. God asserted His supreme sovereignty. **for .. die,**^c "thou wilt have the sentence of death within thee wh. grows on sin as its root .. sin, pain, sorrow are not only forerunners of death, but parts of death."^d The sentence included especially moral and spiritual death.

The Paradise-life, not an unrestricted state.—There is limitation of—I. Action : the calling to dress and keep. II. Enjoyment : not to eat of the tree of knowledge of good and evil. III. The treatment of nature, and especially of the beasts: no enclosing. IV. Human society: regulation of marriage and domestic life.^e—*God's voice to man on his entering into earthly life.* I. That man's earthly sphere of life is furnished with vast and varied blessings. There is—1. The sensational tree ; 2. The intellectual tree ; 3. The social tree ; 4. The religious tree. II. That these blessings are to be used under certain Divine regulations. Regulations, which are—1. Proper ; 2. Liberal ; 3. Needful. III. That the violation of these regulations will entail the utmost ruin—" thou shalt surely die."^f

Traditions of the Fall.—The Persian tradition is to the effect that man, at first, enjoyed a period of happiness and innocence in an elevated region which his god, Ormuzd, had assigned to him ; but it was necessary to his existence in this state, that he should be humble of heart, and humbly obey the Divine ordinances ; pure he must be of thought, pure of word, pure of deed. For a time, the first pair were holy and happy. But at last Ahriman, the evil one, appeared, and beat down their good dispositions ; and, under the influence of his glozing lies, they began to ascribe their blessings to him. Emboldened by this success, Ahriman the liar presented himself again, and brought with him fruit ; of which they ate : and in that instant, of a hundred excellences which they possessed, all but one departed from them ; and they became subject to misery and death.

18—20. (18) **It .. alone,**^a regard being had to his social and moral nature : and also to the fulfilling of the Divine will ; i. 28 ; **help .. him,** *lit.* a help as over against him, before him, so as to meet him, tally and correspond to him as his counterpart. (19) **out .. air,** see on i. 24. **brought .. Adam,**^b by supernatural influence, as aft. they were brought to Noah in the ark. **what .. them,** hence he had the gifts of speech, reason, perception, etc. **whatsoever .. thereof,** the names given, answering prob. to their nature, met with God's approval. (20) **Adam .. him,** ea. other creature had its mate : but the man was alone.

The creation of woman.—Here we have an instance of—I. The Creator's care of man, and His fatherly concern for his comfort,

---

B.C. 4004.

His command."
— *Topics for Teachers.*

g Dr. R. W. Hamilton.

permission and prohibition

a Ep. iv. 28.
b 1 Ti. iv. 4 ; vi. 17.
c Ro. vi. 23 ; 1 Co. xv. 22 ; Ja. i. 5.
d Wordsworth.

"Death is not only the actual separation of soul and body, but includes all that culminates in that separation. A man may, as we say, 'die by inches ;' and may be said, especially if passing fr. a state where death was not the necessary end of his days, to die, when the seeds of death begin to work in him. It is not sufficiently borne in mind that man's exclusion fr. the tree of life wh. could have conferred immortality on him, was the carrying out of this sentence."—*Alford.*

e Lange.
f Dr. Thomas.

the naming of the animals

a Pr. xviii. 22 ; 1 Co. xi. 9.
1 Ti. ii. 13 ; iv. 1—3.

b Ps. viii. 6—8 ; Ge. ix. 2.

"The names given by Adam had, doubtless, their foundati n in the nature of

20 GENESIS. [Cap. II. 21—25.

B.C. 4004. the creatures to wh. they were given. An evidence of man's intuitive knowledge, derived fr. God; and of the origin of language as God's gift." — *Wordsworth*. c *M. Henry*. "Teach him to live unto God and unto thee, and he will discover that women, like the plants in woods, derive their softness and tenderness from the shade." — *W. S. Landor*. **the creation of woman** *a Bush*. *b* 1 Co. xi. 8; He. xiii. 4. *c Delitzsch*. *d* Ma. xix. 5, 6; Ep. v. 29, 30. *e* So Old Latir, a man; vira, a woman. *f* Mal. ii. 14—16; Ro. vii. 2; 1 Co. vii. 10, 11. *g* Ex. xxxii. 25; Is. xlvii. 3; Je. xvii. 13. "Their bodies were the clothing of their inner glory, and this glory (rightly understood) was the clothing of their nakedness."—*Delitzsch*. *v.* 22. Dr. T. *Manton*, a ser. *v.* 24. Dr. S. *Johnson*, S.S., l. 1. *h T. W. Richards, M.A.* "Wherever found, women are the same kind, civil, obliging, humane, tender beings, inclined to be gay and cheerful,	Observe—1. God's pity for his solitude; 2. His resolve to provide society for him. II. The creatures' subjection to man, and his dominion over them. God brought the animals to Adam that he might name them, and so give a proof of—1. His knowledge; 2. His power. III. The creatures' insufficiency to be a happiness for man. Observe—1. The dignity and excellency of human nature; 2. The vanity of the things of this world.*c* *A true helpmeet.*—The Rev. Philip Henry used to give two pieces of advice to his children and others, in reference to marriage. One was, "Keep within the bounds of profession." The other was, "Look at suitableness in age, quality, education, temper," etc. He used to observe, from Gen. ii. 18, "I will make him an helpmeet for him;" that where there is not meetness, there will not be much help. He commonly said to his children, with reference to their choice in marriage, "Please God, and please yourselves, and you shall never displease me;" and greatly blamed those parents who conclude matches for their children without their consent. He sometimes mentioned the saying of a pious gentlewoman, who had many daughters: "The care of most people is how to get good husbands for their daughters; but my care is to fit my daughters to be good wives, and then let God provide for them." 21—25. (21) **deep sleep**, prob. a *trance* or *ecstasy:* so the LXX. **took..ribs**, "the miracle is in the creation, not in the choice of subjects to create from."*a* (22) **made..woman**, *lit*. builded her to a woman. **brought..man**,*b* "Here He [God] appears as the first bridesman."*c* (23) **This..now**, *lit*. this is for this time, this once. The only woman produced in this way. **bone..flesh**,*d* nearness of mar. relation. Husband to care for wife, as for himself. **woman**, Heb. *Isha* **man**, Heb. *Ish*.*e* (24) **Therefore**, *etc*.*f* This *may* have been spoken by Adam: but was more *prob*. the inspired reflection of Moses. But by whomsoever said, it is prophetic of all mankind. (25) **ashamed**,*g* they knew no shame, bec. they knew not sin. *Eve.*—Let us speak of—I. The woman. 1. Her creation; 2. The purpose God had in view in creating her. II. The wonderful institution by which man and woman are made one. It is wonderful that this institution should be found so early in human history. III. The glorious union of which this institution is a type. Adam is a type of Christ; and since Christ was the spouse of the Church, then Eve was a type of the Church. And our conclusion therefore is that the marriage of Adam and Eve, and the marriage institute altogether, is typical of the union between Christ and the Church.*h* *The relation of woman to man.*—The woman was made of a bone; and but one bone. *ne esset ossea*, lest she should be stiff and stubborn. The species of the bone is expressed to be a rib, a bone that might be best spared, because there are many of them: a bone of the side, not of the head; the wife must not usurp authority over her husband: nor yet of the feet; she is not a slave, but a fellow-helper. A bone, not of any anterior part; she is not *prælata*, preferred before the man: neither yet of any hinder part: she is not *post-posita*, set behind the man: but a bone of the side, of the middle, and indifferent part, to show that she is a companion, and "the wife of thy covenant" (Mal. ii. 14). A bone she is from under the arm, to put man in mind of protection

and defence to the woman. A bone not far from his heart, to put him in mind of dilection and love to the woman. A bone from the left side, as many think likely, where the heart is, to teach that hearty love ought to be betwixt married couples.*i*

B.C. 4004.

timorous and modest."—*Ledyard.*
i B. King.

CHAPTER THE THIRD.

1—3. (1) **serpent**, Heb. *nachash;* of wh. the root denotes mental properties, *i.e.* to search, scrutinize. **subtil,***a* "and so a more fit instrument of that old serpent the devil" *b* **he**, the devil in this form. **said,** his *speaking* not surprising to Eve, who knew not the qualities of the var. animals; not being present when they were named: for the same reason she would not be alarmed at his *appearance.* **woman,** the weaker of the two, and alone. **yea .. garden?** throwing her off her guard by showing an acquaintance with the law: yet subtilly conveying a taunt "you dare not:" and rousing desire, and curiosity. (2) **woman .. serpent,** this parley was her ruin. **we .. garden,** she had heard the law fr. her husband: and now corrects the tempter. (3) **touch,** not in the original law. Perh. Adam, to prevent her fr. eating, told her not even to *touch.*

The scriptural account of human apostasy confirmed by history and tradition.—I. Human nature is a ruin. That "we have sinned" is shown by—1. Inspired writings; 2. Our present condition and character; 3. the nature of universal death. II. The instrument of the ruin of human nature was the serpent.*c*—*The Fall.*—In the Fall of man we distinguish three degrees:—I. The preparation made for it. II. The carrying out of the temptation. III. Its immediate effects.*d*

Traditions of Eden.—We have before us the whole history of this transaction in an engraving (see *Creuzer's Symbolik,* pl. 158) from ancient bas-relief; and what is most remarkable, there are two groups at each extremity of the tablet, offering, as it were, a Biblical key to the whole scene. On the one hand, are a man and woman standing naked under a tree: the woman in a drooping and disconsolate posture; the man with one hand raised to the tree, and the other directed towards the woman. It is such a picture that a child would at once say, "That is Adam and Eve!" At the other extremity is a sedate and august figure, seated upon a rock, and strangling the serpent with his outstretched hand.*e*

the first temptation

a 2 Co. xi. 3; Re. xii. 9; xx. 2.

b Trapp.

"Woman was the first sinner; and, behold, in the two greatest falls, and most immediate denials of God, Adam's and Peter's, woman is made the first tempter."—*Bp. Reynolds.*

c Dr. Cox.

"When I cannot be forced, I am fooled out of my integrity. He cannot constrain if I do not consent. If I do but keep possession, all the posse of hell cannot violently eject me; but I cowardly surrender to his summons. Thus there needs no more to be my undoing but myself."—*Fuller.*

d Michow.

e Kitto.

4—7. (4) **ye .. die,***a* *lit.* ye shall not dying die: or, as LXX., ye shall not die the death. (5) **for .. know,** he impugns the veracity of God. **that .. eat,** other and better effects than death shall *immediately* ensue. **then .. opened,** not closed in death, but beholding things with a deeper insight. **gods,** Heb. *Elohim.* **knowing .. evil,** till now only the good was known. (6) **saw,** by looking long, and longingly. **tree .. wise,** assuming the devil's words to be true. **gave .. her,** Adam was thus reached at last. **he .. eat,** out of affection for her, being importuned by her, not perceiving that she was injured. (7) **eyes .. opened,***b* they saw that they had sinned. **naked,** sin brought a sense of shame. **sewed,** twisted, platted. **aprons,** *lit.* things to gird about.

The woman and the serpent.—We have here a sample of—I. The

the first sin

a 1 Ti. ii. 14; Jo. viii. 44. "Clothes are the ensigns of our sin and covers of our shame. To be proud of them is as great a folly as for a beggar to be proud of his rags or a thief of his halter. As the prisoner looking on his irons thinketh of his theft, so we,

B.C. 4004.

looking on our garments, should think on our sins."—Trapp.

b Ro. v. 12; 1 Jo. ii. 16; Ja. i. 14, 15; iv. 7; 2 Co. ii. 11; Ma. vi. 13. "The Genevan Bible (1st ed. 1560) is sometimes called the 'Breeches Bible,' fr. its trans. of v. 7, 'They sewed figge-tree leaves together, and made themselves breeches.'"

c J. A. Macdonald.

v. 4. Bp. Mant, iii. 23; Dr. Alford, ii. 100; S. Smith, ii. 143.

d Humboldt.

fear and shame

a Ps. xciv. 9; cxxxix. 7; Job xxxi. 33; xxxiv. 21, 22; 2 Ch. xxvi. 9; Pr. xv. 3; Jo. xxiii. 24; Am. ix. 3; He. iv. 12, 13; De. v. 25, 26.

b Ps. cxix. 120; Job xxiii. 15; 1 Jo. iii 20; Re. ii. 18.

"Pure nakedness was God's creature, and he was naked b e f. without fear or shame." — *Ainsworth.*

"The bad heart runs fr. God, and would run fr. its own terrors; as the wounded deer fr. the deadly arrow that sticks in its side; but refusing ordinary trial, it is in danger to be pressed to death inevitably."—*Trapp.*

c Ps. xc. 8.

d H. J. Martyn.

e Dr. Sprague.

wisdom of the world. Among the maxims of this wisdom are these—1. That happiness is the end of human existence; 2. That nature is a sufficient source of happiness; 3. That man's chief happiness lies in forbidden objects; 4. That God is what we fancy or desire Him to be. II. The qualities of sin. 1. The elements of all sin are here,—sensuality, covetousness, ambition; 2. Sin originates in unbelief; 3. It wears a specious appearance of goodness. III. The results of sin. It—1. Transforms its victims into Satanic incarnations; 2. Reveals its own deceptiveness; 3. Covers its victims with confusion.*c*

Shirt trees.—"We saw, on the slope of the Cerra Dnida, shirt trees fifty feet high. The Indians cut off cylindrical pieces two feet in diameter, from which they peel the red and fibrous bark, without making any longitudinal incision. This bark affords them a sort of garment which resembles a sack of a very coarse texture, and without a seam. The upper opening serves for the head, and two lateral holes are cut to admit the arms. The natives wear these shirts of Marina in the rainy season; they have the form of the pouches and manes of cotton which are so common in New Grenada, at Quito, and Peru. As in this climate the riches and beneficence of nature are regarded as the primary causes of the indolence of the inhabitants, the missionaries do not fail to say in showing the shirts of Marina, ' in the forests of Oronoko, garments are found ready made upon the trees.'"*d*

8—11. (8) **voice .. walking,** it was the *voice* (not the Lord) *walking:* i.e. it sounded along through the avenues of the garden, growing louder and louder. **cool .. day,** *lit.* in the wind of the day, *i.e.* towards evening. **hid .. garden,***a* guilt-inspired terror: once they would have joyously welcomed that voice. (9) **Adam .. thou?** this was what the voice said. Where was he morally? A sinner vainly flying fr. his Maker. (10) **afraid .. naked,***b* the devil had deceived him with a lie: not so could he deceive God. (11) **who .. naked?** only a heart knowing *evil* could have told thee that. **hast,** *etc.?c* by this question the origin of the fear and shame was urged home.

God's call to Adam.—Our text suggests—I. Man's departure from God. Adam was in a state of—1. Alienation from God; 2. Fear of Him; 3. Delusion about Him; 4. Danger. II. God's concern about man's departure. God is concerned about man's departure from Him, because it involves—1. Evil; and He is "of purer eyes than to behold iniquity; 2. Suffering; and He "is love." III. God's personal dealing with the wanderer.*d* *Where art thou?*—Apply this question to—I. The professing Christian. He ought ever to be—1. At his proper work; 2. In his proper place; 3. In a state of mind to seek the Divine blessing; 4. Where he can meet God in judgment without fear. II. The sinner. He is where he ought not to be. He is—1. In his sins; 2. In the pathway of eternal ruin; 3. In a state of condemnation; 4. Wandering in a land of darkness and gloom; 5. Under God's immediate eye; 6. In the hands of angry Lord.*e*

The Divine omniscience.—Some of the natives of South America, after listening a while to the instructions of the Popish missionaries, gave them this cool answer:—"You say that the God of the Christians knows everything, that nothing is hidden from Him, that He is everywhere, and sees all that is done below. Now, we do not desire a God so sharp-sighted; we choose to live with freedom in our woods, without having a perpetual observer of our actions over our heads."

12, 13. (12) **and .. said,**[a] equivocating. **woman .. tree, you gave the woman, she gave the fruit.** He shifts the blame in guilty fear first upon Eve, but indirectly on God. **I .. eat,** not denying but extenuating: stating *last*, what should have been confessed *first*. (13) **and .. woman,** first Adam, now Eve. to convict both and lead to repentance. **and .. me,**[b] fear, in her case also, would shift the blame.
What is this that thou hast done?—This third chapter of the Bible is the revelation of the original sin. And that, for the present, in three senses. I. The record before us is the history of the first sin. II. The first sin is, also, the specimen sin. All other sins are copies of it. III. Besides this, the first sin is also the infectious sin.[c]
A Mohammedan tradition.—"A certain king, having a pleasant garden, in which were ripe fruits, set two persons to keep it, one of whom was blind and the other lame; the former not being able to see the fruit, nor the latter to gather it. The lame man, however, seeing the fruit, persuaded the blind man to take him upon his shoulders, and by that means he easily gathered the fruit, which they divided between them. The lord of the garden coming some time after and inquiring after his fruit, each began to excuse himself, the blind man said that he had no eyes to see with, and the lame one that he had no feet to approach the trees; but the king, ordering the lame man to be set upon the blind, passed sentence on and punished them both."[d]

14, 15. (14) **cursed,** addressed no question to, but pronounced a woe upon. **upon .. go,** the form thou hast assumed shall be degraded in the eyes of those whom thou hast deceived. They shall henceforth look upon thee with loathing and horror. Impossible to say how far, and in what respect, the form and motion of the serpent may have now been changed. **dust .. eat,** this literally true. The S. swallows dust with its food. It grovels in the dust. (15) **enmity,** thy friendship being so dangerous. **between .. seed,**[a] literally true. Man is everywhere the foe of the serpent. **it .. head,**[b] man shall ultimately destroy the whole serpent race. **thou .. heel,**[c] thou shalt injure the human race but slightly. (*Note.*—There is a higher meaning. The Messiah, the promised seed of the woman, shall destroy the devil and his works: being Himself wounded only in His lower, *i.e.* His human nature).
The first promise.—Consider from these words—I. The grace of which they are the germinal revelation. II. The way in which God is fulfilling the promise. Inferences—(1) Salvation begins with God; (2) No consciousness of guilt, however deep, warrants mistrust of God's mercy; (3) Satan's overtures, however specious, tend only to evil; (4) In Christ, and only in Him, is salvation provided and to be sought for.[d]

Death conquered.—
    Death, the old serpent's son,
      Thou hadst a sting once, like thy sire,
    That carried hell and ever-burning fire;
      But those black days are done;

B.C. 4004

sinful evasions

a Pr. xxviii. 13; Ja. i. 15.
b Ge. vi. 7.
"There is nothing of so ill consequence to the public as falsehood, or (speech being the current coin of converse) the putting false money upon the world; or so dark a blot as dissembling, which, as Montaigne saith prettily, 'is only to be brave towards God and a coward towards man;' for a lie faceth God, and shrinketh from man."—*Lloyd.*
c Dr. *Vaughan.*
d W. R. *Cooper.*

the promised seed

a Ma. xiii. 38; Jo. viii. 44; Ac. xiii. 10; 1 Jo. iii. 8; Is. vii. 14; Lu. i. 31—35; Ga. iv. 4.
b Ro. xvi. 20; Ep. iv. 8; Col. ii. 15; He. ii. 14, 15; 1 Jo. iii. 8; Jo. xvi. 11; xii. 31; Lu. x. 17—20; Re. xii. 17.
c Is. liii. 3, 4, 12; Da. ix. 26; Mal. iv. 1.

Labour. "'Tis the primal curse, but softened into mercy made the pledge of cheerful days, and nights without a groan."—*Cowper.*
d *Analyst.*
"Labour is become necessary

GENESIS. [Cap. iii. 16—21.

B.C. 4004.

to us, not only because we need it for making provisions for our life, but even to ease the labour of our rest, there being no greater tediousness of spirit in the world than want of employment and an inactive life."—*Jeremy Taylor.*

Bp. Taylor.

the punishment of sin

a 1 Ti. ii. 15.
b Ep. v. 22—24; 1 Co. xi. 3; xiv. 34; Col. iii. 18; 1 Ti. ii. 11, 12; Tit. ii. 4, 5; 1 Pe. iii. 1—7.

"Under fallen man, woman has been more or less a slave. In fact under the rule of selfishness the weaker must serve the stronger. A spiritual resurrection only will restore her to her true place as the helpmeet for man."—*Murphy.*

c 1 Sa. xv. 23.

d Ro. viii. 20—22.

e Job v. 7; xiv. 1; Ec. ii. 23.

f Ep. iv. 28; 2 Th. ii. 10.

g 1 Co. xv. 21.

h Is. lxi. 10; Ps. xxxii. 1.

J. *Maskell.*

"The body returns to the earth, fr. whence it was framed, and the spirit ascends to the ether."—*Euripides.*

v. 17, 19. E. *Irving,* iii. 1025.

k Mad. de Gasparin.

Thy foolish spite buried thy sting
　　In the profound and wide
Wound of our Saviour's side:
And now thou art become a tame and **harmless thing**;
　　A thing we dare not fear,
　　Since we hear
That our triumphant God, to punish thee
For the affront thou did'st Him on the tree,
Hath snatch'd the keys of hell out of thy hand,
　　And made thee stand
A porter at the gate of life, thy mortal enemy.
O Thou who art that gate, command that he
　　May when we die,
　　And thither fly,
Let us in the courts of heaven through Thee! Hallelujah.*

16—21. (16) **greatly .. conception,**^{a} pain and sorrow of pregnancy and parturition. **children** *lit.* sons. **they .. thee,**^{b} in all things—even thy desires—he shall rule thee. (17) **because .. tree,**^{c} commands and entreaties of nearest relatives not to usurp the relations of God. **cursed .. ground,**^{d} fr. thy living shall be extorted. **sorrow .. life,**^{e} the sorrow of toil, disappointment, etc. (18) **thorns .. thee,** without cultivation. **eat .. field,**^{f} the poor reward of thy toil. (19) **bread,** Heb. *lehem* = all kinds of food. (20) **Eve,** Heb. *Havah* = life. A name sugg. of honour and hope: pointing to that eternal life wh. the woman's seed procured.^{g} (21) **made,** prompted and taught the doing of it. **coats .. them,** skins of animals offered in sacrifice. Man did not then eat flesh. (*Ill.* Our Great Sacrifice provides us with a dress.)^h

The curse and the blessing of labour.—I. The universal necessity of labour. The earth no longer produces fruit independently of labour. II. The fact, asserted in the text, that labour is a curse. It is part of our punishment for the Fall, that it should be so. III. The manner in which we may lighten this curse, and cause it to be borne. We may not escape from it; but it may be lightened by—1. Religion—personal, practical, and real; 2. The cultivation of knowledge; 3. The maintenance of good health; 4. The practice of economy.*

The groaning of creation.—Cries of pain rise from this Eden of ours. They come from the forest glade, where the hawk pounces upon some quivering thing; from the village, where the peasant takes the new-born lamb from its mother; they come still more from cities,—clamours, sinister laughs, slaughtered cattle, sobs, threats, men who kill, who are killed; tears of those who refuse to be comforted! And those who do not cry out, whom we do not hear, are those that suffer most. Fly from our civilized countries: go to the centre of Africa, what do you find there? A sandy desert so steeped in blood, such wholesale massacres, that travellers of every creed call those negro-lands the kingdom of Satan. On their coasts, caravans of slaves with halters round their necks, beaten, bartered, piled on one another between decks, exposed to sale, dragged off to plantations, married, unmarried, at their master's will, dying under the lash. In Pagan isles, wars, massacres, cannibalism. In China, Persia, India, refined cruelties, of which our nerves cannot bear the recital. In every latitude, human brutality, taking advantage of the helplessness of dumb animals, cowardly cruelty, or cruel kindness!^{k}

22—24. (22) **man . . evil,** prob. meaning is that man had attempted, etc.: such was his object and wish. **and now . . ever,** eating it now with wrong motive; *i.e.* to counteract the sentence. (23) **sent . . Eden,** losing both holiness and happiness. The meek inherit the earth, the ambitious forfeit it. (24) **drove . . man,** forcible ejection of one who was loth to leave. **cherubims,** (*warders*), living creatures: prob. angels. **and . . way,** it flashed in all directions. **keep . . life,** prevent access.

The first outcast.—I. God "*drove* out the man:" then he was reluctant to go. We might have expected that Adam would have been oppressed by—1. A sense of guilt; 2. The idea of forfeiture. But no; God "drove" him out. II. God "drove out the man:" He did not smite him; He loved him still. III. God "drove out the man;" in reality to another, though inferior, Paradise. IV. God "drove out the man;" *God*, not an angel. V. God "drove out the man;" but not without hope.*a*

Milton's Paradise Lost and Regained.—Thomas Ellwood, one of the Society of Friends, was the pupil and friend of Milton, and one of those who read to the poet after the loss of his sight. Having been for some time absent, he paid Milton a visit. "After some common discourse had passed between us," says Ellwood, "he called for a manuscript of his, which, being brought, he delivered to me, bidding me take it home with me, and read it at my leisure, and, when I had so done, return it to him with my judgment thereupon. When I came home, and had set myself to read it, I found it was that excellent poem, which he entitled *Paradise Lost*. After I had, with the utmost attention, read it through, I made him another visit, and returned him his book, with due acknowledgment for the favour he had done me, in communicating it to me. He asked me how I liked it and what I thought of it, which I modestly but freely told him; and after some further discourse about it, I pleasantly said to him, 'Thou hast said much here of Paradise lost; but what hast thou to say of Paradise found?' He made me no answer, but sat some time in a muse; then brake off that discourse, and fell upon another subject."—After some time, Mr. Ellwood visited Milton again, when he showed him *Paradise Regained*, and said in a tone of pleasantry, "This is owing to you, for you put it into my head at Chalfont, which before I had not thought of."

B.C. 4004.

paradise lost
v. 22. Dr. R. Clerke, 289; R. Gell, Essay, 25.

"The placing of these Cherubim at the E. of Eden was indicative of ordinances of worship, and a form of access to the Divine presence still open to man, though he was debarred fr. entrance into paradise."—Alford.

a R. A. Griffin.

"The Almighty placed cherubims and a flaming sword to keep man from returning to Paradise, to the tree of life; but He has placed Himself in all the terror, grandeur, loveliness and majesty of His character between sin and man, to prevent him touching the accursed thing."—*John Bate.*

"Sin and shame are ever tied together with Gordian knots, of such a strong thread spun, they cannot without violence be undone."—*Webster.*

CHAPTER THE FOURTH.

1, 2. (1) **Cain***a* (*possession; acquisition*). **I . . Lord,** lit. I have gotten a man, the Jehovah. They perh. thought this manchild was the promised seed: the destined deliverer. (2) **Abel,** (*vanity, vapour*) name prophetic of his untimely end. They may have been secretly moved to give that name. **Abel . . sheep,** lit. a feeder of a flock. **Cain . . ground,** a husbandman. (The husband and wife, in their new relation of father and mother, bring up their children to industrial pursuits.)

The first murderer.—I. This history (v. 1—16) presents a picture of the baseness of selfishness. Selfishness—1. Overlooks the means employed by others to become great; 2. Destroys the sacredness of natural ties; 3. Considers the virtues of others hostile to itself. 4. Is not scrupulous in injuring the innocent.

birth of Cain and Abel

a Ge. xxxiii. 5; Ps. cxxvii. 3.

v. l. *Meilan, M.A. S.S.* for children, iii. 157.

"As the rose-tree is composed of the sweetest flowers and the sharpest thorns; as the heavens are sometimes fair and some-

GENESIS. [Cap. iv. 3–5.

B.C. 4004.

times overcast, alternately tempestuous and serene; so is the life of man intermingled with hopes and fears, with joys and sorrows, with pleasures and with pains."—*Burton.*
b *Jenkin Jones.*
"How short is human life! the very breath Which frames my words, accelerates my death."
Hannah More.
c *Webster.*

the brothers' sacrifices
a Ex. xiii. 2; Nu. xviii. 17.
b Ex. xxix. 13; Le. iii. 3, 4.
c He. xi. 4; 1 Pe. i. 18, 19.
d Le. ix. 24; 1 K. xviii. 24; 1 Ch. xxi. 26; 2 Ch. vii. 1; Ps. xx. 1, 3; Pr. xxi. 27.
e Ma. xx. 15; Ac. x. 35.

"Had I a careful and pleasant companion, that should show me my angry face in a glass, I should not at all take it ill. Some are wont to have a looking-glass held to them while they wash, though to little purpose; but to behold a man's self so unnaturally disguised and disordered, will conduce not a little to the impeachment of anger."-*Plutarch.*

v. 3, 4. *Bp. Conybeare,* ii. 191.
f *T. Grantham, B.D.*
g *Crittenden.*

II. The injuries done to the good are noticed in heaven. A Witness testifies against every unjust act, who is—1. Conversant with all the circumstances of the case; 2. Truthful in His evidence; 3. An eye-witness. III. An impartial investigation will be made touching these wrongs. 1. A righteous Judge; 2. An opportunity for proving innocence offered; 3. Only integrity can stand the trial. IV. The evil-doer is the greatest sufferer in the end. 1. No prosperity; 2. No home; 3. No peace.*b*

Virtues of industry.—
 The chiefest action for a man of spirit,
 Is never to be out of action; we should think
 The soul was never put into the body,
 Which has so many rare and curious pieces
 Of mathematical motion, to stand still.
 Virtue is ever sowing of her seeds,
 In the trenches for the soldier; in the wakeful study
 For the scholar; in the furrows of the sea
 For men of that profession; of all which
 Arise and spring up honour.*c*

3—5. (3) and .. time, *lit.* at the end of days. Cain .. ground, Adam inculcated the duty of religious worship, as well as industry. offering, Heb. *mincha* = oblation, token of subjection, or submission. (4) Abel .. flock,*a* a sin-offering: and .. thereof,*b* *lit.* the fatnesses of them: *i.e.* the *best* portions. respect .. Abel,*c* he offered with faith in the appointed Lamb of God. offering, wh. was a type of Xt. (5) Cain, who lacked faith. offering, neither rightly selected, nor offered. he .. respect,*d* there was prob. some visible sign of acceptance or rejection. wroth,*e* filled with burning. intense rage: instead of spirit of self-examination and repentance. and .. fell, became gloomy. sullen.

Abel's sacrifice.—Let us—I. Consider the offerings of Cain and Abel, and the way in which they were received by the Almighty. II. Make some observations upon this Scripture narrative. 1. Not all who worship God are acceptable worshippers; 2. If we desire to serve God acceptably, we must serve Him with our best; 3. Our persons must be rendered pleasing to God. or our offerings will not be accepted by Him. III. Deduce from the whole a few practical reflections—1. None can stand before God with acceptance, save through the atoning sacrifice of Christ. 2. The visible Church of God hath ever been a mixed company, consisting of the evil as well as the good; 3. A sacrifice has been appointed of God for the sins of the whole world, and, through it, all who believe shall assuredly be saved.*f*

Man, the child of Mercy.—When God. in His eternal counsel, conceived the thought of man's creation, He called to Him the three ministers who wait constantly upon His throne,—Justice, Truth, and Mercy,—and thus addressed them: "Shall we make man?" Then said Justice, "O God! make him not; for he will trample upon Thy laws." Truth made answer also, "O God! make him not; for he will pollute Thy sanctuaries." But Mercy, dropping upon her knees, and looking up through her tears, exclaimed, "O God! make him: I will watch over him with my care through all the dark paths which he may have to tread." Then God made man, and said to him, "O man! thou art the child of Mercy: go and deal with thy brother."*g*

6—8. (6) **why .. fallen?**[a] question to turn his attention to real cause of rejection. (7) **if .. well, offerest the right** sacrifice, with a right spirit. **shalt .. accepted?**[b] as well as thy bro. **lieth,** *lit.* croucheth. Thy sin, like a beast of prey, ready to spring upon thee. (But some think the meaning is,[c] "if thou doest not well, sin"—*i.e.* a sin-offering—"lieth at the door"—*i.e.* is close at hand. "Sin" sin-offering: as Xt. was "made sin"—*i.e.* a sin-offering—"for us.") **and .. him,** some think this means that Cain, if he did well, should, as the firstborn, have the pre-eminence over his bro.; others, that he should overcome the sin now crouching at the door. (8) **Cain,** rejecting Divine counsel. **talked .. brother,**[e] familiarly, concealing his anger. **Cain .. him,**[d] the first death in the first family: murder the offspring of envy.

The religion of nature, and the religion of the Gospel.—Introduction:—Cain's religion, in common with many false religions, was one—(1) Which had in it *some* good; (2) Of expediency; (3) Which lacked faith. (4) Abounding in self-righteousness. (5) That persecuted others. Abel's religion—(1) Embodied all the good that was in the other; (2) Surpassed it, even in its own excellencies—"more plenteous sacrifice;" (3) Recognized the existence of guilt, and its merited doom; (4) Was actuated by faith; (5) Was approved of by God. Consider, then—I. Natural religion. Look at—1. The principle upon which it is founded—practical goodness. This principle is intrinsically excellent, is one upon which all men should act; is one to which no one can object. 2. The standard by which it is to be tested—the moral law of creation, love to God and man. In order to "do well," the act itself must be perfect; the motive must be good; and the rule must be good; 3. Its reward to its faithful adherents—"shalt thou not be accepted?" Such a religion will command the approval of God; and will secure immortality for all its votaries. Now measure your conduct by this religion; and are you perfect? Think of sin in its nature, its effects, and its ultimate consequences, and see if you have not sinned. And can natural religion justify you? No; something else must be found, and something else is to be found. Look then at—II. Revealed religion. Notice—1. That revealed religion assumes that men are guilty. She also recognizes their liability to punishment; 2. That it has provided a sin-offering,—a substitution of person, of sufferings: (1) The acceptance of this is accompanied with Divine evidence; (2) It is efficient for all purposes for which it is presented; (3) Having accepted it, the sinner is treated as though he himself had suffered. 3. That the sin-offering reposeth at the door. This implies that Xt.'s atonement is accessible to the sinner; that it rests with man to avail himself of it; that men often neglect it; that God exercises great patience towards the sinner; that the sinner cannot go to hell without first trampling on the cross; and that he will be for ever deprived of every excuse for his destruction.[e]

Brotherly love.—A little boy, seeing two nestling birds pecking at each other, inquired of his elder brother what they were doing. "They are quarrelling," was the answer. "No," replied the child, "that cannot be: they are brothers."

9—12. (9) **where .. brother?**[a] this to awaken a sense of guilt. Shows Divine knowledge of human actions. **I .. not,** a

---

B.C. 4004.

the first murder

a Is. i. 18; iii. 10, 11.

b Ro. ii. 11.

c Pr. xxvi. 24, 25.

d 1 Jo. iii. 12—15; Ja. i. 15.

"O envy, the corrosive of all ill minds, and the root of all desperate actions! The same cause that moved Satan to destroy the first man, the same moves the second man to destroy the third. If there be an evil heart there will be an evil eye; and if both these, there will be an evil hand. There never was an envy that was not bloody; if not in act, yet in affection."—*Bp. Hall.*

To be angry about trifles is mean and childish; to rage and be furious is brutish; to maintain perpetual wrath is akin to the practice and temper of devils; to prevent or suppress rising resentment is wise and glorious; to forgive is heavenly and Divine.

v. 7. *Dr. Felton,* 247; *Bp. Stillingfleet,* iv. 36; *Dr. Kitto, Jour.,* 4 :*H. Whishaw, A.M.,* i. 61; *Dr. Gell.Essay,* 31; *Bp. Wordsworth, Christian Boyhood,* ii. 100.

e D. Evans.

the fratricide

a Nu. xxxii. 23;

GENESIS. [Cap. iv. 13–16.

B.C. 4001.

Ps. x. 13, 14; Pr.
xxxviii. 13; Jo.
viii. 44.

b Ps. lxxii. 14;
He. xii. 24; Ro.
vi. 10.

"Heart murder is
the secret wishing or designing
the death of any
man; yea, the
Scripture saith,
'Whosoever
hateth his brother is a murderer' (1 Jo. iii.
15). We have instances of this
kind of murder
in Ahab (1 K.
xxii. 9); Jezebel
(1 K. xix. 2); the
Jews(Mar.xi.18);
David (1 Sa. xxv.
21, 22); Jon. (ch.
iv. 1, 4)."—*C.
Buck.*

*v. 9. H. Melvill,
ii. 354.*

c B. Dale, M.A.

d Johnson.

Cain's punishment

a Job xv. 20—24;
Ps. li. 11; Pr.
xiv. 32; xxviii. 1.
b Ge. ix. 6; Nu.
xxxv. 21.
Thales Milesius,
one of the wise
men of Greece,
being asked what
was the most
difficult in life,
answered, "For
a tyrant to live
to old age." The
application may
be extended to
the cruel, bloodthirsty, and murderers.
Murder is the
act of wilfully
and feloniously
killing a person
upon malice aforethought.—*C. Buck.*
c Dr. Lightfoot.
d Whitecross.

Cain's posterity

falsehood, one sin leads to another. **am .. keeper?** repudiating fraternal regard. Am I to be accountable for one who should take care of himself? (10) **what .. done?** dost thou know the extent of thy crime? **voice .. ground,**[b] the murdered Abel not so voiceless as Cain might deem, concealment is vain. (11) **cursed .. earth,** fr. the ground thus moistened by thy bro.'s blood a curse arises to thee. (12) **tillest .. strength,** *lit.* it shall not add to yield. Cain doomed to harder toils. **vagabond, wanderer,** "a wretched outcast, abhorred and rejected of his kind."

The two brothers (comp. Jo. i. 42).—Observe—I. That earthly relationships involve the duty of spiritual care. II. That they afford peculiar opportunities for the discharge of this duty. III. That, according as the spirit of Christ, or that of selfishness, is possessed, will this duty be fulfilled or neglected. IV. That concerning the performance of this duty an account will be required. V. That earthly relationships, according to the manner in which they are used, become an eternal blessing or bane.[c]

Responsibilities of man.—Of him to whom much is given much shall be required.—Those whom God has favoured with superior faculties, and made eminent for quickness of intention and accuracy of distinction, will certainly be regarded as culpable in His eye for defects and deviations, which in souls less enlightened may be guiltless. But surely none can think without horror on that man's condition, who has been more wicked in proportion as he had more means of excelling in virtue, and used the light imparted from heaven only to embellish folly, and shed lustre upon crimes and infidelity.[d]

13—15. (13) **punishment,** *lit.* sin. **greater .. bear,** greater than can be forgiven. (14) **driven .. earth,** fr. the part I have hitherto cultivated. **face .. hid,** fr. the favoured spot on wh. Thy protecting glance falls. **fugitive .. earth,**[a] fr. all dear and familiar spots. **one .. me,** fr. the time that had elapsed since the creation (v. 4, 5) it is quite possible that there were many men now on the earth. (15) **Lord .. him,** God is ever merciful. **sevenfold,**[b] manifold, utter, complete vengeance. **mark,** not necessarily a mark or brand on Cain. The LXX. says, "God set a sign bef. Cain to persuade him that whosoever should find him should not kill him."

The sparing of Cain's life.—Observe that—I. Abel was happier dying than Cain living. II. The righteousness of God's providences is not to be judged of only according to outward appearances. III. The greatest seeming earthly prosperity may be the greatest punishment.[c]

The effect of remorse.—The cruel Al Montaser, having assassinated his father, was afterwards haunted by remorse. As he was one day admiring a beautiful painting of a man on horseback, with a diadem encircling his head, and a Persian inscription, of which he inquired the meaning, he was told that it signified, "I am Shiunyeh, the son of Kosru, who murdered my father, and possessed the crown only six months." He turned pale, as if struck by a sentence of death. Frightful dreams interrupted his slumbers; and he died at the early age of twenty-five.[d]

16—18. (16) **presence,** His special presence, seat of His worship. **Nod** (*flight, exile*), the land of the wanderer. The *terra incognita* beyond the centre of population. (17) **and .. wife,** who, still faithful to the wretched man, followed him in his wanderings. **Enoch** (*dedicated*), perh. the name is a sign of Cain's repentance. **city .. Enoch,**[a] called it not after his own, now infamous, name. (18) **Irad** (*wild ass*). **Mehujael** (*smitten of God*). **Methusael** (*man of God*). **Lamech** (*powerful*).

The city of Cain.—Cain is a type of the worldling, cut off from God, whose all is in this life, and who has no hope of heaven. I. His thought is of living here always. A city is a settled place of residence, meant to endure long. II. His ambition and pride. Great pomp and state in cities. III. His covetousness. Money made and hoarded in cities. IV. His luxuriousness. Cities are scenes of luxury and vice. There is Satan's seat.[b]

The benefits of cities.—I bless God for cities. Cities have been as lamps of life along the pathway of humanity and religion. Within them Science has given birth to her noblest discoveries. Behind their walls Freedom has fought her noblest battles. They have stood on the surface of the earth like great breakwaters, rolling back or turning aside the swelling tide of oppression. Cities, indeed, have been the cradles of human liberty. They have been the active centres of almost all Church and State reformation. Having, therefore, no sympathy with those who, regarding them as the excrescences of a tree, or the tumours of disease, would raze our cities to the ground, I bless God for cities.[c]

19—22. (19) **two wives,** Lamech doomed to infamy as the first recorded polygamist. **Adah** (*ornament, beauty*). **Zillah** (*shade*). (20) **Jabal** (*a stream*). **father .. cattle,** he inaugurated a nomad, or migratory life; like that adopted by present Bedouins. (21) **Jubal** (*music*) **.. father,** originator, inventor. **harp,** Heb. *Kinoor*, prob. similar in shape to present harp, but of rude construction. **organ,** Heb. *oogab*, mouth-organ, flute, or like the pipe of Pan. (22) **Tubal-cain** (*metal-worker*), prob. the original of the Gk. Vulcan. **Naamah** (*pleasant*)—How sugg. are these names and brief descriptions of primitive life, "in the days when earth was young."

The evils of polygamy.—Polygamy not only violates the constitution of nature, and the apparent design of the Deity, but produces to the parties themselves, and to the public, the following bad effects:—Contests and jealousies amongst the wives of the same husband; distracted affections, or the loss of all affection in the husband himself; a voluptuousness in the rich which dissolves the vigour of their intellectual as well as active faculties, producing that indolence and imbecility, both of mind and body, which have long characterised the nations of the East; the abasement of one half of the human species, who, in countries where polygamy obtains, are degraded into instruments of physical pleasure to the other half; neglect of children; and the manifold and sometimes unnatural mischiefs which arise from a scarcity of women.[a]

23, 24. (23) **hear .. speech,** the last we hear of the posterity of Cain—beginning and ending so far as hist. is concerned, with a manslayer. This address is the oldest snatch of poetry known. **slain .. hurt,** rather obscure: but it appears that L. had been insidiously attacked, or wantonly provoked, and

---

B.C. 4004.

a Ps. xlix. 11.
"Life is made up, not of great sacrifices or duties, but of little things in which smiles and kindness and small obligations given habitually, are what win and preserve the heart and secure comfort."—*Sir Humphrey Davy.*

"The price of life is greater than that any man, how wealthy soever, can compass it. Money is the monarch of this world, but not of the next."—*J. Trapp.*

b *T. G. Horton.*
v. 17. *Philo. Wks.*, i. 286.
c *Dr. Guthrie.*

Lamech
"I believe that the ages which are to follow this will surpass our possibilities of art. The art of to-day should embody the highest life of to-day for the use of to-day; for those who have gone before us need it not, and those who will come after us will have something better."—*J. G. Holland.*

"We speak of profane arts; but there are none properly such;—every art is holy in itself; it is the son of Eternal Light."—*Tegner.*

a *C. Buck.*

"If this life is unhappy, it is a burden to us, which it is difficult to bear; if it is in every re-

B.C. 4004.

spect happy, It is dreadful to be deprived of it; so that in either case the result is the same, for we must exist in anxiety and apprehension."—La Bruyère.
a see Kalisch. It may be trans.: "For a man I have slain for my wound, and a youth for my hurt."—Murphy.
b Carpenter.

seriously wounded.ᵃ He had killed a man in self-defence: we should call this "justifiable homicide." (24) **Cain**, *etc.*, a clear distinction betw. murder and manslaughter.

The ground of Lamech's argument.—The act of Lamech, in taking to himself two wives, had probably excited the jealousy of some young man, says Geddes, who under the impulse of this passion had attacked and wounded Lamech, and whom Lamech in his own defence had slain. To allay the fears of his wives, therefore, he argues, and justly, that if Cain, who had wilfully and maliciously killed his brother, was nevertheless protected from the blood-avenger by the special providence of God, he might confidently expect the same protection, since the person whom he had slain had sought and endangered his life; and that a still heavier punishment than that which was threatened to the avenger of Abel's death, would fall upon the man who should attempt to molest him.ᵇ

birth of Seth and Enos

a Ge. v. 3.

b 1 K. xviii. 24; Ps. cxvi. 17; Joel, ii. 32; Ac. ii. 21; Ro. x. 13; 1 Co. i. 2; Ac. ix. 14; xxii. 16.

c Lightfoot, who supposes that Noah is called in 2 Pe. ii. 5, the eighth person in ref. to these times, viz. the eighth in succession fr. Enos, in whose days the world beg. to be profane.

d C. Simeon, M.A.

e Mrs. Jameson.

25, 26. (25) **Seth**ᵃ (*set, appointed*), who took the place, whence his name, of his slain brother. (26) **Enos**ᵇ Heb. *Enosh* (*sorrowful, miserable*). **began .. Lord**,ᶜ prob. it means that there now began a more marked distinc. betw. the godly and ungodly. Someᶜ think now the Lord began to be called upon in a profane sense.

Institution of public worship.—Consider in what manner we should—I. Confess God. We should—1. Separate ourselves from the ungodly; 2. Make an open profession of our attachment to Christ. II. Worship Him. Publicly: because public ordinances 1. Preserve the knowledge of God in the world; 2. Are the means of perfecting His work in His people's hearts. Address—(1) Those who have others under their control; (2) Those who are acting for themselves.ᵈ

Sloth in worship.—A certain monk in one of the dependent cells at Subiaco was always inattentive to his religious duties, and, at the hour devoted to mental prayer, was seen to leave the choir, and wander forth. Benedict, coming to reprove him, saw that he was led forth by a demon in the shape of a little black boy, who pulled him by the robe (a personification of the demon of sloth). This demon, however, was visible to no other eyes but those of the saint, who, following the monk, touched him on the shoulder with his staff, and exorcised the demon, who, from that hour, troubled the sinner no more.ᵉ

CHAPTER THE FIFTH.

the death of Adam.

a Ps. li. 5; Jo. iii. 6; Job. xiv. 4.
"Grace does not run in the blood, but corruption does. A sinner begets a sinner, but a saint does not beget a saint."—M. Henry.

1—5. (1) **generations**, history and posterity—family tree. **in .. him.** (2) **male .. created**, *see* on i. 26, 27. (3) **begat .. likeness**,ᵃ Adam was made in the likeness of God—and he fell: Seth was begotten in the likeness of Adam. (4) **eight .. years**, on the longevity of the patriarchs, see *Kalisch* Intro. to this chap., and *Bush, in loc.* (5) **and .. died**, words sev. times repeated in this chap. The longest life must end.

The life and death of Adam.—Consider—I. The subject of this brief narration,—Adam, the first of men. Notice him as—1. A compound being. He had both body and spirit; 2. The common

[Cap. v. 6—17.] GENESIS.

head of mankind; 3. The chief of sinners; 4. A subject of God's redeeming mercy; 5. A figure or type of Christ. II. His life: he lived 930 years. Consider it in—1. Its origin; 2. Its progress; 3. Its duration. III. His death—1. A dissolution of first principles; 2. The fruit of sin; 3. A release from the vanity of this world; 4. A certain indication of our own.*

Comparison between man and a book.—Man is like a book: his birth is the Title-page of the book; his baptisme is the Epistle Dedicatory; his groans and crying, are the Epistle to the Reader; his infancy, and childhood, are the Argument, or Contents of the whole ensuing Treatise; his life, and actions, are the Subject, or Matter of the book; his sins, and errours of his life, are the Errata, or faults escaped in the printing; and his Repentance is the Correction of them. Now amongst books (we know) some are large Volumes, in *Folio;* some little ones, in *Decimo sexto;* and some are of other sizes, in *Octavo,* or *Quarto.* Again, some of these are fairer bound, some in a plainer manner; some are bound in strong velame, or leather, and some in thin paper. Some again have Piety for their Subject, and treat of Godlinesse; others are prophane Pamphlets, full of wantonnesse, and folly; but in the last page of every one of them, there stands a word, which is FINIS, implying the end of all.*

6—11. (6) **Seth .. Enos,** *see* on iv. 25, 26. (7) **begat .. daughters,** prob. many, the formula is oft. repeated to indicate the rapid increase of the race; and fulfilment of original promise. (9) **Cainan**ᵃ (*possession*) or Kenan.

Brief records of lives.—Notice—I. The longevity of the antediluvian race. This longevity—1. Might be explained on natural principles; 2. Was for special ends; 3. Contributed to their depravity. II. The poverty of human history. III. The materialising tendencies of sin. IV. The inevitableness of man's mortality. These men lived long, yet of each it is said "he died." V. The blessedness of practical godliness—Enoch.ᵇ

"*And he died.*"—A certain libertine of a most abandoned character, happened one day to stroll into a church, where he heard the 5th chapter of Genesis read, importing that so long lived such and such persons, and yet the conclusion was, "they died." Enos lived 905 years, and he died. Seth 912, and he died —Methuselah 969, *and he died.* The frequent repetition of the words *he died,* notwithstanding the great length of years they lived, struck him so deeply with the thought of death and eternity, that, through Divine grace, he became a most exemplary Christian.

12—17. (12) **Mahalaleel**ᵃ (*praise of God*). (15) **Jared**ᵇ (*descent*) or Jered.ᶜ

The moral characteristics of man.—Every man is a missionary now and for ever, for good or for evil, whether he intends or designs it or not. He may be a blot, radiating his dark influence outward to the very circumference of society; or he may be a blessing, spreading benediction over the length and breadth of the world: but a blank he cannot be. There are no moral blanks; there are no neutral characters. We are either the sower that sows and corrupts, or the light that splendidly illuminates, and the salt that silently operates; but being dead or alive, every man speaks.ᵈ

B.C. 4004.

"The Chinese apply to different ages certain terms. The age ten is called the opening degree; twenty, you'll expired; thirty, strength and marriage; forty, officially apt; fifty, error-knowing; sixty, cycle-closing; seventy, rare bird of age; eighty, rusty-visaged; ninety, delayed; one hundred, age's extremity."—*Sir J. Bowring.*

r. 3. *A. Burgess, Orig. Sin,* ii. 110.
b *Anon.*
c *R. Gore.*

Seth's posterity
a Lu. iii. 37; 1 Ch. i. 2.

"In a Sabbath gathering of Quakers, some years ago, an aged and venerable-looking man arose, and with prophet-like authority said, 'Many say it is a solemn thing to die; but, bethink you all, and bethink you well, it is a solemn thing to live.' That witness was true."—*S. Coley.*

b *Dr. Thomas.*

a 1 Ch. i. 2.
b Lu. iii. 37.
c 1 Ch. i. 2.
"The life of man is summ'd in birthdays and in sepulchres."
—*H. K. White.*
"At twenty years of age, the will reigns; at thirty, the wit; and at forty, the judgment."—*Gratian.*
d *Chalmers.*

Enoch's translation

a Lu. iii. 37; Ho. xi. 5; Jude 14.
b 1 Ch. i. 3.
c 1 Ch. i. 3.
d Ge. vi. 9; xvi. 1; xxiv. 40; Ps. xvi. 8; cxvi. 9; cxxviii. 1; 1 K. iii. 6; 2 K. xx. 3; Lu. i. 6; Ac. ix. 31; Ga. v. 16; 2 Co. v. 7; 1 Jo. i. 6, 7; Il. 6; Am. iii. 3.
e Ho. xi. 5.
f Delitzsch. "We are convinced that the 'taking away' of Enoch is one of the strongest proofs of the belief in a future state, prevailing among the Hebs.: without this belief the hist. of Enoch is a perfect mystery, a hieroglyph without a clue, a commencement without an end." *Ka'isch.*
g R. Balgarnie.
h Bp. Simpson.

Methuselah and Noah

a 1 Ch. i. 3; Lu. iii. 36.
b "As that in his time the race would be relieved fr. the need of eating vegetable food, and hence of the toilsome raising of it.—*Ka'isch.* That the curse in consequence of sin had so increased with the progress of crime as to become an intolerable burden, and that by N. crime and tho curse would be abated."—*Bp. Sherlock.*
c vt. 10; vii. 13, 1 Ch. i. 4; Ge. ix. 20—27.
d 1 Ch. i. 4.
e Dr. Cheever.

B.C. 4004.

18—24. (18) **Enoch**[a] (*dedicated*) or Hanoch.[b] (21) **Methuselah**[c] (*man of the dart*). (22) **walked .. God,**[d] passed his life in intimate communion with God. Walked with as a friend. (24) **and .. him,** was translated.[e] "The dread monotony of 'and he died' is now first broken through."[f]

Every-day religion.—This walking with God implies agreement, trust, friendship, progress in knowledge and holiness. Observe that Enoch "walked with God" without—I. A Bible. Slaves to the letter. Interpret precept into practice. "Sermons in stones, God in everything." II. A church. Deduct chapel-going from our worship, and what is left? III. The sacraments. Every meal should be a sacrament. IV. Saint-fellowship. Times of degeneracy and sin, when the child of God stands alone.[g]

Walking with God.—I. That it is possible for man to walk with God. How is this brought about? The word Enoch means "trained," or "educated." His good training brought with it this happy state. II. That Enoch set himself apart purposely to walk with God. Of what importance is decision! III. That he was enabled to overcome all difficulties by means of faith. Faith, the source of all our triumphs. IV. That he not only exercised this faith for himself, but spent his life in doing good. He was "a preacher of righteousness."

The influence of godliness.—John Smith, the Wesleyan preacher, of England, was distinguished by no remarkable mental power or culture. The beginning of his ministry was a failure, which drove him nearer to Christ, till his power became akin to the miraculous. His presence carried the power of God with it. It was claimed that when he entered an audience an additional spiritual influence could be felt. His word was with power. His life was power, because he walked with God. Rev. Benjamin Abbott was a man of like power, whose influence could only be ascribed to his godliness.

25—32. (25) **Lamech**[a] (*powerful*). (27) **and .. died,** acc. to usual calculation he died in the yr. of the deluge. (29) **Noah** (*comfort*). **saying .. cursed,** of wh. there have been many inconclusive explanations.[b] (32) **Shem**[c] (*name*). **Ham** (*warm, black*). **Japheth**[d] (*widely spreading*).

The longest life and its lessons.—In dwelling upon this text I shall—I. Take a simple survey of the age and manners of the antediluvian world. The youth of the world was the season of man's greatest age; perhaps, also, of man's greatest wickedness. II. Draw some important lessons from this survey: 1. The agglomerative tendencies of human depravity; 2. The vanity of earthly things; 3. The power of an endless life; 4. The great natural wickedness of the heart; 5. That mere duration of years does not constitute a long life, but the fulfilment of life's ends; 6. The danger of religious procrastination.[e]

Death universal.—No sex is spared, no age exempt. The majestic and courtly roads which monarchs pass over, the way that men of letters tread, the path the warrior traverses, the short and simple annals of the poor—all lead to the same place; all terminate, however varied in their routes, in that one enormous house which is appointed for all living. One short sentence closes the biography of every man, as if in mockery of the unsubstantial pretensions of human pride—"The days of the years of Methuselah were 969 years; and he died." There is the end of it: "And he died." Such is the frailty of this boasted man. "It is appointed unto men"—unto *all* men—"once to die."*f*

B.C. 2448.

f Dr. Punshon.

CHAPTER THE SIXTH.

1—4. [Having traced race of Seth; the hist. now descr. the growth of wickedness leading to the flood] (1) **when .. multiply,** at the *beginning* of the increase. (2) **sons .. God,** descendants of Seth :*a* the godly—or *more* godly—race. **daughters .. men,** descends. of Cain. **fair,***b* beautiful. These daus. of C. were the *city dames* of that early time: the Sethites were a pastoral race. **took .. chose,** making beauty of person the basis of the choice. (3) **my .. man,** *lit.* shall not judge, *i.e.* shall not continue to rebuke, condemn. **yet .. years,** time for repentance bef. the flood. (4) **giants,** Heb. *Nephilim,* ref. not so much to bodily stature as to moral qualities—lawless, violent, cruel men. **mighty,** in the chase, exploits, wrong-doing. **renown,** *lit.* men of name. Fame founded on preceding qualities.

A wonderful and alarming fact. We have here—I. A wonderful fact implied. The Holy Spirit strives with man. Here observe— 1. Remarkable human power; 2. Amazing divine condescension; 3. Astounding human obduracy; 4. A merciful reason; 5. A benevolent purpose; 6. A mysterious method. II. An alarming fact stated. The cessation of divine influence. Such a desertion is a calamity—1. Of awful magnitude; 2. Most melancholy, terminating in despair.*c*

The danger of beauty. Gaze not on beauty too much, lest it blast thee; nor too long, lest it blind thee; nor too near, lest it burn thee. If thou like it, it deceives thee; if thou love it, it disturbs thee; if thou hunt after it, it destroys thee. If virtue accompany it, it is the heart's paradise; if vice associate with it, it is the soul's purgatory. It is the wise man's bonfire, and the fool's furnace.*d*

5—8. (5) **wickedness .. earth,** result of unholy alliances, casting off fear of God. withhold. of divine rebuke. **every .. heart,***a* *lit.* the whole fabrication. That wh. the heart forms, and wh. forms character. **continually,** without exception, or cessation. (6) **repented,** *etc.**b* speaking aft. the mann. of men. A change of dispensation, wh. in man's view is a change of inward feeling and purpose. (7) **and .. said,** purposed. **destroy,***c* *lit.* blot out; wipe out. **man .. beast,** man, the head of creation, brings ruin on all beneath him. **grace, favour,** *Chal.**e* found mercy bef. the Lord."

The sinfulness and cure of thoughts. These thoughts may be reduced to three heads—I. In regard of God. 1. Cold; 2. Debasing and unworthy; 3. Accusing; 4. Curious thoughts concerning Him. II. In regard of ourselves. Our thoughts are— 1. Ambitious; 2. Self-confident; 3. Self-applauding; 4. Foolish; 5. Immoderate and unlawful. III. In regard of others—1. Envious; 2. Censorious; 3. Jealous; 4. Revengeful.*d*

Universality of sin. The existence of sin; of sin, as an acknowledged fact—of sin as an acknowledged evil which has not only tainted the nature, but which has poured its corruption upon every part of every man; found everywhere, alike in the crowded

race of Seth and Cain

a In this view most eminent critics are agreed; as *Ainsworth, Lange, Murphy, Wordsworth, etc.:* but some say, "Sons of God" = Angels; so *Alford, Kurtz, etc.*

b "the daus. of the stirring Cainites, distiug. by the graces of nature, the embellis. of art, and the charms of music and song, even though destitute of the loftier qualities of likemindedness with God, would attract attention, and prompt to unholy alliances."—*Murphy.*

c C. W. Evan, B.A.

d F. Quarles.

Noah finds favour with God

a Ge. viii. 21; 1 K. viii. 46; Ps. xiv 2, 3; Ro. iii. 10; Pr. xx. 9; Ec. ix. 3; vii. 20; Ma. xv. 19, 20; Ro. i. 28; iii. 13; De. xxix. 19.

b He. iii. 10; Mal. iii. 6; Ja. i. 17; 1 S. xv. 29; Nu. xxiii 19; Ro. xi. 29.

c 2 Pe. ii. 5; Ex. xxxii. 13, 17 Lu, i. 30; Pr. iii. 1—4.

d S. Charnock.

"How loth is God to strike, that threats so long! Ho tha' delights *i*n re-

b.c. 2448

venge surprises his adversary; whereas he that gives long warning desires to be prevented."—*Bp. Hall.*
r. *S. J. Wesley. Wks.,* vi. 51. *F. B. Maurice,* O.T. 21.
e *Dr. Punshon.*

city streets, and among the scantier tribes of the Savannah; alike where refinement and civilisation gild and soften crime, and where in the swarthy bearded Druse it reigns tameless as the pennon that flutters upon the lance of his djeereed; alike in sordid man and lost woman, in generous youth and smiling babe —in all circumstances, in all countries, in all parallels of latitude, in all diversities of language, there is no escape, and there is no exception from this disastrous uniformity of evil. The fountain has been corrupted, and the streams of necessity must flow polluted and impure. Every mouth must be stopped, for all the world is guilty before God.*e*

the world's condition and Noah's election.

a Joh. i. 1; Ps. xxxvii. 37, 38; Hab. ii. 4; Ez. xiv. 14; Ge. xvii. 1.

b Ge. v. 32, and notes on ix. 24, and x. 21.

c Pr. xv. 3.

d 1 Pe. iv. 7; 2 Pe. iii. 7, 11, 12.

"The cause and origin of all sin is ignorance, folly, and inadvertence. There is a false proposition in the understanding before there is any misapplication in the will; and 'tis through the swimming of the head that the feet slip and lose their station. And yet the sinner is no way excusable for this his deception, because 'tis the ignorance of that which he habitually knows and he might have attended better, and 'twas his fault that he did not."—*Norris.*

e *T. Boston.*
f *Dr. Wardlaw.*

9—13. (9) **generations**, times, history, events. **Noah .. generations,**a upright and sincere in his relations with men. **and .. God,** the cause of the former. (10) **and .. sons,**b they are again named to prepare us to note their place in hist. (11) **corrupt,** in morals depraved, in religion idolatrous. **violence,** wrong-doing, lawlessness, cruelty. (12) **and .. earth,**c He still looks, always looks. **all,** with exception of one family. **had .. way,** had wilfully perverted its right manner of life. (13) **end .. come,**d of human wickedness and Divine forbearance: day of grace ended. **behold .. earth,** grace being scorned, justice will be severely tested.

Cleaving to the Lord in a declining time.—I. The truth of the statement that in the most declining generation, God has still some, though few, that cleave to Him. II. How it is that the declining of a generation comes to be so general, that so very few are left retaining their integrity. 1. The corruption of human nature is the springhead; 2. Neglect of religious education of those growing up notably advances it; 3. Corruption of manners thus prevailing serves to corrupt others; 4. The removal of the good takes away all restraint on it. III. Why some, though few, are still left preserving their integrity, in such a generation. Because—1. God is faithful in His promises; 2. He will not leave Himself without a witness at any time; 3. Therein appears the power of His grace; 4. He preserves them for a seed to better days.*e*

The fears and hopes of the wicked.—He has his fears; they are realised: he has his hopes; they are frustrated and lost. The fears are well founded: the hopes delusive and vain. They are based and built on false and deceitful views of himself and God. They have no foundation in truth. They are like the house built on the sand, which may stand in the summer's sunshine and calm, but gives way with tremendous and utter downfall, before the storm and the flood of winter. "His expectation shall perish." He flattered himself with its stability; but it was while it was untried: in the end he is buried in its ruins. "His hope is as the giving up of the ghost." The vision that has deceived him,— the unreal phantom that has cheated his eyes and allured his wandering steps onward and upward to the gates of hell, shall vanish then in "the blackness of darkness for ever!"—all his fears fulfilled; all his hopes blasted!*f*

the ark

a Used in Asia for ships, in Athens for coffins.

14—17. (14) **ark,** Heb. *tebrah* (word found only in hist. of Moses and Noah)= hollow vessel, chest. **gopher,** woods of pitch: prob. the cypress.*a* **rooms,** nests, cells. **pitch .. pitch,** lit., coat it with a coating. (15) **fashion,** taking the cub. at

21 *in.*, it was 525 ft. long : 87 ft. 6 in. broad : 52 ft. 6 in. high.*b*
Or, taking the cub. at 18 *in.*, it had a tonnage of 43,413 = to twenty ships of 2,100 tons ea.*c* It was prob. not unlike a huge house on a raft. (16) **window**, light: *i.e.* N. was to provide for the lighting of the A. **cubit .. above**, *i.e.* the ridge of the roof was to be a cub. higher than the eaves. **lower .. it**, *i.e.* the ark. (17) **flood**, *etc.*, this explains to N. the use of the A., and the instrument of destruction.

The preaching of the ark.—The ark appears as—I. A memorial of Divine goodness. It reminds us of His regard. 1. For His saints ; 2. For the families of His saints ; 3. For the world. All are invited to enter. II. A testimony to Noah's faith. 1. It was on account of Noah's faith the ark was devised ; 2. Faith built and furnished it ; 3. By faith Noah entered ; 4. Faith sustained him there. III. A symbol of the Saviour. It was—1. A refuge ; 2. A home ; 3. A temple ; 4. A conveyance. IV. A beacon for the sinner. It—1. Proclaims the wilfulness of sinners ; 2. Warns us of the power of sin.*d*

A tradition of the flood.—Mythology represents a woful, bloody, wicked, iron age, when avarice prevailed, the affections were dethroned, war and slaughter desolated the earth, and the gods abandoned it. At this state of things, Jupiter burned with anger, and called a council of the gods. He addressed them, setting forth the awful condition of things upon the earth, and announced his determination to destroy all its inhabitants, and provide a new race, worthy of life, and true worshippers of the gods. He took a thunderbolt, and was about to launch it upon the world to destroy it by fire, when he thought it might enkindle the heavens also. He then resolved to drown it. He made the clouds pour out torrents of rain. He called on Neptune for aid, who unloosed the rivers, and poured the oceans over their shores. Flocks, herds, men, houses, and temples were swept away. Only here and there a hill-top projected above the all-pervading ocean. "The fishes swim among the tree-tops. Where the graceful lambs played but now, unwieldy sea-calves gambol. The wolf swims among the sheep, the yellow lions and tigers struggle in the water. The strength of the wild boar serves him not, nor his swiftness the stag. The birds fall with weary wing into the water, having found no land for a resting-place. At length, Parnassus alone, of all the mountains, over-topped the waves ; and the Deucalion and his wife Pyrrha, of the race of Prometheus, found refuge,—he a just man, and she a faithful worshipper of the gods." Then Jupiter scattered the clouds ; and Neptune caused Triton, with his shell, to sound a retreat to the waters, and they returned to their accustomed courses. Deucalion and his wife went to a surviving temple, to worship, and obtain instruction from the gods. They received instruction, which they understood to mean, that they should go forth, casting stones behind them. They did so ; and the slimy stones began to grow into the human form, like a block in the hands of the sculptor. Those thrown by the man became men, and those by the woman became women. Thus was the earth repeopled with a hardy race, adapted to labour as we find ourselves to be at this day, giving plain indications of our origin.

18—22. (18) **establish**, make sure. **covenant**, testament, promise. **thou .. thee**, 8 souls, 4 married pairs. (19) **two**, *lit.*

B.C. 2118.

a fins in Egypt for mummy cases. It is said that the gates of St. Peter's at Ro., made of cypress, suffered no decay in 1,100 years.

b The Great Eastern is 680 ft. long, 83 ft. broad; 58 ft. deep; light draught, 12,000 tons. The ark was as high as Solomon's temple, five times as long, and twice as wide.

c These would carry 20,000 men, besides cannon, and stores, &c., for six mos.

"A life of the most absolute devotedness to God is the only righteous way of living; no man lives a righteous life that doth not live a devoted life."—*Howe.*

d R. A. Griffin.

"The wicked world could not flout him out of his faith; but that 'moved with fear'(He. xi. 7), he preacheth, and buildeth, and finisheth; every stroke upon the ark being a real sermon (as Nazianzen hath it) to forewarn them to flee from the wrath to come; which yet they did not,—no, not the very shipwrights that made the ark,—but were all buried together, in one universal grave of waters."—*Trapp.*

Noah's obedience

[Cap. vii. 1—6.

B.C. 2448.

a Alford sees a discrepancy in the two accs., and accepts as an explanation Delitzsch's supplement theory; i.e., "The original document spoke of only two of ea. kind taken in by N., the supplements specifies this more clearly fr. sources wh. gave more particulars."
b Anon
r. 18. C. Marriott, M.A., i. 51; Dr. E. Burton, Univ. Ser., 385.
r. 22. Jon. Edwards, Wks., ii. 51; C. Simeon, Wks., i. 75; S. F. Surtees, Noah's Obedience.
c Spencer.

by twos, i.e. by pairs. The number of twos or pairs of ea. kind is given presently vii. 2.ª **to .. alive**, nourish, preserve fr. flood. (20) **come**, their instincts overruled, and guided, by their creator. (21) **food**, herbs, fruits. (22) **according**, persevering for 120 yrs. till the work was done.

Noah's obedience.—I. The rule of Noah's obedience—"all that God commanded." Mankind needs a rule, that should—1. Come forth from God; 2. Be practicable in its requirements; 3. Be plain and circumstantial; 4. Be beneficial. II. Its nature. 1. Pious in principle; 2. Prompt and decided in action; 3. Laborious in exercise; 4. Universal in extent; 5. Persevering in its course; 6. Successful in its objects.b

Mercy in judgment.—It is observable, that the Roman magistrates, when they gave sentence upon any one to be scourged, had a bundle of rods, tied hard with many knots, laid before them. The reason was this,—that whilst the beadle was untying the knots, which he was to do by order, and not in any other hasty or sudden way, the magistrate might see the deportment and carriage of the delinquent,—whether he was sorry for his fault, and showed any hope of amendment,—that then he might recall his sentence, or mitigate his punishment: otherwise, he was corrected so much the more severely. Thus God in the punishment of sinners,—how patient is he! how loth to strike! how slow to anger!c

B.C. 2349.

God invites Noah into the ark

a 1 Pe. iii. 20; Pr. xiv. 26; Ps. xci. 7, 8; Zep. ii. 3; Is. iii. 10, 11; Ps. xxxiii. 18, 10.

"What a wonder of mercy is this that I here see! one poor family called out of a world, and, as it were, eight grains of corn fanned fr. a whole barnfull of chaff."— Bp. Hall.

"Just one week was allowed for N. to embark, and for the world to repent; and what a week was this."—Bush.

b M. Badger.

r. 1. J. Burder, viii. S., iv. 25; D. Lamont, iii. 311 C. Simeon, i. 78; A. Roberts, M.A.,

CHAPTER THE SEVENTH.

1—6. (1) **come .. ark**,ª He was there who gave the invitation: this, a call to prepare to enter. **for**, *etc.* divine testy. to moral character. (2) **clean .. sevens**, some of wh. would be needed for sacrifice. (3) **fowls .. sevens**, or. as LXX. says, seven of the clean and two of the unclean. (4) **yet .. days**, to yet, *etc., i.e.* the seventh day aft. this. (5) **Noah .. him**, as bef. in building the ark; so now in these final preparations. (6) **Noah .. old**, *lit.* a son of 600 yrs.: *i.e.* going on his 600th. yr. **was .. earth**, *i.e.* began to be.

Fathers invited into the ark.—I. There is provision in the ark for thee and for all thy house. II. There is no safety for you or for your children out of it. III. You should enter, and seek to bring all your children in with you, not only because your salvation depends upon it, but because it may be indispensable to theirs. 1. Your children, that are outside, will not believe that there is a storm coming. Who can convince them of their error but you? 2. They need an Almighty arm around them to protect them. What prayers can obtain this so well as yours? 3. They need also the influence of example, as well as of instruction and prayer. Whose example can influence them like that of their father.b

A voice from Assyria.—"The cuneiform inscription which I have recently found and translated gives a long and full account of the deluge. It contains the version or tradition of this event which existed in the early Chaldean period at the city of Erech (one of the cities of Nimrod), now represented by the ruins of Warka. In this newly-discovered inscription the account of the deluge is put as a narrative into the mouth of Xisuthrus or Noah. He relates the wickedness of the world, the command to build the ark, its building, the filling of it, the deluge, the resting of the ark on a mountain, the sending out of the birds, and other matters. The narrative has a closer resemblance to the account transmitted by the Greeks from Berosus, the Chaldean historian, than to the Biblical history, but it does not differ materially from either; the principal differences are as to the duration of the deluge, the name of the mountain on which the ark rested, the sending out of the birds, etc. The cuneiform account is much longer and fuller than that of Berosus, and has several details omitted both by the Bible and the Chaldean historian. This inscription opens up many questions of which we knew nothing previously, and it is connected with a number of other details of Chaldean history which will be both interesting and important. This is the first time any inscription has been found with an account of an event mentioned in Genesis."c

B.C. 2349.

25; *Dr. J. Kitto*, Bibl. Ill., 1. 145; *Bp. Newton*, Wks. i. 165. *v*. 4. *J. Morton*, i. 121.

"For if he had been led by sense, he would have fled as far as Jonah did, ere ever he had gone about it."— *Trapp*.

c *Mr. G. Smith, of the Brit. Museum.*

7—10. (7) **because** .. **flood**, *lit*. fr. the face of : *i.e.* for fear of. (8) **of clean**, *etc.*,a in the proportions ordered. (9) **two** .. **female**, ea. two being a pair in rel. to sex. (10) **after** .. **days**, *lit*. at the seventh of the days.

The judgment of God on the first world.—Look at it as—I. A sign of light for the understanding of the course of the world. II. An everlasting sign of warning. III. A sign of salvation full of the blessing of salvation.b

Effects of judgments.—In the province of Quito, after the tremendous earthquake of 1797, a number of marriages were contracted between persons who had neglected for many years to sanction their union by the sacerdotal benediction. Children found parents by whom they had never till then been acknowledged; restitutions were promised by persons who had never been accused of fraud; and families who had long been at enmity were drawn together by the tie of common calamity. But if this feeling seemed to calm the passions of some, and open the heart to pity, it had a contrary effect on others, rendering them more rigorous and inhuman.c

Noah accepts the invitation

a Is. xi. 6, 7.

b *Lange*.

"The wages that sin bargains with the sinner are life, pleasure and profit; but the wages it pays him with are death, torment, and destruction: he that would understand the falsehood and deceit of sin, must compare its promises and payments together.—*South*.

c *Humboldt*.

11—16. (11) **in** .. **month**, 17th of April or May.a **all** .. **deep**,b *lit*. fountains of the great deep: not necessarily of the sea. **windows**, sluices, flood-gates. LXX. cataracts. **heaven**, the clouds. (12) **rain** .. **nights**, continued falling in an unceasing *torrent* through all that time. (13) **In** .. **day**, precisely. (14) **bird** .. **sort**, *lit*. of every wing. · (15) **they** .. **Noah**, God collected, selected, guided them. (16) **Lord** .. **in**. *lit*.c closed round ab. him. LXX. "shut the ark on the outside of him." *Chal*. "protected over him." Enclosed him, excluded others.

The Lord shut him in.—Noah was shut in—I. Away from all the world. II. With His God. "*Come* thou into the ark," said God: by which He clearly showed that He Himself meant to dwell there. III. So that no evil could reach. Floods did but lift him heavenward, and winds did but waft him on the way. Outside the ark all was ruin ; inside all was rest and peace. IV. That he could not even desire to come out. The same door that shuts him in shuts all others out.d

Wonderful care.—When we think of the labour required to rear the few that are in our households,—the weariness, the anxiety, the burden of life,—how wonderful seems God's work! for he carries heaven and earth, and all realms, in his bosom.

the flood begins

a *Kalisch*.
b Ma. xxiv. 37—, 39; 1 Th. v. 3.
c Ps. xlvi. 1—3; Ma. xxv. 10; Lu. xiii. 24, 25; Jo. x. 27, 28; 1 Pe. i. v.

"The margin has the 'flood-gates of heaven were opened.' In the East, when the rain falls in torrents, the people say, 'the heavens are broken.'"— *Roberts*.

"There is more bitterness following upon sin's ending, than ever there was sweetness flowing from sin's acting. You that see nothing

B.C. 2349.

but *well in its commission, will suffer nothing but woe in its conclusion. You that sin for your profits, will never profit by your sins."—*Dyer*.
d C. H. Spurgeon.
e Beecher.

the flood prevails for forty days
The theory of a universal deluge cannot be reasonably entertained. Astronomy, geology, and zoology, ea. furnish evidence against it. A partial deluge, meets the necessity of the case,—the destr. of man and his immediate surroundings,—does not violate the true sense of Scripture and is the view held by eminent critics; as *M. Poole, Bp. Stillingfleet, Pye Smith, Murphy, Geikie, Hitchcock, Perowne*, etc., etc. As to the words 'all' and 'every' etc., "Universal terms are oft. used to sig. only a very large amount in number or quantity." —*Pye Smith*. To see this, carefully comp. the following passages:— Ge. xli. 57; Ex. ix. 25; with x. 15; De. ii. 25; Ac. ii. 5; Col. i. 23; 2 Ch. ix. 23; 1 K. iv. 34, etc.
a M. Henry.
b Hasse"l.

all creatures in the world die

a Nu. xxiii. 19; Pr. xi. 21; Ma. xxv. 46; Ez. xiv. 14.
"Sin is the only thing in the

Many think that God takes no thought for anything less than a star or a mountain, and is unmindful of the little things of life; but, when I go abroad, the first thing which I see is the grass beneath my feet, and, nestling in that. flowers smaller yet, and, lower still, the mosses with their inconspicuous blooms, which beneath the microscope glow with beauty. And if God so cares for "the grass of the field, which to-day is, and to-morrow is cast into the oven," shall he not much more care for the minutest things of your life, "O ye of little faith"?*e*

17—20. (17) **forty .. earth,** *i.e.* descending on it. **and .. increased,** fed by the fountains and the rain. (18) **prevailed,** overcame absorption and exhalation. **went,** *lit.* walked: *i.e.* with a gentle motion. (19) **upon .. earth,** that part of its surface known to man. **all .. hills,** in that region. **that .. heaven,** that bounded the human horizon. (20) **fifteen .. covered,** *i.e.* the average depth of water on the lowlands, and the summits of the hills of the region were submerged.

The waters of the flood a boon to Noah, but destruction to the world. I. The waters, which broke down everything else, bore up the ark. That which to unbelievers is a savour of death, is to believers a savour of life. II. The more the waters increased, the higher was the ark lifted up towards heaven. Thus sanctified afflictions are spiritual promotions; and as troubles abound, consolations much more abound.*a*

Traditions of the flood.—It is a remarkable fact that among many of the tribes of the North American Indians there are several traditions held respecting the creation and the flood. When referring to this subject a writer in the *Quarterly Review* for March, 1840, says:—"The various nations have different notions of the origin of their race. It is, nevertheless, an extraordinary fact, vouched for by Mr. Catlin, that, of all the tribes he visited, there was no one which did not, by some means or other, connect their origin with "a big canoe," which was supposed to have rested on the summit of some hill or mountain in their neighbourhood. The Mandan Indians carry this vague Mount Ararat impression to a very remarkable extent; for Mr. Catlin found established among them an annual ceremony, held round "a great canoe," entitled in their language, "The settling of the waters," which was held always on the day in which the willow trees of their country came into blossom. On asking why that tree out of all others was selected, Mr. Catlin was informed that it was because it was from it that the bird flew to them with a branch in its mouth; and when it was inquired *what* bird it was, the Indians pointed to the dove, which it appears was held so sacred among them that neither man, woman, nor child would injure it. Indeed, the Mandans declared that even their dogs instinctively respected this bird."*b*

21—24. (21) **flesh .. man,***a* the impossibility of escape beyond a hilly boundary of the deluged district will be clear to any who consider the dreadful violence of this flood-storm, and the difficulty of progress through ordinary storms. (22) **the .. life,** *lit.* the breath of the spirit of life. (23) **every .. substance,** *lit.* every thing that stood up. *i.e.* whatever by the principle of life is capable of maintaining an erect posture. **Noah .. ark,** how strange and startling to them within; the cry, and presently the scene, without. The ark.—the only safe spot in the habitable globe (safety alone in Christ). (24) **waters .. days,** by wh. time not only all life, but all old landmarks, etc., would be "wiped out."

The grandeur of Noah's faith.—Contrast it with—I. The universal apostasy. II. The dreadful judgment. III. Its once great task and labour. IV. The sport of the world. V. The terrors of the flood. VI. The terrors of the animal world enclosed with him—the ark, a lion's den.[b]

Every living creature.—We have some reason to doubt, from the fossil remains of animals now discovered, which have not yet been found alive upon the present earth, whether *every living creature* was included in this strong expression; and, though, from the remarkable circumstance of the similarity of all languages in certain common expressions, and in the universal tradition of the deluge found among the most distant and savage nations, we feel assured that the whole existing race of *man* on the whole earth, has sprung from Noah and his family; we have no evidence to lead us to the same conclusion with respect to quadrupeds, or birds. It appears probable, that we ought to consider the strong expression used in the record, *of every living thing of all flesh,* in the same sense as we find it in various other parts of Scripture; and, indeed, as such expressions are often used in our own, and in other languages, that is, not as literally meaning every *created being* over the whole globe, but merely *a great number.*[c]

B.C. 2349.

world that is contrary to God. God is light, and that is darkness; God is beauty, and that is ugliness and deformity. All sin is direct rebellion against God; and with what notions soever we sugar it and sweeten it, yet God can never smile upon it. He will never make a truce with it. God and sin will never agree together. He that committeth sin is of the devil."—*Cudworth.*

b *Lange.*

c *Fairholme.*

v. 23. *J. B. S. Carwithin,* Bamp. Lec., 73; *J. W. Warter,* ii. 231.

CHAPTER THE EIGHTH.

1—5. (1) **remembered,**[a] practically. Had him in mind, and did him good. **wind .. earth,** a beating, drying wind. **assuaged,** *lit.* settled down. depressed. (2) **fountain .. rain,** *etc.,* as the wind operated, the flood-storm ended. (3) **the .. continually,** *lit.,* going and returning: *i.e.* gradually but ceaselessly settling down. (4) **in .. month,** five clear months after begin. of flood. **upon .. Ararat,** not necessarily on the top of Mt. Ararat wh. is not only 17,750 ft. high; but for at least 4,000 ft. fr. the summit is cov. with perpetual snow. Some spur of A. must be meant. (5) **tops .. seen,** prob. the highlands of Armenia, 3,000 or 4,000 ft. above the sea.

The figures of the coming salvation.—I. The resting of the ark, the firmly-grounded church. II. The emerging of the mountain-tops, the mountains of God as the sign of heaven. III. The flight of the dove, "the longing of the creature." IV. The dove with the olive-leaf, the spirit of life with the announcement of peace. V. The remaining out of the dove, and the opening of the ark, the free intercourse of the church and the consecrated world.[b]

Ararat.—Ararat, the name of a mountainous country in Armenia, on one of the peaks on which it is said that Noah's ark rested after the deluge, Gen. viii. 4. Tavernier says, that there are many monasteries upon one of the mountains of this region, which has obtained the name anciently given to the whole region, which the Armenians call Meresoussar, because the

the waters decrease

a Ge. xix. 29; Ps. xxxvi. 6; Jon. iv. 11; Ma. x. 22.

Ararat *(holy land)* the Heb. word is twice rendered Armenia in the A.V. (2 K. ix. 37; Is. xxxvii. 38). The mt. is called by the natives *Massis;* by the Turks, *Agridagh;* and by the Persians, *Kuh-i-Nuh, i.e.,* Noah's Mt. The region is volcanic. Great earthquake in 1840. Armenians used to say the mt. has never been ascended; but Parrot reached the top in 1829, aft. two efforts; and in 1856, 5 Englishmen succeeded

GENESIS. [Cap. viii. 6—12.

B.C. 2349.

to the astonishment of the people of the country.
b Lange.
"Though the ark be driven in a tempestuous sea, saith one, yet it shall neither sink nor split, while we sail in the thoughts of Almighty God."— *Trapp.*
c Green's Bib. Dict.

ark stopped there. Tournefort says, that the top of Mount Ararat is inaccessible, both from its great height and the snow it is covered with; it lies twelve miles east of Erivan, in a vast plain, having no other mountain near it, and so high as to be seen at the distance of ten days' journey. Sir R. K. Porter, in his Travels, has given a beautiful description of this celebrated mountain. It has two peaks about seven miles apart from each other, and in this space he supposes the ark to have rested. It must, however, be remarked, that whatever distinction was conferred by the resting of the ark, is enjoyed by this mountain only in common with many other eminences in that region. The aspect of this country was very much changed by a series of earthquakes, lasting from June 20 to September 1, 1840.*c*

the raven and the dove

The raven is considered a bird of ill-omen, bec. Noah could learn nothing favourable; while the dove bringing an olive leaf is regarded as an emblem of peace. "In the deluge of pleasure, the dove of piety can find no place where to set the sole of her foot. But punishment will take place where piety can find none."— *Willes.*

a J. G. Owen, B.A.

Peace makes plenty, plenty makes pride, pride breeds quarrel, and quarrel brings war: war brings spoil, and spoil poverty; poverty patience, and patience peace. So peace brings war, and war brings peace.

v. 9. C. E. Kennaway, The Dove and the Ark.

6—9. (6) **end .. days,** fr. first app. of mts. **window,** Heb. *hallon.* not the word trans. window bef. Here some aperture. (7) **raven,** if the waters had suf. subsided it would not return. **went .. fro,** fr. the Ark and back. **until .. ground,** feeding prob. on floating carcases. (8) **dove,** of swift and long-sustained flight, rests on dry places only, feeds on grain. (9) **dove .. foot,** no dry spot: doves fly low, do not affect mts. **returned .. hand,** *etc.,* all this tallies with the domestic nature of the bird.

The dove's return.—Noah "pulled her in unto him into the ark." Notice—I. She did not enter willingly. Fear perhaps kept her back. Sinners do not enter into grace through fear. II. She brought nothing with her. Yet she was still taken in. III. She would be required to go forth at some future time. Converted sinners should become in their turn preachers of righteousness.*a*

The ark and the dove.

There was a noble ark
Sailing o'er waters dark,
 And wide around:
Not one tall tree was seen,
Nor flower, nor leaf of green,
 Nor e'en the ground.

Then a soft wing was spread,
And o'er the billows dread
 A meek dove flew;
But on that shoreless tide,
No living thing she spied
 To cheer her view.

So to the ark she fled,
With weary drooping head,
 To seek for rest.
Christ is the ark, my love,
Thou art the tender dove—
 Fly to His breast.

the dove and the olive leaf

a Ps. xl. 1.

"Peace is the still music of the soul. It is the calm sunset of a summer's sab-

10—12. (10) **stayed,***a* *lit.,* patiently abode. **yet .. days,** there had prob. been one such interval betw. the sending forth of raven and dove. (11) **olive,** grows in Armenia, on lower hills and plains, but not so high on mts., as walnut, apricot, etc. **pluckt off,** *i.e.,* fresh. *lit.,* a newly-pluckt olive-leaf: not a loose leaf or floating twig. There had perh. been time in the region visited by the dove, for the olive tree to shoot. **knew ..**

earth, since they were lower than the tops of trees wh. grew in the plain. (12) **which .. more,** finding now some other place of rest and safety.

The olive branch.—I have been reminded in the South Seas of the olive branches, which, ever since the days of Noah, have been emblematical of peace. One day in 1848, when Captain Morgan, Mr. Nisbet, and I were backing out into deep water, to get clear of some shallow coral patches, and to look for a better passage for our boat, the natives on the shore, thinking we were afraid of them, ran and broke off *branches* from the trees, and waved or held them erect in their raised hands. I afterwards learned that our conjecture at the time was right: it was a sign of peace and friendship. A party, for instance, who had been fighting, and wished to sue for peace, would approach the enemy with green boughs, as the signal of their pacific and friendly intentions.[b]

13—19. (13) **pass .. year,** of Noah's life. **covering,** Heb., *miksch,* used in ref. to cov. of tabern. perh. the ark was cov. with skins: or, if of wood, N. now broke up the planking. **face .. dry,** the dry earth appeared, yet still saturated. (14) **second .. month,** hence the duration of the flood was 1 yr. 10 dys.[a] (15) **and .. saying,** the new race, like the old, begin life with the divine blessing. (16) **forth,** be as confident of safety on leaving, as on entering. (17) **bring .. earth,** there had been no death in the ark. **that .. earth,** indicating the end for wh. they had been preserved. (18) **Noah .. him,** he left, as he entered, at God's bidding. (19) **after .. ark,** an orderly egress, not a tumultuous rush into liberty.

Noah's first consciousness of safety after the deluge.—On the first look-out of Noah upon the dry ground, he would probably be impressed with—I. The greatness of the calamity he had escaped. He would feel with regard to the flood—1. That it was the result of sin; 2. That it was only a faint type of the final judgment. II. The efficacy of the remedial expedient. This expedient—1. Was Divine; 2. Alone was effective; 3. Was only effective to those who committed themselves to it. III. The wisdom of his faith in God. He must have felt that it was wiser to believe in the word of God than to trust to—1. The conclusions of his own reason; 2. The uniformity of nature; 3. The current opinion of his contemporaries.[b]

Table of time of continuance of the flood; and abiding in the Ark.

Yr. of N's life.	mo.	dy.	Event.
600	2	17	The Ark entered: flood begins, vii. 11.
,,	3	27	The 40 dys. rain: the Ark floats, vii. 17.
,,	7	17	The 150 dys. (incl. the 40) the Ark rests, viii. 3, 4.
,,	10	1	The mountains visible, viii. 5.
,,	11	11	The raven sent out, viii. 6, 7.
,,	,,	18	The dove sent out, and returned, viii. 8, 9.
,,	,,	25	The dove sent, and returns with leaf, viii. 10, 11.
,,	12	2	The dove sent, and returns no more, viii. 12.
,,	,,	28	Unaccounted for. Noah waits.
601	1	1	Waters off the earth, viii. 13.
,,	,,	27	Earth dry: Noah leaves the Ark, viii. 14—19.

B.C. 2349.

bath. It is the olive branch—sign of judgment abating. It is Jerusalem, *i.e.,* the vision of peace. It is Melchizedec, king of righteousness, king of peace."—*G. S. Bowes.*

b Dr. Turner.

the earth dried

a Alford; if, however, acc. to *Ainsworth,* the Jewish yr. = 354 (6 of the 12 mos. 30 dys. ea. and 6 mos. 29 dys. ea. = 354) then by adding 11 dys. for the 27th of the 2nd mo. completed, the amount will be 365 days, or one solar year.

"Nature gives to every time and season some beauties of its own; and from morning to night, as from the cradle to the grave, is but a succession of changes so gentle and easy that we can scarcely mark their progress." *Dickens.—*

"Nature has perfections, in order to show that she is the image of God; and defects, in order to show that she is only his image." —*Pascal.*

b Dr. Thomas.

v. 15–17. *Dr. F. Nolan,* Bamp. Lect, 265.

B.C. 2349.

Noah offers sacrifice

a Ex. xx. 24; Ho. xiii. 15.
b Ep. v. 2.
c "The meaning is, that N.'s sacrifice was a grateful and acceptable to the Lord, as sweet odours are to a man."—*Bush. Chal. V.*, "The Lord accepted with favour his oblation." "The favour of satisfaction or delectation."—*Sp. Comly.*
d Je. xvii. 9; Ro. viii. 7, 8.
e Dr. Thomas.
"Men will wrangle for religion; write for it; fight for it; die for it; anything but — live for it."—*C. Colton.*

20—22. (20) **altar,**a prob. of earth. **took**..**fowl**, (*see on* vii. 2) *i.e.* of such as were suitable; as oxen, sheep, goats, doves, pigeons. **and**..**offerings,** *lit.*, ascensions, or rise-offerings: so called bec. they *went up* to the Lord in fire. (21) **smelled**..**savour,**b *lit.*, a savour of rest c (Anthropomorphic). **for**..**youth,**d God mercifully considers the nat. tendency to evil. (22) **while,** *etc.*, the world must at that moment have presented a spectacle of utter desolation as if there were an end of all the seasons.

The moral significance of winter.—I. The evanescent forms of earthly life. II. The stern aspects of nature's God. III. The retributive law of the creation. IV. The probable resuscitation of buried existence. This is a picture of the resuscitation of—1. Christian truth; 2. Conscience; 3. The human body.e

Carnal thoughts and religious worship.—Some years ago, two pious weavers were conversing together, and complaining of the trouble which they found from vain and evil *thoughts* in the solemn duties of religion. Another person of the same business overheard them, and rushing forth, said, "I always thought you two vile hypocrites; but now I know it from your own confessing. For my part, I never had such vain and wicked thoughts in my life." One of the men took a piece of money out of his pocket, and put it into his hand, adding, "This shall be yours, if, after you come from the church the next time, you can say you had not one vain thought there." In a few days he came, saying, "Here, take back your money, for I had not been five minutes in the church before I began to think how many looms could be set up in it."

CHAPTER THE NINTH.

B.C. 2349.

God's blessing on Noah and his sons

a Ge. i. 29.
b Le. xvii. 10, 11; 1 Ti. iv. 40.
"The greatest man is he who chooses right with the most invincible resolution; who resists the sorest temptation from within and without; who bears the heaviest burdens cheerfully; who is calmest in storms, and most fearless under menaces and frowns; whose reliance on truth, on virtue, and on God, is most unfaltering."—*Seneca.*
c Dr. Candlish.

1—4. (1) **blessed,** the second head of the human race commences life with a blessing, as Adam. (2) **fear**..**dread,** *etc.*, supremacy of man reasserted; but *now* on the basis of fear. (3) **every**..**you,** animal food, wh. had never been *prohibited,* is now expressly named and *permitted.* **even**..**herb,**a to this time *prob.* the sole food of man. (4) **flesh**..**life,**b prob. a prohibition ag. eating raw flesh: also ag. the *unnecessary* killing of animals. **which**..**blood,** the *vital* fluid.

The law of nature.—Look at the law—I. For the propagation of life, and increase of inhabitants on the earth—"be fruitful, and multiply." The institution of marriage same as before the flood. II. For the security and preservation of life. 1. Man's dominion over the creatures is to rest mainly on fear and dread; 2. Man's dominion over his fellow-man. The power of the sword is instituted, and is given into the hand of the magistrate. III. For the support or sustenance of life. Animal food is allowed to be eaten under certain restrictions. The former fertility of the earth, found before the fall, is somewhat restored.c

Man's power over the animal creation.—During the Sepoy rebellion in India a party of British soldiers were being towed up the Indus on flats by a steamer. From time to time they stopped, landed, cooked a meal, and rested for a short time. On one of these occasions two of the men were walking along a narrow path, with high, thick, jungly grass on each side. As they proceeded, it came into the mind of one of them that where they were was a suitable resort for tigers. Scarcely had the thought crossed him, when there emerged from the grass, and faced them, an immense tiger. He cried, and ran. The other, by a sort of stupid fascination, stared at the animal. This stare was probably their deliverance. Making off from them, the magnificent fellow leaped over a party of soldiers at cards, snapped up a dog, and left the neighbourhood.*d*

5—7. (5) **blood . . lives,***a* *i.e.*, life-blood: or, perh. "your blood *for* your lives:" *i.e.*, life for life. **at . . beast,** the ox for example.*b* **hand . . brother,***c* every man to regard every other man as his brother. (6) **whoso . . blood,** wilfully, unwarrantably. **by . . shed,***d* in way of legal retribution, not private revenge. **for . . man,***e* "to destroy man's life has in it the sin of sacrilege . . . to destroy the life of such a one is to cut short his time of probation, to abridge his day of grace, to step in betw. him and his moral Governor, to frustrate, as far as may be, God's purposes of love and mercy to his soul."*f* (7) **and you,** *etc.*, instead of taking away human life, increase it, fill the world with it.

The punishment of murder.—According to the Divine law, murder is to be punished with death (De. xix. 11, 12; 1 K. ii. 28, 29). It is remarkable that God often gives up murderers to the terrors of a guilty conscience (Ge. iv. 13, 15, 23, 24). Such are followed with many instances of Divine vengeance (2 S. xii. 9, 10); their lives are often shortened (Ps. lv. 23); and judgment of their sins is oftentimes transmitted to posterity (Ge. xlix. 7; 2 S. xxi. 1).*g*

Murder the chief of crimes.—
Murder but intentional, not wrought
To horrid act, before the eternal throne
Stands forth the first of crimes. Who dare assume,
Unwarranted, Heaven's high prerogative
O'er life and death, with double force shall find,
Turn'd on themselves the mischiefs they design'd.*h*

8—11. (8) **Noah . . him,** the sons to share in the father's blessing, and duty. (9) **covenant,** Heb. *berithi*, usually a "mutual compact," here a "solemn promise." (10) **and . . you,** *etc.*,*a* the prom. made to N. covers all that was given to him. **from . . earth,** "not only those preserved in the ark, but all other animals are to be interested in this promise."*b* (11) **and . . flood,** in the region peopled by yourselves and descendants. **neither,** and in addition **flood . . earth,***c* in any part of it whatever.

The triumphal arch of summer (on v. 8—16).—The text shows us, concerning the rainbow, that it—I. Is a token, or pledge of God's fidelity to His word. II. Is an emblem of the covenant of redemption. III. Is an apt emblem of union and harmony in the midst of diversity. IV. Well represents man's present state of probation and discipline. V. Is a striking emblem of human hopes. VI. Affords us a glimpse of the magnificence of the heavenly world, and the glory of God.*d*

The Rainbow.—
When thou dost shine, darkness looks white and fair;
Forms turn to music, clouds to smiles and air,

B.C. 2348.

d Bib. Trea.

v. 1. *J. H. Pott,* i. 246; *R. Warner,* Old Ch. Prin., i. 219.

law concerning human life
a Ps. ix. 12.
b Ex. xxi. 12, 28.
c "At the hands of the man who shall spill his bro.'s blood will I require the soul (or life) of man." —*Ch. Ver.*
The Go l was the nearest relation of a murdered person, whose duty it was to avenge his kinsman's death with his own hand—See *Cities of Refuge;* Do. xix.; *also Michaelis, Com. on Law of Moses,* ii. 195.
d "with witnesses by the sentence of the judges shall his blood."—*Ch. Ver.*
e Ge. i. 27.
f Speaker's Commentary.
g C. Buck.
h Whitehead.

there shall be no more flood

a Ps. cxlv. 9.

b Speaker's Com. wh. adds, "From wh. we can hardly fail to infer that the destr. of the lower animals was confined to a certain district, and not general throughout the earth."
c 2 Pe. iii. 6, 7; Is. liv. 7—10.

"That are of light,
Born of the shower, and colour'd by the sun;

GENESIS. [Cap. ix. 12—23.

B.C. 2348.

Which spans the heavens when April skies are bright."
J. C. Prince.
d Dr. Hitchcock.
e H. Vaughan.

the rainbow
a Nu. xiv. 4.
"Let us make (i.e. appoint) a captain, etc.;" see also 1 K. ii. 35.

It is a sugg. fact that the rainbow is never seen except in a cloud fr. wh. the rain is at the same time falling. So that if the shower reminds us of the flood; the bow in that same shower cloud shall remind us of the covenant.
b Dr. C. J. Vaughan.

c Milton.

v. 12, 13, Dr. G. Townsend, 238; F. Elwin, i. 104.
v. 13. Dr. F. Lee, Diss., ii. 1; J. P. Hewlett, 105.

the sons of Noah
See McCausland, Adam and the Adamite; and the works of Pritchard, Smith, Pickering, Knox, Laurence, etc., also Birks' Scientific Theories on the Origin of Man. Dr. Duns' Bibl. Nat. Sc., vol. i. Lyell on Antiquity of Man, in Quar. Rev., Oct., 1863. Wood's Letter on Theo. of Devel., and Ant. of Man. Poole, Genesis of Earth and Man.

a A. Helps.

Noah's drunkenness

Rain gently spends his honey-drops and pours
Balm on the cleft earth, milk on grass and flowers.
Bright pledge of peace and sunshine, the sure tie
Of thy Lord's hand, the object of His eye,
When I behold thee, though my light be dim,
Distant and low, I can in thine see Him.
Who looks upon thee from His glorious throne,
And minds the covenant betwixt all and One.*

12—17. (12) **token**, sign to you and the whole world: everywhere visible and intelligible. **for** .. **generations**, a sign as lasting as nature, whose laws produce it: must therefore endure to the end of time. (13) **set**, Heb. *nathatti*, give, often trans. with sense of "appoint" or "constitute."ᵃ **bow** .. **cloud**, the rainbow. **token** .. **earth**, the reminder of a promise to God and man. (14) **bring** .. **earth**, a rain-cloud to water the earth. **that** .. **cloud**, heretofore the terrible "window of heaven." (15) **remember**, this, in condescension to us. He would never forget His word though there were no token. (16) **I** .. **it**, let us think of that when we look upon, and admire the rainbow. (17) **God** .. **Noah**, *etc.*, this v. the summing up of the whole.

The Gospel of the Flood.—Regard the record before us—I. As a fact in history. It has a twofold aspect. It was—1. A judgment. When sin reaches a certain point, it demands God's interposition; 2. A mercy. II. In its uses. Think of it as—1. A type —a type of baptism; 2. A prophecy. It is the prediction of a last flood of fire; 3. A warning. As were the days of Noah, so shall the days of the coming of the Son of Man be.ᵇ

The Rainbow.

Then with uplifted hands, and eyes devout,
Grateful to heaven, over his head beholds
A dewy cloud, and in the cloud a bow
Conspicuous, with three listed colours gay,
Betokening peace with God, and covenant new.ᶜ

18, 19. (18) **sons**, *see* on v. 32. **Ham**, *heat*, perh. so named in all. to the *hot* regions wh. his descs. were to inhab. **Canaan**, Heb. *Kenaan*, fr. rt. *Kâna*, to humble, depress: perh. prophetic of his posterity. (19) **them** .. **overspread**, the whole race deriv. fr. these three.

Man affected by climate.—To understand any people thoroughly, we must know something of the country in which they live, or at least of that part inhabited by the dominant race. The insects partake the colour of the trees they dwell upon, and man is no less affected by the place of his habitation on the earth. Stern, arid, lofty, dignified, and isolated from the men of other nations, the Spaniard was probably the most remarkable European man in the sixteenth century. He had a clearness of conviction, and a resoluteness of purpose, which resembled the sharp atmosphere in which he had lived, that left no undecided outlines; and as, in the landscape, all variety was amply compensated for, by the vast extent of one solemn colour, so, in the Spaniard's character, there were one or two deep tints of love, of loyalty, and of religion, which might render it fervid, bigoted, and ferocious, but never left it small, feeble, or unmeaning.ᵃ

20—23. (20) **Noah** .. **husbandman**, under N. the earth begins again, and man returns to primitive occupations, he ..

[Cap. ix. 24—29.] GENESIS. 45

vineyard, prob. the art of vine-cultivation known bef. the flood.ª (21) **drank .. drunken,**ᵇ N. has been excused on the ground that he was ignorant of the strength of the wine: but prob. the abounding prosperity, and guarantee of safety, induced a culpable laxity.ᶜ **he .. tent,** so habits of intemperance strip off one's clothes and property; and uncover, disclose their mental and moral state. (22) **Ham .. father,** etc.ᵈ prob. told them mockingly. (23) **garment,** prob. the one thrown off by N. and **.. backward,** etc.ᵉ their conduct indicating profound grief, and respect for a father. even in that deplorably fallen state.

Noah's drunkenness, and his son's sin.—From the text (v. 20, 23), we learn—I. That in even the best of lives some fault may be found. 1. Perfection can never be obtained by man in this life; 2. Although the subjects of God's especial mercy, yet we are not precluded from the possibility of sin. This drunkenness was one of Noah's first acts after his preservation from the flood. II. That a sinful act on our part will generally lead to some equally sinful, or even worse, act by another. Noah's drunkenness leads to sensuality on the part of his son. Consider this act of Ham's— 1. In itself. It was an index of a corrupt mind; 2. In its relation to others. Noah's shame is Ham's gratification. 3. In its fruits. Ham and his posterity are henceforth accursed. III. That virtue will at all times meet with its proper reward. Shem and Japheth were rewarded by—1. The testimony of their own hearts; 2. The blessing of their outraged father; 3. The practical approbation of God. God was the rewarder of the brothers; He it was who should enlarge their posterity, and bind them in mutual affection.ᶠ

Degradation of drunkenness.—There is no sin which doth more deface God's image than drunkenness: it disguiseth a person, and doth even unman him. Drunkenness makes him have the throat of a fish, the belly of a swine, and the head of an ass. Drunkenness is the shame of nature, the extinguisher of reason, the shipwreck of chastity, and the murder of conscience. Drunkenness is hurtful to the body. The cup kills more than the cannon: it causes dropsies, catarrhs, apoplexies; it fills the eye with fire, and the legs with water, and turns the body into a hospital.ᵍ

An argument for drinking.—Harootune, a converted Armenian on the Harpoot mission-field, is a strong temperance man. He lives among those who love "native wine." To one who drank a glass of wine, and by way of excuse asked, "Didn't God make grapes?" he indignantly exclaimed, "God made dogs: go eat some dog-carcass! He made poisons too: go eat them, and kill yourself!"

B.C. 2348.

a If not "may it be said that mankind has been worse without wine than with it."—*Alford.*
b Pr. xx. 1; xxiii. 31, 32; Ec. vii. 20; 1 Co. x. 12.
c "Leaving all this in uncertainty, let us learn fr. N.'s intemperance how foul and detestable a vice drunkenness is." *Calvin.*

d Pr. xxx. 17; 1 Cor. xiii. 16.
"The son would never have derided his father in his shame, had he not first banished fr. his mind that reverence and deference wh. by God's command should be in children towards their parents."—*Luther.*
"He who was himself a father, should have been more respectful to him who was his father."—*M. Henry.*

e Ex. xx. 12; Ga. vi. 1; 1 Pe. iv. 8.
f F. Ward.
g T. Watson.
v. 20, 21. *Philo Judæus* Wks., i. 453; *H. Smith*, 159.
v. 22—25. *C. Benson,* Huls. Lect., 247.

24—29. (24) **knew,** being informed of it. **what .. son,** *lit.,* his little son. (25) **said .. Canaan,**ª who was prob. the first to see the state of N., and told his fa. Ham.ᵇ **servant .. brethren,** "The curse, as a matter of world-hist., has more or less foll. all the Hamite races."ᶜ (26) **Blessed,** etc.,ᵈ the prophecy assumes the form of thanksgiving. Abraham and the Jews desc. fr. Shem. (27) **God .. Japhet,** whose name sig. *enlargement.* **shall .. Shem,**ᵉ God? or Japhet? prob. the latter: and it may mean that the posterity of Japhet would learn fr. those of Shem the knowledge of the true God. (28, 29) **Noah .. died,** Noah was born upwards of 80 yrs. bef. *Enos* (9th son of

the curse on Canaan death of Noah
a De. xxvii. 16; Ju. i. 28.
b Origen mentions as a trad. among the Jews, that Canaan first saw the shame of his g.-father and told it to his father.

B.C. 2348.

Hence C. inherited the curse. This solves the dif. that is found in II. sinning and C. being cursed. This view is now adopted by many (see *Speaker's Commentary*). c *Alford.* See also *Kalisch* and *Keil.* d "Instead of making prominent the blessedness of Shem, he makes prominent the source of that blessedness." — *Knobel.*
e Is. lx. 35; Mal. i. 11; Ep. ii. 19.
f R. S. Hollis.

B.C. 1998.

the sons of Japheth
Note the similarity of name. Japheth and Japetus, whom the Gks. and Roms. regarded as the first of human race. Gomer is traced in the *Kimmerians* of Homer, and in the Welsh *Cymri.* Madai is traced in the *Medes,* called in old Persian *Mada.* Javan is identified with the *Ionian* race, whom the old poets called *Iaones:* this name in Eastern tongues designated the whole Grecian people.

the sons of Ham
Nimrod, "a hunting giant." — LXX. "a terrible tyrant." — *Arab.;* "a war-like giant." — *Syr.* "He was a hunter of the children of men in their languages, and he said unto them, depart fr. the religion of Shem,

Adam) died: and lived upwards of 120 yrs. aft. *Jerah* (the father of Abraham) was born.

Predictions respecting the sons of Noah.—In directing your attention to these words, let me remind you of—I. The time and occasion of their utterance. Noah's sin. Ham's wickedness, Shem and Japheth's virtue. II. Their meaning. 1. The order of names is not the order of the age of these sons of Noah, but rather of the development of the truth of the predictions relating to them; 2. These predictions relate to the nations springing from Noah's sons, and not to the sons themselves; 3. They wear a general aspect; 4. In tracing their fulfilment, we must have assistance from the geography of the world; 5. We must also remember that their first division only embraced a small portion of the earth's surface. III. The agreement between these predictions and the great outlines of history. Look at the descendants of—1. Ham, and their servitude; 2. Shem, and their privileges; 3. Japheth, and their enlargement.*f*

CHAPTER THE TENTH.

1—5. (1) **generations,** genealogical records. (2) *The Sons of Japheth,* **Gomer** (*complete, perfection*), **magog** (*region of Gog*) **madai** (*middle land*). **Javan** (*? clay*), **Tubal** (*a flowing forth*). **Meshech** (*a drawing out, possession*). **Tiras** (*desire*). (3) *Sons of Gomer* **Ashkenaz,** (?) **Riphath** (*? a crusher*). **Togarmah** (*? breaking bones. ? Armenian tribe*). (4) *sons of Javan.* **Elishah** (? perh. adopted fr. *Elis* or *Hellas*) **Tarshish** (*? a breaking, subjection*). **Kittim** (**?**) **Dodanim** (*? leaders*). (5) **isles .. Gentiles,** prob. those parts of Europe and A. Minor, to wh. the inhabs. of the E. had access only by sea.

Table of descendants of Japheth, and their countries.—I. GOMER, fr. whom the *Cimmerians* on N. coast of Black S. From these—1. *Ashkenaz,* perh. betw. Armenia and Black Sea; 2. *Riphath,* Riphœan mts.; 3. *Togarmah,* Armenia. II. MAGOG, the Scythians. III. MADAI, the Medes. IV. JAVAN, the Ionians or Greeks, fr. whom—1. *Elishah,* Hellenes proper; 2. *Tarshish,* Tartessus in Spain; 3. *Kittim,* Cyprians, Macedonians; 4. *Dodanim,* the Dolonœi in Epirus. V. TUBAL, the *Tibareni,* in Pontus. VI. MESHECH, the *Muscovites, i.e.,* the Moschi of the Moschian mts. betw. Iberia, Armenia, and Colchis. VII. TIRAS, prob. the Thracians.

6—12. (6) *The sons of Ham* **Cush** (*? black*) **Mizraim** (*bulwark*). **Phut** (*afflicted*). **Canaan** (*servant*). (7) *The sons of Cush.* **Seba** (*? man*), **Havilah** (*terror*), **Sabtah** (*striking*), **Raamah** (*a trembling*). **Sabtechah,** as Sabtah. *sons of Raamah,* **Sheba,** as Seba. **Dedan** (*low ground*). (8) **Nimrod** (*a rebel*), began .. earth, became a conqueror and king. (9) **mighty ..** **Lord,** *etc.* his fame in the chase so great as to become proverbial. (10) **beginning,** foundation, nucleus. **Babel,**[a] see on xi. 9. **Erech** (*length*) prob. the *Orchœ* of Ptolemy, now *wurka:* 82 ms. S.; 43 ms. E. fr. Babylon on the Euphrates. **Accad** (*fortress*), site, as yet, undetermined. **Calneh** (*fort of* the god *Anu*), prob. the mod. *Niffer,* ab. 60 ms. SSE. of Babylon. **Shinar,** *see* on xi. 2. (11) **Out .. Asshur,** *lit.* "he [prob. *Nimrod* is meant] went out into Assyria." **Nineveh,**[b] *see* on

Jon. i. 2; iii. iv. 11. **Rehoboth** (*wide places*), prob. now *Itahalch-malik*. **Calah** (*old age*), site uncertain. (12) **Resen** (*a bridle*), perh. now *Selamiyeh*. **same .. city**, perh. it included Nineveh, Rehoboth, Calah, and Resin, as four places contiguous and called under one name—Nineveh.[c]

Nimrod.—Nimrod was—I. A great hunter. This he began with, and for this he became famous. By this he became a prince. II. A great ruler. "The beginning of his kingdom was Babel." III. A great builder. He built Nineveh. Observe in Nimrod the nature of ambition; it is—1. Boundless; 2. Restless; 3. Expensive; 4. Daring.[d]

Table of descendants of Ham and their countries.—I. CUSH, the Ethiopic and mid-Southern Arabs: fr. whom—1. *Nimrod*, first K. of Shinar; 2. *Seba*, Meröe; 3. *Havilah*, the Chaulotæi in S. Arab.; 4. *Sabtha*: Sabota in S. Arab.; 5. *Ragma*: Rhegma in S.E. of Arabia, or Pers. Gulf. fr. whom—(1) *Sheba*, a tribe in S. Arab.; (2) *Dedan*, island in Pers. Gulf; 6. *Sabtecha*: E. of Ethiopia. II. MIZRAIM, the Egyptians: fr. whom—1. *Ludim*; and 2. *Ananim*; African tribes: 3. *Lehabim*, Libyans; 4. *Naphtuchim*, on Lake of Sirbo; 5. *Pathrusim*, Pathros; 6. *Casluhim*: the Colchians, fr. whom—(1) *Philistim*, Philistines; (2) *Caphtorim*, Cretans. III. *Phut*, the Mauritanians. IV. CANAAN: fr. Sidon to S. end of Dead Sea: fr. whom—1. *Sidonians*, Phœnicia; 2. *Hittites*, S. of Jerusalem; 3. *Jebusites*: in and round Jerus; 4. *Amorites*, E. and W. of Dead S.; 5. *Girgasites*; 6. *Hivites*, valleys of Lebanon; 7. *Arkites*; foot of Lebanon; 8. *Sinites*, country of Lebanon; 9. *Arvadites*, Isle of Aradus; 10. *Zemarites*; town of Sinyra; 11. *Hamathites*, town of Epiphania.

13—20. (13) **Ludim** (fr. *strife*). **Ananaim** (*responding waters*). **Lehabim** (*flames*). **Naphtuhim** (*border people*). (14) **Philistim** (*strangers*). **Caphtorim** (*chaplets*). (15) **Sidon** (*fisher*). **Heth** (*fear*). (16) **Jebusite** (*thresher*). **Amorite** (*mountaineer*). **Girgashites** (*dwellers in loamy soil*). (17) **Hivites** (*villagers*). **Arkite** (*fugitive*). **Sinite** (*dwellers in the marsh*). (18) **Arvadite** (*wanderer*). **Zemarite** (*hill man*). **Hamathite** (*fortress dweller*). **afterwards .. abroad**, they first dwelt in the neighbourhood of Zidon. (19) **border**, inhabited region. **Sidon**, their first possession. **Gerar** (*a lodging place*), see on xx.. 1, 2. **Gaza** (*the strong*). **Sodom** (*? burning or vineyard*). **Gomorrha** (*submersion*). **Ahmah** (*red earth*). **Zeboim** (*roes*). **Lasha** (*fissure*). (20). **these .. nations**, *i.e.* those included in *vv.* 6—20.

Circumstances attendant on man.—Instead of saying that man is the creature of circumstance, it would be nearer the mark to say that man is the architect of circumstance. It is character that builds an existence out of circumstance. Our strength is measured by our plastic power. From the same materials one man builds palaces, another hovels; one warehouses, another villas: bricks and mortar are mortar and bricks, until the architect can make them something else. Thus it is that, in the same family, in the same circumstances, one man rears a stately edifice, while his brother, vacillating and incompetent, lives for ever amid ruins; the block of granite which was an obstacle in the pathway of the weak, becomes a stepping-stone in the pathway of the strong.[a]

B.C. 1998.

and cleave unto the institutes of Nimrod."—*Jerus. Targ.*
Wurka; a vast mound called el-Assagah (*the place of pebbles*) or Irka, or Irak is here. It was prob. a city consecrated to the moon, a kind of necropolis. Gt. numbers of tombs and coffins found here. The arrowheaded acc. of the flood recently discov. and trans. by Mr. Smith, of the Brit. Mus., was a copy, so it states, of an original inscription at this place.
a Ge. xi. 9; Mi. v. 6.
b The Arabs still call the principal mound of ruins *Nimroud*.
c Knobel.
d M. Henry.

"When a man stands in no awe of the disgrace which attends bad actions, and has no concern for his character, there is no way of transgression in which that man may not walk. With a countenance clothed in shamelessness and audacity, he easily proceeds from one bad action to the most profligate attempts."—*Procopius*.
a Carlyle.
"Man is a jewel robbed of its precious stone, with only the costly setting left, and even of that we must exclaim, How is the gold become dim, and the most fine gold changed!"—*Rev. Henry Gill*.

B.C. 1998.

the sons of Shem
"A wise man shall not be deprived of pleasure even when death shall summon him; forasmuch as he has attained the delightful end of the best life—departing like a guest full and well satisfied; having received life upon trust, and duly discharged that office, he acquits himself on departing."—*Epicurus.*

a "He was called Phaleg, bec. he was born at the time of the dispersion of the nations to their sev. countries; for Phaleg among the Hebs. sig. division."—*Josephus.* It may be also noticed that the root of the word is applied (Ps. lv. 9, 10) not to a *physical,* but *moral* division. Hence some think P. lived at the time of the dispersion of Babel.
b *Kingsley.*

a *Bochart.*
b *Michaelis, Rosenmüller, Gesenius, Kalisch.*

c In mod. Arabic, *Isfar*, a series of villages nr. shore of Indian Ocean, in prov. of Hadramaut. Many ruins, and a lofty tn. called *Esh-Shihr.*
"It is only our mortal duration that we measure by visible and measurable objects; and there is nothing mournful in the contemplation for one who knows that the Creator made him to be

21—23. (21) **Shem**..**Eber**, Shem's great honour that he was the ancestor of the Abrahamic race. **brother**..**elder**, ambiguous: but prob. it is "Shem, the elder bro. of Japheth." (22) *The children of Shem.* **Elam** (*age*). **Asshur** (*a step*). **Arphaxad** (*stronghold of the Chaldees*). **Lud** (*? strife*). **Aram** (*high region*). (23) **Uz** (*? fertile land*). **Hul** (*circle*). **Gether** (*? greqs*). **Mash** (*? drawn out*).

Table of the descendants of Shem and their countries.—I. ELAM, Persians. II. ASSHUR, Assyrians. III. ARPHAXAD, N. part of Assyria: fr. whom *Shelah*; fr. whom *Eber* (fr. whom the Hebrews); fr. him (1) *Peleg* and (2) *Joktan*, fr. him the Arab tribes of vv. 26—29. IV. LUD, prob. Ethiopia. V. ARAM, Syria and Mesopotamia: fr. whom—1. *Uz*, N. of Arabia Deserta; 2. *Hul,* prob. Cœlo-Syria; 3. *Gether*, unknown; 4. *Mash*, part of Gordiœan Mts. (Mons Masius), N. of Nisibis.

24, 25. (24) **Salah** (*sending forth*). **Eber** (*passing over*). prob. these were the first to cross the gt. rivers on way to Mesopotamia, and thence to Canaan. (25) **Peleg**ᵃ (*division*). for..**divided**, he was born at the time that the Shemites divided, and occupied their dif. lands: hence his name. **Joktan** (who *is made small*). He is prob. identical with the *kahtan* of the Arabs.

Man the subject of circumstances.—It is a painful fact, but there is no denying it, the mass *are* the tools of circumstance; thistle-down on the breeze, straw on the river, their course is shaped for them by the currents and eddies of the stream of life; but only in proportion as they are *things*, not men and women. Man was meant to be not the slave, but the master, of circumstance: and in proportion as he recovers his *humanity*, in every sense of the great *obsolete* word,—in proportion as he gets back the spirit of manliness, which is self-sacrifice, affection, loyalty to an idea beyond himself, a God above himself, so far will he rise *above* circumstances, and wield them at his will.ᵇ

26—32. (26) **Almodad** (*? extension*). **Sheleph** (*selected*). **Hazamaveth** (court of death). **Jerah** (the moon). (27) **Hadoram** (*noble honour*). **Uzal** (*? wanderer*). **Diklah** (*palm-tree*). (28) **Obal** (*bare of leaves*). **Abimael** (*father of might*). (29) **Ophir** (*abundance*). **Jobab** (*a desert*). these..**Joktan**, fr. vv. 26—29. (30) **Mesha**, the sea-port *Musa* or *Muza*:ᵃ or else the island *Mesene*.ᵇ **Sephar**, now *Zafar* or *Dhafari*.ᶜ (31) These..**nations**, *i.e.* those included in vv. 22—30. (32) These..**nations**, *i.e.* those included in vv. 1—31. and..**flood**, as explained by the tables on pp. 46—48.

The study of man.—In order, however, to pursue this study with success, we should be brought in contact with individuals belonging to the several divisions of the human family. To accomplish this by travelling is impossible. The nation, therefore, if it wishes its own enlightenment, should be at the cost of forming an ethnological institution, with very extensive grounds, on which by degrees might be located specimens in pairs of the various races which could subsist in our climate. They should construct their own dwellings according to the architectural ideas of their several countries; their furniture, dress, ornaments, amusements, food, and mode of life, should be their own. The forms of industry prevalent in their nation or tribe they should be required to practise; and their ideas, opinions, habits, and superstitions should be permitted to perpetuate themselves until extinguished by the spontaneous efforts of civilisation. The Esquimaux, the Red Indian, the Kaffir, the Hottentot, the Negro, the Australian, the New Zealander, the Dyak, the Malay, the wild Goond, the Cingalese, the Beloucheff, the Afghan, the Brahmin, and various other castes or tribes of India, might thus be brought together within the same enclosure. In many ways such an assemblage would serve to throw light on the nature and primitive ideas of our species; and not the least instructive part of the plan would be the study of the way in which civilisation affected the several sections of mankind.*d*

B.C. 1998.

the image of his own eternity, and who feels, that in the desire for immortality he has sure proof of his capacity for it."
—*Southey.*
"A good man enlarges the term of his own existence."—*Martial.*
d J. A. St. John.

CHAPTER THE ELEVENTH.

1—4. (1) **one .. speech,** *lit.* of one lip and one (kind of) words. Prob. the *Heb.* tongue. (2) **they .. east,**ᵃ eastward, *lit.* on the sides of the east. **Shinar** (*land of two rivers*), *Babylonia.*ᵇ (3) **brick,** the country rich in brick-making material, but no stone. **and .. thoroughly,** *lit.* burn them with a burning.ᶜ **slime,** bitumen, asphalte.ᵈ (4) **go to,** *lit.* give. Idiomatic expression. **city,**ᵉ under the influence of ambition, and dissatisfied with simple patriarchal life, they wished to found a great monarchy, of wh. this city was to be the capital. **tower .. heaven,** *i.e.* an exceedingly high tower.ᶠ **name,**ᵍ let us become famous, and found a political power. **lest .. earth,** wh. was the divine intention.

The tower of Babel.—Here we observe—(1) Self-reliance; (2) A desire for self-preservation; (3) Ambition—a city, a tower, and a name. Several practical thoughts are suggested by these words. I. Carefully examine the quality and meaning of every new plan of life. Beware of—1. Appearances; 2. Miscalculations; 3. Oversights. II. Beware of the sophism that heaven helps them that help themselves. III. Regulate ambition by the divine will. IV. If we make great plans, let us make them in God's name, and carry them out in God's strength. See the folly of planning without God. 1. He has all forces at command; 2. He has set a limit to every man's life; 3. He has pronounced Himself against those who dishonour His name. V. Learn what is meant by all the unfinished towers that we see around us. VI. Notice that co-operation with God will alone secure the entire realisation of our plans. Application—(1) We all have plans; (2) Examine them; (3) Remember the only foundation, on which alone men can build with safety.ʰ

The tower of Babel.—It is not necessary to suppose that any real idea of "scaling heaven" was present to the minds of those who raised either the tower of Babel, or any other of the Babylonian temple towers. The expression used in Genesis (xi. 4) is a mere hyperbole for great height (comp. Deut. i. 28, Dan. iv. 11, etc.), and should not be taken literally. Military defence was probably the primary object of such edifices in early times; but with the wish for this may have been combined further secondary motives, which remained when such defence was otherwise provided for. Diodorus states that the great tower of the temple of Belus was used by the Chaldeans as an observatory (ii. 9), and

the tower of Babel

a If Armenia was their first home, they must first have journeyed S.E., and theu have turned from the E. to Shinar.

b Described by Herodotus as a great plain.

c Usual method sun-drying: both kinds found in the ruins here.

d Anc. writers (*Pliny, etc.*) descr. a lake nr. Babylon, with bitumen wh. floated on the surface *Layard* notes that the cement is so tenacious that it is almost impossible to detach an entire brick fr. the mass; see *Alford* and *Kalisch.*

e Da. iv. 30; Ps. xlix. 11—13.

f De. ix. 1.

g Dr. Parker.

v. 1—9. *Dr. W. B. Collyer,* Scrip. Facts, 144.

v. 4. *E. M. Goulburn,* 273.

h "There, doubtless, is something of rebellion against *God's* purposes implied in

B.C. 2247.

their determination. He would have them spread over the whole earth, while they resolved to be gathered in one spot."—*Alford.*
i *G. Rawlinson.*

the confusion of tongues
a "We are not to suppose locomotion in Him who is Omnipresent; but by such sentences as these, in which the Holy Spirit condescends to man's weakness, He teaches us that God does not punish without examination."—*Wordsworth.*
b Ps. ii. 1; xxxiii. 10; li. 4.
c Ps. xcii. 9; Lu. i. 51.
d Acc. to the Gks. the city was named aft. *Belus,* its mythic founder. Eichhorn sugg. that the name was orig. Bab, Beb, "the gate or court of Bel," *i.e.,* Baal or Belus.
v. 4–8. *H. Owen,* Miracles, i, 157; *C. Simeon,* i, 90; *J. Jenkins,* 118.
e *H. J. Browne.*
A perfect Babel, a thorough confusion. "A Babel of sounds," A confused uproar in which nothing can be heard but hubbub.
f *G. Rawlinson.*

the line of Shem
a Note the alteration in length of life bef. and aft. the flood. Noah, 950 yrs.; Shem, 600; Arphaxad, 438; Peleg, 239; Nahor, 148.
b "Many of the names in these genealogies are

the careful emplacement of the Babylonian temples with the angles facing the four cardinal points would be a natural consequence, and may be regarded as a strong confirmation of the reality of this application. M. Fresnal has recently conjectured that they were also used as sleeping places for the chief priests in the summer time. The upper air is cooler, and is free from the insects, especially mosquitoes, which abound below; and the description which Herodotus gives of the chamber at the top of the Belus tower (i. 181) goes far to confirm this ingenious view.*i*

5–9. (5) **Lord .. see,**a anthropomorphic: and suited to the mass of readers in all times. **which .. men,** not "the sons of God." (6) **this .. do,** this is the beginning of their doings. **now .. them,** nothing will be unattempted, though its nature pronounce it wrong, if they are allowed to succeed here. (7) **and .. language,**b and so destroy this political conspiracy. (8) **Lord .. earth,**c made their dispersion unavoidable. **they .. city,** they were no longer *one* people : prob. they were overwhelmed with fear also. (9) **Babel**d (*confusion*).

The confusion of tongues.—Here we have—I. A record of a past event. 1. Ambition satisfying itself : 2. Ambition justly punished. II. A lesson for the present. 1. Are there no towers that you are building, no plans that you are forming without God? Take care, for such will be overthrown ; 2. Is there no wrong ambition in your heart? Crush it at once, lest punishment come upon you.*e*

Traditions of Babel and the confusion of Tongues.—Of this remarkable circumstance in the history of mankind a traditional remembrance seems to have been retained among a certain number of nations. In Babylon itself, especially, the great city of the land of Shinar, there was a belief which is thus expressed by those who had studied its records:—"At this time—not long after the flood—the ancient race of men were so puffed up with their strength and tallness of stature, that they began to despise and contemn the gods, and laboured to erect that very lofty tower which is now called Babylon, intending thereby to scale heaven. But when the building approached the sky, behold, the gods called in the aid of the winds, and by their help overturned the tower and cast it to the ground ! The name of the ruin is still called Babel ; because until this time all men had used the same speech, but now there was set upon them a confusion of many and diverse tongues." It may have been also a recollection of the event, though one much dimmed and faded, which gave rise to the Greek myth of the war between the gods and the giants, and the attempt of the latter to scale heaven by piling one mountain upon another.*f*

10–13. (10) **these .. Shem,** *etc.*, family tree, etc. carried down to Abram : and including duration of life*a* (*see* also x. 22 *ff*). (11) **Arphaxad .. flood,** the first-born of Shem aft. the flood. "After the flood," may = aft. the begin. of flood. (12, 13) **Salah,**b = *extension.* Acc. to Knobel there is a place of this name in N.E. Mesopotamia.

Bad men unfitted for service.—During the course of my life, I have acquired some knowledge of men and manners, in active life, and amidst occupations the most various. From that knowledge, and from all my experience, I now protest that I never knew a man that was bad fit for any service that was good. There was always some disqualifying ingredient mixing with the compound, and spoiling it. The man seems paralytic on that side: his muscles there have lost their tone and natural properties, they cannot move. In short, the accomplishment of anything good is a physical impossibility in such a man. He could not if he would, and it is not more certain than that he would not if he could, do a good or a virtuous action.[c]

14—19. (14) **Eber,**[a] or *Heber*,[b] whence the name,—Hebrew. (18) **Reu** (*friend*, i.e. of God), or *Ragau*,[c] traceable in *Roha*, the Arab name of Edessa in N.W. Mesopotamia.[d]

Difference in men.—The difference of men is very great: you would scarce think them to be of the same species; and yet it consists more in the affections than the intellect. For, as in the strength of the body two men shall be of an equal strength, yet one shall appear stronger than the other, because he exercises and puts out his strength, while the other will not stir nor strain himself:—so it is in the strength of the brain; the one endeavours, and strains, and labours, and studies; the other sits still and is idle, and takes no pains, and therefore he appears so much the inferior.[e]

20—26. (20) **Serug** (*shoot, branch*) or *Saruch*.[a] There is a place called by the Arabs *Sarug*, ab. a day N. of Haran. (22) **Nahor**[b] (*snorting*) or *Nachor*.[c] (24) **Terah** (*station*), who dwelt at *Ur*, and said to have been an idolater.[d] (26) **Abram** (*father*), not the eldest, but named first bec. of superior dignity.[e] **Nahor,** not Nahor of v. 22. Fr. this N. came Rebekah, Leah, and Rachel. **Haran** (*mountaineer*), the father of Lot, Milcah, and Iscah.

The greatness of bad men.—A bad great one is a great bad one: for the greatness of an evil man makes the man's evil the greater. It is the unhappy privilege of authority, not so much to act, as teach wickedness, and by a liberal cruelty to make the offender's sin not more his own than others. Each fault in a leader is not so much a crime as a rule for error: and their vices are made (if not warrants, yet) precedents for evil. To sin by prescription is as usual as damnable: and men run post in their journey, when they go to the devil with authority. When then the vices of the rulers of others are made the rules for vices to others, the offences of all great ones must needs be the greatest of all offences. Either then let me be great in goodness, or else it were good for me to be without greatness. My own sins are a burden too heavy for me, why then should I lade myself with other offences?[f]

27, 28. (27) **these .. Terah,** the hist. now passes to T., since his descs. have to be dealt with. **Lot** (*covering, veil*), nephew of Abram. (28) **Ur .. Chaldees,** Heb. *be-Oor Kasdim.* Site of Ur (*light*) uncertain: by some[a] said to be *Edessa*, i.e. the mod. *Orfah*: by others[b] *Mugeyer* or *Umghier*, where there are yet ruins. Chaldea was the S. part of Babylonia.

Man under spiritual law.—Man is under law; but he is also under more than any mere natural law. The laws which regulate phenomena apply to his conduct, but they do not exhaust his being. He has a spirit and life of his own which transcend nature-conditions, and are not contained by them. Above the system of these conditions there is a higher system of being, and man, in his innermost life, belongs to this higher system. It is his peculiar glory that he does so—that amid ceaseless movements

---

B.C. 2247.

significant, and were prob. given to their bearers late in life, or even historically aft. their death."
—*Speaker's C.*
c *Burke.*

the line of Eber

a Ge. x. 21, 24, 25; Nu. xxiv. 24; 1 Ch. i. 18, 19, 25.

b Lu. iii. 35.

c LXX. and Lu. iii. 35.

d *Alford.*

e *Selden.*

a Lu. iii. 35. He is said to have been the founder of hero-worship. Suidas and others ascribe to him the deification of dead benefactors of mankind. See *Smith's Bib. Dict.*
b There was ano. N., i.e., Abram's bro., the g.-son of this N.
c Lu. iii. 34.
d Jos. xxiv. 2, 15.
e cf. v. 32, with xii. 4. A. was born when Terah was 130 years old; i.e., 350 years aft. the flood, or A.M. 2008.
f *Warwick.*

Terah and Haran

a *Stanley, Jewish Ch.,* i. 7; also anc. trad.

b *Rawlinson.* The name of *Urukh,* a king (2230 B.C.), has been found on the bricks. The temple was dedicated to the moon-god *Hurki;* hence perh. its name. *Ka'isch,* 292; *Loftus: Chaldea,* 126—131.

of matter, before which he is apparently so weak, he is conscious of an existence higher than all matter, and which would survive its wildest crash. He *knows himself*, and that is what nature does not do. There is no play of conscious life in its mighty mutations. But man is characteristically a self-conscious, thinking soul, higher than all nature, and which no subtle development of mere natural conditions can ever explain. This is the eternal basis of Christian Theism, and of all religion that is not mere consecration of earthly energies and passions. This is the only spring of a genuine morality that can survey man as under some higher law of voluntary obedience, and not a mere law of harmony and growth.ᶜ

29—32. (29) **Sarai** (*my princess*), half-sister to A.,ᵃ *i.e.*, dau. of Terah by ano. wife: and 10 yrs. younger than A.ᵇ **Milcah** (*queen*), g.-mother of Rebekah.ᶜ **Iscah** (*? covering*), acc. to Jewish trad. ano. name for Sarai. This unlikely.ᵈ Someᵉ conjecture she was Lot's wife. (30) **Sarai**, *etc.*, now stated to prepare for following hist. (31) **and .. Chaldees**, A. received the call in Ur,ᶠ and seems to have persuaded his father, etc., to accom. him. **to .. Canaan**, this the Divine intention: prob. A. knew not the destination at this time.ᵍ **Haran** (*parched, dry*), or *Charran*.ʰ (32) **Terah .. Haran**, prob. ab. 60 yrs. aft. A. set out thence for Canaan.ⁱ

Stopping short.—Observe—I. Terah was favoured with a revelation of the Divine will. 1. Without it he could not have known God's purpose; 2. He evidently understood it; 3. He was influenced by it; 4. He began to obey God; 5. He proceeded some distance in the right direction. II. The object of the Divine revelation to Terah was not accomplished, Why stay and die in Haran. Perhaps because of—1. Indecision; 2. Unbelief; 3. Love of ease; 4. Love of the world; 5. The suasion of others.ᵏ

Haran.—The conclusion that Haran is identical with *Carrhæ* is liable to very great doubt, so far at least as concerns the Haran in which the members of the Abrahamic family were settled. It has been proposed, therefore, to identify the Mesopotamia of the early Scripture writers, *Aram-naharaim*, Aram of the two rivers with Aram of Damascus, where certainly there were two noted streams, Abana and Pharpar, and to look for the city of Haran in that neighbourhood. It is clear that there must have been some connection between Abraham and Damascus; for Eliezer, "born in his house," is denominated "of Damascus" (Ge. xv. 2, 3). Still further, Jacob, travelling of necessity, on account of his cattle, slowly, reached Mt. Gilead in ten days after leaving Padan-aram. The distance is between three and four hundred miles if the usual theory be adopted; it is, therefore, physically impossible that the journey could have been accomplished in the time specified. Moreover, it is not easy to understand how a pillar on Mt. Gilead could be a boundary-mark between Jacob and Laban, if the latter lived far away beyond the Euphrates. There is, therefore, a high probability that the Haran in question is a place of the name near Damascus, visited in 1861 by Dr. Belsa.ˡ Milton, generally so accurate in his geography, has fallen into the error of placing Haran on the W. bank of the Euphrates (see Par. L., xii. 130, 131). This may be coupled with that other topographical mistake in the Par. R. (iv. 250—253), where he puts Lyceum *within* the walls of Athens."ᵐ

B.C. 2247.

"To make a man virtuous, three things are necessary:—1. Natural parts and disposition. 2. Precepts and instruction. 3. Use and practice, which is able better to correct the first, and improve the latter."
—*Locke.*
c Dr. Tholluck.

Abram leaves Ur

a Ge. xx. 12; mar. with nr. relatives was usual in Terah's fam., xxiv. 3, 4; xxviii. 1, 2.

b xvii. 17.

c Ge. xxii. 20, 23.

d Ge. xx. 12.

e Ewald.

f Ge. xv. 7; Ne. ix. 7; Ac. vii. 2.

g Ac. vii. 3; He. xi. 8.

h Ac. vii. 2, 4, said to be the *Carrhæ* of the Greeks where Crassus fell, defeated by the Parthians (*Plut. Vit. Cras.*)

i Alford.

k Dr. J. Burns.

l See *Notes and Queries*, Feb. and Mar. 1862, pp. 95, 192; and comp. Miss Corbeaux, in *Journ. of Sacr. Lit.*, Jan., 1852, pp. 386, 387.

De Ur Chaldeorum, Crit. Sac. Thes., i. 173 N. Alexander, Hist. Eccles. i. 287; Dr. F. Zee, Diss. ii. 78.

m Bishop *Wordsworth.*

CHAPTER THE TWELFTH.

B.C. 1921.

1—4. (1) **now .. Abram**, in Ur. *see* on xi. 31. **get .. kindred,**[a] this call to A. alone, did not prevent the others fr. going with him. **unto .. thee**, A. knew not the land when he set out : but walked as Providence led. (2) **I .. thee,**[b] abundant increase or multiplication of favours. **thou .. blessing**, through the Jews we have a Bible, a Saviour, the Gospel, *etc.* (3) **thee .. blessed,**[c] the ref. is to Xt. (4) **departed :** *i.e.* fr. Haran, the force of the old call still operating on him. **Abram .. Haran,**[d] an old man with his childless wife setting fr. home, and walking by faith.

The journey of Abram, a type of the journey through life of a good man.—The good man, like Abram—I. Reverently listens to the Divine voice. II. Reposes implicit faith in the sovereignty and fatherhood of God. III. Maintains his faith by continual worship. IV. Often finds his blessings associated with trials. V. Sometimes feels that his faith is tried more severely by the less than by the greater affairs of life.[e]

Prompt obedience.—A story is told of a great captain, who, after a battle, was talking over the events of the day with his officers. He asked them who had done the best that day. Some spoke of one man who had fought very bravely, and some of another. "No," he said: "you are all mistaken. The best man in the field to-day was a soldier who was just lifting up his arm to strike an enemy, but, when he heard the trumpet sound a retreat, checked himself, and dropped his arm without striking the blow. That perfect and ready obedience to the will of his general is the noblest thing that has been done to-day."[f]

5—7. (5) **souls .. Haran**, they must have been here many yrs. Perh. *Eliezer* was one of these souls (*see on* xi. 32). Children born: servants hired. (6) **and .. through**, travelling S. **Sichem**, the place aft. so called, prob. the Sychar of aft. times, now Nablon's (fr. the Gk. Νεαπολις, *i.e.*, new city). **unto .. Moreh**, *lit.*, to the oak (or terebinth) of Moreh. M. was perh. the name of a person, the owner of the land. **Canaanite .. land**, this fact exalts an idea of A.'s faith. (7) **unto .. land,**[a] notwithstanding thy childless state, and the present inhabs. **and .. Lord**, evidence of faith and gratitude : thus he formally took possession.

Abram's journey into Canaan.—I propose to set before you—I. The perfections of God for your admiration. 1. His sovereignty; 2. His power; 3. His faithfulness. II. The virtues of Abram for your imitation. 1. His simple faith; 2. His prompt decision; 3. His self-denying zeal; 4. His prudent care; 5. His persevering diligence.[b]

The first halting-place in the Holy Land.—Abram had now to leave Mesopotamia, and to cross the "Great river," the Euphrates. This separated him entirely from his old home, and hence the Canaanites gave to him the name of the "Hebrew"—the man who had *crossed* the river—the emigrant from Mesopotamia. He now passed through the great Syrian desert; and, though his route is not mentioned in the sacred narrative, we may credit the tradition that he tarried at Damascus, since Eliezer, "the steward

---

Abram and Lot leave Haran

a Lu. xiv. 26, 33.
b Ge. xxii. 16—18;
Mi. vii. 20; Ga. iii. 14.
c Ac. iii. 25, 26;
Ga. iii. 8.
d He. xi. 8—10.
e Dr. Parker.

"The life of some men is very much like a day in November, foggy, chilly, and damp until the afternoon, when it clears off, becomes bright and pleasant, and the sun sets without a cloud, throwing his golden light over the broad expanse of the heavens; an evidence that he is shining on though beyond the ken of mortals this side of the globe."—*John Bate.*
f Oxendon.

Abram enters Canaan

"A. reigned in Damascus, being come with an army fr. the country beyond Babylon called the land of the Chaldeans. But not long aft. leaving this country with his people, he migrated into the Land of Canaan, wh. is now called Judæa." *Nicholaus of Damascus* (*Hist. Bk.* iv.), quoted by *Josephus*, who adds, "that the name of A. was, even in his days, famous in the country of the Damascenes, and a village was pointed out there

of his house," was a native of that place. Quitting Damascus, Abram crossed the Jordan, and, entering the Holy Land, passed into the valley of Shechem or Sichem. His resting-place was marked, like other memorable localities, by an oak or a grove of oaks ("the oak or oaks of Moreh" rather than "the *plain* of Moreh," as in our version), near the "place of Sichem," between mts. Ebal and Gerizim. Here God appeared to him again, and gave him the *second promise*, of the possession of the land by his seed; and here Abram built the first of those altars to Jehovah, which the patriarchs erected wherever they pitched their tents. Thus Sichem became his first halting-place in the Holy Land.*c*

8—10. (8) **removed**, *lit.*, he plucked up (his tent pegs). **Beth-el**, *i.e.*, house of God, called at this time *Luz*;*a* now *Beitan:* ab. 18 ms. S. of Sechem. **Hai**, the ruins called *Medinet Gai* are ab. 5 ms. E. of Beitan. (9) **Abram .. south**, going through the length of the land. (10) **famine**, another trial of faith. **Egypt**, the great granary of anc. times.*b* **sojourn** not to *live* there.

The leadings of Abram.—Consider Abram in his pilgrimage, and glance at—I. The goal to reach which he strove. II. The promises which secured its attainment. III. The dangers under which he stood. IV. The divine service which he rendered.*c*

An incident of famine.—An Algerian paper, the *Echo d'Oran*, has the following: "No historical famine has presented to the saddened eye of humanity so horrible a spectacle as that which is at this moment to be observed among the Arabs. Two days ago, a native woman in the neighbourhood of Misserghin killed her daughter, twelve years of age, and gave the flesh to her other children, and partook of it herself. The legal authorities, hearing of the circumstance, at once proceeded to the spot, and, on entering the hut occupied by these cannibals, learned that the heart, the liver, and the interior portions of the corpse, were eaten, because they would not keep. The mother was occupied in salting the flesh, cut up into pieces, exactly as is done with pork."

11—13. (11) **Egypt**, despotic government, licentious people. **said .. Sarai**, as she lived to 127 yrs., and was now 60, she was in middle life. (12) **say .. wife**, *etc.*,*a* "The Arab life of A. naturally made him wary of danger."*b* (13) **sister**, she was indeed his step-sister, but this was an untruth since it was intended to convey the impression that she was nothing more than a sister. **soul .. thee**, *i.e.*, my life shall be spared when it is seen that I am only thy brother.

Abram in Egypt.—Since Abram was continually dependent upon the grace of God, he must feel his weakness, which betrays him into manifold acts of insincerity and sin. For—I. He acted from fear, when he should still have looked to God. II. He gave out that Sarai was his sister when she was his wife. III. He had great guilt in the sin of Pharaoh. IV. He thought to secure his own safety, while he placed Sarai and her chastity in the greatest peril.*c*

Double-mindedness.—

See the professor labouring, but in vain,
The world and cross together to sustain;
The globe is in his right hand dexterous found,
His left the cross, drags sluggish on the ground;

In vain for him appears the narrow way,
The world has led him from the path astray:
In vain for him shines forth the heavenly light,
The world has risen and obscured his sight;
Two minds he has, both he may call his own,
Sometimes they lead him up, and sometimes down;
Like doubtful birds, that hop from spray to spray,
His will is never at one certain stay;
Too late he learns with deep regret and pain,
He loses both who more than one would gain.*d*

14—16. (14) **beheld .. fair,** A.'s suspicions were correct. (15) **princes,** lords of the court. **Pharaoh,** wh. sig. King:*a* not a prop. name but a title as *Cæsar* among the Roms., or *Czar* among mod. Russ. **commended,** vile panderers and sycophants, who, though officers of state, ministered to the worst passions of the king. **woman .. house,** with the intention of making S. one of his wives. (16) **entreated .. sake,** *etc.*, to compensate him for the loss of his *sister*.

Abram's sin.—Consider—I. The temptation is no ordinary one. Pharaoh was powerful; Abram was weak. II. He sins through unbelief. The falsehood which he put into Sarai's mouth was a grievous sin in itself; and it was sinful, also, as indicating want of trust in God. III. His scheme avails him but little. His policy overreaches itself. IV. God interferes at last to deliver him. He averts the evil, and even turns it to account for God.*b*

Talmudic story about Abraham.—The Talmudists say that Abraham, in travelling to Egypt, brought with him a chest. At the custom-house the officers exacted the duties. Abraham would have readily paid them, but desired they would not open the chest. They first insisted on the duties for clothes, which Abraham consented to pay; but then they thought by his ready acquiescence that it might be gold. Abraham consents to pay for gold. They now suspect it might be silk. Abraham was willing to pay for silk, or more costly pearls—in short, he consented to pay as if the chest contained the most valuable of things. It was then they resolved to open and examine the chest; and, behold as soon as the chest was opened, that great lustre of human beauty broke out which made such a noise in the land of Egypt—it was Sarah herself! The jealous Abraham, to conceal her beauty, had locked her up in this chest.

17—20. (17) **plagues,** *lit.*, strokes, blows. **because .. wife,** God preserves whom men distress. (18) **Pharaoh,** the suddenness and unusual nature of the plagues led P. to connect them with S. **what .. wife,** P. discov. the relations by inquiries prompted by the plagues.*a* (19) **I .. wife,** hence we learn that he had not. **therefore .. wife,** she has never in any sense been mine. (20) **and .. him,***b* that A. might not be molested in any way. **and .. had,** including P.'s presents.

Abram in Egypt.—From the record before us (v. 11—20) we may learn—I. The danger of deceit and equivocation. *Partial* truth is worse than *all* deceit. "I would thou wert cold or hot." II. The proneness to sin in even the best of men. Abraham's faith, though great, did not stand every test. III. The desirability of perfect trust in God. This course is the best as being—1. Least fraught with danger to ourselves; 2. Most calculated to

B.C. 1921.

error and sin."— *Speaker's Com. R. P. Buddicom,* Friend with God, i. 308; *N. Alexander;* Hist. Eccles., i. 368; *Dr. Kitto,* Bibl. Ill. i. 188.
c Cramer.
d W. Holmes.

Sarai introduced to Pharaoh

a Josephus.

"Happiness is not the end of life; character is. This world is not a platform where you will hear Thalberg-piano playing. It is a piano manufactory, where are dust and shavings and boards, and saws and files and rasps and sand-papers. The perfect instrument and the music will be hereafter."— *Beecher.*

b Dr. R. S. Candlish.

Live so that when death comes you may embrace like friends, not encounter like enemies.—*P. Quarle.*

Pharaoh sends Abram away

Acc. to *Josephus* (Ant. i. 8) P.'s priests told the king the reason of the plagues.
a Patrick.
b Ps. cv. 13, 14.

"The candour of the historian is shown by his exhibiting in such strong relief, the dissimulation of Abram, as con-

procure for us the respect of others; 3. The only course that is at all pleasing to God Himself; and therefore—4. The only way by which eternal happiness can be obtained.ᵉ

Degrees of punishment.—The legend of St. Macarius of Alexandria runs thus: "One day, as Macarius wandered among those ancient Egyptian tombs wherein he had made himself a dwelling-place, he found the skull of a mummy, and, turning it over with his crutch, he inquired to whom it belonged; and it replied, 'To a pagan.' And Macarius, looking into the empty eyes, said, 'Where, then, is thy soul?' And the head replied, 'In hell.' Macarius asked, 'How deep?' And the head replied, 'The depth is greater than the distance from heaven to earth.' Then Macarius asked, 'Are there any deeper than thou art?' The skull replied, 'Yes: the Jews are deeper still.' And Macarius asked, 'Are there any deeper than the Jews?' To which the head replied, 'Yes, in sooth! for the Christians whom Jesus Christ hath redeemed, and who show in their actions that they despise his doctrine, are deeper still.'"

CHAPTER THE THIRTEENTH.

1—4. (1) **south,** *i.e.* of Canaan. (2) **rich,**ᵃ "He has now to experience some of the dangers and evils of prosperity."ᵇ (3) **journeys,** encampments. **Bethel,** *etc.*, see on xii. 8. (4) **altar,** the *altar* and the *tent* go together. **there** .. **Lord,**ᶜ returning thanks for deliverance and prosperity.

Calling on the name of the Lord.—It is better that we have no detail respecting this act. We know what is meant. The heart can fill up the vacancy. I. Abram went back to an old scene—back "where his tent had been," back "unto the place of the altar." II. What happened locally also happened morally. In Egypt we saw him equivocate,—now behold, he prayeth. His spiritual sense was not destroyed. Learn—(1) Prayer should testify to the depth of our humiliation, and the reality of our contrition; (2) Much depends upon praying promptly; procrastination is death.ᵈ

The wealth of Abraham.—As Abraham was very rich in silver and gold, as well as cattle, he was able to procure the luxuries of life as well as the modern Arab princes. This might partly be done by an exchange of articles as well as by purchase, for both of which purposes he had many opportunities. Dr. Russell tells us that the people of Aleppo are supplied with the greater part of their butter, their cheese, and their cattle for slaughter by the Arabs, Rushwans, or Turcomans, who travel about the country with their flocks and their herds, as the patriarchs did of old. The patriarchs doubtless supplied the ancient cities of Canaan in like manner with these things. Hamor expressly speaks of their trading with his people (Ge. xxxiv. 21). At the same time that the Arabs receive money for their commodities their expenses are very small, so that their princes are rich in silver and gold as well as cattle, and amass large quantities of these precious metals, insomuch that La Roque remarks that in the time of Pliny the riches both of the Parthians and Romans were, in a manner, melted down among the Arabs, they turning everything into money without parting with any of it again.

Margin notes:

B.C. 1921.
trusted with the straightforward integrity of Pharaoh."—*Speaker's Commentary.*

ᶜ H. Jenkyns.

"God had reproved Pharaoh, and now Pharaoh reproves Abram: It is a sad thing that saints should do that for which they should justly fall under the reproof of the wicked."—*Trapp.*

B.C. 1918.

Abram returns to Canaan

ᵃ Ge. xxiv. 35; Ps. cxii. 1—3; De. viii. 18; Pr. iii. 9—10; x 22.

ᵇ *Speaker's Comty.*

ᶜ Ps. cxlv. 18; xxvi. 8; cxvi. 2, 17.

"I know of no pleasure so rich, none so pure, none so hallowing in their influences, and constant in their supply, as those which result from the true and spiritual worship of God. Pleasant as the cool water brooks are to a thirsty hart, so pleasant will it be to us to approach unto the living God."—*R. Watson.*

ᶜ. 2. *H. Blunt* On Abraham, 50.

ᵈ *Dr. Parker.*

5—7. (5) **Lot,** *etc.*, partook of A.'s prosperity: advantage of association with people of God. (6) **land, impoverished by** recent famine. **bear, nourish, sustain. so .. together, they** needed wider pasturage. (7) **strife .. cattle,** over zeal of servants in their master's interests. **Perizzite,** prob. nomads; villagers. **dwelled .. land,**[a] making fodder more dif. to obtain, and union more needful.

Contentions among Christian brethren.—We remark—I. That it is no uncommon thing for strifes and contentions to arise among the people of God. Here there are two objects worthy of notice—1. The impartiality of the inspired writers in recording the failings as well as the excellencies of believers; 2. That whatever be the contentions of Christians, they themselves are to be blamed, and not the religion with which they are identified. II. That the prevention or suppression of such contentions is an object which every right-minded Christian is deeply anxious to secure. III. That one of the strongest reasons which should induce believers to avoid such contentions, and to cultivate opposite feelings, is to be found in the endearing relationship subsisting between them. 1. Let different Christian communities; 2. Let all members of the same church remember this. Application:—(1) Cultivate more and more the precious grace of Christian love; (2) Be above noticing every trifle; (3) Beware of small beginnings; (4) Think of the effect which a contentious spirit will have upon the ungodly.[b]

Avoiding quarrels.—Gotthold said to one who had left another rather than avenge an insult, "Tell me, my friend, were you climbing a hill, and were a great stone or block to be rolled down towards you, would you consider it disgraceful to step aside, and allow it to rush past? If not, what disgrace can there be in avoiding and giving way to a man instigated by drink or anger, until he has had time for reflection, and his agitated mind finds rest in repentance? He who breaks his will and yields is ascending; he who gives the reins to his passions is falling."[c]

8—13. (8) **Abram,** to whom the whole land belonged, and who might have exercised despotic sway. **let .. herdsmen,** love of peace. **for .. brethren,**[a] the best of all reasons for peace. (9) **is .. thee?** *etc.*, he magnanimously waives his right to make the first selection. (10) **Lot .. Jordan,**[b] they were prob. on the mt. (xii. 8) E. of Bethel. **watered,** important to pastoral people. **even .. Lord,** so called on acc. of its surpassing beauty and fruitfulness. **like .. Egypt,** whose fruitfulness they had seen. **Zoar** (*smallness*) also Bela.[c] (11) **Lot .. east,** satisfied with his choice: his future trouble growing out of his covetousness. **they .. other,** yet not divided in heart on A.'s side. (12) **Abram .. Canaan,** in the heart of the land. **Lot .. Sodom,**[d] approaching the evil place, step by step. (13) **wicked .. exceedingly,**[e] and yet L. did not withdraw fr. their neighbourhood.

Separation rather than strife.—Introduction:—The disputants —(1) Were related to each other: (2) Were professors of the same religious faith: (3) Both differed in the relative amount of their power. Consider Abram's conduct on this occasion as—I. Just. II. Statesmanlike. III. Magnanimous.[f]

From this height, thus offering a natural base for the patriarchal altar, and a fitting shade for the patriarchal tent, Abraham

---

B.C. 1918.

the strife among the herdsmen
a Ne. v. 9; Ph. ii. 14, 15.

"The writer would intimate that, notwithstanding the check which the vicinity of these heathen tribes ought to have given to the spirit of dissension, it still broke forth. So in all ages, enemies of the church are ever on the watch to discover, publish, and triumph over the feuds and jealousies that may arise between its members."—*Bush.*

b Anon.

"Getting money is not a man's business; to cultivate kindness is a great part of the business of life."—*Johnson.*

c C. Scriver.

Abram's generosity
a Ma. v. 9; Ro. xii. 10—18; 1 Jo. iii. 18.
b Ps. cvii. 33, 34; 1 Jo. ii. 15.
c Ge. xiv. 2, 8; prob. at N. end of Dead Sea, and on E. side, and nr. Sodom.
d Ps. xxvi. 5; 1 Co. xv. 33.
e Ez. xvi. 49; 2 Pe. ii. 7, 8.

"Peace is love reposing. It is love on the green pastures, it is love beside the still waters. It is that great calm which comes over the conscience

GENESIS. [Cap. xiv. 1–4.

B.C. 1918.

when it sees the atonement sufficient, and the Saviour willing, It is unclouded azure in a lake of glass; it is the soul which Christ has pacified, spread out in serenity and simple faith, and the Lord God, merciful and gracious, smiling over it."—*Dr. J. Hamilton.*

f *Dr. Thomas.*

g *Stanley.*

the promise to Abram renewed
a Ge. vii. 5.
b Ge. xxii. 17; xxviii. 14; xxxii. 12; xv. 5; Is. xlviii. 18, 19; Je. xxxiii. 22; He. xi. 12; Re. vii. 9.
c Ge. xiv. 34.
d Nu. xiii. 22.
e Ge. xxiii. 2; Jos. xiv. 15; Ju. i. 10; now called *el-Khulil*, 22 ms. S. of Jerus., pop. 7000, of whom 700 Jews. A mile up the valley is a vast oak, said to be the tree of Mamre, under wh. A. pitched his tent.
v. 14–17. *R. P. Buddicom,* Friend with God, i. 360.
v. 15. *A. R. C. Dallas,* Bloom. Lect. I.
v. 18. *Dr. F. Lee,* Diss. ii. 121.
f *Dr. Parker.*

and Lot must be considered as taking the wide survey of the country "on the right hand and on the left," such as can be enjoyed from no other point in the neighbourhood. To the east there rises in the foreground the jagged range of the hills above Jericho; in the distance the dark wall of Moab; between them lies the valley of the Jordan, its course marked by the tract of forest in which its rushing stream is enveloped; and down to this valley a long and deep ravine, now as always, the main line of communication by which it is approached from the central hills of Palestine—a ravine rich with vine, olive, and fig, winding its way through ancient reservoirs and sepulchres, remains of a civilization now extinct, but in the times of the patriarchs not yet begun. In the south and west the view commanded the bleak hills of Judæa, varied by the heights crowned with what were afterwards the cities of Benjamin, and overhanging what in a later day was to be Jerusalem, and in the far distance the southern range on whose slope is Hebron. Northward are the hills which divide Judæa from the rich plains of Samaria.g

14—18. (14) **after .. him,** a divine friend in a heathen land: a friend that sticketh closer than a brother: A. is the sole possessor. (15) **and .. ever,**a another trial of the faith of a childless old man. (16) **and .. earth,** *etc.,*b Divine promises not scarcely but abundantly fulfilled. (17) **arise .. thee,** the owner to inspect his property: to be safe in midst of present occupants. (18) **plain .. Mamre,** oak, or, oak-grove of Mamre, the Amorite A.'s friend and ally.c **Hebron,**d *(alliance),* also called *Kirjath-arba,*e the city of *Arba,* the progenitor of the Anakim.

Tent and altar.—Tent and altar still together! I. The altar is as essential to the man's soul as the tent to his body. The good man neglects neither body nor soul; his life shows how possible it is to have both tent and altar. II. Even Divine promises do not supersede individual worship. III. A man needs his altar as much after receiving the promises as before.f

Advantages of godliness.—A learned philosopher objected to religion, that, if he should adopt it, he should lose all he had in the world. A Christian friend said no one ever lost any thing by serving Christ; and offered to give his bond to indemnify the philosopher for all losses he should suffer on that account. The bond was duly executed, and the philosopher became a praying man. Just before his death, he sent for his Christian friend, and gave him the paper, saying, "Take this bond, and tear it up. I release you from your promise. Jesus has made up to me a hundredfold for all I ever did or suffered on His account. *There is nothing left for you to pay.* Tell everybody how true it is that there is great profit in serving Jesus."

CHAPTER THE FOURTEENTH.

the rebellion of the kings of Siddim
a Rawlinson discov., a name wh. is supposed to be C.'s, *i.e.,* Kudur-Mapula, called

1—4. (1) **Amraphel** *(? guardian of the gods).* **Shinar,** see on xi. 2. **Arioch** *(lion-like).* **Ellasar** *(the heap of Assyria),* prob. *Larsa* or *Larancha,* betw. Ur and Erech; now *Senkereh.* **Chedorlaomer**a *(handful of sheaves).* **Elam** *(? age, eternity),* S. of Assyria, E. of Persia prop., down to and along Pers. gulf. **Tidal**b *(fear, veneration).* **nations,** sev. nomad tribes. (2)

Bera (*? son of evil*). Birsha (*son of wickedness*). Shinab (*father's tooth*). Shemeber (*lofty flight*). (3) Siddim (*a depression full of stones*), perh. the S. end of Dead S. (4) rebelled, this war was to stamp out the rebellion.

The level of the Dead Sea.—As to the exact level of the Dead Sea, that is now satisfactorily ascertained by Captain Wilson's survey. On the 12th of March, 1865, the depression was found to be 1,292 feet below the level of the Mediterranean; but at some periods of the year it rises two feet six inches higher. He also learned from inquiry amongst the Bedouins, that during the early summer the level is lower by at least six feet. Everybody has heard how buoyant and how nauseous are the waters. We tested the buoyancy, but were careful not to test the nauseousness, satisfied with the testimony of our companions on that point. We could not float so easily as some of them; but we all found ourselves very uncomfortable after dressing, as though we had been rubbed with soap or oil; and we were glad to wash away the effect by plunges in the Jordan a few hours afterwards.*c*

5—9. (5) Rephaims*a* (*? giants*). Ashteroth-Karnaim*b* (*Ashteroth of the two horns, horned Astarte*). Zuzims (*restless*). Ham (*noisy, multitude*). Emims (*terrible men*). Shaveh Kiriathaim*c* (*plain of Kiriathaim*) Kiriathaim = *double city*. (6) Horites (*dwellers in caves*). Seir (*bristly*) Mt. range fr. S. of Palestine to head of Elanitic gulf of Red S. El-paran (*the oak of Paran*), Paran*d* = *cavernous region*. (7) En-mishpat (*fountain of judgment*). Kadesh*e* (*sacred*). Amalekites (*a people that licks up*), betw. Palestine, Idumea, and Mt. Sinai: on plateau now called *er-Rakhmah*. Harzezon-tamar (*pruning of the palm*), anc. name of *En-gedi*. (9) four .. five, these kings can have been little more than wild Arab chiefs.

Kenath.—We spent the afternoon, and some hours of the next day in exploring Kenath. Many of the ruins are beautiful and interesting. The highest part of the site was the aristocratic quarter. Here is a noble palace, no less than three temples, and a hippodrome once profusely adorned with statues. In no other city of Palestine did I see so many statues as there are here. Unfortunately they are all mutilated; but fragments of them— heads, legs, arms, torsos, with equestrian figures, lions, leopards, and dogs—meet one on every side. A colossal head of Ashteroth, sadly broken, lies before a little temple, of which probably it was once the chief idol. The crescent moon which gave the goddess the name Carnaim ("two-horned"), is on her brow. I was much interested in this fragment, because it is a visible illustration of an incidental allusion to this ancient goddess in the very earliest historic reference to Bashan. We read here that the kings of the East, on their way to Sodom, "smote the Rephaims in *Ashteroth-Karnaim.*" May not this be the very city?*f*

10—12. (10) slime-pits,*a* *i.e.* bitumen-pits: fell, were defeated. they .. mountain, of whom the K. of Sodom was one, *v.* 17. (11) went .. way, laden with spoil. (12) Lot*b* .. departed, the effect of companionship with the wicked.

To the mountains for refuge.—People retired to the *mountains* anciently when defeated in war: they do so still. Dr. Shaw indeed seems to suppose that there was no greater safety in the hills than in the plains of this country: that there were few or

---

B.C. 1917.

a also Apda-Martu or Ravager of the west.
b In LXX. called *Thargal* = great chief. The Mohammedans have a custom of inscribing texts from the Koran upon their sword blades. They do their missionary work with this emblem of civil power. The pope and the false prophet are alike in this.
c Dr. Stoughton.

the battle in the Vale of Siddim
a "These were the aboriginal inhabs. of Bashan, and prob. of the greater pt. of Canaan."—*Porter, Giant Cities*, ii. But Miss *Corbeaux* identifies them with the shepherd race that once held dominion in Egypt.
b Porter's Cities of Bashan.
c Acc. to Porter, the mod. *Keireiyut*, under S. side of *Jebel Attarus*.
d Elevated desert track, now called et-Tih, which extends fr. wilderness of Shur in the W., to ridge of *Jebel-el-Tih* in S.
e By Stanley identified with Petra; by Rowlands with *Ain-el-Kadeis*.
f Dr. Porter.

the capture of Lot
a Asphalt; hence the Dead S. was called *Lacus Asphaltites*, *i.e.*, Sea of Asphalt.
b Pr. xiii. 20; Ro. iii. 19.

"That wealth,

GENESIS. [Cap. xiv. 13—20.

B.C. 1917.

which was the cause of his former quarrels, is made a prey to merciless heathens; that place, which his eye covetously chose, betrays his life and goods. How many Christians, whilst they have looked at gain, have lost themselves."— *Bp. Hall.*

c *Harmer.*

no places of difficult access: and that both of them lay equally exposed to the insults and outrages of an enemy. But in this point this ingenious writer seems to be mistaken; since, as we find that those that remained of the armies of the kings of Sodom and Gomorrah fled to the mountains, in the days of Abraham ; so d'Arvieux tells us, that the rebel peasants of the Holy Land, who were defeated while they were in that country by the Arabs, in the plain of Gonin, fled towards the mountains, whither the Arabs could not pursue them at that time. So, in like manner, the Archbishop of Tyre tells us that Baldwin IV. of the croisade kings of Jerusalem, ravaging a place called the valley of Bacar, a country remarkably fruitful, the inhabitants fled to the mountains, whither our troops could not easily follow them. This flying to hills and mountains for safety, is frequently alluded to in Scripture.^c

the rescue of Lot

a Ge. xviii. 19.

b Ju. xviii. 29.

"Not one solitary habitation is there [at Laish]. The fountain still pours forth its river of delicious water; but herds of black buffaloes wash and wallow in its crystal pools. You cannot even examine the site with satisfaction, so dense is the jungle of briers, thorns, and thistles which have overspread it."—*Thomson.*

c *A. M. Heathcote.*

"The natural principle of war is to do the most harm to our enemy with the least harm to ourselves, and this, of course, is to be effected by stratagem."— *Washington Irving.*

d *Harmer.*

13—16. (13) **one .. escaped**, prob. of Lot's retainers. **Hebrew** (*the man from beyond*). **Eshcol** (*cluster*). **Aner** (*exile*). (14) **brother**, kin, relative. **armed**, drew out. **trained**, catechized, instructed : prob. in ref. to sacred things.^a **born .. house**, the children of his own followers. **Dan** (*judge*), anc. *Laish :*^b nr. Paneas on way to Tyre; nr. the mound now called *Tell-el-Kady.* (15) **divided .. night**, he and his allies attacked fr. dif. quarters. Time and manner ensured success. **Hobah** (*hiding place*) **left hand**, *i.e.*, to the N., that point being to the *left* of one who looks towards the sunrise. **Damascus** [*N. T.* iii. 81 ff.]. (16) **brought**, *etc.*, Abraham, friend of God, is a friend to man. A friend in need is a friend indeed.

The patriarch-warrior.—Consider—I. The causes of the expedition, which Abram headed, being fitted out. Love to Lot, his nephew. He returns evil for good. What a lesson is this to us. II. The manner of its conducting. Abram shows himself a prince in war, as he is a prince in peace. III. The success that crowned it. Lot is released Learn—(1) War may sometimes be lawful : (2) God helps those who help themselves; (3) All success should be attributed to Him.^c

Arab mode of attack.—The manner in which the Arabs harass the caravans of the East, is described in the same page. Chardin tells us, " that the manner of their making war, and pillaging the caravans, is, to keep by the side of them, or to follow them in the rear, nearer or farther off, according to their forces, which it is very easy to do in Arabia, which is one great plain, and in the night they silently fall upon the camp, and carry off one part of it before the rest are got under arms." He supposes that Abraham fell upon the camp of the four kings, that had carried away Lot, precisely in the same Arab manner, and by that means, with unequal forces, accomplished his design, and rescued Lot. Gen. xiv. 15, he thinks, shows this ; and he adds, that it is to be remembered, that the combats of the age of Abraham more resembled a fight among the mob, than the bloody and destructive wars of Europe.^d

Melchizedec meets and blesses Abram

a 2 S. xviii. 18.

17—20. (17) **King .. return**, *see* on *v.* 10. **Shaveh** (*a plain*) **.. dale**,^a a valley N. of Jerus. (18) **Melchizedec**^b (*King of righteousness*), [*N. T.* v. 38]. **Salem**^c (*peace*), whether *title* or *place* not known. **priest**, Heb. *Cohen*, the first use of the word.

(19) **blessed,** in his function as priest.*ᵉ* **Abram .. God,** his character and prosperity proved him blessed of God. (20) **which .. hand,**ᶠ he piously gives the praise to the God of battles. **gave .. all,**ᶠ *i.e.*, of all the spoil he had recovered: as a tribute of piety to God.

Melchizedec blessing Abram.—I. The respect which Melchizedec paid to Abram. 1. Melchizedec was a person of a most singular and mysterious character; 2. As God's servant, he came forth on a remarkable occasion to honour Abram. Melchizedec blessed Abram for the zeal he had manifested, and God for the success He had given. II. The return which Abram made him. If we consider it we shall find here—1. An acknowledged duty; 2. A hidden mystery.*ᵍ*

Melchizedec.—The typology connected with Melchizedec does not require that he himself should be regarded as any superhuman person, but merely exalts the human circumstances under which he appears into symbols of superhuman things. Everything combines to show that Melchizedec was a Canaanitish king who had retained the worship of the true God, and combined in his own person the offices of priest and king. It is to be observed that there is not used regarding him, nor does he use, the title of Jehovah, but that of the High God, a title found also in the question addressed (Mic. vi. 6) by the Moabitish king Balak to his prophet Balaam; but that Abram, in answering the King of Sodom, probably in his presence, affirms the identity of his covenant-God Jehovah with the High God, possessor of heaven and earth, of whom Melchizedec had spoken.*ʰ*

21—24. (21) **give .. thyself,** influence of A.'s liberality: men of more value than material wealth. (22) **lift .. Lord,**ᵃ *i.e.*, I swear: anc. form of oath-taking: "form of solemn attestation in all nations." **the .. earth,** all I have belongs to Him. (23) **take .. shoe-latchet** [*N. T.* i. 243], conscientiousness in trifles: fidelity in small matters: little sins. **lest .. say,** boastful character of worldlings. **I .. rich,** and not see that all is fr. God. (24) **save .. eaten,** of the victuals rescued (*v.* 11). **let .. portion,** A. will not enforce his rule on others: liberty of conscience.

Abram's refusal of the king of Sodom's offer.—I. The refusal itself. 1. Generous in its nature; 2. Qualified by an oath of solemn import. II. The reasons for this refusal—"lest thou shouldest say," etc. This would be a reflection upon—1. God. As if He could not alone have enriched Abram; 2. Abram himself. He did not undertake this expedition for reward in filthy lucre; 3. Abram's posterity. They would have been constantly taunted by their enemies with the question, "Who made ye rich?" III. The lessons it contains for us—1. Beware of covetousness in any shape; 2. Be careful that you give no occasion for words to be spoken against you.*ᵇ*

Eastern oath-taking.—"The next morning, before sunrise, they were ready to depart for their camp, two or three days' journey distant. We made known to Hassan our uncertainty and apprehension of what would be their behaviour to us, when the chief lifted up his right hand to heaven, and swore by Allah we should suffer no injury while in his power; an oath which is seldom violated by them." *The thread and the latchet.*—This may refer to the red *thread* worn round the neck or the arm, and which

---

B.C. 1917.

b He. vii. 1—3. "But M., he is Shem, the son of Noah, K. of Jerusalem."—*Targum of Jonathan.* So also the Jerus. Targum.
c Ps. lxxvi. 2.
d 1 Ch. xxiii. 13; Nu. vi. 23, 27.
e Ps. cxliv. 1.
f He. vii. 2—4; Ge. xxviii. 22.
g C. Simeon, M.A. "Lo, here an instance of the communion of saints; Melchidec doth all good offices to Abram (a believer, though a stranger), not of courtesy only and humanity, but of charity and piety."—*Trapp.*
h Alford.

Abram refuses any share of the spoil

a Da. xii. 7; Re. x. 5, 6.

"The king of Sodom appears moved by the liberality of Abram to a like generous return. But there is no league between Abram and Sodom, nor will he give his riches to the idolaters about him. This is at least a different spirit from that in which he acquired his riches in Egypt" (xii. 16).—*Alford*

b H. J. Smith.

"'Tis not the many oaths that make the truth; But the plain single vow, that is vow'd true."—*Shakspeare.*

binds on the amulet; or the *string* with which females tie up their hair. The latchet I suppose to mean the *thong* of the sandal, which goes over the top of the foot, and betwixt the great and little toes. It is proverbial to say, should a man be accused of taking away some valuable article, which belongs to another, "I have not taken away even a piece of the *thong* of your worn-out sandals."*c*

B.C. 1917.

c Roberts.

v. 20—22. J. Doughty, Analecta Sacra, 24—27.

B.C. 1913.

CHAPTER THE FIFTEENTH.

God appears to Abram in a vision

a Nu. xxiv. 4—16.

b Is. xli. 10; Ma. x. 28.

c Ps. xxvii. 1; Pr xxx. 5; Ps. xci. 4; v. 2; cxix. 114; lxxxiv. 9, 11.

d The LXX reads, "Thy reward shall be exceeding great."

e Ac. vii. 5; Ps. cxxvii. 3.

"If Abram came into Palestine by the way of Damascus, it is not unlikely that he should have taken his principal retainer from that place."—*Speaker's Commentary.*

f J. *King.*

"Reward a good servant well; and rather get quit of a bad one than disquiet thyself with him."—*Fuller.*

"Servants are good for nothing unless they have an opinion of the person's understanding who has the direction of them."—*Addison.*

g Dr. J. *Hamilton.*

His promise to Abram renewed

a Ho. xi. 12 De. x. 22. III.

b Ga. 6 Ro. iv. 3—22; Ja. ii. 23.

c *Bush.*

1—4. (1) **vision,** *this a waking* vision.*a* **fear not,***b* timely encouragement: might not the defeated kings rally? **shield,***c* protection. **thy .. reward,** *lit.* "thy reward exceeding abundantly."*d* Good works, wh. are of faith, have their reward. (2) **childless,** notwithstanding thy promise. **steward .. Damascus,** *lit.* the heir of my house, etc., Eliezer = *God his help.* (3) **behold,** *etc.,* my property and the covenant will descend not to a *son,* but to a *dependant.* (4) **word .. came,** *etc.,e* Divine condescension: doubts removed: promise re-affirmed: a *son* and no other, the heir.

God the shield and reward of His people.—Consider—I. The doctrine of the text. Observe in what sense God is—1. The defence of His people. He shields them from danger by His Providence, and from sin by His grace; 2. Their portion. He gives them Himself. II. The inference deducible from it. "Fear not." Fear not—1. The enemies which surround you; 2. The dangers that threaten you; 3. The toils that you may be required to undergo; 4. The sacrifices that it may be necessary for you to make. Let fear be replaced by a confidence coming from God.*f*

Eliezer of Damascus.—With Eliezer of Damascus we have always associated in our own minds Melancthon's good servant, John of Sweden. During the thirty-four years that he had the charge of the Reformer's house, notwithstanding boundless hospitality and the many inevitable expenses incident to a public position, no debt was incurred, and wonders were wrought with the limited income. He was the first instructor of Melancthon's children, "and all the goods of his master were in his hand." When he died the students of the university attended his funeral, and on his tomb his master inscribed this epitaph:—

 "Here at a distance from his native land
 Came honest John, at Philip's first command;
 Companion of his exile, doubly dear,
 Who in a servant found a friend sincere:
 And more than friend—a man of faith and prayer;
 Assiduous soother of his master's care:
 Here to the worms his lifeless body's given,
 But his immortal soul sees God in heaven."*g*

5—7. (5) **brought .. abroad,** out of the grove into open glade. **look,** waking vision. *v.* 1. **so .. be,***a* countless and wide-spread as the stars. (6) **believed,** faith rests on the promise. **it,** *i.e.* his faith. **righteousness,***b* "an acceptable, excellent, praiseworthy act."*c* (7) **I .. Chaldees,***d* the same who then called thee, is now with thee to fulfil his promise.

Cap. xv. 8—17.]   GENESIS.   63

to .. it, the purpose for wh. the call was first given is not forgotten.
Abram justified by faith.—I. The faith he exercised. 1. The promise, now given him, was very extensive; 2. The faith he exercised, had respect to the promise in all its parts. II. The benefit he obtained: "it was counted to him for righteousness." The meaning of this is, that his faith, as laying hold of Christ and of His righteousness, was the instrument whereby he was justified.*e*

Merchandise of godliness.—A merchant in a single morning will make a hundred pounds, while poor men work hard for a shilling. The voice of Nature is, "How shall we come to be rich?" Prize the trade of godliness. Works of morality are like the labouring man; but godliness is a full merchant's trade, that brings in hundreds and thousands at a clap. Such a trade would God have us set our hearts upon. As Cleopatra said to Marcus Antonius, it was not for him to fish for gudgeons, but for towns, forts, and castles; so it is not for the godly to be trading for transitory trash, but for eternal life, glory, and immortality.*f*

8—12. (8) **whereby,** .. **know,***a* he asked a sign to confirm his faith: he may have thought of his posterity. (9) **take me,** *i.e.* take and offer to me. **three .. old,** prime of life. (10) **divided .. midst,***b* cut ea. animal in half, longitudinally. **laid .. another,** opposite ea. other leaving a passage betw. **birds .. not,** as aft. prescribed by law.*c* (11) **fowls .. carcases,** birds of prey. **Abram .. away,** covenant not yet ratified. (12) **deep sleep,***d* Heb. *tardamah*, Gk. εκστασις; *i.e.* supernatural trance or extacy. **horror .. darkness,** *lit,* a horror, a great darkness, overwhelming awe, wh. deepens with increasing darkness and silence.

Patriarchal worship.—Observe—I. The nature of primitive worship. 1. Of divine appointment; 2. Sacrificial. II. What it taught—1. The Divine claims on man; 2. Man's guilt and peril. 3. The interposition of God's mercy and grace; 4. The Scriptural way of coming to God; 5. The coming of the great Sacrifice. III. How it was observed. It was—1. Personal; 2. By faith; 3. Open; 4. Sincere.*e*

Abrahamic covenant.—This very solemn form of ratifying a covenant is again particularly mentioned in Je. xxxiv. 18. It consisted in cutting the throat of the victim, and pouring out its blood. The carcass was then divided, lengthwise, as nearly as possible into two equal parts, which being placed opposite to each other at a short distance, the covenanting parties approached at the opposite ends of the passage thus formed, and meeting in the middle took the customary oath. The practice was by no means peculiar to the Hebrews. Traces of it may be found in the Greek and Roman writers, and in the accounts of travellers.*f*

13—17. (13) **stranger .. theirs,** chief ref. is to Egypt. **four .. years,** in round numbers; or more precisely 430 yrs.*a* (14) **nation,** Egypt. **judge,***b* punish. **with .. substance,** great riches. (15) **go .. fathers,***c* a hint of immortality. **peace,***d* by a peaceful death. **in .. age,** *lit.*, in a good hoary age. (16) **fourth .. again,** thus Caleb was 4th fr. Judah: and Moses fr. Levi: so prob. of many others. **for .. full,** God foresaw that they would add sin to sin. It was for their sins they

B.C. 1913.

d No. ix. 7, 8; Ge. xii. 1; xi. 31.
e C. *Simeon, M.A. v.* 5, G. *Br. R. Gell*, Essay, 135; *H. Blunt,* Abra., 112; *R. P. Buddicom*, i. 414; *Dr. Kitto*, Bibl. Ill. i. 228.
"When I gazed into these stars, have they not looked down on me as if with pity from their serene spaces, like eyes glistening with heavenly tears over the little lot of man!"
—*Carlyle.*
f Spencer.

the promise ratified by a covenant
a Ju. vi. 17; Lu. i. 18.
"Dove, lit. the diver; fr. its rapid rising and falling in the air. A.S., *duva, dúfian*, the d. kept in cages is the *collared* pigeon, called the turtle or *ringdove*."—*Topics,* i. 34.
b Jo. xxxiv. 18, 20.
c Le. i. 17.
d Ge. ii. 21.
"There are several species of this bird enumerated by Mrs. Tristam as common in Palestine, such as *Turtur auritus,* the turtle-dove, *Turtur Ægyptiacus,* the palm-dove, or Egyptian turtle, *Columba livia,* the rock-dove, etc."
—*Treas. Bib. Knowledge.*
e Dr. J. Burns.
f Bush.

the smoking furnace and burning lamp
a Ex. xii. 40; Ps. cv. 23, 25; Ainsworth reckons the time fr. Ishmael's mocking of Isaac.
—Abraham en-

B.C. 1913.

ters Canaan and receives the promise, B.C. 1921; Isaac mocked by Ishmael, B.C. 1891; Israel departs from Egypt, B.C., 1491. The difference between the first and last of these dates, is just 430 yrs. Of this period 215 yrs. were passed in sojourning in Canaan, and 215 in Egypt.

b De. vi. 22; Ex. xii. 36; Ps. cv. 37, 38.
c Is. lvii. 1, 2; Job v. 26.
d Ps. xxxvii. 37.
e Ex. xix. 18; He. xii. 29.
f R. A. Griffin.
g Spurgeon.

the terms of the covenant
a Is. xxvii. 12; 1 K. iv. 21.
b Land and Bk., 164.

"What a chimera is man! what a confused chaos! what a subject of contradiction! a professed judge of all things, and yet a feeble worm of the earth! the great depository and guardian of truth, and yet a mere huddle of uncertainty! the glory and the scandal of the universe!"—*Pascal.*

"If a man is not rising upward to be an angel, depend upon it he is sinking downward to be a devil. He cannot stop at the beast. The most savage of men are not beasts: they are worse,—a great deal worse."—*Coleridge.*

were cut off. (17) **behold** .. **furnace,**e an oven of smoke. **and** .. **lamp,** flame or tongue of fire. **that** .. **pieces,** token of a present God ratifying the covenant.

The vocation of the aged saint.—Aged saints—I. Render peculiar assistance to the church. By—1. Their prayers; 2. Their counsels; 3. Their influence. II. Furnish signal examples of the power of Divine grace. Divine grace is seen—1. To be sufficient for saints in every period, and under all circumstances. In prosperity and adversity. Amid conflict and peace. Amid temptations and trials. When friendless, and when many friends are possessed; 2. To lose none of its vitality with the decay of mind and body. III. Attest much of the character of God. A long life of faith and labour shows that God is—1. An abiding source of help and joy; 2. Longsuffering; 3. Wise. Conclusion—(1) Let us be willing to live as long as God wills; (2) Let the aged consider their high vocation.*f*

Godliness no burden to true saints.—The Princess Elizabeth carried the crown for her sister in the procession at Mary's coronation, and complained to Noailles of its great weight. "Be patient," was the adroit answer, "it will seem lighter when on your own head." The outward forms of godliness are as burdensome to an unregenerate man as was the crown to the princess; but let him be born again and so made a possessor of the good things of Divine grace, and they will sit easily enough upon his head, as his glory and delight.*g*

18—21. (18) **made** .. **saying,** *lit.,* cut the covenant. **from** .. **Egypt,** prob. the *Wady-el-Arisch,* wh. is called the stream of E.*a*; or it might be the Nile. (19) **Kenites,** (*smiths* or *dwellers in a nest*) prob. S. and S.W. of Pales. **Kenizzites** (*hunters*). **Kadmonites***b* (*orientals*) prob. E. of Pales. (20) **Hittites,** *see* x. 15. **Perizzites,** *see* xiii. 7. **Rephaims,** *see* xiv. 5. (21) **Amorites,** *see* x. 16. **Canaanites,** including other unspecified tribes. **Girgashites** .. **Jebusites,** *see* x. 16.

The profit of godliness.—There dwelt an old and prosperous couple near London, of whom a charity was asked, to which the wife replied, "Why, sir, we have lost a deal by religion since we first began: my husband knows that very well. Have we not, Thomas?" After a solemn pause, Thomas answered, "Yes, Mary, we have. Before I got religion, Mary, I had an old slouched hat, a tattered coat, and mended shoes and stockings; but I have lost them long ago. And, Mary, you know, that, poor as I was, I had a habit of getting drunk, and quarrelling with you; and that you know I have lost. And then I had a hardened conscience, and wicked heart, and ten thousand guilty fears; but all are lost, completely lost, and, like a millstone, cast into the deepest sea. And, Mary, you have been a loser too, though not so great a loser as myself. Before we got religion, Mary, you had a washing-tray, in which you washed for hire; but since then you have lost your washing-tray. And you had a gown and bonnet much the worse for wear; but you have lost them long ago. And you had many an aching heart concerning me at times; but these you happily have lost. And I could even wish that you had lost as much as I have lost; for what we lose for religion will be an everlasting gain."—William Greehill used to say, "Christians must always profess godliness, and always practise it; their life must always be green, and their fruit always ripe."

CHAPTER THE SIXTEENTH.

B.C. 1898.

1—3. (1) **Egyptian,** who prob. foll. S. fr. Egypt. **Hagar** (*flight*) or Agar.*a* (2) **Lord** .. **bearing,** a childless wife owning God's Providence. **go** .. **her,** though A. was to be the father, it was said that Sarai was to be the mother of the promised seed. **Abram** .. **Sarai,***b* his knowledge and faith were imperfect. (3) **after** .. **years,** A. being 85; and S. 75 yrs. of age.*c* **gave** .. **wife,** as inferior wife, or concubine.

Our aptness to make mistakes.—We were riding along in the afternoon of a lovely but blazing day from Varallo to Riva, and to quench our thirst on the road we carried with us some bottles of an excellent lemonade. The empty bottles were of no use to us, and one of them was given to a friend on the box seat of the carriage to throw away. He happened to be the essence of gentleness and liberality, and seeing two very poor peasant women trudging along with huge empty baskets strapped on their backs, he thought it would delight them if he dropped the bottle into one of their receptacles; a bottle being far more a godsend there than in England. Alas, for our friend's happiness during the whole of the next twenty-four hours! The motion of the carriage made him miss his aim, and the bottle fell on the head of the woman instead of into her basket. There was a shrill cry, and a good deal of blood and speedy faintness. Of course, we were all in an instant binding up the wound with silver, and our friend, we feel sure, used golden ointment, so that the poor old creature would have cheerfully had her head broken ten times to receive such a sum as she obtained by way of solatium; but still the accident saddened us all, and especially our dear tender-hearted friend from whose hand the missile was dropped. How often has his case been ours! We meant to cheer a troubled conscience and instead thereof we wounded it yet more. We intended nothing but love, but our words gave pain; we had miscalculated, and missed our aim. This has both astonished us and caused us the deepest regret. Yet such a blunder has made us the more careful, and has humbled us under a sense of our readiness to err, and moreover it has led us to be still more liberal in the use of that precious treasure of the Gospel, which easily recompenses for all our blundering. Loving reader, be careful with your kindnesses, but be not too much depressed should they fail to comfort. The Lord knows your intentions.*d*

4—6. (4) **her** .. **eyes,***a* the maid elevated to rank of wife (?) becomes insolent. (5) **wrong** .. **thee,** you are the cause of the insult. **Lord** .. **me,** in other words, may God defend the right. (6) **behold,** *etc.*,*b* the vexed husband is gentle. **do** .. **thee,** should he not have stood betw. the maid and his incensed wife? **fied** .. **face,** having no protector in Abram.

Man reflected in history.—Man's twofold nature is reflected in history. "He is of earth," but his thoughts are with the stars. Mean and petty his wants and his desires; yet they serve a soul exalted with grand, glorious aims, with immortal longings, with thoughts which sweep the heavens, and "wander through eternity." A pigmy standing on the outward crust of this small planet, his far-reaching spirit stretches outwards to the infinite.

Sarah gives Hagar to Abram

a Ga. iv. 24.

b Ge. iii. 17.

c cf. xii. 4; xvi. 16; xvii. 17.

"The father of mankind sinned by hearkening to his wife, and now the father of the faithful follows his example. How necessary for those who stand in the nearest relations, to take heed of being snares, instead of helps, to one another."—*Fuller.*

"Let him who gropes painfully in darkness or uncertain light, and prays vehemently that the dawn may ripen into day, lay this precept well to heart: 'Do the duty which lies near thee,' which thou knowest to be a duty! Thy second duty will already have become clearer."—*Carlyle.*

d Spurgeon.

Hagar flees from Sarai

a Pr. xxx. 21—23

b 1 Pe. iii. 7.

"A thousand volumes written against polygamy would not lead to a clearer, fuller, conviction of the evils of that practice than the story

[Cap. xvi. 7—16.

B.C. 1898.

under review."—*Bush.*

c Carlyle.

There are more victims to errors committed by society itself than society supposes.

d Abp. Whately.

Hagar and the angel

a "First mention of 'angel of Jehovah.' In several places it appears that this emissary of Jehovah is none other than an appearance, carrying the power of the Divine presence."—*Alford.*

b See also *Kitto's Pict. Bible.*

c 1 Pe. ii. 18.

d The word *pere*, wild ass, is prob. fr. *para*, = to run swiftly.

e Rosenmuller, Delitzsch. cf. Job i. 3; Nu. xxi. 11; Jos. xv. 8; Zech. xiv. 4.

f Martin Shaw.

v. 6—12. Bp. Newton, Prophecies, i. 21.

v. 10—12. R. Poltchele, i. 145.

v. 11. Dean Delany. Rev. Exam., ii. 113.

v. 12. Dr. Worthington, Boyle L c., i. 419.

Beer-lahai-roi

a Ps. cxxxix. 7; Pr. v. 21.

b Spk. Comm.

and there alone finds rest. History is a reflex of this double life. Every epoch has two aspects—one calm, broad, and solemn—looking towards eternity; the other, agitated, petty, vehement, and confused—looking towards time.*c* *Man and his mistakes.*—In all ages and all countries, man, through the disposition he inherits from our first parents, is more desirous of a quiet and approving, than of a vigilant and tender conscience, desirous of security instead of safety; studious to escape the thought of spiritual danger more than the danger itself; and to induce, at any price, some one to assure him confidently that he is safe, to prophesy unto him smooth things, "and to speak peace, even when there is no peace."*d*

7—12. (7) **angel,**^a Heb. *Maleach* = one sent: a messenger. **fountain,** see ver. 14. **Shur,** perh. *Al-jifar*, N.E. part of Wild. of Paran.*b* (8) **Hagar,** called her by name. **maid,** reminded her of her station, duty, etc. **whence..thou?** fr. a pious house. **and..go?** to a heathen land. (9) **Return,***c* etc., duty oft. calls us to suffer in the way of obedience. (10) **I will,** etc. Who is this who says "I will"? (11) **Ishmael** (*God heareth*). **because..affliction.** God knows, compensates, sanctifies our trials. (12) **wild man,** *lit.* "wild ass among men:"*d* ref. to wild, free, roving life. **hand..him,** exactly descr. Arabs, who are descen. fr. Ishmael. **dwell..brethren,** or, "to the E. of all his brethren."*e*

Ishmael's descendants.—Look at—I. Their character as here foretold. It is said that—1. They should be wild men from their birth. The figure here used is that of the onagra, a wild, untamable animal, thus indicating their roving disposition; 2. Their hands should be against mankind. Enmity on their part against man; 3. Every man's hand should be against them. Enmity on man's part against them. II. The remarkable fulfilment of this prediction. At this day the Bedouin Arabs are at war, so to speak, with mankind, and lead a wild, roving kind of life, in which robbery is a chief point.*f*

The posterity of Ishmael.—The descendants of Ishmael continue to this day to live in hostility to the greater part of mankind. On the margin of the Red Sea and Arabian Gulf commerce has exerted some influence, but the Eastern Arabs, or Nabatheans, are almost entirely freebooters, living by plunder. Although spread over a country thirteen hundred miles long and twelve hundred miles broad, they are comparatively secure, while those who are sometimes hardly enough to follow them either die with thirst or are compelled to return, overcome with fatigue and sickness. Their water is obtained from wells, sunk amid the rocks and plains which they inhabit, and known only to themselves. Notwithstanding the opposition they have met with from the ancient Assyrians, the Medes, the Persians, and the Macedonians, they have, from first to last, maintained their independence. No conqueror has subdued them; and they still, as a memento of Scripture prophecy, dwell in the presence of all their brethren.

13—16. (13) **Lord..her,** who app. in angelic form. **Thou,** etc.,*a* "Thou art a God that seest all things, and am I yet living and seeing, aft. seeing God?"*b* (14) **Beer-lahai-roi.***c* "The well of life of vision: *i.e.*, where life remains after vision of God."*d* **between..Ber-ed,** site of neither place known.*e*

Cap. xvii. 1—5.] GENESIS. 67

(15) **Abram**, *etc.*,*f* he having heard of words of angel fr. Hagar.
(16) **was . . old**, *lit.* "a son of 86 years."
Belief in the Divine omniscience the foundation of a true and earnest life.—This text may be regarded as—I. The basis of a living creed. II. An incentive to a useful and beautiful life. Two things are essential to such a life—1. Sincere love of the truth; 2. Earnest practice of the truth. III. A restraint upon a sinful course. Let these words, "Thou God seest me," preserve you from—1. Unhallowed thoughts; 2. Selfish motives; 3. Formalism and hypocrisy; 4. Despondency and unbelief.*g*
A son's rebuke.—A man who was in the habit of going into a neighbour's cornfield to steal the ears, one day took his son with him, a boy of eight years of age. The father told him to hold the bag while he looked if anyone was near to see him. After standing on the fence and looking around, he returned and took the bag from the child, and began his guilty work. "Father," said the boy, "you forgot to look somewhere else." The man dropped the bag in a fright, and said, "Which way, child?" supposing he had seen some one. "You forgot to look up to the sky, to see if God was noticing you." The father felt this reproof of the child so much, that he left the corn, returned home, and never again ventured to steal, remembering the truth his child had taught him, that the eye of God always beholds us.

B.C. 1898.

c Ge. xxiv. 62; xxv. 11.

d *Rowlands* thinks he has found it at *Moilahhi*, ab. 10 hrs. S. of Ruheibeh. *Moi*, water; being=to *Beer*, well. *Williams, Holy City*, i. 465.

e Ge. xxi. 20.

f *Joseph Carter.*

g *J. R. Goulty. B.S.*

r. 13 *J. Jenkins*, i. 145; *C. Simeon*, i. 131; *Wm. Jay*, i. 28; *J. H. Newman*, iii. 124; *Dr. H. Hughes, Fem. Cha.*, i. 108.

CHAPTER THE SEVENTEENTH.

1—5. (1) **Abram . . nine**, *i.e.* 13 yrs. aft. last-named event. **I . . God**,*a* Heb. *El Shaddai* = mighty. God all-sufficient. Abraham might need to be now reminded of this. **walk . . me**,*b* live as in my sight. **perfect**,*c* upright, sincere. (2) **make**, *lit.* give. It was not betw. *equals*, who could *make* a cov., but God, on the one side, *gave* it. (3) **fell . . face**, profound humility, and adoration. (4) **thou . . nations**,*d* multitude of nations. (5) **Abram**, high father (*ab.* father; *ram*, high). **Abraham**, high father of a multitude.
The establishment of the covenant between God and Abram.—I. The precondition of the establishment of the covenant (xv. and xvi.). II. The contents of the covenant of promise. The name Abraham in—1. The natural; 2. The typical sense. III. The covenant in the wider and narrower sense. IV. The covenant sign.*e*
Change of name.—In Eastern countries a change of name is an advertisement of some new circumstance in the history, rank, or religion of the individual who bears it. The change is made variously; by the old name being entirely dropped for the new, or by conjoining the old with the new, or sometimes only a few letters are inserted, so that the altered form may express the difference in the owner's state or prospects. It is surprising how soon a new name is known, and its import spread through the country. In dealing with Abraham and Sarah, God was pleased to adapt His procedure to the ideas and customs of the country and age. Instead of Abram, "a high father," he was to be called Abraham, "a father of a multitude of nations."*f*

Abram's name changed

a Ex. vi. 3; Jo. i. 18; Ge. v. 22; vi. 9; Job i. 1.

b 1 K. ii. 4; 2 K. xx. 3.

c Ep. iii. 20; Ma. v. 48.

d Ge. xii. 2; xiii. 16; xxii. 17.

e *Lange.*

v. 1. *Dr. Whitby*, 120; *J. Saurin*, i. 243; *J. Abernethy*, i. 248; *J. Reeve*, i. 116; *Dr. Drysdale*, i. 353; *J. Milner*, iii. 268; *Dr. Dwight*, i. 103.

v. 1, 2. *J. Fawcett*, 72; *R. P. Buddicom*, ii. 22.

f *Jamieson.*

[Cap. xvii. 6—14.

B.C. 1898.

Canaan promised to him
a Matt. i. 6—11; see also *Bush in loc.*
b Ho. xl. 16; Lu. i. 54, 55; Go. xxvi. 24; xxviii. 13; Ro. ix. 7—9; De. xiv. 2; xxvi. 18.
c R. Sibbes, D.D.
"Where there is any good disposition, confidence begets faithfulness; but distrust, if it do not produce treachery, never fails to destroy every inclination to evince fidelity. Most people disdain to clear themselves from the accusations of mere suspicion."—*Jane Porter.*
v. 7. R. Sibbes, 2 sers. *J. Davison, Warb. Lect.*, 68.
d Spurgeon.

circumcision instituted
a Ps. ciii. 17, 18.
b Ro. iv. 11; 1 Co. vii. 28, 29; 1 Co. vii. 19; Ph. iii. 3; Col. ii. 2; Ga. v. 6.
c Le. xii. 3; Lu. ii. 21; Ph. iii. 5. That "circumcision drives away the Sabbath," was a Jewish maxim; and acted upon in time of Christ.—Jo. vii. 22, 23.
d Speaker's Com., cf. Ex. iv. 24, 25.
e Osiander.
"Children have more need of models than of critics."—*Joubert.*
v. 9, 10. N. Alexander, Hist. Eccl. i. 405; *C. Simeon,* i. 133.
v. 10. W. Reading, i. 1.

6—8. (6). **kings..thee**, this lit. fulfilled.*a* (7), **for..covenant**, *lit.* covenant of eternity. (8). **land..stranger**, land of thy sojournings. I..**God**,*b* the object of their worship, and the source of their prosperity.

The faithful covenanter.—I. The party covenanting—God. "I will be thy God." II. The parties covenanted with—Abraham and his seed. III. The substance of this covenant—"I will be a God to thee and to thy seed." IV. Its qualities. 1. Sure; 2. Everlasting; 3. Peculiar; 4. Most free; 5. A covenant consisting mostly of spiritual things. V. The condition of the whole. This though not expressed, is implied. "I will be thy God;" therefore thou shalt take Me for thy God.*c*

Trusting the promises.—When a pious old slave on a Virginia plantation was asked why he was always so sunny-hearted and cheerful under his hard lot, he replied, "Ah, massa! I always lays flat down on de *promises*, and den I pray straight up to my heabenly Father." Humble, happy soul! he was not the first man who has eased an aching head by laying it upon God's pillows, or the first man who has risen up the stronger from a repose on the unchangeable word of God's love. Spiritually that man was a Croesus; for all his soul's wealth was in the currency of heaven. If you take a Bank of England note to the counter of the bank, in an instant that bit of paper turns to gold. If we take a promise of God to the mercy-seat, it turns to what is better than gold,—to our own good and the glory of our Father.*d*

9—14. (9) **keep**,*a* faithfully observe thy duty in relation thereunto. (10) **this**, *i.e.* the *sign* of, etc. **circumcised**,*b* Heb. *yimmol*, "shall be cut round about." (11) **token**, sign, evidence of faith on the one part, reminder of promise on the other. (12) **eight days**,*c* child then old enough to bear the operation. (13) **born**, *etc.*, children of thyself, or servants. **he..money**, bondsman. (14) **cut off**, "it is pretty certain that *death* in some form is intended."*d*

The rite of circumcision.—God introduces a sacrament which, viewed in itself alone, might be regarded as involving disgrace. I. But, on this very account, it typifies the deep depravity of men, in which they are involved from the corruption of original sin, since not only some of the members, but the whole man, is poisoned. II. For the same reason, it confirms the promise of the increase of the race of Abraham. III. Through this sign God intends to distinguish the people of his possession from all other nations. IV. He represents in it, the spiritual circumcision of the heart—the new birth.*e*

Securing obedience.—The first rule of the order which St. Francis founded was implicit submission to the superior. The legend says, that one day a monk proved refractory, and must be subdued. By order of St. Francis, a grave was dug deep enough to hold a man: the monk was put into it; and his associates began to shovel in the earth, while the superior looked on, stern as death. When the mould reached the knees of the stubborn monk, St. Francis, stooping down, asked him, "Are you dead yet? is your self-will dead? do you yield?" There was no answer. In the grave there seemed to stand a man with a will as iron as his own. The burial continued, to the middle, to the shoulders, to the lips. Once more St. Francis bent down to repeat his question, "Are you dead yet?" The suffocating monk saw no relenting in the stern countenance of his superior. Resistance was useless. A few moments more, and the earth would cover him. Then the iron will was broken: the funeral was stayed, and the submissive monk replied, "I am dead." The monk is the type of many, some of whom yield in the last extremity, and others go into eternity still raging against the Supreme.

15—17. (15) **Sarai,** *my princess.* **Sarah,** *princess.* "Her limited pre-eminence is to be unspeakably enlarged." (16) **she .. nations,** *lit.* shall be to nations; *i.e.* shall become nations. (17) **fell .. face,** in adoration. **laughed,**[a] transported with joy.

Sarai and Sarah.—Her name always one that indicated dignity. Consider—I. Her old name, "my princess," limited. Sarai to live for her husband only. II. Her new name, "princess," in wider sense. He, the father of the faithful; she, the mother. Now stands in a historical relation to the church.

Joy, gladness, and mirth.—The happy condition of the soul is designated by all these terms; but the *joy* and *gladness* lie more internal; the *mirth* is the more immediate result of external circumstances. What creates *joy* and *gladness* is of a permanent nature; that which creates *mirth* is temporary; *joy* is the most vivid sensation in the soul; *gladness* is the same in quality, but inferior in degree: *joy* is awakened in the mind by the most important events in life; *gladness* springs up in the mind on ordinary occasions: the return of the prodigal son awakened *joy* in the heart of the father; a man feels *gladness* at being relieved from some distress or trouble: public events of a gratifying nature produce universal *joy*; the relief from either sickness or want brings *gladness* to an oppressed heart; he who is absorbed in his private distresses is ill prepared to partake of the *mirth* which he is surrounded with at the festive board.[b]

18—22. (18) **O .. Thee,** perh. he feared the heir would altogether exclude Ishmael fr. the blessing of God. (19) **Isaac,** Heb. *yitzhek,* he shall laugh. **I .. covenant,**[a] already made, and several times re-affirmed. (20) **heard,** prob. all. to meaning of Ishmael.[b] **twelve .. beget,** *lit.* fulfilled.[c] (21) **but .. Isaac,** ref. to the Messiah. **this .. year,** at this very time next year.[d] (22) **left .. him,** for this occasion. **God .. up,** to heaven.[e]

The father's prayer.—I. The person who prayed. Ishmael's father. 1. Who is so suitable as the parent to pray? He above all others knows the child's propensities, weakness, hindrances, and capabilities. Make each a topic: 2. Who is so responsible? You are responsible for the use of the means. If you neglect them, how dreadful your future! 3. Who is so interested? 4. Who is so likely to pray with fervour? They cannot be so dear to others as to you. By your love for them, by their love for you, pray ye for them. II. The petition. 1. He does not pray for temporal good for him, except as it flows out of his spiritual blessing; 2. Nor for great spiritual honours and gifts; 3. His prayer had a twofold object. (1) God's glory; (2) Ishmael's safety. III. Was the prayer answered? In all probability, yes. Address—(1) Praying parents; (2) Inconsistent parents; (3) Unconverted parents.[f]

Philip Henry's promise.—The following remark of Rev. Philip

B.C. 1898.

Experience is the most eloquent of preachers, but she never has a large congregation.

Sarai's name changed
a Jo. viii. 56; Ps. iv. 7.

"True joy is a sober and serene motion; and they are miserably out that take laughing for rejoicing; the seat of it is within, and there is no cheerfulness like the resolution of a brave mind, that has fortune under its feet."—*Seneca.*

"What is joy? A sunbeam between two clouds."—*Mde. Deluzy.*

"True joy is only hope put out of fear."—*Ld. Broöke.*

b G. Crabb.

promise of a son, to be called Isaac
a Ro. ix. 8; Ga. iv. 28.
b Ge. xvi. 11.
c Ge. xxv. 12—16.
d Os. xxi. 2.
e "The angel of God went up."—*Arab.* "The glory of the Lord went up."—*Chal. i.e.* "The visible majesty of Jehovah, the Shekinah, the symbol of the Divine presence."—*Bush.*

"The most affecting thought to me, on the death of my parents, was, that I had lost their prayers."—*Dr. Spring.*
f R. A. Griffin.

B.C. 1898.

"Truly there is nothing in the world so blessed or so sweet as the heritage of children." — *Mrs. Oliphant.*

g Cheever.

Abraham's household circumcised

a Ps. cxix. 60.
b Jos. Ant.. i. 13.
c Ro. iv. 20, 21.
"Fr. this circumstance the Arabians, and other descendants of Ishmael, and indeed all the followers of Mohammed, defer circumcision till the age of thirteen, and when it occurs it is made a festival occasion of great rejoicing." — *Bush.*
v. 24. *J. Donne, Wks.,* v. 325.

Abraham visited by three angels

a cf. v. 22; xix. 1.
b He. xiii. 2.
c 1 Pe. iv. 9.
d xix. 2; xxiv. 32; Ju. xix. 21; 1 Ti. v. 10.
Feet washing, *Topics,* ii. 8.
e J. H. Jones.
"Often has my mind reverted to the scene of the good old patriarch sitting in the door of his tent in the heat of the day. When the sun is at the meridian, the wind often becomes softer, and the heat more oppressive; and then may be seen the people seated in the doors of their huts, to inhale the breezes, and to let them

Henry, after he had been engaged in ardent prayer for two of his children, that were dangerously ill, is so expressive of the *simplicity* and *tenderness* of Christian faith and love, as to recommend itself to the hearts of those who walk with God:—" If the Lord will be pleased to grant me this my request concerning my children, I will not say as the beggars at our door used to do, 'I'll never ask anything of Him again;' but, on the contrary, He shall hear oftener from me than ever; and I will love God the better, and love prayer the better as long as I live."*g*

23—27. (23) **Abraham,** *etc.,* without the least delay.*a* (24) **Abraham** .. **nine,** did not plead age as an excuse for avoiding a *new* and *painful* duty. (25) **Ishmael** .. **old,** hence *Arabs* and *Mohammedans* defer the rite to that age.*b* (26) **selfsame** .. **son,** as prompt to exact as to yield obedience. (27) **all the men,** *etc.,c* the command was obeyed without any limitation.

The safety of obedience.—A pointsman in Prussia was at the junction of two lines of railway, his lever in hand for a train that was signalled. The engine was within a few seconds of reaching the embankment, when the man, on turning his head, perceived his little boy playing on the rails of the line the train was to pass over. " Lie down !" he shouted to the child; but, as to himself, he remained at his post. The train passed safely on its way. The father rushed forward, expecting to take up a corpse; but what was his joy on finding that the boy had at once obeyed his order! He had lain down, and the whole train passed over him without injury. The next day the king sent for the man, and attached to his breast the medal for civil courage.

CHAPTER THE EIGHTEENTH.

1—5. (1) **Mamre,** *see on* xiii. 18, and xiv. 13. *plains* = oak grove. **sat .. day,** what followed was no *night* vision. (2) **three men,** two were angels, and the third was the Lord.*a* **stood,** *etc.,* their appearance sudden. **ran .. them,** eager to tender hospitality. **bowed,** *etc.,* saw a dignity in them, yet knew not who they were.*b* (3) **Lord,** Heb. *Adonai* (plural of excellence). One prob. appeared more dignified than the others. (4) **water .. feet,***c* walking in sandals made this custom necessary.*d* **rest,** *lit.* lean : *i.e.* recline. (5) **comfort .. hearts,** *lit.* support your hearts : *i.e.* refresh all the vital powers and spirits. **after .. on,** he will entertain, but not hinder. **for .. servant,** for rest, etc., nothing more.

Hospitality.—Consider this virtue in—I. Its source : a kind and generous heart. II. Its attendant qualities. 1. Prompt ; 2. Admitting of no refusal ; 3. Unsparing. III. The esteem in which it is held. It is—1. Pleasing to man. 2. Approved of by God. IV. The reward which it brings. 1. An angel may be entertained unawares ; 2. Gratitude in its object is but natural to expect.*e*

Eastern hospitality.—Nothing is more common in India than to see travellers and guests eating under the shade of trees. Even feasts are never held in houses. The house of a Hindoo serves for the purposes of sleeping and cooking and of shutting up the women, but it is never considered as a sitting or dining room.

"On my return to the boat, I found the aga and all his retinue seated on a mat, under a cluster of palm-trees, close to the water. The sun was then setting, and the shades of the western mountains had reached across the Nile and covered the town. It is at this time the people recreate themselves in various scattered groups, drinking coffee, smoking their pipes, and talking of camels, horses, asses, dhourra, caravans, or boats."*f*

6—8. (6) **measures,** *lit.* seahs. A *seah* = ab. 2½ galls. **of .. meal,** finest flour. **cakes .. hearth,** thin cakes placed on ground fr. wh. fire has been removed; and then covered with the hot embers. (7) **Abraham,** he himself made the selection. **dress,** cook, prepare for food. (8) **butter,** clotted cream. **milk,** as a beverage. **stood .. tree,** in watchful attendance.

Position of females in the East.—When we had finished our meals in the family in which I resided at Deir el Kamr, and were risen, the mother, daughter, and daughter-in-law, who had been waiting at the door, came in, and partook of what remained. Thus it is in Syria, and thus it has been, probably, ever since Abraham, "a Syrian ready to perish" (Deut. xxvi. 5), traversed these regions, dwelling in tents; when Sarah, having prepared an entertainment for three heavenly strangers, did not present it, that being Abraham's office; but stood at the tent door, which was behind him.*a*

9—12. (9) **Sarah,** their visit concerned her. **tent,** the tent assigned to her. (10) **according .. life,** *lit.* acc. to the living time. Meaning ambiguous. **Io .. son,** A. must have begun to perceive who his guest was. **which .. him,** she was out of sight. (11) **ceased .. women,** past the time of child-bearing. (12) **laughed,**ᵃ being incredulous, not knowing the speaker. **within herself,** silently.

The position of woman.—I. In ancient times: "behind the door." Position of woman subordinate: waited at table; stood behind her lord and master. This is still the case in heathen and eastern lands. II. In modern times: Christianity recognises her rightful station, brings her from "behind the door," and places her by her husband's side as his friend, help-meet, and counsellor.

I am made to laugh.—A woman advanced in years, under the *same circumstances,* would make a similar observation: "I am made to *laugh.*" But this figure of speech is also used on any *wonderful* occasion. Has a man gained anything he did not expect, he will ask, "What is this? I am made to *laugh.*" Has a person lost anything which the moment before he had in his hand, he says, "I am made to laugh." Has he obtained health, or honour, or wealth, or a *child,* it is said, "He is made to laugh." "Ah, his mouth is now full of *laughter;* his mouth cannot contain all that laughter" (Ps. cxxvi. 2).—*Roberts.*

13—15. (13) **laugh,** His knowledge must have shown A. who He was. (14) **Is .. Lord,**ᵃ *lit.* "Is anything too wonderful for the Lord?" (15) **denied,** prevaricated, under cover of not having laughed aloud. **afraid,** recognising One who knew her altogether. **nay .. laugh,** a mild rebuke for such a sin.

Sarah reproved for her unbelief.—I. The reproof given to Sarah. In it we notice—1. A just expostulation; 2. A convincing interrogatory; 3. A reiterated assurance. II. The instruction to be gathered from it. It teaches us—1. What need we have to

---

B.C. 1898.

blow on their almost naked bodies"-*Roberts.*
v. 1. *H. Blount,* 151; *W. Reading,* iii. 332.
f Be'zoni.

he entertains them

Bread, dif. kinds, and mode of preparation.-*Topics,* ii. 22—26.

Butter. *Robinson's Res.,* ii. 180.

"Let not the emphasis of hospitality be in bed and board; but let truth and love and honour and courtesy flow in all thy deeds."—*Emerson.*

a Jowett.

they renew the promise of a son

a Ge. xvii. 17; Ro. iv. 18—21; He. xi. 11, 12, 19.

"The father laughed, when a son was promised to him, from wonder and joy; the mother laughed when the three men renewed the promise, from doubtfulness and joy. The angel reproved her, because though that laughter was from joy, yet it was not of full faith. Afterwards by the same angel she was confirmed in faith also."—*Augustine.*

Sarah laughed

a Lu. i. 37; Je. xxxii. 17; Ma. iii. 9; xix. 26.

"Of what consequence is it that anything should be concealed from man? No-

GENESIS. [Cap. xviii. 16—26.

a C. 1898.
thing is hidden from God; He is present in our minds and comes into the midst of our thoughts. Comes, do I say?—as if He were ever absent!"—Seneca.

b C. Simeon, M.A.

c. 14. H. Owen, Scrip. Mir., i. 49.

guard against the workings of unbelief; 2. How ready God is to mark the good in our actions, while He casts a veil over the evil which accompanies it; 3. What a mercy it is to have our secret sins detected and reproved; 4. How essential to our best interests is a right knowledge of God.*b*

Divine power and providence.—The Rev. Henry Venn, during a thunderstorm, when his children expressed some alarm at the loudness of the thunder, and the vividness of the lightning, took them up with him to a window, where they could observe most distinctly the progress of the storm. He then expatiated to them upon the power of that God whose will the thunder and lightning obeyed. He assured them that the lightning could injure no one, unless by the express permission of that God who directed it. He taught them to fear His power, and adore His majesty, and finished His address to them by kneeling down and solemnly adoring that God whose perfections they had seen so signally displayed.

the angels go towards Sodom

a "There is a trad. that he went as far as Caphar-berucha, fr. wh. the Dead Sea is visible through a ravine."—Speaker's Com.

b De. xxxii. 40; iv. 9, 10; vi. 7; Jos. xxiv. 15; Ps. cxix. 9; Pr. vi. 20; Ep. vi. 4.

c Ez. xvi. 49, 50; Ja. v. 4.

d Je. xvii. 10; He. iv. 13.

e Mal. iii. 1; Is. ix. 6, LXX.

f J. H. Evans.

"Confidence in another man's virtue is no slight evidence of a man's own." Montaigne.

g Cheever.

16—22. (16) **looked**, sign of their intention. **went.. way**,*a* both fr. courtesy and respect. (17) **said**, a soliloquy. **thing..do**, that I have purposed to do. (18) **seeing**, *etc.*, having bestowed this great mercy, shall I withhold the less. (19) **know**, *etc.*, the disclosure of Sodom's doom will not make him reckless through fear: but act together with my friendly confidence—as a motive to induce greater parental care. **command**, *etc.*,*b* A.'s obedience paved the way to the greatness ref. to in v. 18. (20) **cry**, *see on* iv. 10. **great**, calls aloud for punishment. **grievous**,*c* heavy (21) **altogether**,*d* the whole of the people. **know**, whom to accept for punishment. (22) **men**, the two angels, **Lord**, the third. "The messenger of the covenant."*e*

God's commendation of Abraham.—Observe—I. What the Lord declares concerning Abraham—" I know him." A mere knowledge is not what is here implied; but a knowledge of love. II. The commendation implied in the text—" that he will command," etc. Here we have God's explicit declaration, that it is an important duty of parents to give their children scriptural instruction. III. The great blessings resulting from the proper exercise of parental authority. IV. That the proper exercise of such authority is the medium through which the Lord will fulfil His promise.*f*

A good example.—Sir Thomas Abney was the beloved friend of the celebrated Dr. Watts, who found in his house an asylum for more than thirty-six years. This knight was not more distinguished by his hospitality than his piety. Neither business nor pleasure interrupted his observance of public and domestic worship. Of this a remarkable instance is recorded: upon the evening of the day that he entered on his office as lord mayor of London, without any notice, he withdrew from the public assembly, at Guildhall, after supper, went to his house, there performed family worship, and then returned to the company.*g*

Abraham intercedes for Sodom

a Ja. xii. 1; Ez. xxi. 3; Ho. x. 22.
b Nu. xvi. 22; 2 S xxiv. 17.

23—26. (23) **near**,*a* intimate communion. **destroy..wicked**,*b* in this world the righteous often suffer through the wicked. (24) **fifty**,*c* with the largest charity A. does not suppose there are more than these in wicked Sodom. (25) **that**, *etc.*,*d* " There is no grander testimony on record to the majesty of the moral sense in man."[c] (26) **spare .. sakes,**[f] of how much blessing to the world are the righteous in it!

The power of intercession.—How came Abraham to be qualified for this intercession? Why is it he. and not Lot, who thus intercedes? *Both* were religious men. Observe—I. A man's praying power is not an arbitrary thing, but the result of long antecedent spiritual processes. 1. God does not even impart His confidence to Lot: He merely sends messengers to save him; 2. Suppose that Lot had been made acquainted with Jehovah's purpose, could he have interceded like Abraham? No; he was not prepared to do so. II. The praying power of a man is conditioned upon the circumstances by which he surrounds himself. Abraham at Mamre, Lot at Sodom! This alone explains how much Lot needed Abraham's prayers, and how Abraham was in a position to offer them. III. Even when God vouchsafes to visit man, how much of its spiritual blessing depends upon his own character and circumstances. Lot receives divine guests, but how? In the midst of one of the most hellish night scenes recorded. What a contrast this to Abraham. Was Lot, then, qualified to pray like Abraham? IV. The comparison between the intercession of Abraham and the pleadings of Lot, when the angels sought to deliver him. V. The narrow, selfish, self-willed prayer of Lot was answered: the holy, Christian-like intercession of Abraham was unavailing. Zoar was spared, Sodom destroyed. It is, therefore, no criterion of a right or a wrong prayer, that it does not receive the kind of answer we ask. Conclusion—(1) What a moral sublimity there is in the character of a man like Abraham; (2) What grandeur is there in a good man's intercession![g]

The eye of God.—How dreadful is the eye of God on him who wants to sin! Do you know about Lafayette, that great man who was the friend of Washington? He tells us that he was once shut up in a little room in a gloomy prison for a great while. In the door of his little cell was a very small hole cut. At that hole a soldier was placed day and night to watch him. All he could see was the soldier's *eye:* but that *eye* was always there. Day and night, every moment when he looked up, he always saw that *eye.* Oh! he says, it was dreadful! There was no escape, no hiding; when he lay down, and when he rose up. that eye was watching him. How dreadful will the eye of God be upon the sinner, as it watches him in the eternal world for ever![h]

27—31. (27) **dust,** *etc.,*[a] dust in my origin, ashes in my end.[b] (28) **there .. five,** for the presence of fifty, to need of five. **if I find,** *etc.,* A. gains this concession too. (29) **spake,** and is heard once more. (30) **thirty,** fr. five A. comes to ten: but he leaves off adding "wilt thou destroy," etc." (31) **twenty,** A. takes off another ten.

Abraham's intercession for Sodom.—I. The basis of his intercession. 1. The value of purity; 2. God's justice. II. The earnestness of the intercessor. This is seen in—1. The responsible position he took upon himself; and took upon himself willingly too; 2. The depraved characters for whom intercession was made: 3. His repeated attempts. III. The failure of his intercession. This resulted from—1. His ignorance of sin in all its aspects; 2. From an inadequate conception of God's mercy.[c]

God irresistible.—As you stood some stormy day upon a sea-

B.C. 1898.

[c] Je. v. 1.
[d] Job xli. 20; Is. iii. 10, 11; Ps. lviii. 11; Job xxxiv. 17; Ro. iii. 6; Is. lvii. 1.
[e] *Alford.*
[f] Ez. xxii. 30.
[g] *H. Allon, D.D.*
"If once we are sure God hath done a thing, there is no room left to dispute its equity." — *Halyburton.*
v. 25. J. Donne, *Wks.,* ii. 206; *Abp. Tillotson,* viii. 179.
"Pity is to many of the unhappy a source of comfort in hopeless distresses, as it contributes to recommend them to themselves by proving that they have not lost the regard of others; and heaven seems to indicate the duty even of barren compassion, by inclining us to weep for evils which we cannot remedy."—*Johnson*
"How different is the ready hand, tearful eye, and soothing voice, from the ostentatious appearance which is called pity."—*Jane Porter.*
[h] *J. Todd, D.D.*

[a] Lu. xviii. 1.
[b] Ge. iii. 19; Is. vi. 5; Lu. v. 8; Job iv. 19.
[c] *Jenkin Jones.*
"Pity and forbearance, and long sufferance and fair interpretation, and excusing our brother and taking in the best sense, and passing the gentlest sentence, are as certainly our duty, and owing to every

cliff, and marked the giant billow rise from the deep to rush on with foaming crest, and throw itself thundering on the trembling shore, did you ever fancy that you could stay its course, and hurl it back to the depths of ocean? Did you ever stand beneath the leaden, lowering cloud, and mark the lightning's leap, as it shot and flashed, dazzling athwart the gloom, and think that you could grasp the bolt, and change its path? Still more foolish and vain his thought, who fancies that he can arrest or turn aside the purpose of God, saying, " What is the Almighty, that we should serve Him? Let us break His bands asunder, and cast away His cords from us." Break His bands asunder! How He that sitteth in the heavens shall laugh![d]

32, 33. (32) **oh let,** *etc.*,[a] he trembles for himself as he proceeds, **ten,** to so few are the fifty reduced. **I will not,** *etc.*, so *ten* righteous people would have saved the city! (33) **Lord . . w ly,** A. would feel that he could not urge his intercession further. **and . . place,** his home beneath the oaks at Mamre.

Abraham pleading for Sodom.—From this interesting record we learn—I. That God holds inquest upon the moral condition of a city. II. That God is accessible to human appeal. III. That the few can serve the many. Abraham, one man, can save Sodom: ten righteous men can save a city. IV. That human prayer falls below Divine resources. If Abraham had said " for my sake," who knows what great answer God might not have given?[b]

Where is God not?—During the American war a British officer, walking out at sunrising, observed at some distance an old man, whom he supposed to be taking aim at some game. When come up to him, the officer took him by the arm, and said, " What are you about?" The old man made no reply, but waved his hand expressive of his desire for him to stand at a distance. This not satisfying the inquirer, he repeated the question, when the native again waved his hand. At length, somewhat astonished, the officer said, " You old fool, what are you about?" To which he answered, " I am worshipping the GREAT SPIRIT." The question was then asked, " Where is he to be found?" To which the old man replied, " Soldier! *where is he not?*" and with such energy of expression as made the officer confess he should never forget it to his dying day.

CHAPTER THE NINETEENTH.

1—3. (1) **gate,** gates of anc. cities of E. were used as public promenades, markets, courts of justice, etc. (2) **and he said,** *etc.*,[a] no inns in those days. Strangers dependent on private hospitality. **street,**[b] *lit.* " the broad open place." Not an unusual thing to spend the night in open air. Warm climate. (3) **feast,** *lit.* banquet, *i.e.* more than an ordinary meal.

The angel's visit to Lot.—I. The danger attendant upon a good man in whatever condition. II. Religious contemplation as a security to the soul. III. The method of the Divine interposition. IV. The separation which is to take place when the Divine interposition is rejected.[c]

Eastern Hospitality.—We dismounted at the Oda, a lodging-

B.C. 1898.

person that does offend and can repent, as calling to account can be owing to the law, and are first to be paid; and he that does not so is an unjust person."—*J. Taylor.*

r 27. *T. Mallery, Morn. Ex.,* . 360.

d *Dr. Guthrie.*

a Ju. vi. 39; Is. lxv. 8; Ja. v. 16.

b *J. Parker, D.D.*

r. 32. *Bp. Lowth,* 281; *C. Simeon,* i. 150; *J. Hordern,* 183.

" Pity is a sense of our own misfortunes in those of another man; it is a sort of foresight of the disasters which may befall ourselves. We assist others in order that they may assist us on like occasions; so that the services we offer to the unfortunate are in reality so manyanticipated kindnesses to ourselves." — *La Rochefoucauld.*

"It is easy to condemn; it is better to pity."—*Abbott.*

two angels visit Lot in Sodom

a He. xiii. 2.

b Lu. xxiv. 28.

c *E. Carpenter.*

"The houses of holy men are full of these heavenly spirits whom they know not; they pitch their

house for travellers, in the village of Cooselare, or Cuselare. It was certainly not a palace, for we shared it with our horses, and there were holes, called windows, without glass or shutters; but the hospitality of our hosts more than compensated for everything else. We had trakana soup, pilau, cheese, and petmes, and surprised were we to see our table-cloth, or table-skin, soon after laid, the pancake bread placed all around, and the smoking viands in the midst. It was the more surprising, since we were unexpected guests; and, as the village seemed wretchedly poor, we ventured to ask an explanation, and we learned that our fare was the contribution of many families—the trakana soup was supplied by one, the pilau by a second, the petmes by a third, the bread by a fourth; but all were emulous to feed the famished strangers, with as little loss of time as possible; and these were Turks!*d*

B.C. 1898.

tents in ours. and visit us when we see not; and, when we feel not, protect us. It is the honour of God's saints to be attended by angels."—*Bp. Hall.*
Bp. Cooper, Brief Expos.; Bp. Hall, Contem.; W. Whately, Proto., 211.
d Arundell.

4—8. (4) **before .. down**, they had not long been there. **men .. quarter**, their sin was open, shameless, general. (5) **and they called**, *etc.*,*a* their sin so vile as known only by the name of the city abandoned to it.*b* (6) **shut .. him**, both that his guests might be safe, and not hear of the insults proposed. (7) **and said**, *etc.*, gentle expostulation. (8) **behold**,*c* *etc.*, proposing one sin to avoid another. Mixed character of good men. **therefore .. roof**, for hospitable treatment.

Sin a delusion.—Transport yourself to such scenes as Hogarth painted. Here is a man in a damp, dark cell, seated on a heap of straw, and chained like a wild beast to the wall. He smiles, sings, laughs; the straw is a throne; his bare cell, a palace; these rough keepers, obsequious courtiers; and he himself, a monarch, the happiest of mortals, an object of envy to crowned kings. Strange delusion! Yet is that man not more beside himself who, with a soul formed for the purest enjoyments, delights in the lowest pleasures; who, content with this poor world, rejects the heaven in his offer; who, surest sign of insanity, hates in a heavenly Father and a Saviour those who love him; who, in love with sin, hugs his chains; lying under the wrath of God, is merry, sings, and dances on the thin crust that, ever and anon breaking beneath the feet of others, is all that separates him from an abyss of fire?

the sin of Sodom
a Ro. i. 24—27; Ju. xix. 22; Jude 7; Is. iii. 9.
b Le. xviii. 22.
c Ro. iii. 8.
v. 8. N. Alexander, Hist. Eccl., i. 415.
"Use sin as it will use you; spare it not, for it will not spare you; it is your murderer, and the murderer of the world: use it, therefore, as a murderer should be used."—*R. Baxter.*

9—11. (9) **stand back**, *lit.* "come near, farther off." **this .. sojourn**, wh. was indeed Lot's great mistake. **judge**,*a* this prob. not the only instance. (10) **men**, who knew all, and heard the commotion. **pulled .. door**, rescued the old man. Kindness repaid. (11) **and .. blindness**,*b* Heb. *bassanverim*, dazzled blindnesses.*c*

The scriptural signs that the judgment is near (on v. 9—14). —I. That God abandons men or communities to outbreakings and presumptuous sins. II. That warnings and chastisements fail to produce their effect, and especially when the person grows harder under them. III. That God removes the good from any community: so before the flood, so before the destruction of Jerusalem. IV. The deep security of those over whom it is suspended.*d*

Effects of sin.—We might illustrate the evil of sin by the following comparison: "Suppose I were going along a street, and were to dash my hand through a large pane of glass, what

the men of Sodom struck blind
a Ex. ii. 14.
b 2 K. vi. 18; Ac. xiii. 11.
c "with fatuity of vision " (*Chal*), "with illusions" (*Syr*).
d A. Gosman, D.D. v. 11. J. Saurin, i. 270.
"If the people be led by laws, and uniformity sought to be given them by punishments, they will try to avoid the punishment, but have no sense of

B.C. 1898.

"shame." — *Confucius.*

"Punishment that is the justice for the unjust."
Augustine.
c J. *Inglis*

Lot being warned warns his relatives

a Ma. xiii. 49, 50.

b 2 Pe. ii. 6—8.

c Lu. xvii. 28, 29; 1 Th. v. 3.

d Lu. xxiv. 11; Ex. ix. 21.

e J. *Burns, D.D.*

v. 14. Dr. *Jortin,* iv. 41; W. A. *Gunn,* 116; J. *Mariott,* 371; Bp. *Maltby,* i. 245.

"Whatever is worthy to be loved for anything is worthy of preservation. A wise and dispassionate legislator, if any such should ever arise among men, will not condemn to death him who has done or is likely to do more service than injury to society. Blocks and gibbets are the nearest objects with legislators, and their business is never with hopes or with virtues."—*Landor.*

"It is hard, but it is excellent, to find the right knowledge of when correction is necessary and when grace doth most avail."—*G. Sidney.*

"If thou hast fear of those who command

harm would I receive?"—"You would be punished for breaking the glass."—"Would that be all the harm I should receive?"—"Your hand would be cut by the glass."—"Yes; and so it is with sin. If you break God's laws, you shall be punished for breaking them; and your soul is hurt by the very act of breaking them."*c*

12—14. (12) **here .. besides?** *a* in the city, other than in this house: any connected by marriage. **bring .. place**, better had he never entered it. (13) **for,** *etc.,b* shows God's view of the sin of Sodom. (14) **Lot .. out,** *c* he believed the warning, and warned others. **but .. law,** *d* men of Sodom. His warning too strange to be true.

The city of destruction.—The spiritual city of destruction, like Sodom of old—I. Is under the rule and authority of the devil. II. Is in direct hostility and open rebellion towards God. III. Has its laws and statutes. But these are all evil. Laws—1. Of worldly honour; 2. Pride and arrogance; 3. Polluted, in harmony with base passions. IV. Has its streets and squares. It is divided into four parts—1. The sceptical; 2. The profligate; 3. The worldly; 4. The formally religious. V. Is doomed, and will perish.*e*

The fall of the Ross-berg.—"Good morning, neighbour; we are likely to have a fine day," said a young Swiss peasant to his old neighbour, who was sitting idly at his cottage door, basking in the rays of the early sun. "Time we should have a fine day; it has been wet enough lately," growled the old man. "Have you heard the report?" rejoined the other; "those who were up the earliest this morning declare that they saw the top of old Ross-berg move." "Indeed! like enough, like enough," said the old man; "mark my words, and I have often said so before: I shan't live to see it, but those who are now young will not be as old as I am before the top of yonder mountain lies at its foot." "The saints forbid!" ejaculated the other, crossing himself devoutly; "at least I hope it will not be in my day." This conversation took place at the close of the summer of 1806, in the little village of Goldau, in the canton of Zug. This village was beautifully situated in a fertile valley at the foot of the Rossberg, near the Lake of Zug. Though the season was advanced, everything in nature was verdant as well as luxuriant; for the summer had been unusually wet, though it had now given place to lovely weather, ripening the corn and the grapes, which hung in rich profusion on every side. That harvest and that vintage, however, were never to be gathered in by the simple peasants of the valley. The heavy rains had overcharged the springs of water within the mountain, and loosened the ground above. The upper part of the mountain, formed of rounded pieces of old rock, cemented together by clay, became loosened by the water within, and, giving way, fell headlong into the valley, and buried the entire village, with many of its inhabitants, under its weight. The old man, who had often confidently declared that he expected such an accident, sat composedly in his cottage smoking his pipe, when the young man, running by, told him that the mountain was falling. The old man rose, looked out of doors, said that he had time to fill another pipe, and went back into his house. He suffered for his recklessness. The young man continued flying, and at length escaped, though with difficulty,

Cap. xix. 15—22.]   GENESIS.   77

for he was often thrown down by the trembling of the earth. When he looked back, the old man's house, with its owner, was carried off. Such infatuation seems incredible, yet his conduct is recorded as a matter of fact.

15—17. (15) **when .. arose**, the dawn striking up. **then .. Lot,**[a] who was endangering himself by persuading others. **take .. here**, save whom you can, if you cannot save all you would. **lest .. city,**[b] justice delays while you tarry. (16) **lingered**, not willing to leave any behind. **they .. forth,**[c] using a gentle and merciful violence. (17) **life,**[d] *lit.* thy soul. **plain**, which he had once so coveted. **mountain,**[e] *i.e.* Mts. of Moab.

Escape for thy life.—I. You must escape for your life,—the life, not of the body, but of the soul. 1. The everlasting welfare of your soul is in danger; 2. To effect your deliverance, you must escape yourselves; 3. You must be in earnest; 4. You must sacrifice everything that stands in your way. II. Look not behind. 1. He who has once left this sinful world ought to give up all thoughts of return; 2. Look not behind you, for the sake of your former companions; 3. Look not back to relieve yourself of the sense of guilt which weighs upon you; 4. Look not behind, lest you should never advance beyond your present position. III. Stay not in all the plain. Delay not—1. In hope of a better opportunity; 2. In reliance upon your good intentions; 3. Because you have *begun* to attend to religion; 4. Though you have been brought to feel deeply about religion; 5. For a more thorough conviction of sin; 6. Through discouragement and despondency; 7. Because you *hope* you are a Christian.[f]

Fleeing from sin.—We often say, "Flee from sin as from the face of a serpent." Perhaps very few of you know how a man feels when, for the first time, he finds himself, as I remember finding myself, within a few inches of a serpent—when he sees the cobra di capella rearing its head ready to strike, and knows that one stroke of those fangs is death, certain death. That moment he experiences a varied passion, impossible to describe. Fear, hatred, loathing, the desire to escape, the desire to kill, all rush into one moment, making his entire being thrill. Now, take two men: one is in the face of that serpent; the other is in the presence of the old serpent called Satan, the devil: one is in danger of the sting; the other is in danger of committing sin. Which of the two has most reason to flee? O thou that art tempted to sin this day against God, flee from sin as from the face of a serpent: a far deadlier serpent is that old serpent the devil than the other.[g]

18—22. (18) **Lot said,** *etc.*,[a] he anticipated danger in Moab; as once he had hoped for safety in Sodom. (19) **cannot .. die**, wearied by events of the night, he fears he will not live to reach the mt. (20) **little one**, few people, few sins, unworthy of being the subject of Divine justice. (21) **see .. also,** *lit.* I have lifted up thy face.[b] (22) **cannot .. thither,**[c] the wicked not to be punished till the righteous are safe. **Zoar** (*little*), formerly Bela.[d] Site not known.

Lot delivered out of Sodom.—The advice to escape, which the angels gave to Lot, may be considered as—I. Given to him. It

---

B.C. 1898.

thee, spare those who obey thee."
—*Ben Azai.*

Lot is pressed to leave Sodom

a Nu. xvi. 21, 26, Re. xviii. 4.

b 2 Co. vi. 2.

c He. i. 14.

d Ps. xxxiv. 22; La. iii. 22, Ro. ix. 15, 16.

e Ma. xxiv. 16—18; Re. xviii. 14, 15; Lu. ix. 62; Ph. iii. 13, 14.

"No ceremony that to great ones belongs,—not the king's crown, nor the deputed sword, the marshal's truncheon, nor the judge's robe, become them with one half so good a grace as mercy does."—*Shakespeare.*

f J. Day, D.D.

"Kill sin before it kills you; and though it kill your bodies, it shall not be able to kill your souls; and though it bring you to the grave, as it did your Head, it shall not be able to keep you there."—*Baxter.*

g W. Arthur, D.D.

Lot wishes to find a refuge in Zoar

a Ma. xvi. 22.

b "It was the custom in the E. to make supplication with the face to the ground; when

B.C. 1898.

the prayer was granted, the face was said to be raised."—*Spk.'s Commentary.*
c 1 S. xxvii. 1; Pr. iii. 5, 6; Ho. iv. 15; Ps. cxlv. 19.
d Ge. xiv. 2.
e C. Simeon, M.A.

the fate of Lot's wife
a Ps. xi. 6; Judo 7; 2 Pe. II. 6; Jo xx. 16; xlix. 18; Lu. xvii. 28—30; Ho. xi. 8; Am. iv. 11; Is. i. 9.
b Lu. xvii. 31, 32; He. x. 38, 39.
"There was a trad. wh. identified a pillar of salt nr. the Dead Sea with Lot's wife."—*Jos. Ant.*, i. 11. Lynch found to the E. of Usdum, a pillar of salt, 40-ft. high. It was prob. that to wh. Jos. refers.
c D. Thomas, D.D.

"The essence of justice is mercy. Making a child suffer for wrong-doing is merciful to the child. There is no mercy in letting the child have its own will, plunging headlong to destruction with the bit in its mouth. There is no mercy to society or to the criminal if the wrong is not repressed and the right vindicated. We injure the culprit who comes up to take his proper doom at the bar of justice if we do not make him feel that he has done a wrong thing. We may deliver his body from the prison, but not at the expense of justice,

was—1. Most salutary; 2. Most benevolent. II. Applicable to ourselves. 1. Our condition is very similar to Lot's; 2. The same advice, therefore, is proper for us, as for him. We should have—(1) Personal exertion; (2) Persevering diligence. Address:—(1) Those who are at ease in Sodom; (2) Those who are lingering and deferring their flight; (3) Those who are daily running in the way prescribed.*

Habits of sin.—The Arabs have a fable of a miller, who was one day awakened by having the nose of a camel thrust into the window of a room where he was sleeping. "It is very cold out here." said the camel, "I only want to get my nose in." The miller granted his request. After a while, the camel asked that he might get his neck in; then his fore feet; and so, little by little, crowded in his whole body. The miller found his companion troublesome: for the room was not large enough for both. When he complained to the camel, he received for answer, "If you do not like it, you may leave: as for myself, I shall stay where I am."

23—26. (23) **sun . . earth**, the day broke brightly: the last day for Sodom. (24) **rained . . fire**,a *i.e.* burning brimstone, marks of volcanic eruption, and sulphur still found in the neighbourhood. (25) **overthrew**, *etc.*, many scientific explanations of this. The nature of the region is a present and lasting comment on the text. (26) **but . . back**,b in defiance or forgetfulness of the command v. 17. **and . . salt**, judgment was mingled with mercy.

The lessons of a day.—What lessons did this day bring to Lot? I. The absurdity of letting secular motives govern men's conduct. II. The incongruity between the physical and moral scenery of the world. Sodom a beautiful spot; but look at the men. This suggests—1. The abnormal state of human society; 2. The necessity of a retributive period; 3. That a man's external circumstances are no true signs of character. III. The tremendous force of old associations. 1. Local; 2. Social; 3. Secular. IV. The futility of human reasoning concerning the ways of God. V. The determined antagonism of the Divine government to sin.c

Looking back.—When men or women leave their house, they never look back, as "it would be very unfortunate." Should a husband have left anything which his wife knows he will require, she will not call on him to turn or look back; but will either take the article herself, or send it by another. Should a man, on some great emergency, have to look back, he will not then proceed on the business he was about to transact. When a person goes along the road (especially in the evening), he will take great care not to look back. "because the evil spirits would assuredly seize him." When they go on a journey they will not look behind, though the palankeen or bandy would be close upon them; they step a little on one side, and then look at you. Should a person have to leave the house of a friend after sunset, he will be advised in going home not to look back: "As much as possible keep your eyes closed; fear not." Has a person made an offering to the evil spirits? he must take particular care, when he leaves the place, not to look back. A female known to me is believed to have got her crooked neck by looking back. Such observations as the following may be often heard in private conversation: "Have you heard that Comaran is very ill?" "No; what is the matter with him?" "Matter! why, he has looked back, and the evil spirit has caught him."*d*

27—29. (27) **Abraham .. Lord,** his faith prompted him. (28) **looked .. plain,** to see the fruit of Divine justice. **smoke .. furnace,**ᵃ an awful type of the "lake that burneth with fire and brimstone."*b* (29) **God .. Abraham,** remembered his intercession, and extended his mercy to Lot. **sent .. dwelt,**ᶜ clearly implied that for safety he was indebted, under God, to Abraham.

Lot saved.—Saved—I. In a time of imminent peril: "the midst of the overthrow." II. When all around him was destroyed: the cities where he had dwelt, the property he had gathered. III. For the sake of another: "God remembered Abraham." Learn—(1) Our goodness extendeth not to Thee; (2) If we are saved, it will be for the sake of another; (3) The destruction of sinners will be terrible and complete.

The power of God.—On August 1, 1846, St. George's Church, recently built at Leicester, was entirely destroyed by the effects of a thunderstorm. The steeple was burst asunder, and parts of it were blown thirty feet; while the vane-rod and top part of the spire fell perpendicularly down, carrying with it every floor in the tower. Mr. Highton, in comparing the power of this discharge of lightning with some known mechanical force, states that 100 tons of stone were blown a distance of thirty feet in three seconds; consequently a 12,220 horse-power engine would have been required to resist the effects of this single flash.*d*

30—35. (30) **mountain,**ᵃ whither he should have gone at first. **for .. Zoar,** the moral character of even this *little* town may have alarmed him. **he .. cave,** reduced even to this. (31) **and,** *etc.,* living in Sodom had corrupted them. (32) **come .. wine,**ᵇ even this vile course was a tacit acknowledgment of their father's goodness. (33) **made .. night,** Lot should not have consented so far as this. **and he,** *etc.,* yet is not a voluntary drunkard responsible for the sins he commits in his cups. (34) **firstborn said,** *etc.,* she not only shamelessly avows her sin, but incites her younger sister to the same. (35) **drink .. also,** not a sin of ignorance, he had tested the strength of wine but the night before.

Dwellers in caves.—The mountains of Palestine abound in caves, and it was and is customary for the shepherds to occupy them. Mr. Stephens, in his *Incidents of Travel,* gives an interesting description of what he witnessed in a Bedouin encampment on the road to Gaza. "We were climbing," he writes, "up the side of a mountain, and saw on a little point on the very summit the figure of an Arab, kneeling in evening prayer. He had finished his devotions, and was sitting on the rock when we approached, and found that he had literally been praying on his housetop, for his habitation was in the rock beneath. Like almost every old man one meets in the East, he looked exactly the patriarch of the imagination, and precisely as we would paint Abraham, Isaac, or Jacob. He rose as we approached, and gave us the usual Bedouin invitation to stop and pass the night with him; and leading us a few paces to the brink of the mountain, he showed us, in the valley below, the village of his tribe."

B.C. 1898.

nor to his own injury."—*Chapin.*
d Roberts.

the cities destroyed but Lot saved

a Re. xviii. 9.

b De. xxix. 23; Is. xiii. 19; Je. xlix. 18; Jude 7; 2 Pe. ii. 6.

c Ge. viii. 1; Ps. cxlv. 20; 2 Pe. ii. 6—10.

"The martyrs to vice far exceed the martyrs to virtue, both in endurance and in number. So blinded are we by our passions, that we suffer more to be damned than to be saved."—*Colton.*

d Timbs.

the sin of Lot's daughters

a Ja. i. 8.

b Pr. xxiii. 31—33; 1 Co. x. 12.

"Drunkenness is the way to all bestial affections and acts; wine knows no difference either of persons or sins."—*Bp. Hall.*

"All excess is ill, but drunkenness is of the worst sort. It spoils health, dismounts the mind, and unmans men. It reveals secrets, is quarrelsome, lascivious, impudent, dangerous, and mad. He that is drunk is not a man, because he is, for so long, void of reason that distinguishes a man from a beast."—*W. Penn.*

Moab and Ammon

B.C. 1898.

a De. ii. 9; Nu. xxv. 1—3; xxi. 29.
b De. ii. 19.
c Dr. Bush.

"The character of the reputed ancestors of some men has made it possible for their descendants to be vicious in the extreme, without being degenerate; and there are some hereditary strokes of character by which a family may be as clearly distinguished as by the blackest features of the human face."— *Junius.*

d A. Burgess.

36—38. (36) **thus,** *etc.,* did he never perceive their condition, and inquire the cause? (37) **Moab**ᵃ (*seed of the father*), son of incest and father of a wicked race. (38) **Ben-ammi**ᵇ (*son of my own kindred*), what must Lot have thought of these names given by his daus. to their children?

Lessons from the life of Lot.—I. The duty and advantage of hospitality (Lot and the angels). II. The enormous depravity of wh. human nature is capable (Sodom). III. The care and favour with wh. God regards the good (Lot saved when Sodom was destroyed). IV. Those who are hastening to heaven should not be content to go alone (Lot tried to save his family). V. Sinners when most careless and secure are often nearest to danger (the day on wh. Sodom was destroyed broke brightly). VI. The need of personal exertion and persevering diligence to escape the wrath to come. (Haste thee. Look not behind). VII. We are never out of danger while we are on earth. (The dishonourable end of Lot).ᶜ

Deceitfulness of sin.—It hath many secret ways of insinuating; it is like a Delilah; it is like Jael to Sisera. Sin is a sweet poison, it tickleth while it stabbeth. The first thing that sin doth is to bewitch, then to put out the eyes. then to take away the sense and feeling; to do to a man as Lot's daughters did to him,—make him drunk, and then he doth he knoweth not what. As Joab came with a kind salute to Abner, and thrust him under the fifth rib, while Abner thought of nothing but kindness, so sin comes smiling, comes pleasing and humouring thee, while it giveth thee a deadly stab.ᵈ

CHAPTER THE TWENTIETH.

B.C. cir. 1898.

Abimelech takes Sarah and is warned

a Ge. x. 19.
b Ge. xxvi. 26.
c Williams' Holy City, i. 465.

d Kurtz remarks that she had her youth renewed since the visit of the angels, when a son was promised.

e Ps. cv. 14; Ez. xxxiii. 14, 15.
f 2 K. xx. 3; 2 Co. i. 12.
g Lange.

"The confusion and undesigned inaccuracy so often to be observed in conversation, especially in that of uneducated per-

1—5. (1) **thence,** Mamre. **from . . south,** he also went S. **Kadesh** (*sacred*) in the S. of Canaan. **Shur** (*a fort*), a desert in the S.W. of Canaan. **Gerar** (*a longing place*), nr. Gaza,ᵃ and Beersheba;ᵇ anc. cap. of Philistia; ruins now prob. at Khirbel-el-Gerar.ᶜ (2) **sister,** *see on* xii. 13, *etc.* **Abimelech** (*father king*), a title, as Pharaoh. **sent . . Sarah,** she was 23 or 24 yrs. older than when in Egypt.ᵈ (3) **God . . night,** a revelation fr. God to a heathen. **thou . . man,** the sin of adultery merited death. (4) **had . . her,**ᵉ providentially hindered. **Lord . . nation,** he trusted that his people would not suffer through his sin. (5) **integrity,** *etc.*ᶠ he did not regard concubinage or polygamy as a sin.

Abraham's reaction after his high spiritual experiences.—Consider this repetition of his old fault with regard to—I. Its causes: 1. Recent experience of the corruption of the world; 2. False prudence; 3. Exaggerated confidence; 4. The brotherly relation to Sarah; 5. The probable issue of the case in Egypt. II. Its natural results. 1. Anxiety and danger; 2. Shame before a heathen's princely court. III. Its gracious issue through the interference of God.ᵍ

The disgrace of lying.—Clear and round dealing is the honour of man's nature; and that mixture of falsehood is like alloy in coin of gold or silver, which may make the metal work the better, but it embaseth it. For these winding and crooked courses are the goings of the serpent, which goeth basely upon the belly, and not upon the feet. There is no vice that doth so cover a man with shame as to be found false and perfidious; and therefore Montaigne saith prettily, when he inquired the reason why the word of the lie should be such a disgrace and such an odious charge, saith he, "If it be well weighed, to say that a man lieth, is as much as to say that he is brave towards God, and a coward towards men. For a lie faces God, and shrinks from man."[h]

6—8. (6) **withheld .. me**, God helps the conscientious. **suffered .. her**,[a] laid him under mental restraint, or physical illness. (7) **prophet**, a medium of Divine revelation. **he .. live**,[b] God had proved A.'s power as an intercessor. **and if**, etc., God thus marks His abhorrence of the sin of adultery. (8) **told .. ears**, he would teach the lesson he had learned; and acc. for his subsequent conduct. **men .. afraid**, when they heard how near destruction another's sin had brought them.

God's appearance to Abimelech.—Observe—I. The manner of the revelation—by a dream. II. The substance of the reply. 1. An admission of Abimelech's plea, or an acknowledgment of his integrity of heart; 2. An instruction to him to take notice of God's providence with regard to him.[c]

Providence in regard to sin.—If you ask, how far God's providence is concerned about sin? we reply that it is concerned about it four ways: First, in morally hindering the internal commission of it before it is committed. Secondly, in providentially hindering (at times) the external commission of it, when it has been intentionally committed. Thirdly, in marking, bounding, and overruling it, while it is committed. And, fourthly, in bringing about means of properly pardoning or exemplarily punishing it, after it has been committed.[d]

9—13. (9) **what .. us?**[a] placed us in peril by thy deceit. **what .. thee**,[b] only a great injury could furnish a plea. **hast .. sin?** kingdoms suffer when kings are vile. **deeds .. done**, reproofs are the more terrible when a child of God is the subject of them at the hands of a worldling. (10) **what**, etc., a conscientious man will seek to put away the occasion of another's sinning. (11) **surely .. place**,[c] beware of rash conclusions: or of hastily judging of men's moral character. The man judged was, in this case, better than the man judging. **slay .. sake**,[d] those who do not fear God will have little regard for human rights. (12) **and yet**, etc.,[d] concealing the truth is ofttimes the suggesting of an untruth.[e] (13) **when .. wander**, etc.,[f] he took measures for his own safety. **I .. her**, he screens Sarah while he explains his own conduct.

Abraham reproved for denying his wife.—Consider—I. The offence which he committed. A very grievous sin. Look at—1. The principle from which it sprang—loss of faith; 2. Its natural and necessary tendencies; 3. The fact of its having been before practised by him, and reproved. II. The rebuke given him on account of it. In this we observe much that was—1. Disgraceful to Abraham; 2. Honourable to Abimelech: (1) Moderation; (2) Equity; (3) Virtue. Application:—(1) Shun every species of deception; (2) Guard against relapses into sin; (3) Be thankful to God for His protecting grace; (4) Strive to the uttermost to cancel the effects of your transgressions.[g]

B.C. cir. 1898.

sons, proves that truth needs to be cultivated as a talent, as well as recommended as a virtue."—*Mrs. Fry.*
h *Bacon.*

Abimelech repeats the warning
a Ge. xxxi. 7; Pr. xxi. 1; Lu. xii. 48; Ps. li. 4.
b 1 S. vii. 5; Job xlii. 8; 1 Jo. v. 16; Ja. v. 14, 15.

Prophet, Heb.; *Nabi,* Gk.; *prophetes,* fr. *pro,* before, and *phemi,* to speak; *i.e.* one who speaks of things before they happen. From this place it appears that the above was not the *original* notion of the word.

c *Bp. Sanderson.*

d *J. Fletcher.*

Abimelech reproves Abraham, who excuses his conduct
a Ge. xxvi. 10.
b Ex. xxxii. 21.
c Ps. xxxvi. 1; Pr. xvi. 6.
d Ge. xi. 29; 1 Th. v. 22.

e "He said she was his sister, without denying that she was his wife, concealing the truth, but not speaking what was false."—*Augustine.*
f Ge. xii. 1; He. xi. 8.

g *C. Simeon, M.A.*

"Whenever anything is spoken against you that is not altogether

Gentleness of reproof.—

> You have heard
> The fiction of the north wind and the sun,
> Both working on a traveller, and contending
> Which had most power to take his cloak from him ;
> Which, when the wind attempted, he roar'd out
> Outrageous blasts at him, to force it off,
> Then wrapt it closer on : when the calm sun
> (The wind once leaving) charged him with still beams,
> Quiet and fervent, and therein was constant ;
> Which made him cast off both his cloak and coat :
> Like whom should men do.[h]

Abraham intercedes for Abimelech

B.C. cir. 1898.

true, do not pass it by or despise it because it is false ; but forthwith examine yourself, and consider what you have said or done that may administer a just occasion of reproof."—Plutarch.
h Chapman.

a Lit. "a thousand silverlings." Very little known of coins of this period. Cattle used to represent money with pastoral people; hence the word pecuniary is fr. Lat. pecus, cattle; cattle forming the chief wealth of the Roms., some of whose coins had the figures of animals stamped upon them. Thus, too, we read in many places in Homer of a coat of mail worth 100 oxen; a cauldron worth 20 sheep ; a goblet worth 12 lambs, etc.

b Alford.

"To despise money on some occasions leads to the greatest gain."—Terence.

c Alford.

14—18. (14) **Abimelech .. Abraham**, gifts prob. more fr. respect for Abraham's God, than Abraham himself. (15) **behold**, *etc.*, not unlike the former address of A. to Lot. (16) **brother**, a gentle reproof. a .. **silver**,*a* prob. the value of the sheep and oxen : not money in addition. **behold**, *etc.*, the relation of Abraham to God made him a protection to Sarah (*v.* 7). (17) **Abraham .. Abimelech**, he causes joy where he had caused sorrow. (18) **for**, *etc.*, " God had visited all with incapacity, wh. visitation was now removed."*b*

Supplementary note on v. 16.—The meaning of the latter part of the verse is much disputed. Kalisch renders, " Behold, he is to thee a protection to all who are with thee, and with all, and thou wilt be recognised ;" and explains, " he gave to Abraham for her a thousand shekels of silver (for the property of the wife belonged to the husband), and addressed to her a remark embodying the experience he had just made, and the respect with which it inspired him (*v.* 18); he said that though she might profess Abraham was her brother, he was her protection against every man ; she might be taken by others as his sister, but she would be soon known and convicted of being his wife by the supernatural interference of God." On the other hand Knobel renders, " It (the gift of 1,000 shekels) is to thee a covering of eyes (*i.e.* shall shut thine eyes that they see not, *i.e.* shall blind thee that thou care not for what has happened, *i.e.* shall reconcile and make amends to thee) in ref. to all wh. is with thee and with all (*i.e.* which has happened to thee and thy companions); thus thou art righted (thine injury atoned for)." Similarly Keil, Delitzsch, and Lange. I have therefore preferred this rendering. The LXX. gives it, " These shall be to thee for an honour of thy countenance, and to all the women that are with thee ; and speak the truth in all things." The Vulgate, " This shall be to thee for a veil of the eyes to all that are with thee, and wheresoever thou shalt go ; and remember that thou hast been detected."*c*

CHAPTER THE TWENTY-FIRST.

Isaac is born

a Ga. iv. 23, 28 ; Ge. xvii. 19.

b He. xi. 11.

1—5. (1) **and .. said**,*a* God never forgets His word. (2) **bare .. age**,*b* nothing too hard for God. **at .. time**, *see on* xvii. 21. (3) **Isaac***c* (*laughter ;* or *there shall be laughter, i.e.* joy. (4) **as .. him**,*d* God's faithfulness suggestive of duty of obedience. (5) **and**, *etc.*,*e* " after all delays and difficulties the promised mercies of heaven come at last."*f*

Isaac's birth a great resemblance to the birth of Christ.—I. Both births were announced long before. II. Both occur at the time fixed by God. III. Both persons were named before they were born. IV. Both were miraculously conceived. V. Both births occasioned great joy. VI. The law of circumcision begins (as to its principle) with Isaac, and ceases through Christ.*c*

Unchangeableness of God.—We have passed through one more year. Thank God, we are quit of it! One more long stage in the journey of life, with its ascents, and descents, and dust, and mud, and rocks, and thorns, and burdens that wear the shoulders, is done. The old year is dead. Roll it away. Let it go. God, in His providence, has brought us out of it. It is gone; or rather, its evil is gone: its good remains. The evil has perished, and the good survives. And now we stand on the beginning of the next, the new, the present year. That God who has lifted us out from one into another, out from one path into another, out from one experience into another, never forgot. He never did less, but always more than He promised. He has done exceeding abundantly more than we asked or thought. By His grace we have been what we have been; by His grace we have experienced what we have experienced; and by His grace we shall have our experience in days to come.*h*

6—8. (6) **God .. laugh**,*a* *i.e.* made me to rejoice. (7) **who .. said,** *etc.*, who could have anticipated, or believed the possibility of so strange an event? (8) **weaned,** Heb. *rayiggamel*, of wh. the idea is, *return, requital, restitution,* **and .. feast,** most likely a religious festival.

Divine rejoicing.—God makes us to laugh, *i.e.* to rejoice—I. Unexpectedly: even when expecting sorrow. II. Heartily: the joy that God gives is personal. III. Manifestly: the joy that God gives is diffusive: "all that hear," etc. IV. Righteously: the joy that God gives has a pure source, and a holy object. Learn—The greatest of all human joy is the joy of salvation; and that flows from the cause of Sarah's joy: the Messiah was descended from her son.

Weaning in the East.—When the Persian ambassador was in England, he attributed to the custom of early weaning the greater forwardness of our children in mental acquirements than those of his own country, where male children are often kept to the breast till three years of age, and never taken from it till two years and two months. The practice is nearly the same in other Asiatic countries. In India the period is precisely three years. But everywhere a girl is taken from the breast sooner than a boy: in Persia at two years: in India within the first year. When the child is weaned, the Persians make "a great feast," to which friends and relations are invited, and of which the child also partakes, this being in fact his introduction to the customary fare of the country. The practice is the same amongst the Hindoos (see Morier's *Second Journey,* and Roberts' *Oriental Illustrations*).*b*

9—11. (9) **son,***a* Ishmael was now fr. 15 to 17. yrs. old. **mocking,***b* prob. deriding or teasing Isaac.*c* (10) **cast out,** *etc.,d* she prob. foresaw strife betw. the elder son and the true heir. (11) **grievous,** the father of both had a paternal regard for ea., he was perplexed, and committed his way to the Lord.

B.C. cir. 1898.

c Ge. xvii. 19; Jos. xxiv. 3; 1s. liv. 1.

d Ge. xvii. 10; Ac. vii. 8.

e Ge. xvii. 1, 17.

f Bush.

g H. C. Rambach.

"When real nobleness accompanies that imaginary one of birth, the imaginary seems to mix with real and becomes real too."—*Greville.*

h H. W. Beecher.

Isaac is weaned

a Ps. cxliii. 9; Lu. i. 58.

Wean, fr. A.-S. *awendan,* to convert, transfer, turn fr. one thing to another; hence to wean. *is to turn a child fr. the breast* in order to receive another kind of nourishment."—*Adam Clark.*

"Mothers may learn fr. the example of S. that it is their duty to nurse their own children. The good women of those days thought it their duty to do so, and dry breasts were reckoned a great reproach."—*Orton.*

b Dr. Kitto.

Ishmael mocks Isaac

a Ge. xvi. 15.
b Ga. iv. 29.
c Gesenius thinks it was "playing

[Cap. xxi. 12—16.

B.C. cir. 1898.

"and dancing gracefully," and so attracting the favour of the father, wh. moved the envy of Sarah.

d Gn. iv. 22—31.

e C. Simeon, M.A.

"God's favourites are the world's laughing-stocks" —*M. Henry.*

"Levity of character is the bane of all that is good and virtuous."—*Seneca.*

f Roberts.

Hagar and Ishmael are sent away

a Ro. ix. 7, 8.

b Ge. xvii. 20, 21.

c Leathern bottle prob. made of skin of goat or kid.

d "Still com. in the E. to see women so carry skins of water." —*Robinson, B. R.,* i. 340; ii. 163, 276.

e Jo. viii. 35.

"Our conduct, in many occasions of private life, may admit of a certain courage being exercised, which is not inferior to the warrior's bravery; some occasions require even more perseverance and endurance." —*Cicero.*

the water is spent

"Be thankful, Christian, for the spiritual *refreshments* you have

Abraham casting out Hagar and Ishmael.—Observe—I. The history itself—the expulsion of Hagar and her son. Inquire into—1. The reasons for this; 2. The manner in which it was carried into execution. II. The mystery contained in it. This narrative was designed to show us that the children of promise— 1. Would always be objects of hatred and contempt to the natural man; 2. Alone are members of the true Church; 3. Alone shall finally possess their father's inheritance.*e*

Concubinage in the East.—It is not uncommon for a man of property to keep a concubine in the *same* house with his wife; and, strange as it may appear, it is sometimes at the wife's *request.* Perhaps she has not had any children, or they may have died, and they both wish to have one, to perform their funeral ceremonies. By the laws of *Menu,* should a wife, during the first eight years of her marriage, prove unfruitful; or should the children she has born be all dead in the tenth year after marriage; or should she have a daughter *only* in the eleventh year; he may, without her consent, put her away, and take a concubine into the house. He must, however, continue to support her.*f*

12—14. (12) **let .. grievous,** be no longer sad or perplexed. **Sarah .. voice,** her desire receives Divine confirmation. **Isaac .. called,***a* a clear limitation of promises to descendants of Abraham in the line of Isaac. (13) **and .. also,** *etc.,b* b. assured that even Ishmael shall not be forgotten. (14) **early,** *etc.,* prompt obedience. **bottle,***c* Heb. *hemath, i.e.* a sack. **shoulder,***d* the usual manner of carrying burdens to this day. **and .. away,***e* with as much kindness and generosity as the circumstances allowed. **child,** Heb. *yeled,* boy, lad, stripling. **Beer-sheba,** *see on* v. 31, ab. m. S. of Hebron.

Leather bottles.—Chardin has given us, at large, an amusing account of these bottles, which, therefore, I would here set down. After observing that the bottle given to Hagar was a leather one, he goes on thus: "The Arabs, and all those that lead a wandering kind of life, keep their water, milk, and other kind of liquors in these bottles. They keep in them more fresh than otherwise they would do. These leather bottles are made of goat skins. When the animal is killed, they cut off its feet and its head, and they draw it in this manner out of the skin, without opening its belly. They afterward sew up the places where the legs were cut off, and the tail, and when it is filled, they tie it about the neck. These nations, and the country people of Persia, never go a journey without a small leather bottle of water hanging by their side like a scrip. The great leather bottles are made of the skin of a he-goat, and the small ones, that serve instead of a bottle of water on the road, are made of a kid's skin. Mons. Dandilly, for want of observing this, in his beautiful translation of Josephus, has put goat skin in the chapter of Hagar and Ishmael, instead of a kid's skin bottle, which, for the reasons assigned above, must have been meant."

15, 16. (15) **water .. bottle,** a serious loss in that hot country. **cast .. shrubs,** exhausted by the journey and thirst she laid him there, leaving him fainting and prostrate. (16) **bowshot,** *i.e.* as far as an archer could shoot an arrow. **let .. child,** she believed him to be dying, and could not endure the sight. **lift .. wept,** feeling her misery and helplessness.

Hagar in the desert.—In order to see the lesson of the text (vv. 15 and 19) in its full force, let us consider—I. The position of Abraham's servants. Hagar is called, "a bond woman;" but she was no slave. The *service* of those days was not the *slavery* of modern times. Hagar was in reality lady's maid to Sarah. II. What brought Hagar into the wilderness? The cause of it was the combined sin and folly of Sarah, Abraham, Hagar, and Ishmael. Sarah's presumption in giving Hagar to her husband; Abraham's weakness in yielding; Hagar's contempt of her mistress; Ishmael's mockery. III. Her condition when in the desert. IV. The relief which, though unseen, was at hand. The well was close by when the bottle was empty. Inferences—(1) Sin has driven us into a desert; (2) Hagar is an emblem of our natural condition as fugitives; (3) The resource of the well teaches us that resource in our need is provided—not in answer to our prayers, but in anticipation of our necessities; (4) There never was an affliction but there was a well of water near; (5) How many have left the household of faith and gone into the wilderness.[a]

A bowshot.—This is a common figure of speech in their ancient writings, "The distance of an *arrow*. So far as the arrow flies." The common way of measuring a short distance is to say, "It is a *call* off," *i.e.* so far as a man's voice can reach. "How far is he off?" "Oh, not more than three *calls*," *i.e.* were three men stationed within the reach of each other's voices, the voice of the one farthest off would reach to that distance.[b]

17—21. (17) **God .. lad,** his mother could not hear or help: his voice faint and weak. **the .. God,** *i.e.* the Angel-Jehovah. **for .. his,** ref. to *condition* as well as *place*. (18) **hold .. hand,** support, comfort him. **for .. nation,** he shall not die. (19) **well .. water,** Divine commands are accompanied with aids to obedience. **gave .. drink,** quenched the fever, and refreshed him. (20) **God .. lad,** prospered him. **grew,** to a vigorous manhood. **archer,** not only as a means of living, but acc. to prediction.[a] (21) **Paran,** prob. that now called *El-Tih*, *i.e.* "the wanderings." **and .. Egypt,** custom then in the E. for mothers to choose wives for their sons.[b]

Hagar and Ishmael.—Let us trace out the various heads of our text. I. They thirsted. This reminds us of our condition without Christ. 'Come ye to the waters." This teaches us—1. That religion is satisfying to the soul, as water is to the thirsty body; 2. How naturally the needy soul should turn to Christ. II. They thirsted—but where? Near a well of water. So when the poor sinner thirsts, Jesus is ever near and ready. III. Hagar's eyes were opened; she saw the well. Before, she saw neither the right thing nor looked in the right direction. IV. Seeing the well, they drank and lived. Hearing of Christ is not enough, we must partake of Him also.[c]

A mother's prayers.—A sailor boy was tossed on the deep in a fearful storm. For a time all hope that they could be saved was taken away, but at last they were brought safely to land. Afterwards, recounting the fearful scenes through which they had passed, the sailor boy said that even in the time of their greatest peril he did not despair, for he knew that his mother was at home praying for him.

B.C. *cir.* 1898.

"already received. Bless God that such merciful provision is made in the Gospel for the relief and comfort of necessitous creatures; and, above all, be thankful that you have been engaged to seek and to prize it, while so many are, as it were, dying for thirst in the midst of these overflowing streams."—*Doddridge.*

a *B. Grant, B.A.*

"There is in the heart of woman such a deep well of love that no age can freeze it."—*Bulwer Lytton.*

b *Roberts.*

Ishmael revives and grows to manhood

a Ge. xvi. 12.

b Ge. xxiv. 4, 55; Ex. xxi. 10.

"As great an archer as he was, however, Ishmael did not think he took his aim well in the business of his marriage as he proceeded without his mother's advice and consent."—*M. Henry.*

"When a father dies, the mother begins to look out for a wife for her son, though he may be very young; and her arrangements will generally be acceded to."—*Roberts.*

c *Siegfried.*

Abraham makes a covenant with Abimelech
a Jos. ii. 12.

b Ge. xxvi. 28; 1 S. xxiv. 21; Zec. viii. 23.

Three-fourths of the difficulties and miseries of men come from the fact that most want wealth without earning it, fame without deserving it, popularity without temperance, respect without virtue, and happiness without holiness.

c Bush.

Abraham reproves Abimelech because of the well
"The reproof of a good man resembles fuller's earth; it not only removes the spots from our character, but it rubs off when it is dry."—*Wilkinson.*

Beer-sheba
a "12 hrs. S. of Hebron are the ruins of an anc. town called *Bir-es-Seba*, with two wells of water."—*Robinson, B. R.* i. 204.

b Ps. xc. 2; De. xxxiii. 27; 1 Ti. i. 17.

c Alford. Ge. xxii. 6.

"Public characters cannot always be accountable for the misdeeds of those who act under them;

22—24. (22) **Phichol** (*the mouth of all*), prob. a title. like Abimelech, grand vizier. **God .. doest**, hence A. would be valuable as an ally, invincible as a foe. (23) **that .. me**, *lit.* "if thou shalt lie unto me," usual form of oath in E. **according, etc.**,ᵃ even a heathen sees that kindness should be returned. (24) **and, etc.**,ᵇ one of the earliest treaties on record. Both sides were equally bound.

Abraham's Divine Friend.—God's friendship for Abraham was—I. Constant: "in all that thou doest." II. Practical: material prosperity was one result. III. Conspicuous: even heathens saw and acknowledged it. IV. Influential: made Abraham what he was in himself, and won for him the respect of others.

Mr. Bruce, the traveller, came to a place, called Shekh Ammer, from the Arab Shekh of which place he got a pledge that he should not be molested in his journey across the desert to Cossier. A number of people afterwards assembled at the house. "The great people among them," says the traveller, "came, and after joining hands, repeated a kind of prayer, by which they declared themselves and their children accursed if ever they lifted up their hands against me in the *tell*, a field in the desert: or in case that I or mine should fly to them for refuge, if they did not protect us at the risk of their lives, their families, and their fortunes, or, as they emphatically expressed it, to the death of the last male child among them."ᶜ

25—28. (25) **reproved**, argued, expostulated. **well**, a most valuable property in such a land, among a pastoral people. (26) **and .. said, etc.**, he evidently admitted the justice of the reproof. (27) **and, etc.**, Abraham, as a "prophet" of God, provided the victims for this religious rite. (28) **and, etc.**, prob. to ratify preceding covenant.

Eastern compacts.—Mr. Bruce (*Travels*, vol. i. p. 199), relating the manner in which a compact was made between his party and some shepherds in Abyssinia, says, "Medicines and advice being given on my part, faith and protection pledged on theirs, two bushels of wheat and seven sheep were carried down to the boat."

29—34. (29) **what .. mean, etc.**, the *heathen* was not familiar with *Hebrew* customs. (30) **and, etc.**, their acceptance by Abimelech an acknowledgment of Abraham's ownership of the well. (31) **Beer-sheba**ᵃ ("*well of the oath*," "*well of the seven*"). (32) **they .. Philistines**, *i.e.* Abimelech and Phichol. (33) **grove**, or a tamarisk tree. **and .. God**,ᵇ not only *publicly* made a covenant, but *privately* sought help to keep it. (34) **and .. days**, in which Isaac grew old enough to carry the wood for the offering.ᶜ

The well of the oath.—A sacred spot, and marked—I. By the goodness of God, who supplied water in that thirsty land. II. By a compact of friendship between Abraham and Abimelech. III. By the offering of devotion: "planted a grove;" "called on the name of the Lord." Learn—(1) All good is from God; (2) Friendship is a sacred thing: (3) Promises made in public, and grace sought privately to keep them.

Beersheba.—The name Beersheba (*well of the oath*) was originally given by Abraham to the well which he and his servants had made. Isaac and his servants applied the name to *their*

well also (Gen. xxvi. 25, 32, 33). The city, which in course of time sprang up around these wells, naturally received the same title, which was afterwards extended to the "wilderness" lying farther south; as in Gen. xxi. 14, where the historian applies it by anticipation. Beersheba marked the southern limits of the land of Israel, as Dan did the northern; and both cities became the site of idolatries which were denounced by the prophet Amos (v. 5, viii. 14) with his accustomed vigour and fidelity. Perhaps the grove, which the patriarch had planted under the influence of motives of the purest kind, was made subservient to these corruptions.^{d}

B.C. cir. 1898.

they had need take care, however, what sort of servants they employ, as while matters are unexplained, that which is wrong is commonly placed to their account."-*Fuller.*
d *Groser.*

CHAPTER THE TWENTY-SECOND.

B.C. 1872.

1—3. (1) **things,** events previously recorded, esp. former trials. **tempt,**^{a} try. For A.'s good, not His own information. **and .. am,** "what is thy pleasure" (*Arab.*). (2) **take,** etc.,^{b} words that remind A. of the value of the sacrifice demanded. **Moriah**^{c} (*vision*), prob. the mt. on wh. the temple was built.^{d} (3) **early,**^{e} prompt, as usual: though now the duty was most painful. **saddled,** equipped. **and .. wood,** provided ag. dearth of proper fuel in what might be a desert, mountainous region, or other hindrances to obtaining it. **rose up,** set himself to the work.

A walk to Mount Moriah.—I. At the bottom of the hill there is a finger-post showing the road, and labelled with the name Moriah. II. At the top of the hill we find a pile of ashes. What was burned here, and why was it burned? III. Lying among the ashes we find the sacrificial knife. On one side of the knife is engraved the word "Surrender;" on the other, "Substitution." IV. On the ground we find an eye-glass cased with ram's horn. Through it we see the heathen sacrificing and performing horrid rites on all the hills around. But look, not on the hills, but through the ages, and you will see a crucified Redeemer, who dies to save these heathen.^{f}

Moriah.—The meaning of the name seems clearly to be *Morijah,* "the vision," or "the manifested of Jehovah." .. In 2 Chron. iii. 1 Solomon is said to have built his temple on Mount Moriah: and the Jewish tradition (Josephus, *Antiq.* i. 13, 2, vii. 13, 4) has identified this Mount Moriah of the temple with the mountain in the land of Moriah on which Abraham was to offer his son, whence probably here Onkelos and the Arab. render "the land of worship." No sufficient reason has been alleged against this identification, except that in ver. 4 it is said that Abraham "lifted up his eyes, and saw the place afar off," whereas Mount Zion is said not to be conspicuous from a great distance. Thence Bleek, De Wette, Tuck, Stanley, and Grove have referred to Moreh (Gen. xii. 6), and attempted to identify the site of the sacrifice with "the natural altar on the summit of Mount Gerizim," which the Samaritans assert to be the scene of the sacrifice. Really, however, the words in ver. 4 mean nothing more than this, that Abraham saw the spot to which he had been directed at some little distance off—not farther than the character of the place really admits. The evident meaning of the words,

a Ja. i. 12; 1 Pe. i. 7; De. xiii. 3; 1 Co. x. 13.
b Jo. iii. 16.
c 2 Ch. iii. 1.
d *Jos. Ant.* i. 13, 2, vii. 14, 4.
e Ps. cxix. 60; Ma. x. 37; Lu. xiv. 26.
f *J. Edmond, D.D.*

"That which he must do, he will do; he that had learned not to regard the life of his son, had learned not to regard the sorrow of his wife."—*Bp. Hall.*

"In all temptations and trials, believe that God the Father doth govern your temptations; that the Holy Spirit doth, and shall assist you; that Jesus Christ was tempted to overcome in you; that the saints on earth pray for you—this will uphold and stay thee up though in the depth of troubles."—*Greenham.*

B.C. 1872.

g E. H. Browne, D.D.

behold the fire, but where is the lamb?

a Some think this was a kind of involuntary prophecy.

b He. xi. 17—19.

c Jo. xix. 17.

d Jos. makes Is. 25 yrs. of age; others 33, wh. was the age of Christ at the crucifixion.

e H. T. Miller.

"If Abraham's heart could have known how to relent, that question of his dear, innocent, and pious son had melted it into compassion. I know not whether that word, 'my father,' did not strike Abraham as deep as the knife of Abraham could strike his son."— *Bp. Hall.*

Abraham prevented from offering Isaac

a Ma. xxvii. 2; Is. liii. 7; Ph. ii. 8; Jo. x. 17, 18.

b He. xi. 17—19; Ja. ii. 21—24.

c I S. xv. 22; Mi. vi. 7, 8; Ep. ii. 10.

d Ro. viii. 32.

e Bush. "The original 'I have

"the mount of the vision of the Lord" (see ver. 14), the fact that the mount of the temple bore the same name (2 Chron. iii. 1), the distance, two days' journey from Beersheba, which would just suffice to bring the company to Jerusalem, whereas Gerizim could not have been reached from Beersheba on the third day, are arguments too strong to be set aside by the single difficulty mentioned above, which, in fact, is no difficulty at all.*g*

4—8. (4) **third day**, the time helps to fix the day (Gerizim, for wh. some plead, could not have been reached in so short a time). **saw.. off**, prob. not very far, *i.e.* in the distance, or before him. (5) **abide.. ass**, wh. he would have said if the mt. had been *very far* off. **come.. you**," he seems to have had faith that both would return.*b* (6) **wood.. son**,*c* Isaac must have been strong to carry enough to consume the sacrifice.*d* **fire**, brand, or torch: another proof that the place was not *very* distant. **knife**, A. forgets nothing. The sacrifice is already offered in intention and will. **they.. together**, as it would seem, their last journey. (7) **where.. lamb?** (1) Isaac is ignorant of his father's purpose. (2.) He is familiar with the customary sacrifice. (8) **God.. provide**, A. has unlimited faith in God. Heb. *yireh lo hasseh*, will see for Himself the lamb.

Helps and hindrances of the Christian life.—We observe that in the path of faith—I. Human help is profitable. Essential service was no doubt rendered by these young men. What higher service can the human know than to wait on the Divine? 1. Let the demands of faith be boldly urged; 2. Let the service be cheerfully rendered. II. Human help is limited. III. Human help must receive a timely dismissal. Here is—1. Discernment: these young men would have stopped Abraham's work; 2. Decision: "Abide ye here." IV. The grandest triumphs have been achieved alone.*e*

Carrying fire.—Caravans carry with them the iron grating for the fire; and sometimes, owing to the difficulty experienced in obtaining a light, the charcoal fire which had been used the previous night was carried suspended by a chain, and kept burning. This may have been the case with Abraham, who had been more than a night on the way to Moriah: he laid the wood on Isaac his son, and took the fire in his hand, most likely that which he had kindled in the chill of the evening before, Gen. xxii.

9—12. (9) **altar**, of earth, or loose stones. **bound.. son**,*a* who did not resist. **laid.. wood**, and he finds that the victim is provided. (10) **and**, *etc.*,*b* what shall prevent the consummation of the act? (11) **angel.. Lord**,*c* the Angel-Jehovah, the covenant God. (12) **for**, *etc.*,*d* "The idea is simply that He knew, by a new proof, by having actually made trial of him."*e*

The sacrifice of Isaac.—Here we see exhibited—I. The sacrifice of eternal love. Look at—1. The antiquity of the love between the Father and the Son: 2. Its intensity. II. The method of human salvation. 1. The consummation of the sacrifice was delayed. Even as Abraham for three days contemplated Isaac's death, so for ages did the Father contemplate Calvary. 2. The mortal wound was inflicted by the Father. The accursed knife was Jewish envy, and Roman indifference and scorn. 3. The Son was unresisting.*f*

Timely succour.—God is wise to conceal the succours He intends in the several changes of thy life, that so He may draw thy heart into an entire dependence on His faithful promise. Thus, to try the metal of Abraham's faith, He let him go on till his hand was stretched forth, and then He comes to his rescue. Christ sends His disciples to sea, but stays behind Himself, on a design to try their faith and show His love. Comfort thyself, therefore, with this, though thou seest not thy God in the way, yet thou shalt find Him in the end.*g*

13, 14. (13) **ram**, one separated fr. the flock.*a* **thicket**, in wh. some see a type of the crown of thorns.*b* **offered .. son**, but Isaac was the true type of Jesus, and virtually offered. (14) **Jehovah-jireh** (*the Lord will see, or provide*), see on v. 8.

Jehovah-jireh, or Divine providence.—Abraham's offering of Isaac teaches—I. God's right to our greatest blessings. II. Man's duty in the highest trial. III. God's providence in the greatest emergency. Concerning the latter, consider—that its provisions— 1. Correspond exactly with human wants. With our wants as (1) Creatures—corporeally, intellectually, socially ; (2) Sinners— purifying influences and pardoning grace. 2. Are obtained in connection with individual agency. 3. Are often strikingly memorable.*c*

The ram.—If we might suppose that the ram in this instance had four horns, like some examples occasionally seen among the Asiatic races, as well as in a breed common in the north of Europe, his liability to be caught by the horns in a thick-grown, tangled underwood must have been very great. It is easy to see, by a contemplation of the figure, that a bunch of horns so variously twisted and "crankled" would have involved the animal in fresh difficulties whichever way he turned in attempt- ing to extricate himself. Mohammedan writers say that the horns of the ram in question were fixed upon the Kaaba or temple of Mecca by the early Arabians ; and that, to remove occasion of idolatry, they were taken down by Mohammed.

15—19. (15) **angel**, the same as in v. 11. (16) **by .. sworn**,*a* He could swear by no greater. God's final promise to A., confirming all the rest. **because**, *etc.*. A. inherits the reward of faith. (17) **seed .. enemies**, *i.e.* they shall subdue them. To possess a gate was to hold the city to wh. it pertained. (18) **seed .. blessed***b* (see on xii. 3), they shall find their happi- ness in thy seed, *i.e.* in the Messiah. (19) **they .. together**, the Divine blessing resting on both.

The promise to Abraham.—Notice.—I. Its certainty—" by my- self." By—1. One who is able to perform His promises ; 2. One who is willing to perform His promises ; 3. One with whom non- fulfilment of His word is impossible. II. Its chief points. 1. Prosperity in worldly affairs ; 2. Increase of number ; 3. Exten- sion of dominion ; 4. Ability to lay the world under eternal obligations. III. Its lessons to us. If we have faith and obedience like Abraham, like him we shall also be blessed.*c*

Perpetuated blessings.—It has been asked why the goodness of one man should extend to, and be rewarded in, successive gene- rations, covering the remotest ages, and reaching to the close of our present economy. But is it not a fact that in the world of providence the very same thing occurs? Has not, for instance,

---

B.C. 1872.

known,' denotes an eventual knowing, a dis- covering by actual experi- ment."—*Murphy*.

f R. A. Griffin.
g Gurnall.

Jehovah- jireh
a He. vii. 26.
b Augustine.
c D. Thomas, D.D.

"This became a proverb among the Hebrews, that if any should be in trouble and should desire the help of the Lord, they should say 'In the mount the Lord will see,' that is, as He had mercy on Abraham, so will He have mercy on us."— *Jerome.*

"He that made that beast brings him thither, fas- tens him there. Even in small things there is a great provi- dence." — *Bp. Hall.*

Abraham dwells at Beer-sheba.
a He. vi. 13, 14.
b Lu. i. 72—75 ; Ga. iii. 7—16 ; Ac. iii. 25.
c C. Johnstone.

"Isaac had never been so precious to his father, if he had not been recovered from death; if he had not been as miraculously restored as given. Abraham had never been as blessed in his seed, if he had not neglected Isaac for God. The only way to

B.C. 1872.

find comfort in an earthly thing is to surrender it in a believing carelessness into the hands of God."—*Bp. Hall.*
"Duty by habit is to pleasure turn'd; He is content who to obey has learn'd."
—*Sir E. Brydges.*
d *Dr. Cumming.*

the pedigree of Rebekah

a Ge. xi. 29.

b The land of Uz. The country of Job was prob. so called fr. Huz.

c Fr. whom perh. the Chaldeans were derived."—*Kalisch.*

d See Blunt's *Undesigned Coincidences*, Pt. I. 4, pp. 35—37.

e R. was the dau. of Isaac's first cousin.

"A good name will wear out; a bad one may be turned; a nickname lasts for ever."—*Zimmerman.*

f *Carlyle.*

such a character as Howard, the great philanthropist, left a mark upon the world that cannot be obliterated, and bequeathed influences that live after he has gone up higher? Have not the victories of Wellington, secured at a dread price, left us years of prosperity and peace? Do not millions shine in the light, and are not thousands of hearts warmed by the fires that were kindled in the days of the great Reformation by Luther, by Ridley, Cranmer, Knox, Calvin, and others? And if you find this to be the fact in the world, you should not object to its being declared to be the law of God's administration of the world. The discovery of printing, steam, the electric telegraph, are also illustrations, all tending to show that beneficent discoveries made by fathers break in benedictions upon their children.[d]

20—24. (20) **and**, *etc.*,[a] this is prob. intended to intro. the acc. of the mar. of Isaac. (21) **Huz**[b] (*? light sandy oil*). **Buz** (*contempt*). **Kemuel** (*? assembly of God*). (22) **Chesed**[c] (*gain*). **Hazo** (*vision*). **Pildash** (*? flame*). **Jidlaph** (*weeping*). **Bethuel**[d] (*? man of God*). (23) **Rebekah** (*enchaining*).[e] **Nahor** .. **brother**, his *elder* bro. (24) **concubine**, secondary wife. **Reumah** (*exalted*). **Tebah** (*executioner*). **Gaham** (*? sunburnt*). **Thahash** (*badger or seal*). **Maacha** (*oppression*).

Importance of names.—There is much, nay, almost all, in names. The name is the earliest garment you wrap round the earth, to which it thenceforth cleaves more tenaciously (for these are names that have lasted nigh thirty centuries) than the very skin. And now from without, what mystic influences does it not send inwards, even to the centre, especially in those plastic firsttimes, when the whole soul is yet infantine, soft: and the invisible seed-grain will grow to be an all-over-shadowy tree! Names? Could I unfold the influence of names, which are the most important of all clothings, I were a second great Trismegistus. Not only all common speech, but science—poetry itself— is no other, if thou consider it, than a right *naming*. Adam's first task was giving names to natural appearances. What is ours still but a continuation of the same, be the appearance exotic, vegetable, organic, mechanic, stars, or starry movements (as in science); or (as in poetry) passions, virtues, calamities, God, attributes, gods![f]

CHAPTER THE TWENTY-THIRD.

B.C. 1860.

the death of Sarah

a *Lightfoot.*

b 1 Ch. xxix. 15; Ps. cv. 9—12; He. xi. 9, 10; Ac. vii. 5; He. xi. 13.

"A burial-place is the first land that A. has in Canaan."—*Lightfoot.*

1—4. (1) **Sarah .. old**, S. the only woman whose age is mentioned in the Bible.[a] Her son. Isaac, was now 37 yrs. old. (2) **Kirjath-arba** (*city of Arba*), the Jews interpret it, "city of the four," bec. Adam, Abraham, Isaac, and Jacob were buried there. **Abraham .. her**, either A. was absent fr. home, or prob. he went to Sarah's tent. (3) **sons of Heth**, elsewhere called Hittites. (4) **I .. you**,[b] as a nomad chief he wandered ab. with his flocks. **give .. you**, first mention of a burial.

The purchased grave (on the whole chapter).—Look upon the purchase of the field of Machpelah in its connection with—1. Sarah ; it is a token of respect to the dead. The body deserves such respect, because—1. It has been the man's dwelling-place;

2. It has assisted the soul to express itself ; 3. It is destined for a higher and nobler service. II. Abraham himself. It shows that he prepared for death. 1. It taught him that the highest earthly possessions terminate in a grave ; 2. It implies that he waited for death. III. The Jewish nation. It serves as a monument for their instruction. 1. Its purchase taught them that it would soon be theirs ; 2. Its stillness taught them to be active ; 3. Its solemnity taught them to seek that country where there is no grave.[c]

Funeral customs.—The ancient Greeks were accustomed to lay out the body after it was shrouded in its grave clothes ; sometimes upon a bier, which they bedecked with various sorts of flowers. The place where the bodies were laid out, was near the door of the house : there the friends of the deceased attended them with loud lamentations ; a custom which still continues to be observed among that people. Dr. Chandler, when travelling in Greece, saw a woman at Megara, sitting with the door of her cottage open, lamenting her dead husband aloud ; and at Zante a woman in a house with the door open, bewailing her little son, whose body lay by her dressed, the hair powdered, the face painted and bedecked with gold leaf. This custom of mourning for the dead, near the door of the house, was probably borrowed from the Syrians : and if so, it will serve to illustrate an obscure expression of Moses, relative to Abraham : "And Sarah died in Kirjatharba ; and Abraham came to mourn for Sarah, and to weep for her." He came out of his own separate tent, and seating himself on the ground near the door of her tent, where her corpse was placed, that he might perform those public solemn rites of mourning that were required as well by decency as affection, lamented with many tears the loss he had sustained.[d]

5—9. (5) **saying**, acc. to LXX., "Saying, not so." (6) **mighty prince**,[a] *lit.* a prince of God : in ref. to his wealth. **choice**, *etc.*,[b] either "the choicest of our," etc., or, "in any thou shalt choose." (7) **bowed**, *etc.*, A. returns courtesy for courtesy. The real Christian should never be outdone in true politeness. (8) **if .. mind**, if this be your pleasure, if you are willing. **Ephron** (*fawn-like*). **Zohar** (*whiteness*). (9) **give**, sell, let me have. **Machpelah**[c] (*double cave*), either a cave having two cavities or two entrances. **for .. worth**, a fair price. Heb. *bakkeseph*, for full silver.

Oriental politeness.—The politeness of Abraham may be seen exemplified among the highest and the lowest of the people of the East : in this respect, nature seems to have done for them what art has done for others. With what grace do all classes bow on receiving a favour, or in paying their respects to a superior ! Sometimes they bow down *to the ground*; at other times they put their hands on their *bosoms*, and gently incline the head ; they also put the right hand on the *face* in a longitudinal position ; and sometimes give a long and graceful sweep with the *right hand*, from the *forehead* to the *ground*.[d]

10—16. (10) **audience .. city**, gate of city was the forum, place of justice, business, etc. (11) **Lord .. give**, *etc.*, customary expressions of politeness, still com. in transacting business in the E. (13) **give .. field**, A. insists on *buying* it. (15) **four .. silver**, as the word *shekel*[a] = weight, the value of these 400

B.C. 1860.

c *Jenkin Jones.*

"There is nothing more certain than death, nothing more uncertain than the time of dying. I will, therefore, be prepared for that at all times, which may come at any time, must come at one time or another. I shall not hasten my death by being still ready, but sweeten it. It makes me not die the sooner, but the better."— *Warwick.*

Death only draws up the veil and reveals the glories of heaven to the emancipated soul of the Christian.

d *Paxton.*

Abraham treats for the purchase of the cave of Machpelah

a Ge. xiii. 2, xiv. 14.

b Thomson, L. and B. 578.

c Robinson, B. R. ii. 431 ; Thomson, L. and B. 580 ; Stanley, *Serm. in E. Appen.*

"There are in business three things necessary —knowledge, temper, and time."—*Feltham.*

d *Roberts.*

Abraham buys the cave

a In later times the LXX. and the N. Test. (Ma. xvii. 24) identify

B.C. 1860.
the shekel with the didrachma, wh. would make the shekel nearly ½ ozs. 220 grains of our weight, or a little less in value than half-a-crown of our present money. The fle'd, therefore, would have been purchased for about £52 10s."—*Speaker's Com.*
b "This is the first mention of money in the hist. of the world, but it was uncoined."—*Smith's O. T. Hist.*
c J. Parker, D.D.
"As a tract of country narrowed in the distance expands itself when we approach, thus the way to our near grave appears to us as long as it did formerly when we were far off." —*Richter.*
d Dr. Porter.

the burial of Sarah
a Ge. l. 13; Je. xxxii. 10, 11; Ru. iv. 7—10.
b C. Simeon, M.A. "It buries every error—covers every defect—extinguishes every resentment. From its peaceful bosom spring none but fond regrets and tender recollections. Who can look down upon the grave of an enemy, and not feel a compunctious throb that he should have warred with the poor handful of dust that lies mouldering before him?"— *Washington Irving.*
"The grave is the common treasury to which

"weights" of silver not known. (16) **current .. merchant,** *lit.* silver passing with the merchant.

Buying a grave.—I. Look at Abraham buying a grave. The good man is forced into such commerce as well as the bad; the best man of his age here bargains for a burial-ground. II. The manner in which the children of Heth answered him deserves special notice. III. Learn that man's final requirement of man is a grave. IV. From the fact of Abraham's mourning for Sarah, note, that consecration to God's purposes does not eradicate our deep human love.*c*

Arab politeness.—In making purchases from an Arab, his politeness is almost amazing. When the price is asked, he replies, "Whatever you please, my lord." When pressed for a more definite answer, he says, "Take it without money." One cannot but remember, under any circumstances, Abraham's treaty with the sons of Heth for the cave of Machpelah. Our feelings of romance, however, are somewhat damped when we find that the price ultimately demanded is four or five times the value of the article. An Arab always tells you that his house is yours, his property is yours, he himself is your slave: that he loves you with all his heart, would defend you with his life, etc., etc. This all sounds very pretty, but it would be just as well not to rely too much on it, for fear of disappointment. Nothing, however, is lost by politeness; and so one may seem to believe all that is said, and even utter an occasional *l'llah yutawwel umrak ya sidy !*" (May God prolong your life. O my lord!) by way of showing gratitude. The Arabs are most profuse in the use of titles. Every beggar will address his fellow with "O, my lord!" *ya sidy* (pronounced *seedy*), or "your excellency!" *jenabak*, while the traveller is generally *saadatak* (your highness!).*d*

17—20. (17) **field**, district, portion of land. **sure**, Heb. *yakom*, stood; *i.e.* were made stable, confirmed. (18) **before .. city**, the bargain was ratified in the presence of competent witnesses. (19) **and .. this**, having secured and paid for the land. **before Mamre**, in the face of; or, E. of M. (20) **were .. Abraham**,*a* *lit.*, "stood firm to Abraham."

Abraham purchasing a burying-place in Canaan.—Remark—I. The manner in which the agreement was made. Notice—1. The courteousness of the parties engaged; 2. Their equity; 3. Their prudence. II. The ends for which it was made. Abraham bought the field to—1. Bury his wife; 2. Express his confidence in the Divine promise; 3. Perpetuate among his posterity the expectation of the promised land.*b*

Immorality in trade.—It ought to be so that a little child could take in its hand a sum of money, and go to any store for a commodity, and hand that money over the counter, and, telling what it wants, receive an article as much better than its own uninstructed judgment could choose as the knowledge of the merchant is superior to its knowledge; but I am afraid it would not be safe to go shopping in that way. I am afraid that if you were no judge of material, and bought accordingly, you would have poor garments. I am afraid that if you had no judgment of prices, you would pay inordinately for many things. These merchants, these men that sell goods—how many pretences they weave! What poor articles, with what a good face, do they palm off on their customers! How they suppress the truth!

How they indulge in over-praising or under-valuing, as the case may be! How much there is of systematic commercial deceit and wrong-doing throughout it!*c*

B.C. 1860.

we must all be taxed."—*Burke.*
c H. W. Beecher.

CHAPTER THE TWENTY-FOURTH.

B.C. 1857.

1—6. (1) **old,***a* 137 yrs. at death of Sarah ; and 140 at mar. of Isaac, who was then 40. (2) **servant,***b* prob. Eliezer of Damascus. **hand .. thigh,** form of adjuration mentioned only in one *other* place ;*c* prob. token of entire subjection. (3) **take .. Canaanites,***d* a licentious, heathen, doomed race. (4) **go .. country,***e* Mesopotamia, v. 10. (5) **will .. land,** a natural supposition, commendable caution. (6) **beware .. again,** a wise father will seek to preserve his son fr. ensnaring influences.

Isaac's marriage (on the whole chapter).—I. The selection of the bride. Abraham's command (v. 3) was given because—1. The Canaanites differed from Isaac in their taste ; 2. A bad influence might be exerted on Isaac's mind ; 3. The Canaanites were to be destroyed. II. The means employed to ensure success. 1. Human instrumentality ; 2. Trust in God ; 3. Self-remuneration. III. The spirit in which the marriage was consummated. It was—1. Modest ; 2. Confident ; 3. Loving. Conclusion—(1) Let the youth of our country study this history ; (2) May parents follow the example of Abraham.*f*

Abraham sends his servant to find a wife for Isaac

a Ge. xxi. 5.

b Ge. xv. 2.

c Ge. xlvii. 29.

d Ge. xxvii. 46 ; 1 Co. vii. 37 ; 2 Co. iv. 14.

e De. vi. 13.

f Jenkin Jones.

Marriage in the East.—Among the Jews the father of a family selects wives for his sons, and husbands for his daughters. If a son had a preference for any person as his wife, he asked the father to obtain her from *her* father. But the father could not give the daughter in marriage without the consent of the brothers (Jahn). These are the very rules observed by the Nestorians at the present day. No young man thinks of making a marriage contract for himself. In case the father is dead, the eldest brother takes the father's place. Where the intended bride lives at a distance, the matter is sometimes intrusted to some faithful servant or agent, as was done by Abraham in relation to his son Isaac. This event was remarkably illustrated by the history of a marriage that took place a short time since among the Nestorians in the mountains. Indeed there was such a remarkable coincidence of names and circumstances, that it seemed like acting over again that most interesting part of sacred history. The Nestorian patriarch, Abraham, who was in the place of a father to his younger brother, Isaac, being desirous of procuring a wife for his foster son, sent his most trusty steward to a distant part of the country to obtain one from among his own people. The servant took with him jewels and raiment for the future wife of Isaac, and presents for her near relatives. He was no less prosperous than the servant of his master's namesake, the ancient patriarch, Abraham. But though I became acquainted with all parties in the case, I must leave the reader's imagination to fill up some of its incidents. Only let him substitute *mules* for *camels,* which are not used in this mountainous country, and I may refer to the close of the 24th chapter of Genesis for the sequel. The damsel was brought to the house of this modern patriarch, and "Isaac took her, and she became his wife, and he loved her."*g*

" The homeliest services that we do in an honest calling, though it be but to plough, or dig, if done in obedience, and conscious of God's commandment, is crowned with an ample reward ; whereas the best works for their kind, if without respect of God's injunction and glory, are loaded with curses."—*Bishop Hall.*

" It is not only paying wages, and giving commands, that constitutes a master of a family ; but prudence, equal behaviour, with a readiness to protect and cherish them, is what entitles a man to that character in their very hearts and sentiments."—*Steele.*

g Grant's Nestorians.

b.c. 1857.

he assures him that his way shall be prepared
a Ex. xxii. 20; Ps. xxxiv. 7.
b J. A. Woodhead. "God has set the type of marriage before us throughout all creation. Each creature seeks its perfection through being blent with another. The very heaven and earth picture it to us, for does not the sky embrace the green earth as its bride? Precious, excellent, glorious, is that word of the Holy Ghost, 'the heart of the husband doth safely trust in her.'"—*Luther.*
c Harmer.

the servant departs to the City of Nahor
a "And he took part of all his master's goods in his hand."—LXX., also Vulg. "As though A. had sent a present with the servant to conciliate the bride's family."—*Spkr.'s Com.*
b Ge. xxvii. 43; cf. xi. 31; Ac. vii. 2.
c See Homer, Od., vii. 20. In the form of a girl, Minerva meets Ulysses when ab. to enter the city of the Phœnicians in the evening. See also Robinson, B. R., ii. 368.
d Ne. i. 11; Ps. xxvii. 5; Pr. iii. 5, 6; Ph. iv. 6.
e Ju. vi. 17; 1 S. vi. 7; xiv. 8; xx. 7.

7—9. (7) **he .. thee,**ᵃ A. believes that his servant's way will be opened; and all hindrances will be removed. **thou .. thence,** whom God will select. (8) **if .. thee,** *etc.*, this said to calm the servant's fears. A. has no doubt of the issue. **only .. again,** on no acc. is the servant to promise his kindred to return and bring Isaac thither. (9) **master,** Heb. *adonav,* lord.

Bring not my son thither again.—" Bring not my son thither again"—I. Lest he fall into the habits of his kindred. II. Lest my own labours prove to have been in vain. III. Lest the promises made to me be annulled, and he be eternally lost. IV. Lest thou thyself be ever troubled with the gnawings of an awakened conscience, and a sense of the non-fulfilment of thy duty to me.ᵇ

Eastern oaths.—The present mode of swearing among the Mohammedan Arabs, that live in tents as the patriarchs did, according to *de la Roque,* is by laying their hands on the Koran. They cause those who swear to wash their hands before they give them the book; they put their left hand underneath, and the right over it. Whether, among the patriarchs, one hand was under, and the other upon the thigh, is not certain: possibly Abraham's servant might swear with one hand under his master's thigh, and the other stretched out to heaven. As the posterity of the patriarchs are described as coming out of the thigh, it has been supposed this ceremony had some relation to their believing the promise of God, to bless all the nations of the earth, by means of one that was to descend from Abraham.ᶜ

10—14. (10) **ten .. master,** more prob. than were absolutely needful: he would make a favourable impression. **for .. hand,**ᵃ implying that the camels were well laden: many servants also needed for protection, etc. **unto .. Nahor,** Haran or Charran.ᵇ (11) **kneel,** posture of camel resting. **time .. water,**ᶜ *lit.* at the time of the going forth of the women-drawers of water. (12) **send .. speed,** Heb. *hatcreh,* cause it to happen. (13) **behold,** *etc.,* the season is opportune: all the industrious and healthy daughters of the people will come hither. (14) **and .. pass,**ᵈ he seeks evidence of God's choice. **to .. say,** he would use his judgment in accosting the most likely. **let .. drink,** he would test her amiability by a simple request. **and she,** *etc.,* she shall be willing to do more than I ask. **let .. Isaac,** one of such a temper and so employed would be a suitable wife for a pastoral chief. **thereby .. master,**ᵉ he thinks more of his master than of himself.

A good servant.—Mark—I. The fidelity of this servant. He swore to his master, and disappointed him not. II. His self-forgetfulness. He spares no pain, refuses no toil, and complains of no difficulty. He lost himself entirely in his master. III. His piety. Note how he follows God's guidance, and waits for His hand. IV. His constancy. He gives his whole life to his master. From childhood to old age he had served him.ᶠ

The secret of success.—Edward Lee, of Manchester, Massachusetts, was for several years a sailor, and apparently hardened in sin, but he became converted, and then all his energies were devoted to the service of Jesus Christ. Quitting the sea for the sake of being more useful, he took up his residence in his native village; and the time which could be spared from his labours on the farm, he employed in behalf of God's glory, and the salvation of souls. For thirty years he kept up a weekly prayer-meeting every Thursday afternoon in his own house. It was his rule to visit all the families in the village once in the year, to inquire after their spiritual welfare. The houses of affliction and sorrow were always sure of his visits and his prayers. In his own house, in the field, and on his journeys, wherever he could warn and plead with the impenitent, he was sure to do so. One night, putting up at an inn where a country ball had commenced, he got permission to enter the room, and addressed the company with such moral power and energy that dancing was abandoned, and the evening, begun in mirth and folly, was spent in holy exhortation, and closed with prayer. Mr. Lee gave away one-eighth of his income, yet left enough to support his widow for thirty years after his death. Wonderful example of piety! What was the secret of his high attainments? He was a man of prayer! A few days before he died, he pointed his Christian friends to a spot on the floor, and observed that for more than thirty years, with the exception of ten days' illness, he had risen from his bed at night, and prayed for a dying world's salvation. His minister used to say, "I am but a babe to brother Lee: I prize his prayers more than gold."

15—20. (15) **before**, *etc.*,[a] his fidelity rewarded by a prompt answer. **Rebekah**, *etc.*,[b] *see on* xxii. 20. **shoulder**, a practice com. with the Hebs. (16) **fair .. upon**, not simply good-looking, but appearing good, *lit.* "good of countenance." **virgin .. her**, unmarried, chaste, modest. **went .. well**, steps leading to it. (17) **ran**, *etc.*, his eagerness denotes his hopefulness. (18) **drink**,[c] first pt. of required sign is met. **lord**, she is respectful as well as kind. If the servant was Eliezer, he was prob. an old man. (19) **said**, without being asked: last pt. of the sign. (20) **hasted**, alacrity in kindness. **and .. trough**, carefulness: did not throw it away. **ran .. camels**, spared neither time, trouble, nor toil: showed cheerfulness, strength, etc.

Rebekah.—Rebekah—I. Came of a good stock. II. Was trained in habits of industry. III. Had a virtuous character: looked good, was chaste and modest—did not speak first to the servant. IV. Was courteous, "my lord." V. Was good-natured: cheerfully doing more than requested. Let maidens seek to be like Rebekah.

Drawing water.—" It is the work of *females* in the East to draw water both morning and evening; and they may be seen going in groups to the wells, with their vessels on the hip or the shoulder. In the morning they talk about the events of the past night, and in the evening about those of the day: many a time would the story of Abraham's servant and Rebekah, the daughter of Bethuel, be repeated by the women of Mesopotamia in their visits to the well."[d] "The women among the Orientals are reduced to a state of great subjection. In Barbary they regard the civility and respect which the politer nations of Europe pay to the weaker sex as extravagance, and so many infringements of that law of nature which assigns to man the pre-eminence. The matrons of that country, though they are considered indeed as servants of better station, yet have the greatest share of toil and business upon their hands. While the lazy husband reposes under some neighbouring shade, and the young people of both sexes tend the flocks, the wives are occupied all the day long, either in toiling

B.C. 1857.

f C. J. Vaughan, D.D.

"Marriage is the best state for man in general; and every man is a worse man in proportion as he is unfit for the marriage state."—*Johnson.*

"Nuptial love maketh mankind, friendly love perfecteth it; but wanton love corrupteth and embaseth it." —*Bacon.*

Rebekah

a Is. lxv. 24; Da. ix. 23; Ps. xxxiv. 15.

b Pr. xxxi. 27.

c Pr. xxxi. 26; 1 Pe. iii. 8.

"If it is remembered that camels, though endowed in an almost marvellous degree with the power of enduring thirst, drink, when an opportunity offers, an enormous quantity of water, it will be acknowledged that the trouble to which the maiden cheerfully submitted required more than ordinary patience."—*Kalisch.*

d Roberts.

"Strong are the instincts with which God has guarded the sacredness of marriage."—*Maria M'Intosh.*

B.C. 1857.

"If you wish to marry suitably, marry your equal."—*Ovid.*

e Paxton.

Rebekah's kindness and its reward

a Harmer.

"Hay is not made in the East. Cattle continue at the present day to be fed with chopped straw mixed with barley. The common reader would suppose the 'straw' to be for litter; but straw is never so employed in the East; dung dried and pounded being used for that purpose."—*Pict. Bible.*

"Kindness in woman, not her beauteous looks, shall win my love."—*Shakespeare.*

Rebekah tells her mother

a Ge. xxxii. 10; Ps. xcviii. 3.

"The good wife is none of our dainty dames, showing the presents. It is well for maidens when they can tell their mothers of the gifts made to them. A modest dam., a sympathising mother.

Mothers and daughters.—This relation should be marked by— I. Confidence on the side of the daughter. II. Sympathy on the side of the mother. Learn—(1) Happy the mother whose daughter withholds no secrets from her ; (2) Happy the daughter whose mother is always ready to hear and advise.

Exhortation to duty.—Previous to the battle of Lutzen, in which eighty thousand Austrians were defeated by an army of thirty-six thousand Prussians, commanded by Frederick the Great, this monarch ordered all his officers to attend him, and

---

on their looms, or in grinding at the mill, or in preparing bread or other kind of farinaceous food. Nor is this all ; for to finish the day, 'at the time of evening,' to use the words of the sacred historian, 'even at the time that women go out to draw water,' they must equip themselves with a pitcher or goat's skin, and tying their sucking children behind them, trudge out in this manner, two or three miles, to fetch water."*e*

21—25. (21) **wondering,** *etc.,* anxious ab. her : amazed, etc. held .. peace, thinking perh. that her tongue would betray her. (22) **ear-ring,** *lit.* a ring, prob. nose-ring : still worn in E. **bracelets,** *etc.,* what present more likely to succeed ? (23) **whose .. thou?** he desired to know of her kindred. v. 4. **is .. in?** by this he might judge of the size of the establishment. (24) **and,** *etc.,* her answer resolved his doubts, confirmed his hopes, filled him with joy. (25) **straw,** chaff. **provender,** fodder, barley, beans, etc.

Kindness rewarded.—The reward was—I. Unexpected : Rebekah was not kind for the sake of gain. II. Suitable : adapted to her sex, station, and the customs of her people. III. Valuable : a great return for a small act. Learn—(1) The best reward of kindness is a heart strengthened in love of kindness ; (2) "A cup of cold water" shall not lose its reward ; (3) God will ultimately reward the good, whom men may treat with ingratitude.

Oriental ornaments.—The weight of the ornaments that the servant of Abraham put upon Rebekah appears to us rather extraordinary. Sir J. Chardin assures us as heavy, and even heavier, were worn by the women of the East when he was there. The ear-ring, or jewel for the face, weighed half a shekel, and the bracelets for her hands ten shekels (Gen. xxiv. 22), which, as he justly observes, is about five ounces. Upon which he tells us, "the women wear rings and bracelets of as great a weight as this, through all Asia, and even much heavier. They are rather manacles than bracelets. There are some as large as the finger. The women wear several of them, one above the other, in such a manner as sometimes to have the arm covered with them from the wrist to the elbow. Poor people wear as many of glass or horn. They hardly ever take them off : they are their riches.*a*

26—28. (26) **worshipped,** thanking God for this happy termination of his journey. (27) **I .. way,***a* one must be in the way of duty, obedience, providence, if he would have God to lead him. (28) **ran,** full of wonder at what she had heard ; and joy, bec. of the presents she had received. **her .. house,** women's apartments or tents distinct fr. those of the men. **things,** and

hus addressed them:—"To-morrow I intend giving the enemy battle; and, as it will decide who are to be the future masters of Silesia, I expect every one of you will in the strictest manner do his duty. If any one of you is a coward, let him step forward before he makes others as cowardly as himself,—let him step forward, I say, and he shall immediately receive his discharge without ceremony or reproach. I see there is none among you who does not possess true heroism, and will not display it in defence of his king, of his country, and of himself. I shall be in the front and in the rear; shall fly from wing to wing: no company will escape my notice: and whoever I then find doing his duty, upon him will I heap honour and favour."

29—33. (29) **Laban**[a] (*white*), prob. a youth at this time. (30) **saw.. hands,** *etc.*, the sister had no concealments fr. her bro. (31) **come.. without?** Laban influenced by customs of hospitality, and perh. also by his sister's presents.[b] **for.. camels,** Laban had ordered the servants to do this. (32) **man.. house,** *i.e.* A.'s servant. **he.. camels,** *i.e.* Laban. **water.. feet,** *see* on xviii. 4. (33) **eat.. errand,**[c] he had come a long journey, yet thinks more of his master's interests than his own gratification.

Duty before self-gratification (v. 33).—We find here—I. Self kept in abeyance: this at a time—1. When Eliezer had arrived at the end of a long, anxious, wearying, and perilous journey: 2. When the hospitality of his entertainers had spread a repast before him. II. Duty paramount. He owed a duty—1. To his master, whose business he was upon; 2. To his entertainers, that they should not be kept in unnecessary suspense.

Duty and self-denial.—There is a beautiful legend illustrating the blessedness of performing our duty at whatever cost to our own inclination. A beautiful vision of our Saviour had appeared to a monk, and in silent bliss he was gazing upon it. The hour arrived at which it was his duty to feed the poor of the convent. He lingered not in his cell to enjoy the vision, but left it to perform his humble duty. When he returned, he found the blessed vision still waiting for him, and uttering these words, " Hadst thou stayed, I must have fled."

34—38. (34) **and,** *etc.*, the master's name would at once intro. him. (35) **greatly,**[a] variously, abundantly. **great, rich and powerful. flocks,** *etc.*, elements of wealth that would be well understood by these pastoral people. (36) **Sarah,** they would recall her name. **son.. old,** a hint that Isaac was now young. **him.. hath,** this young man, the sole heir. (37, 38) **swear,** *see* on v. 3.

Abraham's servant (v. 34).—I. *Eliezer's character.* His position humble, a servant; not the less honourable. Angels are servants; Jesus was a servant. This man a pattern servant. 1. *Attached.* Not given to change; rolling stones, etc. Pecuniary gain of change often more than counterbalanced by moral loss. Might have got another master, with less religious gain; 2. *Trustworthy.* Hence his present mission. Seemed to feel that he must be true to the trust reposed. "I am," etc.; 3. *Pious.* His piety probably the source of other elements of character. A man of prayer (v. 12, etc.). He felt accountable to God as well as to Abraham. Away from home, the thought of his

---

B.C. 1857.

parentage, she doth not so remember what she was by birth, that she forgets what she is by match."—*Fuller.*

v. 26. T. *Boston, Wks.,* iv. 453.

"Take the daughter of a good mother."—*Fuller.*

Laban and Eliezer

a Ge. xxvii. 43—45; xxix. 1—30; *etc.*

b Pr. xix. 6.

c Job xxiii. 12; Jo. iv. 34; Ep. vi. 5—8; Ma. vi. 33.

"There is no mean work, save that which is sordidly selfish; there is no irreligious work save that which is morally wrong; while in every sphere of life "the post of honour is the post of duty."—*Chapin.*

" Whoso escapes a duty avoids a gain."—*Theo. Parker.*

Eliezer's address

a Pr. x. 22; xxii. 4.

"I have been formerly so silly as to hope that every servant I had might be made a friend; I am now convinced that the nature of servitude generally bears a contrary tendency. People's characters are to be chiefly collected from their education and place in life; birth itself does

VOL. I. D

B.C. 1857.

master, etc. II. *Eliezer's reward*—1. The satisfaction of his own mind. This an important part of the reward of piety. Conscience at peace; 2. The joy of witnessing the prosperity of a master he loved, and contributing to it; 3. The trust, etc., of his master. The confidence of others in us very comforting; 4. His honourable mention in history; a servant's history in a book for all men, of which God is the author. (1) Well for those who serve to have good masters; (2) Well for us if we serve Abraham's God.

A faithful servant.—The Rev. S. W. Hanna says: "On the 10th of June, 1770, the town of Port-au-Prince was utterly overthrown by a dreadful earthquake. From one of the falling houses the inmates had fled, except a negro woman, the nurse of her master's infant child. She would not desert her charge, though the walls were even then giving way. Rushing to its bed-side, she stretched forth her arms to enfold it. The building rocked to its foundation—the roof fell in. Did it crush the hapless pair? The heavy fragments fell indeed upon the woman, but the infant escaped unharmed: for its noble protectress extended her bended form across the body, and at the sacrifice of her own life preserved her charge from destruction."

39—41, *see on vv. 5—8.*

Eliezer's speech (vv. 34—49).—Eliezer's speech, the first in the Bible, considered as—I. The speech of a servant. II. The speech of a master. III. A speech which turns the heart to the master.ᵃ

Examples of successful men.—The world-renowned Rothschilds ascribe their success to the following rules: "Be an off-hand man: make a bargain at once. Never have anything to do with an unlucky man or plan. Be cautious and bold." John Jacob Astor, when requested to furnish incidents of his life, replied. "My actions must make my life." Stephen Girard's fundamental maxim was, "Take care of the cents: the dollars will take care of themselves." Amos Lawrence said, when asked for advice, "Young man, base all your actions upon a principle of right; preserve your integrity of character; and in doing this, never reckon the cost." A. T. Stewart, the merchant-prince of New York, says, "No abilities, however splendid, can command success without intense labour and persevering application." Nicholas Longworth, the Cincinnati millionaire, says, "I have always had these two things before me: Do what you undertake thoroughly. Be faithful in all accepted trusts."

42—46, *see on vv. 12—14.*

Eliezer's piety (vv. 42—44).—Eliezer, the earthly messenger of Abraham, in the convoy of the heavenly messengers. A picus diplomat, accompanied by the Angel of the Lord. The diplomats of this world are often accompanied by demons. The love and truth of God is a foundation for love and truth among men.ᵃ

Women drawing water.—It is still the proper business of the females to supply the family with water. From this drudgery, however, the married women are exempted, unless when single women are wanting. The proper time for drawing water in those burning climates is in the morning, or when the sun is going down; then they go forth to perform that humble office, adorned with their trinkets, some of which are often of great value. Agreeably to this custom, Rebekah went instead of her

---

Marginal notes:

"but little."—*Shenstone.*

"It is proper for everyone to consider, in the case of all men, that he who has not been a servant cannot become a praiseworthy master; and it is meet that we should plume ourselves rather on acting the part of a servant properly than that of the master, first, towards the laws (for in this way we are servants of the gods), and next towards our elders."—*Plato.*

"The great highroad of human welfare lies along the old highway of steadfast well-doing; and they who are the most persistent, and work in the truest spirit, will invariably be most successful; success treads on the heel of every right effort."—*S. Smiles.*

a *Lange.*

"In everything the ends well defined are the secret of durable success."—*Cousin.*

"The hand that hath made you fair, hath made you good; the goodness that is cheap in beauty, makes beauty brief in goodness; but grace being the soul of your complexion should keep the body of it ever fair."—*Shakespeare.*

"A virtuous

Cap. xxiv. 47—54. GENESIS. 99

mother to fetch water from the well, and the servant of Abraham expected to meet an unmarried female there who might prove a suitable match for his master's son. In the East Indies the women also draw water at the public wells, as Rebekah did on that occasion, for travellers, their servants and their cattle; and women of no mean rank literally illustrate the conduct of an unfortunate princess in the Jewish History by performing the services of a menial. The young women of Guzerat daily draw water from the wells, and carry the jars upon the head; but those of high rank carry them upon the shoulder. In the same way Rebekah carried her pitcher: and probably for the same reason—because she was the daughter of an Eastern prince.

47—49. (47—48*a*), *see* on vv. 22—26. **my .. daughter,** Rebekah was A.'s brother's grand-dau. (49) **if .. master,** if you will respond to his wish. **that .. turn,** *i.e.* go elsewhere to fulfil my mission.

Eastern jewelry.—Nothing is more common than for heathen females to have a ring in the nose; and this has led some to suppose that the jewel here alluded to was put into that member, and not on the face. "I put a jewel on thy *forehead*" (Ezek. xv. 11). The margin has, for forehead, "nose." It does not appear to be generally known that there is an ornament which is worn by females in the East on the *forehead*. It is made of thin gold, and is studded with precious stones, and called *Pattam*, which signifies dignity. Thus, to tie on the *Pattam* is to "invest with high dignity." *Patta-Istere* " is the name of the first lawful wife of the king." In the Sathur-Agaraathe, this ornament is called "*the ornament of the forehead.*" Tyerman and Bennet say of a bride they saw in China: "Her head-dress sparkled with jewels, and was most elegantly beaded with rows of pearls encircling it like a coronet; from which a brilliant angular ornament hung over her forehead, and between her eyebrows."*b*

50—54. (50) **Laban,** a bro. acting as joint guardian of his sister. **Bethuel,** who may have been aged and infirm.*a* **The .. Lord,** this they knew fr. the details to wh. they had listened. **we .. good,** the Lord has already decided. (51) **behold,** *etc.*, acc. to custom the matter was settled by the guardians of R. (52) **worshipped,***b* thanking God for the successful issue of his mission. (53) **jewels,** *etc.*, bridal gifts to confirm the contract. (54) **they .. drink,** pleasure aft. business. **send .. master,** this servant was no loiterer.

Calmness and resolution in duty.—There are few things more beautiful than the calm and resolute progress of an earnest spirit. The triumphs of genius may be more dazzling; the chances of good fortune may be more exciting; but neither are at all so interesting or so worthy as the achievements of a steady, faithful, and fervent energy. The moral elements give an infinitely higher value to the latter, while, at the same time, they bring it comparatively within the reach of all. Genius can be the lot of only a few; good fortune may come to any, but it would be the part of a fool to wait for it; whereas all may work with heartiness and might in the work to which they have given themselves. It is their simple duty to do this. It may seem but a small thing to do. No o...

B.C. 1857.

"mind in a fair body is indeed a fine picture in a good light, and therefore it is no wonder that it makes the beautiful sex all over charms."—*Addison.*

b Paxton.

a Ps. xxxii. 8; xlviii. 14: Pr. iii. 6.

"We all originally came from the woods; it is hard to eradicate from any of us the old taste for the tattoo and the war-paint; and the moment that money gets into our pockets, it somehow or another breaks out in ornaments on our person, without always giving refinement to our manners."—*Whipple.*

b Roberts.

Laban and Bethuel consent

a The Hebs. have a trad. that B. died on the day of Eliezer's arrival; while Josephus speaks of him as dead. —*Ant.* i. 16.

b Ps. cxvi. 1, 2.

"To men addicted to delights, business is an interruption; to such as are cold to delights business is an entertainment. For which reason it was said to one who commended a dull man for his application, 'No thanks to him; if he had no business he

B.C. 1857.

would have nothing to do."—Steele.

c Dr. Tulloch.

Rebekah consents

a Ge. xxxv. 8.

"It is the most momentous question a woman is ever called upon to decide, whether the faults of the man she loves go beyond remedy, and will drag her down, or whether she is competent to be his earthly redeemer, and lift him to her own level."—Holmes.

"Never marry but for love; but see that thou lovest what is lovely."—Wm. Penn.

"It is a mistake to consider marriage merely as a scheme of happiness. It is also a bond of service. It is the most ancient form of that social ministration which God has ordained for all human beings, and which is symbolised by all the relations of nature."—Chapin.

b Roberts.

Isaac meets Rebekah

a Jos. i. 8; Ps. i. 2; lxxii. 12; cxix. 15; cxlili. 5.

b C. H. Spurgeon.

"It is customary for both men and women, when an Emir or great personage is approaching, to

for doing it. Yet just because it is a duty, it will be found bearing a rich reward. The labour of the faithful is never in vain. The fruits will be found gathered into his hand, while the hasty garlands of genius are fading away, and the prizes of the merely fortunate are turned into vanity.*c*

55—60. (55) **brother,** source of authority. **mother,** moved by affection. **let .. ten,** R. was a good dau., of whom they were not anxious to be rid. (56) **hinder,** *etc.,* he perh. is thinking of his master's anxiety for his return. (57) **inquire,** *etc.,* as to the time she preferred for departing. (58) **I will go,** it shall not be told Isaac that she was an unwilling bride. (59) **nurse,** as a female attendant and friend; one who by her relation was dear. Her name was Deborah.*a* (60) **blessed,** *i.e.* invoked a blessing. **seed .. gate,** *see* on Gen. xxii. 17.

Diligence in business (v. 56).—We have here—I. An earnest servant's request: "Hinder me not." Hindrances in the way of duty are often—1. Intentional: proceeding from many motives, as envy, etc.; 2. Unintentional, as here, proceeding from the thoughtlessness of friendship, from the seductive influences of social customs, etc. II. A good man's plea: "seeing," etc. He regarded the Divine blessing—1. As a summons to perseverance; 2. As a sufficient answer to hindrances; 3. As a conclusive argument for proper diligence.

Rebekah and her nurse.—How often have scenes like this led my mind to the patriarchal age! The daughter is about for the *first time* to leave the paternal roof: the servants are all in confusion; each refers to things long gone by, each wishes to do something to attract the attention of his young mistress. One says, "Ah! do not forget him who nursed you when an infant;" another, "How often did I bring you the beautiful lotus from the distant tank! Did I not always conceal your faults?" The mother comes to take leave. She weeps, and tenderly embraces her, saying, "My daughter, I shall see you no more.—Forget not your mother." The brother enfolds his sister in his arms, and promises soon to come and see her. The father is absorbed in thought, and is only aroused by the sobs of the party. He then affectionately embraces his daughter, and tells her not to fear. The female domestics must each *smell* of the poor girl, and the men touch her feet. As Rebekah had her *nurse* to accompany her, so at *this* day the *Aya* (the *nurse*) who has from infancy brought up the bride, goes with her to the new scene. She is her adviser, her assistant, and friend; and to her will she tell all her hopes and all her fears.*b*

61—64. (61) **damsels,** perh. part of her dowry. (62) **Lahairoi,** *see* on Gen. xvi. 14. (63) **meditate,***a* reflect or pray. **eventide,** the still hour. **behold .. coming,** their forms catching the last rays of the setting sun. (64) **she .. camel,** in token of respect to her future husband.

Isaac's meditation (on v. 63).—Very admirable was—I. His occupation. Meditation extracts the real nutriment from the mental food gathered elsewhere. II. The choice of place. In the field we have a study hung round with texts for thought. III. The season. The season of sunset, as it draws a veil over the day, befits that repose of the soul when earth-born cares yield to the joys of heavenly communion.*b*

Meditation of Isaac.—The Hebrew word does not relate to religious meditation exclusively; still less exclusively to direct prayer. The leading idea seems to be an anxious, a reverential, a painful, a depressed state of mind. "Out of the abundance of my complaint," or my meditation—for the word is the same here, only in the form of a substantive—"Out of the abundance of my meditation and grief have I spoken" (1 Sam. i. 16) are the words of Hannah to Eli. Isaac went out into the fields, not directly to pray, but to give ease to a wounded spirit in solitude. What was the occasion of this? One of the last things recorded to have happened before the servant went to Haran, whence he was now returning, is the death and burial of Sarah; no doubt a tender mother to the child of her old age and her only child. What more likely than that her loss was the subject of Isaac's mournful meditation on this occasion? But this conjecture is reduced almost to certainty by a few words incidentally dropped at the close of the chapter; for having lifted up his eyes and beheld the camels coming, it is added, "And Isaac brought her into his mother Sarah's tent:.. and Isaac was comforted after his mother's death" (v. 67). The agreement of this latter incident with what had gone before is not set forth in our version, and a scene of very touching and picturesque beauty is impaired, if not destroyed.[c]

65—67. (65) **what man**, *etc.*, half suspecting perh., since they were nearing their destination. **took .. herself,** an early custom for the bride to veil herself in the presence of her betrothed. (66) **servant .. done,** explaining who the veiled maiden was. (67) **Isaac .. tent,** treating her with delicate attention. **loved,**[a] yet he had small acquaintance with her. **after .. death,** implying that his mother had been a great comforter before.

Giving in our account (v. 66).—Of this we are reminded by the account given by Eliezer to Isaac. I. It was universal: "all things." We shall have to tell the Master all we have done on the journey of life. II. It was candid. He had nothing to conceal. Happy we, if at the last we can meet the Master with joy, and tell Him all things we have done while in the performance of His will.

Circumspection in marriage.—When it shall please God to bring thee to man's estate, use great providence and circumspection in choosing thy wife: for from thence will spring all thy future good or evil. And it is an action of life like unto a stratagem of war—wherein a man can err but once. If thy estate be good, match near home and at leisure ; if weak, far off and quickly. Inquire diligently of her disposition, and how her parents have been inclined in their youth. Let her not be poor, how generous soever ; for a man can buy nothing in the market with gentility. Nor choose a base and uncomely creature altogether for wealth ; for it will cause contempt in others, and loathing in thee. Neither make choice of a dwarf or a fool; for, by the one thou shalt beget a race of pigmies ; the other will be thy continual disgrace, and it will *yirke* thee to hear her talk. For thou shalt find it, to thy great grief, that there is nothing more fulsome than a she-fool.[b]

B.C. 1857.

alight some time before he comes up to them. Women frequently refuse to ride in the presence of men; and when a company of them are to pass through a town, they often dismount and walk."—*Thomson.*

"Meditation is the soul's perspective glass, whereby, in her long removes, she discerneth God, as if He were nearer at hand."—*Feltham.*

c *Blunt's Undesigned Coincidences.*

Rebekah and Isaac are married

a Eph. v. 25, 28.

"When it shall please God to bring thee to man's estate, use great providence and circumspection in choosing thy wife. For from thence will spring all thy future good or evil; and it is an action of life, like unto a stratagem of war; wherein a man can err but once."—*Sir P. Sidney.*

"A man may be cheerful and contented in celibacy, but I do not think he can ever be happy; it is an unnatural state, and the best feelings of his nature are never called into action."—*Southey.*

b *Lord Burleigh.*

CHAPTER THE TWENTY-FIFTH.

children of Keturah
a 1 Ch. 1. 32.
b Perh. the Zamereni, a tribe in Arabia, were desc. fr. him.
c Ge. xxxvii. 28; Ex. ii. 15—21; iii. 1; Nu. xxii. 4.
d Perh. the Ashurites, nr. Gilead, 2 S. iii. 3.
e Perh. those whom Ptolemy calls the Allumæoti in Yemen.
f Is, lx 6.

"Children sweeten labours, but they make misfortunes more bitter; they increase the cares of life, but they mitigate the remembrance of death."—*Bacon.*

g W. Irving.

Isaac made sole heir
a Ga. iii. 29; He. i. 2.
b Of wh. the people were called *Benekedem*, "the children of the East," they were aft. called *Saracens*, or Easterns. "He who sees his heir in his own child, carries his eye over hopes and possessions, lying far beyond his gravestone, viewing his life, even here, as a period, but closed with a comma. He who sees his heir in another man's child, sees the full-stop at the end of the sentence."—*Bulwer Lytton.*
c C. Scriver.

1—4. Keturah (1) (*incense*) called his concubine.*a* Uncertain when he took her. (2) **Zimran***b* (*celebrated in song*). **Jokshan** (*a fowler*). **Medan** (*contention*). **Midian** (*strife*), ancestor of the Midianites.*c* **Ishbak** (*leaving*). **Shuah** (*a pit*). (3) **Sheba** (*an oath, or seven*). **Dedan** (*? low ground*) **Asshurim***d* (*steps*). **Letushim** (*the hammered*). **Leummim***e* (*peoples*). (4) **Ephah***f* (*darkness*). **Epher** (*a calf*). **Hanoch** (*initiating*). **Abidah** (*father of knowledge*). **Eldaah** (*whom God called*). children, descendants.

Family resemblances.—I always consider an old English family as well worth studying as a collection of Holbein's portraits or Albert Durer's prints. There is much antiquarian lore to be acquired; much knowledge of the physiognomies of former times. Perhaps it may be from having continually before their eyes those rows of old family portraits with which the mansions of this country are stocked; certain it is that the quaint features of antiquity are often most faithfully perpetuated in these ancient lines; and I have traced an old family nose through a whole picture-gallery, legitimately handed down from generation to generation, almost from the time of the Conquest. Something of the kind was to be observed in the worthy company around me. Many of their faces had evidently originated in a Gothic age, and been merely copied by succeeding generations; and there was one little girl in particular, of staid demeanour, with a high Roman nose, and an antique vinegar aspect, who was a great favourite of the squire's, being, as he said, a Bracebridge all over, and the very counterpart of one of his ancestors who figured in the court of Henry VIII.*g*

5, 6. (5) gave .. Isaac, made him his heir.*a* (6) concubines, Hagar and Keturah. gifts .. lived, showing that all their expectations should then cease. unto .. country, Arabia.*b*

Family feuds.—Gotthold, hearing that several relatives were soon to meet for the purpose of dividing a considerable inheritance, took occasion to say to them, "Take heed that you do not divide hearts as well as property. The eye of a man often looks askance when others attempt to share with him that of which he would fain appropriate the whole. A philosopher not improperly calls self-love a dissolvent, because it often disunites the hearts of the nearest relatives, and converts their love into hatred. In Paris, not many years ago, two gentlemen at the division of a property of which they had been left joint-heirs, proceeded from words to blows; when one of them killed the other with a pestle, and afterwards cut his own throat. In this way Satan came in for a share. I, myself, was once present at the implementing of a will, when the minds of the relations became exasperated to such a pitch that they broke to pieces the most costly vessels, and tore into shreds beautiful tapestries and hangings; neither wishing to give anything to the other. Nor did they ever afterwards in their lives meet or exchange words. O, cursed wealth! of which the devil makes an apple of discord. O, unhallowed inheritance! which breaks the bond of Christian love, and forfeits the inheritance in heaven."*c*

7—11. (7) days .. years, life to be reckoned rather by days than years. (8) died .. age, as he had been promised 80 years before.*a* was .. people,*b* in the world of spirits. the better country. (9) sons .. Machpelah, they were now old men.*c* which .. Mamre, *see* on Ge. xxiii. 17. (10) there .. wife,*d* the great patriarch by the side of his princess. (11) after .. Isaac: in how many cases the blessing seems to cease with the father's removal! Lahai-roi, *see* on Ge. xxiv. 62.

A good old age (on v. 8).—Consider—I. The present of an old man—his condition to-day. He has—1. Deprivations. He is conscious of many discomforts. and of being deprived of much enjoyment; 2. Trials. He is pained at feeling himself in the way of others; 3. Imperfections: 4. Inabilities. There are things which he cannot do. II. The retrospect—his past—the things behind. These must vary with the person. The retrospect of the aged Christian is very different, necessarily, from that of the aged worldly man. or the aged sinner. But still there are some things common to all. III. The prospect—the future, the things before. Consider, what need there is of a definite, a sure, a well-known and a long-known prospect, to overbear the discomforts of the present, and to counterbalance the reminiscences of the past.*e*

Triumph in death.—John Wesley's death-scene was one of the most peaceful and triumphant in the annals of the Church. Prayer, praise, and thankfulness were ever on his lips. Many golden sentences worthy to be had in everlasting remembrance were uttered during his last hours. He sees only the shadow of his friends around his bed : " Who are these?" "We are come to rejoice with you : you are going to receive your crown." " It is the Lord's doing," he calmly replies, " and marvellous in our eyes. I will write!" he exclaims, and the materials are placed within his reach : but the "right hand has forgot her cunning;" and "the pen of the once ready writer" refuses to move. "Let me write for you, sir," says an attendant. "What would you say?" "Nothing but that *God is with us.*" "Now we have done all. Let us all go." And now, with all his remaining strength, he cries out, "The best of all is, God is with us!" And again, lifting his fleshless arm in token of victory, and raising his failing voice to a pitch of holy triumph, he repeats the heart-reviving words. "The best of all is, God is with us!" A few minutes before ten o'clock on the morning of the 2nd of March. 1791, he slowly and feebly whispered, "Farewell, farewell!" and literally, "without a lingering groan," he calmly "fell on sleep, having served his generation by the will of God."*f*

12—18. (12) generations, posterity. family record, etc. (13) Nebajoth*a* (*heights*). Kedar*b* (*dark-skinned*). Mibsam (*sweet odour*). (14) Mishma (*a hearing*). Dumah (*silence*). Massa*c* (*? patience*) (15) Hadar (*enclosure*). Tema*d* (*south, desert*). Jetur*e* (*enclosed camp*). Naphish (*recreated*). Kedemah (*eastward*). (16) towns, nomadic camp. castle, fixed stations. twelve .. nations, twelve chiefs of tribes. (17) was .. people,*f* there seems to be a hint here of his dying in the faith. (18) they, his descendants. from .. Assyria,*g* prob. fr. Persian Gulf to Egypt. died, Heb. *naphal*, he fell, i.e. his lot was cast.*h*

The Abrahamites or children of Abraham (on vv. 1—4, 12—18). I. Common characteristics, religiousness, spirituality, wide-spread,

B.C. *cir.* 1853.

death and burial of Abraham

a Ge. xv. 15.

b He. xii. 23.

c Isaac was 75, and Ishmael ab. 90, Jacob and Esau, aged 15, may have been present.

d Ge. xlix., 31 ; 1 13.

" Death brings those together who knew not how to associate together on any other occasion, and will bring us all together, sooner or later." —*Fuller.*

"Death is a commingling of eternity with time; in the death of a good man, eternity is seen looking through time."— *Goethe.*

"When a man dies, they who survive him ask what property he has left behind. The angel who bends over the dying man asks what good deeds he has sent before him."— *Koran.*

e Dr. C. J. Vaughan.

f H. More.

descendants of Ishmael

a Fr. whom the Nabathæans, a famous Arab tribe. See Kalisch.

b Song i. 5; Is. xl. ii. 11; lx. 7; Ez. xxvii. 21; Ps. cxx. 5; Je. xlix. 28—33.

c Fr. whom perh. the *Masani* in Arabia Deserta.

B.C. cir. 1853.	

d "Said to be identified with *Teyma*, a small town on borders of Syria, nr. Dumah."—*Mr. Stanley Poole.*
e Fr. whom the Sturæans.
f A.M. 2231; 573 yrs. aft. flood; 48 yrs. aft. d. of Abraham, and when Isaac was 123 yrs. of age.
g 1 S. xv. 7.
h Kalisch, so *Alford*, etc.
i Lange.
k Cawdray.

ruling the world. II. Distinctions: Arabian and Jew, Mohammed and Christ, Mohammedanism and the Christian world.*i* *Ishmael's descendants* (on vv. 12—18). The Ishmaelites the germ of the Arabic people in its historic significance. The country of Arabia. Its history. Mohammedan. The mission of the Mohammedans. Since Ishmael did not subject himself to Israel, he has become subject to the Turk.*i*

The power of children.—As Alexander the Great attained to have such a puissant army, whereby he conquered the world, by having children born and brought up in his camp, whereby they became so well acquainted and exercised with weapons from their swaddling-clothes, that they looked for no other wealth or country but to fight: even so, if thou wouldst have thy children either to do great matters, or to live honestly by their own virtuous endeavours, thou must acquaint them with painstaking in their youth, and so to bring them up in the nurture and admonition of the Lord.*k*

generations of Isaac

a The plain or flat land of Aram, called "the field or plain of Aram."—Hos. xii. 12.

v. 22. *T. Knight*, 285.

v. 23. *Ambrose*, *Op.*, i. 440.

b 1 Ch. v. 20; 2 Ch. xxxiii. 13; Ez. viii. 23; Ps. cxlv. 19; Pr. x. 24; Ma. vii. 7.

c 2 S. viii. 14; Ro. ix. 12.

d Alford.

e C. Simeon, M.A.

"He asked a child, and his prayer is answered by the gift of two sons, and thus Providence, often slower than our wishes, frequently compensates that delay by greatly outdoing our requests and expectations."—*Hunter.*

birth of Jacob and Esau

19—23. (19) **generations,** personal and domestic hist. (20) **Syrian,** *etc.,* i.e. the Aramean of Padan-aram.*a* (21) **intreated**^*b* .. **wife,** earnestly wrestled in prayer in her behalf. **barren,** as his mother Sarah had been; and whose subsequent hist. prob. encouraged him to hope and pray. This barrenness lasted 20 yrs. (22) **if it be so,** *etc.,* this unusual circumstance was the cause of pain and wonder. **and .. Lord,** who, alone could explain. (23) **two .. womb,** i.e. the *founders* of two nations. **the one,** *etc.*^*c* this antenatal struggle was prophetical of the future enmity of the two brothers.*d*

Jacob preferred before Esau (on v. 23).—Observe—I. That God has a right to dispense His blessings according to His own sovereign will. He possesses this right as—1. The Creator; 2. The Governor and Lord of all things. II. That He actually exercises this right. We may daily see this in—1. The dealings of His providence: 2. The dispensations of His grace. III. That all, in whose favour this right is exercised, are bound to acknowledge it with most ardent gratitude. Impious indeed it would be to arrogate the glory to ourselves.*e*

Respect for children.—About three hundred and fifty years ago there lived, in Germany, a worthy schoolmaster whose name was John Trebonius. He was a philosopher and a scholar, and withal somewhat eccentric in his habits; but the world then needed originality, so that this detracted nothing from his worth. It is not much—more is the pity—that history has recorded of this man: but one tradition of him has descended to our times, which furnishes us with no mean index to his real character and principles. It is said of him that he never entered his school without being affected with the most profound reverence. Nothing could induce him to appear with covered head before his boys:—"Who can tell," said he, "what may yet rise up from amid these youths? There may be among them those who shall be hereafter learned doctors, sage legislators—nay! princes of the empire." Far-seeing teacher that! Right well, too, did he merit the honour that God put upon him of being the instructor of Martin Luther, "the solitary monk that shook the world."

24—28. (24) **twins,** more than Isaac asked for. (25) **red, ruddy. hairy,** *lit.* all of him as a mantle of hair. **Esau** (*hairy*).

Cap. xxv. 29—34. GENESIS. 105

(26) **Jacob**[a] (*supplanter*). (27) **cunning**, skilful, expert. **man .. field**, who ranged the wilds. **plain man**, Heb. *ish tam*, a perfect, upright man.[b] (28) **and .. Esau**, *i.e.* loved him especially. **because .. venison**, Isaac, an aged man now, was proud of his hardy, adventurous son. **but .. Jacob**, a well-conducted son who was much at home with her (note the mischief that arose fr. this domestic favouritism).

And the boys grew (v. 27).—I. *They grew bodily.* Natural provision for this. Food, air, exercise increase bulk of body. Explain. Grew in *stature* and in *strength*. II. *They grew mentally.* Natural provision for this. Memory a storehouse for facts. Judgment a mill for grinding them up and digesting them. Some boys are careless, dull, disobedient, self-willed, grow slowly, become men bodily and remain children in mind. Providential provision for mental growth. Books, schools, etc. These boys had not these things. III. *They grew very unlike each other.* Sketch their differences, bodily, mentally, morally. See rest of verse. Brothers often unlike in temper, taste, etc. With all mental and other differences they should be alike pious. "Boy father of the man." IV. *They grew up into history.* Which became the most prominent? Why? The practice of prayer at length made Jacob the better man. He overcame evil. Esau degenerated. Learn—You are all growing bodily: are you growing mentally? Do you grow in wisdom and in grace, and in the favour of God and man? Are you growing like Christ, growing up into Christ, growing more fit for heaven?

The education of children.—In order to form the minds of children, the first thing to be done is *to conquer their will.* To inform the understanding is a work of time, and must, with children, proceed by slow degrees, as they are able to bear it; but the subjecting the will must be done at once. *and the sooner the better;* for, by neglecting timely correction, they will contract a stubbornness and obstinacy which are hardly ever conquered, and not without using such severity as would be as painful to me as the child. In the esteem of the world *they* pass for kind and indulgent, whom I call *cruel* parents, who permit their children to get habits which they know must afterwards be broken. When the will of a child is subdued, and it is brought to revere and stand in awe of its parents, then a great many childish follies and inadvertencies may be passed by. Some should be overlooked, and others mildly reproved; but no *wilful* transgression ought to be forgiven without such chastisement, less or more, as the nature and circumstances of the offence may require. I insist upon conquering the will of children betimes, because this is the only strong and rational foundation of a religious education, without which both precept and example will be ineffectual. But when this is thoroughly done, then a child is capable of being governed by the reason and piety of its parents, till its own understanding comes to maturity, and the principles of religion have taken root in the mind.[c]

29—34. (29) **sod**, boiled. **pottage**, cooked *in a pot,* of the consistency of gruel. (30) **red**, Heb. *min haadom, haadom,* of the red, the red. **Edom** (*red*). (31) **and .. said**, notwithstanding all that is said ag. Jacob, it is prob. he saw that Esau was not the right man to perpetuate the blessings of the covenant. **sell .. day**, shamefully took advantage of *that day* of weak-

B.C. *cir.* 1853.

a Heb. *jaakob,* he shall hold by the foot, fr. *akub,* to supplant, to trip up the heels, and thence, metaphorically, to deceive, to defraud.

b "A man of steady, domestic, moral habits."—*Speaker's Com.* "Indolence is a delightful, but distressing state; we must be doing something to be happy. Action is no less necessary than thought to the instinctive tendencies of the human frame."—*Hazlitt.*

"'There is nothing so terrible as activity without insight,' says Goethe. 'I would open every one of Argus's hundred eyes, before I used one of Briareus's hundred hands,' says Lord Bacon. 'Look before you leap,' says John Smith, 'all over the world.'"—*Whipple.* "Margin, 'Venison was in his mouth.' Has a man been supported by another, and is it asked, 'Why does Kandan love Muttoo?' the reply is, 'Because Muttoo's rice *is in his mouth.*' 'Why have you such a regard for that man?'—'Is not his rice *in my mouth?*'—*Roberts.* c *Mrs. S. Wesley.*

Esau sells his birthright

a De. xxi. 17; Is. xxii. 13; 1 Co. xv. 32; He. xii. 16, 17.

B.C. cir. 1853.

Lentile, fr. *lentille*, Lat., *lens*. The *Ervum lens*, of which the L. is the seed, is of nat. ord. *Leguminosæ*, and sub. ord. *Papilionaceæ*; and not unlike the com. vetch. "There are several varieties recognised, and the red lentil is considered the best. It is generally used as a pottage, or cooked as the Spaniards cook haricot beans, stewed with oil, and flavoured with red pepper. It is by no means an unsavoury dish."—*Tristram, Nat. Hist. of Bible.*

b *Jenkin Jones.*

c *Palgrave's Arabia*, i. 30.

ness. **birthright**, this quiet stay-at-home was an ambitious man! (32) **I .. die**, prob. ref. to his kind of life wh. exposed him to death: or, to his present circumstances. (33) **sold .. Jacob,**[a] whatever the faults of Jacob, it is clear that Esau had no very exalted views of this birthright. (34) **lentiles**, Heb. *Adashim*, still called *addas* in Syria. **despised**, *i.e.* set too light a price on it.

The birthright sold.—There are two characteristics portrayed in these verses:—I. The cunning man: Jacob. 1. He waited for the right opportunity. This was no sudden thought; 2. He employed the likeliest means of gaining his object. Waited for his return from the field; thought he would be hungry, so the pottage is prepared; food, the strongest temptation to a hungry man; 3. He took no account of natural ties. Fraternal feelings were stifled; 4. He made the compact irrevocable. II. The sensual man. Esau—1. Lacked resolution. He would soon have been home; 2. Despised an honourable position; 3. Lost sight of the future. Conclusion—Both characters are unjustifiable.[b]

Red pottage.—By a curious coincidence, Palgrave, when crossing *Edom* into Arabia, had handed to him what looked like a bowl full of coarse red paste, or bran mixed with ochre. This red pottage was not of lentil flour, but Samh, the main subsistence of Bedouins of N. Arabia. It is made of the coarsely-ground seeds of a small herbaceous plant of which the flowers are a bright yellow. "Its taste and quality were pretty well hit off by Salem. who described it, 'not so good as wheat, and rather better than barley meal.'"[c]

B.C. cir. 1804.

Isaac visits Abimelech

a Ge. xv. 18—21; Ps. cv. 8—12.

Famine, great desire for food, Fr. from Lat. *fames*, hunger, akin to Gk. *phagein*, Sans. *thaksh*, to eat.

c. 5. Dr. F. Randolph, Advent, 2, S.S., 31.

b *W. J. Collins.*

"Stars arose, but such stars not like the spangles of the English poet's conception, 'those patines of bright gold,' though that idea is beautiful; but

CHAPTER THE TWENTY-SIXTH.

1—5 (1) **land**, Canaan. **first .. Abraham,** *see on* Ge. xii. 10. **Abimelech**, prob. not the A. of cap. xx. A. was an official title like Cæsar, or Pharaoh; besides 90 years had elapsed. (2) **go .. Egypt**, whither he intended to have gone. **dwell .. of,** God's purpose wiser than man's. (3) **countries,**[a] *lit.* lands. **perform,** *lit.* will cause to stand up. (4) **multiply,** *etc.*, see on Ge. xxii. 17, 18. (5) **because,** *etc.*, the fulfilment of the promises secured by the obedience of faith.

The famine in Canaan.—Observe—I. That there are seasons of distress for God's people equally as for the ungodly. Isaac is not exempt from the famine. Afflictions—1. Test our confidence in the Lord; 2. Exercise and strengthen our faith. II. That in seasons of distress God never forsakes those who trust in Him. God gives a command to Isaac to stay in Canaan, and go not down into Egypt. Although help may be obtained in Egypt, still he must not go thither. III. That perfect trust in God will bring a perfect reward. Obey me, says God, and thou shalt be blest. Here notice—1. The promise God makes; 2. The condition on which it rests—"sojourn in this land;" 3. The reason for it—"because that Abraham," etc. The father's righteousness aids to obtain prosperity for the son.[b]

Neglected duty.—Dr. Judson sent once for an erring convert. "Look here," he said, taking a ruler, and tracing a crooked line upon the floor, "*here* is where you have been walking. You have made a crooked track, have kept near it, and not taken to new roads; and you have, to a certain extent, grown in grace: and now *here* you stand. You know where this path leads. You know what is before you.—some struggles, some sorrows, and, finally, eternal life and a crown of glory. But to the left branches off another very pleasant road; and along the air floats, rather temptingly, a pretty bubble. You do not mean to leave the path you have walked in fifteen years; you only want to step aside and catch the bubble, and think you will come back again: but you *never will*."

6—11. (6) **Gerar,** *see* on Ge. xx. 1. (7) **sister,** he prevaricates like his father. **kill,** *etc.*[a] this, at any rate, illus. the general lawlessness of the age. (8) **saw .. wife,** the liar has constantly to be on his guard against detection. (9) **lest,** *etc.*, better have died, than lied. (10) **what .. us?** tempting to sin. **guiltiness,** shameful crime. (11) **charged,** *etc.*,[b] Isaac suffers by comparison with the noble-minded Abimelech.

Isaac's deceit.—Here we have—I. A sin committed. Cowardly fear led to it, and fear kept it up. There are three faults in Isaac's character exposed by it—1. Cowardliness; 2. Selfishness; 3. Want of reliance on God. II. A sin detected. Every sin will be some day found out. III. A sin reproved. Abimelech, although reproving Isaac, does so with great forbearance, and follows up his reproof with an act of great kindness. Learn—(1) Avoid deceit—"be sure your sin will find you out." (2) Reprove sin with kindness; be merciful to those who err.[c]

The punishment of liars.—When Aristotle, who was a Grecian philosopher, and the tutor of Alexander the Great, was once asked what a man could gain by uttering falsehoods, he replied, "Not to be credited when he shall tell the truth." On the contrary, it is related that when Petrarch, an Italian poet, a man of strict integrity, was summoned as a witness, and offered in the usual manner to take an oath before a court of justice, the judge closed the book, saying, "As to you, Petrarch, *your* WORD is sufficient." From the story of Petrarch we may learn how great respect is paid to those whose character for truth is established; and from the reply of Aristotle the folly as well as wickedness of lying. In the country of Siam, a kingdom of Asia, he who tells a lie is punished, according to law, by having his mouth sewed up. This may appear dreadful; but no severity is too great against one who commits so great a sin. We read likewise that God Almighty struck Ananias and Sapphira dead for not speaking the truth.

12—16. (12) **received,**[a] *lit.* found, *i.e.* more than he looked for. (13) **went forward,**[b] advanced to greater prosperity. (14) **great store,**[c] Heb. *aruddah rabbah, i.e.* much service. (15) **wells,** without wh. pastoral avocations could not be pursued. **which .. father,**[d] and wh. were therefore parts of I.'s property. **the .. them,** the envious injure others without benefit to themselves. (16) **Abimelech,** a just man, yet fearing the results of this outrage. **for .. we,**[e] especially since he possessed Divine protection, of which his prosperity was a plain sign.

Stopping wells.—To stop the wells is justly reckoned an act of hostility. The Canaanites, envying the prosperity of Abraham and Isaac, and fearing their power, endeavoured to drive them out of the country by stopping "up all the wells which their servants had digged, and filling them with earth." The same

---

B.C. *cir.* 1804.

"one could see that they were round orbs that flashed streams of diamond light from out their brightness."—*J. Finn, M.R.A.S.*

Isaac at Gerar

a Pr. xxix. 25; Ecc. vii. 20.

b 1 Ch. xvi. 21, 22; Ps. cv. 14, 15.

"Deceit is the false road to happiness; and all the joys we travel through to vice, like fairy banquets, vanish when we touch them."—*A. Hill.*

"Half the vices in the world rise out of cowardice, and one who is afraid of lying is usually afraid of nothing else."—*J. A. Froude.*

"No lie you can speak or act, but it will come, after longer or shorter circulation, like a bill drawn on nature's reality, and be presented there for payment,—with the answer: no effects."—*Carlyle.*

c J. H. Smith.

Isaac's prosperity

a Ge. xxvi. 3; 1 Ti. iv. 8.

b Pr. x. 22.

c Ecc. iv. 4.

d Ge. xxi. 30.

e Ex. i. 9.

"Here again we see how vanity attaches to every earthly good: prosperity begets envy, and

B.C. cir. 1804.

from envy proceeds injury."—Fuller.

"To bring the best human qualities to anything like perfection, to fill them with the sweet juices of courtesy and charity, prosperity, or, at all events, a moderate amount of it is required,—just as sunshine is needed for the ripening of peaches and apricots."—A. Smith.

f Parton.

wells at Esek, Sitnah and Rehoboth

a Ma. v. 39.

b "Here is an anc. well, now filled up, 12 ft. in diam., built with hewn stone."—Robinson, Phys. Geog., 243; and B. R., 289.

c Dr. Talmage.

"If men wound you with injuries, treat them with patience; hasty words rankle the wound, soft language dresses it, forgiveness cures it, and oblivion takes away the scar. It is more noble by silence to avoid an injury than by argument to overcome it."—J. Beaumont.

"It is often the lot of even the most quiet and peaceable, that, though they avoid striving, they cannot avoid being striven with. In this sense Jeremiah was a man of contention (Jer. xv. 10), and Christ Himself though the

mode of taking vengeance on enemies, mentioned in this passage, has been practised in more recent times. The Turkish emperors give annually to every Arab tribe near the road by which the Mohammedan pilgrims travel to Mecca, a certain sum of money, and a certain number of vestments, to keep them from destroying the wells which lie on that route, and to escort the pilgrims across their country. D'Herbelot records an incident exactly in point, which seems to be quite common among the Arabs. Gianabi, a famous rebel in the tenth century, gathered a number of people together, seized on Bassorah and Caufa; and afterward insulted the reigning caliph, by presenting himself boldly before Bagdad, his capital; after which he retired by little and little, filling up all the pits with sand, which had been dug on the road to Mecca, for the benefit of the pilgrims. Near the fountains and wells the robber and assassin commonly took his station; and in time of war the enemy placed their ambush, because the flocks and herds, in which the wealth of the country chiefly consisted, were twice every day collected to those places, and might be seized with less danger when the shepherds were busily engaged in drawing water.*f*

17—22. (17) **departed**,*a* for the sake of peace. He might have stayed and defended his rights. **valley**, in one of the wadys running towards the S. (18) **which .. father**, A. not only sojourned in the country, but improved it. **for .. Abraham**, to prevent other tribes fr. settling there. **names .. them**, and thus reasserted his claim. (19) **digged**, *etc.*, I. had so increased that what served his father was not enough for him. (20) **ours**, prob. on the ground that the valley was theirs. **Esek** (*contention*). (21) **Sitnah** (*spitefulness*). (22) **for .. not**, prob. out of their territory. **Rehoboth** (*enlargement*), prob. the *wady er-Ruhaiseh*.*b* 8 hrs. S. of Beer-sheba.

Old wells dug out (on v. 18).—Let us try to dig open some of the old wells which we possess. Bring shovel and pickaxe, and dig out the well of—I. The atonement. It is nearly filled up with the *débris* of old philosophies, which now are unwrapped and called original; but we will dig it out. II. Christian comfort. Take away all stoicism and fatality, and dig out this cooling fountain. III. Gospel invitation. Come ye around this old Gospel well; dig it out, and drink of the water of life.*c*

Strife for water.—One morning, when we had been driven by the stress of weather into a small bay, called Birk Bay, the country around it being inhabited by the Budoos (Bedoweens), the hoquedah sent his people on shore to get water, for which it is always customary to pay. The Budoos were, as the people thought, rather too exorbitant in their demands, and not choosing to comply with them, returned to make their report to their master. On hearing it, rage immediately seized him, and, determined to have the water on his own terms, or perish in the attempt, he buckled on his armour, and, attended by his myrmidons, carrying their matchlocks, guns, and lances, being twenty in number, they rowed to the land. My Arabian servant, who went on shore with the first party, and saw that the Budoos were disposed for fighting, told me that I should certainly see a battle. After a parley of about a quarter of an hour, with which the Budoos amused them, till nearly a hundred were assembled, they proceeded to the attack, and routed the sailors, who made a pre

23—25. (23) **went**, *etc.*, a place filled with memories of his father. (24) **fear not**, *etc.*,[a] a timely encouragement to one who encountered so much opposition. (25) **altar**[b] .. **tent** .. **well**, religion, home, occupation: their mutual relations.

The rich contents of the term, God of Abraham (on v. 24).—It declares—I. That the Eternal God has made a covenant with us imperishable beings (Lu. xx. 37, 38). II. The continuity, the unity, the unchangeableness, of the revelation of Jehovah through all times and developments. III. The transmission of the hereditary blessing from the believing father to the believing children.[c]

The favour of God.—When Antigonus was ready to engage in a sea-fight with Ptolemy's armada, and the pilot cried out, "How many are they more than we?" the courageous king replied, "'Tis true, if you count their numbers, they surpass us; but for how many do you value me?" Our God is sufficient against all the combined forces of earth and hell.

26—30. (26) **Ahuzzath** (*possession*). **Phichol** (*the mouth of all*) see on Ge. xxi. 22. (27) **wherefore**, *etc.*, I might well be perplexed by this visit aft. all the recent contention. (28) **we saw**, *etc.*, the prosperity of I. filled them with superstitious fear. (29) **Mat .. hurt**, I. must have been a great man for a *king* to crave this. **as we**, *etc.*, this was not true. They pretend to be oblivious of what I. had suffered from their people. **thou .. Lord**,[a] and, therefore, can well afford to be magnanimous. (30) **and**, *etc.*, this may well remind us of the great feast of good things spread for kings and peoples, and even enemies, by Him whom I. typified.

The favoured one (on v. 29).—I. The Blesser—the Being who blessed Isaac. It was the Lord. 1. The Ruler of all; 2. The Omnipotent; 3. The Infinite in wisdom; 4. The God of unspeakable goodness and mercy; 5. The Immutable. II. The blessed—Isaac. In his character we notice—1. Youthful piety; 2. Filial obedience; 3. A meditative and prayerful turn of mind. III. The blessings. 1. Peace; 2. Worldly prosperity; 3. God's special presence and protection; 4. A happy death.[b]

Treatment of insults.—Sir Walter Raleigh, a man of known courage and honour, being very injuriously treated by a hotheaded, rash youth, who proceeded to challenge him, and, on his refusal, spat in his face. and that, too, in public, the knight, taking out his handkerchief with great calmness, made him only this reply: "Young man, if I could as easily wipe your blood from my conscience as I can this injury from my face, I would this moment take away your life." The youth, with a strong sense of his improper behaviour, fell on his knees, and begged forgiveness.

31—33. (31) **rose .. sware**, the feast being an amicable intro. to a covenant of peace and friendship. (32) **came .. day**, the blessing of God crowned the compact. (33) **Shebah**, *i.e.* he repeated and confirmed the name.

Forgiveness of injuries.—When the late Rev. Dr. Bedell, of Philadelphia, was a child, one of his companions, whom he had offended by some trifle, ran into a blacksmith's shop, and seizing

---

B.C. *cir.* 1804.

| Prince of Peace."
—*Henry.*
d Major Rooke.

Beer-sheba
a Is. xli. 10; He. viii. 5, 6; Ps. xxvii. 1.
b Ge. xii. 7; Ps. cxvi. 17.

"There is no man who has not some interesting associations with particular scenes, or airs or books, and who does not feel their beauty or sublimity enhanced to him by such connections."—*Sir A. Alison.*
c Lange.
d Spencer.

covenant between Abimelech and Isaac

a Zec. viii. 23; Ps. cxv. 13.

"If you desire to be magnanimous, undertake nothing rashly, and fear nothing thou undertakest; fear nothing but infamy; dare anything but injury; the measure of magnanimity is neither to be rash nor timorous."—*Quarles.*

b B. Bailey.

"Great minds erect their neverfalling trophies on the firm base of mercy; but to triumph over a suppliant, by proud fortune captivated, argues a bastard conquest."—*Massinger.*

"Upon the northern side of the Wady-es-Seba are the two deep and ancient wells which gave occasion to this name."—*Robinson's Phys. Geog.*

GENESIS [Cap. xxvii. 1—5.

B.C. cir. 1804.
p. 242; B. R., i. 300.

"Kindness nobler ever than revenge."—*Shakspeare.*

Esau's wives

a Ge. xxv. 20.
b Ge. xxxvi. 2, 5, 14, 18, 25.
c Ge. xxxvi. 24, etc. *q. v.*
d Jo 3. i. 4; 1 K. x. 29; 2 K. vii. 6; cf. also Ge. xv. xvii. 46, with xviii. 1.
e De. vii. 1—4; Ge. xxvii. 46; xx cii. 1.
f He. xii. 16.
g Lange.
h Schroder.

"God has set the type of marriage everywhere throughout the creation. Each creature seeks its perfection in another. The very heavens and earth picture it to us."—*Luther.*

a shovel of hot coals, threw them down his back. As he had to run a considerable distance to his home he was much burned, and many months pass d before it was quite healed. Yet, when his father and friends prepared to have the boy punished who had so cruelly injured him, he earnestly entreated that he might be forgiven, and his friends could only satisfy him by consenting to do so.

34, 35. (34) **Esau..wife,** the age of his father at his marriage.*a* **Judith** (*Jewess*) also called **Aholibamah***b* (*tent of the height*): prob. J. was the original name. **Beeri** (*the wellman*) also called **Anah,***c* **Hittite,** a name = generally, an inhabitant of Canaan.*d* **Bashemath** (*fragrant*). **Elon** (*an oak*). (35) **which,** *etc.,e* 1. His polygamy: 2. His mar. with an idolatrous people: whence E. is called "a fornicator."*f*

Esau's marriage.—Esau's ill-assorted marriage a continuance of the prodigality in the disposal of his birthright. The threefold offence—I. Polygamy without any necessary inducement. II. Women of Canaanitish origin. III. Without the advice, and to the displeasure of his parents. The heart sorrow of the parents over the misalliance of their son.*g* Esau's marriage a self-attestation of his lawful expulsion from the chosen generation, and, at the same time, an actual warning to Jacob.*h*

Ingratitude to parents.—There was once a man who had an only son, to whom he bequeathed every thing. When his son grew up, he was unkind to his father, refused to support him, and turned him out of his house. The old man said to his grandson, "Go and fetch the covering from my bed, that I may go and sit by the wayside and beg." The child burst into tears, ran for the covering, took it to his father, and said to him, "Pray, father, cut it in two: the half of it will be large enough for grandfather; and perhaps you will want the other half when I grow a man and turn you out of doors." The words of the child struck him so forcibly, that he ran to his father, asked his forgiveness, and took care of him until his death.

B.C. cir. 1760.

Isaac would bless Esau

a Pr. xxvii. 1; Ja. iv. 14; Ec. ix. 10; Lu. xii. 40.

Quiver, a case for arrows. Old Fr., *cuivre*; old Ger. *kohhar*; A.S. *cocer*; Ger. *köcher*; Ice., *kogur.*

Venison, flesh of ans. taken in hunting, now app. to deer only. Fr. *venaison*; Lat. *venatis,* a hunting, game; *venor,* to hunt.

b Ge. xxv. 23.
c Ro. iii. 8.

"O sir, you are

CHAPTER THE TWENTY-SEVENTH.

1—5. (1) **old,** some say 137 yrs. old, wh. for var. reasons seems improb. **he..son,** he was prob. ignorant that E. had sold his birthright. (2) **behold,** *etc.,a* but the day seemed *very near* to the old man. (3) **weapons,** *lit.* implements. **quiver,** the Heb. sig. that wh. is *hung* on. **venison,** *lit.* hunt me a hunting, *i.e.* game. (4) **savoury,** tasteful. **that..die,** prob. it was not a savoury morsel he cared for, so much as to be assured by the venison that it was E. who was bef. him. (5) **heard,** and at once took measures on behalf of Jacob. (In judging of her conduct it is right to remember her view of Esau's conduct on his mar. She doubtless felt that such a man was not a suitable representative of the fam. of Abraham. Nor had she forgotten the prediction at his birth.*b* Yet was she not justified in doing evil that good might come.*c*)

Man's ignorance of the day of his death (on v. 2).—Observe that this ignorance—I. Is universal. All are alike in the dark concerning the time of their death. II. Is unblamable. Religious ignorance is criminal; not so this. III. Will never be superseded by knowledge. Notwithstanding the march of intellect and the progress of knowledge, man will never arrive at this discovery. IV. Manifests the wisdom and goodness of God. To know the day of our death would incapacitate alike for present duties and enjoyments. V. Ought to arouse us to religious activity. " Be ye therefore ready also."[d]

The uncertainty of life.—I have read a parable of a man shut up in a fortress under sentence of perpetual imprisonment, and obliged to draw water from a reservoir which he may not see, but into which no fresh stream is ever to be poured. How much it contains he cannot tell. He knows that the quantity is not great: it may be extremely small. He has already drawn out a considerable supply during his long imprisonment. The diminution increases daily, and how, it is asked, would he feel each time of drawing water and each time of drinking it? Not as if he had a perennial stream to go to—" I have a reservoir; I may be at ease." No: "I had water yesterday, I have it to-day; but my having it yesterday and my having it to-day is the very cause that I shall not have it on some day that is approaching. Life is a fortress; man is the prisoner within the gates. He draws his supply from a fountain fed by invisible pipes, but the reservoir is being exhausted. We had life yesterday, we have it to-day, the probability—the certainty—is that we shall not have it on some day that is to come.[e]

6—10. (6) **spake .. son,**[a] whom she loved. (7) **bless,** a blessing that she felt might be inspired and confirmed by God; and estab. Esau in his birthright. (8) **obey,** *etc.,* heed my advice, act acc. to my instructions. (9) **I .. make,** *etc.,* she would know how to disguise the food. (10) **and thou,** *etc.,* at the best, this mother's advice was but a crooked policy. He who had predicted Jacob's supremacy would have secured it in His own, and therefore a better, way.

The blessing fraudulently obtained (on the whole chapter).— Concerning the spirit of doubt and mistrust here manifested by Rebekah, consider that such a spirit—I. Leads men to practise deceit. There are three things which characterise this deception as of the basest kind: it was deceiving—1. A relative; 2. An infirm relative; 3. An infirm relative in spiritual matters. II. Deadens man's moral sensibilities. 1. It creates indifference to his moral culture: 2. It renders him insensible to the greatest danger. III. Involves pain. 1. Loss of peace; 2. Instability; 3. Humiliation.[b]

Influence over children.—The mother of a family was married to an infidel, who made jest of religion in the presence of his own children; yet she succeeded in bringing them all up in the fear of the Lord. I asked her one day how she preserved them from the influence of a father whose sentiments were so opposed to her own. This was her answer: " Because, to the authority of a *father*, I do not oppose the authority of a *mother*, but that of *God*. From their earliest years my children have always seen the Bible upon my table. This holy book has constituted the whole of their religious instruction. I was silent, that I might allow it to speak. Did they propose a question, did they commit a fault, did they perform a good action, I opened the Bible, and the Bible answered, reproved, or encouraged them. The constant reading of the Scriptures has wrought the prodigy which surprises you."[c]

B.C. *cir.* 1760.

old ; nature in you stands on the very verge of her confine ; you should be ruled and led by some discretion, that discerns your state better than you yourself."— *Shakespeare.*

d R. Jones.

" Age imprints more wrinkles in the mind, than it does in the face, and souls are never, or very rarely, seen, that in growing old do not smell sour and musty. Man moves all together, both towards his perfection and decay."—*Montaigne.*

e R. A. Willmott.

Rebekah tells Jacob and advises him

a "Notice Esau *his* son, Jacob *her* son."—*Alford.*

" All frauds, like the ' wall daubed with untempered mortar,' with which men think to buttress up an edifice, always tend to the decay of the system they are devised to support."— *Whately.*

b J. Jones.

" Ah, that deceit should steal such gentle shapes, and with a virtuous visor hide deep vice!"— *Shakespeare.*

" Wiles and deceit are female qualities."—*Æschylus.*

c A. Monod.

GENESIS. [Cap. xxvii. 11–17.

B.C. cir. 1760.

she takes the effect of the deception on herself
a De. xxvii. 18.
b Ps. xxiv. 4, 5; v. 6; Je. xlviii. 10; 1 Th. v. 22.
"Although the devil be the father of lies, he seems, like other great inventors, to have lost much of his reputation by the continual improvements that have been made upon him."—*Swift.*
"Craftiness is a quality in the mind, and a vice in the character."
—*Saurin'-Dubay.*
c *Lange.*
d *Thomson.*

she prepares him for the interview with Isaac
• Martial (*Lib.* xii. *Epig.* 46), alludes to kidskins as used by the Romans for false hair to conceal baldness. The wool of the Oriental goat is much longer and finer than of those of this country."—*Speaker's Com.*
"For all those with whom we live are like actors on a stage; they assume whatever dress and appearance may suit their present purpose, and they speak and act in strict keeping with this character. In this way we find it difficult to get at their real sentiments, or to bring into clear day the truth, which they have hid in a cloud of

11—13. (11) **Jacob said,** *etc.*, you may disguise the food, but not thy son. (12) **seem,** he seems to have feared detection more than the sin. **curse**ᵃ.. **blessing,**ᵇ the presence of the curse would be a greater evil than the absence of the blessing. (13) **upon.. curse,** fr. so promptly assuming the responsibility, it is clear she felt justified in the course she pursued.
Blessing and curse (on v. 12).—The image of the hereditary curse in the light of the hereditary blessing which Isaac ministers: I. How the curse obscures the blessing. II. How the blessing overcomes the curse.ᶜ—*Jacob's persuasion* (on vv. 11–13). —I. The mother's faith, and her wrong view of it. II. The faith of the son, and his erroneous view.ᵉ
Parental duties:—

Behold the fatal work of my dark hand,
That by rude force the passions would command,
That ruthless sought to root them from the breast:
They may be ruled, but will not be oppressed.
Taught hence, ye parents, who from nature stray,
And the great ties of social life betray;
Ne'er with your children act a tyrant's part:
'Tis yours to guide, not violate, the heart.
Ye vainly wise, who o'er mankind preside,
Behold my righteous woes, and drop your pride;
Keep virtue's simple path before your eyes,
Nor think from evil good can ever rise.ᵈ

14—17. (14) **and,** *etc.* it is strange that he should agree to his mother's incurring so grave a responsibility. (15) **goodly,** desirable, *i.e.* suitable. **put.. son,** disguising the man as well as the food. (16) **put.. neck,** in imitation of E., the hairy man. (17) **and,** *etc.*, the time all these preparations required suggestive of the usual distance afield gone by E. upon his hunting expeditions; or they may have commenced bef. he departed.
Influence of truth.—Abd-el-Kader obtained permission from his mother to go to Bagdad and devote himself to the service of God. "At parting she wept; then, taking out eighty dinars, she told me that, as I had a brother, half of that was all my inheritance. She made me promise, when she gave it to me, that I *would never tell a lie,* and afterwards bade me farewell, exclaiming, 'Go, my son: I consign thee to God. We shall not meet again till the day of judgment.' I went on well till I came near to Hamadôm, when our kâfilah was plundered by sixty horsemen. One fellow asked me what I had got. 'Forty dinars,' said I, 'are sewed under my garments.' He laughed, thinking, no doubt, I was joking with him. 'What have you got?' said another. I gave him the same answer. When they were dividing the spoil, I was called by the chief: 'What property have you got, my little fellow?' said he. 'I have told two of your people already,' I replied. 'I have forty dinars sewed up carefully in my clothes.' He ordered them to be ripped open, and found my money. 'And how came you,' said he with surprise, 'to declare so openly what has been so carefully hidden?'—'Because,' I replied, 'I will not be false to my mother, to whom I have promised that I will not tell a lie.'—'Child,' said the robber, 'hast thou such a sense of thy duty to thy mother at thy years, and I am insensible, at my age, of the duty I owe to my God? Give me thy hand, innocent

boy, that I may swear repentance upon it.' He did so. His followers were all alike struck with the scene. 'You have been our leader in our guilt,' said they to their chief : 'be the same in the path of virtue !' And they instantly, at his order, made restitution of the spoil, and vowed repentance on my hand."

18—20. (18) **who .. son?** he seems not to have recognised the voice. (19) **I .. firstborn, etc.**,[a] it is pitiable to note the efforts of critics to explain and excuse here. Who can make less than a lie of this ? (20) **how .. quickly?** with increasing population wild game went farther off : the distance and mountainous region would make a formal hunting expedition a long affair. **because, etc.**,[b] blasphemy added to falsehood : this, the worst feature in the whole infamous transaction.

Jacob deceiving his father (on vv. 18—26).—Jacob sinned—I. In speaking contrary to the truth, and twice passing himself for Esau. II. In really practising fraud by means of strange raiment and false pretences. III. In his abuse of the name of God. IV. In taking advantage of his father's weakness.[c]

Honest Frank.—A young man—we will call him honest Frank —who loved truth, was a clerk in the office of a rich merchant. One day a letter came recalling an order for goods which had been received the day before. The merchant handed it to honest Frank, and, with a persuasive smile, said : " Frank, reply to this note. Say that the goods were shipped before the receipt of the letter countermanding the order." Frank looked into his employer's face with a sad but firm glance, and replied, " I cannot, sir." " Why not, sir ? " asked the merchant angrily. " Because the goods are now in the yard, and it would be a lie, sir." " I hope you will always be so particular," replied the merchant, turning upon his heel and going away. Honest Frank did a bold as well as a right thing. What do you suppose happened to him ? Did he lose his place ? No ; quite different. The merchant was too shrewd to turn away one who would not write a lying letter. He knew the untold value of such a youth, and at once made him his confidential clerk.

21—23. (21) **and Isaac, etc.**, the *voice* and the *time* made the old man suspicious. Perh. he had a habit, founded in reason and observation, of suspecting Jacob—the supplanter. (22) **felt**, was there no pity for the blind old man when he passed his trembling fingers over his son's person ? **voice .. hands**, aroused by one sense, his suspicions are lulled by another. (23) **so .. him**, mentally prob., anticipative of words aft. spoken.

Voice and dress.—Three thoughts are suggested by these verses—I. That dress is no test of the man. Under a labourer's smock a prince may be found. The finest robes may conceal a villain. II. That the most perfect of deceptions there is often a flaw. Jacob's voice and dress are opposed. By the voice his true identity is revealed. III. That admirers of outward show will often be duped. Had Isaac thought more of the voice, and less of the dress, Jacob's scheme would have been frustrated.[a]

Eminent blind men.—Homer, Ossian, Milton, Blacklock, were poets. Sanderson, celebrated mathematician and Lucasian Professor at Cambridge (blind before one year old). Euler, a mathematician. Huber, author of a work on the " Habits of Bees." M. Phefel, of Colmar, also a poet ; his works fill six octavo

---

B.C. cir. 1760.

darkness."— *Polybius.*

Jacob invites his father to eat

a Ep. iv. 25 ; Col. iii. 9 ; Pr. vi. 16, 17 ; xii. 22 ; xiii. 5 ; Ps. ci. 7 ; cxix. 29 ; Pr. xxx. 8 ; Is. lxiii. 8, 11.

b Job xiii. 7 ; Ex. xx. 7.

c *Starcke.*

v. 18, 19. *J. M. Wynyard, B.D.,* 297.

" On the whole, we think, we must be content to leave this humiliating conduct as a blot on the character of Jacob, without apology and without excuse, only observing, that, disgraceful as it was, God could forgive it, and did forgive it, for the sake of a better righteousness than his own."—*Bush.*

Jacob declares himself to be Esau

a *H. Inglis.*

" It is remarked by Bochart (*Hierozoic.* l. ii., c. 51) that in the Eastern countries the goat's hair has often a soft, delicate feel, very much like that upon the human person ; so that Isaac might be without much difficulty, deceived, especially considering that

volumes. Miss Frances Brown, a poetess of considerable excellence. Holman travelled round the world. William Metcalf, builder of roads and bridges. John Metcalf, of Manchester, guide to those travelling through intricate roads by night, when covered with snow; afterwards a projector and surveyor of roads in difficult mountainous parts: most of the roads about the Peak, and near Buxton, were altered by his direction. Laura Bridgman could neither hear, see, nor speak, yet she learned herself a sinner and Christ a Saviour. Milburn was chaplain for some time to the American Congress; is a writer, lecturer, and traveller. Prescott was a famous historian. Goodrich, an excellent writer for the young. Rev. J. Crosse was vicar of Bradford. John Gough, of Kendal, was a famous mathematician, and an accurate botanist and zoologist. Dr. Moyes, of Kirkaldy, was an itinerant lecturer on chemistry and optics, though blind. Lord Cranbourne, blind from his childhood, published a few years ago a history of France for children. Giovanni Gambassio became an excellent statuary. The late king of Hanover was blind; and Zisca the Bohemian general, performed great acts of valour after the loss of his sight.

24—26. (24) **art . . Esau ?** he cannot shake off the suspicion that he is being deceived. **and . . am,** one lie begets many. (25) **brought . . drank,** his suspicious must have spoiled his relish for the feast. (26) **near . . kiss,** this may have been a token of affection; or it may have been with the intention of trying the test of smell. (Isaac's antitype was *betrayed*, but not *deceived*, by a kiss.)

The blind poet's lament.—

 Seasons return, but not to me returns
 Day, or the sweet approach of ev'n or morn,
 Or sight of vernal bloom, or summer's rose,
 Or flocks, or herds, or human face divine;
 But cloud instead, and ever-during dark
 Surrounds me, from the cheerful ways of men
 Cut off, and for the book of knowledge fair
 Presented with a universal blank
 Of nature's works, to me expunged and rased,
 And wisdom at one entrance quite shut out.
 So much the rather thou, celestial light,
 Shine inward, and the mind through all her powers
 Irradiate: there plant eyes, all mist from thence
 Purge and disperse.[a]

27—29. (27) **smell . . field,** the fresh odour of the hills and plains. (28) **give thee,** *etc.*,[a] favourable seasons: together with choice and abundant productions of the earth—*wealth*. (29) **let people,** *etc.*,[b] foreign and hostile nations were to be subject to him—*power*.

Jacob's blessing.—The three different parts of the blessing contain the three prerogatives of the firstborn—I. The double inheritance. Canaan was twice as large and as fruitful as the country of the Edomites. II. The dominion over his brethren. III. The priesthood which walks with blessings, and finally passes over to Christ, the source of all blessing.[c]

Eastern perfumery.—The natives of the East are universally fond of having their garments strongly perfumed; so much so

---

B.C. cir. 1760.

at his advanced age, his sense of touch might be nearly as much impaired as that of vision."—*Bush*.

"To a nice ear the quality of a voice is singularly affecting. Its depth seems to be allied to feeling; at least, the contralto notes alone give an adequate sense of pathos. They are born near the heart."—*Tuckerman*.

"Some frauds succeed from the apparent candour, the open confidence, and the full blaze of ingenuousness that is thrown around them. The slightest mystery would excite suspicion, and ruin all. Such stratagems may be compared to the stars; they are discoverable by *darkness*, and hidden only by *light*."—*Colton*.

v. 24. R. Warner, *Old Ch. of Eng. Principles*, I. 217.

a *Milton*.

Isaac blesses Jacob

a He. vi. 7; De. xxxiii. 13, 28; Ps. lxv. 9–11.

b 1 K. iv. 21; Is. ix. 7; Ge. xxiii. 25; xii. 3; 2 S. viii. 14.

c *Rambach*.

"Pliny observes that land, after a long drought, moistened by the

that Europeans can scarcely bear the smell. They use camphor, civet, sandal wood. or sandal oil, and a great variety of strongly-scented waters. It is not common to *salute*, as in England: they simply *smell* each other; and it is said that some people know their own children by the smell. It is common for a mother or father to say, " Ah, child, thy smell is like the *Sen-Paga-Poo*." The crown of the head is the principal place for smelling. Of an amiable man it is said, " How sweet is the smell of that man ! the smell of his goodness is universal." That delightful traveller, Captain Mangles, R.N., informed me that while on a short visit at the house of Mr. Barker, our consul at Aleppo, he heard Mrs. Barker, who was a Greek lady, say something to her child, accompanied by signs of great endearment. Mr. Barker said to Captain Mangles, " You do not understand her; she says, ' Come hither, my darling, and let me smell thee.' "[d]

30—33. (30) **Esau .. hunting, he** *was* quick with his hunting aft. all. (31) **bless,** if he had sold his birthright he would at least secure the blessing. (32) **and .. said,** prob. in wonder and perplexity. **I .. Esau,** this time there is E.'s voice. (33) **and .. exceedingly,** "His emotions were actually overwhelming."[a] **who?** he now mistrusts his sense of hearing. **yea .. blessed,**[b] however deceived, he could not revoke the blessing.[c]

Esau's late arrival (on vv. 30—36).—Esau comes too late, because he wished to obtain the Divine blessing of promise—I. By hunting (by running and stirring). II. After he had sold it. III. Without comprehending its significance. IV. Without its being intended for him by the Divine decree, and without his possessing any fitness for it.[d]

Blindness a great affliction.—It would be a dreadful thing to me to lose my sight; to see no more the faces of those I love, nor the sweet blue of heaven, nor the myriad stars that gem the sky, nor the dissolving clouds that pass over it, nor the battling ships upon the sea, nor the mountains with their changing lines of light and shade, nor the loveliness of flowers, nor the burnished mail of insects. But I should do as other blind men have done before me; I should take God's rod and staff for my guide and comfort, and wait patiently for death to bring better light to nobler eyes. Oh, ye who are living in the darkness of sin, turn before it is too late to the light of holiness, else death will bring to you, not recreation but retribution. Earthly blindness can be borne, for it is but for a day; but who could bear to be blind through eternity ?[e]

34—36. (34) **cried .. cry,** with deep and poignant grief. **bless .. father,** I have lost my birthright, still let me have the blessing. (35) **hath .. blessing,** the blessing that specially designed for thee. (36) **is .. Jacob,** *etc., lit.* Is it that he is called Jacob, and he supplanteth or outwitteth me these two times? **hast .. me?**[a] or was the blessing, designed for me, and stolen by another, so great that there is nothing left?

Esau, a type of the world (on v. 36).—In making this a subject for examination, we must endeavour to understand—I. Something of the course or career which ended in this deed of recklessness. In order to comprehend Esau's infatuation, we need to know the meaning of the two words, " birthright" and " blessing." The first was typical or nominal the other substantial and real.

B.C. *cir.* 1760.

rain, exhales a delightful odour, with which nothing can be compared; and adds, that ' it is a sign of a fruitful soil when it emits an agreeable smell after having been ploughed.' "—*Bush.*

d *Roberts.*

Esau's return and Isaac's discovery

a *Bush.*
b Ro. xi. 29.
c " The words of the Patriarch, spoken in the fulness of Divine inspiration, are irrevocable, however obtained."--*Alford.*
d *Lange.*

" Grief or misfortune seems to be indispensable to the development of intelligence, energy and virtue. The proofs to which the people are submitted, as with individuals, .. necessary .. to draw .. from their lethargy, to disclose their character." --*Fearon.*

e *H. W. Beecher.*

Esau craves a blessing

a He. xii. 17; *q. v.*

" See on ch. xxv. 26. The words seem to mean, Is there not a connection between the meaning of his name Jacob, and the fact that he thus supplants or outwits me ?"
—*Speaker's Com.*

GENESIS. [Cap. xxvii. 37—46.

B.C. cir. 1760.

"That grief is the most durable which flows inward, and buries its streams with its fountain, in the depths of the heart."— *Jane Porter.*

b A. Boyd, M.A.
c Spurgeon.

II. The end to which this recklessness led. 1. Esau awakes to the consciousness of his foolishness; 2. He finds the past irrevocable.[b]

The vale of tears.—The vale of tears is very low, and descends far beneath the ordinary level; some parts of it, indeed, are tunnelled through rocks of anguish. A frequent cause of its darkness is that, on either side of the valley, there are high mountains called the mountains of sin. These rise so high that they obscure the light of the sun. Behind these Andes of guilt, God hides His face, and we are troubled. Then how densely dark the pathway becomes! Indeed, this is the very worst thing that can be mentioned of this valley; for, if it were not so dark, pilgrims would not so much dread passing through it.[c]

Isaac blesses Esau

a Jos. Wars, iv, 4. 1.

b 1 S. xiv. 47; 2 S. viii. 14; 1 K. xi. 14; 2 K. xiv. 7, 22; 2 Ch. xxv. 11; xxvi. 2.

c 2 K. viii. 20, 22; xvi. 6; 2 Ch. xxviii. 7.

d Lange.

"Giving comfort under affliction, requires that penetration into the human mind, joined to that experience which knows how to soothe, how to reason, and how to ridicule; taking the utmost care never to apply those arts improperly."— *Fielding.*

e Boyd.

37—40. (37) **and .. son?** what can I give to compensate thy loss? (38) **and Esau,** *etc.,* he found no place (in his father's heart) of repentance (turning towards himself), though he sought it carefully with tears. **Esau .. wept,** Esau bitterly repented. (39) **behold,** *etc.,* so far he is blessed equally with Jacob. (40) **sword .. live,**[a] the Edomites long maintained their independence, living by the sword. **and .. brother,**[b] this the relation of the posterity of the two brothers. **and .. pass,** *etc.,* this was literally fulfilled.[c]

Esau's lamentation (on v. 38).—Consider Esau's lamentation as opposed to his father's firmness. I. It is a passion instead of a godly sorrow. II. It is connected with illusion that holy things may be treated arbitrarily. III. It refers to the external detriment but not to the internal loss.[d]

Comfort in sorrow.—I say there is comfort, real and deep, in thinking that the path of sorrow we tread has been beaten smooth and wide by the feet of the best that ever trod this world; that our blessed Saviour was a Man of Sorrows, and that the best of His Church have been suffered to journey by no other path than that their Master went. It is not alone that the mourner travels through this vale of tears; apostles and prophets are of the company; saints and martyrs go with him; and the sorrowful face of the Great Redeemer, though sorrowful now no more, remains for ever with the old look of brotherly sympathy to His servants' eyes and hearts. Nothing hath come to us, nothing will come to us, but has been shared by better men. Search out the human being suffering the sharpest sorrow, and we can match it in the best of the Church of God.[e]

Esau purposes to slay Jacob, who is told of it by Rebekah

a 1 Jo. iii. 15; Ob. 10.
b Ps. lxiv. 5.
c Pr. xix. 21.
d Ge. xxviii. 8; xxiv. 3.

"All the ends of human felicity are secured without revenge, for without it we are permitted to restore our

41—46. From this time there dates a change in the character of the two bros. The noble Esau bec. revengeful. etc.; while the supplanter bec. prayerful, etc. (41) **hated,**[a] with a cold-blooded hate. **the .. hand,** he will spare his father the grief that his purposed crime will occasion. **then .. him,**[b] in purpose even now a murderer. (42) **words .. Rebekah,** some one had heard him speaking to himself. **she .. son,** a mother's love is the son's shield. (43) **flee .. Haran,** her fraud deprived her of her son, whom she prob. never saw again. (44) **tarry .. days,** it proved to be twenty years. (45) **then,** *etc.,*[c] she would watch for the softening of E.'s heart. **why .. day?** ref. to prob. fate of E. if he slew Jacob. (46) **and .. Isaac,** once more hiding the truth from him. **I .. Heth,**[d] she professes to fear that J. may mar. one of them. **if,** *etc.,* she does not propose Jacob's departure; knowing the bare suggestion will suffice,

Esau's hatred of Jacob (on v. 41).—Consider it in—I. Its moral aspect. II. Its typical significance. Want of self-knowledge a cause of this enmity.*—Esau inclined to fratricide* (on v. 41).—I. Incited by envy, animosity, and revenge. II. Checked by piety towards the father. III. Prevented by his frankness and outspoken character, as well as by Rebekah's sagacity.*

The cure of revenge.—A young man who had great cause of complaint against another told an old hermit that he was resolved to be avenged. The good old man did all that he could to dissuade him; but seeing that it was impossible, and the young man persisted in seeking vengeance, he said to him, "At least, my young friend, let us pray together before you execute your design." Then he began to pray in this way: "It is no longer necessary, O God! that Thou shouldst defend this young man, and declare Thyself his protector, since he has taken upon himself the right of seeking his own revenge." The young man fell on his knees before the old hermit, and prayed for pardon for his wicked thought, and declared that he would no longer seek revenge of those who had injured him.

B.C. cir. 1760.

selves; and therefore it is against natural reason to do an evil that no way co-operates the proper and perfective end of human nature. And he is a miserable person, whose good is the evil of his neighbour, and he that revenges, in many cases, does worse than he that did the injury; in all cases as bad."—*J. Taylor.*

e Lange.

CHAPTER THE TWENTY-EIGHTH.

B.C. cir. 1760.

1—5. (1) **Isaac**, alarmed by R.'s suggestion.* **thou . . Canaan**, in this, imitating Abraham.*b* (2) **Padan-aram**, *see* on Ge. xxv. 20. (3) **thou . . people**, *lit.*c a congregation of peoples, prob. ref. to the twelve tribes. (4) **give . . Abraham**,*d i.e.* confirm to thee the bless. he prom. to A. **land . . stranger**, *lit.* land of thy sojournings. (5) **Laban**, *etc., see* on Ge. xxiv. 29.

Jacob's departure from Canaan.—The necessity for separation among the household of Isaac becomes the source of new blessings. I. The feeble Isaac becomes a hero. II. The plain and quiet Jacob becomes a courageous pilgrim and soldier. III. The strong-minded Rebekah becomes a person that sacrifices her most dearly loved.*e*

Unequal marriages.—Alas! how frequently does the dear partner, who should be the counsellor and favourer of everything good and virtuous, prove a tempter and a seducer! How many have given up their principles to please their wives? This thought surely should engage the attention of our younger readers. Your future character and conduct, perhaps your eternal state, may depend on your choice of the companion to whom you are to be united for life. Beware, lest a regard to worldly prospects, your ill-directed fancy, or the solicitations of your lust, draw you into such connections as may, in the issue, be fatal to your souls. Suppose not, that you can withstand every enticement to evil, while you see how many have been overcome. Nor imagine that you shall convert her to the cause of truth, who is yet an enemy to it, but rather fear, lest your own mind should be more and more corrupted. For how can you expect the blessing of God if you act in contradiction to His will and command? Is it less dangerous for you, than it was for the Jews of old, to be thus joined with unbelievers? Or is your religion of less value than theirs, that you are not so much concerned to maintain it?*f*

Isaac sends Jacob to Laban

a Ge. xxvii. 46.

b Ge. xxiv. 3.

c Ps. cxxvii. 3.

d Ge. xii. 2; xvii. 8; He. xi. 13.

e Lange.

v. 3. *R. Gell, Essay,* 171.

v. 5. *H. Blunt, Jacob,* 25.

"Deceive not thyself by over-expecting happiness in the marriage-state. Look not therein for contentment greater than God will give, or a creature in this world can receive, namely, to be free from all inconveniences. Marriage is not, like the hill of Olympus, wholly clear without clouds."—*Fuller.*

f T. Robinson.

B.C. cir. 1760.

Esau marries dau. of Ishmael

a Ep. vi. 1, 2.
b Ge. xxvii. 1.
c "He knows that his wives were displeasing to his father; and he endeavours in his clumsy way to repair the mischief."—*Alford.*
d Ge. xxxvi. 3.
"Let grace and goodness be the principal loadstone of thy affections. For love which hath ends will have an end, whereas that which is founded on true virtue will always continue."—*Dryden.*
e *Frederika Bremer.*

Jacob's dream

a Ho. xii. 12.
b Jo. i. 51.
c He. i. 14.

"Our Lord Himself teaches (Jo. i. 51) that the ladder signified the Son of Man, Him who was now afresh promised as to be of the seed of Jacob (v. 14); Him, by whom alone we go to God (Jo. xiv. 6); who is the way to heaven, and who has now gone there to prepare a place for us."—*Speaker's Com.*
d *R. Thomas, M.A.*
e *Lange.*

"Dreams in their development have breath, and tears, and tortures, and the touch of joy; they leave a weight upon our waking thoughts,"

6—9. (6) **saw**, understood, considered. (7) **obeyed**,ᵃ yet he may have been now 75 years old.ᵇ (8) **pleased**, *lit.* were evil in the eyes of. (9) **went**, prob. thinking to please his father.ᶜ **took**..**had**, *see* on Ge. xxvi. 34, 35. **Mahalath** (*a stringed instrument, a lyre*), also called *Bashemath*,ᵈ perh. M. was a description, and B. the name, *i.e.* a dau. of music named Bashemath.

Counsels for marriage.—Many a marriage has commenced, like the morning, red, and perished like a mushroom. Wherefore? Because the married pair neglected to be as agreeable to each other after their union as they were before it. Seek always to please each other, my children, but in doing so keep heaven in mind. Lavish not your love to-day, remembering that marriage has a morrow and again a morrow. Bethink ye, my daughters, what the word *housewife* expresses. The married woman is her husband's *domestic trust*. On her he ought to be able to place his reliance in house and family; to her he should confide the key of his heart and the lock of his storeroom. His honour and his home are under her protection, his welfare in her hands. Ponder this! And you, my sons, be true men of honour, and good fathers of your families. Act in such wise that your wives respect and love you. And what more shall I say to you, my children? Peruse diligently the Word of God; that will guide you out of storm and dead calm, and bring you safe into port. And as for the rest—do your best!ᵉ

10—12. (10) **went**..**Haran**,ᵃ a long journey, at a great age, to fulfil a parent's wish. (11) **and**..**place**, in the course of his journey; the dist. proves it was not the close of the *first* day's march. **pillows**, head-rest. (12) **ladder**, or way of ascent. A type of Christ.ᵇ **behold**..**it**,ᶜ the way, a communication, a living way. (Through Christ Divine blessings descend to us, and our prayers ascend to God.)

Jacob's vision (vv. 10—22).—Notice—I. The surroundings of the vision. 1. The ambitious schemings of Jacob and his mother to supplant Esau; 2. The struggle in Jacob's soul of faith against ambition. II. The revelation which it contains. It reveals—1. God as the God of providence; 2. The intimate union of the seen and unseen. III. Its effect on the mind of him to whom it was given. A sense of—1. The universal presence of God; 2. Awe possessing the sinner's soul at the revelation of this presence; 3. Penitence at the revelation of God's goodness.ᵈ—*Consecrated night life* (vv. 10—15).—Consider this vision, as to—I. The occasion. In the most helpless situation, the most solemn and glorious dream. II. The form. A Divine revelation in the dream-vision—1. Miracles of sight, symbols of salvation; 2. Miracles of the ear, promise of salvation. III. Its contents. The images of the vision—1. The ladder; 2. Angels ascending and descending; 3. Jehovah standing above the ladder and speaking.ᵉ—*Jacob's dream* (vv. 10—17).—When reading the narrative in the light of the New Testament, the following thoughts are suggested—I. That the moral distance between heaven and earth is great. The idea of height is implied in the word ladder. 1. Heaven is distant from the thoughts of the ungodly; 2. The conceptions of man prove its distance; 3. The conduct of the wicked confirms it. II. That there is a spiritual communication between heaven and earth. This state—I. Confers dignity upon our globe; 2. Imparts honour to man ; 3. Is of Divine origin ; 4. Is not dependent on the outward circumstances of man. III. That through this communication alone can man have a true knowledge of God. Because—1. In it the human and Divine are united ; 2. Through it a covenant relationship is formed between us and God ; 3. By it God's protection is secured to us : 4. It provides for the consummation of our highest conceptions of felicity. IV. That true communion with God produces reverential fear in the heart. The nearer we approach to God, the greater is the filial fear felt.*f*

Various views of dreams.—The Egyptians and Babylonians attached great importance to dreams ; and to interpret them was the work of a distinct and learned profession. The Persians, also, attached great importance to dreams ; and it is reported Cyrus was cast forth at his birth, because a dream of his mother was interpreted to promise him universal empire. In the *Chou-King* of the Chinese, it is in dreams that the Sovereign of heaven makes his will known to the sovereign of earth. In Homer, dreams came from Jove. The Greeks and Romans believed that, in the solitude of caves and groves and temples, the gods appeared in dreams, and deigned to answer in dreams their votaries. Among the Hindoos dreams give a colouring to the whole business of life. *All* dreams are of importance among the North American Indians. The Moslems hold good dreams from God, and bad from the devil.*g*

13—15. (13) behold .. it,*a* as accepting this way of access to Him. I .. Isaac,*b* the same God who is revealed to us by Christ, "the new and living way." (14) seed .. dust, *etc.*,*c* as Isaac desired, the blessing prom. to A. is confirmed to Jacob. (15) I .. goest,*d* the Divine presence fulfils the Divine Word.

Bethel ; or, the true vision of life (vv. 12—18).—In the true vision of life there is a recognition of—I. Our connection with other worlds. Whilst there is nothing in nature, philosophy, or experience, contradictive of the doctrine that the intelligences of other worlds have a connection with man, there is much that is confirmative. There is—1. Analogy ; 2. General impression : 3. Unaccountable impulse. II. God's relation to all. Here the great God is presented as—1. The Sovereign of all. He stood *above* the ladder. Let that ladder stand as the representative of secondary causes, and then we have suggested the great truth that God is above all instrumentalities and moral agents ; 2. The Friend of man. The blessings here promised to the patriarch were, in reality, blessings for humanity. III. A Divine providence over individuals. "I am with thee"—not merely with the universe and with humanity in general, but with *thee;* not with thee occasionally, but "in all places." IV. The solemnity of our earthly position. "How dreadful is this place." The discovery of God's presence introduced—1. A new ; 2. A memorable epoch in Jacob's history.*e*

Scripture views of dreams.—The view of dreams set forth in Scripture, and which pervades the sacred books, is, that God does sometimes make known His will to man, and disclose His purposes in dreams : "God speaketh once, yea twice, yet man perceiveth it not. In a dream, in a vision of the night, when deep sleep falleth upon men, in slumberings upon the bed ; then He openeth the ears of men, and sealeth their instruction, that He may withdraw man from his purpose, and hide pride from man"

B.C. *cir.* 1760.

"they take a weight from off our waking toils, they do divide our being ; they become a portion of ourselves as of our time, and look like heralds of eternity."—*Byron.*

f Jenkin Jones.
"Dreams are the bright creatures of poem and legend, who sport on the earth in the night season, and melt away with the first beam of the sun, which lights grim care and stern reality on their daily pilgrimage through the world."—*Dickens.*
g Dr. Kitto.

God's promise to Jacob

a Perh. what J. saw in his dream was the Shekinah. Onkelos says, "The glory of the Lord."
b Ge. xlviii. 3 ; xxxii. 12.
c Nu. xxiii. 10 ; Ma. viii. 11 ; Ac. ii. 25 ; Ga. iii. 8.
d Jn. vi. 16 ; Is. xliii. 2, 3 ; Je. i. 19 ; Ps. cxxi. 5—8 ; Jos. i. 5 ; 1 K. viii. 57 ; He. xiii. 5.

e Dr. Thomas.
"Whoever we may leave, or whatever we may lose, still we part not from our best friend, nor are we deprived of our most valuable portion. We cannot be lonely, if God be with us. We cannot want, if He provide for us. We cannot err, if He guide us. We cannot perish, if He preserve us. And all this He will

B.C. cir. 1760.

do for those that put their trust in Him."—*Bush.*
f Dr. Kitto.

Beth-el

a Robinson, B.R., ii. 127, ff.; Stanley, Sin. and Pal., 217, ff.

b Ge. xxxi. 13.

"It has been thought by many that this act of Jacob, in setting up a stone to mark a sacred spot, was the origin of cromlechs and all sacred stones. Certainly we find in later ages the custom of having stones, and those too anointed with oil, as objects of idolatrous worship. Clem. Alex. (*Stromat.* Lib. vii. p. 713) speaks of 'worshipping every oily stone,' and Arnobius (*Adv. Gentes*, Lib. i. 39), in like manner, refers to the worshipping of a 'stone smeared with oil, as though there were in it a present power.'"—*Speaker's Com.*

c R. Aitken, M.A.

d Stanley.

Jacob's vow

a Ec. v. 2, 5.
b 1 Ti. vi. 8.
c De. xxvi. 17.
d J. Hales.

* The *order* of what he desired is deserving of notice. It corresponds with our Saviour's rule, to seek things of the greatest importance first. By

(Job xxxiii. 14—17). See also Joel ii. 28, compared with Acts ii. 16, 17. The question is, whether these things have ceased? It may be so. Miracles have ceased; prophecy has closed; why may not significant dreams also have ceased? They may; but have they?*f*

16—19. (16) **place,**^a wh. when he lay down seemed so dark, cheerless, lonesome. **I .. not,** that He was so near. If in *such* a place, God would be in every place. (17) **but .. God,** every place may be for us a holy place. **this .. heaven,** the earthly traveller is always nr. that gate. (18) **stone,**^b that wh. had been for his comfort should bec. the lasting memorial of God's goodness. **oil .. it,** to sanctify, and set apart the place and stone as holy. (19) **Beth-el** (*house of God*), now (*Beitin*) a mass of ruins ab. 12 ms. N. of Jerus. **Luz** (*almond-tree*, or *hazel*), nr. to the place aft. called Beth-el.

The ladder from earth to heaven (vv. 12—19).—Introduction—Notice some of the ladders men employ to get to heaven—the ladders of harmlessness, charitability, morality, ordinances, and creeds. All these are of no avail; you must come to the true ladder. Consider then—I. The ladder here seen. There are four steps in the true ladder to heaven—1. Wisdom; 2. Righteousness; 3. Sanctification; 4. Redemption. II. Jacob's conclusion on seeing this vision—"this is none other but the house of God and the gate of heaven."^c

Jacob's pillar.—The monument, whatever it was, that was still in after ages ascribed to the erection of Jacob, must have been, like so many described or seen in other times and countries, a rude copy of the natural features of the place, as at Carnac in Brittany, the cromlechs of Wales and Cornwall, or the walls of Tiryns, where the play of nature and the simplicity of art are almost indistinguishable. In all ages of primitive history such monuments are, if we may so call them, the earliest ecclesiastical edifices. In Greece there were rude stones at Delphi still visible in the second century, anterior to any temple, and, like the rock of Bethel, anointed with oil by the pilgrims who came thither. In Northern Africa, Arnobius, after his conversion, describes the kind of fascination which had drawn him towards one of these aged stones, streaming and shining with the sacred oil which had been poured upon it. The black stone of the Arabian Caaba reaches back to the remotest antiquity of which history or tradition can speak.^d

20—22. (20) **vow,**^a this the first of wh. we have formal record: **give .. on,**^b mere necessaries are enough, and all we should desire. (21) **so .. peace,** he to his earthly, we to our heavenly Father's house. **then .. God,**^c in preference to all idol gods. (22) **shall .. house,** this shall always be to me a sacred place. **tenth,** for support of religion. This tenth was purely voluntary.

Jacob's vow.—I. The person that here makes the covenant. From him the following excellent lesson may be drawn—that it is no enemy to true state and greatness to have but a small portion of the world's benefit. II. The covenant itself. 1. Its nature; 2. The reasons why Jacob covenanted with God for food and raiment only.^d

Satisfaction of contentment.—Said a venerable farmer, some eighty years old, to a relative who had lately visited him, "I have lived on this farm for more than half a century. I have no desire to change my residence as long as I live on earth. I have no desire to be any richer than I now am. I have worshipped the God of my fathers with the same people for more than forty years. During the time, I have rarely been absent from the sanctuary on the Sabbath, and have never lost one communion season. I have never been confined to my bed by sickness a single day. The blessings of God have been richly spread around me, and I made up my mind long ago that, if I wished to be happier, I must have more religion."*e*

B.C. cir. 1760.

"how much God's favour is better than life, by so much His being with us, and keeping us, is better than food and raiment."—*Fuller.*

e Dr. Haven.

CHAPTER THE TWENTY-NINTH.

B.C. cir. 1760.

1—3. (1) **went .. journey,**^a *lit.* "lifted up his feet." **into .. east,** term app. to Arabs E. of Palestine. (2) **stone .. mouth,** to keep out sand, etc. (3) **and,** *etc.*, perh. this v. describes what was *customary;* and, further on, what was done in this case.

Allegory of the well (v. 3).—Jesus the well of life. The stone, the impotence of human nature to be removed by faith.*b* How Christ has removed the heavy stone of sin and death. The three herds as referring to the three days in which Christ was in the grave.*c*

The stone on the well.—In Arabia, and in other places, they are wont to close and cover up their wells of water, lest the sand, which is put into motion by the winds there, like the water of a pond, should fill them, and quite stop them up. This is the account Sir J. Chardin gives us in a note on Ps. lxix. 15. I very much question the applicableness of this custom to that passage, but it will serve to explain, I think, extremely well, the view of keeping that well covered with a stone from which Laban's sheep were wont to be watered; and their care not to leave it open any time, but to stay till the flocks were all gathered together before they opened it, and then, having drawn as much water as was requisite, to cover it up again immediately, Gen. xxix. 2—8. Bishop Patrick supposes it was done to keep the water clean and cool. Few people, I imagine, will long hesitate in determining which most probably was the view in keeping the well covered with so much care. All this care of their water is certainly very requisite, since they have so little, that Chardin supposes, "that the strife between Abraham's herdmen and Lot's was rather about water than pasturage ;" and immediately after observes, "that when they are forced to draw the water for very large flocks out of one well, or two, it must take up a great deal of time."*d*

4—8. (4) **brethren,** their occupation was one with wh. he had a brotherly sympathy. (5) **son,**^a *i.e.* descendant. (6) **well?** *lit.*, is there peace to him? **Rachel** (*an ewe*). (7) **it .. day,** *lit.*, yet the day is great, *i.e.* a great part of the day remains. **water .. them,** he evidently desired a private interview with R. (8) **cannot,** in the sense of not having the right; or, it not being the custom.

The stone upon the well's mouth (v. 8.)—I. That great treasures are often hidden away from sight and reach. Gold in mountains, precious stones under the ground, pearls lying at the bottom of

Jacob by the well

a Ho. xii. 12.

b Lange.

"Men may change their climate, but they cannot change their nature. A man that goes out a fool cannot ride or sail himself into common sense."—*Addison.*

c Burmann.

"As the Spanish proverb says, 'He who would bring home the wealth of the Indies must carry the wealth of the Indies with him,' so it is in travelling; a man must carry knowledge with him if he would bring home knowledge."—*Johnson.*

d Harmer.

his discourse with the shepherds

a Ge. xxiv. 24, 29.

"What a solemn and striking admonition to youth is that inscribed on the dial, at All Souls, Oxford—*periunt et impuluntur—*

GENESIS. [Cap. xxix. 9-14.

B.C. cir. 1760.

the hours perish and are laid to our charge; for time, like life, can never be recalled. Melanethon noted down the time lost by him, that he might thereby reanimate his industry, and not lose an hour."
N. Smiles.
b J. H. Tasson.
c Roberts.

Jacob's interview with Rachel

a Ex. ii. 16.

b Zec. xiv. 16; xxiv. 48.

c Ge. ii. 23.

"Forbes, in his *Oriental Memoirs*, mentions that in the Brahmin villages of the Concan, women of the first distinction draw the water from wells and tend the cattle to pasture, 'like Rebekah and Rachel.'"—*Bush.*

"Among the Sinai Arabs, a boy would feel himself insulted were anyone to say, 'Go and drive your father's sheep to pasture.' These words, in his opinion, would signify, 'You are no better than a girl.'"—*Burckhardt.*

"It may be interesting to note the fact that in Samoa, nephews, nieces and cousins, are all called brothers and sisters, as in primitive times."—*Dr. Turner.*

the sea. "Truth lies in a well." II. That to obtain these treasures it is necessary that a strong and united effort should be made. The shepherds must wait till all the rest arrive. III. That the treasure of greatest worth is uncovered by the Redeemer for our benefit. Christ rolls the stone of error away from the mouth of the well of wisdom and righteousness.*b*

The day is great.—Are people travelling through places where are wild beasts, those who are timid will keep troubling the party by saying, "Let us seek for a place of safety:" but the others reply, "Not yet;" for "the day is *great*." "Why should I be in such haste! the day is yet *great*." When tired of working, it is remarked, "Why, the day is yet *great*." "Yes, yes, you manage to leave off while the day is yet *great*."*c*

9—14. (9) **came** .. **sheep**, not an unusual occupation for women in the E.*a* **kept**, *lit.* she shepherdised them. (10) **rolled** .. **mouth**, "a light heart makes a strong hand." (11) **kissed**, respectful salutation of E. **wept**, for joy: perh. his thoughts turned to his mother, and her early life, etc. (12) **told** .. **brother,***b* this would explain his kind attentions: brother, in the wider sense, relation, kinsman. **father**, to whom this stranger had referred. (13) **heard**, *lit.* heard the hearing. **and** .. **things**, who he was, whence he had come, and why. (14) **surely** .. **flesh**,*c* yet L. did not treat his own *flesh* well. **month**, *lit.* a month of days, *i.e.* a full month.

The dignity of woman.—A celebrated writer says that the ladies insist that it is highly derogatory from the dignity of the sex that the poet should affirm that it is the perfection of the character of a wife—

"To study household good,
And good works in her husband to promote."

Now, according to my notion of "household good," which does not include one idea of drudgery, or servility, but which involves a large and comprehensive scheme of excellence, I will venture to affirm that, let any woman know what she may, yet, if she knows not this, she is ignorant of the most indispensable, the most appropriate, branch of female knowledge. Without it, however she may inspire admiration abroad, she will never excite esteem, nor ensure durable affection, at home; and will bring neither credit nor comfort to her ill-starred partner. The domestic arrangements of such a woman as filled the capacious mind of the poet, resemble, if I may say it without profaneness, those of Providence, whose under-agent she is: her wisdom is seen in its effects; indeed, it is rather felt than seen; it is sensibly acknowledged in the peace, the happiness, the virtue of component parts; in the order, regularity, and beauty of the whole system, of which she is the moving spring. The perfection of her character, as the divine poet intimates, does not arise from a prominent quality, or a showy talent, or a brilliant accomplishment; but it is the beautiful combination and result of them all. Her excellences consist not so much in acts as in habits; in—

"Those thousand decencies which daily flow
From all her words and actions."

A description more calculated than any I ever met with to convey an idea of the purest conduct, resulting from the best principles; it gives an image of that tranquillity, smoothness, and quiet beauty which is the very essence of perfection in a wife.*d*

15—20. (15) **serve**, Jacob was not an idle guest. (16) **Leah** (*wearied*). (17) **tender-eyed**, feeble, dull, weak ; not fresh and brilliant. **beautiful**, *etc*.,*a* in form and expression, in figure and face. (18) **serve**, he could not give presents, hence will serve. (19) **better .. man**, ref. to relationship. (20) **years .. days**,*b* not that time seemed short, but the labour light.

Jacob and Rachel (vv. 18—20).—Notice the effect of love in making labour light and giving wings to time. In whatever form love shows itself this is its effect—I. When we love our work, how easy it is to us, how swiftly and pleasantly the time passes by! The schoolboy, the teacher, and the preacher know the power of love in making their tasks easy. II. So with obedience. The child who does not love his parents finds obedience very hard. How different with the child who *does* love them! III. So when we enter upon life's hard work. Some of you must toil seven years for a Rachel. Love will make the time fly quickly by, and will sweeten your labour. IV. So with the service of God. His yoke is easy and His burden is light to those who love Him. Our heart must be in our religion, and our religion in our heart, if it is to be to us other than a toilsome drudgery.*c*

The beauty of woman.—Woman may be said almost to enjoy the monopoly of personal beauty. A good-humoured writer thus defines her position in this respect as contrasted with the opposite sex : If you, ladies, are much handsomer than we, it is but just you should acknowledge that we have helped you, by voluntarily making ourselves ugly. Your superiority in beauty is made up of two things : first, the care which you take to increase your charms ; secondly, the zeal which we have shown to heighten them by the contrast of our finished ugliness—the shadow which we supply to your sunshine. Your long, pliant, wavy tresses are all the more beautiful because we cut our hair short ; your hands are the whiter, smaller, and more delicate because we reserve to ourselves those toils and exercises which make the hands large and hard. We have devoted entirely to your use flowers, feathers, ribbons, jewellery, silks, gold and silver embroidery. Still more to increase the difference between the sexes, which is your greatest charm, and to give you the handsome share, we have divided with you the hues of nature. To you we have given the colours that are rich and splendid, or soft and harmonious ; for ourselves we have kept those that are dark and dead. We have given you sun and light ; we have kept night and darkness.*d*

21—24. (21) **wife**, *i.e.* his betrothed. **fulfilled**, he did his part : it was now for Laban to fulfil his word. (22) **feast**, *lit.* a drinking. (23) **and**, *etc.*, the supplanter is outwitted :*a* perh. the "drinking" facilitated the deception. (24) **Zilpah** (*a dropping*), still the cust. in E. for father to give a slave to his dau. on her mar.

Comparisons between the deception practised by Laban upon Jacob, and that which Jacob practised upon Esau.—I. One brother upon another. II. There the younger upon the older ; here the older upon the younger. III. Jacob did not know Leah when he was married to her, just as his father knew him not when he

---

B.C. *cir.* 1760.

d H. More.

Jacob wishes to marry Rachel

a Pr. xxxi. 30.

b Ep. v. 25.

v. 17. "In the E. the clear, expressive, lustrous eye is accounted the chief feature in female beauty. It was compared to the eyes of the gazelle ; see 1 S. xvi. 12. On the contrary, Rachel's beauty was complete ; she was beautiful in form and beautiful in look, both in figure and face."—*Alford.*

vv. 18, 19. "It is still the custom to serve for a wife. Burckhardt found a young man in Hauran who had served eight years for his board, and had then married his master's daughter, but had yet more years to serve for her. And Laban's speech yet indicates the rule of Eastern betrothals."—*Ibid.*

c D. Longwill, M.A.

d Dr. Doran.

Laban gives Leah to Jacob

a Ge. xxvii. 35, 36 ; Ma. vii. 2 ; 1 Co. iii. 19.

v. 24. J. Doughty, *Analecta Sacra,* 59.

"Cheaters must get some credit

B.C. cfr. 1760.

before they can cozen, and all falsehood, if not founded in some truth, would not be fixed in any belief."—Fuller.

b Roos.

"The life even of a just man is a round of petty frauds; that of a knave a series of greater. We degrade life by our follies and vices, and then complain that the unhappiness which is only their accompaniment is inherent in the constitution of things."—Boree.

c Steele.

Jacob marries Rachel
a Ju. xiv. 12.
b De. xxi. 15.

"All my own experience of life teaches me the contempt of cunning, not the fear. The phrase 'profound cunning' has always seemed to me a contradiction in terms. I never knew a cunning mind which was not either shallow or on some point diseased."—Jameson.
"We take cunning for a sinister or crooked wisdom, and certainly there is a great difference between a cunning man and a wise man, not

blessed him. IV. Leah at the instigation of her father, Jacob at the instigation of his mother. V. But he received, notwithstanding his ignorance as to Leah, the wife designed for him by God, just as Isaac blessed him unwittingly as the rightful heir of the promise.*b*

Different conditions of marriage.—The marriage life is always an *insipid*, a *vexatious*, or a *happy* condition. The first is, when two people of no genius or taste for themselves meet together, upon such a settlement as has been thought reasonable by parents and conveyancers, from an exact valuation of the land and cash of both parties. In this case the young lady's person is no more regarded than the house and improvements in purchase of an estate; but she goes with her fortune, rather than her fortune with her. These make up the crowd or vulgar of the rich, and fill up the lumber of the human race, without beneficence towards those below them, or respect towards those above them. The *vexatious* life arises from a conjunction of two people of quick taste and resentment, put together for reasons well known to their friends, in which especial care is taken to avoid (what they think the chief of evils) poverty, and ensure to them riches, with every evil besides. These good people live in a constant constraint before company, and too great familiarity alone. When they are within observation, they fret at each other's carriage and behaviour; when alone, they revile each other's person and conduct. In company, they are in purgatory; when only together, in hell. The *happy* marriage is, where two persons meet and voluntarily make choice of each other, without principally regarding or neglecting the circumstances of fortune or beauty. These may still love in spite of adversity or sickness: the former we may in some measure defend ourselves from; the other is the portion of our very make.*c*

25—30. (25) **morning,** light once more, effects of the feast had passed away. **wherefore .. me,** deceivers like not to be deceived. (26) **it .. country,** but this he was bound in honesty to have said bef. (27) **week,** the mar. week : week of feasting."*a* (28) **gave .. also,** one sin begets another. Laban's treachery, to Jacob's bigamy. (29) **Bilhah** (*bashfulness*). (30) **loved .. Leah,***b* deceived by R.'s beauty ; as by L.'s fraud.

Influence of women.—Good and bad women either sweeten or poison the cup of life, so great is their power of doing much good or much evil. In sacred history we read that such was the influence of the love of Rachel upon the mind of Jacob, that he served Laban fourteen years for her, and they seemed to him but as a few days. Profane history abounds with very remarkable instances of the influence of love upon some men. When women know the power of their sex, and exercise it, the consequences have been very surprising ; the hero, the magistrate, the philosopher, and the prince, think no more of their grandeur or their power; all restraint, all reserve, are laid aside for a time, and puerile freedom of speech succeeds to studied harangues, and the most grave and solemn looks ; the man of business and of retirement, the young and the old, drop their characters before women. The studious man leaves his closet, the merchant his negotiations, and sometimes the general quits the field, and the judge descends from the bench to enjoy the company of their favourite females. But further still, notwithstanding *only men* take the lead and appear as public characters, yet there is reason to believe that all of them are in some degree influenced by women in what they do. Since, therefore, women have such power either directly or indirectly, it is of the greatest importance that they should have a good education, and all possible means made use of, to make them wise, and to keep them strictly virtuous.[c]

31—35. (31) **hated,** less loved. **He,** *etc.,*[a] by which her husband's love might be increased: or she comforted with love of children. (32) **Reuben** (*behold a son*). **now . . me,** L. seems to have been tender-hearted, as well as tender-eyed. (33) **Simeon** (*hearing*). (34) **now . . me,** she is intensely anxious to win her husband's love. Prob. his little love was occasioned by her participating in her father's fraud. **Levi** (*joined*). (35) **now . . Lord,** prob. thinking she would secure J.'s love. **Judah**[b] (*praise*).

Leah and Rachel (*read to* xxx. 2).—Let us consider—I. Leah's quiet behaviour under her trial, and the reward she received for her patience. Leah loved Jacob with a constant and persevering affection. This is very evident from the expressions she makes use of on the successive occasions of the birth of her four children. Though not loved well by Jacob, still she has the better portion. II. Rachel's self-will and impatience, and God's displeasure with her. Her history and experience are a great contrast to Leah's.[c]

The world without children.—
  Ah! what would the world be to us
    If the children were no more?
  We should dread the desert behind us
    Worse than the dark before.

  What the leaves are to the forest,
    With light and air for food,
  Ere their sweet and tender juices
    Have been hardened into wood,—

  That to the world are children;
    Through them it feels the glow
  Of a brighter and sunnier climate
    Than reaches the trunks below.[d]

CHAPTER THE THIRTIETH.

1—4. envied, was jealous. (1) **or . . die,**[a] I am as one dead. (2) **anger,**[b] angry that one so tenderly loved should charge him with being the cause of her childlessness. (3) **bear . . knees,** I will nurse her children as if they were my own.[c] **may . . her,** *lit.,* be built up by her. (4) **gave . . wife,** as Sarah gave Hagar to Abraham.

A true wife.—
  I would not be ambitious in my wish,
  To wish myself much better, yet, for you,
  I would be trebled twenty times myself:
  A thousand times more fair, ten thousand times
  More rich;

B.C. *cir.* 1760.

"only in point of honesty, but in point of ability."—*Bacon.*

c *Scraggs.*

Reuben, Simeon, Levi, and Judah are born

a Ps. cxxvii. 3.

b Ma. i. 2.

"You are my true and honourable wife; as dear to me as are the ruddy drops that visit this sad heart."—*Shakespeare.*

"It very seldom happens that a man is slow enough in assuming the character of a husband, or a woman quick enough in condescending to that of a wife."—*Addison.*

c *D. Longwell, M.A.*

"Woman is like the reed which bends to every breeze, but breaks not in the tempest."—*Whately.*

d *Longfellow.*

B.C. *cir.* 1749.

Rachel envies Leah

a Ge. xxxv. 16—19; Job v. 2.

b Ep. iv. 26; 1 S. i. 5.

c "That she may bear, and I will be the nurse."—*Onkelos.* "I will take her child on my lap as my own."—*Alford.*

b.c. *cir.* 1749.

"She certainly is no true woman for whom every man may not find it in his heart to have a certain gracious, and holy, and honourable love; she is not a woman who returns no love, and asks no protection."— *Bartol.*

c. 3. *Dr. F. Lee, Diss,* ii. 211.

d *Shakespeare.*

Dan, and Naphtali are born
a Ma. iv. 13.
"Above, *v.* 1. Rachel had manifested impatience and neglect of prayer, seeking from Jacob what only could be given of God. Jacob's remonstrance with her, *v.* 2, may have directed her to wiser and better thoughts."
—*Speaker's Com.*
"Her passions are made of nothing but the finest part of pure love. We cannot call her winds and waters sighs and tears; they are greater storms and tempests than almanacs can report. This cannot be cunning in her. If it be, she makes a shower of rain as well as Jove."— *Shakespeare.*
b Bp. Earle.

Gad and Asher are born
a Bp. Browne.
b Bush.

"If a boy is not trained to endure

That only to stand high on your account,
I might in virtues, beauties, livings, friends,
Exceed account: but the full sum of me
Is sum of something: which, to term in gross,
Is an unlesson'd girl, unschool'd, unpractised;
Happy in this she is not yet so old
But she may learn; and happier than this,
She is not bred so dull but she can learn;
Happiest of all, is, that her gentle spirit
Commits itself to yours to be directed,
As from her lord, her governor, her king.
Myself, and what is mine, to you and yours
Is now converted: but now I was the lord
Of this fair mansion, master of my servants,
Queen o'er myself; and even now, but now,
This house, these servants, and this same myself,
Are yours, my lord.*d*

5—8. (6) **Dan** (*judge*), so called, prob. bec. she regarded God as having *decided* in her behalf. (8) **with** .. **wrestlings**, *lit.*, wrestlings of God: here ref. to earnest prayer. **Naphtali** (*my wrestling*), or Nephtalim.*a*

The happiness of children.—A child is a man in a small letter, yet the best copy of Adam; and he is happy whose small practice in the world can only write his character. He is Nature's fresh picture newly drawn in oil, which time and much handling dims and defaces. His soul is yet a white paper, unscribbled with observations of the world, wherewith at length it becomes a blurred note-book. He is purely happy, because he knows no evil, nor hath made means by sin to be acquainted with misery. He arrives not at the mischief of being wise, nor endures evils to come by foreseeing them. He kisses and loves all, and when the smart of the rod is past, smiles on his beater. Nature and his parents alike daudle him, and entice him on with a bait of sugar to a draught of wormwood. He plays yet like a young prentice the first day, and is not come to his task of melancholy. All the language he speaks yet is tears, and they serve him well enough to express his necessity. His hardest labour is his tongue, as if he were loth to use so deceitful an organ; and he is best company with it when he can but prattle. We laugh at his foolish sports, but his game is our earnest; and his drums, rattles, and hobby-horses but the emblems and mockings of men's business. His father hath writ him as his own little story, wherein he reads those days of his life which he cannot remember, and sighs to see what innocence he has outlived. He is the Christian's example, and the old man's relapse; the one imitates his pureness, and the other falls into his simplicity. Could he put off his body with his little coat, he had got eternity without a burden, and exchanged but one heaven for another.*b*

9—13. (9) **gave** .. **wife**, prob. in hope of retaining such marks of love as she had won. (11) **a** .. **cometh**, "rather *good fortune cometh*."*a* **Gad** (a *troop*). (13) **for** .. **blessed**, "all coming generations will felicitate me on my happy lot."*b* **Asher** (*happy*).

The happiness of woman (v. 13).—The happiness of woman illustrated by that of Leah, the elements of whose happiness consisted of—I. The joys of maternity. II. The increase of conjugal affection. III. An obliviousness of personal defects. IV. The anticipation of further congratulations.

Houses without children.—Tell me not of the trim, precisely-arranged homes where there are no children ; " where," as the good Germans have it, " the fly-traps always hang straight on the wall ;" tell me not of the never-disturbed nights and days, of the tranquil, unanxious hearts where children are not ! I care not for these things. God sends children for another purpose than merely to keep up the race—to enlarge our hearts, to make us unselfish, and full of kindly sympathies and affections ; to give our souls higher aims, and to call out all our faculties to extended enterprise and exertion ; to bring round our fireside bright faces and happy smiles, and loving, tender hearts. My soul blesses the Great Father every day, that He has gladdened the earth with little children.[c]

14—16. (14) **days .. harvest**, ab. mo. of May. **mandrakes**,[a] Heb. *dudāim* = love apples : the *Atropa mandragora*, allied to the deadly nightshade (*Atropa belladonna*), narcotic and stimulating. **give**, *etc.*, she evidently shared in the superstition. (15) **and**, *etc.*, it would seem that J. lived with R. at this time.

The mandrake.—This plant is a species of melon, of which there are two sorts, the male and the female. The female mandrake is black, and puts out leaves resembling lettuce, though smaller and narrower, which spread on the ground, and have a disagreeable scent. It bears berries something like services, pale and of a strong smell, having kernels within like those of pears. It has two or three very large roots, twisted together, white within, black without, and covered with a thick rind. The male mandrake is called Morion, or folly, because it suspends the senses. It produces berries twice as large as those of the female, of a good scent, and of a colour approaching towards saffron. Pliny says the colour is white. Its leaves are large, white, broad, and smooth, like the leaves of the beech-tree. The root resembles that of the female, but is thicker and bigger, descending six or eight feet into the ground. Both the smell and the taste are pleasant; but it stupefies those that use it, and often produces phrensy, vertigo, and lethargy, which, if timely assistance is not given, terminate in convulsions and death. It is said to be a provocative, and is used in the East as filters. The Orientals cultivate this plant in their gardens, for the sake of its smell ; but those which Reuben found were in the field, in some small copse of wood perhaps, or shade, where they had come to maturity before they were found. If they resemble those of Persia rather than those of Egypt, which are of a very inferior quality, then we see their value, their superiority, and perhaps their rarity, which induced Rachel to purchase them from the son of Leah.[b]

17—21. (17) **hearkened**, this implies prayerfulness on her part. (18) **hire .. husband**, prob. ref. to her self-denial in giving up Zilpah. **Issachar** (*he bringeth a reward*). (20) **God .. dowry**, except her maiden she went portionless fr. her earthly father. **now .. me**, in pref to R. ; or, regard me as his wife in reality as well as name. **Zebulun** (*dwelling*). (21) **Dinah** (*judgment*), prob. J. had other daus.,[a] but such were not usually named unless of historical importance.

B.C. cir. 1749.

and to bear trouble, he will grow up a girl ; and a boy that is a girl has all a girl's weakness without any of her regal qualities. A woman made out of a woman is God's noblest work ; a woman made out of a man is His meanest."—*Beecher.*

[c] *Mary Howitt.*

the mandrakes

[a] "Now the voluptuous mandrakes, widely exhaling their somniferous odour, breathe and excite to love."—See *Michaelis on Song*, vii. 13. See also *Tristram*, 103, *ff.* "The root is large, spindle-shaped, and oft. divides in a forked manner, having a resemblance to the human form. Hence sometimes called *Anthropomorphon* (man-like)."—*Topics; see also Thomson, L. and B.* 577.

"There are not unfrequently substantial reasons underneath for customs that appear to us absurd."—*Charlotte Brontë.*

[b] *Paxton.*

Issachar, Zebulun, and Dinah are born

[a] Ge. xxxii. 35 ; xlvi. 7.

Dowry, a gift, or endowment. Fr.

n.c. *cir.* 1710.

donaire; Low L., *douarium, dotarium*; L., *doto*, to endow *dos, dotis*, a dowry—*do*; Gk., *didomi*, to give.

"Joy is the mainspring in the whole round of everlasting nature; joy moves the wheels of the great timepiece of the world; she it is that loosens flowers from their buds, suns from their firmaments, rolling spheres in distant space, seen not by the glass of the astronomer."
—*Schiller*.

b *Tennyson.*

Joseph is born

a 1 S. i. 19, 20.

ᵃ Men are almost always cruel in their neighbours' faults; and make others' overthrow the badge of their own ill-masked virtue."
—*Sir P. Sidney.*

b *Starcke.*

The Rev. Moses Browne had twelve children. On one remarking to him, "Sir, you have just as many children as Jacob," he replied, "Yes; and I have Jacob's God to provide for them."

c *Dobell.*

Jacob wishes to return

a *Alford, Bush.*
b *Bp. Browne.*

Leah's dowry (v. 20).—I. What it was not. Not—1. Worldly wealth; 2. Personal charms. II. What it was. 1. Intense affection for her husband; 2. The increase, through her, of his family; 3. The increase of domestic joy. III. Who gave it? 1. Laban gave her nothing, save her handmaiden; 2. It was God who gave her children and her husband's love.

Attributes of woman.—

The woman's cause is man's. They rise or sink
Together. Dwarf'd or godlike, bond or free;
If she be small, slight-natured, miserable,
How shall men grow? ... Let her be
All that not harms distinctive womanhood;
For woman is not undevelop'd man,
But diverse. Could we make her as the man,
Sweet love were slain, whose dearest bond is this,
Not like to like, but like in difference;
Yet in the long years liker must they grow;
The man be more of woman, she of man;
He gain in sweetness, and in moral height,
Nor lose the wrestling thews that throw the world;
She mental breadth, nor fail in childward care,
More as the double-natured poet, each;
Till at the last she set herself to man,
Like perfect music unto noble words.ᵇ

22—24. (22) **and**, *etc.*, who all this time was childless, save in the very secondary sense of having the children of her maid reckoned to her. (23) **God .. reproach**, the ungenerous reproach of man. (24) **Joseph,**ᵃ (*he will add*). **said,** *etc.,* the birth of J. inspired her with faith and hope.

God hath taken away my reproach (v. 23).—Consider why barrenness was considered by Abraham's descendants as a sign of the Divine curse. Because—I. It appeared as if they were excluded from the promise of the enlargement of Abraham's seed. II. They were without the hope of giving birth to the Messiah. III. They had no share in God's universal command, "Be fruitful and multiply."ᵇ

Delightfulness of children.—

Thou, little child,
Thy mother's joy, thy father's hope—thou bright
Pure dwelling, where two fond hearts keep their gladness—
Thou little potentate of love, who comest
With solemn sweet dominion to the old,
Who see thee in thy merry fancies charged
With the grave embassage of that dear past,
When they were young like thee—thou vindication
Of God—thou living witness against all men—
Who have been babes—thou everlasting promise
Which no man keeps—thou portrait of our nature,
Which in despair and pride we scorn and worship—
Thou household god, whom no iconoclast
Hath broken !ᶜ

25—27. (25) **when,** *etc.,* gen. sup. to have been at end of second 7 yrs.' service;ᵃ but this not necessary, it may have been longer.ᵇ **send .. country,** aft. so long an absence he was not anxious to return, to look aft. his birthright, *etc.* (26) **knowest,**

etc., he asks only what was his due. (27) **if .. eyes**, a very questionable thing. **I .. sake**,[c] he cared more for himself than for Jacob, whose value he had learned by experience, *i.e.* by investigation (*lit.* by divination), by insidious inspection.

Laban's lesson (v. 27).—I. The school in which he learns: "I have learned by experience." 1. Experience is the best teacher of man in worldly matters; 2. It is also a universal teacher. Every one must pass through this school; 3. All do not profit alike by its instructions. II. The lesson he learns. 1. That his prosperity is sent by God; 2. That this prosperity is sent to him as an especial blessing; 3. That this prosperity is sent as a blessing consequent on the presence of his kinsman Jacob. III. The lessons we may learn from it. 1. All good is from God; 2. One man, favoured of God, may often be the means of blessing many.[d]

Yearnings for home.—"I long to see home," says the sailor when the ship rocks to and fro from the violence of the storm. "I am going home," thinks the shopman when he bars his heavy doors, and closes his windows at night, tired with the labours of the day. "I must hurry home," says the mother, whose heart is on her baby in the cradle. "Oh, how I long to get home!" says the schoolboy, disconsolate over the hopeless task. "Don't stop me; I am going home," says the bright-eyed girl skipping along the footpath. And "Almost home," says the dying Christian. "I shall soon be home, and then no more sorrow nor sighing for ever. Almost home."[e]

28—33. (28) **appoint**, *lit.* prick down: *i.e.* state precisely. **and .. it**, if any more than this long service is due. (29) **knowest .. served**,[a] with what conscientious diligence. **how .. me**,[b] how carefully tended. (30) **when .. house**,[c] this explains J.'s conduct. He must care for his own family. (31) **thou .. thing**, he would rather rely on God's blessing than L.'s promise. **if .. me**, suffer me to refer the matter to Divine arbitration. (32) **and .. hire**, these were likely to be *very few*.[d] (33) **so .. face**, it will be clearly seen if I have defrauded you.[e]

Since my coming: Heb. "*At my foot*," v. 30.—By the labour of Jacob's *foot*, the cattle of Laban had increased to a multitude. Of a man who has become rich by his own industry, it is said, "Ah! by the labour of his *feet* these treasures have been acquired." "How have you gained this prosperity?"—"By the favour of the gods, and the labour of my *feet*." "How is it the king is so prosperous?"—"By the labour of the *feet* of his ministers."[f]

34—36. (34) **and**, *etc.*, this seemed, for him, a most safe arrangement. (35) **he .. day**, L. proceeds *at once* to take care for himself. **goats .. sheep**, leaving those whose progeny were least likely to be particoloured. (36) **set .. Jacob**, he places the spotted, etc., at a safe distance fr. the rest. **Jacob .. flocks**, and proceeded to win his hire.

Jacob's expedient.—Some acquaintance with the influence of circumstances on the lower animals at breeding-time, sheds much light on this transaction. For example, I have known among sheep a black wether, when pastured at the breeding season with a white flock, show its influence over the females to such a degree as to add to the flock several lambs marked with black, and even one or two wholly black. In pheasant preserves the influence of

---

B.C. 1749.

c Ge. xxxix. 3–5.
"My idea is that there are duties toward our native land, common to every citizen, and even public institutions and education must have such a direction as to enable every citizen to fulfil his duty toward his fatherland."
—*Kossuth.*
d H. Jeyne.

"The love of country produces good manners, and good manners also love of country. The less we satisfy our particular passions, the more we leave to our general."—*Montesquieu.*
e Bowes.

Jacob's expedient for his vindication

a Ge. xxxi. 38–40; Tit. ii. 10.
b Ep. vi. 5–8; 1 Pe. ii. 18; Col. iii. 22–24.
c 1 Ti. v. 8.
d "The colour of the sheep in the E. is gen. white; that of the goats is black."—*Tristram, Nat. Hist. of Bible*, 144.
e Ps. xxxvii. 6.
f Roberts.

Laban approves Jacob's plan

"It is not juggling that is to be blamed, but much juggling; for the world cannot be governed without it."—*Selden.*

"If thou be strong enough to encounter with the times,

B.C. 1749.

keep thy station; if not, shift a foot to gain advantage of the times. He that acts a beggar to prevent a thief is never the poorer; it is a great part of wisdom sometimes to seem a fool."—*Quarles.*

Increase of Jacob's flocks

a The Arabs still call the almond *luz.*

Pill, to peel. "The skilful shepherd *pilled* me certain wands."—*Shakespeare, M. of Ven.,* I. 3. So one who had lost his hair was said to be *pilled,* or bald. "His scalpe all pild, and hee with eld forlore."—*Chaucer.*

b Alford, Bp. Browne.

c "It has been observed that in the whole of this narrative of J.'s stratagems the sacred names do not once occur."—*Alford.*

"Had I miscarried, I had been a villain; for men judge always by events; but when we manage by a just foresight, success is prudence, and possession right."—*Higgins.*

d Dr. Kitto.

r. 37—9. Dr. F. Lee, Cisser, ii., 256; John Doughty, Anal. Sac., 57.

e Trapp.

a white domestic fowl, when shut up with them, is acknowledged in making the plumage of one or more of the young pheasants much lighter than it would otherwise have been; and there are cases on record in which, in breeding horses, it has been found that the first male brought to the female has so impressed her, that his colour made its appearance in all her after foals by males of a wholly different colour. It would be out of place to dwell here on this. These cases are mentioned in the hope that they will indicate the nature of the expedient to which Jacob had recourse in order to enrich himself from the flocks of Laban. The term "ring-straked" is applied to white bands on the limbs or necks of the goats, and to black or brown bands on those of the sheep. The zebra is neither spotted nor speckled, but ring-straked.a

37—43. (37) **poplar,** perh. the *styrax* or *storax* : a shrub, ab. 12 ft. high. **hazel,** Heb. *luz,*a almond. **chesnut,** the plane-tree. **made .. rods,** by stripping off the thin rind or bark. (38, 39) **and,** *etc.,* "The effect prod. is ill. by many writers on nat. hist., and is said to prevail esp. among sheep." (40) **lambs,** these speckled ones in a flock by themselves. **set .. Laban,** the meaning prob. is that those in the flock of Laban were placed to windward of these separated lambs.b **and .. cattle,** thus L. could not charge him with a fraudulent mixture of the flocks. (41, 42) **and,** *etc.,* hence J.'s flock bec. the most healthy and vigorous, as well as most numerous. (43) **increased,**c *lit.* broke forth, expanded.

The poplar, hazel, and chesnut.—*Poplar.*—As the Hebrew word *libnsh* denotes whiteness, and the Septuagint renders it by λευκη, we have no hesitation in thinking that the *Populus alba,* or "white poplar," is here meant. The λευκη, or "white poplar," is mentioned by Theophrastus as growing in Egypt and Syria; and it occurs very frequently in Persia.—*Hazel*—*Luz,* Heb. (*Corylus Avellana*).—From the suffrage of the ancient versions, we collect that *Luz* is rightly translated "Hazel," though the hazel was called "*Nux Pontica,*" as having been brought to Italy from Pontus. It was cultivated near Avellino, a city not far from Naples, whence we have the specific name *Avellana.*—*Chesnut.*—*Armon,* Heb. There seems to be no doubt that the plane-tree is the *Armon* of Scripture, since the Arabic, Greek, Syrian, and Vulgate versions all agree in so considering it. The *Platanus Orientalis* was a very favourite tree among the ancients, as the classical reader well knows. The term Platanus, πλατανος, is from πλατυς, "broad," and applies to the diffusive shade of this delightful tree, which was, in fact, the quality that recommended it to the attachment of Eastern nations. The Hebrew appellation *Armon* comes from a root which signifies to be stripped, and agrees very well with the plane, where the bark spontaneously peels off, and leaves the trunk apparently bare. The chesnut has a wide, spreading top, but its bark, though curiously cleft into oblong cells, does not peel off as in the plane and birch. The Arabic and Syriac terms are essentially the same; *dulba,* Syriac, and *dulb.* Arabic.d—" This was done, partly by force of the fantasy which is much affected with objects of the sight; partly and chiefly by the blessing of God : for he that shall now try the same conclusion, shall find himself frustrated."e

CHAPTER THE THIRTY-FIRST.

B.C. cir. 1739.

1—3. (1) **sons**, who seem as unjust as their sire. **Jacob .. father's**, "a calumnious assertion." **glory**, *lit.* weight, *i.e.* of wealth. (2) **toward .. before,**ᵃ *lit.* as yesterday and the day before. (3) **return**, *etc.*, such is God's command. **I .. thee,**ᵇ hence all opposition will be in vain.

Jacob's resolution to return (vv. 3—16).—Jacob here makes a resolution to return to Canaan. This he makes—1. Upon a just provocation: Laban's sons speak ill of him; Laban looks ill towards him; 2. By Divine direction, and under the convoy of a Divine promise; 3. With the knowledge and consent of his wives.ᶜ

As yesterday and the day before (v. 2).—Heb. "as yesterday and the day before." See also marginal reading of Isa. xxx. 33, Of old, "from yesterday." The latter form of speech is truly Oriental, and means time gone by. Has a person lost the friendship of another, he will say to him, "Thy face is not to me as yesterday and the day before." Is a man reduced in his circumstances, he says, "The face of God is not upon me as *yesterday and the day before.*" The future is spoken of as *to-day and to-morrow:* "His face will be upon me *to-day and to-morrow;*" which means *always.* "I will love thee to-day and to-morrow." "Do you think of me?"—"Yes, to-day and to-morrow." "Modeliar, have you heard that Tamban is trying to injure you?"—"Yes, and go and tell him that neither to-day nor to-morrow will he succeed." Our Saviour says, "Behold, I cast out devils, and I do cures to-day and to-morrow." A messenger came to inform Him Herod would kill Him; but this was His reply, intimating that the power could never be taken from him. Jacob said to Laban, "My righteousness answers for me in time to come;" but the Hebrew has for this, "*to-morrow;*" his righteousness would be perpetual. In Eastern language, therefore, "yesterday and the day before" signify time *past;* but "to-day and to-morrow" time to *come.* (*See* Ex. xiii. 14. Jos. iv. 6., also xxii. 24, margin.)ᵈ

4—9. (4) **sent .. flock**, for a more private interview. (5) **but .. me**, of which the great flock around them was the proof. (6) **power**, ability, skill, time. (7) **deceived**, false promises, fair words, falsehoods **ten times**, *i.e.* many times: a common idiom.ᵃ (8) **if .. thus**, in each case thinking only of his own advantage. **then**, *etc.*, what he intended for *his*, turned out for *my* gain. (9) **God .. me**, God has cared for me, and also reproved him.

The ways of dishonesty.—It is a universal form of dishonesty to try to get goods below their value; and whenever you do that you undertake to cheat. The man who wants to get a thing without giving a fair equivalent wants to be dishonest. If it costs, to make a hat, and give a good living to the man that works upon it, and a moderate profit to the man that sells it, three dollars, and you undertake to buy it for two dollars and a half, you undertake to cheat half a dollar. If you attempt to beat a man down, and to get his goods for less than a

---

God commands Jacob to return
ᵃ De. xxviii. 54.
ᵇ Ge. xxviii. 15, xxxii. 9.

"A certain amount of distrust is wholesome, but not so much of others as of ourselves; neither vanity nor conceit can exist in the same atmosphere with it."—*Mde. Necker.*
ᶜ *M. Henry.*

"It is because we have but a small portion of enjoyment ourselves that we feel so little pleasure in the good fortune of others. Is it possible for the happy to be envious?"—*W. B. Clulow.*

"Of all the passions, jealousy is that which exacts the hardest service, and pays the bitterest wages. Its service is to watch the success of our enemy; its wages, to be sure of it."—*Colton.*
ᵈ *Roberts.*

Jacob's proposal to his wives
ᵃ Nu. xiv. 22; Job xix. 3; Le. xxvi. 26; Ec. vii. 19; Zec. viii. 23; Re. ii. 10.

"Never put much confidence in such as put no confidence in others. A man prone to suspect evil is mostly looking in his neighbour for what he sees in himself. As to the pure, all things are pure, even so to the

B.C. 1739.

Impure all things are impure."
Hare.
"Trust him with little, who, without proof, trusts you with everything, or, when he has proved you, with nothing."—*Lavater.*
b *Beecher.*

he tells them of the command
a *Bush.*
Grisled, now spelled grizzled, of a greyish colour. Fr. *gris;* Ger. *greis; gray.* The *Spk. Comm.* says, " sprinkled as with hail; the *lit.* meaning of the word grisled." Puzzled is in Bacon's *essays* often spelled pusled.
b Ge. xxviii. 18-22.
" Remembrance wakes with all her busy train."
—*Goldsmith.*

they agree to his proposal

" It may, indeed, be said that sympathy exists in all minds, as Faraday has discovered that magnetism exists in all metals; but a certain temperature is required to develope the hidden property, whether in the metal or the mind."—*Lytton.*

v. 13. Dr. H. *Hammond, Wks.,* iv. 496.

Jacob's departure from Laban

a Ge. xxxv. 2. Gilead, a mt. range extending from S. to N. along E. border

fair price, you are attempting to commit burglary as much as though you broke into his shop to take the things without paying for them. There is cheating on both sides of the counter, and, generally, less behind it than before it. You want a man to build you, for two thousand dollars, a house that shall be worth five thousand; and what is the result? You teach that man to cheat you. You make him dishonest. You drive him to the necessity of using poor material, and of deceiving you by filling up holes with putty, and covering defects with paint.b

10—13. (10) **dream,** perhaps it was in a dream that the expedient was suggested to him;a now by a dream he is warned to return. (11) **here .. I,** ready for all God's will. (12) **for .. thee,** hence to compensate J., and punish L., was the change in the property. (13) **I .. Beth-el,**b who comforted thee on that dark night. **where .. me,** J. is reminded of his promise of obedience. **now,** *etc.,* as I have been thy faithful friend; be thou my obedient servant.

A strange vow.—A minister now (1872) living relates the following:—In early life his father felt called to the ministry, but asked God to excuse him, and made a vow to give his eldest son to the work of the ministry. The vow was apparently accepted of God, as the father felt no longer the pressure of this special duty, and prospered in his religious life. Twenty years later the son was converted, and felt that, if he would be religious at all, he must be a minister. He accepted the duty gladly, prepared for it; and, after his ordination, his father said to him, for the first time informing him of the vow, "My son, you have a double duty to do. You have your own work and mine also."

14—16. (14) **is there,** *etc.,* even his daus. had no great love or respect for L.; and nothing to hope for from him. (15) **strangers,** rather than kindred. **sold,** for the fourteen years' hard toil of their husband. **hath .. money,** referring to the portion which, as daus., they may have expected: or the price for which they were sold. (16) **riches .. father,** God did not permit L. to thrive by his unrighteous exactions. **God .. do,** they were willing to fully cast in their lot with one whom God so signally defended, and who had so proved his love for them.

The better inheritance.—Mr. Orpen gives the following account of a deaf and dumb boy, whom he took from the Beggars' Asylum, in Dublin, at which time the boy did not know how to pronounce a single word. He had been well taught by the master at Claremont, and he shortly began to speak. One evening Mr. O. asked him, "Are you happy?" To which he replied in a clear and distinct manner, "I have God for my Father, Jesus Christ for my Redeemer; I have heaven for my inheritance;—I *am* happy."

17—21. (17) **then .. up,** since they were united, he would act while they were in the mind. **sons,** esp. the younger ones. **wives,** careful for their comfort. (18) **carried,** *lit.* drove, led, conducted. **getting,** possessing. (19) **Laban .. sheep,** the time seized for this removal was when L. and his servants were absorbed by this important occupation. **images,**a Heb. *teraphim,* prob. gods, like the *Penates* of classical

Cap xxxi. 22—24.] GENESIS. 133

na'ions; objects of adoration, or instruments of divination. (20) **stole .. Laban,**[b] *lit.* stole away the heart, *i.e.* departed without his knowledge. (21) **river,** Euphrates. **Gilead** as it was afterwards called (vv. 46, 47).

Rachel's theft of her father's teraphim.—Among the many solutions which have been attempted of her conduct, the following may be specified:—1. That the images were of precious metal, and Rachel stole them to compensate for the loss of dowry sustained through Laban's bargain with Jacob; 2. That she thought that by taking the oracles she should deprive Laban of the means of discovering the flight of her husband; 3. That she expected by this act to bring prosperity from the household of her father to her husband; 4. Some conclude that she hoped to cure her father of his idolatrous propensities by depriving him of the instruments; while many, on the other hand, imagine that Rachel and her sister were infected by the same superstitions as their father, and wished to continue the practice of them in the land of Canaan.[c]

22—24. (22) **on .. day,** all so busy with the shearing, and the distance betw. the flocks so great that he could not well hear of it bef. (23) **pursued,** this shows how a formal request for another kind of leaving would have been received. **seven,** Jacob having marched ten days. **overtook,** they were prob. mounted on the swift dromedaries of the E. (24) **God .. dream,**[a] His way of warning the wicked, as well as comforting and instructing the good. **either .. bad,** *lit.* from good to bad. Characteristic of L. to beg with fair speech and advance to rough measures.

Providence in dreams.—Captain Yount, of California, in a mid-winter's night had a dream, in which he saw what appeared to be a company of emigrants arrested by the snows of the mountains, and perishing rapidly by cold and hunger. He noted the very cast of the scenery, marked by a huge perpendicular front of white rock cliff; he saw the men cutting off what appeared to be tree tops rising out of deep gulfs of snow; he distinguished the very features of the persons and the look of their particular distress. He woke profoundly impressed with the distinctness and apparent reality of his dream. At length he fell asleep, and dreamed exactly the same dream again. In the morning he could not expel it from his mind. Falling in shortly with an old hunter comrade, he told him the story; and was only the more deeply impressed by his recognising, without hesitation, the scenery of the dream. This comrade came over the Sierra by the Carson Valley Pass (in California), and declared that a spot in the Pass answered exactly to his description. By this the unsophisticated patriarch was decided. He immediately collected a company of men with mules and blankets, and all necessary provisions. The neighbours were laughing, meantime, at his credulity. "No matter," said he, "I am able to do this, and I will, for I verily believe that the fact is according to my dream." The men were sent into the mountains one hundred and fifty miles distant, directly to the Carson Valley Pass. And there they found the company in exactly the condition of the dream, and brought in the remnant alive. A gentleman present, when the captain told me, said, "You need not doubt this, for we Californians all know the facts, and the names of the families

---

B.C. 1739.

of Canaan. Known by dif. names in dif. parts; it reaches fr. Hermon to Arabia Petrea.

[b] This flight of J. occurred A.M. 2266, 610 yrs. aft. the flood; in the 158th yr. of Isaac's age, and 98th of Jacob's. —*Bush.*

v. 17, 18. *T. Seaton, Duty of Ser.,* 156.

[c] *Bush.*

Laban pursues Jacob
a Ge. xx. 3; Job. xxx. 15.
"Dreams are the children of an idle brain, begot of nothing but vain fantasy; which is as thin of substance as the air, and more inconstant than the wind."—*Shakespeare.*
"If we can sleep without dreaming, it is well that painful dreams are avoided. If while we sleep we can have any pleasing dreams, it is, as the French say, *tant gagne,* so much added to the pleasure of life." —*Franklin.*
"Metaphysicians have been learning their lesson for the last 4,000 years, and it is high time that they should now begin to teach us something. Can any of the tribe inform us why all the operations of the mind are carried on with undiminished strength and activity in dreams, except the judgment, which

B.C. 1739.

alone is suspended and dormant?'—Colton.
b Dr. Bushnell.

and overtakes him in Gilead

a "The laws of true friendship are expressed by the rule — welcome the coming guest, speed the parting."—Homer, Od. xv. 83.
b To, ies, ii. 122.

c Pr. xxvi. 24, 25.

d Ju. xviii. 24.

"Parting and forgetting? What faithful heart cau do these? Our great thoughts, our great affections, the truths of our life, never leave us. Surely they cannot separate from our consciousness; shall follow it whithersoever that shall go; and are of their nature divine and immortal."—Thackeray.

See T. Saurin, Disc. Hist. i. 411

e Morton's New Canaan.

the search for the gods

a Ex. xx. 12; Le. xix. 32.

"Cunning has only private selfish aims, and sticks at nothing which may make them succeed. Discretion has large and extended views, and, like a well-formed eye, commands a whole horizon; cunning is a kind of shortsightedness, that discerns the minutest objects which are near at hand, but is not able to dis-

brought in, who look upon our venerable friend as a kind of Saviour." Their names he gave, and the places where they reside, and I found afterwards that the California people were ready everywhere to second his testimony.*b*

25—30. (25) Jacob .. **mount**, for him a mt. of safety. (26) **what .. done**, the guilty are prone to accuse others. It was bec. of what *he* had done that Jacob fled. **and .. daughters**, but if so, they were J.'s wives. **as .. sword**, not true; they went of their own free will. (27) **that .. away**, if so willing to send them away, why the pursuit? **mirth, feasting, and song**: old custom.*a* **tabret**.*b* Heb. *toph*, a kind of tambourine. (28) **kiss**,*c* sheer hypocrisy. **thou .. doing**, would it have been wiser to have remained? (29) **it .. hurt**, an empty boast to a man who had God for his helper: L. must have felt this after the dream to which he referred. (30). **because .. house**, but chiefly to be free from oppression. **yet .. gods**,*d* how, in the hurry of pursuit, had he missed them? Perh. he had gone to consult them in ref. to this journey.

An Indian marriage.—Winnepuskit, otherwise called George, Sachem of Sangus, married a daughter of Passaconaway, the great Pennacook chieftain, in 1662. The wedding took place at Pennacook (now Concord, N.H.), and the ceremonies closed with a great feast. According to the usages of the chiefs, Passaconaway ordered a select number of his men to accompany the newly-married couple to the dwelling of the husband, where, in turn, there was another great feast. Some time after the wife of Winnepuskit, expressing a desire to visit her father's house, was permitted to go, accompanied by a brave escort of her husband's chief men. But when she wished to return, her father sent a messenger to Sangus, informing her husband and asking him to come and take her away. He returned for answer that he had escorted his wife to her father's house in a style that became a chief, and that now, if she wished to return, her father must send her back in the same way. This Passaconaway refused to do; and it is said that here terminated the connection of his daughter with the Sangus chief.*e*

31—35. (31) Jacob, astounded at this charge of theft. **for .. me**, a hint to L. that he knew him for a violent and unjust man. (32) **with .. live**, one who was dishonest and idolatrous, unworthy of life in his esteem. **for .. them**, otherwise he *might* have been ready in her defence. (33) **and .. tent**, where he would have been glad to have found them. **Rachel's**, guilty, yet least suspected. (34) **furniture**, prob. the litter wh. the camel carried for her convenience, and wh. she made use of as a couch in the tent. (35) **let .. lord**, a respectful address, but sugg. of the sternness of his character. **and .. images**, suffering the vexation of losing his gods, being deceived, and exposing himself to censure for making what appeared a false charge.

Filial reverence.—Children in the Eastern countries cultivate and express for their parents the most profound respect. "During a feast I remarked that the Amin-ad-douleh's son, Abdallah Khan, a man seemingly about thirty years old, the possessor of considerable wealth, and governor of Ispahan, but seldom appeared among the guests; and only seated himself as one of the humblest, when invited by the words, or encouraged by the looks of his father. This reserve, however, was not caused by any ill-will or deficiency of kindness subsisting on either side; but arose from the filial respect which, in every stage and condition of life, the Persians are thus taught to express.[b]

36—39. (36) **wroth,** with this charge of theft, aft. all that had preceded. **chode,** disputed, pleaded. **what,** *etc.*,[a] he who had deceived others, is now himself deceived. (37) **what.. stuff?** gods or aught else. **judge,** decide, arbitrate. (38) **thy.. young,** through neglect of mine in the lambing season. **and ..eaten,**[b] I have not taken the usual rations or perquisites. (39) **I..loss,** *etc.*, like a com. hireling shepherd rather than as one of the fam.

Jacob's onerous duties.—When, after twenty years' service, Jacob withdrew secretly from Laban, and was pursued and overtaken by him, the son of Isaac vindicated his conduct and retorted the reproaches of Laban with a manly warmth which interests us greatly in his favour. Dwelling upon his care of the flocks, he says, among other things, "That which was torn of beasts I brought not unto thee ; I bore the loss of it ; of my hand didst thou require it." That Laban should thus have exacted that Jacob should make good all casualties to the flock was most ungenerous, and contrary to all known usages of pastoral life, which exonerate the shepherd when he is able to afford such evidence as shall satisfy the owner that the animal is really dead, and has not been sold by the shepherd for his own advantage. For this the carcass itself is the best evidence, as Jacob intimates ; but time and distance will often render its production difficult. Jacob himself was sometimes three days' journey distant from Laban, and in that time the dead carcass would, in an Eastern climate, have become most offensive ; besides that, it would have required the services of a man and a beast six days, going and returning, to take it to Laban. It might also happen that the production of the animal, or even of its skin, which is the next best evidence, would be impossible through its having been carried away. or wholly or in great part consumed by some beast of prey. The experience of this led to the production of some part of the animal being taken as sufficient evidence of its loss through misadventure. Hence the anxiety of the shepherds to rescue from ravenous beasts at least some part of the sheep, to satisfy the owner as to its loss.[c]

40—42. (40) **day..night,** exposed to all extremes of heat and cold in the discharge of his duties. **my..eyes,** through exhaustion and anxiety. (41) **six..cattle,** time occupied by his expedient; *see* on xxx. 32—43. **thou..times,** *see* v. 7. (42) **except..Abraham,**[a] to whom alone I am indebted for what I have. **and..Isaac,** *i.e.* God, who is the object of Isaac's fear. **thou..empty,** notwithstanding thy pretence. **God.. yesternight,** Jacob appeals to L.'s confessed vision or warning.

The climate of Palestine.—"A fine day at this time of year shows the country in its best cloak. A little later in the season every blade of grass will be withered up; the shrubs on the hills will be blackened and parched; the plain will be covered with an impenetrable veil of white mist, known to the African

B.C. 1739.

cern things at a distance." — *Addison.*

[b] *Ouseley.*

Jacob vindicates his conduct

Wroth, *wrathful, angry,* A.S. *wradh.* Chode pa. t. of chide, A.S. *cidan,* to scold.

[a] "All this virtuous indignation is founded on Rachel's lie."—*Alford.*

[b] Ez. xxxiv. 1—5.

"Wrong is wrong: no fallacy can hide it, no subterfuge cover it so shrewdly but that the All-seeing One will discover and punish it."—*Rivarol.*

"We make ourselves more injuries than are offered to us; they many times pass for wrongs in our own thoughts, that were never meant so by the heart of him that speaketh. The apprehension of wrong hurts more than the sharpest part of the wrong done."—*Feltham.*

[c] *Kitto.*

and ascribes his prosperity to God

[a] Ps. cxxiv. 1—3; Ex. iii. 7; Is. viii. 13; Jude ix. Yesternight, the night *last* past. Yester, relating to yesterday, the last day. A. S. *gistran,* yesterday; Ice. *ges,* L. *heri,* orig. *hes,* Gk. *chthes,* Saus. *hyas.*

traveller by the appropriate name of 'smokes.' Above head the sky will be that pitiless glare of changeless blue, never to be relieved by a single speck of cloud till the welcome rains of autumn begin to cool the scorched soil and burning rocks. These fine days of early spring are rare, however, and we must often look for cold pelting rains, mists, hail, and even snow—though the latter very rarely, and only on the central range. While I am writing these lines hail is falling, and dense fogs, accompanied by sharp showers at intervals, are hurried up by the violent equinoctial gale from the south-west, which threatens every moment to tear the frail cotton shelter from over my head and hurl it into the neighbouring valley. Stout guy ropes and piles of stones on the tent-pegs have as yet succeeded in baffling Æolus, though for three nights and days we have been obliged to be on the alert every instant to save our tents from wrack and ruin. Only a few days ago the weather was like a fine June day in England. Such are the changes of temperature to be found in this country from Petra to Damascus. Just two years ago I was snowed up near the former place, at an elevation of 4,500 feet, and three weeks later in Moab, being only 1,500 feet lower, I sighed for a lump of snow to put in my tea, the thermometer standing at 105° Fahr. in the shade. At Damascus (2,340 feet, in the Salahíyeh suburb) snow is rare, though sleet is not uncommon in winter. In summer the thermometer ranges up to 100° Fahr. in the shade, and there is at times a difference of as much as 30° between the dry and wet bulbs."[b]

43—47. (43) **answered**, he still has the effrontery to reply. **are .. is**, these words in *italics* may be read in the past tense—*were, was*. **what can**, *etc.*, it was prob. only his conscious inability that prevented him making some attempt. (44) **make**, *etc.*, *lit.* cut, *see* on xv. 18. (45) **stone**, to mark the site. (46) **stones .. heap**, on wh., aft. they had eaten, the pillar was prob. erected. (47) **Jegar-sahadutha**, Aramaic (Chaldee or Syriac), and **Galeed**, Hebrew; both terms mean the same; *i.e.* heap of witness.

These daughters are my daughters (v. 43).—Laban now turns again, and gives way to the natural affections of a father. Consider the circumstances which tended thus to calm his mind. I. The seven days' journey. II. The Divine warning. III. The mortification resulting from his fruitless search. IV. Jacob's self-defence and the truth of his reproaches. His courage and anger gradually give way to fear and anxiety.[a]

Heaps of stones.—The traveller in Palestine frequently remarks in the open country pyramidic piles of small stones of different heights. These, as I proceed to explain, have significations differing with their shapes. When they are from five to six feet high, and arranged in a line with a certain regularity, they are meant to mark the spot where a battle has taken place between two hostile tribes. When, however, they are formed of five or more stones, and are placed on the boundary of some property, they signify that there two litigants have come to terms, and erected them in token of their agreement, and no one dares to remove these land-marks. Sometimes small heaps surround fields, where the crops are growing or have just been reaped, or are placed upon piles of logs or hewn timbers, signifying that they are private property, so that no one ventures to take them. I have no doubt that this custom was mainly derived from the ancient owners of the soil, for we find many instances of it in the Bible. Laban and Jacob raised a heap of stones as a witness of the covenant between them. Jacob after his vision took the stone which had served for his pillow and "set it up for a pillar" (Ge. xxviii. 18). He that removes his neighbour's landmark is cursed (De. xxvii. 17). Joshua set up twelve stones in the Jordan and twelve others taken from the bed of the river, at Gilgal, in memory of the miracle wrought there for Israel (Jos. iv. 9, 20—22). Again, at the close of his life, he "set up a great stone under an oak," as a witness unto the people, lest they should deny their God (Jos. xxiv. 26, 27). We may also remember that from the earliest times altars were formed in a similar manner (Ge. viii. 20; xii. 7, 8; xxvi. 25).*b*

48—50. (48) **witness**, those who made it and saw it made will testify to its purpose. (49) **Mizpah**,*a* (*watch-tower*) perh. same with *Ramath-mizpeh*,*b* and *Ramoth-gilead*. There were sev. Mizpchs.*c* **watch** .. **another**, certainly L. had need to be "watched." (50) **afflict**, hypocritical profession of a tender regard for the daus. he had "sold."

Mizpah.—There were several places of this name in Palestine. The word, taken in one form, means a high place affording an extensive prospect; and in another, a watch-tower or beacon, as in the present text; whence we may conclude that the names were given to towns in elevated situations, or where watch-towers existed, or where commemorative heaps had been formed to mark the site of some important occurrence. A town built near the scene of the transaction between Jacob and Laban took the name which had been given to the heap of stones. It is mentioned in Ju. xi. and xii., and from the 29th v. of the former chap. it seems to have been "Mizpah of Gilead," to distinguish it from other towns of the same name. It belonged to the half-tribe of Manasseh beyond Jordan, and was the residence of Jephthah. In after times the Ammonites obtained possession of it, and it was in their hands when Judas Maccabæus utterly destroyed it with fire.*d*

51—55. (51) **heap**, wh. J. cast equally with L. (52) **harm**, he draws the limit here. (53) **the .. father**, but their father Terah was an idolater.*a* **sware .. Isaac**, *i.e.* by the only true God, who was the object of Isaac's reverential homage. (54) **sacrifice .. bread**, a religious festival: happy termination of what threatened to be a feud. (55) **blessed**, but of what value and force would be the blessing of such a man? **Laban .. place**,*b* wh. he had been more wise not to have left. Jacob's place no more.

Memorial pillars.—The covenant proposed by Laban and consented to by Jacob was, that seeing (as he alleged) the property was his, it should not be allowed to be shared by others, by Jacob's taking any wives besides his daughters; and that they were neither of them to pass the boundaries defined by these memorials for harm to the other. In this point of view they became boundary monuments, analogous to others of the like kind found in various countries. Witness that mentioned in the treaty of peace between England and Scotland, as recited by Holinshed:—"That Malcomb shall enjoy that part of Northum-

---

B.C. 1739.

to be nice, even to superstition, in keeping thy promises; and therefore thou shouldst be equally cautious in making them."
—*Fuller.*

"Those who can command themselves command others."—*Hazlitt.*

b Pierotti.

Galeed and Mizpah

a Ju. xi. 29; 1 S. vii. 6.

b Jos. xiii. 26.

c As with us there are sev. "beacons" and "beacon-hills."

"Duties are ours; events are God's. This removes an infinite burden from the shoulders of a miserable, tempted, dying, creature. On this consideration only can he securely lay down his head and close his eyes."—*Cecil.*

d Dr. Kitto.

Jacob and Laban separate

a Jos. xxiv. 2.

b Pr. xvi. 7.

"Let our parting be full as charitable as our meeting was; that the pale, envious world, glad of the food of other's miseries, civil dissensions and nuptial strifes, may not feed fat with ours."—*Middleton.*

"Abruptness is an eloquence in parting, when spinning out the

B.C. 1739.

time is but wearing of new sorrow."—*Suckling*.
" Let us not unman each other, part at once; all farewells should be sudden, when for ever."—*Byron*.
c *Dr. Kitto*.

berland that lieth between Tweed, Cumberland, and Stainmore, and do homage to the kings of England for the same. In the midst of Stainmore there shall be a crosse set up, with the king of England's image on the one side, and the king of Scotland's on the other, to signify that one is on his march to England, and the other to Scotland. The crosse was called the Roi-crosse, that is, the crosse of the kings." The intention of the cross, and the pains taken to defend it, as Sir Walter Scott remarks, indicate that it was intended to be a landmark of importance. In this case the two images represented the two contending parties, shown by a different kind of memorial in the transaction between Jacob and Laban.*c*

CHAPTER THE THIRTY-SECOND.

Mahanaim

a Ps. xci. 11; He. i. 14.

b Lu. ii. 13; Ps. ciii. 20, 21; Jos. xxi. 28.

c *Lange*.

"God holds them chain'd in fetters of His power; that without leave, one minute of an hour, they cannot range."— *Du Bartus*.

d *Beecher*.

See *Swanston's Sermons*, 1.

1, 2. (1) **Jacob .. way**, still homeward bound, after an absence of twenty yrs. **angels .. him,***a* prob. in a vision, yet may have been otherwise. (2) **Mahanaim***b* (*two camps*), prob. they were on the right hand and left hand, seeming to surround him.

Hosts of angels.—Consider why the angels are called hosts. I. From their multitude. II. From their order. III. From their power for the protection of the saints, and the resistance and punishment of the wicked. IV. From their rendering a cheerful obedience as becometh a warlike host.*c*

Surrounded by angels.—I did not see, early in the morning, the flight of those birds that filled all the bushes and all the orchard trees, but they were there, though I did not see their coming, and I hear their songs afterwards. It does not matter whether you have ministered to you yet those perceptions by which you perceive angelic existence. The fact that we want to bear in mind is, that we are environed by them, that we move in their midst. How, where, what the philosophy is, whether it be spiritual philosophy, no man can tell, and they least that think they know most about it. The fact which we prize and lay hold of is this, that angelic ministration is a part, not of the heavenly state, but of the universal condition of men, and that, as soon as we become Christ's, we come not to the home of the living God, but to the " innumerable company of angels."*d*

Jacob's message to Esau

a Ge. xiv. 6; De. ii. 12.

b Ge. xxv. 30.

c Ge. xxvii. 29.

d Pr. xv. 1.

"To be a finite being is no crime, and to be the Infinite is not to be a creditor. As man was not consulted he does

3—5. (3) **and .. Esau**, Laban gone, an angry brother now to be dealt with. In the journey of life one diff. succeeds another. **Seir** (*hairy, bristly*). mt. range anc. inhab. by Horites.*a* The N. of Seir now *Jebal;* the S., *esh-Sherah*. **the .. Edom** (*red*). so called fr. Esau, who aft. possessed it, having sold his birthright for the *red* pottage.*b* (4) **commanded**, he had sent, some time bef.: Jacob had not yet crossed the Jabbok. **lord**, language of conciliation. Jacob was strictly E.'s lord.*c* **and .. now**, without coming to claim my inheritance. (5) **I .. women-servants,***d* now a rich man disinterestedly seeking reconciliation, not a desperate man under stress of poverty.

Jacob under trial (on the whole chapter).—I. Trials are generally the result of transgressions. Learn hence—1. When tempted to transgress, to see not only the shining seduction, but also the dark retribution behind; 2. In trial not to murmur against God's providence, but to measure rightly our own perversity. II. While God righteously permits the transgressions of His people to bear their appropriate fruit of trials, for those trials He graciously prepares them (vv. 1, 2.) III. In trial, the most efficacious of all resources is a prayerful committal of ourself to the providence of God (vv. 9—11). Three excellent things in Jacob's prayer—1. A grateful acknowledgment of past mercies; 2. A humble confession of unworthiness; 3. A believing pleading of God's promises. IV. Prayerful invocation, in trial, of God's providential care does not exclude the employment of all lawful means suggested by human prudence (vv. 7, 8; 13—23). V. There is no final issue from trials until pardon of the transgressions to which they are due is won from God (vv. 24—31).[e]

Bear, forbear, forgive.—The attachment of the Rev. John Eliot, usually called "the apostle to the Indians," to peace and union among Christians was exceedingly great. When he heard ministers complain that some in their congregations were too difficult for them, the substance of his advice would be, "Brother, compass them! Brother, learn the meaning of those three little words—bear, forbear, forgive." His love of peace, indeed, almost led him to sacrifice right itself. When a bundle of papers was laid before an assembly of ministers, which contained the particulars of a contention between parties who he thought ought at once to be agreed, he hastily threw them into the fire, and said, "Brethren, wonder not at what I have done; I did it on my knees this morning before I came among you."

6—8. (6) **and .. Jacob**, *i.e.* to his camp on the N. of the Jabok. **he .. thee**, they seem to have brought no reply, save that he would come. **and .. him**, the band by the aid of wh. he was prob. subjugating Seir. (7) **afraid**, not knowing the purpose of his bro. **distressed**, perplexed, straitened; notwithstanding Mahanaim. **and .. bands**, he prudently prepares for the worst. (8) **said .. escape**, this, an Arab expedient; and an ill. of the old cunning of the man.

Forgiveness, a necessary virtue.—Man has an unfortunate readiness, in the evil hour, after receiving an affront, to draw together all the moon-spots on the other person into an outline of shadow, and a night-piece, and to transform a single deed into a whole life; and this only in order that he may thoroughly relish the pleasure of being angry. In love, he has fortunately the opposite faculty of crowding together all the light parts and rays of its object into one focus, by means of the burning glass of imagination, and letting its sun burn without its spots; but he too generally does this only when the beloved and often censured being is already beyond the skies. In order, however, that we should do this sooner and oftener, we ought to act like Winckelmann, but only in another way. As he, namely, set aside a particular half-hour of each day for the purpose of beholding and meditating on his too happy existence in Rome, so we ought daily or weekly to dedicate and sanctify a solitary hour for the purpose of summing up the virtues of our families, our wives, our children, and our friends, and viewing them in this beautiful crowded assemblage of their good qualities. And, indeed, we should do so for this reason, that we may not forgive and love too late, when the beloved beings are already departed hence, and are beyond our reach.[a]

B.C. 1739.

not flud himself a party in a bargain, but a child in the household of love. Reconciliation, therefore, is not the consequence of paying a debt, or procuring atonement for an injury, but an organic process of the human life."—*John Weiss.*

[e] *Pulpit Analyst.*

"Be circumspect in your dealings, and let the seed you plant be the offspring of prudence and care; thus fruit follows the fair blossom, as honour follows a good life."—*H. Ballou.*

the messenger's return

"This plan seems not to have been first invented by Jacob: but it may be conjectured that large caravans used at that time to take this precaution against hostile attacks. Sir H. Blount relates in his *Travels*, that he travelled with a caravan which had divided itself in like manner into two troops; one of which that went before, being attacked by robbers, had an action with them, and were plundered, whereas the other escaped uninjured."—*Rosenmuller.*

[a] *Richter.*

[Cap. xxxii. 9—19.

B.C. 1739.

Jacob's prayer

a Ge. xxxi. 3; xxviii. 13.

b Ps. 1. 15; xci. 15; Ph. iv. 6; 1 S. xxx. 6; 2 Ch. xx. 12.

c 2. S. vii. 18; Ge. xxiv. 27; Is. lxiii. 7; Job viii. 7.

d Is. xliii. 26; He. x. 23.

e. 9, 10. *S. Lowell*, 224; *G. Lambert*, 187; *W. A. Gunn*, 62; *R. P. Buddi, Com.*, ii. 290.

e *Jenkyn Jones*.

"When a pump is frequently used, the wa er pours out at the first stroke, because it is high; but if the pump has not been used for a long time, the water gets low, and when you want it, you must pump a long while; and the water comes only after great efforts. It is so with prayer. If we are instant in prayer, every little circumstance awakens the disposition to pray, and desire and words are always ready; but if we neglect prayer, it is difficult for us to pray, for the water in the well gets low."—*F. Neff.*

f *T. Grantham, B.D.*

g *Knight.*

Jacob sends a present to Esau

a Pr. xviii. 16. Milch, *that is milked* (milk, *lit.* to stroke, to handle); A.S., *meolc*

9—12. (9) **said**, aft. making provision for safety, he betakes himself to prayer. **the .. saidst,** *etc.*,*a* he pleads his obedience to the command; and the promise too. (10) **worthy .. servant,***b* nor are better men than Jacob worthy of God's mercies. *lit.* "I am less than all the mercies." **staff ..** **Jordan,** the staff was all his substance once. **become,***c* by the blessing of God. **two bands,** *v.* 7. (11) **smite .. children,** *lit.* smite me, *even* the mo. with the children : implying that if they were killed he would have nothing. (12) **saidst,***d* admitting his own unworthiness, he casts himself on the Divine word.

Jacob's prayer.—We shall look upon the spirit pervading this prayer. It is a spirit of—I. Reverence. II. Humility. The sense of God's greatness, and of his own weakness humbled him. III. Thankfulness. When comparing the present with the past, his heart is filled with thankfulness to God for the great wealth given him. IV. Dependency upon God. To save himself from Esau he hopes not, unless the Lord comes to his help. V. Great confidence in God. He rests himself on the promises given him, and feels assured that deliverance in some way or other will be given him.*e Jacob's prayer.*—I. The circumstances under which this prayer was offered. Jacob's separation from Laban, return to Canaan, meeting with Esau, and his fear thereat. Its component parts—1. An address to the Almighty ; 2. A humble acknowledgment of his own unworthiness and of God's abundant mercy and loving-kindness ; 3. An earnest petition for deliverance from an impending danger. III. Some lessons of instruction that we may derive from it—1. That prayer is the best resource in every period of trouble and perplexity ; 2. That the language of the heart, and not merely of the lip, is what God looks upon with favour; 3. That we should keep firm hold of God's promises.*f*

Valuing prosperity.—A king was sitting in a vessel with a Persian slave. The boy began to cry, and would not be pacified. The king's diversion was interrupted. A philosopher, who was in the ship, said. "If you will command me, I will silence him." The king replied, "It will be an act of great kindness." The philosopher ordered them to throw the lad into the sea ; and, after several plunges, they laid hold of the hair of his head, and dragged him into the ship. When he got out of the water, he sat down quietly in a corner of the vessel. The king was pleased, and asked how this was brought about. The philosopher replied, "At first, he had never experienced the danger of being drowned ; neither knew he the safety of a ship." In like manner, he knoweth the value of prosperity who hath encountered adversity. O thou! who hast satisfied thine hunger, to thee a barley-loaf is beneath notice ; that seems loveliness to me which in thy sight appears deformity. To the nymphs of paradise, purgatory would be hell; but ask the inhabitants of hell whether purgatory is not paradise.*g*

1 —19. (13) **there,** N. of Jabbok at its union with the Jordan. **took .. hand,***a* not that which was nearest at hand : but, prob. that wh. he carefully selected. (14) **two,** *etc.,* 550 head of cattle : a princely gift: sugg. of Jacob's wealth, of his fear of his bro., and of his desire for reconciliation. (15) **thirty ..** **camels,** these, on acc. of milk, esp. valuable. (16) **every ..**

Cap. xxxii. 20-26.] GENESIS. 141

themselves, *i.e.* of each kind. **put..drove**, that any good impression on Esau's mind might be deepened by successive arrivals. (17) **and**, *etc.*, sent select messages as well as gifts. (18) **servant..lord**, by respectful terms seeking to disarm resentment. (19) **second**, *etc.*, giving definite instructions in each case.

Eastern flocks and herds.—From the present which Jacob made to his brother Esau, consisting of five hundred and eighty head of different sorts, we may form some idea of the countless numbers of great and small cattle which he had acquired in the service of Laban. In modern times, the numbers of cattle in the Turcoman flocks which feed on the fertile plains of Syria are almost incredible. They sometimes occupy three or four days in passing from one part of the country to another. Chardin had an opportunity of seeing a clan of Turcoman shepherds on their march, about two days' distance from Aleppo. The whole country was covered with them. Many of their principal people, with whom he conversed on the road, assured him that there were four hundred thousand beasts of carriage, camels, horses, oxen, cows, and asses, and three millions of sheep and goats. This astonishing account of Chardin is confirmed by Dr. Shaw, who states that several Arabian tribes, who can bring no more than three or four hundred horses into the field, are possessed of more than so many thousand camels, and triple the number of sheep and black cattle. Russell, in his history of Aleppo, speaks of vast flocks which pass that city every year, of which many sheep are sold to supply the inhabitants. The flocks and herds which belonged to the Jewish patriarchs were not more numerous.*b*

20—23. (20) **appease,***a* *lit.* I will cover (*i.e.* pacify) his face. **accept**, *lit.* will lift up my face. (21) **night**, one of the most memorable nights on record. (22) **Jabbok,***b* wh. flows into the Jordan on the E. side, about half-way betw. Dead S. and S. of Galilee. (23) **brook**, or *wady.*

The river Jabbok.—The Jabbok lies on the east of the Jordan, and takes its rise among the mountains in the south-east of Gilead. The natives call it *Nahr-el-Zerkah*, or Zerkah, from a village of that name in the neighbourhood. It flows with a rapid course for about fifty miles, over a rocky bed, towards the Jordan, which it enters about forty miles to the south of the Sea of Tiberias. The waters of the stream are clear, and agreeable to the taste, while the banks are well wooded with wild olive and almond trees, tall reeds and shrubs. Buckingham says that when he crossed the river it was ten yards wide, and that the stream, being deeper than the Jordan and quite as rapid, was forded with difficulty. It separated the kingdom of Sihon from that of Og, king of Bashan (Deut. ii. 36, 37). When Jacob was returning from Haran, with his family and flocks, he crossed over the ford Jabbok, and there, hard by the rippling stream, in the silence of the night, he wrestled with an angel, and received in his change of name a token of God's favour.*c*

24—26. (24) **alone**, not crossing himself till all was safely over. **man**, but a supernatural being, an angel.*a* (25) **he..thigh,***b* socket of the hip-joint, this, that Jacob, though a conqueror, might be humbled. (26) **let..breaketh**, Jacob is

---

B.C. 1739.

a melean, to milk; Ger. *milch—melken*, to handle; akin to L. *mulgeo*, to milk; *mulceo*, to stroke; Gk. *amelgo*, to squeeze.

"It passes in the world for greatness of mind, to be perpetually giving and loading people with bounties; but it is one thing to know how to give, and another thing not to know how to keep. Give me a heart that is easy and open; but I will have no holes in it; let it be bountiful with judgment, but I will have nothing run out of it I know not how."—*Seneca.*

"To reveal its complacence by gifts is one of the native dialects of love."—*Sigourney.*
b Paxton.

Jacob sends his company over the Jabbok

a Heb. *akapperah panav; tr. kaphar*, t) cover, the term usually employed under the law to sig. "making atonement." The LXX. reads "I will propitiate his countenance."
b Jos. xii. 2.

"A gift—its kind, value, and appearance; the silence or the pomp that attends it; the style in which it reaches you—may decide the dignity or vulgarity of the giver."—*Lavater.*
c Bib. Treasury.

Jacob wrestles with the angel

B.C. 1739.

a Ho. xii. 3, 4; Ep. vi. 12 The Jews held this was Esau's guardian A., or the A. that protected his country. Many think the "man" was a created A. The fathers held that the A. was one of the manifestations of the Eternal Son; an anticipation of this incarnation. Perh. this is the right view; see vv. 23, 30.
b 2 Co. xii 7.
c Is. lxiv. 7; xviii. 1; Ma. xv. 28; Lu. xxiv. 28, 29.
v. 26, A. Buchanan, 366; Lord A. Hervey, II. 244; Bp. Cowper, 203.
d J. C. Jones.

e R. A. Griffin.

f D. Longwill, M.A. "For the most part we should pray rather in aspiration than petition, rather by hoping than requesting; in which spirit also we may breath a devout wish for a blessing on others upon occasions when it might be presumptuous to beg it."—Leigh Hunt.

g J. Jones.

h Dr. J. Wotherspoon.

"Faith builds in the dungeon and the lazar-house its sublimest shrines; and up, through rods of stone, that shut out the eye of heaven; ascends the ladder where the angels glide to and fro, prayer."—Lytton. "Prayer is not eloquence, but earnestness; not the definition of helplessness, but

reminded of the work that needs his presence. **said .. me,**' without that blessing, how should the work succeed: with it, he would be in time.

Jacob and the angel (vv. 24—29).—I. Jacob praying. 1. The text shows us that Jacob was alone when God appeared to him; 2. We are also informed that it was night; 3. Further, the narrative teaches us that he was sunk in a deep fear. II. Jacob wrestling. 1. There was bodily wrestling; 2. There was mental wrestling; 3. The struggle was a long one. III. Jacob prevailing. 1. He earnestly desires a blessing; 2. His prayer is answered.*d*

The advent at Peniel (vv. 24—30). This narrative reminds us of—I. The traits of prevailing prayer. 1. Boldness; 2. Faith; 3. Perseverance. II. The season of most earnest pleading. 1. When alone; 2. After doing a worthy action; 3. In the night. III. The trials of importunate believers. 1. The apparent unwillingness of God; 2. The infirmities of the flesh. IV. The comforts of praying hearts. Jacob wrestled with One who—1. Gave him strength; 2. Had all power to bless; 3. Meant to give way. V. The victory of courageous wrestling. Jacob—1. Gained a royal name; 2. Was brought into high fellowship with God; 3. Was strengthened to meet Esau; 4. Secured lasting renown.*e* *The supplanter become a prince* (vv. 24—29).—We see here—I. Jacob helplessly hanging upon God. Jacob's thigh being paralysed, he clings helplessly to the man of God. This is expressive of the inward change; he relies no longer on his mean cunning, he is no longer Jacob. II. Jacob prevailing mightily as a prince with God. He prevailed through his helpless clinging to God. "When I am weak, then I am strong." III. Jacob invested with the true glory and blessedness of a prince.*f* *Jacob at Peniel* (vv. 24—32).—Consider—I. Jacob's wrestling. It was—1. A personal contest; 2. A protracted contest; 3. A contest with an unknown person. II. Jacob's victory. It was—1. A partial victory; 2. A victory by which he obtained a better name; 3. A victory ever to be remembered.*g* *Importunity in prayer* (vv. 24—29).—Introduction founded on the history. I. Explain this holy wrestling in prayer. Wrestling implies some resistance to be overcome. Some of the chief obstructions which must be overcome are—1. A sense of guilt whelming the soul; 2. A frowning providence discouraging the mind; 3. Unbelieving thoughts and inward temptations; 4. Coldness and slothfulness of the heart; 5. Discouragement through Divine delays. II. The reasonableness of importunity in praying—1. It strengthens in our minds a sense of God's glory; 2. Our unworthiness vindicates it; 3. The inestimable value of the blessings to be obtained requires it. III. Its advantages—1. It prepares for blessings in many cases; it is itself the actual possession of them; 2. It has the promises of success; 3. Memorable examples confirm its worth. IV. Improvement—1. How many have cause to mourn their lack of this spirit; 2. Its absence is one cause of the low state of religion; 3. As you would persevere in prayer,—be watchful and circumspect,—observe the course of Providence,—be much in intercession for others.*h*

Importunity in prayer.—Wrestling and importunity in prayer is in many cases itself the possession of the very mercies we desire. It is the exercise of almost every gracious disposition.

To increase in sanctification, to have his graces strengthened, his corruptions subdued, is the habitual and prevailing desire of every real believer. But how can this be more effectually obtained than by fervent prayer? How, and where, can any gracious disposition be either more improved or more clearly discerned than when it is in exercise? Faith, love, penitential sorrow, trust, and resignation, are the very essentials to a wrestling believer.[i]

27—29. (27) **name**? a question that would be a reminder of character. (28) **name** .. **Israel**,[a] *i.e.* princely prevailer with God. **men**,[b] he prevailed with men as the result of prevailing with God. (29) **wherefore**, *etc.*,[c] I had a reason for asking thy name; what is *thy* reason? or, is not my name clear to thee? **blessing**, the blessing more fully revealed then. **there**, the place of prayer was the place of blessing.

Jacob's wrestling (vv. 24—29).—There is before us the record of an inward spiritual struggle, as real now as then; as real in every earnest man as it was in Jacob. We take these points—I. The nameless secret of existence. 1. The contrast observable between this and a former revelation made to Jacob's soul; 2. The end and aim of Jacob's struggle—to know God; 3. That this desire of Jacob was not the one we should naturally have expected on such an occasion. II. The revelation of that secret to the soul. 1. It was revealed by awe; 2. The revelation was made in an unsyllabled blessing; 3. Its effect was to change Jacob's character. Jacob becomes Israel.[d]

Prevailing prayer.—Prayer is the work of God's Spirit in us, and therefore cannot be in vain. Faithful prayer was never lost, nor never shall be, while God is true. It hath strongly produced means, qualified and fitted means, wonderfully protected means, united means, prospered means. If we cease not begging, God will not cease giving. Go on to seek God, He cannot hold out long. Prayers and importunities will break His heart, extort and force mercy from Him. We have wearied Him by sin; let us weary Him by prayer. We have been impudent in transgressions; be impudent in seeking forgiveness. We have been bent to perpetual backsliding; let us be constant in suing for deliverance,—so shall we be as Jacob.[e]

30—32. (30) **Peniel** (*the face of God*). **and** .. **preserved**,[a] the vision instead of destroying, preserved life: prob. ref. to safety in prospect of meeting Esau. (31) **sun** .. **him**, bright herald of joyous day, aft. night of anxiety and prayer. **he** .. **thigh**, his physical defect a reminder of that memorable night. (32) **the** .. **shrank**, Heb. *nasheh*, the sciatic nerve (*nervus ischiadicus*) called *nasheh* by the Arabs to this day.

God seen and yet unseen (v. 30; comp. Ex. xxxiii. 20).—I. Consider the Scriptures that testify of God's invisibility. 1. His invisibility is affirmed (Col. i. 15; He. xi. 27); 2. The utter impossibility of seeing Him is affirmed (1 Tim. vi. 16; Jo. i. 18, v. 37). II. Observe how God did reveal Himself. 1. By an audible voice to Abraham and others; 2. By magnificent symbols; 3. In human or angelic form. III. Note that God has revealed Himself more truly and favourably in His Son Jesus Christ. Learn—(1) The folly and wickedness of all images to represent God;

B.C. cir. 1739.

"the feeling of it; not figures of speech, but compunction of soul."—*H. More.*

i *J. Wotherspoon.*

Jacob's name is changed to Israel

a Ho. xii. 3—5.
b Ge. xxxiii. 4.
c Ju. xiii. 18.
d F. W. Robertson, M.A.

"Prayer among men is supposed a means to change the person to whom we pray; but prayer to God doth not change Him, but fits us to receive the things prayed for."—*Stillingfleet.*

"We pray for trifles without so much as a thought of the greatest blessings; and we are not ashamed, many times, to ask God for that which we should blush to own to our neighbour."—*Seneca.*

e *W. Sedgwicke.*

Peniel
a Ex. xxiv. 10, 11; De. v. 24; xxxiv. 10; Ju. vi. 22; xiii. 22; Is. vi. 5; Ex. xxxiii. 20; Jo. i. 18; Col. i. 15; 1 Co. xii
b Dr. Burns.

"The custom prevailing among the Jews to this day of abstaining religiously from eating this sinew seems a lasting monument of the historical truth of this

B.C. 1739.

wonderful event in the life of Jacob."—Spk r.'s Com.
"We, ignorant of ourselves, beg often our own harm, which the wise powers deny us for our good; so find we profit by losing of our prayers."
—*Shakespeare.*
c *Dr. Ryland.*

(2) The grossness of all material symbols; (3) The blessedness of seeing God in Christ.[b]

Deeds of prayer.—Prayer has divided seas, rolled up flowing rivers, made flinty rocks gush into fountains, quenched flames of fire, muzzled lions, disarmed vipers and poisons, marshalled the stars against the wicked, stopped the course of the moon, arrested the sun in its rapid race, burst open iron gates, recalled souls from eternity, conquered the strongest devils, commanded legions of angels down from heaven. Prayer has bridled and chained the raging passions of man, and routed and destroyed vast armies of proud, daring, blustering atheists. Prayer has brought one man from the bottom of the sea, and carried another in a chariot of fire to heaven. What has not prayer done?[c]

CHAPTER THE THIRTY-THIRD.

the meeting of Jacob and Esau

a *Jenkyn Jones.*
v. 1, 2. *Dr. H. Hughes. Fem. Char.* i. 210.
"There are ceremonious bows that throw you to a greater distance than the wrong end of any telescope."
—*Ruffini.*

"All ceremonies are in themselves very silly things, but yet a man of the world should know them. They are the outworks of manners and decency, which would be too often broken in upon if it were not for that defence which keeps the enemy at proper distance."—*Chesterfield.*

b *Col. Johnson.*

Jacob introduces his wives and children to Esau

a Ge. xxxii. 28;

1—3. (1) **looked**, now without fear. **Esau..men**, an Arab chief at the head of a great band of warriors. **handmaids**, Zilpah and Bilhah. (2) **Rachel..hindermost**, the dearest in the safest place. (3) **bowed..brother**, these salutations of respect and humility followed ea. other at intervals.

The brothers reconciled.—This chapter relates the reconciliation of Jacob and Esau. Concerning this we notice that it was—I. A reconciliation after a long separation. II. A most desirable reconciliation. Desirable on account of—1. The happiness of their aged parents; 2. Their own families; 3. Their own spiritual well-being. III. A reconciliation which brought to sight the best traits of their character; 1. Prayerfulness; 2. Humility; 3. Disinterestedness.[a]

Approaching Royalty in the East.—"We saw the king," he says, "seated upon his throne, in an upper room, open, and supported by pillars. When we came to the end of the walk turning toward and fronting the king, we made two low bows, as did also the minister, whose motions we observed and repeated; then advancing to the first cross-walk, we made another bow; proceeding thence until we arrived within about fifty yards of the building, we again halted and made two bows. Here we took off and left our slippers, and walked in the cloth boots to another turning and bowed again. We now came to a small door, from which a flight of steps led up to the open room. These were covered with blue glazed tiles. At the head of the stairs was the door of the king's sitting-room; on advancing to which, fronting the king, we made two bows, rather low, and severally entered the room, keeping close to the wall on the left. When we had taken our stations here, we each made a low bow and arranged ourselves standing. There were six pauses and nine bows; the number of both diminishes with the increase of rank in the person admitted to an audience."[b]

4—7. (4) **ran**, comp. this with J.'s slow and ceremonious approach. **fell..him**,[a] perfect reconciliation. **wept**, in fulness of joy: but fr. dif. causes. (5) **who..thee?** lit. who are these to thee? i.e. in what relation do they stand to thee? **graciously**,[b] all he was and had was of grace. (6, 7) **Then**, *etc.*, it has been noted that E. made no reply, kind or otherwise, to these salutations: perh. he was overwhelmed with surprise.

Reconciliation of Esau and Jacob.—I. The resentments of brethren are usually exceedingly deep. 1. The disappointment of the two parties is greater than in enmity between comparative strangers; 2. The aggravating circumstances are more numerous; 3. The foundations of their regard are overthrown. II. However deep the resentment of any one may be, we may hope by proper means to overcome it. The means we should use are—1. Prayer to God; 2. A conciliatory conduct to man. III. When once a reconciliation is effected, extreme caution is necessary to preserve and maintain it. We must aim at this by—1. Mutual kindness and endearments; 2. Abstaining from all mention of past grievances; 3. Guarding against that kind or degree of intercourse that may rekindle animosities. Application:—Are there any who—(1) Are involved in disputes? Follow after peace. (2) Desire reconciliation with an offended friend? Be willing rather to make, than exact submission. (3) Have an opportunity of promoting peace? Embrace it gladly, and exert yourselves impartially.[c]

Eastern salutations.—Here comes another caravan, of twenty camels at least. Such a shaking of hands! Foremost is our sheikh, who advances to the old grey-bearded—I cannot say grey-headed (for who can see an Arab's bare head?) Sheikh Beshârah. from Sinai, probably the same who was Dr. Robinson's guide. The sheikhs take each other by the right hand; then, throwing the left round each other's necks, they kiss five times on either cheek. They then inquire after the health of themselves and their friends. How like does this seem to the sons of Isaac,—" And Esau ran to meet him, and embraced him, and fell on his neck and kissed him." Here are the same four things:—they run to meet, they embrace, they fall on the neck, they kiss. So in the case of Laban, "when Laban heard the tidings of Jacob his sister's son, he ran to meet him, and embraced him, and kissed him" (Gen. xxix. 13). Still more does the meeting of Sheikhs Sulimân and Beshârah remind us of Aaron and Moses—" He went and met him in the mount of God and kissed him,"—for this is the region in which the two brothers met, and their mode of salutation was the same.[d]

8—12. (8) **what .. met?** ref. to the presents; wh. fr. magnitude he had perh. thought was all his bro. had. **lord,** J. still adopts this form of address. (9) **brother,** in exchange for *lord.* **keep .. thyself,** generosity: he would not have J. think he was influenced by these presents. (10) **present,** thus convince me we are at one again. **for .. face,** that sight is well worth all I offer. (11) **blessing,**[a] a sugg. that his gift might bring a blessing. **enough,** *see* Heb., E. says. *yesh li rab,* "I have much," and J. *yesh li kol,* "I have all."[b] (12) **let,** *etc.*, E. proposes to make J.'s way his. **I .. thee,** prob. intending to be his bro.'s escort.

Presents in the East.—It is the custom of the East, when one invites a superior, to make him a present after the repast, as an acknowledgment of his trouble. Frequently it is done before it, as it is no augmentation of honour to go to the house of an inferior. They make no presents to equals, or those who are below themselves.[c] Not to receive a present, is at once to show

B.C. 1739.

Ps. xxxiv. 4; Pr. xvi. 7; xxi. 1.

b Ps. cxxvii. 3; 1 Ch. xxviii. 5; Oe. xli. 52.

c C. Simeon, *M.A.*

' Sir, you are very welcome to our house, it must appear in other ways than words, therefore, I scant this breathing courtesy." — *Shakespeare.*

" Absence, with all its pains, is by this charming moment wiped away."*- Thomson.*

" Ah me! the world is full of meetings such as this,—a thrill, a voiceless challenge and reply, and sudden partings after!" *Willis.*

" The joys of meeting pay the pangs of absence; else who could bear it?"—*Rowe.*

"There are moments of mingled sorrow and tenderness, which hallow the caresses of affection." — *W. Irving.*

d Dr. Bonar.

Esau declines the present

a 2 K. v. 15.

b "Jacob had all, because he had the God of all." —*Trapp.*

" The Christian's inheritance will leave him riches enough, and his prerogative bounty enough, after all the abatements that his generosity prompts him to make."—*Bush.*

c Burder.

B.C. 1739.

Roberts.

Jacob and Esau separate
a *Harmer.*
b *Roberts.*
c *Ibid.*
"Gentle feelings produce profoundly beneficial effects upon stern natures. It is the spring rain which melts the ice-covering of the earth, and causes it to open to the beams of heaven."—*F. Bremer.*
"A more glorious victory cannot be gained over another man than this, that when the injury began on his part, the kindness should begin on ours."—*Tillotson.*

El-Elohe-Israel
a Jos. xiii. 27; Ju. viii. 4, 5; Ps. lx. 6; cviii 7.
b Jo. iii. 23; Ac. vii. 15, 16; Ge. xxxiv. 2.
c *Robinson. B.R.*, iii. 322; *Wilson, Lands of Bib.*, ii. 72.
d Jos. xxiv. 32; Jn. iv. 5.
e The *Kesitah* was perh. a coin with the impression of a lamb upon it. f Ge. xxxii. 28.
g *Lange.*
"Religion is the final centre of repose—the goal to which all things tend; apart from which man is a shadow, his very existence a riddle, and the stupendous scenes of nature

that the thing desired will not be granted. Hence, nothing can be more repulsive, nothing more distressing, than to return the gifts to the giver. Jacob evidently laboured under this impression, and therefore pressed his brother to receive the gifts, if he had found favour in his sight.*d*

13—16. (13) **men .. die**, Esau's men would move too fast for Jacob's cattle. (14) **softly**, gently. **according**, *etc.*, the cattle and children were to decide the pace. (15) **let .. lord**, he and his bro. were at peace; that was all he needed. (16) **so**, *etc.*, a bright day in the hist. of the two bros.

Pastoral life in the East.—"Their flocks," says Chardin, speaking of those who now live in the East after the patriarchal manner, " feed down the places of their encampments so quick, by the great numbers which they have, that they are obliged to remove them too often, which is very destructive to their flocks, on account of the young ones, which have not strength enough to follow."*a*

Travelling in the East.—People having taken a journey, say, "We came to this place according to the walking of our feet," "It was done according to the foot of the children;" which means, they did not come in a palankeen, or any other vehicle, but on foot. From this it appears that the females and the children performed their journey on foot, and that according to their strength.*b*

Presents in the East.—As Esau had received valuable gifts from his brother, he wished to make some present in return; and having received cattle, it would not have looked well to have given the same kind of gift that he had received; he therefore offered some of his people (who were no doubt born in his house) as a kind of recompense for what he had received, and as a proof of his attachment.*c*

17—20. (17) **Succoth**,*a* (*booths*) site not identified. (18) **Shalem**,*b* (*safe, peace*) site uncertain:*c* prob. not a place, and we should read "and J. came *in peace* to the city of Shechem." **Shechem**, see on xii. 6. (19) **bought**,*d* *etc.*. a proof of his faith that the whole land would one day be his. **money**, Heb. *kesitah*,*e* *i.e.* lamb. (20) **El-Elohe-Israel**,*f* (*God, the God of Israel*). Jacob had to this time called God " the God of Abraham:" this title sugg. that J. felt he was accepted of God.

Jacob at Succoth.—The settlement at Succoth.—I. How promising; a happy return! Prosperous acquisition of the parcel of land; peaceful relations with the Shechemites: religious toleration. II. How seriously endangered: through Jacob's carelessness. He does not return early enough to Bethel to fulfil his vow. Probably he even considers the altar at Shechem a substitute. His love for Rachel makes him tolerant to her teraphim. III. How fearfully disturbed (ch. xxxiv.). Dinah, Simeon and Levi. IV. The happy conclusion caused by Jacob's repentance and God's protection.*g*

Early coins.—There is very great reason to believe that the earliest coins struck were used both as weights and money, and indeed this circumstance is in part proved by the very names of certain of the Greek and Roman coins. Thus the Attic *mina* and the Roman *libra* equally signify a pound; and the στατηρ (*stater*) of the Greeks, so called from weighing, is decisive as to this point.

[Cap. xxxiv. 1—5.] GENESIS. 147

The Jewish shekel, was also a weight as well as a coin: three thousand shekels, according to Arbuthnot, being equal in weight and value to one talent. This is the oldest coin of which we anywhere read, for it occurs (Gen. xxiii. 16), and exhibits direct evidence against those who date the first coinage of money so low as the time of Crœsus or Darius, it being there expressly said, that Abraham weighed to Ephron four hundred shekels of silver, *current money with the merchant.* Having considered the origin and high antiquity of coined money, we proceed to consider the *stamp* or *impression* which the first money bore. The primitive race of men being shepherds, and their wealth consisting in their cattle, in which Abraham is said to have been rich, for greater convenience metals were substituted for the commodity itself. It was natural for the representative sign to bear impressed the object which it represented; and thus accordingly the earliest coins were stamped with the figure of an ox or a sheep: for proof that they actually did thus impress them, we can again appeal to the high authority of Scripture: for there we are informed that *Jacob bought a parcel of a field for a hundred pieces of money.* The original Hebrew translated pieces of money, is *kesitoth*, which signifies lambs, with the figure of which the metal was doubtless stamped.[h]

B.C. cir. 1732.

"which surround him as unmeaning as the leaves which the sibyl scattered in the wind."—*R. Hall.*

"Nothing but religion is capable of changing pains into pleasures."—*Stanislaus.*

"Religion is a necessary, an indispensable element in any great human character. There is no living without it. Religion is the tie that connects man to his Creator, and holds him to his throne."— *D. Webster.*

h *Maurice, Indian Ant.*

CHAPTER THE THIRTY-FOURTH.

1—5. (1) **Dinah**,[a] not less than fifteen yrs. old. **see**,[b] know, bec. acquainted with. (2) **Hamor** (*an ass.*) **prince**, his station flattering to her vanity. **defiled**, *lit.* humbled. (3) **and .. damsel**, *i.e.* "tried to gain her affections,"[c] *lit.* "spake to the heart of the damsel." (4) **get .. wife**, this not simply for reparation, but fr. affection. (5) **and .. peace**, *i.e.* took no measures. **until .. come**, when he would consult with them.

Early marriages in the East.—Voltaire objects, in like manner, to the probability of the Old Testament history, in the account given us there of the dishonour done to Dinah, the daughter of Jacob, by a Hivite prince in Canaan (Gen. xxxiv. 1, 2), who he supposes was too young to have suffered such an injury, or to have excited the affections of Shechem. The two following citations will prove there was nothing incredible in it, and that an ardent young Eastern prince may be supposed to have been guilty of such a fact. The first citation shall be from Niebuhr's account of Arabia: "I have heard speak in Persia of one that was a mother at thirteen: they there marry girls at nine years of age; and I knew a man whose wife was no more than ten years old when the marriage was consummated." The other is from Dr. Shaw's travels and observations. Speaking of the inhabitants of Barbary, he says, "The men, indeed, by wearing only the tiara, or a scull cap, are exposed so much to the sun, that they quickly attain the swarthiness of the Arab; but the women, keeping more at home, preserve their beauty until they are thirty: at which age they begin to be wrinkled, and are usually past childbearing. It sometimes happens that one of these girls is a mother at eleven, and a grandmother at two-and-twenty." If they become mothers at eleven, they might easily become the

Dinah is seduced by Shechem

a Ge. xxx. 12.

b Tit. ii. 4, 5; Ge. xlvii. 46; see also *Jos. Ant.* i. 21.

c *Alford.*

"Woman's thoughts are ever turned upon appearing amiable to the opposite sex; they talk, and move, and smile with a design upon us; every feature of their faces, every part of their dress is filled with snares and allurements. There would be no such animals as prudes or coquettes in the world, where there not such an animal as man."—*Addison.*

"O, if the loving closed heart of a good woman should open before a man,

b.c. 1732.

how much controlled tenderness, how many veiled sacrifices and dumbvirtues would he see reposing therein!"
—*Richter,
d Harmer.*

conference of Hamor and Jacob
a Percy.
"Secrecy of design, when combined with rapidity of execution, like the column that guided Israel in the desert, becomes the guardian pillar of light and fire to our friends, a cloud of overwhelming and impenetrable darkness to our enemies."—*Colton.*
"I will govern my life and my thoughts as if all the world were to see the one and to read the other; for what does it signify to make a thing secret to my neighbour, when to God all is open?"—*Seneca.*

Shechem proposes to marry Dinah
a Ep. iv. 25.
b They pretended to have scruples of conscience, ab. the mar. of their sister with a heathen.—*Bush.*

"I have heard some of the first judges of whist say, that it was not those who played best by the true laws of the game that would win most, but those who played best to the false play of others; and I am

objects of attachment at ten, or thereabouts; and this cannot be supposed to be very extraordinary, when the daughter of such a one is supposed to become a mother too by eleven. It cannot then be incredible that Shechem should cast his eyes on Dinah at ten years of age, and should desire to marry her at that age, if human nature in the East then was similar, in that respect, to what it is now. But she might be considerably older than ten when this affair happened, for aught that is said in the book of Genesis relative to this matter.*d*

6—10. (6) **Hamor..him**, but their friendly interview was rudely interrupted. (7) **because..done**, these the words of the historian, not of Jacob's sons. (8) **longeth**, fr. intense affection. (9) **marriages**, *etc.*, to him there seemed no reason ag. this. (10) **dwell..trade**, peaceful residence and profitable trade offered as inducements.

The power of love.—Gilbert Becket, who was afterwards a flourishing citizen, was, in his youth, a soldier in the crusades, and, being taken prisoner, became slave to an emir, or Saracen prince. He obtained the confidence of his master, and met and was loved by the emir's daughter. After some time, he effected his escape. The lady with her loving heart followed him. She knew but two words of the English language—*London* and *Gilbert*; and, by repeating the first, she obtained a passage in a vessel, arrived in England, and found her trusting way to the metropolis. She then took to her other talisman, and went from street to street, pronouncing "Gilbert." A crowd collected about her wherever she went, asking a thousand questions; and to all she had but one answer, "Gilbert, Gilbert!" She found her faith in it sufficient. Chance, or the determination to go through every street, brought her at last to the one in which he who had won her heart in slavery was living in a prosperous condition. The crowd drew the family to the window: his servant recognised her: and Gilbert Becket took to his arms and his bridal-bed his far-come princess, with her solitary fond word.*a*

11—14. (11) **let..eyes**, I pray you grant my request. **what..give**, to seal the compact. (12) **dowry**, present to the parents. **gift**, present to the bride. (13) **deceitfully,***a* **smoothly, dissembling.***b* (14) **uncircumcised**, they demanded submission to this rite to facilitate their revenge.

Purchasing wives in the East.—In the remote ages of antiquity, women were literally purchased by their husbands; and the presents made to their parents or other relations were called their dowry. The practice still continues in the country of Shechem; for when a young Arab wishes to marry, he must purchase his wife; and for this reason, fathers, among the Arabs, are never more happy than when they have many daughters. They are reckoned the principal riches of a house. An Arabian suitor will offer fifty sheep, six camels, or a dozen of cows; if he be not rich enough to make such offers, he proposes to give a mare or a colt, considering in the offer the merit of the young woman, the rank of her family, and his own circumstances. In the primitive times of Greece, a well-educated lady was valued at four oxen. When they agree on both sides, the contract is drawn up by him that acts as cadi or judge among these Arabs. In some parts of the East, a measure of corn is formerly mentioned in contracts for their concubines, or temporary wives, besides the sum of money which is stipulated by way of dowry. This custom is probably as ancient as concubinage, with which it is connected; and if so, it will perhaps account for the prophet Hosea's purchasing a wife of this kind for fifteen pieces of silver, and for a homer of barley, and a half-homer of barley.^c

15—19. (15) **this**, proposal of marriage. (16) **we .. people**, which proposition promised prospective advantages. (17) **daughter**, *i.e.* the dau. of our house. **and .. gone**, we will have no further connection with you. (18) **pleased**, *lit.* were good in the eyes of. This sugg. of power of Jacob, and number of his retainers; otherwise he would have been defied rather than conciliated. (19) **and .. thing**, "force of love, and hope of profit." **he .. father**, he stood high in rank; had therefore much influence.

Constancy of love.—A short time previous to the death of the Marchioness of Tavistock, and when she was preparing to go to Lisbon for the recovery of her health, a consultation of physicians was held at Bedford House; and one of the gentlemen present requested, while he felt her pulse, that she would open her hand. Her frequent refusals occasioned him to take the liberty of gently forcing the fingers asunder; when he perceived that she had kept her hand closed to conceal the miniature-picture of the marquis. "O madam!" observed the physician, "my prescriptions must be useless if your ladyship is determined to keep before your eyes an object which, although deservedly dear to you, serves only to confirm the violence of your illness." The marchioness replied, "I have kept the picture either in my bosom or my hand ever since the death of my lamented lord; and thus I am determined to preserve it till I fortunately drop after him into the grave.^a

20—24. (20) **gate**, called a public meeting at the usual place of assembly. (21) **these**, *etc.*, they saw great advantage fr. so small a concession. (22) **as .. people**, as if the outward rite made the only difference. (23) **shall .. ours?** with Hamor the motive was love; with them, gain: dif. men, dif. motives impel to similar acts. (24) **every .. city**, their assent was unanimous.

The characteristics of a cheat.—A cheat is a freeman of all trades, and all trades of his fraud and treachery are his calling, though his profession be integrity and truth. He spins nets like a spider out of his own entrails, to entrap the simple and unwary that light in his way, whom he devours and feeds upon. The common ignorance of mankind is his province, which he orders to the best advantage. He is but a tame highwayman, that does the same thing by stratagem and design which the other does by force, makes men deliver their understandings first, and after their purses. Oaths and lies are his tools that he works with, and he gets his living by the drudgery of his conscience. . . . He can put on as many shapes as the devil that set him on work, is one that fishes in muddy understandings and will tickle a trout in his own element, till he has him in his clutches, and after in his dish, or the market. He runs down none but those which he

---

B.C. 1732.

sure it is true of the great game of the world."—*Greville.*

c *Paxton.*

and agrees to the conditions

"Lo, herein was their deceit. How often is religion pretended, made a state and stalking-horse to wordly and wicked aims and respects! A horrible profanation: as when Naboth was put to death at a fast; Henry VII., emperor, poisoned in the sacramental bread, by a monk."—*Trapp.*

a *Percy.*

the subjects of Hamor are circumcised

"Were the king at noon-day to say, 'This day is night,' it would behove us to reply, 'Lo, there are the moon and seven stars.'"—*Saadi.*

"By a kind of fashionable discipline, the eye is taught to brighten, the lip to smile, and the whole countenance to emanate with the semblance of friendly welcome, while the bosom is unwarmed by a single spark of

B.C. cir. 1732.

genuine kindness and goodwill."—*W. Irving.*
"A few drops of oil will set the political machine at work, when a ton of vinegar would only corrode the wheels and canker the movements."
—*Colton.*
a Fuller.

the revenge of Simeon and Levi
a Ge. xxxv. 5.

Spoil, lit. *that wh. is stripped off.* Lat. *spolium,* akin to Gk. *skulon,* in pl. *skula,* arms stripped off an enemy, fr. *skulto,* to flay.

"Dissipation leads to seduction; seduction produces wrath; wrath thirsts for revenge; the thirst of revenge has recourse to treachery; treachery issues in murder; and is followed by lawless depredation."—*Bush.*

"One murder made a villain; millions, a hero. Numbers sanctified the crime!"
—*Bp. Porteus.*

b Rosenmuller.

Jacob reproves his sons

a Ge. xlii. 36.

c C. Simeon, M.A.

"Of a man who has lost his honour, whose fame has entirely gone, it is said, Ah! he has lost his smell—where is

is certain are *feræ naturæ*, mere natural animals, that belong to him that can catch them. He can do no feats without the co-operating assistance of the chouse, whose credulity commonly meets the impostor half way, otherwise nothing is done: for all the craft is not in the catching (as the proverb says), but the better half at least in being catched. He is one that, like a bond without fraud, covin, and further delay, is void and of none effect, otherwise does stand and remain in full power, force, and virtue. He trusts the credulous with what hopes they please at a very easy rate, upon their own security, until he has drawn them far enough in, and then makes them pay for all at once. The first thing he gets from him is a good opinion, and afterwards anything he pleases.*a*

25—29. (25) **came . . sore,** they were incapable of resistance. **two . . brethren,** sons of the same mother: these were the leaders, but the rest prob. joined (*v.* 13). **boldly,** *lit.* in confidence. (26) **they . . sword,** these are named, being the chief offenders. **took . . out,** maid, wife, widow—three short chapters in her young life. (27) **sons,** perh. it was at this point that the rest joined the two. (28, 29) **wealth,** including *all* their property. **spoiled . . house,***a* furniture, etc.

Satisfaction for family wrongs.—Among the Bedouin Arabs, the brother finds himself more dishonoured by the seduction of his sister than a man by the infidelity of his wife. As a reason, they allege, "that a wife is not of the family, and that they are obliged to keep a wife only as long as she is chaste; and if she is not, she may be sent away, and is no longer a member of the family; but that a sister constantly remains a member of the family; and even if his sister became dissolute, and was defiled, nobody could hinder her from still being his sister." (D'Arvieux.) This is confirmed by Niebuhr. "I learnt at Basra, that a man is not allowed to kill his wife, even on account of adultery; but that her father, brother, or any of her relations were suffered to do it without being punished, or at least paying a small sum as an atonement, because her relations had been dishonoured by her bad behaviour; but that, after this satisfaction, nobody is permitted to reproach the family. They remembered examples of it in Basra and Bagdad; in this latter place, a rich merchant, a few years since, had found a young man with a relation of his, and not only hewed her in pieces on the spot, but also, by witnesses and money, caused the young man, who was the son of a respectable citizen, to be hanged the same night by the magistrates.*b*

30—31. (30) **troubled,** not only grieved but endangered. **and . . number,***a* I, men of number, *i.e.* capable of being numbered. (31) **said,** *etc.,* note the pride and revenge in this reply.

Slaughter of the Shechemites.—In considering the answer which Jacob's sons made to his reproofs, we notice—I. The provocation they had received. II. The manner in which they resented it. Their conduct is characterised by—1. Hypocrisy; 2. Profaneness; 3. Cruelty. III. Their vindication of their conduct. In their answer we see—1. Offended pride: 2. Invincible obduracy.*b*

Reputation.—
Dost thou know what reputation is?

Upon a time, Reputation, Love, and Death,
Would travel o'er the world; and 'twas concluded
That they should part, and take three several ways.
Death told 'em they should find him in great battles;
Or cities visited with plagues; Love gives them counsel
To inquire for him 'mongst unambitious shepherds,
Where dowries were not talk'd of; and sometimes
'Mongst quiet kindred, that had nothing left 'em
By their dead parents. But, says Reputation,
Do not forsake me: for it is my nature,
If once I part from any man I meet,
I am never found again![c]

B.C. 1732.

the sweet smell of former years?' 'Alas!' says an old man, 'my smell is for ever gone.'"—*Robert.*

[c] *Webster.*

v. 30. *Dr. Arnold,* 341; *It Reading,* iii 141

CHAPTER THE THIRTY-FIFTH.

1—5. (1) **Bethel,** *see* on xxviii. 12—19. (2) **put .. gods,**[a] they had just spoiled a heathen city. **clean,**[b] ceremonial, typical of spiritual purity. (3) **distress,**[c] when flying fr. a bro.'s anger. (4) **ear-rings,** perh. worn as charms, or symbols of an idolatrous nature. (5) **terror,**[d] God filled the minds of the people with terror.

Lessons from the life of Jacob (vv. 1—3).—Consider—I. Every spiritual history has its special places where memory loves to linger, and where spiritual power pertains. II. Special mercies demand special remembrance. Note—1. The tenderness and delicacy of God's dealing with Jacob; 2. That, generally, emphasis is laid more upon remembrance of mercies than of sorrows. III. The text may be applied to a devout remembrance of the time and circumstances of our early Christian life. IV. Bethel was the scene of "vows" which had been partially neglected and forgotten. V. The picture of a man of activity and business retiring to spend the leisure of age amidst the contemplations of religion, and the memories of its power, is given by these words. Then let us, too, "dwell" in those memories and places where heaven descends to earth, and earth rises to heaven.[e] *Vows called to remembrance* (v. 1).—Let us—I. Review the transactions to which these words refer. II. Draw forth some of the instruction implied in them—1. How soon the influence of impressive scenes wears away; 2. God will remind His people of forgotten duties. He does this by—(1) His Providence, (2) His Word, (3) His ministers; 3. Gracious characters are alive to Divine intimations; 4. Holy preparations become the service of God; 5. There may be wickedness in a religious family; 6. Our religious concern should not be confined to ourselves only; we are to engage our families to accompany us in the exercises of devotion; 7. Deliverance claims service—prayer answered is to become praise. III. 'Apply the text—1. Have some of you been advanced in wealth? Look back to former days, and praise God; 2. Have some of you been led back from "the valley of the shadow of death?" Remember your vows then made; 3. Are there backsliders here? Return to God; 4. Are there Christians present? Look forward to a heavenly country. Be stedfast in the faith.[f] *The Divine Benefactor* (vv. 1—3).—This passage teaches us three things respecting the bestowment of mercies.

Jacob journeys to Bethel

[a] Ge. xxxi. 19; Jos. xxiv. 15—23; 2 Co. iv. 16.
[b] Ex. xix, 10; Ps. xviii. 31; Ez. xviii. 31; xxxvi. 25; Ho. x. 22.
[c] Ge. xxxii. 7; xxviii. 20—22;
[d] De. xi. 25; Ex. xv. 6; Jos. ii. 9, v. 1; 1 S. xi. 7.
[e] *Dr. Deane.*
[f] *W. Jay.*

"True religion, as revealed in the Scriptures, may be compared to a plum on the tree, covered with its bloom. Men gather the plum, and handle it, and turn and twist it about, till it is deprived of all its native bloom and beauty; the fairest hand would as much rob the plum of its bloom, as any other."—*Cecil.*

"It has been said that men carry on a kind of coasting-trade with religion. In the voyage of life they profess to be in search of heaven, but take care not to ven-

B.C. cir. 1732.
ture so far in their approximations to it, as entirely to lose sight of the earth; and should their frail vessel be in danger of shipwreck, they will gladly throw their darling vices overboard, as other mariners their treasures, only to fish them up again when the storm is over."—*Colton.*

g *J. F. Woodhouse.*
h *Dr. Kitto.*

Allon-bachuth

The Jews have a trad. that it was at this spot, Bethel, that Jacob heard of his mother's death; so that the name given to the oak ref. to her as well as to Deborah.

a *Jenkyn Jones.*

If Deborah was ab. 40 when she left Mesopotamia with Rebekah, she could not have been much less than 180 now.

"A grave matron she was; of great use while she lived, and much missed when she died. This is not every man's case."—*Trapp.*

v. 7. *Bp. Wolly, A. Ser., 1673.*

the covenant renewed to Jacob

The recipients of temporal mercies are sometimes—I. Admonished by their benefactor. In the text God reminds Jacob of his vow, and—1. Points out the future place of his residence; 2. Specifies a particular work for his accomplishment; 3. Refers to a past event in his history. III. Obedient to Him. Three things show the sincerity of Jacob's submission. There is—1. An immediate response to the Divine command; 2. A generous proposal for Divine worship; 3. A holy preparation for Divine communion. III. Grateful to Him. Jacob—1. Proclaims God's supremacy; 2. Acknowledges His faithfulness; 3. Recognises His presence.g

Ear-rings.—Had these ear-rings been simply ornamental, they certainly would not need to have been given up with the "strange gods." It would therefore seem that they bore the figures of false gods, or some symbol of their power. Such ear-rings are still to be found in India and other countries of the East, and are regarded as charms or talismans to protect the wearer against enchantments and against enemies. It seems that the Israelites were not in after times free from the objectionable practice, for Hosea (ii. 13) represents Jerusalem as having decked herself with the ear-rings of Baalim.h

6—8. (6) **Luz**, see on xxviii. 19. (7) **El-beth-el** (*the God of Beth-el*) i.e. the God of the house of God. (8) **Deborah** (*bee*), here we learn the name of the nurse ref. to in xxiv. 59. **Allon-bachuth**, (*the oak of weeping*).

Jacob at Bethel. (vv. 6—15).—I. That men are liable to suffer losses in this world, even when obeying God's commands. II. That when obeying God's word, we may expect to meet God Himself (v. 9). Meeting Him—1. Is to have a greater knowledge of ourselves; 2. Is to have a clearer revelation of Him; 3. Will increase our usefulness; 4. Gives us an assurance of the future. III. That meeting God is a memorable event (v. 14).a

A beautiful death.—A preacher, having been sent for to visit a Western cabin, found a father and his dying daughter surrounded by evidences of luxury and taste. He asked the daughter if she knew her condition. "I know that my Redeemer liveth," said she in a voice whose melody was like the sweetest Æolian tones. A half-hour passed, and she spoke in the same deep, rich, melodious voice: "Father, I am cold: lie down beside me." And the old man lay down by his dying child; and she twined her emaciated arms around his neck, and murmured in a dreamy voice, "Dear father, dear father!"—"My child," said the old man, "doth the flood seem deep to thee?"—Nay, father, for my soul is strong."—"Seest thou the thither shore?"—"I see it, father; and its banks are green with immortal verdure."—"Hearest thou the voices of its inhabitants?"—"I hear them, father, as the voices of angels falling from afar in the still and solemn night-time; and they call me. Her voice too, father: Oh! I heard it then."—"Doth she speak to thee?"—"She speaketh in tones most heavenly."—"Doth she smile?"—"An angel smile; but a cold, calm smile. But I am cold, cold, cold! Father, there's a mist in the room. You'll be lonely, lonely. Is this death, father?"—" It is death, Mary."—"Thank God!" So she passed away.

9—12. (9) **God .. him**,a Jacob had now returned to the spot associated with the blessing and the vow of many yrs. bef. (10)

Cap. xxxv. 13—15.] GENESIS. 153

name,*b* he is solemnly reminded of his change of name. (11) nation .. nations,*c* *lit.* a nation, even a church of nations. (12) land,*d* *etc.*, the covenant to Abraham is renewed to Jacob.

God's arm sufficient (v. 11).—I. God can create. He can create—1. What He wills; 2. When He pleases; 3. As He will, and for His own pleasure. II. He can also make, that is, adapt, fashion, and mould all He creates. We can make but we cannot create. III. He can control all He creates and makes. Far below this is our position. He—1. Sees; 2. Knows; 3. Is with; 4. Is above, all things. IV. He can destroy. V. He can retain His own life from everlasting to everlasting. VI. He can do all things, and therefore—VII. He can redeem.*e*

God is the chief good.—

"Without Thy presence earth gives no refection;
Without Thy presence, sea affords no treasure;
Without Thy presence, air's a rank infection;
Without Thy presence, heaven itself no pleasure;
If not possessed, if not enjoyed in Thee,
What's earth, or sea, or air, or heaven to me?

"The highest honours that the world can boast,
Are subjects far too low for my desire;
Its brightest beams of glory are at most
But dying sparkles of Thy living fire;
The proudest flames that earth can kindle, be
But nightly glow-worms if compared to Thee.

"Without Thy presence, wealth is bags of cares
Wisdom but folly; joy, disquiet, sadness;
Friendship is treason, and delights are snares;
Pleasures but pain, and mirth but pleasing madness,
Without Thee, Lord, things be not what they be,
Nor have their being when compared with Thee.

"In having all things and not Thee, what have I?
Not having Thee, what have my labours got?
Let me enjoy but Thee, what further crave I?
And having Thee alone, what have I not?
I wish not sea nor land; nor would I be
Possessed of heaven, heaven unpossessed of Thee."*f*

13—15. (13) **went**, *etc.,a* prob. it was the depart. of some visible manifestation. (14) **pillar**, *etc.*, perh. the old one had fallen down, or been removed: or this may have been the reconsecration of the old. (15) **called .. Beth-el**, as he is reminded of his new name, so he revives the new name he had given to Luz.*b*

*Our Father.—*Those who have ever traversed the plains of Mexico have seen the cactaceæ family. The cactus has an ungainly leaf, fat and thick, and full of thorns, so that when men see it growing, they say, "It is a clumsy and hateful thing that is ugly to look upon, and that pierces you whenever you touch it." Wait. When at last that plant, which grows in arid places, where hardly any weed will grow, with thick and succulent leaves, and a tough skin, and which stands almost without root through the whole year,—when at last it has come to the point where it is developed, is there in the whole kingdom of beauty a blossom that is for exquisiteness of form and tint equal to the

---

B.C. 1732.

a Ge. xxviii. 12; xxxi. 11; xxxii. 1; 24.
b xxxii. 28.
c Ge. xlviii. 3, 4.
d Ge. xii. 7; xxvi. 34.

"A sweet allayment of his late heaviness for Deborah, and a gracious preparative to the ensuing loss of Rachel."—*Trapp.*
e S. Martin.

"In vain do they talk of happiness, who never subdued an impulse in obedience to a principle. He who never sacrificed a present to a future good, or a personal to a general one, can speak of happiness only as the blind do of colours."—*H. Mann.*

"The common course of things is in favour of happiness; happiness is the rule, misery the exception. Were the order reversed, our attention would be called to examples of health and competency, instead of disease and want."—*Paley.*
f Quarles.

Beth-el
a Ge. xvii. 22.
b Ge. xxviii. 19.

"The glory of the Lord went up,"—*Chal.* "The light or splendour of God went up."—*Arab.* and *Ethiop.*

"A prince who loves and fears religion is a lion who stoops to the hand that strokes, or to the voice that appeases him. He who fears and hates religion is like the savage beast that growls

B.C. 1732.

and bites the chain, which prevents his flying on the passenger. He who has no religion at all is that terrible animal who perceives his liberty only when he tears it in pieces, and when he devours."—*Montesquieu.*
c H. W. Beecher.

death of Rachel

a In the LXX. *hippodrome, i.e.,* the length of a *horse-race course,* which, Michaelis says, among the people of the E. was ab. a mile.

b Ge. xxx. 24.

c Mi. v. 2; Ma. ii. 6.

d There can be no doubt that the sqr. building surmounted by a dome, of Muhammedan origin, marks the site of this pillar. *Porter, Sy. and Pal.* i. 70; *Thomson, L. and B.* 644; *Robinson, B. R.* i. 156; ii. 322; *Stanley, Sin and Pal.* 149; *Bonar's L. of Promise,* 116; 178.

e 1 Sa. x. 2.

f A. F. Smith.

g Buchanan.

v. 16. *Crit. Sac. Theo. Nov.,* 1. 207.

v. 18. *Dr. Kitto, Bibl. Illus.*, i. 349.

v. 19. *House of Mourning,* 411.

"If the internal griefs of every man could be read, written on his forehead, how many who now excite envy would appear to be objects of pity!"—*Metastatio.*

cactus blossom? It is the very perfection of beauty growing out of the very emblem of homeliness. And as it is with the vegetable kingdom, so it is with many developments of the Divine kingdom. God's providence looks like a cactus leaf—like an arid plant growing uselessly in the wilderness. But wait till it blossoms, and see how glorious is its beauty. The Lord Himself was declared to be a root out of a dry ground, in whom was no form or comeliness; and yet out of this has blossomed the infinite glory of the Saviour and Brother which makes us children of the common Father. The glory of the world, and the wealth and beauty of it, are not enough to illustrate the fulness of the meaning of that one word which the Lord's Prayer begins with, and which every man on earth may utter—" Our Father."*e*

16—20. (16) **but .. way,**^a *lit.* a little space of ground. **Ephrath** (*fruitful*). (17) **fear .. also,** timely comfort: a reminder of her former desire.*b* (18) **Ben-oni,** (*son of my sorrow*) **Benjamin,** (*son of my right hand*). (19) **was .. way,** ab. a mile from **Beth-lehem,***c* (*house of bread*) about 6 m. S. fr. Jerus. (20) **and,** *etc.,d i.e.* when Moses wrote this hist.*e*

The pillar of death.—From these verses, we note—I. That no human joy is unmixed with sorrow. Rachel bears a son; but loses her own life. II. That the greatest revelation of God and communion with Him may be followed by the greatest trial. Jacob has a vision of, and a visitation from God, almost together. III. That it is a good thing to keep the dead in remembrance by some especial token. It serves both to—1. Keep their names and characters in our memory; 2. Remind us of our own future destiny.*f*

The tomb of Rachel.—Not far from Bethlehem a small solitary structure upon the open moor attracted our notice. It was the tomb of Rachel. The present building has been recently repaired, and is now the property of the Jews, having been purchased for his nation by Sir Moses Montefiore. It cannot well be doubted, however, that the tomb which it encloses is really that of the venerable mother of the tribes of Israel. Scripture all but identifies the spot. It is "near to Ephrath," and is in the direct route from Bethel to that place. The pillar placed upon the tomb by Jacob still remained when Moses wrote the book of Genesis, and when the people of whom Rachel was the mother were already about to enter into permanent possession of the land. Josephus, in speaking of it, instead of using the rather indefinite expression of the Scripture narrative, "near to Ephrath," employs the more precise expression, "over against Ephrath:" suggesting the idea that down to his time the place continued to be familiarly known. The ridge on which it stands is the summit-level, or watershed, between the Dead Sea and the Mediterranean. On its eastern side one of the smaller valleys, branching up from the great Wady Tâamirah, makes a deep cleft in the country between Mar-Elias and Bethlehem: and the ridge or backbone of the district along which the Bethlehem road runs takes a rather sharper bend as it advances southward round the head of this valley. It forms, in other words, a bow or curve, of which a straight line stretched right across the valley between the tomb and Bethlehem or Ephrath would be the string. The evidence, therefore, which supports the tradition amounts as nearly as possible to a demonstration.*g*

Cap. xxxvi. 1–3.] GENESIS. 155

21—26. (21) **Edar,**[a] (*flock*) "He was on his way to Hebron, and his first stage aft. his sore bereavement was but a short one."[b] (22) **Reuben,** *etc.*, for this crime he lost his birthright.[c] Israel, *etc.*, sorrow upon sorrow for the old man. now .. twelve, as follow. (23) **Leah,** *etc.*, see xxix. 32—35; xxx. 18—20. (24) **Rachel,** *etc.*, see xxx. 22; xxxv. 18. (25) **Bilhah,** *etc.*, see xxx. 6—8. (26) **Zilpah,** *etc.*, xxx. 11, 12. these .. Padan-aram, Benjamin excepted.

Joy in the family.—Among those who rose for prayers one night at a school-house meeting, were three adult children of an aged father, a member of my church. The old man's heart was deeply moved as he saw them rise; and, as soon as the opportunity was given for remarks, he was on his feet. I shall not soon forget the scene. The Holy Spirit was present with power, the room silent, and many cheeks wet with tears. With a full heart and tremulous voice, that white-haired father urged all to come to Jesus; and then, turning to his children, he said with a simple earnestness that thrilled every heart, "Oh, my children ! do come to Christ now!" I rode home with the family that night in the great farm-wagon; and, as we crept slowly along those prairie slopes in the beautiful moonlight, the old man still preached Jesus to his weeping children. It seemed as if he could not cease. We knelt together once more at the family altar before retiring. In a few days, all those children were rejoicing in a new-found Saviour.

27—29. (27) and .. **father,** it is prob. that Jacob visited his blind old father bef. this. **Mamre,**[a] see xiii. 18. **Arba,** see xxiii. 2. (28) **and,** *etc.*, he survived Jacob's return twelve yrs. (29) **was .. people,**[b] a hint of another world in wh. "*his people*" lived. **sons .. him,** they meet, reconciled, at their father's grave. (So Isaac and Ishmael had buried Abraham.)

Note on Isaac.—Isaac really survived Jacob's return to Hebron 12 years. This may be seen as follows : Isaac was 60 when Jacob was born (ch. xxv. 26), consequently Jacob was 120 at his father's death. But he was 130 at his migration (ch. xlvii. 9), which therefore was ten years after. At that time Joseph was between 39 and 40 (comp. chap. xli. 46, 47, and xlv. 6). But seeing he was 17 when he was sold into Egypt (xxxvii. 2), and 23 years elapsed between that and Jacob's migration, Isaac must have survived Joseph's selling into Egypt between 12 and 13 years. Hence it also follows that Joseph was sold immediately on Jacob's coming to Hebron.[c]

CHAPTER THE THIRTY-SIXTH.

1—3. (1) **Esau .. Edom,** see on xxv. 30. (2) **Adah,** (*ornament, beauty*) or Bashemath.[a] **Aholibamah,** (*tent of the height*) or Judith. **Anah** (*answer*) or Beeri. (3) **Bashemath,** (*fragment*) or Mahalath.

Inconsistency in the family.—I have been in his family, said Christian the Talkative, and have observed him both at home and abroad; and I know what I say of him is the truth. His house is as empty of religion as the white of an egg is of savour. There is neither prayer nor sign of repentance for sin; yea, the brute in his kind serves God far better than he. He is the very

---

B.C. 1732.

Reuben's deed of shame

[a] M. iv. 8. Jerome says this "tower of the flock" was ab. a m. fr. Bethlehem, and was the place of the shepherds. It was prob. a watch-tower for the protection of flocks ag. robbers and wild beasts. See 2 K. xviii. 8; 2 Ch. xxvi. 10, xxvii. 4.

[b] *Bonar.*

[c] Ge. xlix. 3–4; 1 Ch. v. 1; 1 Co. v. 1.

v. 24. *J. Doughty, Anal. Sac.,* 65.

death of Isaac

[a] Jos. xiv. 15; xv. 13.

For Hebron see Porter Hd. Bk. for Syria i. 64.

[b] Ge. xxv. 7, 8; He. xi. 13.

[c] *Alford.*

B.C. *cir.* 1796.

the generations of Esau

[a] Ge. xxvi. 34. prob. one set of names were those borne bef. marriage; the others aft.; by the Edomites.— Anah was prob. called Beeri; or, *well-finder,* fr. the

stain, reproach, and shame of religion to all that know him: it can hardly have a good word in all that end of the town where he dwells, through him. Thus say the common people of him,— "A saint abroad, and a devil at home." His poor family find it so. He is such a churl! such a railer at, and so unreasonable with his servants, that they neither know how to do for or to speak to him. Men that have any dealings with him say it is better to deal with a Turk than with him; for fairer dealings they shall have at his hands. This Talkative, if it be possible, will go beyond them, defraud, beguile, and overreach them. Besides, he brings up his sons to follow his steps; and, if he finds in any of them a "foolish timorousness" (for so he calls the first appearance of tender conscience), he calls them fools and blockheads, and by no means will employ them in much, or speak to their commendation before others. For my part, I am of opinion that he has by his wicked life caused many to stumble and fall; and will be, if God prevents not, the ruin of many more.*b*

4—8. (4) **Eliphaz***a* (*God his strength*). **Reuel** (*friend of God*). (5) **Jeush**, (to whom God *hastens*). **Jaalam** (whom God *hides*). **Korah** (*baldness*). (6) **country**, into a land or country; *i.e.* another land. **from** .. **Jacob**, *lit.* fr. before; *i.e.* bef. his arrival. (7) **riches**, *etc.*, so the prosperity of Esau was an advantage to Jacob. (8) **thus** .. **Seir**, *etc. see* on xiv. 6.

The cost of prosperity.—"What is the value of this estate?" said a gentleman to another with whom he was riding, as they passed a fine mansion and through rich fields. "I don't know what it is valued at; I know what it cost its late possessor." "How much?" "His soul." A solemn pause followed this brief answer. The person to whom it was given was not seeking first the kingdom of God and His righteousness. The late possessor referred to was the son of a pious man who supported his family by the labour of his hands. The son early obtained a subordinate position in a mercantile establishment in this city. He was then a professor of religion. He continued to maintain a reputable profession till he became a partner in the concern. He then gave increasing attention to business, and less to religion. Ere he was an old man, he had become exceedingly wealthy and miserly, and no one who knew him had any suspicion that he had ever been a professor of religion. He purchased a large landed estate, built the costly mansion referred to above, and died. Just before he died, he said, "My prosperity has been my ruin."*b*

9—14. (9) **father**, *i.e.* founder. (10) **sons**, *etc.*, *see* on v. 4. (11) **Teman** (*south, desert*) fr. whom the Temani, or Temanites.*a* **Omar** (*? eloquent*). **Zepho***b* (*watch-tower*). **Gatam** (*one puny and thin*). **Kenaz***c* (*a hunt*). (12) **Timna** (*inaccessible*). **Amalek***d* (*? a people that licks up*), fr. whom the Amalekites. (13) **Nahath** (*rest*). **Zerah** (*? a rising of light*). **Shammah** (*astonishment*). **Mizzah** (*fear*). (14) **Zibeon** (*dyed*). **Jeush** (whom *God hides*). **Jaalam** (to whom *God hastens*). **Korah***e* (*baldness*).

Providence among nations.—"A few drops of water, more or less," says Victor Hugo, "prostrated Napoleon." He meant that the battle of Waterloo was begun at eleven o'clock in the morning, because there was rain on the previous night, and Napoleon could not move his artillery over the heavy mud-plain until near noon, and that five hours' delay turned the fate of Europe; for Blucher did not arrive with his allies till the forces of the Iron Duke were all but defeated. In the same spirit, we believed, in the midst of our struggle, that nothing but Providence, immediately interfering in the crisis-hours of our destiny, could have saved us. You can never forget how, just at the nick of time, the little *Monitor* came down against that terrible monster which might have destroyed Washington, and raised the blockade. In Hampton Roads was fought, that day, a battle which revolutionised the navies of the world, while one great nation wept for joy, and all the nations wondered.*f*

15—19. (15) **dukes,** Heb., *alluph*, chief, leader, guide, answering to present *emir* or *sheikk* (see previous vv. for meaning of names).

Pride of ancestry.—
I look down upon him
With such contempt and scorn, as on my slave;
He's a name only, and all good in him
He must derive from his great grandsire's ashes:
For had not their victorious acts bequeath'd
His titles to him, and wrote on his forehead,
"This is a lord," he had lived unobserved
By any man of mark, and died as one
Amongst the common rout.*a*

20—25. (20) **sons** . . **Horite,** whom Esau conquered.*a* **Lotan** *b* (*covering*). **Shobal** (*flowing*). (21) **Dishon** (*antelope*). **Ezer** (*help*). (22) **Hori** (*a dweller in caverns*). **Heman** *c* (*destruction*). (23) **Alvan** *d* (*tall, thick*). **Manahath** *e* (*rest*). **Ebal** (*stony*). **Shepho** *f* (*smoothness*). **Onam** (*strong, stout*). (24) **Ajah** (*hawk, falcon*). this . . **Anah,** *g* lit. this was that A. that found the hot springs while, *etc.* (25) **Aholibamah,** wife of Esau.

Mules (v. 24).—The Syriac renders the greatly disputed word as "waters," and is followed by St. Jerome, who translates *aquas calidas*, "warm springs or waters," and in his note makes a remark on the diversity of opinions which prevails on the subject, and says that the word has, in the Punic language, the signification which he assigns. Gesenius concurs in this interpretation; and we are certainly disposed to conclude, with Dr. Boothroyd, that waters of some kind or other are intended. The probability is, that Anah, while feeding his father's asses, discovered a copious spring or lake, and this would certainly, in that arid region, be considered an event of sufficient importance to be recorded; and it might be the asses that led him to make the discovery, as these animals, as well as camels, have the reputation of being very sagacious in the discovery of water. Dr. Boothroyd renders it thus: "It was this Anah that found the waters in the wilderness, as he fed the asses of Zibeon, his father."*h*

26—30. (26) **Hemdan** (*pleasant*). **Eshban** (*wise man*). **Ithran** (*excellence*). **Cheran** (*lyre*). (27) **Bilhan** (*bashful*). **Zaavan** (*restless*). **Akan** (*? distortion*). (28) **Uz** (*? fertile land*). **Aran** (*wild goat*). (29, 30) for names see previous vv.

*Individual responsibility in nations.—*Men come to think that

---

B.C. cir. 1796.

tress of same name N. E. of Petra.

d Ex. xvii. 8—16; Nu. xxiv. 18—20; De. xxv. 17—19.

e There is a tribe of Arabs called Kuraych.

f C. D. Foss.

"Titles of honour are like the impressions on coin, which add no value to gold and silver, but only render brass current." -*Sterne.*

"A great and fatal weight on him doth lie, the greatness of his own nobility."— *Seneca.*

a Beaumont and Fletcher.

a De. ii. 12—22.

b A tribe called Leviathan, nr. Petra.

c Homaina, a place S. of Petra.

d Alawin, a tribe N. of Akaba.

e Manychiates W. of Petra. See Ptolemy, v. 17, 3.

f A hill called Shafeh N. of Akaba. Robinson B.R. i. 256.

g Called also Beeri, i.e. the wellfinder.

h Kitto.

v. 24. J. Doughty, Anal. Sac., 65.

"Title and ancestry render a good man more illustrious, but an ill one more contemptible.

the guilt of sins committed in concert is distributed; and that, if there be a thousand men banded and banded together in wickedness, each shall have but the one-thousandth part of guilt. If a firm succeeds, the gain is distributed to each partner; but, if it fails, each one may be held for the whole loss. Whoever commits a sin will bear the sins, whether alone or with a thousand: whoever commits or connives at public sin will bear the blame. Public guilt always has private indorsement; and each man is liable for the whole note.*d*

31—39. (31) **these**, *etc.*, hence some*a* have sup. that these words were written *aft.* kings reigned in Israel. They are prob, in all. to xxxv. 11, but see below. (32) **Bela** (*swallowing up*). **Beor** (*torch*). **Dinhabah** (*robber's den*). (33) **Jobab**b (*a desert*). **Zerah** (*a rising of light*). **Bozrah**c (*fortress*), now *el-Busarieh*, a small vil. of 50 houses, in midst of ruins S.E. of Dead S. (34) **Husham** (*haste*). **Temani** (*south. desert*), desc. of Teman, v. 11, 15. (35) **Hadad** (*clamour*). **Bedad** (*separation*). field, country. **Avith** (*ruins*). (36) **Samlah** (*garment*). **Masrekah** (*vineyard of noble vines*). (37) **Saul** (*asked for*). **Rehoboth** (*streets* or *wide places*). **by . . river**, prob. Euphrates: to dis. fr. R. of x. 11. (38) **Baal-hanan** (*lord of grace*). **Achbor** (*mouse*). (39) **Hadar** (*ornament*), also called Hadad.*d*

Supplementary note on v. 31.—There is, however, nothing inconsistent with the Mosaic origin of the whole passage. In the last chapter (xxxv. 11) there had been an emphatic promise from God Almighty (El-Shaddai) to Jacob that "kings should come out of his loins." The Israelites, no doubt, cherished a constant hope of such a kingdom and such a kingly race. Moses himself (Deut. xxviii. 36) prophesied concerning the king that the Israelites should set over them; and hence it was not unnatural that, when recording the eight kings who had reigned in the family of Esau up to his own time, he should have noted that as yet no king had risen from the family of his brother Jacob, to whom a kingly progeny had been promised. The words in the original are: "before the reigning of a king to the sons of Israel;" and might be rendered, "whilst as yet the children of Israel have no king;" there being nothing in the words expressive of a past tense, or indicating that before the writing of the sentence a king had reigned in Israel.*e*

40—43. (40) **dukes**, some of whom, as leaders of tribes, were prob. contemporaneous. **Alvah** (*wickedness*). **Jetheth** (*nail, tent-pin*). (41) **Elah** (*terebinth*). **Pinon** (*darkness*). (42) **Mibzar** (*fortress*). (43) **Magdiel** (*praise of God*). **Iram** (*belonging to a city*). **in .. possession,** *i.e.* their firm, fixed, abiding possession.

Safeguard of nations.—France tried to get on without a God in the time of her first Revolution; but Napoleon, for reasons of State, restored the Catholic religion. M. Thiers gives this singular passage in his history. Napoleon said, "For my part, I never hear the sound of the church-bell in the neighbouring village without emotion." He knew that the hearts of the people were stirred by the same deep yearnings after God which filled his own; and so he proposed to restore the worship of God to infidel France. The *savans* of Paris ridiculed the proposal, laughed it to scorn, declared it was weakness in him to yield to a superstition that had for ever passed away; that he needed no such aid to government; and that he could do what he pleased. "Yes," said he; "but I act only with regard to the real and sensibly felt wants of France." Negotiations were opened with the Pope; and the Romish worship was set up, amid the enthusiasm of the nation. The historian utters this reflection: "Whether true or false, sublime or ridiculous, men must have a religion." Later, and with deeper meaning, Perrier, successor to Lafayette as prime-minister to Louis Philippe, said on his death-bed, "France must have religion." So I say to-day, concerning that better faith, which overthrows what Romanism sets up, which breaks the shackles Romanism binds on, which is the only security of national permanence,—America must have religion.*a*

B.C. 1796.

"Kings do with men as with pieces of money; they give them what value they please, and we are obliged to receive them at their current and not at their real value."—*La Rochefoucauld.*

a C. D. Foss.

CHAPTER THE THIRTY-SEVENTH.

B.C. cir. 1728.

1—4. (1) **Jacob**, having bought the birthright. **dwelt.. strange,***a* *lit.* in the land of his father's sojournings. (2) **generations**, family hist. **Joseph..old**, at wh. time Isaac was living. **feeding..brethren**, *lit.* was tending his brethren in the flock. **lad..wives**, with *these* in particular. **and..report**, an acc. of their ill-doings: this was part of his duty as overseer. (3) **because..age,***b* *lit.* son of old age to him; perh. it means son of wisdom, wise son: wisdom and age being related. **and..colours,***c* prob. to sig. distinction, office. (4) **hated,***d* instead of imitating his example.

Joseph's coat of many colours (v. 3).—It may remind us—I. Of the dress which earthly parents prepare for their children. Respecting which consider—1. They toil to procure it, working hard and long. 2. They exercise thought in selecting. Have to consider size, season, material, appearance. 3. They have to inspect it often. How it has been used; how it wears; does it need repair. 4. They have to renew it often. The best will wear out or be out-grown. (See 1 Sam. ii. 19.) II. Of the robe which our Heavenly Father prepares for those who love Him. 1. We need clothing for the soul, as well as for the body (1 Pet. iii. 3, 4; v. 5). God knows what things we have need of, even if we are unconscious of our need (Rev. iii. 17). 2. We cannot make, or purchase, soul-clothing. We must receive it as a free gift. Only God can give it (Rev. iii. 18). 3. For earnest, persevering, asking—accompanied by watching—we may obtain the robe of righteousness, the garment of salvation. This robe Jesus wrought for us. 4. This robe will fit well, look well, wear for ever. It is a white robe. White includes all the colours (explain). Hence it is a coat of many colours. 5. It is a court dress (explain) in which to enter the great King's presence. Learn—(1) Be careful of clothes. Those who cannot earn them may lessen their parents' expenses and labour and anxiety by taking care of them. (2) Keep your soul-clothes unspotted from the world. Beware of sin-stains, and of self-righteous cleansing and patching. (See the hymn by Dr. Watts, "Awake, my heart; arise, my tongue.")

Family training.—"Another manifest principle observed by Mrs. Wesley in the education and training of her family, was

the history of Joseph

his coat of many colours

a Ge. xvii. 8; He. xi. 9.

b Ge. xliv. 20.

c The LXX. and Vulg. say, a garm. of dif. pieces, patchwork; hence, of dif. colours. Other V.S. as *Aquila, Syriac, etc.,* say a tunic with fringes reaching to hands and feet. See *Jos. Ant.* vii. 8, 1, and *cf.* 2 Sa. xiii. 18.

d Ep. vi. 4.

"It is the curse of service; preferment goes by letter and affection, not by the old gradation, when each second stood heir to the first."—*Shakespeare.*

"At almost every step in life we meet with young men from whom we anticipate wonderful things, but of

B.C. 1728.

whom, after careful inquiry, we never hear another word. Like certain chintzes, calicoes and ginghams, they show finely on their first newness, but cannot stand the sun and rain, and assume a very sober aspect after washing-day."— Hawthorne.

c J. Kirk.

his dreams

the sheaves

a Ge. xlii. 6, 9; xliii. 26; xlv. 14.

Sheaf, the stalks of grain, shoved and bound together. A.S. sceaf, Ger. shaub, A.S. sceofan, Ger. schieben, to shove.

b Dr. Thomas.

"What the tender and poetic youth dreams to-day, and conjures up with inarticulate speech, is to-morrow the vociferated result of public opinion, and the day after is the character of nations."— Emerson.

"Nothing so much convinces me of the boundlessness of the human mind as its operations in dreaming."— W. B. Clulow.

"Every one turns his dreams into realities as far as he can; man is cold as ice to the truth, hot as fire to falsehood."— La Fontaine.

c Dryden.

that of thorough impartiality. There was no pet lamb in her deeply interesting flock; no Joseph among her children to be decked out in a coat of many colours, to the envy of his less loved brethren. It was supposed by some of her sisters that Martha was a greater favourite with Mrs. Wesley than the rest of her children, and Charles expressed his ' wonder that so wise a woman as his mother could give way to such a partiality, or did not better conceal it.' This, however, was an evident mistake. Many years afterwards, when the saying of her brother was mentioned to Martha, she replied, ' What my sisters call partiality was what they might all have enjoyed if they had wished it, which was permission to sit in my mother's chamber when disengaged, to listen to her conversation with others, and to hear her remarks on things and books out of school-hours.' There is certainly no evidence of partiality here. All her children stood before her on a common level, with equal claims, and all were treated in the same way."*c*

5—8. (5) he.. brethren, a more crafty person would have concealed it. they.. more, without perfectly understanding it, they saw it pointed to his advancement. Perh. regarded it as the result of ambitious day-dreams. (6) he.. them, in guileless confidence. (7) behold, *etc.*,*a* imagery related to most familiar objects. shalt.. us, they understood this to be the general drift of the dream.

The dreams of Joseph (v. 5—11).—Look at these dreams as illustrating—I. The visions of youth. A tendency to brighten the future belongs to youth. This tendency serves to—1. Increase the amount of man's happiness on this earth; 2. Supply a mighty stimulus to our mental powers; 3. Intimate what human nature would have been had there been no sin. II. The jealousies of society. Three remarks about this jealousy. It is—1. Very general: 2. An unhappy feeling; 3. Unchristian. III. The destiny of virtue. Glory is ever the destiny of virtue. 1. There is much in a virtuous life itself to ensure advancement; 2. Advancement is pledged by God Himself to a virtuous life. Learn in conclusion:—(1) The fate of eminence; (2) The path of glory.*b*

Human views of dreams.—

Dreams are but interludes which fancy makes;
When monarch reason sleeps, this mimic wakes:
Compounds a medley of disjointed things,
A court of cobblers, and a mob of kings:
Light fumes are merry, grosser fumes are sad,
Both are the reasonable soul run mad:
And many monstrous forms in sleep we see,
That neither were, nor are, nor e'er can be.
Sometimes forgotten things, long cast behind,
Rush forward in the brain, and come to mind.
The nurse's legends are for truths receiv'd,
And the man's dreams but what the boy believ'd.
Sometimes we but rehearse a former play,
The night restores our actions done by day,
As hounds in sleep will open for their prey;
In short, the farce of dreams is of a piece,
Chimeras all, and more absurd or less.*c*

9—11. (9) **and .. dream,** imaginary dif., but meaning the same. Repetition confirms the certainty of the event predicted. **sun .. moon,** ref. to father and mother: first dream ref. to brethren alone. (10) **rebuked,** if for *dreaming,* this was unjust, since Joseph could hardly be responsible for his dreams: if for *relating* the dream, Jacob showed want of faith. (11) **father .. saying,**[a] *lit.* kept the word: *i.e.* laid it to heart.

The brethren and father of Joseph (v. 11).—We observe—I. That both brethren and father were worshippers, in the dream which they heard related. II. That, if any might naturally be angry with Joseph for so dreaming, it was the father. III. That sundry matters of interest account for the difference in the feelings of the father and brethren; but chiefly the faith in God that Jacob possessed.

Interpretation of dreams.—Many people find out more mysteries in their sleep than they can well expound waking. If they dream of a green garden, they shall hear of a dead corpse; if they dream they shake a dead man by the hand, then there is no way but death. It is superstition, folly, to repose any such confidence in dreams; but, if any man desire to profit by them, let him consider in what direction these usually carry him, so by his thoughts in the night, he shall learn to know himself by day. Be his dreams lustful, he may ask if his heart runs after concupiscence; are they turbulent, they may indicate a contentious disposition; are they revengeful, they point out malice; run they upon gold and silver, they argue covetousness. Generally, men answer to such waking, as their thoughts do sleeping.[b]

12—14. (12) **Shechem,** ab. sixty ms. N. fr. Hebron, where Jacob then was. (13) **said .. I,** sugg. of his habit of obedience. (14) **see .. well,** *lit.* see the peace, etc. Jacob might judge the neighbourhood of Shechem an unsafe place.

Joseph's filial obedience (v. 13).—Ready at his father's bidding to—I. Set out on a long journey. II. Set out on a long journey through enemies' country. III. Set out on a long journey to brethren who hated him (comp. with Jesus).

The Vale of Shechem.—Having crossed the hill, we entered the rich vale of Shechem, or Nablous, clad with olives, full of gardens and orange groves, with palm trees, and watered by plenteous rills. It was the brightest and most civilised scene we had met with. Passengers on horse and foot, many of them unarmed, were travelling to and fro; camels, in long file, laden with cotton bales, were mingled with asses bearing firewood and baskets of cotton husks to the city; and wild horsemen were galloping in and out as they skilfully threaded their way among the laden beasts. Jays and woodpeckers laughed among the olive trees, and a fox slunk past us to his hole; while the home-like caw of the jackdaw, whose acquaintance we had not before made in the country, was re-echoed from the poplar trees and the minarets.[a]

15—18. (15) **wandering,** *etc.,* he would not return without information of his brethren. His father would be anxious. (*They* showed less thought presently.) (16) **tell .. flocks,** flocks of such size could hardly be unnoticed. (17) **let .. Dothan,** either bec. of danger: or of scant herbage. **Dothan**[a] (*two cisterns or wells*), on S. edge of plain of Esdraelon; ab.

B.C. cir. 1729.

Joseph's second dream
a Lu. ii. 19.

"Dreaming is an act of pure imagination, attesting in all men a creative power which, if it were available in waking, would make every man a Dante or a Shakespeare."—*F. H. Hedge.*

"As dreams are the fancies of those that sleep, so fancies are but the dreams of those awake."—*T. P. Blount.*

"Dreams are like portraits; and we find they please because they are confessed resemblances."—*Crabbe.*
b *Spencer.*

he is sent to seek his brethren

"As ships meet at sea a moment together, when words of greeting must be spoken, and then away upon the deep; so men meet in this world: and I think we should cross no man's path without hailing him, and if he needs giving him supplies."—*Beecher.*

"The world is so corrupt that a reputation for honesty is acquired by not doing wrong."—*De Levis.*

a *Dr. Tristram.*

they conspire against him
a 2 K. vi. 13.
b Ps. xxxvii. 32.

"Combinations of wickedness

VOL. I. F

twelve ms. N. of Samaria; site now called *Tell Dothaim*. (18) **when..off,** and recog. him by his coat. **they..him,**[b] *lit.* they craftily conspired, etc.

Stages of crime (v. 18).—"They conspired against him to slay him." Let us inquire into the various processes that at last resulted in this deliberate scheme of murder. I. Envy. This vice was the first symptom. They envied Joseph. II. Hatred. Envy, long indulged in, developes into open hatred. III. Treacherous conspiracy. The brothers conspire in secret, after the manner of all criminals. Wickedness can never bear the light of day. IV. The plan of murder itself. This is the culminating point. Learn—1. The danger of secret and small vices; 2. The tendency of all sin to increase in magnitude.

Allurements of sin.—We have heard of a singular tree, that forcibly illustrates the deceitfulness of sin. It is called the Judas tree. The blossoms appear before the leaves, and they are of brilliant crimson. The flaming beauty of the flowers attracts innumerable insects; and the wandering bee is drawn to it to gather honey. But every bee that alights upon the blossoms imbibes a fatal opiate, and drops dead from among the crimson flowers to the earth. Beneath this enticing tree, the earth is strewed with the victims of its fatal fascinations. That fatal plant that attracts only to destroy is a vivid emblem of the deceitfulness and deadliness of sin. For the poison of sin's bewitching flowers there is but one remedy: it is found in the "leaves of the tree of life" that groweth on Mount Calvary.[c]

19—22. (19) **dreamer,** *lit.* lord of dreams. Spoken in contempt. (20) **pit,**[a] none deep enough to conceal their crime fr. God. **say,** *etc.,* they would be murderers of their bro., and liars to their father. **we..dreams,** this they did *see,* some twenty years hence. (21) **delivered,**[b] *i.e.* it was his intention to do so. (22) **to..again,** at some convenient time.

Joseph and his dreams (vv. 19, 20).—I. The causes of the unkind feelings with which Joseph was regarded by his brethren. 1. His piety; 2. His father's fondness for him; 3. The dreams that he dreamt. II. The consequences to which the indulgence of such feelings led. These were awful in the extreme. III. The object which the brethren of Joseph contemplated in the accomplishment of the evil designs to which their hatred prompted them.

Hidden sin.—Certain great iron castings have been ordered for a railway bridge. The thickness has been calculated according to the extent of the span and the weight of the load. The contractor constructs his moulds according to the specification, and, when all is ready, pours in the molten metal. In the process of casting, through some defect in the mould, portions of air lurk in the heart of the iron, and cavities like those of a honeycomb are formed in the interior of the beam; but all defects are hid, and the flaws are effectively concealed. The artisan has covered his fault; but he will not prosper. As soon as it is subjected to a strain, the beam gives way. Sin covered becomes a rotten hollow in a human soul; and, when the strain comes, the false gives way.[c]

23—28. (23) **stript,** *etc.,* thus they sought to degrade him: taking away the proofs of a father's love. (24) **took,** *etc,*[a] yet

---

b.c. cir. 1729.

would overwhelm the world by the advantage which licentious principles afford, did not those who have long practised perfidy grow faithless to each other."—*Johnson.*

"Conspiracies no sooner should be formed than executed."—*Addison.*

"Conspiracies, like thunderclouds, should in a moment form and strike, like lightning, ere the sound is heard."—*J. Dow.*

c Dr. Cuyler.

v. 17, 18. *Bp. Wordsworth, Christian Boyhood,* ii. 52.

their plot and Reuben's purpose

a Pr. xxvii. 4; Ma. xxvii. 14.

b Ge. xlii. 22.

"On him that takes revenge revenge shall be taken, and by a real evil he shall dearly pay for the goods that are but airy and fantastical; it is like a rolling stone, which, when a man hath forced up a hill, will return upon him with a greater violence, and break those bones whose sinews gave it motion."—*Bp. J. Taylor.*

c Dr. W. Arnot.

Joseph is sold to the Ishmaelites

he whom they intended to starve lived to feed them in a time of famine. (25) they .. bread,^{b} their hungry bro. in the pit hard by. Reuben had left them meanwhile, v. 29. company, caravan. Ishmaelites, or Midianites,^{c} vv. 28 and 36. spicery, perh. *storax*. gum of the styrax tree. balm, gum of *opobalsam* or balsam tree : used for healing wounds. myrrh, or *ladanum*, a gum wh. exudes fr. a shrub, the *cistus ladaniferus*. Egypt, Cairo is still the seat of the myrrh trade. (26) profit,^{d} the spirit of *Judas* in this Judah. (27) come .. flesh, a pretence of mercy for the sake of gain. content, *lit.* hearkened. (28) drew .. Joseph, who might think they relented. sold, the son becomes a slave. they .. Egypt, torn fr. his earthly father, his heavenly Father accom. him thither.

The execution of the plot against Joseph.—I. They stripped him. Thus, in imagination, they degraded him from the birthright. II. They went about to starve him, throwing him into a dry pit. III. They slighted him in distress, eating bread before his very face. IV. They sold him. This plan was—1. Proposed by Judah through compassion ; 2. Acquiesced in by the others from policy. They thought if he were sold for a slave, he would never be a lord.^{e}

The selling of Joseph by his brethren (v. 28).—I. from what sources this horrible deed arose. II. How the Divine mouth remains silent, whilst the Divine hand so much the more strongly holds. III. The types that lie concealed herein.^{f}

The company of Ishmaelites.—These were coming, says Kiel, along the road which leads from Beisan, past Jenin, and through the plain of Dothan to the great caravan road running from Damascus to Legum, Ramleh, and Gaza into Egypt. These traders are called by two or three names, which shows that these tribes (the descendants of Ishmael, Medan, and Midian) resembled each other, not only in their common parentage, but also in their mode of life and frequent change of abode. There is nothing improbable in the fact that these descendants of Abraham should have so far increased by this time, as more than a hundred years must have elapsed since Ishmael was expelled from his father's house. The burden of the camels was, probably, first, gum tragacanth ; secondly, balm, or balsam ; and, thirdly, labdanum, the fragrant resin of the cistus rose.

29—33. (29) and .. pit, prob. he had gone to devise means of Joseph's escape. behold .. pit, having been sold meanwhile. and .. clothes, cust. sign of grief. (30) and .. brethren, evidently he was not present at the sale. and .. said, *etc.,* as the eldest bro. he felt responsible. (31) and .. coat, *etc.,* to conceal their crime, and acc. for absence of Joseph. (32) they .. father, the old man waiting for his son. this .. found, one crime begetting another, now falsehood. know .. no, who should know so well. (33) an .. him, the thing they wished to suggest. Joseph .. pieces, he could not suspect them of so foul a crime.

The character of Reuben.—In his farewell benediction in later days, Jacob declared this his eldest son was " unstable as water," or, as Craik points out, rather "impetuous as the water-floods." He was a man moved by sudden impulse : hence, in this incident, he is seen almost beside himself with grief, and expresses himself in extravagant language ; though at one time he had

B.C. *cir.* 1729.
a Ge. xlii. 21.
b Pr. xxx. 20; Am. vi. 6.
c Medan and Midian, songs of Abraham by Keturah ; Ishmael his son by Hagar. The Ishmaelites and Midianities were neighbours and prob. united for commercial purposes.
d Ge. iv. 10.
e M. Henry.
f Taube.
"There is an inward world which none see but those who belong to it; and though the outside robe be many - coloured, like Joseph's coat, inside it is lined with camel's hair or sackcloth, fitting those who desire to be one with Him who fared hardly in the wilderness, in the mountain, and on the sea."—*Newman.*
" That execrable sum of all villanies commonly called a slavetrade."—*Wesley.* v. 26—28. *J. Saurin, Disc.,* i. 439 ; *Ibid, Dissertations,* 253.

his coat is shown to Jacob

"Cruelty is no more the cure of crimes than it is the cure of sufferings. Compassion, in the first instance, is good for both ; I have known it to bring compunction when nothing else would."—*Landor.*

" Let me be cruel, not unnatural ; I will speak daggers to her, but use

GENESIS. [Cap. xxxviii. 1–5.

B.C. *cir.* 1729.

none; my tongue and my soul in this be hypocrites."—*Shakespeare.*

Jacob mourns for Joseph who is sold to Potiphar

a Re. vi. 12.

"Of permanent griefs there are none, for they are but clouds. The swifter they move through the sky, the more follow after them; and even the immovable ones are absorbed by the other, and become smaller till they vanish."
—*Richter.*

"Excess of grief for the deceased is madness; for it is an injury to the living, and the dead know it not."—*Xenophon.*

b Paxton Hood.

evidently taken part in the general dislike shown by Jacob's sons to the favoured child. Judah also desired to save his life, from a dread of incurring the guilt of fratricide, yet he was willing to get Joseph out of the way. But Reuben, though thus affected at the moment, had not courage afterwards to disclose the crime committed by his brothers.

34–36. (34) **sackcloth,**ᵃ made sometimes of camel's hair. **and .. days,** they unmoved by his grief. (35) **daughters,** prob. daus.-in-law: only one daughter named—Dinah. **grave,** Heb. *sheolah,* Gk. *Hades, i.e.* the invisible world. **thus .. him, inconsolable.** (36) **Potiphar** (*consecrated to the sun*). **captain,** *etc., lit.* prince of the executioners, or, commander of the body guard.

Jacob mourning for Joseph (v. 35).—"Thus," etc.—I. In relation to time: "many days." II. In relation to degree: "refused to be comforted." III. In relation to cause. 1. The loss of Joseph: 2. The lurking suspicion that his other sons knew something more about Joseph than they professed.

Nursing troubles.—"Some people are as careful of their troubles as mothers are of their babies: they cuddle them, and rock them, and hug them, and cry over them, and fly into a passion with you if you try to take them away from them; they want you to fret with them and to help them to believe that they have been worse treated than anybody else; if they could, they would have a picture of their grief, in a gold frame, hung over the mantel-shelf for everybody to look at. And their grief makes them ordinarily selfish—they think more of their dear little grief in the blanket and in the cradle than they do of all the world beside: and they say you are hard-hearted if you say, don't fret. 'Ah! you don't understand me—you don't know me—you can't enter into my trials.'"ᵇ

B.C. *cir.* 1727.

birth of Er and Onan

a 1 S. xxii. 1; Jos. xii. 15; 2 S. xxiii. 13; 1 Ch. xi. 15; 2 Ch. xi. 7; Mi. i. 15.

b Ge. xxiv. 3.

c Ge. xlvi. 12; Nu. xxvi. 19; 1 Ch. ii. 3.

d Jos. xv. 14; Mi. i. 14.

"When love is well timed, it is not a fault to love; the strong, the brave, the virtuous, and the wise, sink in the soft captivity together.—*Addison.*

CHAPTER THE THIRTY-EIGHTH.

1–5. (1) **and .. time,** while and before those events were proceeding in Egypt. **Judah,** going from sin to sin. **down,** *i.e.* southward. **Adullamite,** native of Adullamᵃ (*justice of the people*). **Hirah** (*noble birth*). (2) **Shuah**ᵇ (*wealth*). (3) **Er** (*watchful*). (4) **Onan**ᶜ (*strong, stout*). (5) **Shelah** (*petition*). **Chezib** (*false*), or Achzibᵈ (*deceit*), a city in the plain of Judah.

Sin, a quicksand.—It sometimes happens on the coast of Britain or Scotland, that a person walking on the strand will suddenly find difficulty in walking. The shore is like pitch, to which the soles of his feet cling. The coast appears perfectly dry; but the footprint that he leaves is immediately filled with water. Nothing distinguishes the sand which is solid from that which is not. He passes on unaware of his danger. Suddenly he sinks: he looks at his feet; the sand covers them. He wishes to turn back; but with every effort sinks more deeply. With indescribable terror, he finds he is involved in a quicksand. He throws down his burden: but it is already too late. The slow burial of hours continues. The sand reaches to his waist, to his chest, to his neck: now only his face is visible. He cries. The sand fills his mouth, and all is silent; his eyes, then the night of death. What a striking emblem of the danger of sin!

B.C. *cir.* 1727.

6—11. (6) **Tamah** (*a palm tree*). (7) **and .. him,**[a] by a signal stroke of Divine judgment: a man too wicked to live: how many wicked now live. (8) **and .. brother,**[b] aft. incorporated into the Jewish code. (10) **wherefore .. also,**[c] God branding the sin with Divine indignation. (11) **then .. said,** *etc.*,[d] prob. Judah thought her the cause of his son's death. **till .. grown,** who was prob. too young to marry.

Only one sin.—If but one sin be unsold, the man continues still a bondslave of hell. By one little hole a ship will sink into the bottom of the sea. The stab of a penknife to the heart will as well destroy a man as all the daggers that killed Cæsar in the senate house. The soul will be strangled with one cord of vanity, as well as with all the cart-ropes of iniquity: only the more sins, the more plagues and fiercer flames in hell; but he that lives and dies impenitent in one, it will be his destruction. One dram of poison will dispatch a man, and one reigning sin will bring him to endless misery.[e]

their sin and death

[a] Nu. xxxii. 23; Ec. xii. 14; Job xxxiv. 22; Pr. xv. 3; Nu. xxvi. 19.

[b] De. xxv. 5; Ma. xxii. 24; Mk. xii. 19; Lu. xx. 28.

[c] Ge. xlvi. 12.

[d] Ru. i. 13; Le. xxii. 13.

[e] R. Bolton.

12—15. (12) **and .. time,** *lit.* and the days were multiplied, *i.e.* several yrs. had passed. **Timnath**[a] (*portion assigned*), now *Tibneh*, S. of Zorah, near Wady Surar. (13) **behold .. sheep,** wh. would occupy him some time. (14) **sat .. place,**[b] *lit.* in the gate of Enaim. **for .. she,** *etc.,* she believing him old enough. (15) **harlot,** *lit.* consecrated, *i.e.* to the impure worship of Astarte. **because .. face,** whence he prob. thought she was under a vow.

The power of women.—Whatever may be the customs and laws of a country, the women of it decide the morals. Free or subjugated, they reign, because they hold possession of our passions. But their influence is more or less salutary, according to the degree of esteem which is granted them. Whether they are our idols or companions, courtesans or beasts of burthen, the reaction is complete, and they make us such as they are themselves. It seems as if Nature connected our intelligence with their dignity, as we connect our morality with their virtue. This, therefore, is a law of eternal justice; man cannot degrade woman without himself falling into degradation: he cannot raise them without himself becoming better. Let us cast our eyes over the globe, and observe those two great divisions of the human race, the East and the West. One half of the ancient world remains without progress or thought, and under the load of a barbarous cultivation; women there are slaves. The other half advances toward freedom and light; the women are loved and honoured.[c]

the story of Tamar

she deceives Judah

[a] Ju. xiv. 1—5; see *Thomson, L. and B., pp.* 566, 567.

[b] Pr. vii. 12; ix. 14, 15.

"Ah, how much suffering might be spared sometimes by a single abstinence, by a single no, answered in a firm tone to the voice of seduction."—*Lavater.*

"Endeavour to have as little to do with thy affections and passions as possible; and labour to thy power to make thy body content to go of thy soul's errands."—*J. Taylor.*

[c] *Martin.*

16—19. (16) **go to,** *etc.,* question—yet was not harlotry a sin? **and she said,** *etc.,* sustaining her assumed character by demanding payment. (17) **pledge,** a man capable of this sin will break his word. (18) **signet,** signet-ring or seal, or seal sometimes worn round the neck. **bracelets,** cord to which the seal was attached. **staff,** perh. a symbol of authority. (19) **laid .. her,** by wh. she had concealed herself fr. Judah. **put .. widowhood,** and returned to Judah's house as if nothing had happened.

The signet-ring.—The signet used by kings and persons of rank

she takes a pledge of him

"All animals are more happy than man. Look, for instance, on yonder ass: all allow him to be miserable; his evils, however, are not brought on by himself and his

GENESIS. [Cap. xxxviii. 20–33.

B.C. cir. 1727.

own fault; he feels only those which nature has inflicted. We, on the contrary, besides our necessary ills, draw upon ourselves a multitude of others."
—*Menander.*

"As surely as God is good, so surely there is no such thing as necessary evil. For by the religious mind, sickness and pain and death are not to be accounted evils. Moral evils are of your own making, and undoubtedly the greater part of them can be prevented."-*Southey, a Dr. Paxton.*

Judah tries in vain to redeem the pledge

"Judah now fears lest he shall be beaten with his own staff, lest his signet shall be used to seal his reproach; resolving not to know them, and wishing they were unknown of others. Nature is not more forward to commit sin, than willing to hide it."—*Bp. Hall.*

"Chastity consists in a fixed abhorrence of all forbidden sensual indulgences, a recollection of past impurities with shame and sorrow: a resolute guard over our thoughts, passions, and actions for the future; a steady abstinence from the distant approaches of evil

in the East was a ring which served all the purposes of sealing. All the Orientals, instead of signature by sign manual, use the impression of a seal on which their name and title (if they have one) is engraved. Among intriguing and malicious people, it is so easy to turn the possession of a man's seal to his disgrace, by making out false documents, that the loss of it always produces great concern. This shows how much Judah put himself in the power of Tamar, when he gave her his signet; and one reason of his anxiety, " Let her take it to her, lest we be ashamed," may therefore mean something beyond the mere discovery of the immoral action; " Lest by some undue advantage taken of the signet, I may be endangered." In an Indian court, the monarch still takes the ring from his finger, and affixes it to the decree, and orders the posts to be despatched to the provinces, as in the reign of Ahasuerus. When an eastern prince delivers the seal of empire to a royal guest, he treats him as a superior; but when he delivers it to a subject, it is only a sign of investiture with office. Thus the king of Egypt took off his ring from his hand, and put it upon Joseph's hand, when he made him ruler over all his dominions; and the king of Persia took off the ring which he had taken from Haman and gave it unto Mordecai.ᵃ

20—23. (20) **but . . not**, not seeking her in the house of Judah. (21) **openly**, *lit.* at Enaim. (22) **harlot**, *see* v. 14. (23) **let . . her**, *i.e.* the pledged. **shamed**, *lit.* lest we be for a contempt. **behold**, *etc.* I have done my best to redeem the pledge.

The legend of St. Margaret.—Her story is singularly wild. She was the daughter of a priest of Antioch, named Theodosius; and in her infancy, being of feeble health, she was sent to a nurse in the country. This woman, who was secretly a Christian, brought up Margaret in the true faith. The holy maid, while employed in keeping the few sheep of her nurse, meditated on the mysteries of the Gospel, and devoted herself to the service of Christ. One day, the governor of Antioch, whose name was Olybrius, in passing by the place, saw her, and was captivated by her beauty. He commanded that she should be carried to his palace, being resolved, if she were of free birth, to take her for his wife; but Margaret rejected his offers with scorn, and declared herself the servant of Jesus Christ. Her father and all her relations were struck with horror at this revelation. They fled, leaving her in the power of the governor, who endeavoured to subdue her constancy by the keenest torments. They were so terrible, that the tyrant himself, unable to endure the sight, covered his face with his robe; but St. Margaret did not quail beneath them. Then she was dragged to a dungeon, where Satan, in the form of a terrible dragon, came upon her with his inflamed and hideous mouth wide open, and sought to terrify and confound her; but she held up the cross of the Redeemer, and he fled before it. Or, according to the more popular version, he swallowed her up alive, but immediately burst; and she emerged unhurt: another form of the familiar allegory, the power of sin overcome by the power of the cross. He returned in the form of a man to tempt her further; but she overcame him, and placing her foot on his head, forced him to confess his foul wickedness and to answer to her questions. She was again brought before the tyrant, and, again refusing to abjure her faith, she was further tortured; but

Cap. xxxviii. 24—30.] GENESIS.

the sight of so much constancy in one so young and beautiful only increased the number of converts: so that in one day five thousand were baptised, and declared themselves ready to die with her. Therefore the governor took counsel how this might be prevented; and it was advised that she should be beheaded forthwith. And, as they led her forth to death, she thanked and glorified God that her travail was ended; and received joyfully the crown of martyrdom, being beheaded by the sword.*a*

B.C. *cir.* 1727.

"desires and indecency."—*J. Beaumont*

a Mrs. Jameson.

24—26. (24) **burnt.**" This punishment afterwards reserved for the daus. of priests. (25) **sent .. saying,**^b *etc.*, leaving it to his conscience to vindicate her. (26) **she .. I,** *i.e.* less blamable. **because .. son,** had he done right she would not have done wrong. **and .. more,**^c abstinence from sin best proof of true repentance.

Which is the most guilty? (v. 24)—Society has usually little pity for the harlot. Her sisters scorn the fallen. Judah filled with pious (? self-righteous) indignation voted for the burning of Tamar. He acknowledged that she had been "sinned against," as well as "sinning." The scene reminds one of the N. T. story of the adulteress and her accusers; some of whom perh. had sinned after Judah's fashion; but had left no evidence in the woman's hands.

Reform of an abandoned woman.—The legend of St. Mary of Egypt runs thus: Towards the year of our Lord 365, there dwelt in Alexandria a woman whose name was Mary, and who in the infamy of her life far exceeded Mary Magdalene. After passing seventeen years in every species of vice, it happened that one day, while roving along the seashore, she beheld a ship ready to sail, and a large company preparing to embark. She inquired whither they were going. They replied, that they were going up to Jerusalem, to celebrate the feast of the true cross. She was seized with a sudden desire to accompany them. On their arrival at Jerusalem, she joined the crowds of worshippers who had assembled to enter the church; but all her attempts to pass the threshold were in vain: whenever she thought to enter the porch, a supernatural power drove her back in shame, in terror, in despair. Struck by the remembrance of her sins, and filled with repentance, she humbled herself, and prayed for help: the interdiction was removed; and she entered the church of God, crawling on her knees. Thenceforward she renounced her wicked and shameful life; and, buying at a baker's three small loaves, she wandered forth into solitude, and never stopped or reposed till she had penetrated into the deserts beyond the Jordan, where she remained in severest penance, living on roots and fruits, and drinking water only. Her garments dropping off, she was miraculously clothed. The three small loaves lasted through the forty-eight years of her hermitage. A lion helped to dig her grave, and, when her body was committed to it, retired gently, according to the report of Father Zosimus, who saw it, and rejoiced at the grace shown to the penitent.

Tamar's sentence and Judah's exposure

a Le. xxi. 9; 2 S. xii. 5; Ma. vii. 1, 2; De. xxii. 21.

b Nu. xxxii. 23; Ro. ii. 1, 3, 21, 22.

c Job xxxiv. 32; Jo. viii. 11.

"There is no den in the wide world to hide a rogue. Commit a crime, and the earth is made of glass. Commit a crime, and it seems as if a coat of snow fell on the ground such as reveals in the woods the track of every partridge and fox, and squirrel and mole."—*Emerson.*

"Most people fancy themselves innocent of those crimes of which they cannot be convicted."—*Seneca.*

"Guilt, though it may attain temporal splendour, can never confer real happiness. The evident consequences of our crimes long survive their commission, and, like the ghosts of the murdered, for ever haunt the steps of the malefactor."—*W. Scott.*

27—30. (27) **travail,** labour, child-bearing. (28) **midwife,** *etc.*, thus careful to mark the first-born. (29) **Pharez**^a (*a breach*), called also Perez.^b (30) **Zarah**^c (*rising*), called also Zerah.^d

Woman's need of Christianity.—If there be anyone in this world

birth of Pharez and Zarah

a Ge. xlvi. 12; Nu. xxvi. 20, 21; Ru. iv. 12, 18; 1

B.C. cir. 1727.

Ch. ii. 4, 5; iv. 1; ix. 4.

b 1 Ch. xxvii. 3; Ne. xi. 4 6.

c Ge. xlvi. 12.

d Nu. xxvi. 20; Jos. vii. 18, 21; xxii. 20; 1 Ch. ii. 4, 6; ix. 6; Ne. xi. 24.

who more than another cannot afford not to be a Christian, it is a woman. If there be any one whose beauty fades as a flower and whose grace needs the sustenance of the ineffable : if there be anyone whose power is in beauty, in purity, in goodness, it is a woman. If there be any one more than another upon whom blight falls more rudely ; if there be any one more than another who is more burdened with grief or more wrung with sorrow, it is a woman. I marvel to see a woman that is not a Christian. The ladder between your souls and God is not half so long as that between our souls and God. God made woman to be better than man, and the perversion is in proportion when she is worse.

CHAPTER THE THIRTY-NINTH.

B.C. cir. 1729.

Joseph becomes Potiphar's house-steward

a 1 S. xviii. 14; Ac. vii. 9.

b Ps. i. 3.

c Ge. xxx. 27.

d W. Blackley, B.A.

"What Anacharsis said of the vine may aptly enough be said of prosperity. She bears the three grapes of drunkenness, pleasure, and sorrow ; and happy is it if the last can cure the mischief which the former work. When afflictions fail to have their due effect, the case is desperate." — *Bolingbroke.*

e *Roberts.*

Potiphar's wife

a Pr. i. 10; ii. 10—18 ; vii. 25—27.

b *Herod*, ii. iii.; *Did.* i. 59.

c Pr. vi. 29 ; Le. xx. 10.

d Ge. xx. 6 ; Ne. v. 15; 2 S. xii. 13; Ps. li. 4.

e Pr. i. 15 ; v. 8;

1—6. (1) **and**, *etc.*, see on xxxvii. 36. (2) **and .. man,**^a *lit.* a man causing to prosper. **house .. Egyptian**, *i.e.* a domestic servant. (3) **and .. saw,**^b *etc.*, the success of Joseph's administration was manifest. (4) **grace**, favour. **served**, ministered. **overseer**, steward. **all .. hand**, proof of confidence. (5) **and .. time**, change for the better in the affairs of Potiphar. **blessed .. sake,**^c not for Potiphar's sake : a master enriched by a faithful servant. (6) **left .. eat**, Potiphar's confidence exempted Joseph from making minute returns. **and .. favoured,** *lit.* was fair of form and fair of aspect.

Joseph carried down into Egypt (v. 1).—I. The circumstances under which Joseph went down to Egypt. He was brought down—1. Not by his own choice ; 2. With the prospect of servitude before him ; 3. Really, though not then apparently, by God. II. The lessons we may learn from the contemplation of these circumstances. 1. To acknowledge God in all our ways ; 2. To confide in him under all circumstances; 3. To repress every bad feeling of the heart ; 4. To recognise the Providence of God attending those that love Him.^d

The authority of Joseph.—All respectable men have a head servant called *kanika-pulli,* that is, "an accountant," in whose hands they often place all they possess. Such a man is more like a relation or a friend than a servant ; for on all important subjects he is regularly consulted, and his opinion will have great weight with the family. When a native gentleman has such a servant, it is common to say of him, " Ah ! he has nothing : all is in the hand of his *kanika-pulli.*" "Yes, yes, he is the treasure-pot." "He knows of nothing but the food which he eats."^e

7—10. (7) **and .. things,**^a *etc.*, licentiousness of Egyptian women proverbial.^b (8) **wotteth, knoweth. he .. hand,** great confidence should beget corresponding fidelity. (9) **there .. I,** to whom I must give account. **neither .. wife,**^c whom therefore I should regard with the greater respect. **how .. God?**^d a greater sin than a crime against his master. (10) **hearkened**, consented. **or .. her,**^e would not trust himself in the way of temptation.

Sin the greatest of all evils (v. 9).—Sin is the most pernicious and destructive evil. 1. Considered in itself. It—1. Is a rebellion against the sovereign majesty of God, who gives the life of authority to the law ; 2. Vilifies the ruling wisdom of God, who presented the law to men; 3. Is contrary to the unspotted holiness of God; 4. Is contempt and abuse of His excellent goodness; 5. Disparages His impartial goodness; 6. Implicitly denies His omniscience; 7. Slights His power. II. Relatively to us. Consider the evils that are consequential to it—such as proceed from it—1. By emanation. It has tainted men with pollution—has degraded him from his native dignity—and has broken the soul's peace; 2. As its penal effects—the fall of angels, and of man.*f*

A motherless boy.— When I was a little child, said a good man, my mother used to bid me kneel beside her, and to place her hand upon my head while she prayed. Before I was old enough to know her worth, she died, and I was left much to my own guidance. Like others, I was inclined to evil passions, but often felt myself checked, and, as it were, drawn back by the soft hand on my head. When I was a young man, I travelled in foreign lands, and was exposed to many temptations; but, when I would have yielded, that same hand seemed to be upon my head, and I was saved. I appeared to feel its pressure as in the days of my happy infancy, and sometimes there came with it a voice in my heart—a voice that must be obeyed—"Oh, do not this wickedness, my son, nor sin against thy God."

11—15. (11) **that.. business**, temptation should not force him fr. duty. **none.. within**, sinners shall not lack opportunities: this made appearances against Joseph. (12) **fled**,*a* we must sometimes fly from, and sometimes fight, temptation. (13) **when she saw**, *etc.*, she would have revenge if not her desire. (14) **she.. house**, lust changes to hatred. **see.. us**, note this woman's infernal cunning. **I.. voice**, she pretends to great chastity. (15) **garment**, circumstantial evidence against Joseph.

Circumstantial evidence.—An old lady kept a shop in a row of houses bordering on La Place St. Michel in Paris. She was generally known to have a quantity of money in the house. She had only one servant, a boy who had been with her for a long time. She slept at the back of the shop. on the ground floor; and the boy on the fourth story, which could only be approached from outside the house. He used to lock up the shop at night, and carry away the key. One morning, the door was observed to be open earlier than usual; and as no one was seen moving, some of the neighbours looked in. The door was not broken. They found the old lady dead in her bed. having received several wounds, as it seemed, from a knife; and a knife, covered with blood, was lying in the middle of the shop floor. In one hand of the corpse was a thick lock of hair, and in the other hand a cravat. The knife and cravat undoubtedly belonged to the shop-boy; and the lock of hair exactly resembled his. He was charged with the crime, and confessed it, and was broken on the wheel. A short time afterwards, another boy, in a wine-shop near, being taken up for another offence, on his death-bed confessed to the crime. He was well acquainted with the shop-boy accused of the crime, and often dressed his hair. He had, little by little, collected enough hair from the comb he used to make into a stout lock; and he had put it into the deceased's hand. He had procured one of the other boy's cravats, and his knife; and he had taken in wax an impression of the key.*b*

B.C. *cir.* 1729.

2 Th. iii. 14; 2 Ti. ii. 22; Ps. l. 1; Phi. v. 22; Ma. vi. 13; 1 Co. x. 13.

Wot, wotteth, pr. t. of *wit*, A.S. *wittan*, to know, of wh. the first and third persons sing. are wat.
"Men are not made truly religious by performing certain actions which are externally good; but men must have righteous principles in the first place, and then they will not fail to perform virtuous actions."- *Luther.*
f Dr. W. Bates.

Joseph is falsely accused

a Ec. vii. 26; Pr. vi. 5.
"Heaven has no rage like love to hatred turned, nor hell a fury like a woman scorned." — *Wm. Congreve.*
"Vice is attended with temporary felicity, piety with eternal joy."—*Bayard.*
"Do anything but love; or if thou lovest and art a woman, hide thy love from him whom thou dost worship; never let him know how dear he is; flit like a bird before him; lead him from tree to tree and from flower to flower; but be not won, or thou wilt, like that bird when caught and caged, be left to pine neglected and perish in forgetfulness."—*L. E. Landon.*
b Westminster Review.

Joseph is cast into prison

B.C. *clr.* 1729.

a Ex. xx. 16; De. v. 20; Pr. xix. 9; Ps. cxx. 3; Jas. iii. 8.

b Is. liv. 17; Ma v. 11, 12; 1 Pe. iii. 14—17.

c Ps. lxxvi. 10; Pr. vi. 34.

d Ps. cx. 18; 1 Pe. ii. 19.

e B. W. Noel, M.A

"They are not easily kept in the path of duty by harshness; distrust, bolts, and iron grating do not produce virtue in women and girls. It is honour which must keep them to their duty, and not severity."—*Molière.*

f Caussin.

he finds favour with the jailer

a Pr. xvi. 7; Ps. xxxvii. 5, 6; cvi. 46; cxii. 4; Da. i. 9.

b J. J. Cort, M.A.

"Virtue is more to man than either water or fire. I have seen men die from treading on water and fire, but I have never seen a man die from treading in the paths of virtue."—*Confucius.*

"The virtue of a man ought to be measured not by his extraordinary exertions, but by his every-day conduct."—*Pascal.*

c T. à Kempis.

16—20. (16) **she . . her,** nursing revenge: concocting her plan. (17) **saying,**^a *etc.*, as if reproaching her husband for exposing her to insult. (18) **and . . pass,**^b *etc.*, leaving me an example of injured innocence! (19) **that . . kindled,**^c against Joseph, though this is not said. (20) **prison,**^d roundhouse or dungeon, of wh. Potiphar had the official care.

The example of Joseph set before the young (vv. 20, 21).—Let us attend to—I. The troubles which came upon Joseph. Hated by his brothers, sold into Egypt, cast into prison on a false charge. II. His consolations in his trouble. "The Lord was with him."—1. By His grace. Joseph was under the government, and also under the comfort, of God's Spirit; 2. In His Providence. God made His good dispositions win the affection of the governor of the gaol. Conclusion :—To follow Joseph's good example—1. Obtain the converting grace of God. 2. Cherish purity of heart.^e

Power of a holy woman.—Great is the power of a woman when she applies herself to virtue. Behold at one instant (Matt. xv.) how one of that sex assails God and the devil: prevailing with the one by submission, and conquering the other by command! And He which gave the wild sea arms to contain all the world finds his own arms tied by the chains of a prayer which Himself did inspire. She draws unto her by a pious violence the God of all strength, such was the fervency of her prayer, such the wisdom of her answers, and such the faith of her words. As He passed away without speaking, she hath the boldness to call Him to her. To be short, she is stronger than the patriarch Jacob; for when he did wrestle with the angel, he returned lame from the conflict: but this woman, after she had been so powerful with God, returns straight to her house, there to see her victories, and possess her conquests.^f

21—23. (21) **but . . Joseph,** divine compensation. **and . . mercy,**^a fr. an unexpected quarter. **keeper . . prison,** *lit.* captain of the roundhouse. (22) **keeper . . prison,** made him an under-jailer. **and . . it,** he set them their appointed tasks. (23) **looked . . hand,** having like Potiphar confidence in Joseph. **the . . prosper,** *see* v. 3.

Joseph blessed in the prison (vv. 21—23).—Consider—I. Joseph as a prisoner for righteousness' sake. It was thus with Jeremiah, with John, with Paul and Silas, and with Daniel. Trial, in one form or another, is the portion of all the saints. II. God's presence and blessing with him in his confinement—"the Lord was with Joseph," etc. His gracious presence ensures a blessing.^b

The benefits of adversity.—It is good for man to suffer the adversity of this earthly life: for it brings him back to the sacred retirement of the heart, where only he finds he is an exile from his native home, and ought not to place his trust in any worldly enjoyment. It is good for him also to meet with contradiction and reproach : and to be evil thought of, and evil spoken of, even when his intentions are upright, and his actions blameless: for this keeps him humble, and is a powerful antidote to the poison of vainglory ; and then chiefly it is that we have recourse to the witness within us which is God, when we are outwardly despised, and held in no degree of esteem and favour among men. Our dependence up n God ought to be so entire and absolute, that we should never think it necessary, in any kind of distress, to have recourse to human consolations.^c

CHAPTER THE FORTIETH.

B.C. cir. 1720.

1—4. (1) **butler**, cup-bearer. **baker**, bread-maker (these were high officials in the court of Egypt). (2) **officers**, eunuchs (a term of wide meaning in the E.). (3) **ward**, guard. (4) **charged**, *lit.* made to visit them. **served**, distributed rations, etc. **season**, *lit.* days, perh. a year as the Jews understood the term.

Religion in adversity.—I. A good man in a bad place. 1. He had not been guilty of any crime. Many good men have been in prison (Bunyan, Baxter, etc.); 2. The plots of the wicked seem to succeed for a season. Success lifts them up and makes their fall the greater (Absalom, etc.). II. A good man in prison not forsaking his religion.—1. Might have said, " If I had not been so scrupulous I should not be here ;" 2. Did not grow morose or churlish; maintained a cheerful disposition, and integrity of purposes ; 3. Made himself useful to his jailer ; 4. Was friendly and faithful to fellow-prisoners. III. A good man in adversity befriended by his God.—1. God not forget his friend in adversity ; 2. God could reach him even there ; 3. God reached him through others—butler and baker, and by means of their dreams; 4. God's mercy was slow but sure.

Bunyan in prison.—The following anecdote is told respecting the jailer and Mr. Bunyan :—It became known to some of his persecutors in London that he was often out of prison. They set an officer to talk with the jailer on the subject; and in order to discover the fact, he was to get there in the middle of the night. Bunyan was at home with his family, but so restless that he could not sleep. He therefore acquainted his wife, that though the jailer had given him liberty to stay till the morning, yet, from his uneasiness, he must immediately return. He did so, and the jailer blamed him for coming in at such an unseasonable hour. Early in the morning the messenger came, and interrogating the jailer, said, "Are all the prisoners safe?" "Yes." "Is John Bunyan safe?" "Yes," "Let me see him." He was called and appeared, and all was well. After the messenger was gone, the jailer, addressing Mr. Bunyan, said, "Well, you may go in and out again just when you think proper, for you know when to return better than I can tell you."

5—8. (5) **each..dream**, *i.e.* corresponding with the event. (6) **sad**, troubled, meaning of dream *perplexed* them. (7) **wherefore..day?** Joseph's sympathy speedily aroused; not rendered unfeeling by injustice. (8) **interpreter**, diviner, astrologer. **do..God?**[a] he would lead their mind away from the human to the Divine revealer of secrets.

Sadness (v. 7).—"Wherefore," etc. Here is—I. Irrepressible sadness betraying itself. II. Sympathy with sadness expressing itself. III. The remover of sadness declared. IV. Sadness proved to be without reason to the innocent; and less than it should be to the guilty.

The philosophy of adversity.—It was a high speech of Seneca (after the manner of Stoics), that the good things which belong to prosperity are to be wished, but the good things that belong to adversity are to be admired : " *Bona veram secundarum optabilia,*

Pharaoh's butler and baker

"Let no man think lightly of good, saying in his heart, it will not benefit me. Even by the falling of water-drops a waterpot is filled; the wise man becomes full of good, even if he gather it little by little."—*Buddha.*

J. Saurin, *Disc. Hist.,* i. 455; also *ibid. Diss.* 270; Dr. Kitto, *D. B. I.* i. 386.

"Goodness does not more certainly make men happy, than happiness makes them good. We must distinguish between felicity and prosperity; for prosperity leads often to ambition, and ambition to disappointment; the course is then over, the wheel turns round but once; while the reaction of goodness and happiness is perpetual."—*Landor.*

they are perplexed with dreams
a Ge. xli. 16; Da. ii. 28.

"It is pleasant to be virtuous and good, because that is to excel many others; it is pleasant to grow better, because that is to excel ourselves; it is pleasant to mortify and subdue our lusts, because that is

B.C. cir. 1720.

victory; it is pleasant to command our appetites and passions, and to keep them in due order within the bounds of reason and religion, because this is empire."—Tillotson.

"A good deed is never lost; he who sows courtesy reaps friendship, and he who plants kindness gathers love; pleasure bestowed upon a grateful mind was never sterile, but generally gratitude begets reward."—Basil.

"Adversity has the effect of eliciting talents, which in prosperous circumstances, would have lain dormant."—Horace.

b Lord Bacon.

the butler relates his dream

"Ask the man of adversity how other men act towards him; ask those others how he acts towards them. Adversity is the true touchstone of merit in both; happy if it does not produce the dishonesty of meanness in one, and that of insolence and pride in the other."—Ld. Greville.

a Kitto.

v. 10, 11. *Il. Glorer, A Ser., 4to. (1664).*

Joseph interprets it
a Re. i. 20, xvii.

adversarum mirabilia." Certainly, if miracles be the command over nature, they appear most in adversity. It is yet a higher speech of his than the other (much too high for a heathen), "It is true greatness to have in one the frailty of a man and the security of a God." "*Vere magnum habere fragilitatem hominis, securitatem Dei.*" This would have done better in poesy, where transcendencies are more allowed: and the poets, indeed, have been busy with it; for it is, in effect, that strange thing which is figured in that strange fiction of the ancient poets, which seemeth not to be without mystery; nay, and to have some approach to the state of a Christian: "That Hercules, when he went to unbind Prometheus (by whom human nature is represented) sailed the length of the great ocean in an earthen pot or pitcher, lively describing Christian resolution, that saileth in the frail bark of the flesh through the waves of the world." But to speak in a mean, the virtue of prosperity is temperance, the virtue of adversity is fortitude, which in morals is the more heroical virtue. Prosperity is the blessing of the Old Testament: adversity is the blessing of the New, which carrieth the greater benediction, and the clearer revelation of God's favour. Yet, even in the Old Testament, if you listen to David's harp, you shall hear as many hearse-like airs as carols; and the pencil of the Holy Ghost hath laboured more in describing the affliction of Job than the felicities of Solomon. Prosperity is not without many fears and distaste; and adversity is not without comforts and hopes. We see in needle-works and embroideries, it is more pleasing to have a lively work upon a sad and solemn ground, than to have a dark and melancholy work upon a lightsome ground: judge, therefore, of the pleasure of the heart by the pleasure of the eye.[b]

9—11. (9) **vine**, art of wine-making known in Egypt from time of pyramids. (10) **and .. branches**, *etc.*, the wonder was that the vine budded and produced ripe fruit so rapidly. (11) **and .. hand**, *etc.* I was cup-bearer once more. **I .. cup**, the wine also rapidly made. **gave .. hand**, sign of restoration to royal favour.

The vine in Egypt.—Herodotus says that the culture of the vine was unknown in Egypt. But he was certainly mistaken; for every kind of evidence concurs to confirm the statement of Scripture. Indeed, other ancient writers even say that the Egyptians claimed for their Osiris the honour of being the first who cultivated the vine, and extracted wine from its fruit; and Athenæus, Strabo, Pliny, and Clement of Alexandria, specify districts in which it was grown. Modern travellers still find the vine cultivated in some places; and vine-branches, laden with ripe grapes, are among the ornaments of ancient Egyptian architecture. Egyptian paintings also have been found representing the vintage, with men occupied in pressing the ripe fruit. It is, nevertheless, true that the soil of Egypt is not generally favourable to the culture of the vine, and it does not appear that it throve well except in some more elevated spots. The quantity of wine afforded by the vines of Egypt was so small that wine was never, as in Greece, a common drink.[a]

12—15. (12) **are**,[a] *i.e.* they signify. (13) **yet .. days**, a short space would prove the truth or otherwise of the interpreta-

tion. **lift . . head,**[1] restoration of joy, honour, etc. (14) **think
. . thee,** *lit.* remember me with thee. **mention**[c] **. . Pharaoh,**
as a wise man able to interpret dreams. **bring . . house,** *i.e.*
cause me to be brought out. (15) **indeed . . away,** *lit.* stealing.
I was stolen . . the Hebrews, so, by faith, he calls Canaan.
here, in Egypt. **done . . dungeon,**[d] nothing deserving of
such a punishment.
Traces of God in prison.—I. Divine light. II. Holy love. III.
Divine monitions. IV. Hope of deliverance. *God's government
in its great issues.*—Consider His government of—I. The smallest
things. II. The proudest events. III. The most fallible judgments of men. IV. The darkest prisons. V. The nightly life.
VI. Hopes and fears in human need.[e]
Lifting up the head.—The ancients, in keeping their reckonings or accounts of time, or their list of domestic officers or
servants, made use of tables with holes bored in them, in which
they put a sort of pegs, or nails with broad heads, exhibiting the
particulars, either number or name, or whatever it was. These
nails or pegs the Jews call *heads,* and the sockets of the heads
they call *bases.* The meaning therefore of Pharaoh's *lifting up
his head is,* that Pharaoh would take out the peg, which had the
cup-bearer's name on the top of it, to read it, *i.e.* would sit in
judgment, and make examination into his accounts; for it seems
very probable that both he and the baker had been either suspected or accused of having cheated the king, and that, when
their accounts were examined and cast up, the one was acquitted,
while the other was found guilty. And though Joseph uses the
same expression in both cases, yet we may observe that, speaking
to the baker, he adds, *that Pharaoh shall lift up thy head from
off thee i.e.* shall order thy name to be struck out of the list of his
servants, by taking thy peg out of the socket.[f]

16—19. (16) **good,** favourable to the dreamer. **three . .
head,** baskets of white bread, or baskets full of holes, or baskets
of peeled osiers. (17) **all . . Pharaoh,** *lit.* food for Pharaoh,
the work of the baker. **birds . . head,** (comp. the wine in one
case handed to the king, in the other his bakemeats caught
away). (18) **are,** *see* v. 12. (19) **lift . . head,** ill. by the bakemeats lifted off thy head. **birds . . thee,** thou shalt be denied
the rites of sepulture.
Birds carrying off food.—That which seems a strange incident
to us is a very common one in such countries as Egypt, where
the air teems with animal life. It may be doubted whether, in
this case, the birds were kites, which make nothing of carrying
off large joints wholesale, or lesser birds, which were content to
pick away what they could not carry off. We incline to the
former supposition, as we observe, from the mural paintings, that
the Egyptians had not much taste for made dishes, but had their
tables supplied chiefly with joints and large birds (such as geese)
dressed whole, and very convenient, therefore, for kites to carry
off. Their doing this is a matter of constant occurrence, and it
is still a common complaint that such a man has lost his dinner
from its having been seized and carried off by a kite, as he bore
it upon his head, or even in his hands, in the open air. Those
who have read *The Thousand and One Nights*—and who
has not?—will remember some instances of this. There is, for
example, the case of Cogia Hassan Alhabbal, which is no doubt

B.C. 1720.

9, 10; Lu. xxii. 19.
b Ps. iii. 3; Je. liii. 31.
c Jos. ii. 12; 1 Co. vii 21.
d 1 Pe. iii. 17.

"It is only great souls that know how much glory there is in being good."—*Sophocles.*

"Good-nature is that benevolent and amiable temper of mind which disposes us to feel the misfortunes and enjoy the happiness of others, and, consequently, pushes us on to promote the latter and prevent the former; and that without any abstract contemplation on the beauty of virtue, and without the allurements or terrors of religion."—*Fielding.*
e *Lange.*
f *Stackhouse.*

the baker's dream and its interpretation

"It is when our budding hopes are nipped beyond recovery by some rough wind, that we are the most disposed to picture to ourselves what flowers they might have borne if they had flourished."
—*Dickens.*

"The setting of a great hope is like the setting of the sun. The brightness of our life is gone, shadows of the evening fall

B.C. cir. 1720.

around us, and the world seems but a dim reflection itself,—a broader shadow. We look forward into the coming lonely night; the soul withdraws itself. The stars arise, and the night is holy."—Longfellow.

a Dr. Kitto.

Pharaoh's birthday

a Ma. xiv. 6; Mk. vi. 21.

b Ma. xxv. 19.

c Job xix. 14; Ps. xxxi. 12; Am. vi. 6.

d C. Simeon, M.A.
"Verily, I swear, it is better to be born lowly, and range with humble livers in content, than to be perked up in a glistering grief, and wear a golden sorrow."
—*Shakespeare.*

"Every anniversary of a birthday is the dispelling of a dream."
—*Zschokke.*

"I am satisfied that we are less convinced by what we hear than by what we see."—*Herodotus.*

e Roberts.

such as the writer of the tale knew to have often occurred. "I went to the shambles, and bought something for supper. As I was carrying the meat I had bought home in my hand, a famished kite flew upon me, and would have taken away my meat, if I had not held it very fast; but the faster I held the meat, the more the bird struggled to get it, drawing me sometimes on one side, sometimes on another, but would not quit the prize, till unfortunately, in my efforts, my turban fell to the ground; the kite immediately let go its hold, and seizing the turban before I could pick it up, flew away with it." Two friends to whom he told this, felt no surprise at the attack on the meat, but were astonished that the bird made off with the turban. One said, "What have kites to do with turbans? They only seek for something to satisfy their hunger." But the other thought even this part of the affair probable, and "told a great many as surprising stories of kites, some of which he affirmed that he knew to be true."*a*

20—23. (20) **birthday**,*a* note also another birthday. **made servants**,*b* commemorative of the event: also token of royal favour. **lifted .. servants**, to serve as an encouragement and a warning to the rest. (21) **restored**, *etc.*, his character vindicated. (22) **hanged**, *etc.*, his crime having prob. been proved. (23) **butler .. him**,*c* yet God quickened his memory at the right time.

Ingratitude of Pharaoh's butler (*v.* 23).—We observe—I. That gratitude is but a feeble principle in the human mind. Corrupt practices are too strong in the heart—ambition, pride, covetousness, envy, wrath, revenge, hope, and fear. II. That its operations are rather weakened than promoted by prosperity. III. That the want of it is hateful in proportion to the obligations conferred upon us.*d*

Birthdays in the East.—The king "gave a feast unto his servants." Great men give an entertainment to their domestics on the first day of ploughing, when they all come together in their master's house, and have great enjoyment. His pleasure consists chiefly in hearing himself praised. The guests refer to feats of former days, when the host was young, when he was shaved for the *first* time, when he put on the ear-rings, or when he was married. They talk over the events of those days, and refer to the exploits of their master. He listens with delight, and lives his youthful days again. Should there be anything which his servants formerly did that is worthy of being referred to, they too are reminded of it, and they feel themselves highly honoured by such attention.*e*

B.C. cir. 1715.

Pharaoh's dreams

the first dream

a Cows, A.-S., *cunn,* gen of *cy,* pl. of *cu,* cow; Scot., *kye.*

CHAPTER THE FORTY-FIRST.

1—4. (1) **end .. years**, *i.e.* fr. the time that Joseph was put into, or the butler taken out of, prison. **river**, the Nile. (2) **kine**,*a* the cow sacred to Isis or Athor, the Venus Genetrix of Egypt. **meadow**, *lit.* among the sedge, or in the reed-grass, or rank grass, by the river side. (3) **seven .. river**, *note.* the river associated both with plenty and famine. **stood .. river**, but the first seven had eaten up the grass. (4) **and .. kine**, being without food. **d .. kine,** the great wonder of the dream. **awoke,** perplexed, wondering.

Pharaoh dreaming (vv. 1—7).—Consider—I. The physical causes of dreams. Thoughts during the day: various states of health. II. The moral significance attached to them in ancient times. They were often the medium by which God communicated with man, and hence remarkable dreams were regarded in the light of Divine revelations. III. The lessons we may gather from these dreams of Pharaoh. From them note—1. The providential care of God towards men; 2. The means He uses to advance His faithful servant's estate. Joseph's prosperity begins with Pharaoh's sleeping thoughts.[b]

The kine coming out of the river.—I couldn't understand Pharaoh's other dream respecting the fat and lean cattle which he said he saw "come up out of the river ... and they fed in a meadow." The figure, or things dreamt, seemed contrary to nature. But in going along the Nile, the puzzle was solved in the following manner:—Being seated on the deck of the steamer, I heard the Arabs belonging to the vessel shouting and making a great noise; then the steam whistle sent forth its shrillest shriek, and, as the engineers were English, I heard the familiar words, "Ease her," and shortly afterwards, "Stop her." Wondering what was amiss, I went to the front, and saw from twenty to thirty black knobs sticking out of the water, nearly as large as the crown of a hat. When the vessel got closer to them they began to rise and assume the form of buffaloes which had gone into the river with the double object of cooling their bodies and freeing themselves from their great tormentors, the flies of Egypt. When first seen there was nothing visible but the noses of these animals; but when they raised their bodies they moved very leisurely to the bank, and walked out into the meadow, in the same way as seen by Pharaoh in his dream.[c]

5—7. (5) **seven .. stalk,** prob. the *triticum compositum*, or Egyptian wheat. (6) **east wind,** prob. the S.E. wind, or *chamsin*, wh. blows fr. Arabia. **sprung .. them,** prob. fr. the same stalk. (7) **thin .. ears,** the thin ears absorbing the others without increasing in bulk. **behold .. dream,** which dwelt in his memory and perplexed his mind.

Rapidity of thought in dreaming.—A very remarkable circumstance, and an important point of analogy, is to be found in the extreme rapidity with which the mental operations are performed, or rather, with which the material changes on which the ideas depend are excited in the hemispherical ganglia. It would appear as if a whole series of acts, that would really occupy a long lapse of time, pass ideally through the mind in one instant. We have in dreams no true perception of the lapse of time—a strange property of mind! for if such be also its property when entered into the eternal disembodied state, time will appear to us eternity. The relations of space as well as of time are also annihilated; so that while almost an eternity is compressed into a moment, infinite space is traversed more swiftly than by real thought.[a]

8—13. (8) **troubled,**[a] smitten as with a hammer: stunned. **magicians,** sacred scribes: professed interpreters of hidden things. **and .. Pharaoh,**[b] God, the *only* revealer of secrets. (9) **faults,** (1) forgetfulness of Joseph; (2) offence against

B.C. *cir.* 1715.

"Animals of the buffalo kind in hot countries seem almost amphibious; they delight to stand for hours in the water, with their bodies immersed, except the head." —*Kitto.*

"Dr. Royle thinks that the word translated meadow is a plant, perhaps the *cyperus esculentus*, or some species of panicum, wh. forms excellent pasture in warm countries."

b A. W. Pemie, B.A.

c Heycock.

See *Dr. Kitto, Royal Dreams, &c.,* in *Daily Bibl. Illus.,* i. 411.

the second dream

"The south-east wind, here called the east wind, blowing in March and April, is one of the most injurious winds, and of longest continuance, while the shelter that Egypt has from it, by means of the Mokatten chain of mountains is only partial, and by no means extends to the whole country." —*Havernick.*

a Dr. F. Winslow.

Joseph is remembered by the butler

a Job vii. 13, 14

B.C. cir. 1715.

b Is. xxix. 14.

"I have only to take up this, or this, to flood my brain with memories."— *Mlle. Deluzy.*

"Memory can glean, but can never renew. It brings us joys faint as is the perfume of the flowers, faded and dried, of the the summer that is gone."—*Beecher.*

"A scent, a note of music, a voice long unheard, the stirring of the summer breeze, may startle us with the sudden revival of long-forgotten feelings and thoughts."— *Talfourd.*
v. R. *J. C. Dieteric, Antiquitates,* 126.

c *Bibl. Treas.*

Joseph is sent for

a Ps. cxiii. 7; 1 S. ii. 8.

b Ps. xxv. 14.

c Dn. ii. 20; Ac. iii. 12; 2 Co. iii. 5; Dn. ii. 22, iv. 2.

"'On the monuments, when it was intended to convey the idea of a man of low condition, or a slovenly person, the artists represented him with a beard' *(Wilkinson,* iii. 357; *Hengstenberg,* p. 30). Joseph, therefore, when about to appear before Pharaoh, was careful to adapt himself to the manners of the Egyptians."
—*Spk. Comm.*

Pharaoh. **day,** time Divinely chosen : memory Divinely prompted. (10, 11) The butler rehearses the prison incident. (12) **Hebrew,** the faith of Joseph prevented him fr. being ashamed of a name that was despised in Egypt. (13) **restored,** *i.e.* predicted the restoration, etc.

The remembrance of sin (v. 9).—I find in these words—I. The recognition of the true moral character of a past act. We are reminded here—1. That injury to man—whether in the form of omission or commission—is a sin against God ; 2. That the forgetting of this principle results in people sometimes thinking they have nothing, or very little, to repent of. II. The confession of a sin. 1. The lateness of the confession ; resulting from (1) Forgetfulness ; (2) Fear ; (3) Ignorance. 2. The confession, though late, was honest and full. III. The causes that led to this confession being made—" this day." Why this day ? 1. An overruling providence so ordered it ; 2. The law of the association of ideas : Pharaoh's dream reminded the butler of his own.

Egyptian magicians.—The two designations probably apply to the same class of persons. They were called "scribes," and had their Egyptian names from the styles or writing implements they carried. Belonging also to the priestly class, they occupied themselves with the sacred arts and sciences of their nation, being concerned in hieroglyphic writings, astrology, the interpretation of dreams, foretelling of events, and, lastly, magic. But, as Delitzsch observes, they all failed to interpret Pharaoh's vision, although they might have found a clue to it even in their own religious symbols ; for the cow was the symbol of Isis, the goddess of the all-sustaining earth, and represented the earth, agriculture, and food. And, moreover, the Nile, through its periodical inundations, was the souce of the fertility of Egypt.c

14—16. (14) **they .. hastily,**a *lit.* caused him to run. **shaved,** a Hebrew adopting Egyptian customs : no sacrifice of principle involved. **and .. raiment,** Joseph in no hurry : unruffled calmness : not unduly elated. **and .. Pharaoh,** having fitted himself for the king's presence. (15) **that .. it,**b *lit.* thou wilt hear a dream to interpret it. *i.e.* the interpretation was to Joseph as easy as the hearing. (16) **it .. me,**c modesty of Joseph comp. with presumption of astrologers. **God,** whom Joseph never forgets. **give .. peace,** a clear interpretation that shalt restore Pharaoh's peace of mind.

Joseph shaving himself.—Carefully considered, this is one of many passages in which the truth of the Scripture narrative is attested by an incidental and slight allusion to remarkable customs, which no mere inventor would think of noticing, or notice without explaining. Shaving was a remarkable custom of the Egyptians, in which they were distinguished from other Oriental nations, who carefully cherished the beard, and regarded the loss of it as a deep disgrace. This was the feeling of the Hebrews ; but here Joseph shaves himself in conformity with an Egyptian usage, of which this passage conveys the earliest intimation, but which is confirmed, not only by the subsequent accounts of Greek and Roman writers, but by the ancient sculptures and paintings of Egypt, in which the male figure is usually beardless. It is true that in sculpture some heads have a curious rectangular beard, or rather beard case, attached to the chin ; but this is proved to be an artificial appendage by the same head being represented sometimes with and at other times without it; and still more by the appearance of a band which passes along the jaws, and attaches it to the cap on the head, or to the hair. It is concluded that this appendage was never actually worn, but was used in sculpture to indicate the male character.[d]

17—24. (17, 18) See vv. 1—4. (19) **such .. badness,** where he must have seen many bad ones. (20) See v. 4. (21) **it .. them,** *etc.*, ill. so with some men who are not benefited by the best food—mental, spiritual. (22, 23) See vv. 5—7. (24) **but .. me,** not fearing the Lord, His secret was not with them.

The dreams of Pharaoh.—Introduction :—The dreams—(1) Were formed of elements with which the dreamer was somewhat familiar ; (2) Were a Divine communication to the mind of a heathen ; (3) Brought trouble into the heart of a monarch ; (4) Could only be interpreted by a devout Theist. Notice, as suggested by these dreams—I. The revolution of providence. "Seven years of plenty," followed by "seven years of famine." Change—1. Promotes our spiritual discipline ; 2. Reminds us of God's activity ; 3. Inspires us with a feeling of our dependence upon Him. 4. Gives a meaning to the Bible. II. The advantages of wisdom. Joseph's wisdom—1. Invested him with a chastened humility of soul ; 2. Enabled him to solve the distressing inquiries of the monarch ; 3. Exalted him to supremacy in the kingdom. III. The duty of rulers. They should be—1. Philanthropic ; 2. Forecasting ; 3. Economical. Learn :—(1) How great is the Governor of the world ; (2) How worthless the world is without religion ; (3) How important it is to be in fellowship with the great God.[a]

Fantasies of dreams.—
Still when the golden sun withdraws his beams,
And drowsy night invades the weary world,
Forth flies the god of dreams, fantastic Morpheus,
Ten thousand mimic phantoms fleet around him,
Subtle as air, and various in their natures ;
Each has ten thousand thousand diff'rent forms,
In which they dance confused before the sleeper,
While the vain god laughs to behold what pain
Imaginary evils give mankind.[b]

25—28. (25) **the .. one,** *i.e.* one in purport. **God .. do,**[a] the dream a picture of Divine Providence. (26) **are,** see xl. 12. (28) **this,** *etc.*, i.e. I have told Pharaoh the Divine purpose only.

Mercy of God to heathen people (v. 28).—I. This is seen in that He left not Himself without a witness among them (Ac. xiv. 7) as prophets (Jonah, Daniel), dreams (Pilate's wife, and here Pharaoh). II. Mercy to the heathen subservient to the cause of His own people. As now, a famine is revealed to forward the cause of Israel (historical ills.).

Dreaming.—About the age of fourteen I was almost every night unhappy in my sleep from frightful dreams. Sometimes hanging over a frightful precipice, and just ready to drop down; sometimes pursued for my life, and stopped by a wall, or a sudden loss of all strength ; sometimes ready to be devoured by a wild beast. How long I was plagued with such dreams I do not now recollect. I believe it was for a year or two at least; and I think they had not quite left

---

B.C. *cir.* 1715.

d Dr. *Kitto.*

Pharaoh relates his dreams to Joseph

"To make anything very terrible, obscurity seems, in general, to be necessary. When we know the full extent of any danger, when we can accustom our eye to it, a great deal of the apprehension vanishes." — *Burke.*

"Generally he perceived in men of devout simplicity this opinion: that the secrets of nature were the secrets of God,—part of that glory into which man is not to press too boldly."—*Bacon.*

a Dr. *Kitto.*

b Rowe.

Joseph interprets the dreams

a Re. iv. 1.

"One might as well attempt to calculate mathematically the contingent forms of the tinkling bits of glass in a kaleidoscope as to look through the tube of the future and foretell its pattern." —*Beecher.*

"Futurity is impregnable to mortal ken: no prayer pierces

B.C. 1715.

through heaven's adamantine walls. Whether the birds fly right or left, whatever be the aspect of the stars; the book of nature is a maze, dreams are a lie, and every sign a falsehood."—Schiller.

"God will not suffer man to have the knowledge of things to come; for if he had prescience of his prosperity, he would be careless; and, understanding of his adversity, he would be senseless."—Augustine.

b T. Reid.

the famine predicted

a Ge. xlvii. 13.
b Nu. xxiii. 19; Is. xlvi. 10; 1 Ki. xl. 9; Job. xxxiii. 14; Ps. lxii. 11.

"One month in the school of affliction will teach thee more than the great precepts of Aristotle in seven years; for thou canst never judge rightly of human affairs unless thou hast first felt the blows and found out the deceits of fortune."—Fuller.

"Adversity has the effect of eliciting talents which, in prosperous circumstances, would have lain dormant."—Horace.

c Milton.

Joseph's advice to Pharaoh

me before I was sixteen. In those days I was much given to "castle-building;" and in my evening solitary walk, which was generally all the exercise I took, my thoughts would hurry me into some active scene, where I generally acquitted myself much to my own satisfaction; and in these scenes of imagination I performed many a gallant exploit. At the same time, in my dreams I found myself the most arrant coward that ever was. Not only my courage, but my strength failed me in every danger; and I often rose from my bed in the morning in such a panic, that it took some time to get the better of it. I wished very much to get rid of these uneasy dreams, which not only made me very unhappy in sleep, but often left disagreeable impressions on my mind for some part of the following day. I thought it was worth trying whether it was possible to recollect that it was all a dream, and that I was in no real danger. I often went to sleep with my mind as strongly impressed as I could with this thought, that I never in my lifetime was in any real danger, and that every fright I had was a dream. After many fruitless endeavours to recollect this when the danger appeared, I effected it at last, and have often, when I was sliding over a precipice into the abyss, recollected that it was all a dream, and boldly jumped down. The effect of this commonly was, that I immediately awoke. But I awoke calm and intrepid, which I thought a great acquisition. After this, my dreams were never uneasy, and in a short time I dreamed not at all. During all this time I was in perfect health.*b*

29—32. (29) **plenty** .. **Egypt**, the largest corn-producing country in the world at that time. (30) **all .. forgotten,** as past benefits are forgotten in present sorrow, **and .. land,**ᵃ *i.e.* the people of the land. (31) **grievous,** *lit.* very heavy; yet Egypt was oft. called the granary of the world. (32) **doubled .. established,**ᵇ repetitions in Scripture suggestive of confirmation of facts stated.

Present trouble obliterating the memory of past mercy (v. 30).— I. In the case before us. Care and hunger in time of famine induced forgetfulness of previous plenty. II. So in their troubles men forget their happy past. Jacob had had some bright seasons, yet called his days few and evil.

The nature of dreams.—

Know that in the soul
Are many lesser faculties, that serve;
Reason as chief: among these Fancy next
Her office holds: of all external things
Which the five watchful senses represent,
She forms imaginations, airy shapes,
Which Reason, joining or disjoining, frames
All what we affirm, or what deny, and call
Our knowledge or opinion: then retires
Into her private cell, where nature rests.
Oft in her absence mimic Fancy wakes
To imitate her; but misjoining shapes,
Wild work produces oft, and most in dreams;
Ill matching words and deeds long past or late.ᶜ

33—36. (33) **now,** *etc.,* Joseph, taught of God, advises Pharaoh. **man,** whom Pharaoh was to choose, while God guided the king. **discreet,** *etc.,* suitable human qualities, fitting instruments of Divine Providence. **set** .. **Egypt**, a responsible official rather than an irresponsible and divided council. (34) **him** .. **land**, *i.e.* Pharaoh's viceroy to appoint *overseers*. **take**, purchase. **fifth part**, in addition to usual revenue, wh. was prob. a tenth. **in** .. **years**, *i.e.* year by year. (35) **hand**, authority. **and** .. **cities**, as fortified granaries, safe fr. clamorous and hungry mobs. (36) **food** .. **store**, prudential forethought an evidence of trust in Providence.

Self-imposed taxes.—" Friends," says he, " the taxes are indeed very heavy; and, if those laid on by the government were the only ones we had to pay, we might more easily discharge them; but we have many others, and much more grievous to some of us. We are taxed twice as much by our idleness, three times as much by our pride, and four times as much by our folly; and from these taxes the commissioners cannot ease or deliver us by allowing an abatement. However, let us hearken to good advice, and something may be done for us; ' God helps them that helps themselves,' as poor Richard says."a

Legend of the devil and the tax.—A large sum of money having been collected by Edward, king and saint, for the tribute called *Danegelt*, it was conveyed to the palace, and the king was called to see it. At the sight thereof, he started back, exclaiming, that he beheld a demon dancing upon the money, and rejoicing. Thereupon, he commanded that the gold should be restored to its owners, and released his subjects from that grievous tribute.b

37—40. (37) **good**, suitable to the occasion. **eyes**, judgment, opinion. (38) **can** .. **is**, his equal, not to say his superior. **in** .. **is**,a wh. made Joseph what he was. (39) **God** .. **this**, the king acknowledges the source of Joseph's wisdom. **there** .. **art**, God being the special Teacher of no other. (40) **house**, affairs. **unto** .. **ruled**,b *lit.* at thy mouth shall all my people **kiss**, *i.e.* in token of reverence, submission, obedience. **only** .. **thou**, so far as relates to the kingly office.

Joseph's exaltation (vv. 39, 40).—Look at his exaltation—I. As considered in itself. Grounded in his destiny. Accomplished by his innocent sufferings and his good account. Carried out by God's grace and wisdom as a Divine miracle in His most special providence. Its principal object the preservation of Israel and of many nations. Its further object, Israel's education in Egypt. Its imperishable aim the glory of God, and the edification of the people of God by means of the fundamental principle,—through humiliation to exaltation. II. In its typical significance: the seal of Israel's guidance in Egypt, of the guidance of all the faithful, of the guidance of Christ as the model of our Divine instruction.c

The kiss of obedience.—" Alluding," says Wilkinson, " to the edict granting official power to Joseph, to be issued in the form of a firman, as in all Oriental countries; and all who should receive that order would kiss it, according to the usual eastern mode of acknowledging obedience and respect for the sovereign." The Hon. Robert Curzon, in his *Visit to the Monasteries of the Levant*, remarks on that of Somopetra:—" Except Dionysion, this was the only monastery where the *agoumenos* (head) kissed the letter of the patriarch and laid it upon his forehead ; the sign of reverence and obedience which is, or ought to be, observed with the firmans of the Sultan and other Oriental potentates."

B.C. *cir.* 1715.

"Taxing is an easy business. Any projector can contrive new impositions, any bungler can add to the old; but is it altogether wise to have no other bounds to your impositions than the patience of those who are to bear them?"—*Burke.*

v. 38. J. *Saurin, Disc. Hist.* i. 463; *Bp. Mant.* ii. 21; and ii. 1.

a Dr. *Franklin.*

b *Mrs. Jameson*

Joseph is made viceroy of Egypt

a Nu. xxvii. 18; Job. xxxii. 8; Pr. ii. 6; Ps. lxxxiv. 11.

b Job xxxi. 27; cf. 1 S. x. 1; 1 Kī. xix. 18; Ps. ii. 12.

"The wonder is not that the world is so easily governed, but that so small a number of persons will suffice for the purpose. There are dead weights in political and legislative bodies as in clocks, and hundreds answer as pulleys who would never do for politicians." —*Simms.*

" The Egyptians, on taking anything from the hand of a superior, or that is sent from him, kiss it ; and, as the highest respect, put it to their foreheads." —*Bp. Pococke.*

c *Lange.*

B.C. cir. 1715.

Joseph's change of name and marriage

a Ps. cv. 21, 22.

b Est. iii. 19; Da. v. 29; Ac. v. 9, 10.

c Acc. to *Origen* and *Jerome* " native Egyptian," wh. would sig. a proclamation of naturalisation.

d Acc. to *Coptic*, "a revealer of secrets;" acc. to *Gesenius*, "sustainer of the age;" acc. to *Vulgate*, "the saviour of the world;" prob. the true meaning is, "the food of the living."

e Jer. xliii. 13.

"Honours soften fatigue. It is easier riding in a gilded and embossed saddle. Atlas, while he sustains the world upon his shoulders, is himself sustained by the admiration his feat excites."—*Bovee*.

f C. Simeon, *M.A.*

g Dr. *Buchanan*.

Joseph gathers the corn

a "In the tomb of Amenemho, at Beni Hassan, there is a painting of a great storehouse, before the door of which lies a large heap of grain already winnowed. Near by stands the bushel with which it is measured, and the registrar

41—45. (41) **sat,**ᵃ *lit.* I have given, *i.e.* established. (42) **ring,**ᵇ signet-ring, special symbol of authority. **linen,** *i.e.* the byssus or fine linen of Egypt: the priestly dress. **chain,** to denote distinction : mark of royal favour. (43) **second.. bad,** next to the royal chariot in splendour. **bow.. knee,**ᶜ Heb. *abrech,* meaning of word not known: *see* marg. A. V. (44) **lift .. foot,** prov. express.=complete subjection. (45) **Zaphnath-paaneah**ᵈ (*revealer of mysteries*). **Asenath** (*she is of Neith,* the Egyptian Minerva). **Potipherah** (*devoted to Ra, i.e.* the sun). **On,** Heliopolis (*the city of the sun*) or Bethshemesh,ᵉ on E. bank of Nile, few ms. N. of Memphis; a red granite obelisk still marks the site.

Joseph's advancement (v. 41).—Observe—I. That we can be in no state, however desperate, from whence God cannot speedily deliver us. II. That God is never at a loss for means whereby to effect His gracious purposes. III. That we are never in a fairer way for exaltation to happiness than when we are waiting God's time, and suffering His will. Learn—1. To submit with cheerfulness to all the dispensations of providence; 2. To be thankful to God for the governors whom He has been pleased to set over us; 3. To be thankful, above all, for our adorable Emmanuel.*ᶠ*

Heliopolis.—Six or seven miles from Cairo, the eye lights on the spot where stood of old that On or Heliopolis, the far-famed city of the sun, the daughter of whose high-priest became the wife of Joseph. Some traces of the temple still remain. There is a pool of water, with a few willows weeping over it—that pool was the spring, or fountain of the sun. There is a solitary obelisk rising amid ruins, and surrounded by garden shrubs that have been growing wild for ages. That obelisk, and another, the base of which alone remains, confronted the ancient temple of On; and there it has stood for well-nigh four thousand years. It was there when Abraham came down into Egypt to escape the famine that desolated Canaan. It may have been beneath its shadow that Joseph first beheld his future wife Asenath. Often must Moses have stood beside it. . . . Herodotus makes mention of its existence; so that it was already old before any other history than that which the Bible contains had yet been written. Plato, the greatest of the sages of ancient Greece, made a pilgrimage to see it. It has survived the dynasties of the Pharaohs, the Ptolemies, and the Cæsars, and bids fair to survive that of the Mohammeds too.ᵍ

46—49. (46) **was .. old,** having now been thirteen years in Egypt. **went .. Egypt,** in the discharge of the duties of office. (47) **handfuls,** *i.e.* in great abundance. (48) **food .. same,** that there might not be far to carry it, and for convenience of distribution. (49) **for .. number,** the quantity exceeded the power of Egyptian computation.

The young minister of state (v. 46).—I. His rise to power. 1. Without influence or friends; 2. Through trial; 3. By force of character; 4. By the blessing of God. II. His administration. 1. For the time apparently oppressive : heavy taxation; 2. For the ultimate advantage of all. III. His title, " the preserver of life." Compare with power, rule, and title of Christ.

The fertility of Egypt.—This I witnessed. I plucked up at random a few stalks out of the thick corn-fields. We counted the number of stalks, which sprouted from single grains of seed, carefully pulling to pieces each root, in order to see that it was but one plant. The first had seven stalks ; the next three ; the next nine ; then eighteen ; then fourteen. Each stalk would bear an ear.[b]

B.C. cir. 1715.

who takes the account."—*Kitto*.
b *Jowett*.

50—52. (50) **two .. came,** *i.e.* during the yrs. of plenty. (51) **Manasseh** (*causing to forget*) : he forgot[a] his sorrow, but prob. remembered Canaan. (52) **Ephraim** (*doubly fruitful*). **for .. affliction,** the season of affliction oft. the time of spiritual fruitfulness.

Manasseh (v. 51).—" God hath made me to forget "—I. All the hatred of my brethren, and their treachery towards me. II. All the consequences of that hatred—my selling for a slave, my imprisonment without cause. III. All the sorrow and toil that I have ever endured. *Ephraim* (v. 52).—" God hath caused me to be fruitful " in—I. Wealth. My riches are boundless. II. Honour and dignity. I am second in the land. III. Wisdom. IV. The esteem of those around me. I have saved them through the help of God.[b]

Manasseh.—The explanation is given in the name which Joseph gave to his son Manasseh, *i.e.* forgetting ; " For God," saith he, " hath made me to forget all my toil, and all my father's house." Joseph's conduct was not unfilial. The naming of his son shows that his father's home was not forgotten ; and while he retained that true and earnest love, which by-and-by was to be exhibited, he acquiesced in the Divine will, and was content to wait God's time to be delivered from this long silence, just as he had waited God's time to deliver him from prison.[c]

birth of Manasseh and Ephraim
a Job xi. 16.

" The domestic relations precede and, in our present existence, are worth more than all our other social ties. They give the first throb to the heart and unseal the deep fountains of its love. Home is the chief school of human virtue. Its responsibilities, joys, sorrows, smiles, tears, hopes, and solicitudes form the chief interest of human life."— *Channing.*
b *M. A. Stoddard.*
c *Bibl. Stud.*

53—57. (53) **ended,** times of prosperity intermittent. (54) **and .. lands,**[a] they had no Joseph to instruct them. **but .. bread,** through the " preserver of life." (55) **people .. bread,** so men in soul-famine cry to the great King for mercy. **go .. do,** Jesus our Teacher and Saviour. (56) **all .. earth,** *i.e.* the known world. **Joseph .. Egyptians,** ill. Jesus dispenses the bread of life. (57) **all .. corn,** hunger drove men fr. great distances and through many difficulties: Canaan amongst these countries.

Egyptian granaries.—Egypt was noted for its superabundant harvest, but the people do not appear to have been in the habit of storing up the surplus produce until taught the lesson by Joseph, in anticipation of the seven years of famine. Of the labours rendered by him in collecting the produce of the country during the years of plenty we may form a clear idea from the many representations given us of the vast granaries in which corn was stored. These granaries appear to have been erected apart from the house, and enclosed within a separate wall. Some of them had vaulted roofs, which were filled through an aperture near the top, to which the men ascended by steps, and the grain, when wanted, was taken out from a door at the base. Several of this kind exist at old Cairo, the erection of which tradition ascribes to Joseph. The lesson taught the Egyptians seems to have been learned by the Romans, who formed granaries in seasons of plenty to secure food for the poorer citizens, and all who wanted it were provided with corn from these reservoirs, in necessitous times, at the expense of the treasury. There were 120 such storehouses in Rome. Even in our country, in the time of James I., twelve new

the famine begins

a " In the year of the Hejira 444, a famine took place in Egypt on account of a deficiency in the increase of the Nile, which at the same time extended over Syria, and even to Bagdad." — *Kitto.*

v. 55—57. *A. Roberts, M.A., S.S. on Histories of Scripture,* 174.

Although the area of Egypt capable of cultivation is about 16,000 sq. ms. only, or ab. half the area of Ireland, E. was in anc. times one of the granaries of the world. See note on Acts xxvii. 5—8.

granaries were built at Bridewell, in which 6,000 quarters of corn were stored, to prevent the sudden dearness of this article arising from the very rapid increase of population.[b]

CHAPTER THE FORTY-SECOND.

1—4. (1) **why .. another ?**[a] 1. Looks of vacuity, they had nothing to suggest; 2. And of fear, they must have heard of Egypt. (2) **heard**, fr. passing caravans; he had prob. also seen his neighbours departing. **corn**, lit. a breaking. i.e. a breaking of hunger. (3) **went .. Egypt**, and to fulfil the dream. (4) **Benjamin**, now a man, and a father.[b] **brother**, they are called Joseph's brethren not Jacob's sons: Joseph now being the central person in the history. **lest .. him**, twenty yrs. had not obliterated the memory of Joseph.

Corn in Egypt (v. 2).—Here we are reminded—I. That Divine relief often comes from unexpected quarters. II. That as Joseph was sent to Egypt—as he said, "to preserve life"—so Jesus, of whom he was an eminent type was ordained to be the world's Saviour, and the dispenser of spiritual life. III. That as Joseph had to be applied to by the people individually, that their wants might be met; so, if we would have our spiritual wants supplied, we must go personally to Christ. IV. That just as Joseph—the brother they had so cruelly wronged—was the only one in the world who could help them; so this Saviour, whom we have in the old time despised and rejected, or whom we have treated with indifference, is the only being in the universe to whom we can go in our soul's extremity.

Cowardly fear.—The very worst thing you can do is to lock the closet door when you think probably there is a skeleton within. Fling it wide open; search with a paraffine lamp into every corner. A hundred to one, there is no skeleton there at all. But from youth to age we must be battling with the dastardly tendency to walk away from the white donkey in the shadow, which we ought to walk up to. I have seen a little child, who had cut her finger, entreat that it might just be tied up, without ever being looked at: she was afraid to look at it. But when it was looked at, and washed and sorted, she saw how little a thing it was for all the blood that came from it; and about nine-tenths of her fear fled away.[c]

5—8. (5) **among .. came**, fr. Canaan and elsewhere. (6) **bowed .. earth**,[a] the dream fulfilled. (7) **spake .. them**,[b] lit. spake hard things with them. **said**, to test their penitence. (8) **Joseph .. brethren**, prob. he was expecting them. **but .. him**, they did not recognise the Heb. shepherd in the Egyptian prince.

Joseph knew his brethren, but they knew not him (v. 8).—From the text, consider—I. Our heavenly Joseph's knowledge of us. This was most blessedly perfect long before we had a being in the world. He never mistook His chosen, but always beheld them as objects of His infinite affection. II. Our ignorance of our royal brother. Out of this ignorance grew a host of sins. We withheld our hearts from Him; we mistrusted Him; and we rebelled against Him. We have but begun to study Him; but He knoweth us altogether.[c]

Side notes:

B.C. cir. 1715.
b *Bibl. Treas.*

B.C. cir. 1707.

the sons of Jacob sent to buy corn

a "Youth is one while witless, another while shiftless; as at feasts so at other meetings, old men should be vowels, young men mutes, or at most but semi-vowels."—*Trapp.* cf. Job xxxii. 7.

b Ge. xlvi. 21.

"The more weakness, the more falsehood; strength goes straight; every cannon-ball that has in it hollows and holes goes crooked. Weaklings must lie."—*Richter.*

"Fear hath the common fault of a justice of peace, and is apt to conclude hastily from every slight circumstance, without examining the evidence on both sides."—*Fielding.*

c Dr. Boyd.

they are recognised by Joseph

a Ge. xxxvii. 7.
b Pr. xviii. 19.
c C. H. Spurgeon.

"The Orientals bring their forehead to the ground, and before resuming an erect position, either kiss the earth or the feet or border of the garment of the king or prince,

Recognition.—That identity of persons, and recognition after death are indeed facts, may be clearly comprehended also from the definite and distinctive position of man in the sight of God. "Fear not, I have redeemed thee, I have called thee by thy name" (Isa. xliii. 1). "I will not blot out his name out of the book of life, but I will confess his name before My Father and before His angels" (Rev. iii. 5). St. Paul speaks of those whose names are in the book of life; and St. James of those whose names are not in the book of life. And numerous other passages might be quoted to show that the Christian especially will stand before God in heaven as personally and as individually known and distinguishable from his fellow-beings as he now stands before God and man on earth. The deduction is obvious; where individuality exists, recognition is a necessary consequence. If, with our present limited faculties, men know each other after long absence, and change from youth to age, is it possible that redeemed man, with the enlarged perceptions of a higher existence, can fail to recognise the earthly friends who were the faithful solace of their life's pilgrimage?[d]

9—13. (9) **remembered .. them,** he had never forgotten, but now sees their fulfilment. **ye .. come,** to take advantage of its defenceless state. (10) **lord .. servants,** what terms for brethren to use. (11) **we,** *etc.,* not likely that one man would allow ten of his sons to undertake the perilous duties of spies. (12) **and,** *etc.,* he professes not to be convinced, to lead to further explanations. (13) **youngest .. father,** they might have added, He will not trust him with us. **and .. not,** implying that he was dead, as prob. they believed him to be.

The memory of sin.—A rich landlord once cruelly oppressed a poor widow. Her son, a little boy of eight years, saw it. He afterwards became a painter, and painted a life-likeness of the dark scene. Years afterwards he placed it where the man saw it; he turned pale, trembled in every joint, and offered any sum to purchase it that he might put it out of sight. Thus there is an invisible painter drawing on the canvas of the soul a life-likeness reflecting correctly all the passions and actions of our spiritual history on earth. Eternity will reveal them to every man. We must meet our earth-life again.

14—16. (14) **Joseph .. them,** he professes not to believe they are the sons of one man. (15) **proved,** tried tested. **by .. Pharaoh,**[a] a strong asseveration.[b] **except .. hither,** he would assure himself of the safety of Benjamin. (16) **send .. you,** leaving them to select the messenger: whom he would perceive to be the son in whom the father had most confidence.

Joseph and his brethren (on v. 14—24).—Consider some of the leading ideas suggested by these verses.—I. The unfailing fulfilment of the Divine word. Joseph's brethren bow before him. II. The reproaching power of a guilty conscience. III. The unerring certainty of the punishment of sin. IV. The suspicion that always attaches to men who have sinned greatly, whether they be guilty or not. V. The merciful love of injured virtue.[c]

By the life of Pharaoh.—Extraordinary as the kind of oath which Joseph made use of may appear to us, it still continues in the East. Mr. Hanway says, the most sacred oath among the *Persians* is "by the king's head;" and among other instances of

B.C. *cir.* 1707.

before whom they are allowed to appear."—*Kitto.*

"Were we to take as much pains to be what we ought to be as we do to disguise what we really are, we might appear like ourselves without being at the trouble of any disguise at all."—*La Rochefoucauld.*

d *W. Merry.*

Joseph charges them with being spies

"Memory is the primary and fundamental power, without which there could be no other intellectual operation."—*Johnson.*

"Memory, like books which remain a long time shut up in the dust, needs to be opened from time to time; it is necessary, so to speak, to open its leaves, that it may be ready in time of need."—*Seneca.*

Joseph demands proof of their honesty

a Jas. v. 12.

b "Had he said, 'As the Lord liveth,'his speech would have betrayed him."—*Bush.*

c *W. S. Bailey.*

"If we have need of a strong will in order to do good, it is more necessary still for us in order not to do evil: from which it

B.C. cir. 1707.

often results that the most molest life is that where the force of will is most exercised."—*Count Molé.*

v. 11–14. *J. H. Gurney, M.A., S.S. on O.T. Hist., 83.*

d *Burder.*

he orders that one shall remain as hostage

a "I should have handled them more roughly." —*Luther.*

b Le. xxv. 43; Ne. v. 15.

"Be stirring as the time, be fire with fire, threaten the threatener, and outface the brow of bragging horror; so shall inferior eyes, that borrow their behaviours from the great, grow great by your example and put on the dauntless spirit of resolution."— *Shakespeare.*

Simeon is chosen

a Job xxxvi. 8, 9; Nu. xxxii. 23; Hos. v. 15.

b Pr. xxviii. 13–xxi. 13; Mu. vii. 2; Jas. ii. 13.

c Ge. ix. 5; Pr. ix. 12.

d *C. Simeon, M.A.*

"He who is conscious of secret and dark designs, which, if known, would blast him, is perpetually shrinking and dodging from public observation, and is afraid of all

it we read in the travels of the ambassadors, that "there were but sixty horses for ninety-four persons. The *mehemander* (or conductor) swore *by the head of the king,* (which is the greatest oath among the Persians), that he could not possibly find any more." And Thevenot says, "his subjects never look upon him but with fear and trembling; and they have such respect for him, and pay so blind an obedience to all his orders, that how unjust soever his commands might be, they perform them, though against the law both of God and nature. Nay, if they swear *by the king's head,* their oath is more authentic, and of greater credit, than if they swore by all that is most sacred in heaven and upon earth."d

17–20. (17) **together,** mercy in midst of judgment, for companionship. **ward..days,**a to promote repentance; and reflection. (18) **Joseph..day,** he visits them in prison. **for.. God,**b and will therefore be merciful: his fear of God spared them; their lack of it sacrificed him. (19) **go..houses,** his thoughtful care of their families. (20) **so..verified,** they may have wondered how he should know him to be their brother. **and..so,** *i.e.* they agreed to do so.

The effect of mercy.—A soldier in our army heard of the severe sickness of his wife. He applied for leave of absence, but was refused. He left the army; but, before he got away, was retaken, and brought in as a deserter. He was tried, found guilty, and summoned before the commanding officer to receive his sentence. He entered the tent, saluted, and stood perfectly unmoved while the officer read his fearful doom.—"To be shot to death with musketry on the next Friday." Not a muscle of his face twitched, not a limb quivered. "I deserve it, sir," he replied respectfully: "I deserted from my flag. Is that all, sir?"—"No," replied the officer: "I have something else for you;" and, taking another paper, he read aloud the doomed man's pardon. The undaunted spirit which severity had failed to move was completely broken down by clemency. He dropped to the ground, shaking, sobbing, and overcome: and, being restored to his regiment, proved himself grateful for the mercy shown him, and was soon promoted for good conduct.

21–24. (21) **we..brother,**a they see in this the hand of a retributive providence. **saw..hear,** this presents a vivid picture of the scene by the pit's mouth. **therefore..us,**b and is no more than we deserve. (22) **spake..hear?** (see xxxvii. 21, 22). **therefore..required,**c by a God of justice. (23) **knew'..them,** he addressed each other in Hebrew, **for.. interpreter,** as if he knew not their language. (24) **Simeon ..eyes,** passing over Reuben who had sought to save him, and taking the next eldest.

The power of conscience (v. 21).—We shall show—I. The general office of conscience. It is given by God, to operate as—1. A guide; 2. A judge. II. Its insensibility when dormant—1. Wonderful was its insensibility in the sons of Jacob. Look at their conspiracy against Joseph, their deception of Jacob; 2. Yet this is in reality what we may see in ourselves, and in all around us. Behold the profane, the sensual, the worldly, the self-righteous, the professors of religion. III. Its power, when awake. 1. Some, it inspires only with terror; 2. On others, it operates with a more genial influence; 3. On all, its testimony is as the voice of God Himself. Advice—(1) Seek to maintain a good conscience before God; (2) Do not, however, rest too confidently in testimonies of its approbation; (3) Look forward to the future judgment.*d*

Conscience reviewing.—When it comes night, and the streets are empty, and the lights are out, and the business and the driving and gaiety are over, and the pall of sleep is drawn over the senses, and the reason and the will are no longer on the watch, then conscience comes out solemnly, and walks about in the silent chambers of the soul, and makes her survey and her comments; and sometimes sits down and sternly reads the records of a life that the waking man would never look into, and the catalogue of crimes that are gathering for the judgment. And as conscience reads and reads aloud, and soliloquises, you may hear the still small deep echo of her voice reverberated through the soul's most secret unveiled recesses. Imagination walks tremblingly behind her; and now, they two alone pass through the open gate of the Scriptures into the future and eternal world, for thither all things in man's being naturally and irresistibly tend; and then, as conscience is still dwelling upon sin, imagination draws the judgment, and the soul is presented at the bar of God, and the eye of the Judge is on it, and a hand of fire writes as on the walls of the universe, " Thou art weighed in the balance, and found wanting." Then whatever sinful thoughts or passions, words or deeds, the conscience enumerates and dwells upon, the imagination, with prophetic truth, fills eternity with corresponding shapes of evil.*e*

25—28. (25) **restore .. sack,** ill. the bread of life a free gift. **and .. way,***a* over and above what they had purchased. (26) **they .. thence,** leaving Simeon behind, and oppressed with the memory of strange treatment. (27) **inn,** *lit.* lodging-place, prob. camping-ground, not *caravanserai* or *chan,* wh. prob. did not at that time exist. (28) **their .. failed,***b* *lit.* went out. *i.e.* they had no courage left. **what .. us?** in all that had happened they saw the finger of God.

Demetrius and the Athenians.—It is related of Demetrius (surnamed the *Conqueror of Cities*), that having received a marked and undoubted provocation, he laid siege to the city of Athens. The inhabitants made a desperate resistance; but were at last obliged to surrender, in consequence of great scarcity of provisions. Demetrius then ordered them, with the exception of the women and children, to be assembled together in one place, and to be surrounded with armed soldiers. Every one was in the greatest fear, conscious how much they had injured him, and expecting every moment to be put to death. It is not surprising that they were overwhelmed with joy and admiration, when they heard him with a magnanimity honourable to human nature, thus address them:—" I wish to convince you, O Athenians, how ungenerously you have treated me; for it was not to an enemy that your assistance was refused, but to a prince who loved you, who still loves you, and who wishes to revenge himself only by granting your pardon, and being still your friend. Return to your own homes; while you have been here my soldiers have been filling your houses with provisions."

29—34. (29) **told .. them,** in Egypt and on the way. (30—

B.C. *cir.* 1707.

around him, and much more of all above him."—*Wirt.*

"Think not that guilt requires the burning torches of the Furies to agitate and torment it. Their own frauds, their crimes, their remembrances of the past, their terrors of the future, — these are the domestic furies that are ever present to the mind of the impious." — *R Hall.*

"Let wickedness escape us it may at the bar, it never fails of doing justice upon itself; for every guilty person is his own hangman."—*Seneca.*

e Dr. Cheever.

returning they find the money in the sack's mouth

a Mа. v. 44, 45; Ro. xii. 17—21.

b Gk., "their heart was astonished;" Chal., "the knowledge of their heart departed;" Arab., "their hearts were much disturbed."

"Conscience is, at once, the sweetest and most troublesome of guests. It is the voice which demanded Abel of his brother, or that celestial harmony which vibrated in the ears of the martyrs and soothed their sufferings."—*Mde. Swetchine.*

they relate their

B.C. cir. 1707.

adventures to Jacob
a Pr. xiii. 15, xxii. 5.

"Fear is implanted in us as a preservative from evil; but its duty, like that of other passions, is not to overbear reason, but to assist it; nor should it be suffered to tyrannise in the imagination, to raise phantoms of horror, or to beset life with supernumerary distress."—*Johnson.*

"Fear is far more painful to cowardice than death to true courage." —*Sir P. Sidney.*
b Dr. Boyd.

Jacob's complaint
a 1 S. xxvii. 1; Job. vii. 7; xlii. 10; Ps. xxxiv. 19; Ro. viii. 28; 2 Co. iv. 17.

b Is. xlvi. 4.

"Misfortune is never mournful to the soul that accepts it; for such do always see that every cloud is an angel's face. Every man deems that he has precisely the trials and temptations which are the hardest of all others for him to bear; but they are so, simply because they are the very ones he most needs."— *Mrs. Child.*

"Misfortune makes of certain souls a vast desert through which rings the voice of God."— *Balzac.*

33)*a* see vv. 9—16 (34) **so..land,** the deliverance of their brother was to secure their return to Egypt.

The ridiculousness of fear.—My friend Jones told me, that, after several months of extremely hard headwork, which had lowered his nervous system, he found himself getting into a way of vaguely dreading what might come next, and often received his letters in the morning with many anticipations of evil. But, happily, a friend came to visit him who carried all this about a hundred degrees farther; who had come through all his life expecting at least an earthquake daily, if not the end of the world. And Jones was set right. In the words of Wordsworth, "He looked upon him, and was calmed and cheered." Jones saw how like a fool his friend seemed, and there came a healthy reaction; and he opened his letter-box bravely every morning, and was all right again. Yes: let us see the Helot drunk, and it will teach us to keep sober. My friend Gray told me, that, for some little space, he felt a growing tendency to scrubbiness in money matters; but, having witnessed pinching and paring (without the least need for them) carried to a transcendent degree by some one else, the very name of economy was made to stink in his nostrils; and he felt a mad desire to pitch half-crowns about the streets wherever he went. In this case the reaction went too far; but, in a week or two, Gray came back to the middle course, which is the safest and best.*b*

35—38. (35) **sack,** Heb., *sack,* same word as in Eng. **afraid,** full of apprehension. (36) **bereaved,** he connects them with the absence of Joseph and Simeon. **ye..away,** farther than Egypt he suspected. **against,***a* *lit.* upon me, *i.e.* a burden too heavy to bear. (37) **saying,** *etc.,* his own sons shall be pledges for the safety of Jacob's. (38) **alone,** of the children of his dear Rachel. **grey hairs,***b* he would have them consider the few comforts left him in his old age.

Jacob's despondency (v. 36).—I. The complaint. The Church is heir to the cross. "Those whom God afflicts in mercy, and Satan in malice," says an old writer, "must needs have many sorrows." Especially the complaint of the text seems applicable when inward and outward troubles meet. II. Its cause: 1. Ignorance of the nature and design of Divine dispensations; 2. Forgetfulness of Divine consolations; 3. False reasoning upon one's spiritual condition. III. Its cure: 1. A sense of the mighty power and all-sufficiency of God; 2. A conviction of the Divine wisdom; 3. A firm belief in the infinite rectitude of the Most High; 4. A persuasion of the love of God; 5. A clear view of the Gospel method of salvation; 6. An earnest, and foretaste, of future bliss. *All these things are against me* (v. 36).—These words I. Remind us of the common course pursued by men in trouble. In Jacob's case, something must be set down to 1. His great age; 2. His peculiar constitution of mind; 3. His faith in God; *i.e.,* in one side of the Divine character. Rather religious *fear,* than faith. At such times as these men are apt to complain and to despond. They remember not that " fair weather cometh out of the north." II. Suggest to us the more excellent way. We have need of 1. Patience; 2. Consideration; 3. Faith: think of "the bright light which is in the clouds." Learn (1) The excellence of faith in God; (2) How blessed must be the heavenly state.

The lost boat.—A South Sea islander who had been converted through the efforts of a good missionary, was once attempting to cross from one island to another, when a gale arose and swept him far out at sea. For eight weeks he was tossed up and down, enduring the greatest privations and sufferings; but at last his boat was thrown upon a reef, and he and three surviving companions were saved. The natives of the island showed them great kindness, and with hearts overflowing with thankfulness to God for His wonderful preservation, they were ready to proclaim His Word to these willing listeners. He preached Christ to them faithfully, and began schools, all the time praying earnestly for a missionary to be sent to them. As early as he could he went to the island of Samoa, six hundred miles away; and told them of this field the Lord had so wonderfully opened. They sent a good missionary back with him and two native helpers, and what was their surprise and pleasure to find that all spoke the Samoan language. They could go to work at once, and teach them to read the Bibles and tracts prepared in the dialect of that island. What a blessing that little wrecked boat cast up on their shores had brought to them. How wonderfully God works, by all the agents of nature, to accomplish his pleasure with regard to Christ's kingdom. He had guided that little bark in all its wanderings. He had preserved it amidst all dangers. He had even selected the two men who were to be preserved alive in it, and who were to proclaim His Gospel in that still darkened land. So our seeming disasters often work out the highest good for ourselves as well as others. If we get spiritual good out of them, then are they blessings, however trying to the heart and flesh. Let us learn to look upon them in the true light, and not cry out in despair, "All these things are against me," when God lays His hand upon us. There is comfort for every sorrow, if we will but take it, and it is a comfort without stint or measure.

B.C. *cir.* 1707.

"It is seldom that God sends such calamities upon man as men bring upon themselves and suffer willingly." —*Bp. J. Taylor.* v. 38. *H. Grove,* i. 411; *D. Wilcox,* 1. 125; *J. Jenkins,* f. 230; *J. H. Newman,* v. 322.

"Is a man placed in great difficulty, and does he make a solemn promise, in which another person is also involved; he will say, 'Ah! if I do not this thing, then kill my children.' 'Yes, my lord, my children shall die if I do not accomplish this object.' 'Ah! my children, your lives are concerned in this matter.'"— *Roberts.*

CHAPTER THE FORTY-THIRD.

1—5. (1) **famine .. land,** the seven yrs. dragged slowly on. (2) **go .. food,** he said not a word of Benjamin. (3) **Judah,** Reuben having tried ineffectually. **did .. protest,** *lit.* protesting he protested. (4) **if .. we,** *etc.*, the only condition on which they would undertake the journey. (5) **but if,** *etc.*, we may as well perish in Canaan as in Egypt.

Famines in the East.—Twice only, in the eleventh and in the twelfth centuries of the Christian era, such a catastrophe is described by Arabian historians, in terms which give us a full conception of the calamity from which Joseph delivered the country. The first lasted, like that of Joseph, for seven years. Of the other the most fearful details are given by an eyewitness:—"Thus the year presented itself as a monster, whose wrath must annihilate all the resources of life and all the means of subsistence. The famine began. Large numbers emigrated. The poor ate carrion, corpses, and dogs. They went further, devouring even little children. The eating of human flesh became so common as to excite no surprise. The people spoke and heard of it as of an indifferent thing. As for the number of

B.C. *cir.* 1707.

Jacob proposes the return of his sons to Egypt

"If all men would bring their misfortunes together in one place, most would be glad to take his own home again, rather than to take a proportion out of the common stock." —*Solon.*

"There is a certain sort of man whose doom in the world is disappointment, who excels in it,

188　　　　　　　　　　GENESIS.　　　　　　[Cap. xliii. 6—10.

B.C. cir. 1707.

and whose luckless triumphs in his meek career of life, I have often thought, must be regarded by the kind eyes above with as much favour as the splendid success and achievements of coarser and more prosperous men."—Thackeray.

a *Dr. Stanley.*

they demand the company of Benjamin
a Phil. 1s, 19.

"Beware of suretyship for thy best friend. He that payeth another man's debt seeketh his own decay. But if thou canst not otherwise choose, rather lend thy money thyself upon good bonds, although thou borrow it; so shalt thou secure thyself, and pleasure thy friend."—*Lord Burleigh.*

"Every human being has a work to carry on within, duties to perform abroad, influences to exert, which are peculiarly his, and which no conscience but his own can teach."—*Channing.*

b *Lange.*

"Much misconstruction and bitterness are spared to him who thinks naturally upon what he owes to others, rather than what he ought to expect from them."—*Mde. Guizot.*

"The margin has, for words,

the poor who perished from hunger and exhaustion, God alone knows what it was. A traveller often passed through a large village without seeing a single living inhabitant. In one village we met the families of each house extended dead, the husband, the wife, and the children. In another where, till late, there had been four hundred weaving shops, we saw, in like manner, the weaver dead in his cornpit, and all his dead family round him. We were here reminded of the text of the Koran, "One single cry was heard," and "they all perished." The road between Egypt and Assyria was like a vast field sown with human bodies, or rather like a plain which has just been swept by the scythe of the mower. It had become as a banquet-hall for the birds, wild beasts, and dogs, which gorged on their flesh." These are but a few of the horrors which Abd-el-Latif details, and which may explain to us how "the land of Egypt fainted by reason of the famine."a

6—10. (6) **Israel**, he who *prevailed* with God argues ineffectually with man. (7) **asked**, *lit.* asking he asked, *i.e.* close scrutiny. **state .. brother**, this the first we hear of Joseph's inquiries. **we .. tenor**, *lit.* acc. to the mouth, *i.e.* as to the nature of his questions. **could .. know**, had they known it they would have made fewer admissions. (8) **lad**, Heb. not *yeled*, lad ; but *naar*, young man. **die .. ones**, better the life of one to be in peril than the lives of many. (9) **surety**,a while Reuben pledged his children, Judah pledged himself. **bear .. blame**, *lit.* I will be a sinner to thee. (10) **lingered**, through fear. **surely .. time**, wh. shows that they had eked out to the utmost the corn previously bought.

Israel's character.—We here (v. 6—14) recognise Israel's character, especially in the following traits :—I. Not to his other sons does he entrust Benjamin, not even to Reuben, but only to Judah, whose honesty and strength seem to inspire him with courage. II. He again employs his old weapon, the sending of presents ; this time sending quality, not quantity. III. With a severe uprightness does he require his sons to return the money found in their sacks. IV. He entrusts to them Benjamin *as their brother*. V. He commits himself to the protection of Almighty God. VI. He resigns himself to God's providence, even at the risk of becoming childless.b

Anxious fear.—It is curious to think how often these needless fears, which cause so much unnecessary anxiety and misery, are the result of pure miscalculation ; and this miscalculation not made in a hurry, but deliberately. I have a friend who told me this. When he was married, he had exactly five hundred pounds a year, and no means of adding to that income. So, as he could not increase his income, his business was to keep down his expenditure below it. But neither he nor his wife knew much about household management ; and he was a good deal victimised by his servants. After doing all he could to economise, he found, at the end of the third month of his financial year, that he had spent exactly one hundred and twenty-five pounds. Four times one hundred and twenty-five pounds he calculated, made six hundred pounds a year : which was just one hundred more than he had got. So the debtor's prison appeared to loom in view, or some total change in his mode of life, which it seemed almost impossible for him to make, without very painful circumstances :

and for weeks the thought almost drove him distracted. Day and night it never was absent. At length, one day, brooding over his prospects, he suddenly discovered that four times one hundred and twenty-five made just five hundred, and not six hundred; so that all his fears were groundless. He was relieved. he told me; but somehow his heart had been so burdened and sunk by those anxious weeks, that, though the cause of anxiety was removed, it was a long time before it seemed to recover its spring.*c*

11—14. (11) **best .. land,** *lit.* of the song of the land, *i.e.* that on account of which the land was praised: "fruits celebrated in song." **balm,** *see* xxxvii. 25. **honey,** prob. not of bees, but juice of grapes boiled down to syrup. **spices .. myrrh,** *see* xxxvii. 25. **nuts,** pistachia-nuts. (12) **take .. money,** *lit.* money of repetition. **oversight,** rather than a design as feared at first. (13) **take .. brother,** a reluctant consent. (14) **Almighty,***a* all things possible to God. **mercy,** *lit.* bowels. **bereaved,** *etc.,* blending of sorrow and resignation.

The pressure of want, and its power in the hands of Providence. —I. How inexorable in its demands. Jacob is to deliver up Benjamin. II. How full of grace in its designs. By it alone can Jacob's house be delivered from the burden of deadly guilt.*b*

Bereaved indeed.—That Joseph was not dead, after all, makes no difference in our estimate of the father's grief. Entirely convinced of the death, as entire was his fellow-feeling with a modern's note of explanation, varying in but one little word. after allowing for the difference of an unrecovered and unburied corpse—

"But he is in his grave, and oh,
The difference to me!"

Nor does it matter that possibly in after years a faint surmise of doubt as to Joseph's actual death may have feebly possessed him : for it is noteworthy that although he plainly tells his remaining sons, "Me have ye bereaved of my children: Joseph is not, and Simeon is not"—and hence his dread of their taking Benjamin away. Yet is he represented as saying a chapter later, "The one went from me, and I said, surely he is torn in pieces, and I saw him not since:" words which admit of the recognition of a doubt, however dim and comfortless. At the time his conviction was, "Joseph is without doubt rent in pieces." And therefore did he not only refuse to be comforted when all his sons and all his daughters rose up to comfort him; but he declared that he would go down into the grave unto his son mourning.

"It is too true an evil; gone he is;
And what's to come of my despised time
Is nought but bitterness."

15—18. (15) **and .. Joseph,** with the evidence of their truthfulness. (16) **bring .. home,** they are now taken to Joseph's house. **slay,** *lit.* kill a killing. **dine,** eat. (17) **man .. house,** they become the guests of their banished brother. (18) **afraid***a* **.. house,** expecting a severer examination, and an excuse for punishment. **that .. us,** *lit.* that he may roll himself upon us.

Terrors of a guilty conscience (v. 18).—A guilty conscience—I.

B C. cir. 1707.

'mouth.' Send a messenger with a message to deliver, and ask him on his return, what he said, he will reply, 'According to your mouth!'"-*Roberts.*

c Dr. Boyd.

Jacob consents, and sends a present

a Ne. i. 11; Ps. xxxvii. b.

"The iron hand of necessity commands, and her stern decree is supreme law, to which the gods even must submit. In deep silence rules the uncounselled sister of eternal fate. Whatever she lays upon thee, endure; perform whatever she commands."-*Gőethe.*

v. 11—14. J. H. Gurney, M.A., 53; Bp. Wilson, iii. 13; R. Warner, ii. 16.

"When God will educate a man, He compels him to learn bitter lessons. He sends him to school to the necessities rather than to the graces, that by knowing all suffering he may know also the eternal consolations."—*Celia Burleigh.*

b Lange.

c F. Jacox, B.A.

Joseph invites his brethren to dine with him

a Ps. liii. 5.

"What a strange thing an old dead

190   *GENESIS.*   [Cap. xliii. 19-28.

B.C. 1707.

sin laid away in a secret drawer of the soul is! Must it some time or other be moistened with tears, until it comes to life again, and begins to stir in our consciousness, as the dry wheat animalcule, looking like a grain of dust, becomes alive if it is wet with a drop of water?"—*Holmes.*

b Roberts.

they tell Joseph's steward the story of the money

a Ge. xviii. 4; xxiv. 32.

"It is with honesty in one particular as with wealth,—those that have the thing care less about the credit of it than those who have it not. No poor man can well afford to be thought so, and the less of honesty a finished rogue possesses the less he can afford to be supposed to want it."—*Colton.*

Joseph inquires concerning his father

"It is a proof of boorishness to confer a favour with a bad grace; it is the act of giving that is hard and painful. How little does a smile cost!"—*La Bruyère.*

"He gives not best that gives most; but he gives most who

Always dreads the worst. II. Misinterprets passing events. III. Betrays a craven fear.

"*Fall upon us.*"—The margin has this, "Roll himself upon us." (Job xxx. 14.; Psa. xxii.; S. xxxvii. 5.; Prov. xvi. 3.) For to say a man rolls himself upon another, is the Eastern way of saying he falls upon him. Is a person beaten or injured by another: he says of the other, "He rolled himself upon me." Of the individual who is always trying to live upon another, who is continually endeavouring to get something out of him, it is said, "That fellow is for ever rolling himself upon him." So, also, "I will not submit to his conduct any longer; I will beat him, and roll myself upon him." Has a man committed an offence, he is advised to go to the offended, and roll himself upon him. A person in great sorrow, who is almost destitute of friends, asks in his distress, "Upon whom shall I roll myself?" When men or women are in great misery, they wring their hands and roll themselves on the earth. Devotees roll themselves round the temple, or after the sacred car.*b*

19—25. (19) **steward . . house,** the slave has now servants under him in his own house. **they . . house,** fearing to enter. (20) **O sir,** *etc.,* they wished to clear themselves of all suspicion. (21) **our . . weight,** not rejected because deficient. **we . . hand,** as not belonging to us. (22) **we . . sacks,** *i.e.* we did not purloin it. (23) **and he said,** *etc.,* the steward was evidently in his master's secret. **I . . money,** doing with it as I was bid. **he . . them,** happy reunion of the brothers. (24) **water . . feet,** cust. rite of hospitality.*a* (25) **ready,** arranged it. **present,** see v. 11. **heard . . there,** prob. were informed by the steward.

The money found in the sacks.—According to this verse, the sons of Jacob tell Joseph's steward that they had opened their sacks at the inn, and found every man's money then, whereas it would seem, from the account in chap. xlii., only one sack was opened at the inn, and the rest found their money on opening their sacks at home. Keil observes that there is no real difficulty. The one sack opened at the inn had the money in its mouth, the rest, surprised at this, also opened their sacks, but found no money; it was only on emptying their sacks that they discovered theirs. So he proposes to translate, "A man's money was in the mouth of his sack"—*every* not being in the Hebrew.

26—28. (26) **bowed . . earth,** dream fulfilled once more. (27) **Is . . well?** *lit.* is there peace to your father? (28) **they . . alive,** good news fr. a far country. **bowed . . obeisance,** token of respectful homage.

Home news (v. 27).—I. The great prince thinking of his shepherd-father. A hint to young men who get on in the world. II. A brother interested in his brethren's welfare.

Friendliness in adversity.—As it is with the deer that is hunted, when the huntsman goes into the park, he rouses the whole herd, and they all run together; but if one be shot, and they see the blood run down, they will soon push him out of their company. Or, as a man being in his travel upon the road, and there being a sun-dial set up in the way, if the sun shine, he will step out of his way to take notice of it; but if the sun do not shine, he will go by a hundred times and never regard it. So let but the sun of prosperity shine upon a man, then who but he? he shall have friends more than a good many; but if a cloudy day come, and take away the sunshine, he may easily number his acquaintance. And so when a man goes on in the credit of the world, he shall be welcome into all companies, and much made of by every one; but if he come once to be shot, and disgrace put upon him, then he shall soon perceive a cloud in every man's face, no one so much as regarding him.*a*

29—31. (29) **God..son,** express. denoting not diff. of age but rank. (30) **bowels,***a* *i.e.* heart, feelings. **he..there,** privacy: tears of joy. (31) **he..face,** to remove signs of tears, **and..himself,** regaining his self-composure. **set on bread=** let the dinner be served.

Joseph's state of soul at the appearance of Benjamin (v. 30).— I. His joy. II. His deep emotion. III. His doubt, and the modes of testing it. 1. The feast; 2. The cup; 3. The claim to Benjamin. If at the first meeting with his brethren Joseph had to struggle with his ill-humour, he has now to contend with the emotions of fraternal love.*b*

Eastern salutations.— The forms of salutation in the East wear a much more serious and religious air than those in use among the nations of Europe. "God be gracious unto thee, my son," were the words which Joseph addressed to his brother Benjamin. In this country it would be called a benediction; but Chardin asserts that, in Asia, it is a simple salutation, and used there instead of those offers and assurances of service which it is the custom to use in the West. The Orientals, indeed, are exceedingly eloquent in wishing good and the mercy of God on all occasions to one another, even to those they scarcely know; and yet their compliments are as hollow and deceitful as those of any other people. This appears, from Scripture, to have been always their character: "They bless with their mouths, but they curse inwardly." These benedictory forms explain the reason why the sacred writers so frequently call the salutation and farewell of the East by the name of blessing.*c*

"God be gracious unto thee, my son," was the address of Joseph to his brother Benjamin; and in this way do people of respectability or years address their inferiors or juniors. "Son, give me a little water." "The sun is very hot; I will rest under your shade, my son."*d*

32—34. (32) **set..himself..themselves..Egyptians,** caste-exclusiveness in Egypt. **Egyptians..Hebrews,** *i.e.* it was contrary to custom wh. is "the king of men."*a* **that.. Egyptians,** who regarded peculiar religious ceremonies in eating. Prob. Joseph had respect to the feelings of his brethren.*b* (33) **firstborn..youth,** they were arranged acc. to age. **men ..another,** wondering how their age had been discovered. (34) **took..him,** the choicest food fr. the chief table.*c* **five,** the Egyptian special number.*d* **drank..merry,***e* *lit.* they drank freely.

Mysterious selections (v. 34).—Some persons in the world have five times as much as others. These differences in human circumstances—I. Often excite wonder. II. Are often the effect of a Divine purpose. III. Need not prevent the real enjoyment of those who have least: they all "were merry," yet only one had the sign of great favour.

B.C. cir. 1707.

gives best. If then I cannot give bountifully, yet I will give freely; and what I want in my hand, supply by my heart. He gives well that gives willingly." —*A. Warwick.* *a* Spencer.

Joseph recognises Benjamin

a Jer. xxxi. 20; 1 Ki. iii. 26. Yearn, to "feel earnest desire; A.S. geornian— georn, desirous; Ice., girna, to desire; giarn, desirous.
"Joy is the happiness of love. It is love exulting. It is love aware of its own felicity, and resting in riches, which it has no fear of exhausting. It is love taking a view of its treasures, and surrendering itself to bliss without foreboding."—*Rev. J. Hamilton.*
"He who can conceal his joys is greater than he who can hide his griefs."—*Lavater.*
b Lange.
c Dr. Paxton.
d Roberts.

the banquet and Benjamin's mess

a Pindar.
b Ex. viii. 26.
c 1 S. ix. 23.
Mess, food served up; It., *messa*; *messo*, a messenger, a course at table; Lat., *mitto*, *missum*, to send.
d Ge. xli. 34; xlv. 22, xlvii. 2, 24; Is. xix. 18.

"The reason is

B.C. cir. 1707.

stated to have been, that the Egyptians recognised only five planets."—*Alford.*

e "*Inebriati sunt.*"—*Vulg.*

"A well-governed appetite is a great part of liberty."—*Seneca.*

f Wilkinson.

Egyptian chairs.—"The house of a wealthy person was always furnished with chairs. Stools and low seats were also used, the seat being only from eight to fourteen inches high, and of wood, or interlaced with thongs: these, however, may be considered equivalent to our rush-bottomed chairs, and probably belonged to persons of humble means: and many of the *fauteuils* were of the most elegant form: they were made of ebony and other rare woods, inlaid with ivory, and very similar to some now used in Europe. The legs were mostly in imitation of those of an animal; and lions' heads, or the entire body, formed the arms of large *fauteuils*, as in the throne of Solomon, 1 Kings x. 19. Some, again, had folding legs, like our camp stools."*f*

B.C. cir. 1707.

Joseph orders his cup to be put into Benjamin's sack

a In Jer. xxxv. 5, pots; in Ex. xxv. 31. xxxvii. 17, it—the calix of sculptured flowers. "The Egyptians drank out of brazen cups." — *Havernick.*

b "Not that Joseph practised any kind of divination; but as the whole transaction was merely intended to deceive his brethren for a short time, he might as well affect divination by his cup, as he affected to believe they had stolen it."— *Clarke.*

c Delitzsch.

CHAPTER THE FORTY-FOURTH.

1—5. (1) **steward .. house,** *lit.* him that was over his house. (2) **cup,***a* bowl. **he .. spoken,** the steward was in Joseph's confidence. (3) **soon .. light,** that they might travel in the cool of the day. (4) **when .. city,** so that the event would not be publicly observed. **wherefore .. good,** reminding them of the good they had received fr. Joseph. (5) **divineth,***b* *lit.* reminding them of it, i.e. learns experimentally by means of it.

The more haste the less speed (v. 3).—I. The hasty start: 1. Early morning; 2. Glad to leave Egypt behind; 3. Hopes of soon arriving at home; 4. Joy at success of their mission. Benjamin safe. II. The unexpected overtaking: 1. The race is not to the swift; 2. Man proposes, God disposes; 3. Providence sometimes checks the rapid progress of men.

Divining cups.—This cup, or goblet, which is described as a well-known possession of Joseph's, is called a divining vessel. The word literally means to "whisper" or "mutter incantations," and it was applied to a kind of divination which proceeded by signs or symbols. There were two ways by which the goblet was used. In the first, they poured clean water into it, and then looked into the water for representations of future events. In the second, they filled the vessel with water, and then dropped into it pieces of gold, silver, or precious stones, and, by the appearances which these produced, prognostics were formed. But we cannot infer for certain from the reference to this cup, that Joseph had adopted this Egyptian practice, which would have been a censurable act on his part. It is likely that the steward only meant to imply thereby that it was an article which was sacred.*c*

they are pursued and charged with theft

"Honest policy is a good friend, both to our safety and to our usefulness. The serpent's head (provided it be not akin to the old serpent) may

6—9. (6) **spake .. words,** with assumed roughness of manner. (7) **God .. thing,** they professed to live in the fear of God. (8) **behold,** *etc.,* they appeal in self-vindication to this proof of honesty. (9) **both .. bondmen,** a hasty speech of wh. they soon repented.

The honesty of the dishonest (v. 9).—I. Marked by hasty speech: violent self-vindication, vaunting promises. II. Marked by much thoughtlessness: possibility of circumstantial evidence overlooked. III. When the dishonest defend an action which they may have performed honestly, or repudiate an unjust charge, they do so unnaturally, and betray their real character.

Scrupulous honesty.—A Russian was travelling from Tobolsk to Beresow. On the road, he stopped over night at the hut of an Ostiack. In the morning, on continuing his journey, he discovered that he had lost his purse, containing about one hundred rubles. The son of the Ostiack, a boy of fourteen years of age, found the purse while out hunting; but, instead of taking it up, he went and told his father, who was equally unwilling to touch it, and ordered the boy to cover it with some bushes. A few months after, the Russian returned, and stopped at the same hut; but the Ostiack did not recognise him. He related the loss he had met with. The Ostiack listened very attentively; and, when he had finished, "You are welcome," said he. "Here is my son, who will show you the spot where it lies. No hand has touched it but the one which covered it, that you might recover what you had lost."[a]

10—13. (10) **now .. words,** rash speech taken advantage of. (11) **speedily,** with the promptitude of conscious honesty. (12) **began .. youngest,** though he knew where it was: he keeps up the appearance of justice. (13) **they .. clothes,** overwhelmed with sorrow and wonder that the cup was found at all, and more especially here. **laded .. city,** though at liberty to depart they would learn the fate of Benjamin.

The cup found in Benjamin's sack (v. 12).—Consider—I. That there is sorrow, and sorrow on a vast scale. 1. Sorrow was sent into the world as a preventive of greater sorrow; 2. It gives occasion to the exercise of many an else impossible virtue; 3. Yet this would be a lame excuse indeed for it, if it stood alone; 4. It can hardly be deemed right that such suffering as man endures should—even for the beneficent results that may flow from it—be inflicted on an innocent being. Then why should there be sorrow at all? We answer, because of sin. II. Why that sorrow should so often smite us in the most sensitive place. Or, to take up the parable of the text, why should the cup be in Benjamin's sack? It was put there—1. Because no other would serve so well; 2. To bring the brethren to a better mind ever after; 3. To give Joseph the opportunity to make himself known to his brethren; 4. To lead them out of the land of famine into the land of plenty. Learn—(1) To think more kindly of God and His dispensations: as you see how much reason you have to expect sorrow, how little right to look for joy; (2) To understand the lesson the lesser sorrows are meant to teach, lest you need the greater; (3) To take care lest you not only lose the joy but lose the good the loss of joy was meant to give.[a]

The reward of honesty.—The religious tradesman complains that his honesty is a hindrance to his success; that the tide of custom pours into the doors of his less scrupulous neighbours in the same street, while he himself waits for hours idle. My brother, do you think that God is going to reward honour, integrity, highmindedness, with this world's coin? Do you fancy that he will pay spiritual excellence with plenty of custom? Now, consider the price that man has paid for his success. Perhaps mental degradation and inward dishonour. His advertisements are all deceptive; his treatment of his workmen tyrannical; his cheap prices made possible by inferior articles. Sow that man's seed, and you will reap that man's harvest. Cheat, lie, advertise, be unscrupulous in your assertions, custom will come

B.C. cir. 1707.

"well become a good Christian's body, especially if it have a dove's eye in it."—*M. Henry.*

"If the thing you desire be good, I will do it without any bribe, because it is good: if it be not honest, I will not do it for all the goods in the world."—*Epaminondas.*
a *Percy.*

the cup is found

"Irritated one day at the bad faith of Madame Jay, Mirabeau said to her: 'Madame Jay, if probity did not exist, we ought to invent it as the best means of getting rich.'"—*Dumont.*

"The next natural beauty in the world is honesty and moral truth. For all beauty is truth. True features make the beauty of a face, and true proportions the beauty of architecture; as true measure that of harmony and music. In poetry, which is all fable, truth is still the perfection."—*Shaftesbury.*

a *J. B. Figgis.*

"Honest and courageous people have very little to say about either their courage or their honesty. The sun has no need to boast of his brightness, nor the moon of her effulgence."—*H. Ballou.*

B.C. 1707.

b F. W. Robertson.

they are brought before Joseph

a Spk. Comm.

Nu. xxxii. 23.

"The sacred cup is a symbol of the Nile, into whose waters a golden and silver patera were annually thrown."
—*Pliny.*

"Honesty needs no disguise nor ornament. Be plain."—*Otway.*

v. 16. T. Close, On Gen., 301.

c Roberts.

Judah's intercession

a Ge. xxxvii. 3.
b Alford.

"Has a beloved son been long absent, does the father anxiously desire to see him, he says, 'Bring him, bring him, that the course of my eyes may be upon him.' 'Ah, my eyes, do you again see my son? Oh, my eyes, is not this pleasure for you?'"—*Roberts.*

"A sentence well couched takes both the sense and the understanding. I love not those cart-rope speeches that are longer than the memory of men can fathom." — *Feltham*

c Roberts

he recalls the former visit

to you. But if the price is too dear, let him have his harvest, and take yours. Yours is a clear conscience, a pure mind, rectitude within and without. Will you part with that for his? Then, why do you complain? He has paid his price: you do not choose to pay it.[b]

14—17. (14) **for .. there**, awaiting their return. (15) **wot .. divine?** he "here adapts himself and his language to his character as it would naturally appear in the eyes of his brethren."[a] (16) **Judah,** as esp. interested in the safety of Benjamin. **what .. ourselves?** his words show the utmost perturbation of mind. **iniquity,**[b] he cannot regard this as an accident, nor perceive any human purpose. **we . found,** they will not separate themselves fr. Benjamin. (17) **God .. so,** punish the innocent with the guilty. **but .. found,** and he alone. **he .. servant,** Benjamin to whose safety they were pledged. **get .. father,** without Benjamin as once they had gone without Joseph.

Prostration.—In 1823 two globe-lamps were stolen from the Wesleyan chapel in Trincomalee. Being convinced that it was some of the workmen, the constable was directed to fetch the men immediately. About ten o'clock at night they were all brought on the premises. Seeing one of them much agitated, I inquired of him if he did not think I knew something about it. He fell at my feet like a person dead, and cried out, "True! true! I have done it! I have done it!"[c]

18—21. (18) **Judah,** who pleaded for the slavery of Joseph now an advocate for the liberation of Benjamin. **came .. him,** stepping forward in advance of the rest. **let .. servant,** now pleading for one who appears to be guilty. (19) **saying .. brother,** he recalls a former interview. (20, 21) **and w's said,**[a] etc., "it hence appears that it was the exact state of the case, or Judah would not have ventured to appeal to Joseph's recollection of it."[b]

The chief speaker.—In India a company of people have always some one amongst them who is known and acknowledged to be the chief speaker; thus, should they fall into trouble, he will be the person to come forward and plead with the superior. He will say, "My lord, I am indeed a very ignorant man, and am not worthy to speak to you: were I of high caste, perhaps my Lord would hear me. May I say two or three words?" Some of the party will then speak in an encouraging tone. "Yes, yes, our lord will hear you." He then proceeds,—"Ah, my lord! your mercy is known to all; great is your wisdom; you are even as a king to us; let, then, your servants find favour in your sight." After this introduction, like that of Judah, he relates the whole affair, forgetting no circumstance which has a tendency to exculpate him and his companions; and everything which can touch the feelings of the judge will be gently brought before him. As he draws to a conclusion his pathos increases, his companions put out their hands in a supplicating manner, accompanied by other gesticulations; their tears begin to flow, and with one voice they cry, "Forgive us this time, and we will never offend you more."[c]

22—26. (22) **if .. die,** compared with his own case Joseph would now see that their hearts were changed towards their father. (23) **except .. more**, his presence therefore is a proof of our dire necessity. (24—26) They assured Joseph that they had faithfully reported his words.

Want of paternal affection.—A mulatto youth one day called on a respectable gentleman of Baltimore, and, with tears in his eyes, begged for assistance. "My father and mother," says he, "are about to sell me to Georgia." "Your father and mother!" replied the gentlemen with surprise: "what right have they to sell you?" "My father," answered the boy, "is a white man, Mr. ——, a merchant in this place. My mother is a yellow woman. She has had several children by him, all of whom have been sold to Georgia but myself. He is this moment bargaining with a slave-trader for me." The gentleman promised his assistance, but too late; the bargain was already made. The unfortunate youth was immediately borne off, in spite of tears, execrations, and entreaties, handcuffed and chained, and driven like a brute to a distant market.

B.C. 1707.

"It was necessary that Judah should remind the Egyptian lord that it was by his express command their father had been compelled to consent to the departure of Benjamin."—*Kitto*.

"The man who melts with social sympathy, though not allied, is than a thousand kinsmen of more worth."—*Euripides.*

27—29. (27) **wife**, he speaks of Rachel with an affection that excluded the rest fr. his thoughts. (28) **surely .. pieces,** " fr. these words prob. for the first time Joseph learns what had been Jacob's belief as to his son's fate."ᵃ (29) **and if,** *etc.*, see xlii. 38.

Filial and fraternal affection.—A short time since, just at sunset on a summer's day, I went to the grave of a dear sister of mine. Her two little boys went with me. When we had arrived there, I saw four little rose-bushes standing, two at the head, and two at the foot of the grave, bending over, as if to meet and hang over the grave. "That is her grave—our mother's grave." said one of the boys. "And those rose-bushes?" said I, as the tears started in my eyes. "Those," said the eldest, "brother and I and father set soon after she was laid there. Those two at the head she planted in the garden herself, and we took them up and set them there, and call them 'Mother's bushes.'" "And what do you remember about your dear mother, my boys?" "Oh! everything." "What in particular?" "Oh, this uncle, that there never was a day since I can remember in which she did not take us to her closet, and pray with us, unless she was sick on the bed." Never did that sister seem so dear to me as at that moment: and never did my heart feel so full a hope in the words which were engraved on the tombstone:—

"No mortal woes
Can reach the peaceful sleeper here,
While angels watch her soft repose."ᵇ

he describes his father's reluctance to part with Benjamin

a Spk. Comm.

"Affection. in a philosophical sense, refers to the manner in which we are affected by anything for a continuance, whether painful or pleasant; but in the common sense, it may be defined to be a settled bent of mind towards a particular being or thing." — *C. Buck.*

b Dr. J. Todd.

30—34. (30) **life .. life,**ᵃ *lit.* his soul is bound up in his (the lad's) soul. (31) **servants .. grave**, a politic taking of the consequences upon themselves.ᵇ (32) **surety,** *see* xliii. 9. (33) **servant .. brethren**,ᶜ " whatever sufferings may betide me I will firmly endure them, if by so doing I may ransom my brother."ᵈ (34) **evil .. father,** *lit.* wh. shall find my father, *i.e.* the sorrow wh. shall consume him.

Paternal and filial affection (v. 30).—I. This fact (which we often find illustrated) may be viewed from the father's side. We see fathers whose lives seem to be bound up in their sons' lives. 1. This is often altogether apart from the character of the son. The father loves him, though he may be very foolish

he offers to be bondman in place of Benjamin

a Gk. "His soul hangeth on this man's soul." *Chal.* "His soul is beloved unto him as his own soul."

b "Judah is fearful of giving offence by plainly stating that the

and wicked (David and Absalom); 2. It is seen in the father's earnest and continued labour that the son may be clothed and educated; 3. It is also seen in the father's solicitude when his son is ill. He gives up work; helps to watch and nurse. The neighbours see something is amiss; they ask. "My son is ill." And, as of Jesus once, people say of the father, "Behold! how he loved him!" II. This fact may also be viewed from the son's side. 1. Elder children should be especially tender to the younger, for the father's sake as well as their own. He has a peculiar fondness for the young and helpless; 2. All children should be kind and dutiful to their parents, seeing how one life may be bound up in another; 3. This may recall the love of God for His only Son, and suggest our duty to that Son for the Father's sake.*e*

The insolvent negro.—A negro of one of the kingdoms on the African coast, who had become insolvent, surrendered himself to his creditor, who, according to the established custom of the country, sold him for a slave. This affected his son so much that he came and reproached his father for not selling his children to pay his debts; and, after much entreaty, he prevailed on the captain to accept him, and liberate his father. The son was put in chains, and on the point of sailing to the West Indies, when the circumstances coming to the knowledge of the governor, he sent for the owner of the slaves, paid the money that he had given for the old man, and restored the son to his father.

CHAPTER THE FORTY-FIFTH.

1–3. (1) **Joseph**, clearly perceiving their love for their father and brother. **cause .. me**, the scene too sacred for merely curious eyes. **Joseph .. brethren**,*a* they being known to him all along. (2) **and .. aloud**, *lit.* gave forth his voice in weeping. (3) **I am Joseph**, the most astounding words they had heard in Egypt. **doth .. live?** his first question is concerning his father. **and .. him**, their memory silenced them. **for .. presence**, not knowing but he would avenge himself.

The lost brother found (v. 3).—I. The time having come for him to reveal himself, he commanded all to go out—1. That none of his subordinates might see the great minister of state unmanned; 2. That none might witness the abject repentance of his brethren, and learn their crime. II. The disclosure itself. 1. I am Joseph (ill. "I am Jesus whom thou persecuted"); 2. His first question. III. Its effect. 1. Silence (ill. "and he was speechless"); 2. Confusion of face; 3. Fear. They knew not what might be done to them.

Loud manifestations of feeling.—"This is exactly the genius of the people of Asia, especially of the women. Their sentiments of joy or of grief are properly transports; and their transports are ungoverned, excessive, and truly outrageous. When any one returns from a long journey, or dies, his family burst into cries that may be heard twenty doors off; and this is renewed at different times, and continues many days, according to the vigour of the passion. Especially are these cries long in the case of

---

B.C. 1707.

death which threatened their father might be considered as caused by the Egyptian's unjust and unfounded suspicions."—*Raphall.*

c Ex. xxxii. 32.

d Kitto.

e The Hive.

"There is so little to redeem the dry mass of follies and errors from which the materials of this life are composed that anything to love or to reverence becomes, as it were, the Sabbath for the mind."—*Lytton.*

B.C. *cir.* 1707.

Joseph reveals himself

a Ge. xlii. 8; Ac. vii. 13.

"He was not willing that any should be witnesses of his own passion, or his brethren's former faults."—*Kidder.*

"The very society of joy redoubles it; so that, whilst it lights upon my friend it rebounds upon myself, and the brighter his candle burns the more easily will it light mine."—*South.*

b Chardin.

"It is said of Joseph, 'He wept aloud;' in the original, 'gave

death, and frightful; for their mourning is right-down despair, and an image of hell. I was lodged, in the year 1676, at Ispahan, near the Royal Square: the mistress of the next house to mine died at that time. The moment she expired, all the family, to the number of twenty-five or thirty people, set up such a furious cry, that I was quite startled, and was above two hours before I could recover myself. These cries continue a long time, then cease all at once; they begin again as suddenly at daybreak, and in concert. It is this suddenness which is so terrifying, together with a greater shrillness and loudness than one would easily imagine. This enraged kind of mourning, if I may call it so, continued forty days; not equally violent, but with diminution from day to day. The longest and most violent acts were when they washed the body, when they perfumed it, when they carried it out to be interred, at making the inventory, and when they divided the effects. You are not to suppose that those that were ready to split their throats with crying out wept as much; the greatest part of them did not shed a single tear through the whole tragedy." *b*

4—8. (4) **come .. you,**[a] they prob. shrank back afraid. **and .. near,** trembling but hoping against hope. **brother,** hitherto a brother disguised. **whom .. Egypt,** fr. whom therefore ye may justly expect punishment. (5) **for .. life,**[b] sin overruled by Divine mercy, and made subservient to the ends of infinite benevolence. (6) **earing,** ploughing. (7) **preserve .. earth,** *lit.* to make you a remnant in the earth. **save .. deliverance,** *lit.* to preserve your lives to a great deliverance. (8) **so .. God,** he interprets his painful past by the light of Providence. **father,** as a nourisher or adviser.

The duty of self-forgiveness (v. 5).—Let us consider our sins in —I. Their aspect towards God. Viewed on this side, they bear the inscription—acts of enmity and rebellion. They were designed, and carried through, and completed, in defiance of His will. At the same time, if these sins are repented of, and if we have true faith in the blood of the Redeemer, there is an appointed balm for this wound. II. Their effects upon man. "One sinner destroyeth much good." One sin is like a leak in a ship—it lets in many more.[c]

The widow and the Turk.—During the struggle of the Greeks to retain their liberty, a body of Turks were, in 1824, encamped in a part of Greece, and committed every kind of outrage upon the inhabitants. One of these barbarians, an officer, had pursued a Greek girl, who took refuge in the house of a widow. The widow met him at the door, and mildly attempted to dissuade him from forcing his way in to seize the girl. Enraged, he drew his sabre; but when in the act of attempting to cut down the widow, it snapped in two pieces before it reached the victim. The wretch paused, yet drew a pistol to accomplish his purpose, but it missed fire; and when in the act of drawing a second, he was forcibly dragged away by one of his companions, who exclaimed, "Let her alone. Do not you see that her time is not yet come?" Resolved, however, on taking some revenge, he carried off her infant child to the camp; but, as though Providence designed to frustrate all his designs on this occasion, whilst he was asleep, the child was carried back to the widow by one of his own men.[d]

B.C. 1707.

forth his voice in weeping.' In this way in the East do they still speak. 'How loudly did he give forth his voice, and weep!' 'That child is for ever giving forth its voice.' The violence of their sorrow is very great, and may be heard at a considerable distance."—*Roberts.*

"Joys are our wings, sorrows are our spurs."—*Richter.*

he comforts his brethren

a Is. xl. 2; 2 Co. ii. 6, 7.

b Ge. l. 20; Ps. cv. 17—19.

Ear, to plough. A. S. *erian*; L. *aro*; Gk. *aroo*—root *ar*, to plough.

v. 4. *J. Willison,* 159; *Dr. J. Langhorne,* i. 93; *Dr. S. Carr,* iv. 213.

c *Hemilist.*

"The decrees of Providence are inscrutable, in spite of man's short-sighted endeavours to dispose of events according to his own wishes and his own purposes; there is an intelligence beyond his reason, which holds the scales of justice and promotes his well-being, in spite of his puny efforts."—*J. Morier.*

"There's a divinity that shapes our ends, rough-hew them how we will."—*Shakespeare.*

d *Cheever.*

B.C 1707.

he sends a message to his father

"It is more beautiful to overcome injury by the power of kindness than to oppose to it the obstinacy of hatred."—*F. Maximus.*

"Let your best love draw to that point which seeks best to preserve it."—*Shakespeare.*

"Kind hearts are more than coronets, and simple faith than Norman blood."—*Tennyson.*

he embraces all his brethren
a Ac. vii. 14, 15.
b Ps. xxx. 5.
"The cheapest of all things is kindness, its exercise requiring the least possible trouble and self-sacrifice. 'Win hearts,' said Burleigh to Queen Elizabeth, 'and you have all men's hearts and purses.'"—*Smiles.*
"When people meet after long absence they fall on each other's shoulder or neck, and kiss or smell the part. A husband, after long absence, kisses or smells the forehead, the eyes, the right and left cheeks, and the bosom, of his wife."—*Roberts.*
c *Arvine.*

Pharaoh's command to Joseph
a Nu. xviii. 12, 29. Stuff (Ge. xxxi. 37; 1 S. x. 22; xxv. 13, etc.), furniture, baggage of an army or

9—11. (9) **say..him**, the bearers of ill news shall be the messengers of glad tidings. (10) **Goshen**, N.E. of Lower Egypt: region in Egypt nearest to Palestine. (11) **lest..poverty**, he preferred personal care to the precarious sending of occasional supplies.

Poor relations (v. 11).—I. Their condition: poor, needy. II. Their prospects: the worst still to come, five years more of famine. III. Their helper: a brother—1. Whom they had wronged; 2. Grown rich and great, who was not ashamed to own them.

God's providential care of His people.—Mr. Perkins was often in great straits. Once he had only threepence left. His niece, on hearing it, was greatly affected; but he said cheerfully, "Fear not, God will provide." In a little time a gentleman's servant knocked at the door, who brought him a present of a haunch of venison, together with some wheat and malt. Upon this, he took his niece by the hand, saying, "Do you see, child, here is venison, which is the noblest flesh, and the finest of the wheat for bread, and good malt for drink. Did not I tell thee God would provide for us?" They who trust in Providence shall not be forsaken.

12—15. (12) **Benjamin**, who as a witness Jacob would more readily believe. **mouth..you**, in your own language by an interpreter no longer. (13) **tell..seen**,^a that his father might be filled with confidence and share in their joy. (14) **feel..wept**, loving his brother for his own and his father's sake. (15) **kissed..them**,^b not bestowing all his love on Benjamin alone. **after..him**, mutual congratulations, perfect reconciliation, home news, bright anticipations.

Reconciliation (v. 15).—I. Not solicited by the guilty parties: the injured made the first overture. II. Not urged by circumstances; as nearness of death, etc. III. Not marked by any reservation. It was full and complete: so full that his brothers thought it impossible; and, seventeen years after, begged the assurance of Joseph's forgiveness.

Kindness to poor relations.—As one of the water-bearers at the fountain of the Fauxbourg St. Germain, in Paris, was at his usual labours in August, 1766, he was taken away by a gentleman in a splendid coach, who proved to be his own brother, and who, at the age of three years, had been carried away to India, where he made a considerable fortune. On his return to France he made inquiry respecting his family; and hearing that he had only one brother alive, and that he was in the humble condition of a water-bearer, he sought him out, embraced him with great affection, and brought him to his house, where he gave him bills for upwards of a thousand crowns per annum.^c

16—20. (16) **fame**, report, history. **it..well**, *lit.* it was good in the eyes of Pharaoh. (17) Pharaoh considerately meets Joseph's probable delicacy in inviting strangers, by inviting them himself. (18) **give..Egypt**, a royal recompense to Joseph. **eat..land**,^a the very best of the productions. (19) **wagons**, wheeled vehicles anc. used in Egypt. (20) **regard..stuff**, be not parsimoniously anxious to gather all together, and thus delay the journey. **good..yours**, the good of the future should exempt us fr. anxiety concerning present things.

Royal bounty (v. 20).—I. What Pharaoh did to Joseph was for Joseph's sake. What he did for Joseph's brethren was not for their sake, but Joseph's. II. What the Great King does for us is for the sake of our Brother, not for our own.

Ancient waggons.—" The Hebrew word seems to be fairly rendered by the word 'waggons.' Wheel carriages of some kind or other are certainly intended; and as, from other passages, we learn that they were covered, at least sometimes, the best idea we can form of them is, that they bore some resemblance to our tilted waggons. With some small exception, it may be said that wheel carriages are not now employed in Africa or Western Asia; but that they were anciently used in Egypt, and in what is now Asiatic Turkey, is attested not only by history, but by existing sculptures and paintings. It would seem that they were not at this time used in Palestine, as, when Jacob saw them, he knew they must have come from Egypt. Perhaps, however, he knew this by their peculiar shape."[b]

21—24. (21) **gave .. way**, for the journey to and fro. (22) **gave .. raiment**, such presents still common in the E. **Benjamin .. raiment**,[a] as an evident token to Jacob that he sympathised with him in his love to Benjamin. (23) **sent .. manner**, *etc.*, as a pledge and foretaste of better things in store. (24) **see .. way**, *lit.* be not stirred, *i.e.* do not fall into contentions; do not give way to criminations and recriminations.[b] Joseph had not forgotten their old quarrelsome disposition.

Christian candour (v. 24).—I. The true nature and extent of the caution suggested in the text. Compliance with it is not prevented by—1. Difference of opinion; 2. Diversity of temper; 3. A knowledge of the faults of others. II. Some proper motives to induce us to comply with it. 1. We are brethren; like the patriarchs we have one Father; 2. This advice is given us by our own dear Brother; Joseph here cautions his brethren; 3. We are all guilty; the brothers were all guilty in their former treatment of Joseph; 4. We all hope to be forgiven, as they were forgiven; 5. Like them, we are all sojourners in a strange land; 6. Like them, we are all travelling to the same home.[c]

Changes of raiment.—" The vizier entered at another door, and their excellencies rose to salute him after their manner, which was returned by a little inclining of his head: after which he sat down on the corner of his sofa, which is the most honourable place; then his chancellor, his kiahia, and the chiaouz bashaw came and stood before him, till coffee was brought in; after which, M. de Châteauneuf presented M. de Ferriol to him, as his successor, who delivered him the king his master's letters, complimenting him as from his majesty and himself, to which the vizier answered very obligingly. Then, after some discourse, which turned upon the reciprocal readiness of propension towards the continuance of a good intelligence between the Porte and the court of France, which M. de Ferriol assured them that the king his master was well disposed to cultivate sincerely, they gave two dishes of coffee to their excellencies, with sweetmeats, and after that perfumes and sherbet. Then they clothed them with *caffetans* (or *caftans*) of a silver brocade, with large silk flowers; and to those that were admitted into the apartments with them, they gave others of brocade, almost all

B.C. 1707.

traveller.

"Therefore away, to get our stuff aboard."— *Shakespeare.*

"The people are fashioned according to the example of their king; and edicts are of less power than the model which his life exhibits."— *Claudian.*

b Dr. Kitto.

Joseph's parting injunction

a 2 Ki. v. 22; Zech. iii. 4.

b Bush. Gk. "do not be angry;" *Chal.* "do not contend."

c Dr. Manton.

"A tender-hearted and compassionate disposition which inclines men to pity and feel the misfortunes of others, and which is, even for its own sake, incapable of involving any man in ruin and misery, is of all tempers of mind the most amiable; and though it seldom receives much honour, is worthy of the highest."— *Fielding.*

"The last, best fruit which comes to late perfection, even in the kindliest soul, is tenderness toward the hard, forbearance toward the unfortunate, warmth of heart toward the cold, philanthropy toward the misanthropic."— *Richter.*

GENESIS. [Cap. xlvi. 1–7.

B.C. 1707.

d De la Mo raye.

they return to Jacob

a Lu. xxiv. 11, 34, 41; Ps. cxxvi. 1.

b Ge. xlvi. 30.

c *T. Grantham, B.D.*

"'Tis strange—but true: for truth is always strange: stranger than fiction."—*Byron.*

"Though it be honest, it is never good to bring bad news. Give to a gracious message an host of tongues; but let ill tidings tell themselves, when they be left."—*Shakespeare.*

v. 26—28. *H. Blunt*, 156; *Bp. Conybeare*, i. 423; *Dr. T. F. Dibdin*, 189.

"There are joys which long to be ours. God sends ten thousand truths, which come about us like birds seeking inlet; but we sr shut up to them; and so they bring us nothing but sit and sing awhile upon the roof, and then fly away."—*Beecher.*

d *W. Jay.*

silk. except some slight gold or silver flowers, according to the custom usually observed towards all foreign ministers."*d*

25—28. (25) **came . . father**, and to his great delight Benjamin was safe. (26) **fainted**,*a* *lit.* was weakened. *i.e.* could scarcely believe so strange a tale. (27) **saw . . revived**, his doubts removed and his soul was cheered by what he saw. (28) **said . . enough**, I am convinced and satisfied. **see . . die**,*b* the sight of the prosperity of one so dear will make death easy.

Joseph and his brethren (vv. 26, 27).—I purpose, in considering this text, to—I. Point out to you the truths which this history illustrates and confirms. 1. That the Providence of God regulates the minutest matters; and that He doeth all things according to His will, both in heaven and earth; 2. That wicked men, though following their own devices, and actuated solely by their own evil inclinations, do but bring to pass the secret purposes of the Most High; 3. That God's people are often tried by great and long-continued affliction: 4. That, however long or soundly conscience may sleep, when God is pleased to arouse it, the most stout-hearted sinner will be struck with terror and alarm. II. Direct your attention to some of the lessons of instruction with which it may furnish us. We may learn from it—1. To put full and entire trust in the promises of God; 2. To maintain uprightness and integrity in all our dealings, and to combine an active use of means with an earnest prayer for blessing upon them; 3. That, as Joseph behaved towards his brethren, so God often deals with His people, and with the same object—namely, to make them sensible of their sins, and to effect their humiliation; 4. Not to be overcome of evil, but to overcome evil with good.*c*

Welcoming death.—A child at school welcomes every messenger from home to him; but he desires most the messenger that comes for him. Joseph sends to Jacob, and for him, at once; and his father not only heard the words, but saw the waggons. "Oh! these are really to carry me to him: I shall soon see my son, and die in peace." Such a messenger, Christian, is death to you. "Come," says God, "you have toiled long enough; you have feared long enough; you have groaned long enough; your warfare is accomplished; enter the rest which the Lord your God giveth you. Come; for all things are now ready." "But the swelling river rolls between." Fear not. The ark of the covenant will go before you, and divide the waves, and you shall pass over dry-shod. And then let the streams reunite, and continue to flow on, you will not wish them to reopen for your return. What is misery to others is joy to you. "I shall go the way whence I shall not return."*d*

CHAPTER THE FORTY-SIXTH.

B.C. 1706.

God encourages Jacob to go into Egypt

a Ge. xxviii. 10, 13, xxvi. 23—25, xxxi. 42.

1—7. (1) **Beersheba . . Isaac**,*a* a place hallowed by sacred memories. (2) **Israel . . Jacob**,*b* called by his old name bec. he would not at first *prevail* in Egypt. (3) **fear . . Egypt**, seasonable encouragement. (4) **down . . again**,*c* the Divine presence a guarantee of safety. **Joseph . . eyes**, *i.e.* when dying, Joseph should close his eyes. (5) **sons . . father**,*d* they cared for him

Cap. xlvi. 8—15.] GENESIS. 201

as the chief thing they brought fr. Canaan. (6) **goods,**e leaving behind only what was valueless or immovable. (7) **daughters,** wh. implies that there were more than the one named. all .. **Egypt,** in all seventy souls.

Fear not to go down into Egypt (v. 3).—I. The position in which Jacob was placed. He must have shuddered at the thought of going to dwell among heathen strangers. 1. It was a new scene and likely to be a trying one; 2. Yet the way was evidently appointed for him, and therefore he resolved to go. II. What is frequently the position of believers now: they are called to perils and temptations altogether untried. At such seasons let them—1. Imitate Jacob's example; then shall they have—(1) His companion; (2) His promise. 2. Exercise his confidence.*f*

The dying father.—In the East, a father, at the point of death, is always very desirous that his wife, children, and grand-children should be with him. Should there be one at a distance, he will be immediately sent for, and until he arrive, the father will mourn and complain. "My son, will you not come? I cannot die without you." When he arrives, he will take the hands of his son, and kiss them, and place them on his eyes, his face, and mouth, and say, "Now I die."*g*

8—15. (8) **names .. Egypt,** how long would the list be of those who went out of Egypt? (9) **Hanoch**a (*initiated*). **Phallu**a (*distinguished*) or Pallu. **Hezron**b (*enclosed*). **Carmi** (*vinedresser*). (10) **Jemuel**c (*day of God*) or Nemuel. **Jamin** (*prosperity*). **Ohad** (*united*). **Jachin** (*firmness*) or Jarib. **Zohar** (*whiteness*) or Zerah. **Shaul** (*desired*). (11) **Gershon**d (*expulsion*) or Gershom. **Kohath**e (*assembly*) fr. whom descended the Kohathites, one of the three grt. fams. of the tr. of Levi. **Merari**f (*unhappy*). (12) **Er .. Canaan,** see xxxviii. 6—10. **Hamul** (*spared*). (13) **Tola** (*a worm*). **Phuvah** (*mouth*) also Pua*g* and Puah.*h* **Job** (*? desire*) or Jashub*i* (*he turns*). **Shimron** (*watch post*). (14) **Sered** (*fear*). **Elon** (*an oak*). **Jahleel** (*hoping in God*). (15) all .. three, *k* including Jacob, but exclusive of Er, Onan, and prob. Leah herself.

Different phases of history.—To be entirely just in our estimate of other ages is not only difficult—it is impossible. Even what is passing in our presence we see but through a glass darkly. The mind as well as the eye adds something of its own, before an image, even of the clearest object, can be painted upon it; and in historical inquiries, the most instructed thinkers have but a limited advantage over the most illiterate. Those who know the most approach least to agreement. The most careful investigations are diverging roads; the further men travel upon them, the greater the interval by which they are divided. In the eyes of David Hume, the history of the Saxon princes is "the scuffling of kites and crows." Father Newman would mortify the conceit of a degenerate England by pointing to the sixty saints and the hundred confessors who were trained in her royal palaces for the calendar of the blessed. How vast a chasm yawns between these two conceptions of the same era! Through what common term can the student pass from one into the other? Or, to take an instance yet more noticeable, the history of England scarcely interests Mr. Macaulay before the revolution of the seventeenth century. To Lord John Russell the Reformation was the

B.C. 1706.

b Nachmanides, Raphall.
c Ge. xxviii. 15; Ex. iii. 8.
d Ac. vii, 15.
e Ge. xlv. 20.
f C. H. Spurgeon.

"Who is it that called time the avenger, yet failed to see that death was the consoler? What mortal afflictions are there to which death does not bring full remedy? What hurts of hope and body does it not repair? This is a sharp medicine, said Raleigh, speaking of the axe, 'but it cures all disorders.'"—*Simms.*

g Roberts.

the names of the Children of Israel

the children of Leah

a Ex. vi. 14; Nu. xxvi. 5; 1 Ch. v. 3.
b Nu. xxvi. 6; 1 Ch. v. 3.
c Nu. xxvi. 12; 1 Ch. iv. 24.
d 1 Co. vi. 16.
e Ex. vi. 16, 18; Nu. iii. 17, 19, 27.
f Ex. vi. 16, 19; 1 Ch. vi. 1, 16.
g Nu. xxvi. 23.
h 1 Ch. vii. 1.
i Nu. xxvi. 24; 1 Ch. vii. 1.
k "History presents the pleasant features of poetry and fiction, the majesty of the epic, the moving accidents of the drama, the surprises and moral of the romance. Wallace is a rude Hector; Robinson Crusoe is not stranger than Crœsus; the Knights of Ashby never burnish the page of Scott

GENESIS. [Cap. xlvi. 16—22.

B.C. 1706.

with richer lights of lance and armour, than those Carthaginians, winding down the Alps, east upon Livy." — *Willmott.*
k Froud.

the children of Zilpah
a Nu. xxvi. 15.
b Nu. xxvi. 16
c Nu. xxvi. 17.
d Nu. xxvi. 44.
e 1 Ch. vii. 30.
f Nu. xxvi. 46.
"It was a charming fancy of the Pythagoreans to exchange names when they met, that so they might partake of the virtues each admired in the other. And, knowing the power of names, they used only such as were musical and pleasing."—*A. B. Alcott.*
"Favour or disappointment has been often conceded as the name of the claimant has affected us; and the accidental affinity or coincidence of a name, connected with ridicule or hatred, with pleasure or disgust, has operated like magic."-*Disraeli.*
"With the vulgar and the learned, names have great weight. The wise use a writ of inquiry into their legitimacy when they are advanced as authority." — *Zimmerman.*
g Carlyle.

the children of Rachel
a Nu. xxvi. 38, 40; 1 Ch. vii. 6, 7, viii. 1, 3.

first outcome from centuries of folly and ferocity; and Mr. Hallam's more temperate language softens without concealing a similar conclusion. The writers have all studied what they describe. Mr. Carlyle has studied the same subject with powers at least equal to theirs, and to him the greatness of English character was waning with the dawn of English literature; the race of heroes was already failing: the era of action was yielding before the era of speech.*k*

16—18. (16) **Ziphion** (*a looking out*) or Zephon.*a* **Haggi** (*festive*). **Shuni** (*quiet*). **Ezbon** (*a worker*) or Ozni.*b* **Eri** (*watching*). **Arodi** (*wild ass*) or Arod.*c* **Areli** (*lion of God*). (17) **Jimnah**.*d* (*good fortune*) or Imna.*e* **Isuah**.*e* (*level*). **Beriah** (*son of evil*). **Serah** (*princess*) or Sarah.*f* **Heber** (*society*). **Malchiel** (*God's king*). (18) *whom* .. daughter, *see* xxix. 24.

The province of history.—Under the green foliage and blossoming fruit-trees of to-day, there lie, rotting slower or faster, the forests of all other years and days. Some have rotted fast, plants of annual growth, and are long since quite gone to inorganic mould; others are like the aloe, growths that last a thousand or three thousand years. You will find them in all stages of decay and preservation; down deep to the beginnings of the history of man. Think where our alphabetic letters came from, where our speech itself came from: the cookeries we live by, the masonries we lodge under! You will find fibrous roots of this day's occurrences among the dust of Cadmus and Trismegistus, of Tubalcain and Triptolemus; the tap-roots of them are with Father Adam himself and the cinders of Eve's first fire! At the bottom there is no perfect history; there is none such conceivable. All past centuries have rotted down, and gone confusedly dumb and quiet, even as that seventeenth is now threatening to do. Histories are *as* perfect as the historian is wise, and as he is gifted with an eye and a soul! For the leafy blossoming present time springs from the whole past, remembered and unrememberable, so confusedly as we say:—and truly the art of history, the grand difference between a Dryasdust and a sacred poet, is very much even this: —To distinguish well what does still reach to the surface, and is alive and frondent for us; and what reaches no longer to the surface, but moulders safe underground, never to send forth leaves or fruit for mankind any more: of the former we shall rejoice to hear; to hear of the latter will be an affliction to us: of the latter only pedants and dullards, and disastrous malefactors to the world, will find good to speak. By wise memory and by wise oblivion; it lies all there! Without oblivion there is no remembrance possible. When both oblivion and memory are wise, when the general soul of man is clear, melodious, true, there may come a modern *Iliad* as memorial of the past: when both are foolish and the general soul is overclouded with confusions, with unveracities and discords, here is a "Rushworthian chaos."*g*

19—22. (19) **Rachel** .. **wife**, his wife par excellence. (20) **Manasseh** (*who makes forget*). **Ephraim** (*very fruitful*). (21) **Belah** (*destruction*) or Bela.*a* **Becher** (*first-born*). elsewhere omitted.*b* **Ashbel** (*fire of Baal*). **Gera** (*a seed*). **Naaman** (*pleasantness*). **Ehi** (*my brother*). also Ariram*c* and

Aher,[d] and Aharah.[e] **Rosh** (*chief*). **Muppim** or perh. Shuphan (*? serpent*) and Shephuphan.[f] **Huppim** (*coverings*). **Ard** (*? fugitive*). (22) **fourteen**, *i.e.* Rachel's two sons and their children.

What is in a name?—An answer to this question depends upon the name which you mean. A name is generally the synonym of a thing, a place, or a person; or, in other words, to make mention by name of a certain thing, or place, or person, is to call up before the mind all those things which we know to belong to each respectively. Hence, when you utter the name of some things, that name includes the characteristics of those things, so far as known by those that hear the name. You say, "A moss rose." In that name is contained, in my mind, all that I remember of the thing itself, its fragrance, beauty, &c. Give me the name of some places, and I see in that name the size, locality, population, &c., of those places, as I know them either from observation or reading. Give me the name of some men, and I immediately think of virtue, intelligence, charity, eloquence, &c., as associated with them; the name of other men, and the opposite associations are awoke within me. Speak or write the name of God, and what grand ideas are couched within it! The name of Jesus, what endless beauties, mercies, &c., are embodied there! The "new name" which is given to the Christian conqueror, how full of gracious and happy meaning! As there is so much importance in a name, every man ought to guard his name. Every Christian should be jealous to retain his name in untarnished honour and purity. As no heir can claim the inheritance if he have not the *proper* name, so no man can claim heaven if he have not the *right* name in his heart, and in the Lamb's Book of Life.[g]

23—27. (23) **Hushim** (*the hasting*) or Shuhan.[a] (24) **Jahzeel** (*whom God allots*). **Guni** (*coloured*). **Jezer** (*imagination*). **Shillem** (*requital*) or Shallum.[b] (25) **Laban** . . **daughter**, *see* xxix. 29. (26) **all** . . **six**, if to this number, 66, we add his sons' wives, 9 (Simeon's and Judah's wives being dead, and Joseph's in Egypt), there is perfect harmony with the statement of Stephen.[c] (27) **all** . . **ten**, *i.e.* Joseph and his father and two sons.

Small beginnings (v. 27).—Only 70 souls; yet—I. The foundation of a nation. II. Destined presently to overturn the power and pride of Egypt. III. Designed, in the providence of God to give to the world its only inspired teachers and its great Redeemer.

Writing history.—Many writers, including now an imperial historian, have attempted to weigh and measure the share that individual men and accidents have in the course of human affairs. How far has the world really been affected by Alexander, or by the cold bath that cut him off in his very youth; by the day's march of Claudius Nero, that drove the Carthaginians out of Italy, and led to the ruin of their state; by the mighty genius, or the assassination, of Julius Cæsar; by the arrow that pierced Harold, or the bullet that killed Charles XII., of Sweden; by the passions of our Henry VIII.; by the obstinacy of Charles I., or by the religious convictions of James II.; by the cold ragout which is said to have deprived Napoleon of one victory, or the timely arrival of the Prussians, which extinguished all hope of

B.C. 1706.

b Nu. xxvi. 38, 41; 1 Ch. viii. 1.
c Nu. xxvi. 38.
d 1 Ch. vii. 12.
e 1 Ch. viii. 1.
f 1 Ch. viii. 5.

"In honest truth, a name given to a man is no better than a skin given to him; what is not natively his own falls off, and comes to nothing."—*Landor.*

"The present state of things is the consequence of the past; and it is natural to inquire as to the sources of the good we enjoy, or the evils we suffer. If we act only for ourselves, to neglect the study of history is not prudent, if entrusted with the care of others, it is not just."—*Johnson.*

g J. Bate.

the children of Bilhah

summary

a Nu. xxvi. 42.

b 1 Ch. vii. 13.

c Ac. vii. 14.

"To study history is to study literature. The biography of a nation embraces all its works. No trifle is to be neglected. A mouldering medal is a letter of twenty centuries. Antiquities which have been beautifully called history defaced, compose its fullest commentary. In these wrecks of many storms, which time washes to the shore, the scholar looks

B.C. 1706.

patiently for treasure."—Willmott.

d The Times.

meeting of Joseph and Jacob

a "A word almost reserved for Divine appearances; and Knobel thinks it is used here as according with the royal pomp with which Joseph was invested."—Alford.

"There appears much joy in him, even so much that joy could not show itself modest enough without a badge of bitterness. A kind overflow of kindness,—there are no faces truer than those that are so washed."—Shakespeare.

b As men say, "See Naples and die," meaning that there is nothing more beautiful to be seen.

c Saturday Review.

De numero familiæ Jacobæ, Crit. Sac. Thes. i. 246.

his advice to his brethren

"The Egyptians detested the very sight of a shepherd, from a remembrance of the injuries which they had recently sustained from the pastoral kings;

another? History must deal with persons and things, and it must also clothe them with dramatic interest and importance, but philosophers are apt to think them only the superficial indications of an irresistible current below. A despot is murdered, but the despotism remains. A great soldier falls, but the nation is not less warlike.*d*

28—30. (28) **to Goshen**, *i.e.* in order that Joseph might point out to Judah the land of Goshen. (29) **made .. chariot**, *lit.* bound his chariot, *i.e.* harnessed his horses to it. **presented**,*a* appeared. (30) **now .. alive**, he had lived to see all he wished in this world.*b*

The land of Goshen (v. 28).—I. The temporary abode of Israel in Egypt, and yet most fruitful. II. The scene of a wonderful miracle (darkness). III. The scene of an extraordinary gathering. IV. The scene of a triumphant departure.

The "ifs" of history.—If something had happened which didn't happen, what would have happened afterwards? is a kind of speculation which is now much in fashion. Of course no one can answer positively the above inquiry. Yet, in looking back upon the course of history, it is impossible not to dwell for a moment upon some of the more important crises, and to remark how small a difference might have made an incalculable change. We know the usual sayings about the decisive battles of the world. If Themistocles had lost the battle of Salamis, if Asdrubal had won the battle of the Metaurus, if Charles Martel had been beaten by the Saracens, would not the subsequent history of Europe and the world have been altered, and a great many fine philosophical theories have been destroyed before their birth? Even the strictest believer in universal causation may admit without prejudice to his opinions that the most trivial circumstances may be of cardinal importance. The reluctance to admit the doctrine about great events springing from trivial causes results from another consequence of the theory. Where the fate of a few persons is concerned, no one cares to dispute it. When Noah was in the ark, the most trifling error of steering might (in the absence of providential interference) have shipwrecked the whole human race. Now, the logical difficulties raised by Necessitarians apply just as much to a party of twenty as to twenty millions. The importance of small cases does not affect their theory more in one case than the other. But philosophers are unwilling to allow that the fate of whole countries and many generations can depend upon these petty accidents, because it would obviously render all prediction impossible, and at least have the future of mankind dependent upon the chance of the necessary hero arising at the critical moment.*c*

30—34. (31) **shew**, inform. (32) **shepherds .. cattle**, Joseph does not conceal his extraction. (33) **what .. occupation?** he would never dream that they were men without a trade. (34) **for .. shepherd**, who for the most part led a nomadic life. **abomination**, object of contempt, scorn. **Egyptians**, who lived in cities.

Egyptian antipathy to shepherds.—The extensive tract of country which borders on Egypt, and is inhabitated by the wandering tribes who live by their flocks, was never entirely subject to the dominion of the Pharaohs. From their whole mode of life and feelings towards the Egyptians, they could scarcely be looked upon by the latter in other light than that of enemies. This hatred against them is mentioned by Herodotus. (II. 128.) It is a mistake to suppose that the raising of cattle was the reason of this aversion of the Egyptians. This could not be; for they themselves raised multitudes of cattle, and considered some of them even sacred. Rosenmuller, therefore, supposes that the shepherds of Arabia Deserta, the wandering and warlike tribes east of Egypt, with whom they confounded the sons of Jacob, were those alone who were hated by the Egyptians.[a]

B.C. 1706.

"for when the sons of Jacob stood before Pharaoh, these oppressors had only vacated the country about 36 years."

[a] *Weekly Visitor.*

CHAPTER THE FORTY-SEVENTH.

B.C. 1706.

1—4. (1) **Joseph .. Pharaoh**, loyal to the king as well as kind to his family. (2) **some .. five**, not a *selected* five. (3) **what .. occupation?** the question Joseph expected. **they said**, *etc.*, their reply indicates their confidence in the wisdom of Joseph. (4) **for .. flocks,** two years of famine had exhausted their own land.

Pharaoh's question to the brethren of Joseph (v. 3).—The words of the text—I. Imply that each of us has, or is intended to have, an occupation. Even as regards the present life, each of us are considered to be employed in something; and, surely, with regard to things of higher moment, we have a work entrusted to us. II. Lead us to inquire into the nature of this occupation, with respect to different classes of individuals. Look at—1. The man whose whole time is taken up in the accumulation of earthly wealth; 2. He whose thoughts and time are engrossed with the pursuit of worldly glory; 3. He who devotes himself to earthly pleasures and sinful enjoyments; 4. The Christian. What is his occupation? He is "about his Father's business." Brethren, let this occupation be yours.[a]

Importance of an occupation.—Seventeen years ago there was a fair girl so pure, so lovely, so refined, that she still rises to my mind as almost akin to angels. She was wooed and ultimately won by a handsome young man of considerable wealth. He sported a fine team, delighted in hunting, and kept a fine pack of hounds. He neither played cards, drank wine, nor used tobacco. He had no occupation, no calling, no trade. He lived on his money, the interest of which alone would have supported a family handsomely. I never saw the fair bride again until a few days ago. Seventeen years had passed away, and with them her beauty and her youth; her husband's fortune and his life, during the latter part of which they lived in a log-cabin on the banks of the Ohio River, near Blennerhasset's Island; a whole family in one single room, subsisting on water, fat bacon, and corn bread. The husband had no business capacity. He was a gentleman of education, of refinement, of noble impulses; but when his money was gone, he could get no employment, simply because he did not know how to do anything. For a while he floundered about, first trying one thing, then another, but "failure" was written on them all. He, however, finally obtained a situation: the labour was great, the compensation small; it was that or starvation; in his heroic efforts to discharge his duty acceptably he overworked himself and died, leaving his widow and six girls in utter desti-

Pharaoh inquires their occupation

[a] *S. Coates, M.A.*

"He that hath a trade hath an estate; and he that hath a calling hath a place of profit and honour. A ploughman on his legs is higher than a gentleman on his knees."— *Franklin.*

"There is nothing so useful to man in general, nor so beneficial to particular societies and individuals, as trade. This is that *alma mater*, at whose plentiful breast all mankind are nourished."— *Fielding.*

"I protest against the unfair distribution of the world's work, which can only be well done when every man and woman is fitted to work, left free to choose the field in which to work, and condemned by public opinion if they refuse to work."—*Celia Burleigh.*

B.C. 1706.

b *Dr. Hall.*

Pharaoh gives them the land of Goshen

a Pr. xxii. 29.

b "Prob. the aged patriarch, with the conscious dignity of a prophet and the heir of the promises, prayed for blessings upon Pharaoh."
—*Spk. Com.*

c *Thomson.*

meeting of Pharaoh and Jacob
a Ge. xxxv. 28; Job. xiv. 1; Ge. xxv. 7.
b He. xiii. 14; 1 Pe. ii. 11; Ps. xxxix. 5; xc. 10, 12; Jas. iv. 15; He. xi. 13; 1 Ch. xxix. 15; Ps. cxix. 19.
"The Jews speak of Jacob's seven afflictions: (1) the persecution of Esau; (2) the injustice of Laban; (3) the result of his wrestling with the Angel; (4) the violation of Dinah; (5) the loss of Joseph; (6) the imprisonment of Simeon; (7) the departure of Benjamin for Egypt. They might well have added the death of Rachel and the incest of Reuben."—*Schumann.*
c *W. Champneys, M.A.*
d *Tract Journal.*

Joseph provides for his brethren

a 1 Ti. v. 4, 8.

tution. In seventeen years the sweet and joyous and beautiful girl had become a broken-hearted, careworn, poverty-stricken widow, with a houseful of helpless children.*b*

5—7. (5) **saying,***a* etc., words of congratulation. (6) **land** .. thee, to select from. **Goshen** .. **dwell**, settled in a border province they might serve as a protection for Egypt. **activity,** ability or prowess. (7) **Jacob .. Pharaoh**, this a visit of ceremony: the former one of business. **blessed,***b* i.e. saluted.

Filial piety.—

"Have I, then, no tears for thee, my father?
Can I forget thy cares, from helpless years,
Thy tenderness for me? An eye still beam'd
With love? A brow that never knew a frown?
Nor a harsh word thy tongue? Shall I for these
Repay thy stooping venerable age
With shame, disquiet, anguish, and dishonour?
It must not be, thou first of angels! Come,
Sweet filial Piety, and firm my breast!"*c*

8—10. (8) **how .. thou?** the king impressed with the venerable aspect of the patriarch. (9) **pilgrimage,** *lit.* sojournings. **few,***a* as comp. with those of his ancestors. **evil,** full of sorrow. **have .. been,** he reckoned life by days as well as years. **have .. pilgrimage,***b* old as I appear, my ancestors have yet lived to a greater age. (10) **went .. Pharaoh,** to die in Goshen seventen yrs. after.

Few and evil are the days of life (v. 9).—In discoursing on the words of the text, I would address myself to—I. Those who do *not* serve God. Shall we say that the days of your lives have been many or few? Are you ready to meet your God? II. Those who *do* serve Him. 1. What do you think of the days you passed before you knew God, or rather were known of God. Were they many or few, if you measure them by the good done in them. 2. What shall we say of those you have spent since you knew Him? As you look back, you say, with aged Israel, "Few and evil have the days of the years of my life been."*c*

*Difference in the aged.—*Mrs. G—— was one day visiting an aged man, a friend of her father, and one who was associated with him in early life. Though differing widely in sentiment, the two old men still felt a deep interest in each other. Mr. S—— had been one of those who run after the world and overtake it. All that it can give he had obtained. Now, he inquired of the state of his friend, whom he knew to be in circumstances of far less external comfort than himself. As he listened to the story of his patience in suffering, and of the cheerfulness with which he could look forward either to a longer pilgrimage in this world or to the hour of death, his conscience applied the unexpressed reproach, and he exclaimed, "Yes, yes; you wonder I cannot be as quiet and happy too; but think of the difference: he is going to his treasure, and I—I must leave mine."*d*

11—12. (11) **placed,** caused to dwell. **Rameses,** a city wh. may not now have existed, but named by anticipation. (12) **according .. families,***a* i.e. acc. to the mouth of the little ones, i.e. their number and their wants.

*Abd-el-Kader's intercession.—*Amongst the incidents connected with the life of that extraordinary man, Abd-el-Kader, there is one which shows with what an extraordinary power of eloquence he was endowed, even while yet little more than a boy. It seems that his father, Sidi Ma-hi-el Din, who was one of the most celebrated marabouts, or priests, of the province of Oran, organised a conspiracy, the object of which was to free the Arabs from the dominion of Turkey, and to form their straggling and dispersed tribes into one mighty nation, his favourite son being pointed out as their destined leader and liberator. Before the time for striking the decisive blow had arrived, however, the conspiracy had become known to the Bey Hassan, who was governor of the province; and he resolved to rid himself and his master of their powerful enemy. The marabout, Ma-hi-el Din, was entrapped into the power of the Bey, and thrown into prison to die. To rescue him, either by stratagem or by force of arms, was impossible; and all had been lost but for the daring resolve and subduing eloquence of his son. Abd-el-Kader, at the imminent hazard of his own life, presented himself before the tribunal of the Bey, and there he pleaded the cause of his father with such power, that he at once obtained an order for his liberation. "By Allah and Mahomet," exclaimed the impassioned youth, "I entreat thee to return to me my father. I summon thee, in the name of four powerful tribes of the provinces, to restore to liberty the marabout, Ma-hi-el Din, chief of the Hachim Rhaeriee, of whom thou hast acknowledged the innocence."

What a noble sight must that have been! There stands the son, like another Demosthenes, his stature erect; his eye at one moment lit up with the fire of indignation, and the next beaming with the mild rays of affection. The Bey was subdued by the eloquence of the noble youth, and the father was set at liberty, upon condition that he should at once quit the country.

B.C. cir. 1706.

"You are so to put forth the power that God has given you; you are so to give, and sacrifice to give, as to earn the eulogium pronounced on the woman, 'She hath done what she could.' Do it now. It is not a safe thing to leave a generous feeling to the cooling influences of a cold world. If you intend to do a mean thing, wait till to-morrow; if you are to do a noble thing, do it now,—now!"—Guthrie.

"The office of liberality consisteth in giving with judgment."—Cicero.

v 12. Dr. W. Paley, 147.

13—17. (13) **no .. land,** *i.e.* none comparatively. **fainted,** the people prostrated and spiritless. (14) **brought .. house,** an honest prime minister. (15) **give,** the buyers become beggars. (16) **cattle,** this a wise measure resulting in the preservation of the cattle. (17) **horses,** first mention of the horse in the Bible.

The horse.—Heb. words trans. horse in Bible are *sus* = heavy H. for war-chariot, and *parash* = H. for riding, esp. cavalry. The original country of H. not known. In regard to claim of Arabia, see Kitto on Jos. xi. 6. Until then H. not named, save in Egypt (Ge. xlix. 17; Ex. ix. 3, xv. 21; De. xvii. 16). Nothing said of Arab use of H. during period of wanderings on confines of Arabia, yet other animals are named; and kings of Arabia rode on camels (Jud. viii. 21). Strabo (time of Christ) describes Arabia as without H. This may explain why Moses did not contemplate that the Jews would ever go to Arabia, but Egypt, for H. (De. xvii. 16), and why Solomon, 460 yrs. after, obtained his cavalry from that country (1 K. x. 28, 29). By time of Mohammed II. were numerous and valued in Arabia; hence his saying, "as many grains of barley as are contained in the food we give to a H., so many indulgences do we daily gain by giving it."[a]

18—22. (18) **ended .. year,** *i.e.* from the failing of their money. **lands,** wh. they were no longer able to cultivate. (19) **die .. land,** we by starvation, and our land perish through lack of tillage. **desolate,** barren and depopulated. (20) **bought ..**

the history of the famine

the cattle bought

"This gives the force to the strong,—that the multitude have no habit of self-reliance or original action."—Emerson.

Horse = the neighing animal. A. S. *hors*; old S. *hros*; Ger. *ross*; old Ger. *hros*; Ice. *hross*; Sans. *hresh* = to neigh.

a Topics.

the land bought

"The amelioration of the condition of man-land, and thus secured its better cultivation. (21) **removed .. thereof,**[a] brought them fr. outlying districts near to the stores of corn, to furnish them more easily with food, and with occupation. (22) **land .. not,**[b] in this he was prob. overruled by the king.

Egypt under Mehemet Ali.—The author of *The Boat and Caravan*, writing in 1846, remarked, "Strictly speaking there is but one proprietor of land in Egypt, and that is the all-powerful and all-engrasping Mehemet Ali. By a late edict he has appropriated the whole country to himself, so that Egypt is now as much the property of its ruler as it became after the great famine in the days of Joseph. The people have not, however, been turned out of their possessions, except where it has pleased the Pacha to take the land under his own care. In that case the fellah is not permitted to seek some other residence, but must remain as a labourer in the Pacha's service. Mehemet Ali is not content, as Pharaoh was, with a fifth of the produce; he takes the lion's share. If a fellah lets any portion of the land which he is permitted to retain, he will get, it may be, seventy piastres rent for a portion equal to an acre, of which nearly two-thirds goes to the Government in taxes."[c]

23—26. (23) **seed .. land,** wh. they might have neglected had it not been another's and they servants upon it. (24) **fifth .. own,** an act of liberality and good policy. (25) **thou .. lives,** hence we gratefully obey. (26) **law .. part,** ever after though the land became the people's the fifth part of the produce went into the coffers of the State.

The monuments and the history of Egypt.—It is hardly possible to imagine a greater contrast than is presented between the *Monuments* and the *History* of Egypt. The monuments tell of a native monarchy flourishing among the great empires of the East; its kings little less than demi-gods; its priesthood endued with a sanctity revered in distant lands; its chariots and horses pouring out to battle under the banners of a thousand gods; the nations of the earth bringing tribute; and art and luxury carried to an extent only possible to a numerous population, with abundant material resources and a high mental development. On the date and duration of this splendid period the monuments are dumb. They witness what ancient Egypt was; they know nothing of her rise, progress, or decay. Their testimony is confirmed by the position of Egypt in the Holy Scriptures, where her rulers are found showing hospitality to the father of the faithful, or reducing his descendants into bondage. Still, we only know that Egypt was a great power before Israel was a nation. It gleams out of a remote antiquity with a splendour that cannot be denied; but the splendour is a prehistoric memory, separated from authentic chronology by a gulf which nothing but the Bible can span. All we know of it is, that it existed before Moses, and perished about the close of the Old Testament. With the first page of secular history, Ancient Egypt is already dead. The Pharaohs have become a tradition, the temples and altars are shrouded in mystery, the fleets and armies have disappeared, the people are reduced to inexorable servitude.[a]

27—31. (27) **dwelt,** *etc.,* anticipatory, *see* Ex. i. 7. (28) **so .. years,**[a] *see* v. 9. (29) **must die,**[b] as all *must.* **put ..**

B.C. *cir.* 1706.

kind, and the increase of human happiness ought to be the leading objects of every political institution, and the aim of every individual, according to the measure of his power, in the situation he occupies."—*Hamilton.*

a Ge. xli. 48.

b Ezra vii. 24.

Dr. Kitto. *D. Bib. Ill.*, i. 433.

c *Bib. Treas.*

Joseph gives seed to sow the land

"A statesman, we are told, should follow public opinion. Doubtless, as a coachman follows his horse; having firm hold on the reins, and guiding them."—*Hare.*

"A generous nation is grateful even for the preservation of its rights, and willingly extends the respect due to the office of a good prince into an affection for his person."—*Junius.*

"The rude reproaches of the rascal herd for the selfsame actions, if successful, would be as grossly lavish in their praise."—*Thomson.*

a Canon Trevor.

approaching death of Jacob

thigh, *see* Ge. xxiv. 2. **bury** . . **Egypt**,*c* he firmly believed his posterity would inherit the land of Canaan. (30) **bury** . . **place**,*d* Machpelah. I . . **said**, a son's solemn promise to a dying father; sacredly kept. (31) **swear**, to give his father the fullest satisfaction. **Israel** . . **head**,*e* prob. worshipping God.

Goshen.—" It lay along the Pelusian arm of the Nile, on the east of the Delta, and was the part of Egypt nearest Palestine. This tract is now comprehended in the modern province Esh-Shurkiyeh, which extends from the neighbourhood of Abu Zabel to the sea, and from the desert to the former Tanaic branch of the Nile, thus including also the valley of the ancient canal. If the Pelusiac arm, as is commonly assumed, were navigable for fleets in ancient times, the Israelites were probably confined to its eastern bank; but if we are at liberty to suppose that the stream was never much larger than the present, then they may have spread themselves out upon the Delta beyond, until restrained by larger branches of the Nile. During my stay in Cairo I made many inquiries respecting this district, to which the uniform reply was that it was considered as the best province in Egypt. Wishing to obtain more definite information, I ventured to request of Lord Prudhoe, with whom the Pacha was understood to be on a very friendly footing, to obtain for me a statement of the valuation of the provinces of Egypt. This, as he afterwards informed me, could not well be done; but he had ascertained that the province of the Shurkiyeh bears the highest valuation, and yields the largest revenue."*f*

B.C. *cir.* 1706.

a Job xiv.14, Ps. xxxiii. 4.
b De. xxxi. 14; 1 Ki. ii. 1.
c Ge. l. 25.
d Ge. l. 12, 13.
e He. xi. 21.

"We hold death, poverty, and grief for our principal enemies; but this death which some repute the most dreadful of all dreadful things, who does not know that others call it the only secure harbour from the storms and tempests of life, the sovereign good of nature, the sole support of liberty, and the common and sudden remedy of all evils?"—*Montaigne.*
f Dr. Robinson.

CHAPTER THE FORTY-EIGHTH.

B.C. 1689.

1—4. (1) **that** . . **Joseph**, occupied with affairs of State. Joseph still kept up communications with his kindred. **look** . . **Ephraim**, prob. intending that they should share in Jacob's dying blessing. (2) **strengthened**, revived by the tidings of Joseph's approach. (3) **Luz**,*a* Bethel. (4) **and said**, *etc.*, Jacob repeats the promise to strengthen the faith of Joseph.

Jacob's great experience.—" God appeared to me at Luz," This one, first, and great appearance of God was memorable in all his life because it was the first. Others came after, without a doubt. Dreams and visions, supplementary intimations, he had. But there is something in a full first experience which nothing can ever rival or supersede. Many results come so gradually that we watch their unfolding as we do that of a flower whose seed we plant, and all of whose stages we watch and help, and whose blossoming, though it be a pleasure, is never a surprise. But now and then a great experience comes, unexpected and unsought. It touches the greater chords of the soul, and lifts it above the common level of emotion, outruns all former knowledge, and fills the soul and overflows it, and amazes it with its own capacity of joy, or love, or grief, or fear, or awe. In the presence of its own intense and surpassing emotions the soul is conscious of nothing else in life. It seems to itself to be the height and centre of the universe, and all other things fall off and grade away from it. The reality of immortality, the indestructibleness of the soul's life, is revealed to it in some of these

Joseph's interview with his dying father
a Ge. xxviii. 19; xxxv. 6, 9.

" Friend to the wretch whom every friend forsakes, I woo thee. Death! Life and its joys I leave to those that prize them. Hear me, O gracious God! At Thy good time let Death approach; I reck not, let him but come in genuine form, not with Thy vengeance armed, too much for man to hear."
—*Bp. Porteus.*

" All that nature has prescribed must be good; and as death is natural to us it is absurdity to fear it."—*Steele.*

B.C. cir. 1689.
b H. W. Beecher.

Jacob adopts the sons of Joseph
a Jos. xiii. 7; xiv. 4.

b Dr. Lange.
"There is not a more repulsive spectacle than an old man who will not forsake the world, which has already forsaken him."—*Tholuck.*

"I think that to have known one good old man—one man who, through the chances and mischances of a long life, has carried his heart in his hand, like a palm-branch, waving all discords into peace—helps our faith in God, in ourselves, and in each other more than many sermons."—*G. W. Curtis.*

"There is nothing more disgraceful than that an old man should have nothing to produce us as a proof that he has lived long except his years."—*Seneca.*

c Rogers.

higher and transcendent experiences, that seem not to have come from natural causes, but to have been let down from above by Divine inspiration.*b*

5—7. (5) **mine,** as if lit. so. **as .. mine,**ª shall share equally with my own children in patrimonial rights. (6) **issue .. thine,** if Joseph had any we do not hear of it. (7) **Rachel,** *etc.,* the old man recounts to his son the story of his mother's death and burial.

The settlement of the birthright in Israel (v. 5.)—Settled—I. In correspondence with the facts, or the diverse gifts of God. II. As a prevention of envy on the one side, or of pride on the other. III. As an indication of the Divine source of the true, or spiritual birthright. IV. As a preparation for the universal priesthood of the people of God.*b*

Age rejoicing with youth.—

"Stamped with its signet, that ingenuous brow,
And 'mid his old hereditary trees,
Trees he has climbed so oft, he sits and sees
His children's children playing round his knees.
Then happiest, youngest, when the quoit is flung,
When side by side the archers' bows are strung:
His to prescribe the place, adjudge the prize,
Envying no more the young their energies
Than they an old man, when his words are wise;
His a delight how pure, without alloy:
Strong in their strength, rejoicing in their joy!
Now in their turn assisting, they repay
The anxious cares of many and many a day;
And now by those he loves relieved, restored,
His very wants and weaknesses afford
A feeling of enjoyment. In his walks,
Leaning on them, how oft he stops and talks,
While they look up! Their questions, their replies,
Fresh as the welling waters, round him rise,
Gladdening his spirit : and, his theme the past,
How eloquent he is! His thoughts flow fast:
And while his heart (oh, can the heart grow old!
False are the tales that in the world are told!)
Swells in his voice, he knows not where to end;
Like one discoursing of an absent friend."*c*

and proposes to bless them

"O, the eyes' light is a noble gift of heaven! All beings live from light; each fair created thing, the very plants, turn with a joyful transport to the light."—*Schiller.*

"Sight is by much the noblest of the senses. We receive our

8—11. (8) **behold,** as he was blind this prob. means that he understood others to be present. (9) **bring .. them,** did this remind Jacob of the time when he obtained the blessing fr. his blind father. (10) **dim .. see,** but the inner man was full of light. (11) **and lo,** *etc.,* God is better to us than our hopes.

Ancient aids to vision.—Cicero said that he had seen the entire Iliad, which is a poem as large as the New Testament, written on skin so that it could be rolled up in the compass of a nutshell. Now, this is imperceptible to the ordinary eye. Very recently the whole contents of a London newspaper were photographed on a paper half as long as the hand. It was put under a dove's wing and sent into Paris, where they enlarged it and read the news. This copy of the Iliad must have been made by some such process. Pliny says that Nero, the tyrant, had a ring with a gem in it which he looked through and watched the sword play of the gladiators more clearly than with the naked eye. So Nero had an opera glass. Mauritius, the Italian, stood on the promontory of his island, and could sweep over the entire sea to the coast of Africa with his *nauscopite*, which is a word derived from two Greek words, meaning to see a ship. Evidently Mauritius, who was a pirate, had a marine telescope. The signet of a ring in Dr. Abbott's museum, said to belong to Cheops, who lived five hundred years before Christ, is about the size of a quarter of a dollar, and the engraving is invisible without the aid of glasses. In Parma is shown a gem once worn on the finger of Michael Angelo, of which the engraving is two thousand years old, in which there are the figures of seven women. A glass is needed to distinguish the forms at all. Layard says he would be unable to read the engravings on Nineveh without strong spectacles, they are so extremely small. Rawlinson brought home a stone about twenty inches long and ten wide, containing an entire treatise on mathematics. It would be perfectly illegible without glasses. Now, if we are unable to read it without the aid of glasses, you may suppose that the man who engraved it had pretty strong spectacles. So, the microscope, instead of dating from our time, finds its brothers in the Books of Moses.*a*

12—14. (12) **brought..knees**, *i.e.* Jacob's. **he..earth**, in respect to his father, and in reverence to the blessing. (13) **Ephraim..him**, the eldest son to Jacob's right hand. Joseph assigned them to their proper places as the adopted sons of Jacob, giving to Manasseh his proper place as the eldest. (14) **stretched..head**, passing Ephraim. **left..head**, crossing the other hand. **wittingly**, knowingly, intentionally. **for..born**, therefore a strange act but with a purpose.

The blessing of Jacob as given to Ephraim and Manasseh (v. 14). —I. The names. II. The fulness. III. The certainty.—*Lange.*— *The precedence of Ephraim* (v. 14).—How God sometimes prefers the younger to the elder, we may see in the case of Shem preferred to Japheth, in the case of Isaac who was preferred to Ishmael, of Jacob who was preferred to Esau, of Judah and Joseph who were preferred to Reuben, of Moses who was preferred to Aaron, and, finally, of David who was preferred to all his brethren.*a*

Laying on of hands.—Imposition of hands was a Jewish ceremony, introduced, not by any Divine authority, but by custom; it being the practice among those people whenever they prayed to God for any person, to lay their hands on his head; it was also employed as a mark of favour. The right hand was regarded as the more honourable of the two; thus, when Jacob laid his right hand upon the head of Ephraim, it was expressive of what he designed. The priests attended to the same practice when anyone was received into their body. The form of blessing the people used by Aaron and his sons is recorded, Numb. vi. 23—27. *Maimonides* says that "The priests go up into the desk after they have finished the morning daily service, and lift up their hands above, over their heads; except the high priest, who does not lift up his hands above the plate of gold on his forehead; and one pronounces the blessings word for word." Our Saviour observed the same custom when conferring His blessing on children, but when healing the sick, sometimes added prayers

---

B.C. 1689.

notices from the other four, through the organs of sensation only. We hear, we feel, we smell, we taste, by touch. But sight rises infinitely higher. It is refined above matter, and equals the faculty of spirit."—*Sterne.*

"The balls of sight are so formed that one man's eyes are spectacles to another to read his heart with."— *Johnson.*

a O. W. Holmes.

Joseph brings his sons to Jacob

a Starcke.

"Notwithstanding the precaution Joseph took, Jacob designedly shifted his hands, so as to confer the greater honour on the younger son." — *Philippson.*

"God, from whom the blessing proceeded, directed him in this case to cross hands. Nor is this the only instance in which the order of nature is made to give way to that of grace; for of this Jacob himself had been an example."—*A. Fuller.*

"We, like Joseph, are for setting Manasseh before Ephraim; but God, like Jacob, puts His hands across, and lays His right hand upon the worst man's head, and His

B.C. 1689.

left hand upon the best, to the wonder and amazement even of the best of men."—*Bunyan.*
b Bibl. Treas.

Jacob blesses Joseph

a Ps. xxxvii. 3; Ma. vi. 31, 32; 1 Tī. vi. 8.

b Ge. xvi. 7; xxxii. 24—30; Mal. iii. 1.

c "Considered as my sons."—*Maurer.*

d "The issue of Joseph by his two sons amounted in the time of Moses to 85,200, a number surpassing that of any of the rest of the tribes."—Nu. xxvii. 34, 37.

"May they be worthy of having their names coupled with my own and those of Abraham and Israel."—*Rapha't.* "May my name be named through them."—*Knobel.*

"A proper secrecy is the only mystery of able men; mystery is the only secrecy of weak and cunning ones."—*Chesterfield.*

e Job Orton.

v. 15, 16. D. S. *Deyling, Obs.,* ii. 98; J. *Milner, M.A.,* 1. 20; J. P. *Hewlett,* 359; Dr. C. J. *Vaughan,* 199 (1851).

v. 16. F. *Miller,* 244.

---

to the ceremony. The Apostles likewise laid hands on those upon whom they bestowed the Holy Ghost; and they themselves underwent the imposition of hands afresh, when entering upon any new design. In the ancient church, imposition of hands was even practised on persons when they married, and the same custom is still observed by the Abyssinians.*b*

15—18. (15) **he . . Joseph,** in blessing his sons. **God . . day,***a* lit. who acted as the shepherd towards me, feeding and leading. (16) **angel . . evil,***b* the Angel of the covenant. **let . . them,** let them be called by my name.*c* **let . . earth,** *lit.* let them multiply like fish.*d* (17) **displeased,** men often displeased with what they do not understand. **held . . head,** as men sometimes think to improve upon the Divine will. (18) **put . . head,** he perh. thought that through blindness his father had made a mistake.

Jacob's acknowledgment of the Divine care, and blessing his grandchildren, recommended to the imitation of aged Christians (v. 15).—We shall—I. Illustrate the words of the text. Here are two things observable. 1. Jacob's recollection and acknowledgment of the Divine goodness and care. He acknowledges God as the God of His pious ancestors, and as his own constant preserver and benefactor; 2. His prayer for his grandchildren. He blessed Joseph; either himself, *beside* his children, or *in* his children. II. Consider what lessons of instruction aged Christians may draw from them. It is their duty—1. To recollect and acknowledge their long experience of God's goodness and care. Acknowledge His goodness in providing a supply for all your wants, and in raising you up friends. Such a course will —(1) Promote and cherish your gratitude to God; (2) Tend to prevent your murmuring under the burdens and infirmities of age; (3) Promote your continual activity in God's service; (4) Encourage your prayers and your hope. 2. To bless and pray for their descendants. This—(1) Is a becoming expression of your faith and trust in God, and regard for your children; (2) Will be likely to make a good impression upon their hearts, and so qualify them for the Divine blessing; (3) Is the way to procure the Divine blessing for them. Reflections: (1) Let children desire and value the prayers and blessing of their aged, dying parents; (2) Let the children of good men labour to secure the blessing for themselves.*e*

Fecundity of fishes.—Fish are the most prolific of all creatures. This is, of course, more noticeable in some species than in others, and is more obvious to our notice in the immense shoals of herrings, pilchards, and mackerel, upon our own shores. Many other species are probably equally prolific; but not being of gregarious habits, are not seen together in such vast numbers, and are in consequence less easily taken. But any one who attempts to estimate the number of eggs in the roes of various kinds of fish may form some faint conception of the degree in which the sea generates "reptiles with spawn abundant." The old microscopist, Leuwenhock, gave estimates which the mind could scarcely grasp. The greater accuracy of modern research has somewhat moderated his statements: but enough remains to fill the mind with astonishment. Thus, the roe of a codfish has been found to contain nine millions of eggs: of a flounder, nearly a million and a half; of a mackerel, half a million; of tenches, three hundred and fifty thousand; of the carp, from one to six hundred thousand; of the roach and sole, a hundred thousand; of herrings, perches, and smelts, twenty and thirty thousand; lobsters, from seven to twenty thousand; shrimps and prawns, above three thousand.*f*

19—22. (19) **said,** *etc., i.e.* this act is intentional, not accidental or an error. **he .. great,** *i.e.* Manasseh is not forgotten. **but .. nations,**[a] he spoke with prophetic light. (20) **set .. Manasseh,** assigning the pre-eminence to Ephraim. (21) **behold .. you,**[b] earthly fathers die. the Heavenly Father lives. **bring .. fathers,** whither the earthly father cannot guide. (22) **given .. brethren,**[c] *i.e.* Joseph had a double portion in the persons of his sons. **which .. bow,**[d] inexplainable; perh. Jacob had to recover it after purchase by force of arms; or by faith he realised the future conquest of Canaan.

Death contemplated (v. 21).—What do these words, "Behold, I die," thus uttered, imply? They imply—I. An absorbing crisis. Death is an absorbing crisis, if you consider—1. Its nature; 2. Its cause: it is the result of sin; 3. Its consequences: at death, the death of grace is over. II. An awakening consideration. "Behold." That word suggests to us suitable preparation. In prospect, then, of that amazing hour, we ought—1. To review our past lives; 2. To realise our dying hour; 3. To think of our future prospects.[e]

Imperfection of history.—Nothing is more delusive, or at least more wofully imperfect, than the suggestions of authentic history, as it is generally, or rather universally, written; and nothing more exaggerated than the impressions it conveys of the actual state and condition of those who live in its most agitated periods. The great public events of which alone it takes cognisance, have but little direct influence upon the body of the people; and do not, in general, form the principal business or happiness or misery even of those who are in some measure concerned in them. Even in the worst and most disastrous times— in periods of civil war and revolution, and public discord and oppression, a great part of the time of a great part of the people is spent in making love and money—in social amusement or professional industry—in schemes for worldly advancement or personal distinction, just as in periods of general peace and prosperity. Men court and marry very nearly as much in the one season as in the other, and are as merry at weddings and christenings—as gallant at balls and races—as busy in their studies and counting-houses—eat as heartily, in short, and sleep as soundly—prattle with their children as pleasantly—and thin their plantations and scold their servants as zealously, as if their contemporaries were not furnishing materials thus abundantly for the tragic muse of history. The quiet under-current of life, in short, keeps its deep and steady course in its eternal channel, unaffected or but slightly disturbed by the storms that agitate its surface; and while long tracts of time, in the history of every country, seem to the distant student of its annals to be darkened over with one thick and oppressive cloud of unbroken misery, the greater part of those who have lived through the whole acts of the tragedy will be found to have enjoyed a fair average share of felicity, and to have been much less affected by the shocking events of their day, than those who know nothing else of it than that such events took place in its course.*f*

B.C. 1689.

f Dr. Kitto.

Jacob blesses Ephraim and Manasseh

a Nu. l. 33, 35; De. xxxiii. 17; Re. vii. 4.

b Ge. xxviii. 15; xlvi. 4; De. xxiii. 14; Ge. l. 24; De. xxxi. 8; Josh. xxiii. 14.

c 1 Ch. v. 2; Ez. xlvii. 13.

d Ge. xv. 16; Ju. xi. 20—23; Josh. xvii. 14—18; Am. ii. 9, 10.

"Talent and worth are the only eternal grounds of distinction. To these the Almighty has affixed His everlasting patent of nobility. Knowledge and goodness,—these make degrees in heaven, and they must be the graduating scale of a true democracy."—*Miss Sedgwick.*

"A nation's character is the sum of its splendid deeds; they constitute one common patrimony, the nation's inheritance. They awe foreign powers, they arouse and animate our own people."—*H Clay.*

"National progress is the sum of individual industry, energy, and uprightness, as national decay is of individual idleness selfishness, and vice."—*S. Smiles.*

e C. Clayton, M.A

f J. frey.

CHAPTER THE FORTY-NINTH.

Jacob blesses his other sons
a He. i. 1, 2; Am. iii. 7; Nu. xxiv. 14; Ac. ii. 17.

Reuben
b Spk. Comm.
c "The fig. is taken fr. water in a boiling caldron, foaming and bursting over its bounds." —*Knobel.*
d De. xxvii. 20; Ju. v. 15.
"The characteristic peculiarity of the founder of each tribe was to find its reflection in his posterity." —*Havernick.*
"I hate to see things done by halves. If it be right, do it boldly; if it be wrong, leave it undone." —*Gilpin.*
e Spurgeon.
"There is nothing more to be esteemed than a manly firmness and decision of character. I like a person who knows his own mind and sticks to it; who sees at once what is to be done in given circumstances, and does it."—*Hazlitt.*
f Roberts.

Simeon Levi
a Ge. xxxiv. 25—30.
b Nu. xxvi. 14. Simeon not mentioned in Moses' blessing. De. xxxiii.; Nu. xviii. 23; Josh. xxi. 3.
c J. A. Willis.

1—4. (1) **Jacob.. sons**, by messengers. **last days**," "in the future generally, but with special ref. to times of Messiah."*b* (2) **gather.. Jacob**, imagine the scene. **hearken.. father**, a father's dying words, benediction and prophecy. (3) **the.. strength,** *i.e.* the first-fruits of my vigour. (4) **unstable as water**,*c lit.* thou boilest over like water. *i.e.* a man of sudden passions, impetuous. **thou.. excel**, go beyond thy brethren in power. **because**, *etc..d* see xxxv. 22.

Instability (v. 4).—I propose briefly to notice—I. The common and unavoidable instabilities, which necessarily attach themselves to the best of Christians. How unstable are we in—1. Our frames of mind; 2. Our faith; 3. Our love. II. The character of a Christian who is noted for glaring instability: but who, notwithstanding, has sufficient of godliness to bid us hope that he is a child of God. Such as he are "unstable as water" in—1. Doctrine: they believe the last man they hear; 2. All religious enterprise; 3. Their friendships; 4. Their moral character. III. The mere professor, who cannot excel in any way whatever. He is the most pious, formalistic hypocrite all the world over. IV. The unstable sinner, who makes no pretension of religion whatever. Let me remind him that though he makes no profession of religion now, there was a time when he did.*e*

The firstborn.—" It is generally believed that the firstborn son is the strongest; and he is always placed over his brethren. To him the others must give great honour, and they must not sit in his presence without his permission, and then only *behind* him. When the younger visits the elder, he goes with great respect, and the conversation is soon closed. Should there be anything of a particular nature, on which he desires the sentiments of his elder brother, he sends a friend to converse with him. The younger brother will not enter the door at the same time with the elder; he must always follow. Should they both be invited to a marriage, care will be taken that the oldest shall go in the first. The younger will never approach him with his wooden sandals on: he must take them off. He will not venture to speak to the wife of the elder, except on some special occasion. When the father thinks his end is approaching, he calls his children, and, addressing himself to the oldest, says, 'My strength, my glory, my all is in thee.' From this may be gained an idea of the importance which was attached to the 'birthright.'"*f*

5—7. (5) **instruments.. habitations**,*a i.e.* prob. their swords are instruments of violence. (6) **secret,** council: he disclaims any participation in their act. **digged.. wall,** hamstrung an ox. (7) **divide.. scatter**,*b i.e.* I predict their decision.

The folly and wickedness of anger (v. 7).—Consider—I. The nature of this passion. It is—1. Foolish; 2. Sinful; 3. The prelude to great crimes. II. The effects which followed it in this particular case. 1. The destruction of a city; 2. The massacre of a tribe. III. The punishment which the cruel wrath of the brothers brought upon themselves. 1. Loss of blessing; 2. Division among the tribes.*c*

Capricious anger.—Richard II. showed his affection as a hus-

Cap. xlix. 8--15.] GENESIS. 215

band, and his weakness as a man, in cursing the palace of Sheene, and ordering it to be destroyed, merely because it was the place of his amiable queen's death.[d]

8—12. (8) **Judah .. praise,**[a] *lit.* Judah, thou, thy brethren shall praise thee. Jacob speaks *to* Judah and *of* the others. **hand .. enemies,**[b] victorious warriors. **father's .. thee,**[c] Judah elevated to be the royal tribe. (9) **Judah .. whelp,**[d] lion, the king of beasts. (10) **sceptre,**[e] kingly office. **lawgiver,**[f] scribe. **from .. feet,** *i.e.* fr. among his posterity. **Shiloh,** the pacificator, the giver of peace. **unto .. be,**[g] *lit.* unto him shall be the obedience of the nations. (11) **foal .. vine,** the fathers said that the vine = the Jews, and the wild ass the Gentile converts; prob. this is a picture of the peace and plenty of Messiah's days. (12) **red .. milk,**[h] *lit.* his eyes shall be redder than wine, and his teeth whiter than milk: by some thought to be a ref. to the land flowing with milk and honey, and abounding in vineyards.

Shiloh (v. 10).—I. Using the word prophecy in its predictive sense, this is the language of unquestionable prophecy. II. This prophecy contains a revelation of Christ. The name here given to the Saviour we understand to signify "The Peaceful One." III. This revelation of Christ is connected with the announcement of the particular time when He was to appear. IV. This announcement is connected with a statement showing in what way His people will come to Him. "To Him shall the gathering of the people be." This is at once predictive and descriptive. 1. It predicts the allegiance Christ will certainly receive; 2. It describes the quality of this allegiance. V. This statement suggests an inquiry into the design of Christ in gathering the people to Himself. In harmony with His title as "The Peaceful One," His grand design is to give them rest. Rest, by—1. Reconciling them to God; 2. Effecting the spiritual union of man with man; 3. Leading us to perfect rest in another world.[i]

Sceptre.—A staff of authority which kings, governors, and rulers of provinces held in their hands as emblems of authority. The royal sceptre was transmitted from father to son, and hence Jacob declares that "the sceptre shall not depart from Judah," meaning that the sovereignty of which it was the symbol should remain in the family of that patriarch. Homer notices the hereditary transmission of the sceptre, in the description of Agamemnon's address to the army:—

"The king of kings his awful figure raised,
High in his hand the golden sceptre blazed:
The golden sceptre of celestial frame,
By Vulcan formed, from Jove to Hermes came;
To Pelops he the immortal gift resigned;
The immortal gift great Pelops left behind
In Atreus' hands, which not with Atreus ends,
To rich Thyestes next the prize descends:
And now the mark of Agamemnon's reign,
Subjects all Argos and controls the main."[k]

13—15. (13) **haven .. ships,**[a] *lit.* shore of the sea, and he shall be for a shore of ships, *i.e.* a landing-place for ships. **and .. Zidon,**[b] *lit.* his side shall be towards Zidon. (14) **is .. ass,** *lit.* an ass of bone. **couching .. burdens,** *lit.* crouching down

---

B.C. cir. 1689.
d Recreat. Rev.

Judah
a De. xxxiii. 7; Hos. xi. 12.
b Nu. x. 14, Jn. i. 1—4; Ps. xviii. 40.
c 1 Ch. v. 2; Phil. ii. 10; He. x. 13.
d Re. v. 5; Nu. xxiii. 24, xxiv. 9
e Nu. xxiv. 17.
f Ps. lx. 7.
g Ma. xxi. 9; Is. lx. 1—5, liv. 4, 5, xi. 10, xlii. 1, 4; Mk. xvi. 15.
h De. xxxiii. 28; Ex. iii. 8; 2 Ki xviii. 31, 32.

"They that govern most make least noise. You see when they row in a barge, they that do drudgery work, slash, and puff, and sweat; but he that governs sits quietly at the stern and scarce is seen to stir."—*Selden*.

i C. Stanford.

"An established government has an infinite advantage by that very circumstance of its being established—the bulk of mankind being governed by authority, not reason, and never attributing authority to anything that has not the recommendation of antiquity."—*Hume*.

k Taylor's Bib Cy.

Zebulun
Issachar
a Josh xix. 10.
b De. xxxiii. 18, 19.

between the cattle-pens. (15) **rest,**[c] *i.e.* his place of rest. **became .. tribute,** *i.e.* he submitted to the drudgery of a servant.

The ass.—The ass is not more remarkable for his power to sustain, than for his patience and tranquility when oppressed by an unequal load. Like the camel, he quietly submits to the heaviest burden; he bears it peaceably, till he can proceed no farther; and when his strength fails him, instead of resisting or endeavouring to throw off the oppressive weight, he contentedly lies down, and rests himself under it, recruits his vigour with the provender that may be offered him, and then, at the call of his master, proceeds on his journey. To this trait in the character of that useful animal, the dying patriarch evidently refers, when, under the afflatus of inspiration, he predicts the future lot and conduct of Issachar and his descendants. "Issachar is a strong ass, couching down between two burdens. And he saw that rest was good, and the land that it was pleasant, and bowed his shoulder to bear and became a servant unto tribute." This tribe, naturally dull and stupid, should, like the creature by which they were characterised, readily submit to the vilest master and the meanest service. Although, like the ass, possessed of ability, if properly exerted and rightly directed, to shake off the inglorious yoke of servitude, they would basely submit to the insults of the Phœnicians on the one hand, and the Samaritans on the other. Issachar was a strong ass. "able," says a sprightly writer, "to refuse a load, as well as to bear it; but like the passive drudge which symbolised him, he preferred inglorious case to the resolute vindication of his liberty; a burden of tribute, to the gains of a just and well-regulated freedom; and a yoke of bondage, to the doubtful issues of war."[d]

Dan

16—18. (16) **shall .. people,**[a] *lit.* the judger shall judge. (17) **adder,** Heb. *shephiphon,* the *coluber cerastes* of Linnæus. about fourteen inches long, and one inch thick, poisonous and dangerous. **that .. heels,**[b] horses are filled with terror at the sight of one. (18) **waited .. Lord,**[c] the great salvation for which Jacob waited as distinguished fr. the lesser deliverance of his posterity.

The believer waiting for God's salvation (v. 18).—We may consider this passage as expressive of—I. The living saint's character. He is one who is "waiting for the salvation of God." II. The dying saint's comfort. Jacob's peace, hope, and joy, were now, in his dying circumstances, derived from having waited for, and being in immediate prospect of enjoying, the salvation of God. To him, death was no new subject; the grave no strange country; salvation no unknown theme; heaven not an unlooked for home. He avows therefore his hope, his trust, and his confidence.[d]

The cerastes.—"I saw one of them," he says, "at Cairo crawl up the side of a box in which there were many, and there lie still as if hiding himself, till one of the people who brought him to us came near him; and though in a very disadvantageous posture, sticking as it were perpendicularly to the side of the box, he leaped nearly the distance of three feet, and fastened between the man's forefinger and thumb, so as to bring the blood. The fellow showed no signs of either pain or fear; and we kept him with us full four hours, without applying any kind of remedy, or his seeming inclined to do so."[e]

B.C. 1689.

[c] Josh. xix. 17—22.

"The trident of Neptune is the sceptre of the world."—*A. Lemierre.*

"Nature seems to have taken a particular care to disseminate her blessings among the different regions of the world, with an eye to their mutual intercourse and traffic among mankind, that the nations of the several parts of the globe might have a kind of dependence upon one another, and be united together by their common interest."—*Addison.*

[d] Dr. Paxton.

[a] Jud. xiii. 2, 24. xv. 20, xvi. 21, 30.

[b] "Straight onward spires he glides, and bites the horses' leg or cattle's sides."

[c] Ps. xxv. 5, cxix. 166, 174, cxxx. 5, 6; Is. xxv. 9, xxvi. 8; Lu. ii. 25, 38.

"Men of genius do not excel in any profession because they labour in it, but they labour in it because they excel."—*Hazlitt.*

[d] W. Snell.

[e] Russell.

19—21. (19) **troop .. last,**[a] troops shall press on him, but he shall press upon their rear, *i.e.* Gad would follow and harass the retreat of Arab tribes. (20) **bread .. dainties,**[b] allusion to fertility of territory of Asher: it was rich in corn, wine, and oil. (21) **is .. loose,**[c] timid, swift of foot. **he .. words,** more famous in council than war.

Lines of circumvallation.—These words (v. 19) may be used as graphically descriptive of the defeat of Christ followed by His successes. The human heart is defending itself against Christ, and it has run out several lines of circumvallation; these must, one be one, be taken. There is the line of—I. Prejudice against ministers and churches. II. Social influences—evil companionship, etc. III. The intellectual difficulties of religion—infidelity, scepticism, and the like. IV. Pernicious habits. V. The pride and rebellion of the natural heart.[d]

Importance of words.—What is it which makes men different from all other living things we know of? Is it not speech—the power of words? The beasts may make each other understand many things, but they have no speech. These glorious things—words—are man's right alone, part of the image of the Son of God—the Word of God, in which man was created. If men would but think what a noble thing it is merely to be able to speak in words, to think in words, to write in words! Without words we should know no more of each others' hearts and thoughts, than the dog knows of his fellow dog. without words to think in; for if you will consider, you always think to yourself in *words*, though you do not speak them aloud; and without them all our thoughts would be mere blind longings, feelings which we could not understand ourselves. Without words to write in we could not know what our forefathers did—we could not let our children after us know what we do.[e]

22—26. (22) **is .. bough,**[a] ref. to prosperity of house of Joseph. **even .. well,**[b] rendered even more fruitful by situation. **whose .. wall,** ref. to great increase of Joseph's posterity. (23) **archers,**[c] *lit.* lords of arrows, or arrowmasters. **have .. him,** Joseph himself seems here to be pointed at; if so, a prob. ref. to his early trials. (24) **bow .. strength,**[d] his resolution and perseverance invincible. **arms .. strong,** sense obscure; prob. ref. to the strength and firmness of Joseph. **from thence,** *i.e.* from the mighty God of Jacob. (25) **even .. father,** or, fr. the God of thy father. **with .. above,**[e] *i.e.* rain and dew. **deep .. under,**[f] productions of soil. **blessings .. womb,**[g] strong and numerous offspring. (26) **blessings .. hills,** *i.e.* Jacob's blessing on Joseph greater than Abraham's and Isaac's on Jacob's, and lasting as the mountains. **separate .. brethren,**[h] advanced to pre-eminence by the providence of God.

Joseph's blessing.—In this blessing we have four leading ideas. —I. Fruitfulness, or temporal prosperity. Here is—1. The fruitfulness itself—"a fruitful bough"; 2. The source of this fruitfulness—"a well:" note the great value of wells in the East; 3. Its great extent—its "branches run over the wall"; 4. Its strong supports—it leans upon a wall. II. Persecution consequent upon prosperity. Here we have—1. Hatred; 2. Persecution of mind; 3. Persecution of body. III. Triumphant endurance of persecution—"his bow abode in strength." His faith rises superior to all trials. It—1. Supports him in the present; 2.

B.C. 1689.

Gad, Asher, Naphtali

[a] De. xxxiii. 20; 1 Ch. v. 18.

[b] De. xxxiii. 24; Josh. xix. 24, 26; Is. xxxv. 2. See also Stanley, "Sin. and Pal." 265.

[c] De. xxiii. 23.

[d] *Dr. Talmage.*

"I conceive that words are like money, not the worse for being common; but that it is the stamp of custom alone that gives them circulation or value. I am fastidious in this respect, and would almost as soon coin the currency of the realm as counterfeit the King's English."—*Hazlitt.*

[e] *C. Kinsley.*

Joseph

[a] De. xxxiii. 13—17.

[b] Ps. i. 3.

[c] Ge. xxxvii. 4, 24, 28; Ps. cxviii. 13.

[d] Ps. xviii. 32, 34, xxvii. 14; Job xxix. 20; Col. i. 11.

[e] v. 24.

[f] De. viii. 7.

[g] Ps. cxxviii. 3.

[h] De. xxxiii. 16; Ge. xxxvii. 4.

"A good inclination is but the first rude draught of virtue, but the finishing strokes are from the will: which, if well disposed, will by

B.C. 1689.

degrees perfect; if ill disposed, will by the superinduction of ill habits quickly deface it." — *South.*

"For some men, like unskilful jockeys, give up their designs when they have almost reached the goal; while others, on the contrary, obtain a victory over their opponents by exerting, at the last moment, more vigorous efforts than before."—*Polybius.*

i *J. Hoatson.*

k *Bibl. Treas.*

Benjamin—Summary

a Jud. xx. 14—25.

b Ld. Lindsay saw a wolf near Mt. Carmel, and Monroe saw one in the plains of Philistia.

"It deserves to be considered that boldness is ever blind, for it sees not dangers and inconveniences. Whence it is bad in council though good in execution. The right use of bold persons, therefore is that they never command in chief, but serve as seconds, under the direction of others. For in council it is good to see dangers, and in execution not to see them unless they are very great." —*Bacon.*

c *Dr. Parton.*

Obtains strength for him wherewith to combat his future troubles. IV. Great and general blessings following this endurance.—1. Blessings of heaven—dew and rain to cheer the thirsty land; 2. Blessings of the deep—fountains and wells of water; 3. Blessings in the increase of descendants; 4. Blessings greater than any yet enjoyed by his forefathers; 5. Blessings durable as the hills themselves.¹

Israel's strength.—Herder (*Briefe*, page 84) says, Jacob recurs to the history of his life. He had wrestled with the Mighty, who had given him the name of Israel. He who was the strong God of Jacob had strengthened Joseph. The good God of Jacob who had watched over the naked stone, when he was persecuted, alone, and in a strange place, was the guardian God of his son in similar circumstances of desertion, solitude, and absence from home. Hence, on this idea, he renders the passage :—

"Yet his bow abode firm,
His hands and his arms were strengthened
By the hands of the Almighty God of Jacob,
By the name of Him who watched
Israel on his stone.
By thy father's God, who helped thee,
By God the Shaddai, who further blesses thee
With blessings of heaven from above."¹

27, 28. (27) **ravin**,ᵃ plunder, destroy. **wolf**,ᵇ once abundant, now seldom seen, in Palestine. **morning .. spoil**, allusion to the rapacious habits of wolves, as ill. of boldness and ferocity of Benjamin. (28) **tribes**, to whom the blessings had respect rather than to their founders. **one .. them**, *i.e.* the blessing fulfilled corresponded with the blessing predicted.

The wolf.—The wolf is weaker than the lion or the bear, and less courageous than the leopard; but he scarcely yields to them in cruelty and rapaciousness. So Benjamin, although not destitute of courage and address, nor disinclined to war, possessed neither the strength, nor the manly spirit of Judah, whose symbol was the lion's whelp; but yet he was greedy of blood, and delighted in rapine; and in the early periods of Jewish history, he distinguished himself by an active and restless spirit, which commonly, like the wolf among lambs and kids, spent itself in petty or inglorious warfare, although it sometimes blazed forth in deeds of heroic valour, and general utility. He had the honour of giving the second judge to the nation of Israel, who delivered them from the oppressive yoke of Moab; and the first king who sat on the throne of that chosen people, whose valour saved them from the iron sceptre of Ammon, and more than once revenged the barbarities of the uncircumcised Philistines upon their discomfited hosts. In the decline of the Jewish commonwealth, Esther and Mordecai, who were both of this tribe, successfully interposed with the King of Persia for the deliverance of their brethren, and took their station in the first rank of public benefactors. But the tribe of Benjamin ravened like wolves, that are so ferocious as to devour one another, when they desperately espoused the cause of Gibeah, and in the dishonourable and bloody feud, reduced their own tribe to the very brink of ruin, and inflicted a deep wound on the other members of the state.ᶜ

Cap. l. 1–6.] GENESIS. 219

29–33. (29) **he .. them,** they were to share in the duty enjoined on Joseph. **bury, entomb.** (30) **cave,** *etc.*, he specifies the spot minutely to show that it will not suffice simply to carry him to Canaan. (31) **there .. Leah,** doubtless he would like to have said Rachel also. (32) **purchase .. Heth,** a reminder that the burial-place was really theirs. (33) **when .. sons,** these his last words: he died soon after. **gathered .. bed,** sitting to bless he now laid down to die. **was .. people,**[a] *i.e.* he was *now* gathered to his people in the better country.

Jacob's death-bed (v. 33).—Three things here deserve our attention:—I. His affection for the living. This was—1. Impartial: He gathered them all together; 2. Religious: He invoked the benediction of God upon them. II. His sympathy with the dead. The feeling which he now expresses concerning his burial, suggests—1. That there is something in man stronger than logic; 2. That the dead exert a powerful influence upon the living. III. His magnanimity in all things. Two things alone can explain his calmness: faith in—1. His future existence; 2. The happiness of that existence.[b]

Death-bed instructions.—" In the prospect of death, the head of a family summons his relations around his bed. He instructs them about the state of his affairs, and how his property was acquired, and how to be disposed of. He is most particular to furnish them with proofs respecting the acquisition of his pawns and slaves; mentions the names of the witnesses to the transactions; the circumstances under which they took place, and the sums paid for them, in order that his successor may be enabled to defend his rights, in the event of their attempting to obtain their liberty or redemption at the death of their master. He also recounts the names of his debtors, with the sums which they owe to him, as well as the debts which he owes to others. His death-bed declarations, made in the presence of responsible witnesses, are always received as evidence in the event of litigation afterward. Having made these arrangements, he calmly resigns himself to death, apparently unconcerned about a future state."[c]

B.C. 1689.

Jacob's dying charge
a Ho. xii. 23; Ps. xxxviii. 37.
"O, if the deeds of human creatures could be traced to their source, how beautiful would even death appear; for how much charity, mercy, and purified affection would be seen to have their growth in dusty graves!"—*Dickens.*
"Death comes equally to us all, and makes us all equal when it comes. The ashes of an oak in a chimney are no epitaph of that, to tell me how high or how large that was; it tells me not what flocks it sheltered while it stood, nor what men it hurt when it fell. The dust of great persons' graves is speechless too; it says nothing, it distinguishes nothing."—*Donne.*
b Dr. Thomas.
c Cruickshank.

CHAPTER THE FIFTIETH.

B.C. 1689.

1—6. (1) **Joseph .. face,** *etc.*, and closed his eyes, as Jacob had been promised, see xlvi. 4. (2) **Physicians,** Heb. *ropheim,* healers. **embalm,**[a] Joseph having an eye to the removal of the body. (3) **forty .. embalmed,** the time occupied in the process. **Egyptians,** out of respect for Joseph. **mourned .. days,**[b] the cust. royal mourning in Egypt. (4) **spake .. Pharaoh,** to the chief officers of his court. (5) **father .. swear,** but for a father's wish it might seem strange to Pharaoh that Joseph should wish to bury any of his kindred out of Egypt. (6) **go .. swear,** he regarded a promise to a dying father as sacred.

Embracing the dead.—The embracing of the dead then, and during the reciting of this service, takes place; for, as soon as the priests departed, many came, and, laying their hands on the two sides of the open coffin, kissed the cheeks and forehead of the deceased with much emotion. When a bishop dies, and is

Jacob embalmed
a 2 Ch xvi. 14.
b Nu. xx. 29; De. xxxiv. 8.
"What is grief? It is an obscure labyrinth into which God leads man, that he may be experienced in life, that he may remember his faults and abjure them, that he may appreciate the calm which virtue gives."—*L. Scheffer.*

B.C. 1689.

"Great grief makes sacred those upon whom its hand is laid. Joy may elevate ambition glorify, but sorrow alone can consecrate."
— H. Gresby.

a Jowett.

d Dr. Porter.

Joseph buries his father

a Herodotus ii. 85.

b 1 Sa. xxxi. 13; Job ii. 13; Ac. viii. 2.

"The Stoics, who thought the souls of wise men had their habitations about the moon, might make slight account of subterranean depositions, whereas the Pythagoreans and trans-corporating philosophers, who were to be after buried, held great care of their interment, and the Platonic rejected not a due care of the grave."—Sir T. Browne.

"An angel's arm can't snatch me from the grave,— legions of angels can't confine me there."—Young.

c M. Henry.
d Topics.

and returns to Egypt

"We adorn graves with flowers and redolent plants, just emblems of the life of man, which has been compared in the Holy Scriptures to those fading

laid out in this manner in the church, all the congregation throng to perform this ceremony.*

Filial affection in the East.—We dismounted at the door of a spacious tent in the centre of the encampment. No sooner had our sheikh touched the ground than he was affectionately embraced by his son, a fine boy of about fifteen. This scene at once brought to my mind some incidents recorded in Scripture, and seemed, in fact, to realise the interesting narratives of patriarchal times. The youth placed his hands on his father's neck, and kissed each cheek, and then they leaned their heads for a few seconds, while embracing, on each other's shoulders. Precisely similar was the scene at the meeting of Jacob and his son Joseph, nearly four thousand years ago.*d*

7—10. (7) **went** .. **Egypt**, one of the most extraordinary funeral processions on record (8) **house** .. **house**, *i.e.* all the adults among the kindred of Jacob. (9) **went** .. **horsemen**, Egyptian respect for the great prime minister. **and** .. **company**, *lit.* the encamping host was very heavy. (10) **the** .. **Atad**, *lit.* the threshing-floor of thorns. **which** .. **Jordan**, *i.e.* to the W. of Jordan. **there** .. **lamentation**, Egyptians in their mourning exhibited grt. external demonstrations of sorrow.*a* **made** .. **days**,*b* the Jewish mourning.

Jacob's funeral.—I. It was a stately funeral. He was attended to the grave, not only by his own family, but by the courtiers, and all the great men of the kingdom. who, in token of their gratitude to Joseph, show this respect to his father. II. It was a sorrowful funeral. Note, that the death of good men is a loss to any place, and ought to be lamented.*c*

Embalming.—Art invented by Egyptians, 2000 yrs. B.C.; prob. derived origin. fr. idea that preservation of body was needful for return of soul to human form after completing its cycle of existence of 3,000 or 10,000 yrs. Physical and sanitary reasons may also have led to it. The legend of Osiris, whose body, destroyed by Typhon, was found by Isis, and embalmed by his son Anubis, gave a religious sanction to the rite, all deceased persons being supposed to be E. after the model of Osiris in the *Abuton* of Philæ. Many nations adopted E. Persians used wax; Assyrians, honey. Alexander the Gt. was E. in wax and honey. Roman bodies also. After 500 A.D. it fell into disuse as general practice. Yet there have been cases, as Napoleon I. It does not appear that the Jews practised the systematic E. of the Egyptians. Still some process was employed tending to soothe surviving friends by arresting or delaying natural corruption. In some cases, too, the later Jews E. a body in honey, after having covered it with wax.*d*

11—14. (11) **Abel-mizraim**, the mourning of the Egyptians. (12, 13) **and his sons**, *etc.*, see xlix. 29—32. (14) **returned** .. **Egypt**, and there they waited and multiplied till the time of the Exodus.

Burial of the dead.—The general tendency of mankind to bury dead out of sight [*Bury.* fr. A.S. *birgan*, to conceal; Ger. *bergen*]. To accomplish this, three great methods. 1. Closing up body in earth or stone; 2. Burning of body, and entombing of cinders; 3. Embalming (for *Embalming*, see p. 32). Incremation (burning) practised in Greece and Rome. Cinerary urns have been found in many parts. "Some of the grandest buildings in the world have been tombs; such are the pyramids, the castle of St. Angelo. the tomb of Cæcilia Metella, and many temples scattered over Hindustan and other E. countries. Upon (*epi*) the mound (*taphos*) beneath wh. the ashes of a Greek were placed. it was customary for the public orator to pronounce a panegyric, the pith of wh. was afterwards inscribed on the spot, hence the origin of epitaph. The Gks. had their burial-places at a dist. fr. towns; the Roms. nr. highways, hence necessity for inscription on tombs. First Christian burial-place in A.D. 596; in cities, 742; in consecrated places, 750; in churchyards, 758. Early Christians in catacombs at Rome. *Cemetery*, a sleeping-place; fr. Gk. *koimo*, to lull to sleep.[a]]

15—18. (15) **saw** .. **dead,** and all paternal restraint removed. **Joseph** .. **us.** they could not think he would love them for their own sake. **will** .. **him,** they judged him by their own standard of revenge. (16) **messenger,** some think Benjamin. **thy** .. **command,** of which command we have no record, though they may not have invented it. (17) **forgive** .. **sin,**[a] commanded or not it was a fitting request. **and** .. **him,** wept for joy at their repentance and obedience to their father. (18) **fell** .. **face,** *see* xxxvii. 7—10.

Joseph's brethren fulfilling the prophecy respecting them (v. 18). —I. The means they used to conciliate his favour. 1. They plead the dying request of their revered father; 2. They unite with it their own most humble and earnest entreaties. II. The effect produced on Joseph's mind. 1. Grief; 2. Joy. Learn— (1) To ask forgiveness of those whom we have injured; (2) To forgive those who have injured us.[b]

Influence of forgiveness.—A worthy old coloured woman was walking quietly along a street in New York, carrying a basket of apples, when a mischievous sailor, seeing her, stumbled against her, and upset her basket, and then stood to hear her fret at his trick, and enjoy a laugh at her expense. But what was his astonishment when she meekly picked up the apples without any resentment in her manner, and giving him a dignified look of mingled sorrow, kindness, and pity, said, "God forgive you, my son, as I do!" That touched a tender chord in the heart of the rude jack tar. He felt ashamed, self-condemned. and repentant. The tear started in his eye; he felt that he *must* make some reparation. So, heartily confessing his error, and thrusting his hands into his pockets, and pulling out a lot of loose "change," he forced it upon the wondering old black woman, exclaiming, "God bless you, kind mother! I'll never do so again."

19—21. (19) **for** .. **God** [a] it is His to avenge, not mine. (20) **ye** .. **me,** that was certainly your purpose. **but** .. **good,** He has brought good out of evil. **bring** .. **alive,**[b] Joseph was compensated for the wrongs done him by the good he had been the means of doing. (21) **now** .. **not,** that I will avenge the past. **nourish** .. **ones,**[c] a promise of protection. **spake** .. **them,** *lit.* he spake to their hearts.

Evil overruled for good.—What more contrary to *good* than *evil?* or what more opposeth *happiness* than *sin?* Yet the evil of Joseph's brethren, God disposed to good, and the greatest sin

B.C. 1689.

beauties whose roots, being buried in dishonour, rise again in glory." —*Evelyn.*
"Without settled principle and practical virtue, life is a desert; without Christian piety the contemplation of the grave is terrible."—*Sir Wm. Knighton.*
a *Topics.*

his brothers crave his forgiveness

a Jas. v. 16; Pr. xxviii. 13.

"Nothing in this low and ruined world bears the meek impress of the Son of God so surely as forgiveness."—*A. Cary.*

"Of him that hopes to be forgiven, it is indispensably required that he forgive. It is, therefore, superfluous to urge any other motive. On this great duty eternity is suspended; and to him that refuses to practise it, the throne of mercy is inaccessible, and the Saviour of the world has been born in vain."—*Johnson.*

b *C. Simeon, M.A.*

Joseph comforts his brethren
a De. xxxii. 35; Job. xxxiv. 29; Ro. xii. 19.
b Ro. viii. 28; Ps. lxxvi. 10.
c Ma. v. 44, 45; Ro. xii. 20, 21.
"A cockle - fish may as soon

that ever was, "the crucifying the Lord of Life," by the Divine counsel, produced the greatest blessing. Nay, the bitter waters shall be made sweet by salt, and the sacrifice shall burn when water is poured upon it. Our very afflictions, as over-mastered and ruled by God, have this injunction upon them to further our salvation. Our wounds are remedies; and those who contradict the precepts of the Almighty obey His providence.*d*

22—26. (22) **he .. house,** all the posterity of Jacob. **Joseph .. years,** measured by events one of the longest lives on record, of which 93 yrs. were passed in Egypt. (23) **Machir**^a (*sold*). **were .. knees,**^b the old man not only nursed them, but considered them his own. (24) **Joseph .. said,**^c *etc.*. dying he comforts others, and manifests his own faith in God. (25) **ye .. hence,**^d he participated in the desire and in the faith of Jacob. (26) **embalmed,** to preserve him from corruption to the time of their departure. **coffin,** lit. ark or chest.

Joseph's dying assurance to his brethren (v. 24).—I. The reflection which Joseph makes upon his present circumstances. "I die." II. The assurance he gives his brethren that God would visit them. III. The further assurance, that God would bring them into the land of Canaan. Application—(1) To aged Christians. 1. Frequently speak and think of dying; 2. Reflect that God will visit, and care for, your posterity, when you are gone; 3. Remind your children of this fact, for their encouragement, when you are dying. (2) To those in younger life, who are the children of good men. 1. Encourage yourselves with the thought that God will visit you; 2. Pray earnestly for His visits; 3. Be prepared to receive Him.*e*

Ancient coffins.—When Joseph died, he was not only embalmed, but *put in a coffin.* This was an honour appropriated to persons of distinction, coffins not being universally used in Egypt. Maillet, speaking of the Egyptian repositories of the dead, having given an account of several niches that are found there, says, "It must not be imagined that the bodies deposited in these gloomy apartments were all enclosed in chests, and placed in niches; the greatest part were simply embalmed and swathed after that manner that every one hath some notion of; after which they laid them one by the side of another without any ceremony; some were even put into these tombs without any embalming at all, or such a slight one, that there remains nothing of them in the linen in which they were wrapped but the bones, and those half rotten." Antique coffins of stone, and sycamore wood, are still to be seen in Egypt. It is said that some were formerly made of a kind of pasteboard, formed by folding and gluing cloth together a great number of times. These were curiously plastered and painted with hieroglyphics.*f*

B.C. 1689.

crowd the ocean into its narrow shell, as valu man ever comprehend the decrees of God!"—*Bp. Beveridge.*

d E. Corbett.

the death of Joseph

a Nu. xxvi. 29; De. iii. 15; Josh. xiii. 41; xvii. 1, 3; Jud. v. 14.

b Ps. cxxviii. 4, 6.

c Ge. xvii. 8; xlviii. 21; He. xi. 13.

d Ex. xiii. 19; Josh xxiv. 32.

e Job Orton.

"His coffin laid up by them, ready to be carried away according to his dying request whenever God should restore them to the promised land, would have taught them to keep apart from Egypt and its idolatries, looking for a better country, which God had promised to their fathers."—*Spk. Comm.*

"The heavens do not send good haps in handfuls, but let us pick out our good by little, and with care, from out much bad, that still our little world may know its king."—*Sir P. Sidney.*

f Thevenot.

THE SECOND BOOK OF MOSES,
CALLED
EXODUS.

Introduction.

THE SECOND BOOK OF MOSES, CALLED EXODUS.

I. Title. By the Jews, and in the Heb. Xptures, this bk. is called Ve-Aleh Shemoth ("*these are the names*") fr. the opening words (i. 1): or in brief Shemoth *(the names)*. The title in the A. V. is derived fr. the LXX. and relates to the principal event wh. it records. Ἔξοδος *(Exodus)* = departure: (fr. ἐξ. ex—out; and ὁδός, odos—a way) *i.e.* the departure of the children of Israel fr. Egypt. **II. Author**, MOSES. We have this on the authority of our Lord, who, citing this bk., calls it "the book of Moses" (Mk. xii. 26, see also Lu. xx. 37); indeed 25 passages are quoted fr. it by Xt. and His Apostles, besides making 19 allusions to its sense *(Rivet)*. "In fact no critic of any weight, either in France or Germany, who admits the supernatural character of the transactions, rejects the authorship of Moses" *(Spk. Comm.)*. 1. *Moses could have written the Pentateuch.* The most sceptical of mod. objectors do not deny the existence of Moses, nor that he was the leader of his own people out of Egypt into Canaan. 2. *The concurrent testy. of subsequent times proves that Moses did write the bks. now known by his name.* Beginning with the earliest bks. of the Old Test. we can trace a constant stream of reference and quotation to the laws, the history, and the words of Moses, wh. show them all to have been well known and universally accepted. 3. The internal evidence points to Moses and to him only as the writer of the Pentateuch. (1) The author of the Pent. and the giver of the Levitical law had an intimate acquaintance with Egypt, with Palestine, its laws, and its religion. (2) The hist. and the law of the Israelites both bear marks and tokens of their long passage through the wilderness, and long residence in it. (3) The language and the legislation of the Pent. has Canaan only in prospect. (4) "The language of the Pent. is such as to suit the age and character of Moses" *(ibid)*. **III. Time**, *uncertain:* but after the giving of the law on Mt. Sinai, and the erecting of the Tabernacle; since, "things cannot be historically related until they have actually taken place, and the author of this bk. was evidently an eye and ear witness of the events he has narrated" *(Horne)*. **IV. Scope,** it embraces a hist. of the events that occurred during 145 yrs. (fr. A.M. 2369 to 2514 inclus. *i.e.* fr. the death of Joseph to the building of the tabernacle. Fr. d. of Joseph to b. of Moses 63 yrs.; fr. b. of Moses to the Exodus 81 yrs.; fr. Exodus to erection of tabernacle 1 yr.; total 145 yrs. "The scope of the bk. is to exhibit the accomp. of the promises to Abraham; that fr. him a nation should spring, wh., aft. a sojourn of sev. cents. in a state of degradation in a foreign land, should triumphantly be brought forth, and established in the country destined for its permanent occupation (Ge. xv. 5, 13). The whole hist., too, presents a vivid adumbration of the church militant, in her redemption fr. spiritual bondage, and her passage through the wilderness of this world" *(Litton)*. "As to the gen. scope of this bk., it is plainly to preserve the memorial of the great facts of the national hist. of Israel in its earlier periods, to wit, their deliv. from Egypt, the kindness and faithfulness of God in their subsequent preservation in the wilderness, the delivery of the law, and the establishment of a new and peculiar system of worship" *(Bush)*. "The scope of Exodus is to preserve the memorial of the departure of the Israelites fr. Egypt, and to represent the ch. of God *afflicted* and *preserved;* together with the providential care of God towards her, and the judgments inflicted on her enemies." *(Horne.)*

Synopsis.

(According to Horne.)

PART I.—Account of the transactions previously to the Departure.
1. The oppression of the children of Israel ....i.
2. The youth and transactions of Moses ....ii.-vi.
3. The hardening of Pharaoh's heart and the plagues ....vi.-xi.

PART II.—The narrative of the Departure of the Israelites ...xiv.-xviii.

PART III.—Transactions subsequent to their Exodus.
1. Passage of the Red Sea.......xiv.-xv.-22.
2. Various miracles wrought on behalf of the Israelites ....xv. 23-xvi.-xvii.
3. Arrival of Moses' relatives ....xviii.

PART IV.—The promulgation of the law on Mount Sinai.
1. The preparation of the people and the covenant ....xix.
2. The moral law ....xx.
3. The judicial law..................xxi-xxiii.
4. The ceremonial law ....xxiv.-xxxi.-xxxv.-xl.
   Idolatry of Israelites, &c....xxxii.-xxxiv.

(According to B'unt.)

I.—Connecting links of patriarchal hist. betw. Jacob and Moses ....i.
II.—Personal hist. of Moses fr. birth to his commission ....ii.-iv.
III.—Last days of sojourn in Egypt and Exodus ....v.-xiv.
IV.—First year in wilderness ....xv.-xix.
V.—The giving of the law ....xx.-xxxiv.
VI.—The Tabernacle ....xxxv.-xl.

(According to Nicholls.)

I.—The oppressed state of Israelites in Egypt aft. death of Joseph ....i.
II.—The birth of Moses, and the preparation for his office..........................ii.-vi.

III.—Their deliverance, and the destruction of their enemies..........................vii.-xiv.
IV.—Their entrance into the wilderness, and provision for guidance, &c. ...xv.-xviii.
V.—Their covenant with God; made, broken and renewed ....xix.-xxxiv.
VI.—The hist. of the Tabernacle......xxxv.-xl.

(According to Bush.)

I.—The oppression ....i.
II.—Early life of Moses ....ii.
III.—Legation of Moses ....iii.-iv. 29.
IV.—Mission of Moses ....iv. 29-x. 21.
V.—The Passover ....xii. 21.
VI.—Conclusion of Plagues...x. 21-xii. 21-31.
VII.—The Exodus..............xii. 31-37, 40-42
VIII.—Wanderings to Sinai ....xii. 37-40- xix. 1, 2.
IX.—Moses called to the Mount..........xix.
X.—The moral law ....xx.
XI.—Judicial and ceremonial law xxi.-xxxi.
XII.—Idolatry, &c., of Israelites......xxxii.- xxxiv.
XIII.—Offerings for Tabernacle xxxv.-xxxix.
XIV.—Tabernacle erected, &c..................xl.

(According to Ayre.)

PART I.—Historical.
1. The state of Israel..........................i.
2. Preparation for deliverance ....ii.
3. Moses' commission ....iii. iv.
4. Negotiations with Pharaoh ...v.-xii. 30.
5. The Exodus ....xii. 31-xix. 2.

PART II.—Legislative.
1. Preparation for establishment of theocratic covenant ....xix. 3-25.
2. Promulgation of moral law ....xx.
3. Judicial ordinances ....xxi.-xxiii.
4. Ratification of covenant ....xxiv.
5. The Tabernacle ordered ......xxv.-xxxi.
6. Apostasy of Israel ....xxxii.-xxxiii.
7. The Tabernacle erected ......xxxiv.-xl.

CHAPTER THE FIRST.

B.C. 1706.

first colony of Israelites in Egypt

a De. x. 22.
b Alford; see also *Spk. Comm.* in loc.
c Go. l. 26.

"The very titles of the first two books in the Bible remind us that the history of man is little more than a narrative of his entrance into the world and his exit from it."—*Scott.*

"We die every day; every moment deprives us of a portion of our life, and advances us a step toward the grave; our whole life is only a long and painful sickness."—*Massillon.*

See *Bp. Hall* cont. *T. Baurin, Dis. Hist.*, ii. 1.

d U. R. Thomas.

Pharaoh oppresses the Israelites

a This continued for 23 yrs. more, in all 94 yrs. fr. Jacob's first coming into Egypt."—*Lightfoot.*
b Ec. ix. 15; He. vi. 10.
c "He speaks as if he had looked through a multiplying glass."—*Trapp.*
d Ps. li. 1, 4, x. 2, lxxxiii. 3, 4; Job v. 13; Pr. xxi. 30.

1—6. (1—4) **now .. names,** see Ge. xxix. 32 to xxx. 13. (5) **seventy,**ᵃ *i.e.* 11 sons + 4 sons of Reuben, 6 of Simeon, 3 of Levi, 3 and 2 grandsons of Judah, 4 of Issachar, 3 of Zebulun, Dinah, 7 sons of Gad, 4 and one daughter of Asher and 2 grandsons, 10 sons of Benjamin, 1 of Dan, 1 of Naphtali = 66 in all + Joseph and 2 sons, and Jacob himself.ᵇ (6) **Joseph**ᶜ .. **generation,** *i.e.* 54 yrs. after the death of Jacob.

The death of a whole family (v. 6).—We shall look at these words as recording the death of a whole family, and notice that it was—I. A very large family: "Joseph and all his brethren." II. A very diversified family: "Joseph and all his brethren" are words few and easily recorded; but each one of those twelve had a history distinct from every other. They were diversified in—1. Their sympathies; 2. Social position. III. A very tried family. 1. Very early in the history we read of a sad trial, a bereavement, and that of a mother; 2. There was also discord among the brothers; 3. They were all also afflicted with a grievous famine, that threatened their lives. IV. A very influential family. In addition to the influence, beneficial as it was vast, which Joseph wielded over Egypt, each of the twelve was the source and head of a tribe. V. A very religiously privileged family. The instructions of their childhood, the example of such a father, and the blessings that fell from his dying lips, convince us of this. From the whole subject we gather—(1) A rebuke to family pride: the most influential must succumb to death; (2) A warning against seeking satisfaction in family joys: death will shiver and shatter all; (3) A lesson as to the right use of family relationships: live together as those who must die; (4) Some strong reasons for expecting family meetings after death. 1. Such different characters cannot admit exactly the same fate. Extinction is either too good for the sinner, or else a strange reward for the saint; 2. Family affection seems too strong to be thus quenched. Let us then anticipate family reunions.ᵈ

7—11. (7) **children,** *etc.*, the idea is amazing and unparalleled increase.ᵃ (8) **arose,** 40 yrs. before birth of Moses. **up .. king,** prob. Raameses II. **which .. Joseph,**ᵇ did not regard his services. (9) **said .. people,** *i.e.* his counsellors. **more .. we,** *i.e.* more in proportion to space occupied.ᶜ (10) **wisely, craftily.**ᵈ **and .. land,** their presence a source of revenue and power. (11) **taskmasters,**ᵉ superintendents of the public works. **treasure-cities,** store-cities, magazines, depôts of ammunition, etc. **Pithom** (*abode of Atum*), perh. Patumos.ᶠ **Raameses**ᵍ (*son of the sun*), perh. *Abu Keshed,* N.E. of Heliopolis.

The bitter lives (vv. 7—14).—I. God's blessing makes fruitful—1. The promise to Abraham. Gen. xvii. 2—8; 2. The number of the Israelites in Egypt, vv. 9, 10. II. Note the mistakes committed through prejudice—1. The Egyptians hated and spurned the Israelites: therefore, ultimately, lost the blessing of their presence; 2. Statesmanship fails in placing policy before principle ; 3. Cruelty begot enmity ; kindness would have won. III. Selfishness soon forgets past favours. A new ruler disregarded the claims of Joseph's seed. This world works for present and prospective favours. IV. Here is a type of the growth of sin. The Israelites came into the best part of Egypt : first pleasant, then doubtful, then oppressed, then finally enslaved. 1. Sin yields bitter fruit ; 2. We have taskmasters in our habit ; 3. Life becomes a burden : sorrows of servitude. V. Note the reason for this affliction—1. They were becoming idolatrous, Josh. xxiv. 14 ; Ezek. xx. 5—8 ; 2. Bitterness *now* would help to prevent return to Egypt ; 3. We sometimes find sorrow here that we may look above. VI. God's favour here contrasted with man's opposition. Pharaoh failed ; the Israelites multiplied. VII. Affliction helps us—1. As afflicted, so they grew : 2. Christ purgeth us for more fruit ; 3. Self-denial is the path to power.[h]

Egyptian cruelty.—While staying at Alexandria, we passed a public building in course of erection. A great number of women and children of both sexes were carrying away the earth excavated for the foundation. Some labourers had loosened the soil, and the poor creatures then scraped it with their hands into circular baskets, which they bore away on their backs : they were barefooted, and very slenderly covered with rags. Several taskmasters, who have not ceased out of Egypt since the time of the Pharaohs, stood at invervals, holding a scourge of cords, which was not spared if any of the people, as they passed by crouching under their burdens, seemed to slacken in their work. They had all been pressed into the service by the Pasha's officers, and were paid at the miserable sum of half a piastre a day.[i]

12—14. (12) **grieved,**[a] filled with loathing and fear. (13) **rigour,**[b] *lit.* fierceness. (14) **mortar,** clay. **brick,** common in Egypt at all times, esp. under 18th dynasty.

Increase notwithstanding persecution (v. 12).—Here we have— I. Persecution, a source of increase : " the more they afflicted them, the more they multiplied." II. Renewed persecution consequent on this increase : " they were grieved,"—they made " the children of Israel to serve with rigour." Learn—1. The folly of fighting against God ; 2. The uses of affliction ; 3. The support given by God to His people during affliction.[c]

Brick-making in Egypt.—At one place the people were making bricks with straw cut into small pieces, and mingled with the clay to bind it. Hence it is that, when villages built of these bricks fall into rubbish, which is often the case, the roads are full of small particles of straw, extremely offensive to the eyes in a high wind. They were, in short, engaged exactly as the Israelites used to be—making bricks with straw, and for a similar purpose—to build extensive granaries for the Bashaw : treasure-cities for Pharaoh.[d] *Bitter lives.*—Of a bad man it is said, in the East, " He makes the lives of his servants bitter." Also, " Ah ! the fellow : the heart of his wife is made bitter." " My soul is bitter." " My heart is like the bitter tree."[e]

15—17. (15) **spake . . midwives,**[a] of whom two are named, either bec. of their disobedience to the king, or bec. they were directors of the others. **Shiphrah** (*beauty*). **Puah** (*mouth*). (16) **stools,** perh. the laver in which the infant was

B.C. cir. 1700.

e Ge. xv. 13; De. xxvi. 6; Ps. lxxxi. 6.

f *Herod.* ii. 158; hence near the site of *Abbaseh*, at the entrance of the Wady-et-Tumeylat.

g Ge. xlvii. 11.

h *Dr. Fowler.*

" During this long residence in Egypt God had not held any visible intercourse with the Israelites."— *Pretyman.*

" Man is, beyond dispute, the most excellent of created beings, and the vilest animal is a dog; but the sages agree that a grateful dog is better than an ungrateful man." —*Saadi.*

i *Foat and Caravan.*

they increase and are still more oppressed

a Ps. cv. 24.

b Ex. ii. 23, vi. 9; Ac. vii. 19, 34.

c *S. J. Taylor.*

v. 12. *Dr. Conep.*, n. 173.

v. 13, 14. *R. P. Buddicom,* i. 25.

" There is a frightful interval between the seed and the timber." —*Johnson.*

d *Jowett.*

e *Roberts.*

the midwives ordered to kill the male children

a We learn fr.

B.C. 1706.

Plutarch that some of the nations of antiquity had schools established among them where females were taught the obstetrical art.
b *Gesenius.*
c Nu. v. 15; Pr. xvi. 6; Dan. iii. 18, vi. 13; 1 Pe. ii. 17; Ac. v. 29.
"All the other passions condescend at times to accept the inexorable logic of facts; but jealousy looks facts straight in the face, ignores them utterly, and says that she knows a great deal better than they can tell her."—*Helps.*
d *Bush.*

the people ordered to cast them into the river.
a Pr. xi. 18; Ec. viii. 12; 1s. iii. 10; He. vi. 10.
b 1 Sa. ii. 35; 2 Sa. vii. 11.
c *Spk. Comm.*
d Ac. vii. 19.
"The people's safety is the law of God."—*Jas. Otis.*

e *Part n.*

B.C. *cir.* 1573.

birth of Moses
a Ex. vi. 16—20.
b Nu. xxvi. 59.
c Ac. vii. 20.
d He. xi. 23.
e Heb. *gome,* wh. indicates its absorbing power; Gk. *biblos,* whence the word Bible.
f Ex. xv. 20; Nu. xxvi. 59.

washed.*b* **son.. live,** that only the daughters might grow up and become wives of the Egyptians. (17) **but.. God,***c* in contrast to the Egyptians who thought only of themselves.

The stools.—There have been great difficulties started in the nature and use of the instruments here rendered *stools* (Heb. *stones*). According to the rendering of the established version, it would seem that they were designed for procuring a more easy delivery for women in labour. But besides that stone seats were obviously very unfit for such a purpose, the Hebrew word plainly signifies a vessel of stone for holding water (Ex. vii. 19). A far more probable interpretation, we think, is made out by referring the pronoun *them,* not to the mothers, but to the children. The sense of the passage would then be this :—" When ye see the new-born children, for the purpose of being washed, laid in the troughs or vessels of stone for holding water, ye shall destroy the boys." A passage from Thevenot seems to confirm this construction. "The kings of Persia are so afraid of being deprived of that power which they abuse, and are so apprehensive of being dethroned, that they destroy the children of their female relations, *when they are brought to bed of boys, by putting them into an earthen trough,* where they suffer them to starve:" that is, probably, under pretence of preparing to wash them, they let them pine away or destroy them in the water.*d*

18—22. (18) **why.. alive,** he must have had the midwives watched. (19) **lively,** robust. **delivered.. them,** true, but not all the truth. (20) **God.. midwives,***a* specially favoured them. (21) **that.. houses,***b* a prov. express. = "they married Hebrews, and became mothers in Israel."*c* (22) **and.. people,** whose natural hatred of the Hebrews would make them willing executioners. **river,***d* the Nile.

The midwives.—Oriental women suffer little from parturition; for those of better condition are frequently on foot the day after delivery, and out of all confinement on the third day. They seldom call midwives, and when they do, they are sometimes delivered before they come to their assistance; the poorer sort, while they are labouring or planting, go aside, deliver themselves, wash the child, lay it in a cloth, and return to work again. The same facility attended the Hebrew women in Egypt; and the assertion of the midwives seems to have been literally true.*e*

CHAPTER THE SECOND.

1—4. (1) **man,** Amram.*a* **daughter,** Jochebed.*b* (2) **son,** having already a son and a daughter. **goodly,***c* *lit.* fair to God, *i.e.* exceedingly beautiful. **she.. months,***d* fr. all eyes save those of her family. (3) **bulrushes,***e* prob. the paper-reed (*papyrus nilotica*), triangular stalk, about 10 ft. high, of wh. the cellular tissue was pieced together and made into a long roll for writing purposes. **slime.. pitch,** *lit.* asphalted it with asphalte, *i.e.* to make it water-tight. **flags,** tall flowering rushes (*alga nilotica*). (4) **sister,***f* Miriam. **stood,** *etc.,* doubtless directed by her mother.

The infancy of Moses (vv. 1—11).—I. The concealment of Moses. The cruelty of Pharaoh; the affection of the mother, who was willing to expose herself to death for her child. II. His rescue (vv. 5, 6). III. His restoration (vv. 7—9)*a*.—*Childhood of Moses.*—Notice three things :—I. Helpless infancy. Moses in the ark. A beautiful sight. Unconscious of any danger (*ill.* infant in cradle). Mother far away. No one to help the child. Yes, ONE. Unseen dangers have lurked around our infancy. We may never know how near we have been to peril. II. Sisterly affection. Miriam afar off. Yet she watched the ark. "To wit, etc." Anxious to know her little brother's fate. A very pretty sight to see one child caring for another. The elder sister nursing, and tending, and watching the infant. III. Filial obedience. While love aided her in doing this, probably her mother incited her. She obeyed. Afar off, but not too far. Had she stayed away, or played, or forgotten her duty, Moses might have been taken, and his mother not known by whom. Parents may be helped by dutiful daughters. Learn—1. Have compassion on the very young ; 2. Help parents without waiting for the command.

The ark of bulrushes.—Bitumen is often mentioned in the Bible, but under the name of pitch, in our translation. The Egyptians employed it largely in embalming their dead. The mother of Moses also " daubed " her ark of bulrushes with slime and with pitch, as we have it, but in the Hebrew she *bitumed* it with bitumen and tar, or pitch. This is doubly interesting, as it reveals the process by which they prepared the bitumen. The mineral, as found in this country, melts readily enough by itself ; but then, when cold, it is as brittle as glass. It must be mixed with tar while melting, and in that way it forms a hard, glassy wax, perfectly impervious to water. I once covered the roof of a room, that leaked like a sieve, with such a preparation, spreading it while the rain descended in torrents, and yet with perfect success. The basket of bulrushes for the infant Moses, when thoroughly bitumed, was well adapted to the object for which it was made. Our translation of this passage is deficient in clearness. The bulrush—gomeh—is the Egyptian papyrus. Taboth—ark—is the Arabic word for coffin. Slime and pitch are bitumen and tar. The whole was made like a coffin, to deceive the watchful officers of government with the appearance of a funeral. This, too, would appeal more tenderly to the daughter of Pharaoh, and there is a sort of typical signification in it. The Saviour of Israel was laid in a coffin, and taken from a watery grave ; the Saviour of the world rose from a rock sepulchre in Jerusalem.*h*

5—8. (5) **daughter,** said to be Thermuthis.*a* **wash .. river,** prob. a religious ablution : the Nile was adored as an emanation of Osiris. (6) **wept,** its tears touched her woman's heart. **this .. children,** no Egyptian child would be found in such a place. (7) **then .. sister,** who now, as if moved by curiosity, joined them. **nurse .. women,** no Egyptian woman would have undertaken the task. **that .. thee ?** *i.e.* under thy protection. (8) **maid,** the Heb. implies a grown girl. **called .. mother,** thus the mother's purpose was fulfilled ; her stratagem succeeded.

The weeping babe (v. 6).—This babe had—I. A very cruel king. Pharaoh, proud, hard-hearted, selfish, cruel. II. A very tender mother. Her name and circumstances. Moses born—a beautiful

B.C. cir. 1573.

g C. Morris.
"To make our reliance upon Providence both pious and rational, we should, in every great enterprise we take in hand, prepare all things with that care, diligence, and activity, as if there were no such thing as Providence for us to depend upon; and again, when we have done all this, we should as wholly and humbly rely upon it, as if we had made no preparations at all.'—*South.*
"If God but cares for our inward and eternal life, if by all the experiences of this life He is reducing it and preparing for its disclosure, nothing can befall us but prosperity. Every sorrow shall be but the setting of some luminous jewel of joy. Our very mourning shall be but the enamel around the diamond; our very hardships but the metallic rim that holds the opal, glancing with strange interior fires."— *Beecher.*
h Dr. Thomson.

he is found by Pharaoh's daughter

a Josephus.

"The fact of the princess disobeying her father's command in adopting the babe, so far from being a difficulty, as some have made it, is the very impress of truth itself. If

B.C. cir. 1573.

there is a thing too strong for man's laws, it is woman's heart. Witness Antigone burying her brother."—*Alford.*

b *J. Bolton.*

c *Roberts.*

v. 6 *Dr. T. Lawson,* 325; *J. Hewlett,* i. 93; *M. Anderson,* 3.

he receives his name.

a Ps. xviii 15.

b *Dr. Payson.*

c *Dr. Robinson.*

"We know that the gifts which men have do not come from the schools. If a man is a plain, literal, factual man, you can make a great deal more of him in his own line by education than without education, just as you can make a great deal more of a potato if you cultivate it than if you do not; but no cultivation in this world will ever make an apple out of a potato."—*Beecher.*

"Education, briefly, is the leading human souls to what is best, and making what is best out of them; and these two objects are always attainable together, and by the same means; the training which makes men happiest in themselves also makes them most serviceable to others."—*Ruskin.*

d *Watson Smith.*

child. Her love and fear. What she had at last to do. III. A very loving sister. Her name. Her willingness to watch by the river. What came of her good sense; what she lived to see Moses do. A lesson for elder brothers and sisters. IV. A very kind benefactor. The princess and her care. How she *might* have treated the poor little Hebrew child. The name she gave him, and what she did for him afterwards. The joy in the home of his parents. Learn :—Nothing is too hard for the Lord.*b*

Outdoor bathing.—All this is very natural. Wherever there is a river or a tank which is known to be free from alligators, there females go in companies to some retired place to bathe. There are so many ceremonies and so many causes for defilement among the Hindoos, that the duty has often to be attended to. In the Scanda Purana, the beautiful daughter of Mongaly is described as going to the river with her maidens to bathe.*c*

9—10. (9) **nurse . . me,** with the princess's protection no need for further secrecy. **I . . wages,** a mother paid for nursing her own child ! (10) **she . . daughter,** at what age not known. **he . . son,** adopted. **Moses,** fr. Heb. vb. *mashah,a* to draw out.

Children to be educated for God (v. 9).—I. What is implied in educating children for God. 1. A realising, heartfelt conviction that they are His property ; 2. A cordial, solemn dedication of them to be His for ever ; 3. Regard for the glory of God in our whole treatment of them ; 4. Educating them for His service. This implies that we pay more attention to—(1) The soul than to the body ; (2) The heart than the mind ; (3) Eternity than to time. II. The reward which God usually bestows on those who thus educate their children for Him. 1. The pleasure which attends the attempt. 2. Their happiness when their labours are crowned with success.*b* *A child's rescue* (v. 9). Consider—I. The perils which surrounded the life here saved. It was the life of—1. An infant ; 2. A proscribed ; 3. An outcast child. II. Who it was that saved it. 1. Primarily, of course, it was God ; 2. Instrumentally, however, He made use of four agents in the rescue. (1) A believing mother ; (2) A wealthy princess ; (3) An intelligent child ; (4) An affectionate nurse. The first and last are one and the same person, though in different offices. III. Its value. The child was worth something for—1. Its beauty ; 2. Its gifts ; 3. Its preciousness ; 4. Its purpose ; 5. Its destiny. Learn :—(1) The power of humanity ; (2) The best kind of monuments ; (3) The greatest reason for thanksgiving.*c* *The birth of Moses and its lessons* (vv. 1—11). Consider Moses as illustrating God's method of raising up souls on earth for Divine service. Observe—I. God gives and sends such as they are needed. II. That they may be fitly prepared for their work, they are "made like unto their brethren." III. The very people that sought to destroy Israel are made instrumental in rearing Israel's defender and avenger. IV. In the raising up of Moses we have a most instructive exemplification of the doctrine and working of Divine Providence. V. In Pharaoh's daughter and the part she takes, we note that human nature is one, and that all classes and nations are destined to become one in God's reconciling and saving plan.*d*

Children.—I am fond of children. I think them the poetry of the world, the fresh flowers of our hearths and homes ; little conjurors, with their "natural magic," evoking by their spells what delights and enriches all ranks, and equalises the different classes of society. Often as they bring with them anxieties and cares, and live to occasion sorrow and grief, we should get on very badly without them. Only think, if there was never anything anywhere to be seen but great grown-up men and women! How we should long for the sight of a little child! Every infant comes into the world like a delegated prophet, the harbinger and herald of good tidings, whose office it is "to turn the hearts of the fathers to the children," and to draw "the disobedient to the wisdom of the just." A child softens and purifies the heart, warming and melting it by its gentle presence; it enriches the soul by new feelings, and awakens within it what is favourable to virtue. It is a beam of light, a fountain of love, a teacher whose lessons few can resist. Infants recall us from much that engenders and encourages selfishness, that freezes the affections, roughens the manners, indurates the heart; they brighten the home, deepen love, invigorate exertion, infuse courage, and vivify and sustain the charities of life. It would be a terrible world, I do think, if it was not embellished by little children!*e*

B.C. *cir.* 1573.

"Education commences at the mother's knee, and every word spoken within the hearing of little children tends towards the formation of character. Let parents bear this ever in mind."— *H. Ballou.*

v. 9. *Dr. F. Payson,* iii. 294; *Bp. Dehon,* ii. 427; *Dr. H. Hughes,* i. 230.

e T. Binney.

11—15. (11) **grown,** *lit.* had become great, *i.e.* in reputation, etc. M. was now about 40 yrs. of age.*a* **burdens,** labours, servitude. **Egyptian,** prob. one of the taskmasters. (12) **slew .. sand,***b* oppression maketh a wise man mad. (13) **two .. together,***c* their burdens increased by internal strife. **him .. wrong,** *lit.* the wicked person. *i.e.* the aggressor. **fellow,***d* neighbour, companion. (14) **who .. us?** his friendly interference rejected: a hint that he should mind his own business; this was his business. **intendest .. Egyptian?** a hint that if M. interfered he would be informed against. (15) **when .. thing,** *i.e.* that Moses had killed an Egyptian. **Midian,***e* so called from fourth son of Abraham by Keturah:*f* S. of Dead Sea and the land of Moab.

he kills an Egyptian and flies from Egypt

a Ac. vii. 22—25; He. xi. 24, 26.

b Ge. ix. 6.

c Mal. ii. 10; Ac. vii. 26—29, 35.

d Ma. v. 9; Mk. ix. 33.

e He. xi. 27.

f Ge. xxv. 1, 2.

Homiletic hints.—Moses remembers his afflicted kinsmen. I. Uncorrupted by the royal court. II. Sympathy for his brethren. III. He showed his sympathy by identifying himself with them. —The violent death—I. Not a murder: Egyptian law required the third party to interfere in case of mortal combat, under pain of death. II. Patriotism: defence of a countryman. — The demand for Divine credentials coming unauthenticated was rejected. A teacher's credentials are the fruits of his teaching. —All men are commissioned to reprove wrong. — The Hebrew quarrel — I. Multiplied their enemies. II. Weakened Israel. III. Banished Moses. Divisions defeat the Church.—Moses, as— I. A judge dooming his enemies. II. A peacemaker among his countrymen.—The great choice for God manly, too old for sentimentalism, too young for satiated ambition.*g*

g Dr. Fowler.

"It is the custom of tyrants to oppress their subjects, that they might not be obliged to maintain a guard, and that the people, chained down by daily labour, might not have time to contrive plans of rebellion."—*Aristotle.*

Tyrannical oppression.—The king of Ceylon often employs his people on immense works, which can scarcely be accomplished in several years, that he may accustom them to servitude, and thus prevent them from rebelling against him, which they, perhaps, would do if they had less employment. For this reason he never suffers his people to be idle, but is always thinking of some new employment for them. Tarquin the Proud, out of mistrust, employed the Roman people in hard labour, particularly in digging the subterraneous canals or drains in the city of Rome.*h*

"There is no happiness for him who oppresses and persecutes; no, there can be no repose for him. For the sighs of the unfortunate cry for vengeance to Heaven." — *Pestalozzi.*

h R. Knox.

B.C. cir. 1573.

he settles in Midian and marries

a In Arabic version *Imam*.
b Ge. xxix. 10; 1 Sa. ix. 11.
c Nu. x. 29.
d Josephus conjectures that Reuel was his propername, and Jethro (*excellency*) was his official designation.
e Nu. xii. 1.
f Ac. vii. 29.
g W. R. Cooper.

16—22. (16) **priest**,[a] prob. one who combined in himself the offices of prince and priest, like Melchisedec. (17) **shepherds .. away**, with rustic coarseness. **Moses .. flock**,[b] as Jacob assisted Rachel. (18) **Reuel** (*friend of God*), or Raguel,[c] poss. the same with Jethro.[d] **how .. day?** whence it seems they were often interfered with by the shepherds. (19) **Egyptian**, so they deemed M. fr. his costume and speech. (20) **why .. bread**, Eastern hospitality; gratitude to benefactors. (21) **content**, willing. **Zipporah**, (*a little bird*).[e] (22) **Gershom**[f] (*expulsion*, or *a stranger there*).

Women at wells.—The above passage receives an excellent Western illustration from the ancient Homeric hymn to Ceres. Thus the simple usages of society, derived from one patriarchal source, remain the same in all countries, till a pseudo-civilisation destroys them. The following are the lines referred to :—

"Four gentle nymphs, light moving o'er the plain,
Approach; four brazen urns their arms sustain,
Great Celeus was their sire—he bade them bring
The limpid water from Parthenia's spring;
Lovely they seemed as heaven's immortal powers;
Youth's purple light and beauty's opening flowers
Glowed on their cheeks."[h]

Pharaoh dies

a Ac. vii. 30; Ex. vii. 7.
b Jas. v. 4; Ps. xii. 5.
c Nu. xx. 16; De. xxvi. 7.
d Ge. xv. 13–18, xlvi. 4, xxvi. 5.
e Spk. Comm.
f Ex. vi. 5; Ps. cv. 8, 42, cvi. 44, 45; Ne. ix. 7, 9; Ex. iv. 31.
g Dr. W. Landels.

"I never could believe that Providence had sent a few men into the world, ready booted and spurred to ride, and millions ready saddled and bridled to be ridden."—R. Rumbold.

"Fishes live in the sea, as men do a-land; the greatones eat up the little ones."—Shakespeare.

h J. Timbs.

23—25. (23) **in time**,[a] nearly 40 yrs. and .. **bondage**,[b] their burdens not reduced on the death of the king. **cry .. God**,[c] showing that they retained the religion of their forefathers. (24) **remembered .. Jacob**,[d] *i.e.* "was moved by their prayers to give effect to the covenant."[e] (25) **respect**,[f] **knew**, *i.e.* recognised them as the seed of Abraham, to whom the covenant belonged.

The bondage (v. 23).—What was the purpose of this bondage? Some say—(1) That it was purely vicarious; (2) That it was designed to typify the bondage of sinners in their unsaved condition, and to show the need they have of deliverance. Let us look for the reasons for the bondage in the Israelites themselves. As a nation they had to be trained for a particular mission. And it requires no very acute discernment to perceive how this bondage was likely to conduce to their mission's fulfilment. I. It was an ill. to them of the treatment which the Church might expect from the world, fitted to promote in them the isolation which it was necessary they should maintain. II. It tended to promote that mutual sympathy which is the necessary bond of national life. III. It showed the teaching and practice of the human principles of the Divine law, in the face of the oppression, and violence, and cruelty, which were then prevalent throughout the world.[g]

The great pyramid at Gizeh.—Mr. Tite, the architect, states the original dimensions of the Great Pyramid, near Gizeh, to have been 764 square feet at the base, and 480 feet of perpendicular height; covering 43 acres, 1 rood, 22 perches of ground. It consumed 89,028,000 cubic feet of stone; and Mr. Tite adds, that it could not now be built for less than thirty millions sterling! The joints of the large casing blocks of granite were so fine as to be scarcely perceptible, not thicker than paper; and the mortar was so adhesive that the stones in some cases broke through their substance rather than give way at their jointing.[h]

CHAPTER THE THIRD.

B.C. 1491.

1—3. (1) **Jethro** (*excellence*), **his .. law,** or brother-in-law : kindred by marriage. **backside,** *i.e.* westward.^a **Horeb**^b (dryness), name of district of wh. Mt. Sinai was the southern extremity. (2) **bush,** Heb. *seneh* = bramble-bush. prob. the thorny acacia (*mimosa nilotica*). **and .. consumed,**^c the more wonderful from the nature of the plant.^d (3) **I .. aside,**^e for a season from my occupation as shepherd. **great, wonderful, mysterious. burnt,** eaten up : Moses a scientific inquirer.

The burning bush (vv. 1—6).—Consider—I. The employment in which Moses was engaged. II. The sight which he witnessed. This was a representation of the Church—1. In its lowly condition ; 2. In the persecutions to which it has been exposed ; 3. Its wonderful preservation. III. The resolution he made. IV. The prohibition he received. We see here—1. The reverence required ; 2. The reason assigned : it was holy ground. V. The announcement he heard. These words were—1. Highly instructive ; 2. Peculiarly encouraging.^f *The burning bush* (vv. 1—6). —Consider—I. What this sight was designed to represent : the Israelitish Church of that time, which was in a very lowly and despised condition. 1. The angel in the bush signified the presence of the Lord with the Church ; 2. His appearance in a flame of fire showed the terrible trials to which the Church, for her sins, was exposed ; 3. The circumstance of the bush burning, and not being consumed, was a token that the Church should not perish under her persecutions. II. The practical lessons we may gather from this subject. 1. The vast importance of being ourselves numbered with the true Church ; 2. The comfort which every member of that Church may take to himself, from the general promise here made to the people of God, as a brotherhood and community.^g *The burning bush* (vv. 1—6).—I will endeavour to—I. Show what was intended by the burning bush. It was intended to represent the state and condition of—1. The people of Israel in Egypt ; 2. The Church of God both before and after the manifestation of Christ in the flesh ; 3. Every individual in the Church. II. Account for the miracle thus exhibited. Christ was in the bush, and therefore it was not consumed—1. It was His presence with the afflicted Israelites that prevented their destruction ; 2. It is His presence that still preserves, and ever has preserved, His Church in the world ; 3. It is His presence that preserves, not only His Church collectively, but every individual in it. III. Point out some useful reflections which this subject may lead us to make. It may—1. Afford matter for encouragement respecting the present state of the Church. There may be some things which discourage, but there are others which may well fill our tongues with joy ; 2. Afford encouragement to individual believers. " Be not afraid nor dismayed by reason of the multitude of your enemies, for the battle is not yours, but God's ;" 3. Lead us to reflect upon the difference between God's people and others. If God be a wall of fire for the protection of His people, what is He to His enemies ? What, but a " consuming fire "?^h

the burning bush

^a The E. is the region which is looked upon as bef. a man, the W. behind him, the S. and N. as the right and left hand acc. to the Heb. system of orientation.

^b Phil. iv. 11 ; 1 Cor. vii. 20, i. 27—29.

^c " The symbol of the Scotch Church is likewise a burning bush with the words beneath it : 'Nec tamen consumebatur.'" —*Kitsch.*

^d Ac. vii. 30 ; Mk. xii. 26 ; Is. lxiii. 9 ; De. xxxiii. 16 ; Is. x. 17, xliii. 2 ; Ps. cxxix. 2.

^e Jas. iv. 8 ; Ps. cxi. 2 ; Dan. xii. 26, 27.

^f *Anon.*

^g *J. Slade, M.A.*

" There are more things in heaven and earth than are dreamt of in your philosophy." — *Shakespeare.*
" There are different kinds of curiosity : one of interest, which causes us to learn that which would be useful to us ; and the other of pride, which springs from a desire to know that of which others are ignorant."—*Rochefoucauld.*

^h *T. Grantham, B.D.*

B.C. 1491.

God speaks to Moses

a Ge. xlvi. 2.

b Ex. xix. 12.

c Josh. v. 15; Ec. v. 1; Jo. xiii. 10; Eph. ii. 18, iii. 12; He. x. 22.

d Spk. Comm.

e He. xl. 16; Ma. xxii. 32; Mk. xii. 26; Lu. xx. 37.

f Is. vi. 1—5.

"The desire of Moses to be taught, as indicated by his drawing near, is especially worthy of note. It often happens that God meets us in vain because we perversely spurn so great grace. Let us learn from the example of Moses, as often as God, by any sign, invites us to Himself, sedulously to attend, nor stifle the offered light by our sluggishness."—*Calvin.*

g Dr. Thomas.

"I think we cannot too strongly attack superstition, which is the disturber of society; nor too highly respect genuine religion, which is the support of it."—*Rousseau.*

"The greatest burden in the world is superstition, not only of ceremonies in the Church, but of imaginary and scarecrow sins at home."—*Milton.*

h Bibl. Treas.

Moses commanded

4—6. (4) **saw . . see,** reward of sanctified curiosity. **God . . bush,**a the fire is explained by the voice. (5) **draw . . hither,**b *i.e.* nearer than thou art. **shoes,** sandals. **for . . ground,**c *lit.* ground of holiness: "the reverence due to holy places thus rests on God's own command."d (6) **I . . father,**e Moses regarded the Patriarchs as his ancestors. **hid,** with his hands or robe. **afraid,**f conscious weakness and sinfulness.

Moses and the burning bush, a picture of a true student and the Bible (vv. 2—6).—Introduction :—The circumstances connected with this extraordinary incident suggest four general facts—1. That God's purposes are punctual in their accomplishment ; 2. That these purposes, in relation to the world, are generally accomplished by the agency of man ; 3. That the men whom God employs for the carrying out of His plans, He qualifies by a special revelation ; 4. That this special revelation is frequently symbolical in its character. We shall now regard Moses and the bush as an emblem of a true student and the Bible. Observe him—I. Directing his earnest attention to the Divine revelation. He does this—1. Under an impression of its greatness ; 2. In order to ascertain its import. II. Holding intercourse with God through it. God's communications—1. Depended upon his attention ; 2. Were consciously personal to him ; 3. Were directive and elevating. This language (v. 6) would suggest to him—(1) That his holy ancestors were still in existence ; (2) That the promises which God made to them were about to be fulfilled. III. Realising the profoundest impressions through it. These impressions are—1. Peculiarly becoming in sinful intelligence ; 2. Necessary to qualify men for God's work ; 3. Consonant with the highest dignity and enjoyment.g

Putting off the shoes.—We were encamped on a rising ground just in front of a rajah's tomb. It was probably the anniversary of his death, and we were much amused in watching the honours paid to his memory. In the early morning, crowds of visitors arrived from all the neighbouring villages, each one provided with some offering of respect, which was carried inside the building, and there deposited. The tomb being elevated on about twenty stone steps, we were enabled the better to observe the ceremonies performed. One of the first arrivals was that of a man seemingly of high degree. He was richly clothed, much decked out with ornaments of gold and precious stones, and was most probably some near relative of the deceased. He rode up on horseback, his horse's neck being adorned with garlands of strongly-scented, white, and everlasting flowers. His first act on dismounting was the loosening of his shoes, which were left at the bottom of the steps. Then, barefoot, this great personage ascended the steps, bowing, and touching first the step, and then his forehead, all the way up. He then entered the tomb with limes in his hand (a fruit always offered as a mark of respect), and garlands of flowers. Servants followed, bearing on their heads baskets of fruits, which were also with much reverence carried within. The horse all this time, as if perfectly accustomed to such scenes, quietly awaited his master's return. It would be difficult to say how many pairs of shoes there were at one time around the steps.h

7—10. (7) **taskmasters,** oppressors. **know,**a feel for, commiserate with. **sorrows,**b grief, trials. (8) **I . . down,**c anthropological. **hand,** power. **unto . . honey,**[d] *i.e.* a land of pasturage and flowers. **Canaanites,** *etc., see* Ge. x. 15 ff. and xv. 20. (9) **behold,** *etc.*, repetition to fix the reason of the deliverance in the mind of Moses. (10) **I . . Pharaoh,**[e] M. an ambassador fr. the King of kings to the King of Egypt. **my . . people,** notwithstanding their condition they are yet the people of God.

I know their sorrows (v. 7).—Shall not we be comforted as we discern that our dear Friend knows all about us? He is—I. The Physician; and if He knows all, there is no need that the patient should know. II. The Master: His knowledge is to serve us instead of our own; we are to obey, not to judge. III. The Head. All understanding centres there; and all understanding and knowledge centres thus in our Lord.[f] *The angel in the burning bush.*—This narrative (read vv. 1—14) is a chain of glorious wonders. Let us examine it link by link. Here we see —I. An old man called to go out on the great errand of his life. His education lasted eighty years: forty in college, court, and camp; and forty in the peaceful wilderness. II. The burning bush from which that call was sounded. This was—1. A sign to indicate the peculiar presence of God; 2. A symbol of His people [for enlargement on this point, *see* outlines on vv. 1—3]. III. The angel who uttered this call. We see at the first glance that He is Divine. We next learn that He is an angel; and we further find from a chain of Scripture proofs that He is Christ. IV. The covenant under which the Angel gave him his commission: that made with Abraham, Isaac, and Jacob. V. The Angel's name: "*I Am that I Am.*" This asserts—1. His real; 2. His underived; 3. His independent; 4. His eternal; 5. His unchangeable; 6. His infallible, existence. VI. The effect to be wrought by the remembrance of His name. 1. It is intended to inspire profoundest reverence for the Being to whom it belongs; 2. It reveals the infinite sufficiency of a Christian's portion; 3. It gives encouragement to evangelical enterprise.[g]

Divine sympathy.—"I know their sorrows" (Ex. iii. 7). Man cannot say so. There are many sensitive fibres of the soul the best and tenderest *human* sympathy cannot touch. But the Prince of sufferers, He who led the way in the path of sorrow, "knoweth our frame." When crushing bereavement lies like ice on the heart, when the dearest earthly friend cannot enter into the peculiarities of our grief, Jesus can—Jesus does. He who once bore my *sins,* also carried my *sorrows.* That eye now on the throne was once dim with weeping. I can think, in all my afflictions, "He was afflicted;" in all my tears, "Jesus wept."[h]

11—13. (11) **who am I,**[a] *etc.*, not fear but humility. (12) **token,** sign, *i.e.* not the bush wh. he had seen, but the promise now spoken. **ye . . mountain,**[b] Israel was long encamped at the base of Sinai. (13) **what . . them?** it may be more difficult to convince Israel than to persuade Pharaoh.

God's presence with His ministers (v. 12).—The mission of Moses resembles that of every Christian minister, in that—I. He was sent to his brethren. II. When he went to them, he found them in a state of bondage and oppression: their spirits crushed, their minds degraded. III. He found that he only provoked them by his endeavours to deliver them. IV. Promises were

B.C. 1491.

to visit Pharaoh
a Ne. ix. 9; Is. lxiii. 9; Act. vii. 34; Job xxiii. 10; Ps. cxliii. 3.
b Ex. ii. 23—25.
c Ge. l. 24; Phil. i. 6.
d Nu. xiii. 27; De. xxvi. 9; viii. 7—9; i. 25.
e Ps. cv. 26, 27; Mic. vi. 4.
f *Spurgeon.*
g *C. Stanford.*

"To commiserate is sometimes more than to give; for money is external to a man's self, but he who bestows compassion communicates his own soul."—*Mountford.*

"It is by sympathy we enter into the concerns of others, that we are moved as they are moved, and are never suffered to be indifferent spectators of almost anything which men can do or suffer. For sympathy may be considered as a sort of substitution, by which we are put into the place of another man, and affected in many respects as he is affected."—*Burke.*
h *Macduff.*

Moses asks for credentials

a Je. i. 4—7; Pr. xxix. 25; Eph. vi. 10.

b Josh. i. 5; Ro. viii. 31; 2 Cor. xii. 9.

c *H. Raikes, M.A.*

"The modest

B.C. 1491.

man has everything to gain, and the arrogant man everything to lose; for modesty has always to deal with generosity, and arrogance with envy."—Rivarol.

"Let us be careful to distinguish modesty, which is ever amiable, from reserve, which is only prudent. A man is hated sometimes for pride; when it was an excess of humility gave the occasion."—Shenstone.

d E. Bayley, D.D.

"It is remarked that the modest deportment of real wise men, when contrasted to the assuming air of the young and ignorant, may be compared to the differences of wheat, which, while its ear is empty, holds up its head proudly, but as soon as it is filled with grain, bends modestly down, and withdraws from observation."—J. Beaumont.

the name of God

a Ex. vi. 3; Jo. viii. 38; He. xiii. 8; 2 Cor. i. 20; Re. i. 4; xvi. 5.

b Spk. Comm.

c R. Thomas, M.A.

"How calmly may we commit ourselves to the hands of Him who bears up the world,—of Him

given to support him under his disappointments. View the promise in the way of—1. Encouragement. God will be with every minister—(1) As a guide; (2) To strengthen and support him under trial; (3) To comfort and console him; 2. Caution. While each pastor rests on the consolation of this privilege, he must not forget the call to watchfulness and holiness which is inseparably connected with it.*c* *The pastor's question, and the people's answer* (v. 13; read also Deut. v. xxvii.).—These two passages contain—I. The pastor's question, "What shall I say unto them?" In answering this question, there must be borne in mind—1. The essence; 2. The proportion: 3. The harmony, of Scripture. Since Scripture occupies itself with two great thoughts, God and man; answer may thus be given:—Declare to thy people on the authority of God, their responsibility as men, and their ruin as sinners; preach not the Law alone, but also the Gospel. II. The people's answer. This ought to be like that of the Jews of old: "Speak thou unto us all that the Lord our God shall speak unto thee" [see notes on this passage in vol. ii.]. This implies that they hear—1. Willingly; 2. Attentively; 3. Thoughtfully; 4. Honestly; 5. Prayerfully.*d*

The prayerfulness of Washington.—In 1777, while the American army lay at Valley Forge, a good old Quaker, of the name of Potts, had occasion to pass through a thick wood, near head-quarters. As he traversed the forest, he heard at a distance before him, a voice, which, as he advanced, became more and more fervent and interesting. Approaching with slowness and circumspection, he beheld, under a thick-set bower, apparently formed for the purpose, the commander-in-chief of the armies of the United States, on his knees, in the act of devotion before the Ruler of the universe. At that moment, when Potts, who was concealed by the trees, came up, Washington was interceding for his beloved country, with tones of gratitude, that laboured for adequate expression; he adored the exuberant goodness which, from the depth of obscurity, had exalted him to the head of a great nation, now placed in great difficulty. He utterly disclaimed his own ability for the arduous conflict. He wept at the thought of the ruin which his mistakes might bring on his country, and implored the aid of the Divine arm. As soon as the general had finished, Potts retired. He returned to his house, and threw himself into a chair, by the side of his wife, under the influence of feelings which, for a time, refused him utterance.

14. I .. Am,*a* "the words express absolute, and, therefore, unchanging and eternal being."*b*

The vision of Moses (vv. 1—14).—I. The surroundings of this vision. 1. It was given to Moses while engaged in his lawful calling: 2. It was given to a man already prepared for conspicuous service by a remarkable providence co-operating with maternal sagacity. II. The revelation it contained. The underived character of the Divine nature—the power of God—His competency for what He has undertaken—are here expressed. III. Inferences deducible. 1. God uses mediators when He reveals Himself to men; 2. The true knowledge of God is the power of deliverance to the enslaved.*c* *I Am.* The immutability of our Lord is evinced in—I. The dignity and majesty of His person. II. His Almighty power. Our text leads us more especially to reflect upon the constancy with which that power is exercised in the defence and preservation of His Church. III. His great office of Redeemer. We are kept by His power "through faith unto salvation." IV. His compassion and sympathy. God not only feels for, but also with, the oppressed. V. His faithfulness. The history of the Church in all ages is one record of His presence shown in the exercise of power influenced by love, regulated by wisdom, and therefore always adapted to her condition, and conducive to her welfare.*d* *The immutability of God.*—The proof of the doctrine—that God is unchangeable—may be deduced from two sources—I. From what we know of His other attributes. To suppose any attribute of God to cease entirely, is to suppose that He ceases to be God. To suppose any to increase is to suppose that He is now, in some degree, imperfect. But He is perfect; and the least change in a perfect and infinite being is inconceivable. II. From explicit and repeated declarations of the Bible. (*See* Mal. iii. 6; Tit. i. 2: Jas. i. 17; Ps. cii. 27.) Inferences :—1. All conceptions of God which apply time and succession to His existence are erroneous; 2. God has no *new* purposes; 3. The certainty of final salvation to true believers is thus a reasonable doctrine, grounded on God's promises; 4. When God is said to repent, it implies no change in His character or purposes. He speaks thus to adapt Himself to our ideas; 5. God's immutability is no discouragement, but the best encouragement, to prayer; 6. This doctrine is one full of comfort to God's people; 7. It is also one full of terror to His enemies.*e* *I Am that I Am.*—We have here—I. The chief inquiry of man as a responsible agent (v. 13). Who sends me? What is His name? II. The highest revelation to man as a speculative thinker.—God's name. "*I Am.*" 1. Not Atheism: God Himself speaks; 2. Not Pantheism: God's personality is declared; 3. Not mere Deism: God descends to take an interest in men's affairs. III. The highest authority of man as a moral worker—"I Am hath sent me."*f*

15—18. (15) **name,***a* that by wh. God makes Himself known. **memorial,***b* that by wh. God is worshipped by His people. (16) **elders,***c* persons of influence, teachers, rulers (*sheikhs*): these would instruct the rest. (17) **said,** and therefore resolved. **land,** *etc., see* v. 8. (18) **they,** the elders. **hearken,** believe and obey. **thou .. Egypt,** Moses should enter the presence of Pharaoh, surrounded by the elders of Israel. **and .. him,** *etc.,* so much of the whole truth was he to tell Pharaoh, and no more.

The promised land (v. 17).—Consider the earthly Canaan as—I. A land of nourishment: "milk." 1. Food for babes; 2. Pleasant and strengthening to men. II. A land of pleasure: "honey," implying enjoyment of sweet pleasures. III. A land of abundance: "flowing." Both nourishment and pleasure shall abound, no stint of either. IV. The type of a better and heavenly inheritance. The earthly Canaan may flow with milk and honey; but will it continue for ever?*d*

The climate of Palestine.—"The inhabitants rejoice in the happiest clime. The warmth of the summer enables tropical plants to grow on the plains of Palestine; thus the date-palm and the fig (the edible species and the sycamore fig) found a home in Southern Syria, in sheltered spots. The strip of coast

B.C. 1491.

who has created, and who provides for the joys even of insects, as carefully as if He were their Father!"—*Richter.*

d J. Field, M.A.

e E. Porter, D.D.

"Many people have their own god; and he is much what the French may mean when they talk of *le bon Dieu,*— very indulgent, rather weak, near at hand when we want anything, but far away, out of sight, when we have a mind to do wrong. Such a god is as much an idol us if he were an image of stone."—*Hare.*

f Anon.

Moses receives instructions

a Ps. cxxxv. 13; cxi. 5; Hos. xii. 5.

b "The name declares the objective manifestation of the Divine nature; the memorial, the subjective recognition by man."—*Wordsworth;* see *Keil.*

c Nu. xi. 16.

d W. Coombs.

"I cannot but take notice of the wonderful love of God to mankind, who, in order to encourage obedience to His

B.C. 1491.

laws, has annexed a present as well as a future reward to a good life; and has so interwoven our duty and happiness together, that, while we are discharging our obligations to the one, we are, at the same time, making the best provision for the other."—Melmoth.

e Meyen.

the obstinacy of Pharaoh and departure of Israel predicted

a Ex. vii. 3, 4, v. 2.

b Ex. vii. 5; De. vi. 22; Nc. ix. 10; Ps. cxxxv. 9; cxxxvi. 11, 12.

c Ex. xi. 3, Pr. xvi. 7; Dan. i. 9.

d Ge. xv. 14.

e Ps. ii. 8, Pr. xxii. 7; De. xxviii. 12.

f Ex. xii. 35, 36; Job xxvii. 17; Pr. xiii. 22; Ez. xxxix. 10.

v. 19, 20. *R. P. Buddicomb,* i. 112; *Bp. Armstrong,* 239.

v. 22. *Dr. T. Edwards,* 41; *W. Jacobson,* 1.

"The individual and the race are always moving, and as we drift into new latitudes new lights open in the heaven more immediately over us."—Chapin.

g Carpenter.

h C. Buck.

tended to diminish the extremes of temperature, and thus palms grow, and still grow, in the maritime plain. Palestine was also able to boast a large number of more northern plants, belonging strictly to the warmer temperate zone, on the edge of which Northern Palestine is situated. Hence it gained many beautiful evergreen trees and shrubs, myrtles, laurels, cistuses, and other important plants of Southern Europe, not to speak of the vine and pomegranate. It gained also—and this is the point to which we would now direct special attention—a large number of aromatic shrubs. So numerous are these, that Palestine has been included with the other countries bordering the Mediterranean, in the kingdom or region of labiate and caryophylleous plants. Labiate plants form an order remarkable for aromatic properties, and include such plants as thyme and marjoram, sage and lavender. To this peculiarity in its geographical botany Palestine owes the excellence of its honey. The rich flavour of this sweet product, deemed worthy to be compared to the aromatic honey of the classic Hybla and Hymettus, is due to the fact that both Palestine and Greece lie in the same plant region."*e*

19—22. (19) **that .. go**,*a* they are prepared against disappointment. **no .. hand**, *i.e.* unless by a mighty hand: the influence of God's judgments. (20) **I .. hand**,*b* of wisdom and power. **smite**, Egypt to be punished as well as Israel delivered. **after .. go**, when he can resist no more. (21) **favour**,*c* respect. **ye .. empty**,*d* as poor slaves without worldly substance. (22) **borrow**,*e* ask, demand; such the usual sense of the word. **jewels**, articles, vessels, valuable effects. **put .. daughters**, for the young people to carry. **ye .. Egyptians**,*f* who have these many years spoiled you: retribution.

Israel borrowing of the Egyptians.—This narrative has given rise to several objections; the conduct of the Israelites has been characterised as ungenerous, dishonest; and as it was induced by the command of God, unbelievers have not been sparing in their remarks upon that also. It may be confidently affirmed, however, that the texts, properly understood, are open to no objection, and that the command and the compliance therewith may be shown to be perfectly just. In the first place, the Hebrew word which our translators have rendered borrow, simply signifies to *ask*, to *require*, to *demand*. In the three passages relative to the transaction (chap. iii. 22; xi. 2; xii. 35), the Septuagint has, *shall ask*; and in the two former, the Vulgate has, *shall demand*; and so, indeed, it was in the English Bible, till the edition of Becke, in 1549; the Geneva, Barker's, and some others, having *aske*. The injunction, therefore, was, that the children of Israel should ask or demand of the Egyptians a recompense for their past services: or, it may be, a restoration only of that property of which they had been despoiled. It seems manifest, as Mr. Bryant has suggested, from the expression used in chap. xii. 33, " They sent them out of the land in haste," that the Egyptians never expected or wished for the return of the Israelites; and, consequently, they could not expect the return of the jewels and raiment.*g*

Persecution is threefold.—1. *Mental*, when the spirit of a man rises up and opposes another. 2. *Verbal*, when men give hard words and deal in uncharitable censures. 3. *Actual* or *open*, by the hand, such as dragging of innocent persons before the tribunal of justice (Matt. x. 18).*h*

CHAPTER THE FOURTH.

B.C. 1491.

1—5. (1) **they..voice,** *i.e.* the elders. (2) **rod,**[a] staff of authority. (3) **serpent,**[b] prob. the cobra. **Moses..it,** he started back. (4) **and..hand,** his obedience showed his strong faith. (5) **that..believe,**[c] when the elders see this sign repeated.

The wonder-working rod (v. 2).—Consider—I. What this rod was while Moses used it in a natural way. Simply a useful walking-stick, a shepherd's crook. Property, like this rod, has an earthly value. II. What it was when cast on the ground? It became a serpent. Human passions, when degraded, become as a serpent. Intellect, wrongly employed, becomes a serpent, as in Byron's case. Property, misused, becomes a serpent. III. What the rod became when taken and used as Jehovah bid His servant to employ it. It became—1. A rod. So long as Moses fled from it, so long it was a serpent. Grasping it, it changed back to a rod; 2. A wonder. It became consecrated to the highest uses.[d]

Evidence and testimony.—Evidence is whatever makes *evident*; *testimony* is that which is derived from an individual, namely, *testis* the *witness*. Evidence serves to inform and illustrate; testimony serves to confirm and corroborate; we may give evidence exclusively with regard to things; but we bear testimony with regard to persons. In all lawsuits respecting property, rights, and privileges, *evidence* must be heard in order to substantiate or invalidate a case; in personal and criminal indictments the *testimony* of witnesses is required either for or against the accused party.[e]

6—9. (6) **bosom,** fold of the dress. **hand..snow,**[a] the worst kind of leprosy. (7) **and he said,** *etc.*,[b] the instantaneous production and cure of this dread disease was a sign to the Israelites of their danger, if they resisted the command, and of their deliverance if they obeyed it.[c] (8) **they..latter,** *i.e.* probably: if not, a third is given. (9) **water..blood,** a pledge that Moses' power should prevail over the Nile, which was the boast of Egypt.

Evidence.—Evidence, in its most general sense, means the proofs which establish, or have a tendency to establish, any facts or conclusions. It may be divided into three sorts, mathematical, moral, and legal. The first is employed in the demonstrations which belong to pure mathematics; the second is employed in the general affairs of life, and in those reasonings which are applied to convince the understanding in cases not admitting of strict demonstration; the third is that which is employed in judicial tribunals for the purpose of deciding upon the rights and wrongs of litigants.[d]

10—13. (10) **eloquent,** *lit.* a man of words. **but..tongue,**[a] he prob. had an impediment in his speech, or perh. in the last forty yrs. he had lost the Egyptian language. (11) **and..said,** *etc.,* implying that He who created the organs of speech could remove imperfections if needful. (12) **teach..say,**[b] as well as give the power to say it. (13) **send..send,**[c] the reluctance of Moses finally overcome.

Moses declining the commission given him (v. 10).—I. There is

---

God gives Moses two proofs of his authority

[a] Ge. xxxviii. 18; Mic. vii. 14.

[b] "This was the symbol of royal and Divine power on the diadem of every Pharaoh." —*Spk. Comm.*, see *Tristram, Nat. Hist.*, p. 271.

[c] Jo. iii. 2.

[d] R. Thomas, M.A.

"The incredulous are the most credulous. They believe the miracles of Vespasian, in order not to believe those of Moses." —*Pascal.*

"Miracle is the pet child of faith."—*Goethe.*

[e] G. Crabb.

[a] Nu. xii. 10; 2 Ki. v. 27.

[b] De. xxxii. 39; Ma. viii. 3.

[c] *Spk. Comm.*

"The sign imported, perhaps, that the time was now at hand when God would judge the Egyptians for the death of the Hebrew infants, whose blood they had shed in the waters." —*Bush.*

[d] *Maunder.*

Moses complains that he is not eloquent

[a] Jer. i. 6.

[b] Lu. xii. 11, 12; Is. l. 4; Ac. vii. 22.

240 EXODUS. [Cap. iv. 14—20.

B.C. 1491.
c Jon. i. 3.
d C. Simeon, M.A.

"No man ever did or will become truly eloquent without being a constant reader of the Bible, and an admirer of the purity and sublimity of its language." — *F. Ames.*

"Eloquence is in the assembly, not in the speaker." — *Wm. Pitt.*

v. 13, Dr. T. Donne, i. 79.
e J. Timbs.

in man a backwardness to engage in God's service. II. We are prone to cloak this backwardness with vain excuses. III. However satisfactory our excuses may appear to ourselves, they will only bring upon us the Divine displeasure. Advice :—1. Beware of self-deception ; 2. Learn what are the duties to which you are called ; 3. Yield not to any discouragements in the way of duty.*d*

Eloquence of Demosthenes.—Demosthenes, when a youth, corrected his defective elocution by speaking with pebbles in his mouth ; he prepared himself to overcome the noise of the assembly by declaiming in stormy weather on the sea-shore of the Phalerum ; he opened his lungs by running, and extended the power of holding breath by pronouncing sentences in marching up-hill; he sometimes passed two or three months without interruption in a subterranean chamber, practising night and day, either in composition or declamation, and shaving one half of his beard, in order to disqualify himself from going abroad. In his unremitting private practice he acquired a graceful action by keeping watch on all his movements while declaiming before a tall looking-glass. More details are given by Plutarch. from Demetrius, the Phalerean, who heard them himself from Demosthenes ; and the subterranean chamber, where he practised, was shown at Athens, even in the time of Plutarch.*e*

Aaron appointed as spokesman
a Nu. xxii 33; De. xviii. 18; Jo. xvii. 8.
b Ex. vii. 1, 2.
c Dr. Fowler.

"Eloquence. to produce her full effect, should start from the head of the orator, as Pallas from the brain of Jove, ready armed and equipped. Diffidence, therefore, which is so able a mentor to the writer, would prove a dangerous counsellor for the orator." —*Colton.*

"He has oratory who ravishes his hearers while he forgets himself." *Lavater.*
d Swinton.

14—17. (14) **anger**.. Moses, bec. of his reluctance though he now complied. **know** .. **well**, implying that M. was to be a man of deeds. **behold** .. **thee**, *i.e.* is on the eve of setting out. **when** .. **heart**, after so long a separation and now learning thy mission. (15) **thy mouth**,*a* thou shalt speak to him what I teach. **his mouth**, he shall repeat what you utter. **teach** .. **do**, both the works and the words shall be from God. (16) **spokesman** .. **people**,*b* being familiar with Hebrew. (17) **rod** .. **signs**, the rod of Moses mightier than the sceptre of Pharaoh.

Homiletic hints.—Moses' sin and loss. He doubted God in his diffidence, in spite of the signs and promises. The priesthood was transferred to Aaron. Our excuses always involve loss. A duty involves the needed strength. We must trust ; God did not remove Moses' infirmity of speech ; but He went with him. God is with the mouth of His servants. He is with them for defence. Obey Him, and He will be with your mouth.*c*

The copious meaning of words.—The copiousness of meaning which words enwrap is indeed more than all that was said on thought. Children of the mind, they reflect the manifold riches of man's faculties and affections. In language is incarnated man's unconscious, passionate, creative energy. There is an endless, undefinable, tantalising charm in words. They bring the eternal provocations of personality. They come back to us with that alienated majesty which a great writer ascribes to our own thoughts. They are the sanctuary of the intuitions. They paint humanity, its thoughts, longings, aspirations, struggles, failures, —paint them on a canvas of breath, in the colours of life.*d*

Moses returns to Egypt
a Spk. Comm.
b Ex. ii. 15, 23; Ma. ii. 20.
c Ex ii 21, 22; xviii. 1.

18—20. (18) **let me go**, *etc.*, Moses not exalted above human duties. **return** .. **Egypt**, Moses' mission was a secret between him and God.*a* (19) **which** .. **life**,*b* for killing the Egyptian. (20) **sons**,*c* Gershom and Eliezer. **rod** .. **hand**, the staff of the shepherd becomes the sceptre of the shepherd's king.

Sense of duty.—You may think a sense of duty a very cold

[Cap. iv. 21—26.] EXODUS.

and uninviting thing. But only try it, and you will be astonished to find how it will evoke and sustain ardour. England not long since lost her greatest hero. Full of years and honours, Wellington went down to his grave. A nation mourned him. They mourned him because he had done so much, and done it so bravely and well for his country. He had faced perils by sea and by land. He had borne summer heat and winter cold. He had stood in "the imminent deadly breach," and lifted up an unshrinking front when the air was blackened with fiery shot and bursting shell. He had trodden down his country's foes, and driven her would-be invader into dreary exile. He had maintained her cause against foreign treachery and domestic anarchy. Well, what was it that upheld this man through his wondrous career? What mighty motive lay at the root of his stern, but unimpeachable fidelity? Why, that same cold and uninviting thing—as you deem it—a sense of duty. Duty was his watchword. Duty to a human master—to a king—a ruler. He never boasted higher motive—perhaps never thought of it. If, then, duty to an earthly superior can operate so powerfully, and evoke such steady, cheerful lifelong endurance, what may it be supposed, when properly realised, a sense of duty to God will do.*d*

21—23. (21) see .. **Pharaoh**, that P. may be without excuse. **harden,**^a suffer to grow hard as a punishment for his resistance. (22) **firstborn,**^b as comp. with other nations more beloved, as a firstborn among sons. (23) **refuse .. firstborn,**^c dear to thee as Israel to Me.

Love in the threatenings.—A shepherd, foreseeing a snowstorm that will drift deep in the hollows of the hill, where the silly sheep seeking refuge would find a grave, prepares shelter in a safe spot, and opens its door. Then he sends his dog after the wandering flock to frighten them into the fold. The bark of the dog behind them is a terror to the timid sheep, but it is at once the sure means of their safety and the mark of the shepherd's care. Without it the prepared fold and the open entrance might have proved of no avail. The terror which the shepherd sent into the flock gave the finishing touch to his tender care and effect to all that had gone before. Such, precisely, in design and effect are the terrible things of God's Word ; not one of them indicates that He is unwilling to receive sinners. They are the overflowings of Divine compassion. They are sent by the Good Shepherd to surround triflers on the brink of perdition, and compel them to come into the provided refuge ere its door be shut. The terrors of the Lord are not the salvation of men, but they have driven many to the Saviour. No part of the Bible could be wanted. A man shall live by every word that proceedeth out of the mouth of God.*d*

24—26. (24) **inn**, resting-place. **sought .. him**, perh. he had a dangerous illness wh. he perceived to be from God. (25) **took .. stone**, stone regarded by Egyptians more pure and precious than metal. **cast .. feet**, sign of her abhorrence of the rite. **surely .. me,** per. she felt that thus she had saved her husband's life. (26) **A .. art,**^a *lit.* a husband of blood: ref. to the rite.

A true woman.—Of all Shakespeare's women who best exem-

B.C. 1491.

"There is a sanctity in suffering when meekly borne. Our duty, though set about by thorns, may still be made a staff, supporting even while it tortures. Cast it away, and, like the prophet's wand, it changes to a snake."— *D. Jerrold.*

"Let men laugh when you sacrifice desire to duty if they will. You have time and eternity to rejoice in."— *Theo. Parker.*

d C. M. Merry.

God tells him what to do in Egypt
a Ex. viii. 15 ; De. ii. 20; Josh. xi. 20 ; 2 Ch. xxxvi. 13 ; Job. ix. 4 ; Pr. xxix. 1 ; Dan. v. 20 ; Is. lxiii. 17; Jas. i. 13, 14; Zech. vii. ; xi. 12; Jer. v. 3; 1 Sa. v. 6 ; De. xv. 7; Ro. ii. 5 ; He. iii. 8, 13 ; Ro. i. 28 ; 2 Th. ii. 10, 11; Jo.xii.37—40; Ac. xxviii. 26, 27; Ro. ix. 18—23; Ezek. xxxvi. 26.
b De. xiv. 1, 2; Hos. xi. 1 ; Ma. ii. 15 ; Ro. ix. 4 ; Jer. xxxi. 9; 2 Co. vi. 8; Jas. i. 18.
c Ex. xii. 29.
v. 21. T. Manton, iv. 519.
d Arnot.

Zipporah
a Ge. xvii. 14 ; Josh. v. 2, 3.

"Opposition always inflames the enthusiast, never converts him."—*Schiller.*

B.C. 1491.

"The happiness and misery of men depend no less on temper than fortune."—*Rochefoucauld.*

"There seems to have been some hesitation on the part of Zipporah; but the alternative was death or obedience."—*Bryant.*

r. 25. *J. Mede,* i. 69.

b *Gent's Mag.*

meeting of Moses and Aaron, they gather the elders of Israel

a Ex. iii. 18.

b *Dr Fowler.*

"If we set aside supernatural assistance, Moses and Aaron stand unsupported, without one requisite towards the completion of their purpose."—*Bryant.*

"It is one of the worst of errors to suppose that there is any other path of safety except that of duty."—*Nevins.*

v. 27. E. M. *Goulburn*, 205.

"There is little pleasure in the world that is true and sincere besides the pleasure of doing our duty and doing good. I am sure no other is comparable to this."—*Tillotson.*

c *Webster.*

…plify womanly obedience with womanly rationality, womanly submission with womanly spirit, and a truly feminine gentleness with genuine moral courage and philosophy—is Imogen. She has a heavenly patience, yet no tameness; she has holiest meekness and fortitude, yet no mean subserviency. Her very first speech contains the key to her character; there is in it the philosophy of courage to endure, a religious regard for duty, the purest and warmest fervour of love, and the most hopeful faith.

"My dearest husband,
I something fear my father's wrath; but nothing
(Always reserv'd my holy duty) what
His rage can do on me. You must be gone,
And I shall here abide the hourly shot
Of angry eyes: not comforted to live,
But that there is this jewel in the world
That I may see again."

That is accurately the philosophy of womanhood: bravery beneath daily infliction, gathered from hope and loving constancy.*b*

27—31. (27) **said**, perh. in a vision. **met**..**God**, Horeb, Aaron now about 83 years of age. **kissed**, Orient. form of salutation. (28) **words**..**him**, *i.e.* wh. God had charged him to do. (29) **gathered**..**Israel**, hence there must have been some organisation in Israel at this time. (30) **did**..**people**, *i.e.* the elders. (31) **people**, perh. the elders called meetings of the people. **heard,**a fr. Aaron and the elders. **visited**, in mercy. **looked**, compassionately. **they**..**worshipped**, faith, gratitude, hope.

The believing people (vv. 29—31).—Note that—I. God always furnishes sufficient evidence to justify belief. Moses was a stranger to the people: Aaron doubtless well known. He had a welcome message—deliverance. Miracles in outward form: miracles typical in character: rod changed to a serpent and back, Moses changed from a shepherd to a ruler; cleansing of leprosy, the purifying of the human for Divine use. II. Hearing precedes believing. God sent Aaron to speak. Ministers sent to preach. III. The Israelites manifest their faith publicly. We must confess Christ in token of faith. IV. God prepares the way for the reception of His truth. Aaron called to meet Moses. God's Spirit precedes and accompanies the truth we utter. V. Faith secures deliverance. By it the Israelites secured theirs. So must we by ours. It is unto us according to our faith.*b*

The sense of duty.—There is no evil that we cannot either face or fly from, but the consciousness of duty disregarded. A sense of duty pursues us ever. It is omnipresent, like the Deity. If we take to ourselves the wings of the morning, and dwell in the uttermost parts of the sea, duty performed or duty violated is still with us, for our happiness or our misery. If we say, the darkness shall cover us—in the darkness, as in the light, our obligations are yet with us. We cannot escape their power nor fly from their presence. They are with us in this life, will be with us at its close; and in that scene of inconceivable solemnity which yet lies further onward, we shall still find ourselves surrounded by the consciousness of duty, to pain us wherever it has been violated, and to console us so far as God may have given us grace to perform it.*c*

CHAPTER THE FIFTH.

B.C. 1491.

1—4. (1) **Moses .. Pharaoh,** prob. accompanied by the elders. **let .. wilderness,**^a saying what he was bid. (2) **know .. Lord,**^b your God is not Egypt's god. (3) **let .. God,** see Ex. iii. 18. (4) **let,** hinder. **get .. burdens,** they are contemptuously ordered to proceed with their work.

God entitled to our obedience (v. 2).—We ought to obey God, because He is—I. The benevolent Creator of the Universe. II. The constant Preserver of His creatures. III. The Perfect Governor of all. IV. The merciful Redeemer of sinners.^c— *Speak, Lord* (v. 2).—I. Who is the Lord? 1. Creator; 2. Benefactor; 3. Redeemer; 4. King. II. How may we hear His voice? In—1. Nature; 2. Providence; 3. Our spiritual perceptions; 4. The Bible.^d

Moses and Aaron before Pharaoh.—Pharaoh's heart hardened. —Hardened by threats which provoked his pride, and by forbearance which led him to presume. Yet warning and mercy ought to lead to repentance. The same sun melts the ice, but hardens the clay. *The rival wonders.*—The contention may seem puerile to our notions, but the Egyptians would think otherwise. The lesson was adapted to those who heard it. *Courage and fidelity of Moses and Aaron.*—Egypt was the great empire of the world, and Pharaoh the child of the sun, the favourite of the gods, the great presiding genius of Egypt. We may compare the moral courage of the Hebrew brothers with that of the Scythian ambassador before Alexander. Mutius Scævola before Porsenna, Knox before Queen Mary and her lords. *The obstinacy of pride.* —*Flecti non frangi* ("To be bent, not broken") is a common motto. Pride disdains either to bend or break. It is the spirit of Satan. See the lines which Milton puts into the mouth of the arch-fiend, in *Paradise Lost.*

5—9. (5) **many,** notwithstanding all efforts to reduce the number. **make .. burdens,** by exciting the hope amongst them of this pilgrimage. (6) **taskmasters,** exactors, overseers. (7) **straw,** needful to make the clay hold together until it was dried. **let .. themselves,** hence the burden increased as the straw became scarcer. (8) **tale,** number, amount. **for .. idle,** a pretence for increasing their burdens. **let .. God,** thus he would cure them of their religious desires. (9) **let .. words,** *lit.* words of lying: he regarded them as lying, canting hypocrites.

Bricks without straw.—Some of the most ancient buildings in Egypt were constructed of bricks, not burned but dried in the sun. They were made of clay, or more commonly of mud, mixed with straw chopped in small pieces. An immense quantity of straw must have been wanted for the work in which the Israelites were engaged, and their labours must have been more than doubled by this requisition. In a papyrus of the 19th dynasty the writer complains, "I have no one to help me in making bricks, and no straw." The expression at that time was evidently proverbial—whether or not as a reminiscence of the Israelites may be questioned. They had to go into the fields,

a Ex. iii. 18.
b Job xxi. 15.
c Dr. Coffin.
d W. W. Wythe.

they appeal to Pharaoh

"The sun by the action of heat makes wax moist and mud dry, hardening the one while it softens the other, by the same operation producing exactly opposite results; thus, from the long-suffering of God, some derive benefit and others harm, some are softened, while others are hardened."—*Theodoret.*

"In this first application to Pharaoh, we observe that proper respectful submission which is due from subjects to their sovereign."— *Dodd.*

Pharaoh's refusal and increased cruelty

Tale, that which is told; told or counted off; number, reckoning. A.S. *talu;* Dutch, *taal;* A.S. *tal,* number, tælean, to reckon; fr. tell, to number.

"The bricks of the first pyramid at Dashour are of fine clay from the Nile, mingled with chopped straw. The intermixture gives the bricks an astonishing durability."— *Kitto.*

"Tyranny and

b.c. 1491.

"anarchy are never far a-sunder." — *Benthem.*
"Tyranny sways, not as it hath power, but as it is suffered." — *Shakespeare, a Speak. Com.*

bricks without straw

a "Their sufferings must have been severe; since at that season the pestilential sand-wind blows over Egypt some fifty days, hence its name *Chamsin*." — *Spk. Com.*

"It will be known to our readers, that even at present the rule of the stick is generally prevalent in many parts of the East. Neither rank, learning, nor old age can protect against the ruthless tyranny of the stick." — *Kalisch.*

the Israelites remonstrate

Minish, Lat. *minuere*, to diminish, through the O. Fr. *menuiser*, wh. corresponds with the Ital. *minuzzare*.

a C. Simeon, M.A. "Tyranny, in a word, is a farce got up for the entertainment of poor human nature; and it might pass very well if it did not so often turn into a tragedy." — *Hazlitt.*
"Power, unless managed with gentleness and discretion, does but make a man the more hated,

after the reaping was done, to gather the stubble left by the reapers, who then, as at present in Egypt, cut the stalks close to the ears. They had then to chop it into morsels of straw before it could be mixed with clay. This implies that some time must have elapsed before Moses went again to Pharaoh, and it also marks the season of the year—viz., early spring, after the harvest, probably the end of April. Their sufferings must have been severe, since at that season the pestilential sand-wind blows over Egypt some fifty days.*a*

10–14. (10, 11) **taskmasters .. spake,** *etc.,* the myrmidons of a despot, quite willing to do his behest; jacks-in-office. (12) **stubble,** short straw left after reaping.*a* (13) **hasted,** pressed, drove. **fulfil .. tasks,** *lit.* the matter of a day in his day. (14) **officers .. Israel,** Hebrews by birth. **beaten,** made responsible for the amount of work done.

Death of tyrants.—Hearing a whole choir of birds chirping merrily together, my curiosity was excited to inquire into the occasion of their convocation and merriment, when I quickly perceived a dead hawk in the bush, about which they made such a noise, seeming to triumph at the death of an enemy. I could not blame them for singing the knell of one who, like a cannibal, was wont to feed upon their living bodies, tearing them limb from limb, and scaring them with his frightful appearance. Over this bird, which was so formidable when alive, the most timid wren or titmouse did not now fear to chirp and hop. This occurrence brought to my mind the case of tyrants and oppressors. When living, they are the terror of mankind; but when dead, they are the objects of general contempt and scorn. "When the wicked perish, there is shouting" (Prov. xi. 10). The death of Nero was celebrated by the Romans with bonfires and plays: birds ate the naked flesh of Pompey: Alexander lay unburied thirty days: but a useful and holy life is generally closed by an honourable and lamented death.

15–19. (15) **wherefore .. servants?** demanding impossible results. (16) **fault .. people,** they perh. did not believe that the command was Pharaoh's. (17, 18) **he .. said,** *etc.,* a fair example of a despot's conduct. (19) **did .. case,** when the whip fell on their own shoulders. **minish,** obsol. wd. = diminish.

The opposition made to religion (vv. 17, 18).—I. What that sacrifice is which God requires at our hands—1. A humble; 2. A believing; 3. A thankful; 4. An obedient, heart. II. The light in which it is regarded by an ungodly world. With—1. Contempt; 2. Calumny; 3. Oppression. Address—(1) The opposers of true religion: (2) Those who meet with persecution for righteousness' sake.*a*

The officers' appeal to Pharaoh.—"*Lit. But* [or *And*] *sin of thy people.*" This clause has been variously rendered and understood. The ancient versions take "sin" here in the sense of iniquity or injustice. *And thou dost injustice to thy people,* or, *thy people are treated unjustly.* But the "people" here are evidently in contrast with those who speak of themselves as "the servants" of Pharaoh; and as the latter are the Hebrews, the former must be Pharaoh's own people, the Egyptians. Adopting this reference, the words may mean, "We make our complaint to thee because thy people sin in maltreating us thus, and it is for thee to see that their sin is corrected;" or they may mean, "By thus acting thy people are contracting guilt, which may bring punishment on them and thy kingdom;" or they may mean, "By thus dealing with us thy people sin against us," *i.e.* treat us iniquitously. This last way of understanding the words brings out a meaning much the same as that of the older versions, without, like them, departing from the proper reference of the terms. Some interpreters take "sin" here as a verb, and render, "And thy people sin."[b]

20—23. (20) **they .. Pharaoh**, *i.e.* the officers of v. 15: M. and A. prob. waiting to hear the result of the interview. (21) **because .. Pharaoh**, a most unjust crimination. **put .. us**, a prov. express. = give a plausible pretext for destroying us. (22) **Moses,** *etc.*, the leader of the people carries their griefs to head-quarters. (23) **for .. since**, *etc.*, M. in the impetuosity of his feelings verges upon irreverence.

The burdens increased.—Note that—I. Benefactors may expect misrepresentation. Moses was censured; Christ rejected by His own. The enemy will slander. Our hope is in working only for God. II. Sin asks to be let alone. Pharaoh blamed Moses; Ahab blamed Elijah; the Jews blamed the disciples. III. Sin becomes more terrible with age. Pharaoh grew more exacting, and the people weaker; he answers prayers with falsehoods and insults. Sin toys with youth, but scourges manhood. IV. All appeal must be made to God. Moses turned to God; he did not censure the elders. V. It is darkest just before day. Sin grows worse till it breaks down. It threatens in order to drown conscience.[a]

Danger of murmuring.—I have read of Cæsar that, having prepared a great feast for his nobles and friends, it so fell out that the day appointed was so extremely foul, that nothing could be done to the honour of the meeting: whereupon he was so displeased and enraged, that he commanded all them that had bows to shoot up their arrows at Jupiter, their chief god, as in defiance of him for that rainy weather; which when they did, their arrows fell short of heaven, and fell upon their own heads, so that many of them were very sorely wounded. So all our murmurings, which are as so many arrows shot at God Himself, will return upon our own pates' hearts: they reach not Him, but they will hit us: they hurt not Him, but they will wound us. Therefore it is better to be mute than to murmur: it is dangerous to provoke a "consuming fire."[b]

B.C. 1491.

No intervals of good humour, no starts of bounty, will atone for tyranny and oppression."—*J. Collier.*
[b] *Dr. W. Alexander.*

they censure Moses and Aaron

[a] *Dr. Fowler.*

"It is harder to avoid censure than to gain applause; for this may be done by one great or wise action in an age. But to escape censure a man must pass his whole life without saying or doing one ill or foolish thing."—*Hume.*

"To arrive at perfection, a man should have very sincere friends, or inveterate enemies; because he would be made sensible of his good or ill conduct either by the censures of the one or the admonitions of the others."—*Diogenes.*

vv. 22, 23. *F. D. Maurice, Old Test.,* 140.
[b] *T. Brooks.*

CHAPTER THE SIXTH.

1—3. (1) **for .. hand**,[a] *i.e.* compelled by the power of God. (2) **Lord**,[b] Jehovah. (3) **by .. Almighty**, El-Shaddai. **but .. them**,[c] *i.e.* its full meaning was not disclosed.

The Divine name.—Early English history informs us that some bloodthirsty persecutors were marching on a band of Christians. The Christians, seeing them approaching, marched out towards them, and, at the top of their voices, shouted "Hallelujah, hallelujah!" (Praise Jehovah.) The name of the Lord being

God encourages Moses

[a] Ex. iii. 20; xii. 21, 33, 39.
[b] Ge xvii. 1; Jo. viii. 58; Rev. i. 4.
[c] Ge. xxviii. 16; Ex. iii. 14; Ps. lxviii. 4; lxxxiii. 18.

b.c. 1491.

"They that deny a God destroy man's nobility; for certainly man is like the beasts in his body; and if he is not like God in his spirit, he is an ignoble creature."—*Bacon*.

He repeats His ancient covenant
a Ge. xv. 18; xxvi. 3; xxxv. 12.
b Ps. cv. 8 12; cvi. 44, 45; Lu. i. 68, 72—75.
c De. xxvi. 8; Ps. cxxxvi. 10—12; Ex. xv. 12; De. vii. 8.
d De. iv. 20; vii. 6; xxvi. 18; 2 Sa. vii. 24; Jer. xxxi. 31—34; Hos. i. 10.
e Nu. xxiii. 19; 1 Sa. xv. 29.

"It is the nature of every artificer to tender and esteem his own work; and if God should not love His creature it would reflect some disparagement upon His workmanship, that He should make anything that He could not own. God's power never produces what His goodness cannot embrace. God, oftentimes, in the same man, distinguishes between the sinner and the creature; as a creature He can love him, while as a sinner He does afflict Him."—*South*.
f Dr. Stanley.

the Israelites do not believe Moses
a Ac. vii. 25.

presented, the rage of the persecutors abated. Josephus says that the Great Alexander, when on his triumphal march, being met near Jerusalem by the Jewish high priest, on whose mitre was engraved the name Jehovah, "approached by himself, and adored that name," and was disarmed of his hostile intent. There was significance and power in the glorious old name as written by the Jews. But the name of Jesus is now far more mighty in the world than was the name of Jehovah in these earlier ages.

4—8. (4) **covenant**,[a] *lit.* have erected, have made to stand. **give .. strangers**, *i.e.* in persons of descendants. (5) **remembered**,[b] wh. suffering Israel may have thought I had forgotten. (6) **Lord .. Egyptians**, I will do this as surely as I am the unchangeable Lord. **with .. arm**,[c] *i.e.* by putting forth special and vigorous effort. (7) **people**,[d] nation. **I .. God**, to gather, build up, protect. **know**, by incontrovertible signs. (8) **land .. Jacob**,[e] *see* Ge. xxii. 16 ff.

The plagues of Egypt.—It is impossible, as we read the description of the plagues, not to feel how much of force is added to it by a knowledge of the peculiar customs and character of the country in which they occurred. It is not an ordinary river that is turned into blood; it is the sacred, beneficent, solitary Nile, the very life of the State and of the people, in its streams, and canals and tanks, and vessels of wood, and vessels of stone, then, as now, used for the filtration of the delicious water from the sediment of the river-bed. It is not an ordinary nation that is struck by the mass of putrefying vermin lying in heaps by the houses, the villages, and the fields, or mutiplying out of the dust of the desert sands on each side of the Nile valley. It is the cleanliest of all the ancient nations, clothed in white linen—anticipating, in their fastidious delicacy and ceremonial purity, the habits of modern and Northern Europe. It is not the ordinary cattle that died in the field, or ordinary fish that died in the river, or ordinary reptiles that were overcome by the rod of Aaron. It is the sacred goat of Mendes, the ram of Ammon, the calf of Heliopolis, the bull Apis, the crocodile of Ombos, the carp of Latopolis. It is not an ordinary land, of which the flax and the barley, and every green thing in the trees, and every herb of the field, are smitten by the two great calamities of storm and locust. It is the garden of the ancient Eastern world, the long line of green meadow and corn-field, and the groves of palm, and sycamore, and fig-tree, from the cataracts to the Delta, doubly refreshing from the desert which it intersects, doubly marvellous from the river whence it springs. If these things were calamities anywhere, they were truly "signs and wonders"—speaking signs and oracular wonders—in such a land as "the land of Ham." In whatever way we unite the Hebrew and the Egyptian accounts, there can be no doubt that the exodus was a crisis in Egyptian as well as in Hebrew history—"a nail struck into the coffin of the Egyptian monarchy."[f]

9—13. (9) **anguish, shortness**: their hope could not reach so far; they had become dejected and discouraged. (10, 11) **spake**, *etc.*, this the second appeal to Pharaoh. (12) **children .. me**,[a] my own countrymen do not believe. **how .. me**, who am a foreigner, one of a nation of slaves. **who .. lips?** of slow utterance, of feeble speech. (13) **spake**, *etc.*, ref. to vv. 10, 11.

The despondency of Israel (v. 9).—Let us consider—I. The conduct of the Israelites on this occasion. The testimony of Moses was, it every respect, worthy of credit, nor could anything be conceived more suited to their necessities. Yet would not the people receive, or even "hearken to" his words. II. The instruction to be derived from it. We may notice from hence—1. The weakness of the human mind; 2. The proper office of faith; 3. The excellency of the Gospel dispensation.[b]

Causes of sorrow.—We fancy that all our afflictions are sent us directly from above; sometimes we think it in piety and contrition, but oftener in moroseness and discontent. It would be well, however, if we attempted to trace the causes of them: we should probably find their origin in some region of the heart which we never had well explored, or in which we had secretly deposited our worst indulgences. The clouds that intercept the heavens from us come not from the heavens, but from the earth.[c]

14—20. (14) **heads**, governors, chiefs, elders. **of.. houses**,[a] *i.e.* the houses of Moses and Aaron. **sons**, *etc.*, see Ge. xlvi. 9. (15) **the.. Simeon**, *etc.*, see Ge. xlvi. 10. (16) **of .. Levi**, see Ge. xlvi. 11. (17) **Libni**[b] (*white*). **Shimi**[c] (*renowned*), or Shimei. (18) **Amram**[d] (*red*), father of Moses, Aaron, and Miriam. **Ighar** (*oil*). **Hebron** (*alliance*). **Uzziel** (*might of God*). (19) **Mahali** (*sickly*), also Ma. **Mushi** (*felt out by Jehovah*). (20) **Jochebed**[e] (whose *glory is Jehovah*). **his..wife**, at this time not within the prohibited degrees of sanguinity.

The study of history.—To study history is to study literature. The biography of a nation embraces all its works. No trifle is to be neglected. A mouldering medal is a letter of twenty centuries. Antiquities, which have been beautifully called history defaced, compose its fullest commentary. In these wrecks of many storms, which time washes to the shore, the scholar looks patiently for treasures. The painting round a vase, the scribble on a wall, the wrath of a demagogue, the drollery of a farce, the point of an epigram—each possesses its own interest and value. A fossil court of law is dug out of an orator: and the Pompeii of Greece is discovered in the Comedies of Aristophanes.[f]

21—27. (21) **Korah**[a] (*ice, hail, or baldness*), also Core.[b] **Nepheg** (*sprout*). **Zithri**, incorrectly printed for Zichri (*remembered, renowned*). (22) **Mishael** (*who is what God is?*). **Elzaphan** (*whom God protects*), also Elizaphan.[c] **Zithri** (*protection of Jehovah*). (23) **Elisheba** (*God her oath*). **Amminadab** (*kindred of the prince*). **Naashon**[d] (*enchanter*). **Nadab**[e] (*spontaneous, liberal*). **Abihu**[f] (to whom *He. i.e.* God, is *father*). **Eleazar**[g] (whom *God helps*). **Ithamar**[h] (*palmcoast*). (24) **Assir** (*captive*). **Elkanah** (whom *God created*). **Abiasaph** (*father of gathering*). or Ebiasaph. (25) **Putiel** (*devoted to God*). **Phinehas**[i] (*mouth of brass*). (26, 27) **these..said**, v. 14. **armies**,[k] not a confused multitude but organised host.

National characteristics.—A nation cannot be affected by any vice or weakness without expressing it, legibly and for ever,

B.C. 1491.

b C. Simeon, M.A.
"Sorrow is a kind of rust of the soul, which every new idea contributes in its passage to scour away. It is the putrefaction of stagnant life, and is remedied by exercise and motion."—*Johnson.*

"Sorrow breaks seasons and reposing hours, makes the night morning, and the noontide night."—*Shakespeare.*
c W. S. Landor.

the houses of Moses and Aaron
a "The genealogy of Moses and Aaron, following upon the solemn mention of the eminent brothers.... The genealogy mainly concerns Aaron, as the elder brother; and the progenitor of the Jewish priesthood."—*Alford*; see also *Spk. Comm., Bush*, etc.
b Nu. iii. 18.
c Nu. iii. 18; 1 Ch. xxiii. 7, 10.
d Nu. iii. 19; xxvi. 58, 59; 1 Ch. vi. 2, 3, xxiii. 12, 13, xxiv. 20.
e Ex. ii. 1—10.
f Willmott.

a Nu. xvi., xxvi. 9—11, xxvii. 3.
b Ju. ii.
c Nu. iii. 30.
d Nu. i. 7, ii. 3, vii. 12, 17, x. 14; Ru. iv. 20; Lu. iii. 32.
e Nu. iii. 2, 4, xxvi. 60, 61; 1 Ch. xxiv. 1, 2.
f Nu. iii. 2; Ex. xxiv. 1, 9, 10; Lev. viii. 9.
g Ex. xxviii. 1; Nu. iii. 32, xx. 28,

EXODUS. [Cap. vii. 1–7.

B.C. 1491.
xxvi. 1, xxvii. 18
—23; Josh. xiv.
1, xvii. 4, xxi. 1,
xxiv. 33.
h Nu. xxvi. 60;
Ex. xxviii. 1,
xxxviii. 21.
i Nu. xxv. 6—16,
xxxi. 6; Ps. cvi.
30; Josh. xxii.
13, 34; Jud. xx.
28. Traditionary
tomb of P. shown
at *Awertoh*, 4 ms.
fr. Nablous.
k Nu. xxxiii. 1, 2;
Ps. lxxvii. 20;
Ex. xlii. 18.

"Nationality is
the aggregated
individuality of
the greatest men
of the nation."
Kossuth.

"Man is physically as well as
metaphysically a
thing of shreds
and patches, borrowed unequally
from good and
bad ancestors,
and a misfit
from the start."
—*Emerson*.
l Ruskin.

Moses' commission and hesitation
a Jer. xxiii. 28;
Mu. xxviii. 20; 1
Sa. iii. 18.

"Whenever I
contemplate
man in the actual world or the
Ideal, I am lost
amidst the infinite multiformity of his life,
but always end
in wonder at the
essential unity of
his nature."—*H.
Giles*.
b Spencer.

B.C. 1491.

**age of Moses
and Aaron**
a Ex. iv. 16; Lu.
xxi. 15; Jer. i. 10.

either in bad art or by want of art; and there is no national virtue, small or great, which is not manifestly expressed in all the art which circumstances enable the people possessing that virtue to produce. Take, for instance, your great English virtue of enduring and patient courage. You have at present in England only one art of any consequence—that is iron-working. You know thoroughly well how to cast and hammer iron. Now, do you think in those masses of lava which you build volcanic cones to melt, and which you forge at the mouths of the Infernos you have created—do you think on those iron plates your courage and endurance are not written for ever, not merely with an iron pen, but on iron parchment? And take a..so your great English vice—European vice—vice of all the world—vice of all other worlds that roll or shine in heaven, bearing with them yet the atmosphere of hell—the vice of jealousy, which brings competition into your commerce, treachery into your councils, and dishonour into your wars—that vice which has rendered for you and for your next neighbouring nation the daily occupations of existence no longer possible, but with the mail upon your breasts and the sword loose in its sheath; so that, at least, you have realised for all the multitudes of the two great peoples who lead the so-called civilisation of the earth—you have realised for them all, I say, in person and in policy, what was once true only of the rough border riders of your Cheviot hills—

"They carved at the meal
With gloves of steel,
And they drank the red wine through the helmet barr'd."

Do you think that this national shame and dastardliness of heart are not written as legibly on every rivet of your iron armour as the strength of the right hands that forged it?'

28—30. **and .. pass**, *etc.*, these vv. a rep. of vv. 10—12, the intervening genealogy being parenthetical. **all .. thee**,[a] no more, no less.

Examples of humility.—The wisest of all the philosophers made this profession : "This I know, that I know nothing.' Origen, the most learned of all the Greek fathers, made this confession : " I am not ignorant of my own ignorance." And the most judicious of all the Latin fathers was the humblest ; for, in his heat of contention with Jerome, he acknowledged him his better. Though the dignity of a bishop exceed that of a priest, yet Priest Jerome is greater than Bishop Augustine. Theodosius was the noblest of all the Roman emperors. His motto was, "Malo membrum esse ecclesiæ quam caput imperii." It was greater honour to him to be a member of the Church than the head of the Empire. And Paul, though nothing inferior to the chief of the Apostles, yet was least in his own eyes.[b]

CHAPTER THE SEVENTH.

1—7. (1) **made**, appointed. **thee .. Pharaoh**, doing the works of a god. **prophet**,[a] interpreter, spokesman. (2) **all .. thee**, withholding nothing. (3) **harden**, as the result of protracted obstinacy. **wonders**, persuasive signs. (4) **shall**, **will**, predictive. **that,** *etc.*. *lit.* and I will give my hand. (5) **know** . . **Lord,**[b] by indubitable signs. (6) **did** . . **they,** the obedience of faith. (7) **and Moses,** *etc.*,[c] their venerable appearance would inspire confidence in their wisdom.

God hardening Pharaoh's heart (v. 3).—We shall endeavour to—I. Explain the conduct of God, as it is stated in the text.— 1. He left Pharaoh to the influence of his own corruptions ; 2. He suffered such events to occur as should give scope for the exercise of those corruptions ; 3. He gave Satan permission to exert his influence over him. II. Vindicate it. It was—1. Righteous, as it respected the individual himself ; 2. Merciful, as it respected the universe at large. It has shown us—(1) The extreme depravity of the human heart. (2) Our need of Divine grace. (3) The danger of fighting against God. (4) The obligations we lie under to God, for the long-suffering He has already exercised towards us.[d]

Hardness of heart.—Lightfoot says : "I have heard it more than once and again, from the sheriffs who took all the gunpowder plotters, and brought them up to London, that every night when they came to their lodging by the way, they had their music and dancing a good part of the night. One would think it strange that men in their case should be so merry." More marvellous still is it that those between whom and death there is but a step, should sport away their time as if they should live on for ages. Though the place of torment is within a short march of all unregenerate men, yet see how they make mirth, grinning and jesting between the jaws of hell ![e]

8–13. (8, 9) **when** . . **you,** they are forewarned of Pharaoh's demand, and instructed what to do. **thou** . . **Aaron,** Moses as a God in the presence of Pharaoh was to issue commands. **serpent,** not *nahash* but *tannin, i.e.* large serpent or dragon, perh. crocodile. (10) **they** . . **commanded,** Pharaoh having demanded a sign. (11) **sorcerers,** wizards, jugglers : he prob. regarded M. and A. as mere jugglers, and confronted them with the skilful wizards of his court. **now** . . **enchantments,** still a common trick in the E.[a] (12) **for** . . **rod,** serpents numbed, appearing like rods. **and** . . **serpents,**[b] *i.e.* the serpents resumed their usual appearance and motions. **but** . . **rods,** his only remaining. (13) **and** . . **heart,** or, Pharaoh's heart was hardened : he was doubtless confounded, though not convinced.

The two kingdoms (vv. 10–13).—I. The monarchs : God and Satan. II. Their agents : angels and devils. III. Their characters : righteousness and sinfulness. IV. Their fruit : happiness and misery. V. Their work : blessing and cursing. Choose ye between them. *The double system of wonders and miracles.*— I. At the exodus, Moses and the magicians. II. In the time of the prophets, David and Saul. III. In the time of Christ, the apostles, and those possessed with demons. IV. In later times the Church and the man of sin.[c]

A good heart.—There was a great master among the Jews, who bid his scholars consider and tell him what was the best way wherein a man should always keep. One came and said that there was nothing better than a *good eye,* which is, in their language, a liberal and contented disposition. Another said, a *good companion* is the best thing in the world. A third said, a *good neighbour* was the best thing he could desire ; and a fourth pre-

---

B.C. 1491.

[b] Ps. ix. 16.

[c] Ac. vii. 23, 30; De. xxix. 5 ; xxxi. 2; xxxiii. 7.

[d] C. Simeon, M.A.

"The human heart is like a millstone in a mill; when you put wheat under it it turns, and grinds, and bruises the wheat into flour; if you put no wheat in, it still grinds on ; but, then, it is itself it grinds, and slowly wears away."—*Luther.*

"The wrinkles of the heart are more indelible than those of the brow." — *Mde. Deluzy.*

[e] *Spurgeon.*

Aaron's rod becomes a serpent

[a] "It is a common trick to handle venomous serpents, and benumb them, so that they are motionless and stiff as rods." — *Spk. Comm.*

[b] Ge. xli. 8; De. ii. 2 ; 2 Ti. iii. 8.

[c] *Dr. Fowler.*

"The heart of a man is a short word,—a small substance, scarce enough to give a kite a meal; yet great in capacity, yea, so indefinite in desire that the round globe of the world cannot fill the three corners of it. When it desires more, and cries, 'Give, give!' I will set it over to the infinite good, where the

B.C. cir. 1191.

more it hath, it may desire more, and see more to be desired."— *Bp. Hall.*
"If wrong our hearts, our heads are right in vain."— *Young.*
d *Bp. Patrick.*

the ten plagues

the first plague

the Nile changed into blood

a Ex. v. 2.

b Rev. xvi. 4, 6. Wonderful fertility of this idolatrous land is illus. by the fact that though Egypt contains 115,200 sq. geog. miles, only 9,582 watered by Nile; and of these only 5,626 under cultivation.

c *Richardson.*

a Ps. lxxviii. 44; cv. 29; Jo. ii. 7, 9.

b *G. Wellford, M.A.*

"The water of the Nile was sent, as a present fit for royalty to receive, to distant kings and queens. In the present day, the Arabs will even excite thirst by eating salt, in order to gratify themselves with it. On journeys and pilgrimages nothing is spoken of with so much enthusiasm as the delight of again drinking of the great river on their return. They are accustomed to

ferred a man that could foresee things to come; that is, a *wise person.* But, at last, came in one Eleazar, and he said, a *good heart* was better than them all. True, said the master, thou hast comprehended in two words all that the rest have said. For he that hath a good heart, will be both contented, and a good companion, and a good neighbour, and easily see what is fit to be done by him. Let every man then seriously labour to find in himself a sincerity and uprightness of heart at all times, and that will save him abundance of other labour.*d*

14—18. (14) **hardened,** Heb. *kâbed,* is heavy. (15) **he .. water,** prob. to pay religious adoration to the Nile. (16) **Lord .. thee,***a* proved as well as said. (17) **in .. Lord,** dispensing with entreaties, M. now uses threats. **they .. blood,***b* the sacred river deemed a god. (18) **fish .. die,** destruction of an important article of diet. **and .. stink,** putrescent. **lothe .. river,** *lit.* shall be wearied to drink, *etc., i.e.* wearied by efforts to purify the water.

The water of the Nile.—The water is fresh, without any brackish intermixture; but the overflowing stream being then at its height, was deeply impregnated with mud; that, however, did not deter the thirsty mariners from drinking of it profusely. I shall never forget the eagerness with which they let down and pulled up the pitcher, and drank of its contents, whistling and smacking their fingers, and calling out "*Tayeep! tayrep!*" Good! good! as if bidding defiance to the whole world to produce such another draught. Most of the party, induced by their example, tasted also of their far-famed waters, and pronounced them of the finest relish, notwithstanding the pollution of clay and mud with which they were contaminated: a decision which we never had occasion to revoke. The water in Albania is good, but the water of the Nile is the finest in the world.*c*

19—21. (19) **stretch .. waters,** *etc.,* wave it towards the waters of Egypt. **streams,** tributaries of Nile. **rivers,** canals. **ponds,** cisterns, tanks. **pools,** reservoirs. **vessels .. stone,** filtering apparatus, etc. (20) **and .. blood,***a* waters previously stained with the blood of Hebrew innocents. (21) **fish .. died,** *see* v. 18.

The plague of blood.—The circumstances to be noticed in the first plague inflicted on Egypt are the following:—I. This was not the first notice given to Pharaoh of the will of God, that His people should be free from their captivity in Egypt. He had received a warning, and that warning had been enforced by a miracle, before any judgment was inflicted on him. II. This first plague was inflicted on the "waters that were in the river"—in the river Nile. III. It was performed "in the sight of Pharaoh, and the sight of his servants." The negotiation between the servants of God and Pharaoh was a public affair. IV. It was imitated by the magicians. God had His design in this; He intended to try the king's disposition. V. Its effect was to harden Pharaoh's heart. There was on his part—1. A great want of serious consideration; 2. A wilful avoiding of the truth; 3. Companionship with wickedness. Improvement:—(1) Contemplate the power of God. (2) Remember the mutability of all earthly things. (3) Beware of inattention and hardness of heart under God's reproofs.*b*

The Nile turned into blood.—This miracle bore a certain resemblance to natural phenomena, and therefore was one which Pharaoh might see with amazement and dismay, yet without complete conviction. It is well known that before the rise the water of the Nile is green, and unfit to drink. About the end of June it becomes yellow, and gradually reddish, like ochre. This effect has been generally attributed to the red earth brought down from Sennaar, but Ehrenberg proves that it is owing to the presence of microscopic cryptogams and *infusoria*. Late travellers say that at such seasons the broad turbid tide has a striking resemblance to a river of blood. The supernatural character of the visitation was attested by the connection of the change with the words and acts of Moses, and by its effects. It killed the fishes, and made the water unfit for use.*c*

22—25. (22) **magicians .. enchantments**, but the effect not described : perh. the miracle was imitated on a small scale. (23) **neither .. also**, to consider and learn. (24) **digged .. drink**, *see "lothe,"* v. 18. (25) **seven .. river**, time enough for all Egypt to suffer intensely for lack of water.

Insensibility (v. 22).—Subjects to which it is of supreme importance that our affections should be directed, and concerning which no charge of insensibility should be against us.—I. That great alteration of the soul, without which it plainly is not, and cannot be right and safe towards God, and in its own highest interests. II. The right and effectual manner of apprehending and feeling with respect to the work of our Redeemer : a full sense that without Him all is lost, and a cordial committing of the soul to Him. III. The being placed in a right state of mind towards our fellow-creatures. IV. The being habitually in such a state that it shall be of no *essential* importance *when* the end of life may come.*a*

Notes on the first plague.—(1) The Nile the *only* river in Egypt ; and excepting what water could be obtained by digging, the only source from which water could be obtained ; (2) The Nile held sacred, as also the fish and crocodiles found in it. Thus what was idolised was smitten. Show how this may be the case with people now, even with children. (3) Pharaoh had stained the waters of the Nile with the blood of the children of Israel. Now the river should be a reproof to him.—Here see a retributive justice. So God speaks to us—"Be sure your sin will find you out." (4) The removal of the plague after seven days. Hence see the forbearance of God, and the duty of man to submit.

B.C. *cir.* 1491.

say that if Mahomet had once tasted the stream, he would have asked an immortality on earth, that he might enjoy it for ever."—*Topics.*

c Spk. Com.

a J. Foster.

"On some hearts, 'God's warnings make no more lasting impression than the paddle-wheels on the water—creating a violent agitation for a few minutes, leaving a whitened track for a brief space longer, which melting away from view, all becomes as it had been before.'"

"Obstinacy is ever most positive when it is most in the wrong."—*Med. Necker.*

"Pride is a vice not only dreadfully mischievous in human society, but perhaps of all others the most insuperable bar to real inward improvement."—*Mrs. E. Carter.*

CHAPTER THE EIGHTH.

1—7. (1) **go**, *etc.*, God speaks bef. He strikes. (2) **smite .. borders**, = the entire land. **frogs**, two species in Egypt, the *rana nilotica* and the *rana mosaica* ; this latter now called *dofda.a* (3) **river .. abundantly**, *lit.* shall swarm with frogs. **bedchamber**, recesses on the ground-floor. **ovens**, earthen pots sunk in the ground. (4) **frogs .. servants**, the Egyptians were a scrupulously clean people. (5, 6) **frogs**, a harmless animal multiplied becomes an intolerable nuisance. (7) **magicians**, *etc.*, they seem to have had power to increase the plague,

B.C. 1491.

the second plague

frogs are sent

a "This corresp. to the Heb. wd. used in this and no other passage, except in the Psalms taken

EXODUS. [Cap. viii. 8–15.

B.C. 1491.

for it; it is not a gen. design., but restricted to the species, and prob. of Egyptian origin; they are small, do not leap much, are much like toads, and fill the whole country with their croakings. They are gen. consumed by the ibis, which thus preserves the land fr. the stench desc. r. 14."—*Spk. Com.*
b *M. Henry.*
c *Spk. Comm.*

a Ex. ix. 28; x. 17; 1 Ki. xiii. 6; Ac. viii. 24.

b Is. xlvi. 9; Ps. lxxxvi. 8; Jer. x. 6, 7; De. xxxiii. 26; xxii. 31; 2 Sa. vii. 22; 1 Ch. xvii. 20.

c Mn. v. 44; 1 Sa. xii. 23.

d Jas. v. 6.

e Is. xxvi. 10; Ec. viii. 11.

f *J. Thornton.*

"Obstinacy is certainly a great vice; and in the changeful state of political affairs, it is frequently the cause of great mischief. It happens, however, very unfortunately, that almost the whole line of the great and masculine virtues- constancy, gravity, magnanimity, fortitude, fidelity, and firmness — are closely allied to this disagreeable quality, of which you have so just an abhorrence; and in their excess all these virtues very easily fail into it."—*Burke.*

but not to remove it: prob. God permitted the increase but not the abatement of the annoyance.

The plague of frogs.—God plagues Egypt with these contemptible instruments—I. To magnify His own power. He has the whole creation under command; He is the Lord of small things as well as of great. II. To humble Pharaoh's pride, and chastise his insolence. What a mortification it must have been to this haughty monarch, to see himself brought to his knees, and forced to submit to such despicable means.^{b}

The magicians and the frogs.—Pharaoh's first symptom of yielding arose from the fact that the magicians were only able to increase the plague, and not to remove it. A late commentator, Hirsch, gives the following explanation, which is ingenious, and not improbable. He assumes that the words, " the magicians did so," mean that they imitated the action of Aaron, stretching out their rods, but using magic formulæ with the intention of driving away the frogs, the result being not only a frustration of their object, but an increase of the plague.^{c}

8—15. (8) **intreat,** *etc.,*^{a} first signs of relenting. **He .. me,** why could not his enchanters remove them? (9) **glory .. me,**^{b} in appointing me the time when I shall intreat for thee. (10) **to-morrow,** by fixing the time he would be able to connect M. with the event. (11) **they .. only,** as great a miracle to restrain their movements as to multiply their number. (12) **because .. frogs,**^{c} *lit.* upon the word of the frogs, *i.e.* on the subject of the frogs. **which .. Pharaoh,** *i.e.* wh. he had appointed to Pharaoh. (13) **villages,**^{d} courts, *i.e.* courtyards of houses and walled enclosures. (14) **heaps,** sugg. of immense number. **stank,** the smell should keep Pharaoh in mind respecting his promise. (15) **respite,** breathing-space. **he .. them,**^{e} he could imagine nothing worse than had been already endured.

The hardening nature of sin (v. 15).—I. When God issues out His terrible threatenings against sinners, He is wont to suspend the execution of His sentence, and give them an interval for repentance. II. It proves a state of most dreadful depravity when men take occasion, from the very compassion and mercies of God, to harden themselves in sin. III. God perfectly knows all the deeds of wicked men before they are done, and all their designs before they are conceived. IV. The signs by which it may be known that any man is given up to hardness of heart. The heart is desperately hardened when—1. Men sin knowingly and deliberately; 2. They hate and shun those who faithfully warn and reprove them, and affectionately labour to reclaim them; 3. The opportunities given for repentance are perverted to the purpose of adding sin to sin.^{f}

The frog season—America.—The frog season is now at its height. Thousands of frogs born in the spring swarm the marshy ground. The dealers sell easily 1,200 per day, and the consumption of four hotels which have the delicacy in their bills of fare will probably add 500 to that amount. Several smaller grocery stores sell daily from 25 to 50 pairs, so that not less than 2,000 are eaten in Buffalo every day. Already over 100,000 have been sold, and the remaining two months of the season will increase that amount to nearly 300,000. The best time to catch these croakers is early in the morning, or about noon. Persons going " frogging " prepare themselves with a stout stick three feet long, crooked at the lower end, a basket, a jack knife, and a piece of strong cord. When arrived upon the ground, a novice will be bewildered by the hundreds of moving, croaking objects surrounding him, but recovering himself, he proceeds to work bunglingly; as his nerves become steadier, so will his blows, which should be struck directly upon the head or neck with considerable force, so as to kill completely. When a basketful is obtained, they are taken to the bank of the river, the legs cut off and skinned, then strung on a string and floated in the river to be kept fresh. In this manner a diligent person may kill and prepare 500 in a short time. A boy or man might make 1,000 dollars (£200) a season.^g

16—19. (16) **dust**, dry country, much dust. **lice**, gnats or mosquitoes prob. (17) **lice** .. **Egypt**, "it is as though the very dust were turned into lice."^a (18) **magicians**^b .. **not**, here they are effectually restrained. (19) **this** .. **God**,^c it is divine, and no work of mere magic. **hardened**, notwithstanding what his own magicians even said.

The plague of the lice.—Consider—I. The infliction of this plague. 1. No notice or warning was given on this occasion. The absence of expostulation indicated an increase of wrath, and may be accounted for by the broken promise of Pharaoh; 2. The plague was inflicted by means of a very small insect. Behold in this a display of Almighty power. II. The fruitless attempt of the magicians to imitate it. Here we see the power of these men limited and restrained. III. The hardening of Pharaoh's heart under it. This was more inexcusable than before, and more indicative of a reprobate state.^d

Notes on the third plague.—Some of the ancients suppose that *gnats*, or some animals resembling them, were meant; whereas our translators, and many of the moderns, understand the original word כִּנִּים *kinneem*, as signifying *lice*. Bishop Patrick, in his commentary, supposes that Bochart has sufficiently proved, out of the text itself, that our version is right, since gnats are bred in fenny places, he might have said with truth, and with much greater energy of argument, in water, whereas the animals Moses here speaks of were brought out of the dust of the earth. A passage I lately met with in Vinisaur's account of the expedition of our King Richard the First into the Holy Land may, perhaps, give a truer representation of this Egyptian plague, than those that suppose they were *gnats*, or those that suppose they were *lice*, that God used on that occasion, as the instrument of that third correction. Speaking of the marching of that army of Croisaders, from Cayphas to where the ancient Cæsarea stood, that writer informs us, that each night certain worms distressed them, commonly called *tarrentes*, which crept upon the ground, and occasioned a very burning heat by most painful punctures. They hurt nobody in the day-time, but when night came on they extremely pestered them, being armed with stings, conveying a poison which quickly occasioned those that were wounded by them to swell, and was attended with the most acute pains.^e

20—24. (20) **early** .. **Pharaoh**, the anxious king had risen early to invoke the help of his god. (21) **else**, *etc.*,^a another gracious warning before the judgment. (22) **sever** .. **there**, a new feature in the plagues with which the land was visited, *i.e.* a

B.C. 1491.

"Obstinacy is the strength of the weak. Firmness, founded upon principle, upon the truth and right, order and law, duty and generosity, is the obstinacy of sages."—*Lavater*.

g Buffalo Express.

the third plague

lice are sent
a Sir S. Baker, who descr. the lice as a sort of tick, not larger than a grain of sand, which, when filled with blood, expands to the size of a hazel nut.

b 2 Ti. iii. 8, 9.
c 1 Sa. vi. 3, 9; Ma. xii. 28; Lu. xi. 20.
d G. Welford, M.A.

"There is something in obstinacy, which differs from every other passion. Whenever it fails, it never recovers, but either breaks like iron, or crumbles sulkily away, like a fractured arch. Most other passions have their periods of fatigue and rest, their sufferings and their cure; but obstinacy has no resource, and the first wound is mortal."—*Johnson*.

"There are few, very few, that will own themselves in a mistake."—*Swift*.

e Harmer.

the fourth plague

flies are sent
a Is. vii. 18.

B.C. 1491.

b Ex. ix. 4, 6, 26; x. 23; xi. 6, 7; xii. 13.
c "The same, according to Bochart, as was styled by the Romans, *musca canina*, and by the Greeks, κυνομυια, "the dog-fly." So Bathe, De Wette, Rosenmuller.
The Heb. *zebub* =(acc. to Bruce) the zimb, an Arabic word—the fly in general, and not any particular species. It is a dipterous insect, exceedingly destructive to cattle in Abyssinia, as the tsetse fly of Dr. Livingstone, with which it is prob. identical.
d Pierotti.
a De. vii. 25, 26; xii. 31.
"I consider it a mark of great prudence in a man to abstain from threats or any contemptuous expressions, for neither of these weakens the enemy, but threats make him more cautious, and the other excites his hatred, and a desire to revenge himself."—*Machiavelli*.
Zimb is found only where the soil consists of a rich black loam; but all the inhabitants along the S. shores of the Red Sea, etc., are compelled to remove their cattle in the rainy season to the nearest sands, in order to prevent their destruction by this pest.
b Pierotti.
a Dr. Smith.
"I believe that obstinacy, or the

distinction between Israel and Egypt. **end** .. **earth**, having a special care for my own people. (23) **division**, *lit.* I will put redemption. (24) **grievous**, heavy. **flies**,*c* of various kinds: perh. esp. the dog-fly, of wh. the bite is exceedingly painful.

Flies in the East.—These insects sometimes cause no slight suffering in Palestine, as I can vouch from my own experience. However large or however small they be, they attack alike, restless and rabid foes, and make themselves insufferable in a thousand ways in every season and place, in the house and in the field, by day and by night. I have never, indeed, seen them in such quantities as Moses predicted (Ex. xxiii. 28; De. vii. 20), and as there must have been when two kings of the Amorites were driven from their country by them (Jos. xxiv. 12). According to the Talmud they stung their enemies in the eyes, inflicting a mortal wound. Still, frequently, in 1857 and 1869, while I was encamped near the tents of the Bedawin, in the neighbourhood of the Jordan and to the south of Hebron, flies were brought in such numbers by the east wind, that all, beasts and men, were in danger of being choked by them, as they crept into our ears, noses, and mouths, and all over our bodies. My servant and I were the first to fly from this pest, as we were spotted all over like lepers with the eruption caused by their bites; the Bedawin themselves were not slow to follow our example.*d*

25—29. (25) **go .. land**, a compromise: they might sacrifice, but in the land of Egypt. (26) **it .. do**, it is not so appointed: he would accept no half measures. **abomination .. God**,*a* bold language, *i.e.* things deemed sacred by the Egyptians an abomination in the sight of God. **lo .. us**, our sacrifice of what they deem sacred would be abominable to them. (27) **as .. us**, we will obey God: we reject Pharaoh's concession. (28) **only .. away**, he will not yield unconditionally, but would keep Israel still within reach. (29) **but .. more**, the king had deceived once (v. 15): this, a hint that there might be worse to come.

Flies in the East.—I am not the only person who has experienced this nuisance; for Eugene Roger, who travelled in Palestine during the seventeenth century, informs us that during his stay at Nazareth a swarm of small black flies, called *bargash*, invaded the plain of Esdraelon, where a tribe of Bedawin, to the number of 600, tents, were encamped, who suffered greatly from them. The flies, therefore, still infest Palestine as they did of old, except that they are not now so numerous as to compel the chiefs of the villages or tribes (answering to the kings of the Pentateuch and Joshua) to evacuate the country before them. The Philistines had a special deity whom they invoked against these pests, Baalzebub, the god of flies (2 Ki. i. 2, 16), whose principal temple was at Hebron. The reason of this is evident at the present day, for the ancient country of the Philistines is infested with insect plagues, as I experienced, together with His Excellency Surraya Pasha, in the summer of 1859.*b*

30—32. (30) **Moses .. Lord**, *see* vv. 8—12. (31) **there .. one**, this as great a wonder as the plague itself. (32) **neither .. go**, so much for a king's word.

An ungrateful heart.—Flints may be melted (we see it daily), but an ungrateful heart cannot; no, not by the strongest and the noblest flame. The greatest favours to such an one are like the motion of a ship upon the waves; they leave no trace, no sign behind them: they neither repel nor win upon him. All kindnesses descend upon such a temper, as showers of rain, or rivers of fresh water falling into the main sea: the sea swallows them all, but is not at all changed or sweetened by them."

A right heart.—"When Sir Walter Raleigh had laid his head upon the block," says an eloquent divine, "he was asked by the executioner whether it lay aright. Whereupon, with the calmness of a hero and the faith of a Christian, he returned an answer, the power of which we all shall feel when our head is tossing and turning on death's uneasy pillow: 'It matters little, my friend, how the head lies providing the heart be right.'"*b*

B.C. 1491.

dread of control and discipline, arises not so much from self-willedness as from a conscious defect of voluntary power; as foolhardiness is not seldom the disguise of conscious timidity." *Cicero.*

"An obstinate man does not hold opinions, but they hold him."—*Pope.*
b R. Steele.

CHAPTER THE NINTH.

B.C. 1491.

1—4. (1) **Hebrews,**^a called also Jews^b fr. the patriarch Judah. (2) **wilt .. still,** forcibly detain them. (3) **camels,** only once bef. named in connection with Egypt.^c **murrain,**^d pestilence. (4) **there .. Israel,**^e the grt. distinction betw. Israel and Egypt still preserved.

the fifth plague
the cattle destroyed

Antiquity of the ass and horse.—The horse is not depicted on the ancient Egyptian monuments, but the ass is represented on the very oldest monuments of Egypt. Its form occurs frequently in the tombs of the old empire, at Gizeh, Sakkarah, and Abouzir. There is a highly curious bas-relief on the tomb of Ti (fifth dynasty), on which we see a drove of asses, a plaster cast of this having been sent over by M. Mariette to the Universal Exhibition of 1867. From the beginning of the fourth dynasty the ass was an animal as frequent in Egypt as it is now. In the inscription of the tomb of Shafra Ankh at Gizeh, published by M. Lepsius, a herd of 760 asses is mentioned as having been reared on the estates of the deceased, who was a high functionary at the court of the founder of the second pyramid of Gizeh (fourth dynasty). In other still unpublished tombs, discovered by M. Mariette, M. Lenormand has remarked inscriptions in which landed proprietors boast of possessing thousands of asses.*f*

a Gen. xiv. 13.
b Est. iii. 6; Gen. xxix. 35; xlix. 8.
c Gen. xii. 16.
d Le. xxvi. 21; Ps. lxviii. 21; Re. xvi. 9.
e Ex. viii. 22; Mal. iii. 18.

"Civilisation may be said to be ever in proportion to the number and variety of the animals which man has subdued to his service."—*Craufurd.*

f J. Timbs.

5—7. (5) **time .. morrow,** the king had time for reflection. (6) **all .. died,** *i.e.* some of all sorts,^a see vv. 19—25. (7) **behold .. dead,**^b the diff. is now manifest to Pharaoh. **and .. hardened,** notwithstanding his knowledge increases.

Destruction of the cattle.—Hyperbolical probably for many, as is indicated in v. 20. In Samoa this is a very common form of speech. If two or three houses fall in a gale, the tale goes that "all are down, not one standing." Or if a number of the people are suffering from an epidemic, the report spreads that "the whole land is covered with beds."*c*

All i.e. some of all kinds.—This verse has been said to contradict verse 20, where it is said some of the cattle of Egypt remained alive, and were preserved from a subsequent plague by the servants of Pharaoh; but the fact is, that nothing is more common among writers, both sacred and profane, than the use of the word *all,* not in an *absolute,* but a *relative,* a *comparative* sense, as implying *many,—some of all sorts.*^d

a "This peculiar usage of the word 'all,' as denoting some of all kinds, instead of the absolute totality of the number spoken of, is of great importance to a right understanding of the sacred Scriptures throughout."—*Bush.*
b Mn. x. 20; 1 Co. ix. 9, 10.
c Dr. Turner.
d Carpenter.

EXODUS. [Cap. ix. 8-16.

b.c. 1491

the sixth plague

boils are sent

a De. xxviii. 27; Re. xvi. 2.
"Kalisch mentions a barbarous custom of burning human victims in certain cities of Egypt consecrated to the evil genius Typhon, and scattering their ashes in the air, 'in hope that with the dust the blessings of heaven would spread over the country.' If this were so, it would, at least, give significance to the act here enjoined."—*Alford.*

r. 12. *T. Boucdler*, ii. 323; *Dr. J. Williams*, 111.

b Roberts.

a Mic. vi. 13.

b Pr. xvi. 4; Ro. ix., 22, 23; Ps. lxxvi. 10; Neh. ix. 10.

c Spk. Comm.
d C. Simeon, M.A.
"What a lesson, indeed, is all history and all life to the folly and fruitlessness of pride! The Egyptian kings had their embalmed bodies preserved in massive pyramids, to obtain an earthly immortality. In the seventeenth century they were sold as quack medicines, and now they are burnt for fuel The Egyptian mummies, which Cambyses or

8—12. (8) **Take**, *etc.*, this time a judgment without a warning. **ashes..furnace**, prob. of some smelting-furnace or lime-kiln. **let..Pharaoh**, he prob. met him in the morning by the river, and does this without addressing him. (9) **boil..ulcer. breaking..blains**, running and itching sores. (10) **and**, *etc.*, note the boldness and promptitude of obedience. (11) **magicians..boils**, first defeated, now routed. (12) **and..Pharaoh**, here for the first time we read that the Lord hardened Pharaoh's heart, *i.e.* He judicially gave him up to obduracy of mind.

The use of afflictions.—Two painters were employed to fresco the walls of a magnificent cathedral. Both stood on a rude scaffolding, constructed for the purpose, some distance from the floor. One, so intent upon his work, forgetting where he was, stepped back slowly, surveying critically the work of his pencil, until he had neared the edge of the plank on which he stood. At this moment his companion, just perceiving his danger, seized a wet brush, flung it against the wall, spattering the picture with unsightly blotches of colouring. The painter flew forward, and turned upon his friend with fierce upbraidings, till made aware of the danger he had escaped: then, with tears of gratitude, he blessed the hand that saved him. Just so, sometimes we get so absorbed with the pictures of the world, unconscious of our peril, when God in mercy dashes out the beautiful images, and draws us, at the time we are complaining of His dealings, into His outstretched arms of love. *Throwing ashes in the air.*—When the magicians pronounce an imprecation on an individual, a village, or a country, they take ashes of cow's dung (or from a common fire), and *throw them in the air*, saying to the objects of their displeasure, such a sickness, or such a curse, shall surely come upon you.*b*

13—16. (13) **rise**, *etc., see* viii. 20. (14) **will..send**,*a etc.*, *i.e.* I will send greater plagues than before. (15) **pestilence, deadly plague**. (16) **and..deed**, *etc.*,*b* the meaning is, God permitted him to live and hold out till His own purpose was accomplished.*c*

Pharaoh's elevation to the throne of Egypt (v. 16).—This declaration we will—I. Explain. Its substance may be considered as expressing the following truths.—1. That God allots to every man his station in life; 2. That He foreknows how every man will act in the situation to which he is called: 3. That, whilst He leaves to every man the free exercise of his will, He overrules the actions of all for the accomplishment of His own eternal purposes; 4. That by all, whatever their conduct be, He will eventually be glorified. II. Improve. 1. For the establishment of sound doctrine : 2. For the enforcement of a holy practice.*d*

The significance of the plagues.—These plagues are all significant, proving the power of God, and rebuking idolatry. 1. The Nile—blood: an object of worship turned into an object of abhorrence. 2. The sacred frog itself their plague. 3. Lice, which the Egyptians deemed so polluting, that to enter a temple with them was a profanation, cover the country like dust. 4. The gad-fly (*Zebub*), an object of Egyptian reverence, becomes their torture. 5. The cattle, which were objects of Egyptian worship, fall dead before their worshippers. 6. The ashes, which the priests scattered as signs of blessing, become boils. 7. Isis and Osiris, the deities of water and fire, are unable to protect Egypt, even at a season when storms and rain were unknown, from the fire and hail of God. 8. Isis and Serapis were supposed to protect the country from locusts. West winds might bring these enemies; but an east wind the Egyptian never feared, for the Red Sea defended him. But now Isis fails; and the very east wind he reverenced becomes his destruction. 9. The heavenly hosts, the objects of worship, are themselves shown to be under Divine control. 10. The last plague explains the whole. God's firstborn Egypt had oppressed; and now the firstborn of Egypt are all destroyed. The first two plagues, it will be noticed, were foretold by Moses, and imitated by the Egyptians. The rest they failed to copy, and confessed that they were wrought by the finger of God.*e*

17—21. (17) **exaltest**, proudly self-confident, haughty defiance of the Lord. (18) **rain** .. **hail**, in Egypt rare and usually innoxious. **since** .. **now**, *i.e.* since Egypt became a nation, *see* v. 24. (19) **Send** .. **field**, *etc.*, God mercifully gives Pharaoh the opportunity of saving some of his people and their cattle. (20) **feared**, *etc.*, by this time there had sprung up in the minds of many a belief in the word, and a dread of the power of God. (21) **left** .. **field**,*a* where they perished through lack of faith. *A land storm.—*

    A boding silence reigns,
Dread through the dun expanse; save the dull sound
That from the mountain, previous to the storm,
Rolls o'er the muttering earth, disturbs the flood,
And shakes the forest-leaf without a breath. Prone, to the lowest vale, aërial tribes
Descend; the tempest-loving raven scarce
Dares wing the dubious dusk. In rueful gaze
The cattle stand, and on the scowling heavens
Cast a deploring eye; by man forsook.
Who to the crowded cottage hies him fast,
Or seeks the shelter of the downward cave.*b*

22—26. (22) **all .. Egypt**, the tempest not only fierce but universal. (23) **thunder**, *lit.* voices. **fire**,*a* lightning. **ran .. ground**, *lit.* walked earthwards. (24) **fire .. hail**,*b* *i.e.* continuous sheets of lightning. (25) **smote**, doing extensive damage. **all .. beast**, *i.e.* some of all sorts, *see* v. 6. (26) **only**,*c* *etc.*, the distinction still preserved.

Hail in Egypt.—I do not apprehend that it is at all necessary to suppose, that all the servants and all the cattle of the Egyptians, that were abroad at the time the hail fell, which Moses threatened, and which was attended with thunder and lightning, died; it is sufficient to suppose they all felt the hailstones, and that several of them were killed. This was enough to justify the words of Moses, that it should be a "grievous hail, such as had not fallen before in Egypt from its foundation." For though it hails sometimes in Egypt as well as rains, as Dr. Pococke found it hailed at Fioume, when he was there in February; and thunders too, as Thevenot says it did one night in December, when he was at Cairo; yet fatal effects are not wont to follow in that country, as appears from what Thevenot says of this thunder, which, he tells us, killed a man in the castle there,

---

B.C. 1491.

time hath spared, avarice now consumeth. Mummy is become merchandise."—*Whipple.*

"It is pride which fills the world with so much harshness and severity. We are rigorous to offences as if we had never offended."—*Blair.*
e Dr. Angus.

the seventh plague

hail is sent

a Pr. xxii. 3; Jonah iii. 5.

"Prudence is a quality incompatible with vice, and can never be effectively enlisted in its cause."—*Burke.*
"Prudence is that virtue by which we discern what is proper to be done under the various circumstances of time and place."—*Milton.*

b Thomson.

a Ps. cv. 32; cxlviii. 8; Josh. x. 11; Is. xxx. 30; Ezek. xxxviii. 22; Rev. viii. 7.
b Ps. lxxviii. 47, 48.
c Ex. viii. 22; ix. 5; x. 23; xi. 7; xii. 13; Is. xxxii. 18, 19.

"Divine Providence tempers His blessings to secure their better effect. He keeps our joys and our fears on an even balance, that we may neither presume nor despair. By such compositions God is pleased to make both

b.c. 1491.

our crosses more tolerable and our enjoyments more wholesome and safe."—W. Wogan.
"He who sends the storm steers the vessel."— T. Adams.
d *Harmer.*
a Job xxxiv. 31, 32; Pr. xxviii. 13; 2 Ch. xii. 6, 7; Dan. ix. 14.
b Ps. xxiv. 1; 1 Co. x. 28.
c Is. xxvi. 10.
d *Spurgeon.*
"He who bridles the fury of the billows knows also how to put a stop to the secret plans of the wicked. Submitting with respect to His holy will, I fear God, and have no other fear."—Racine.

a *Kalisch.*
b *Alford.*
c Now called *doura* by the natives.
"Sweet spring, full of sweet days and roses, a box where sweets compacted lie."—G. Herbert.
"Every green herb, from the lotus to the darnel, is rich with delicate aids to help incurious man."—Tupper.
d *Bibl. Treas.*

a 2 Ch. xxxiii. 23; Ec. viii. 11.
b *Different words are used in this and the following verse: here the word means 'heavy,' i.e. obtuse, incapable of forming a right judgment; the other, which is more frequently used in this narrative, is stronger and implies a stub-*

though it had never been heard before that thunder had killed anybody at Cairo. For divers people then to have been killed by the lightning and the hail, besides cattle, was an event that Moses might well say had never happened there before, from the time it began to be inhabited. I will only add, that Moses, by representing this as an extraordinary hail, supposed that it did sometimes hail there, as it is found in fact to do, though not as in other countries: the *not raining* in Egypt, it is well known, is to be understood in the same manner.d

27—30. (27) **said.. time,**a *i.e.* I at this time acknowledge my sin. **Lord,** he recognizes the God of the Hebrews. (28) **mighty thunderings,** *lit.* voices of God. (29) **that.. Lord's,**b God the Lord of the whole earth contrasted with Egyptian notion of local deities. (30) **I.. God,**c a knowledge of coming wickedness no hindrance to Divine mercy.

Confession of sin (v. 27).—Seven texts to this sermon. Consider—I. The hardened sinner. Under terror, Pharaoh says, "I have sinned." II. The double-minded man: Balaam (Num. xxii. 34). He says "I have sinned," and feels that he has, and feels it deeply too, but he is so worldly-minded that he "loves the wages of unrighteousness." III. The insincere man: Saul (1 Sam. xv. 24). He is moulded everlastingly by the circumstance passing over his head. IV. The doubtful penitent: Achan (Josh. vii. 20). V. The despairing repentant: Judas (Ma. xxvii. 4). VI. The repentant saint: Job (Job vii. 20). VII. The blessed confession: the prodigal son (Lu. xv. 18).d

31, 32. (31) **flax,** Egypt the linen-market of the anc. world.a **bolled,** *i.e.* in blossom, or had its *ball-like* seed-vessels on it.b (32) **rie,** or spelt c *(triticum spelta)*: rye not grown so far south; bread of spelt the usual food of anc. Egyptians.

Egyptian flax and barley.—That is, one of the two named was maturing and the other about to mature. The flax was bolled, *i.e.* in blossom. Comparing this with the next verse, we ascertain on reference to the climatology of Egypt that this infliction took place in January or February. The cultivation of flax was of great importance: linen was preferred to any material, and exclusively used by the priests. Pliny specifies four kinds which were used in Egypt. The texture was remarkably fine, in general quality (as we find from relics yet extant) equal to the best now made, and in the evenness of its threads actually superior to that of modern manufacture.d

33—35. (33) **rain.. earth,** pouring rain a most unusual thing. (34) **he.. more,**a prob. ref. to his confession, v. 27. **hardened**b **.. servants,** showing how a wicked king may corrupt a people. (35) **as.. Moses,** *see* v. 30.

The heart the seat of spiritual disease.—Some malady which you do not understand troubles and alarms you. The physician is called. Thinking that the illness proceeds from a certain inflammatory process on a portion of your skin, you anxiously direct his attention to the spot. Silently, but sympathisingly, he looks at the place where you have bidden him look, and because you have bidden him look there, but soon he turns away. He is busy with an instrument on another part of your body. He presses his trumpet tube gently to your breast, and listens for the pulsations which faintly but distinctly pass through. He looks and listens there, and saddens as he looks. You again direct his attention to the cutaneous eruption which annoys you. He sighs and sits silent. When you reiterate your request that something should be done for the external eruption, he gently shakes his head, and answers not a word. From this silence you would learn the truth at last, you would not miss its meaning long. O miss not the meaning of the Lord when He points to the seat of the soul's disease; "Ye will not come." These, His enemies, dwell in your heart.*c*

B.C. 1491.

"born resolution."—*Spk. Com.*
"All our actions take their hues from the complexion of the heart, as landscapes their variety from light."
— *Bacon.*
c Dr. Arnot.

CHAPTER THE TENTH.

B.C. 1491.

1—6. (1) **hardened,** *lit.* made heavy: judicial treatment. that .. **him,** as lessons for all time. (2) **tell,***a* *etc.*, statement of far-reaching purpose of God. (3) **how .. refuse,** "even now Pharaoh's will is supposed to be *free*."*b* **humble,***c* acknowledge the greatness and power of the God of the Hebrews. (4) **locusts,***d* Heb. *arbeh*, either the *Acridium peregrinum*, or *Adipoda migratoria*. Locusts belong to the *saltatorial orthoptera* (leaping flyers with straight wings), the largest of wh. are fr. two to two and a half fr. long, expanse of wings fr. four to six inches. (5) **face .. earth,** *lit.* the eye of the earth, *i.e.* all the eye looks upon. (6) **which .. day,** *i.e.* such locusts never seen before for *numbers* and *size*.

Delaying repentance.—We will—I. Show wherein true humiliation consists. It consists in—1. A deep and ingenuous sorrow for sin, as contrasted with forced acknowledgments; 2. An unreserved obedience to God, as contrasted with partial compliances. II. Expostulate with those in whom it is not yet wrought. Consider the guilt, the folly, and the danger of delaying your humiliation before God. Encouragements :—1. It is never too late; 2. It is never too soon.*e*

The plague of locusts.—The herbage which the storm had spared was now given up to a terrible destroyer. After a fresh warning—

"The potent rod
Of Amram's son, in Egypt's evil day,
Waved round her coasts, called up a pitchy cloud
Of locusts, warping on the eastern wind,
That o'er the realm of impious Pharaoh hung
Like night, and darkened all the land of Nile."

Approaching thus, the swarm alights upon fields green with the young blades of corn; its surface is blackened with their bodies and in a few minutes it is left black, for the soil is as bare as if burnt with fire. Whatever leaves and fruit the hail had left on the trees were likewise devoured; and the houses swarmed with the hideous destroyers. No plague could have been more impressive in the East, where the ravages of locusts are so dreadful that they are chosen as the fit symbol of a destroying conqueror. The very threat had urged Pharaoh's courtiers to remonstrance, and he had offered to let the men only depart, but he had refused to yield more, and had driven Moses and Aaron from his presence. Now he recalled them in haste, and asked them to forgive his sin "only this once," and to entreat God to take away "this death only." A strong west wind removed the locusts as an east

the eighth plague

the locusts

a De. iv. 9; Ps. xliv. 1; Joel i. 3.
b Wordsworth.
c Pr. xviii. 12; 1 Ki. xxi. 29; Jas. iv. 10; Job. xlii. 6; 1 Pe. v. 6; 2 Ch. vii. 14.
d Ma. iii. 4; Mk. i. 6, see B. M, N. T. i. 113, 243; see also Le. xi. 22; Ps. lxxviii. 46; cix. 23; Joel i. 4; ii. 25; De. xxviii.13; Ps. cv. 34; Pr. xxx. 27; Is. xxxiii. 4; Na. iii. 15; Re. ix. 3, 7.

"The earth, with its bright colours, and lovely flowers, and vegetation, shines like a beautiful eye, and looks up to man. The locusts are to it what blindness is to the eye."—*Wordsworth.*

"God hath treasures of plagues for the obstinate; neither can He be, as the poet feared of his Jupiter, possibly exhausted."— *Trapp.*

e C. Simeon, M.A.
f Smith's O. T. Hist.

B.C. 1491.

Moses and Aaron driven from Pharaoh's presence
a Roberts.
"The greater a man is in power above others, the more he ought to excel them in virtue. None ought to govern who is not better than the governed."— *P. Syrus.*
"Power safely defied touches its downfall."— *Macaulay.*

the locusts are sent
a Wordsworth, who adds, "the wind was worshipped in Egypt under the name of Kneph."
b Trapp.
c "They covered all the land so that the sunbeams could not pierce to it, and the land was obscured." — *Chaldee.*
d Mr. Petherick.
"Man supposes that he directs his life and governs his actions, when his existence is irretrievably under the control of destiny."—*Goethe.*

the plague removed
a 2 Ki. iv. 40.
"A thorough and mature insensibility is rarely to be acquired, but by a steady perseverance in infamy."—*Junius*
"There are two ways of attaining an important

wind had brought them; but their removal left his heart harder than ever.*f*

7—11. (7) **snare,** cause of our being led into fresh calamities: the real snare was their sin. (8) **but .. go?** *lit.* who and who (are) going. (9) **young daughters,** *i.e.* all of us. **flocks .. herds,** *i.e.* all we have. (10) **Lord .. go,** *i.e.* may the Lord favour you as I will. **evil .. you,** the meaning is either, "you purpose evil," or "I will practise evil." (11) **now .. men,** he would retain the others as hostages for the men's return. **driven .. presence,** contemptuously.

Driven out.—Among natives of rank, when a person is very importunate or troublesome, when he presses for something which the former are not willing to grant, he is told to be gone. Should he still persist, the servants are called, and the order is given, "Drive that fellow out." He is then seized by the neck, or taken by the hands, and dragged from the premises; he all the time screaming and bawling as if they were taking his life. Thus to be driven out is the greatest indignity which can be offered, and nothing but the most violent rage will induce a superior to have recourse to it.*a*

12—15. (12) **all .. left,** *see* ix. 6—25. (13) **east wind,** "another element is now also enlisted against Pharaoh."*a* **land .. night,** without intermission, otherwise the locusts had not been wafted across the Red Sea. (14) **and .. Egypt,** "as a formidable army."*b* (15) **darkened,** the eye of the earth as it were blinded.*c*

Locusts.—"Shortly before our arrival at Helbé, our passage was literally stopped by the most extraordinary flight of locusts I ever witnessed. An immense quantity of these insects flew in so compact a mass across our path that they appeared like a wall about twelve feet high, and of such density that not a ray of light was emitted through it. On the top of this dense column individual specimens might be distinguished as they sportively elevated themselves; and the noise they made whilst rushing through the air was not unlike the roaring of the sea. The column appeared endless, and was attacked by the camel-men and Takroori pilgrims with all sorts of missiles, without, however, effecting a breach, or producing the slightest deviation in their flight. As soon as they had passed, the damage became apparent by the great number of the killed and wounded, which, roasted on the spot, were greedily devoured. Curiosity tempting me, I partook of several of them; and were it not for the crispness imparted by the fire, the taste was not unlike that of vegetable marrow."*d*

16—20. (16) **called .. haste,** *lit.* hastened to call. (17) **death,***a* *i.e.* deadly plague. (18) **intreated,** Moses once more an intercessor. (19) **strong .. wind,** blowing from the *west.* **and .. sea,** Arabia spared. (20) **so .. go,** his hardness returned when the plague departed.

Locusts.—It is hard to conceive how wide the mischief extends, when a cloud of these insects comes upon a country. They devour to the very root and bark, so that it is a long time before vegetation can be renewed. How dreadful their inroads at all times were, may be known from a variety of authors, both ancient and modern. They describe them as being brought by one wind, and carried off by another. They swarm greatly in Asia and Africa. In respect to Europe, Thevenot tells us, that the region upon the Boristhenes, and particularly that inhabited by the Cossacks, is greatly infested with locusts, especially in a dry season. They come in vast clouds, which extend fifteen and sometimes eighteen miles, and are nine to twelve in breadth. The air, by their interposition, is rendered quite obscure, however bright the day may have been before. In two hours they devour all the corn, wherever they settle, and often a famine ensues. At night, when they repose upon the earth, the ground is covered with them four inches deep, or more : and if a carriage goes over them, and they are mashed under foot, the smell of them is scarcely to be borne, especially when they are reduced to a state of putrefaction. They come from Circassia, Mingrelia, and Tartary, on which account the natives rejoice in a north or northeast wind, which carries them into the Black Sea, where they perish. The vast region of Asia, especially the southern part, is liable to their depredations. China is particularly infested with them; and the natives use various means to obviate the evil, which is generally too powerful to be evaded. But the most fearful accounts are from Africa, where the heat of the climate, and the nature of the soil in many places, contribute to the production of these animals in astonishing numbers.[b]

21—23. (21) **Moses,** does not go in to Pharaoh. **darkness,** chief object of worship among the Egyptians was the sun-god.— *Ra.* **darkness**[a] .. **felt,** *lit.* that may be grasped. (22) **thick darkness,**[b] *i.e.* of preternatural density. (23) **neither .. place,** *lit.* fr. that wh. was under him, *i.e.* his bed, meaning that no one could attend to his affairs. **light .. dwellings,**[c] as preternatural as the darkness without.

Light in the dwellings of Israel.—We may regard the text as emblematical of the difference between a child of God and a worldling in—I. Temporal things. It is true that there is a general similarity outwardly between God's dealings with His people and His enemies. But this rule applies only to the outward surface of things. II. Spiritual things. The unrenewed man is blind as to the condition of his soul before God. How different is the condition of a follower of Christ. III. Eternal things. On one side is "thick darkness;" on the other, joys inconceivable. Which will you choose?[d]

Plague of darkness.—"We remained two months at Khartoum. During this time we were subjected to intense heat and constant dust-storms, attended with a general plague of boils. Verily, the plagues of Egypt remain to this day in the Soudan. On the 26th June (1865) we had the most extraordinary dust-storm that had ever been seen by the inhabitants. I was sitting in the courtyard of my agent's house at about half-past four P.M. : there was no wind, and the sun was as bright as usual in this cloudless sky, when suddenly a gloom was cast over all,—a dull yellow glare pervaded the atmosphere. Knowing that this effect portended a dust-storm, and that the present calm would be followed by a hurricane of wind, I rose to go home, intending to secure the shutters. Hardly had I risen when I saw approaching, from the S.W. apparently, a solid range of immense brown mountains, high in air. So rapid was the passage of this extraordinary

---

B.C. 1491.

end.—force and perseverance. Force falls to the lot only of the privileged few, but austere and sustained perseverance can be practised by the most insignificant. Its silent power grows irresistible with time."— *M de. Sicitchine.*

"Woe to falsehood! it affords no relief to the breast, like truth: it gives us no comfort, pains him who forges it, and, like an arrow directed by a god, flies back and wounds the archer."—*Goethe. b Burder.*

the ninth plague

darkness

a Ju. 13.

b Ps. cv. 28.

c Ex. viii. 22; ix. 26; Eph. v. 8.

"It is probable, too, that they were prevented by the heavy and humid state of the atmosphere from availing themselves of any kind of artificial light."—*Bush.*

d A. Townsend, B.D.

"He moved that thick air from his countenance, often waving his left hand before him: this labour was the only thing that annoyed him."—*Dante.*

"And through the palpable obscure find out his uncouth way."—*Milton.*

"Yet from those

B.C. 1491.

flames no light, but rather darkness visible."— *Milton.*
"Of darkness visible so much He lent as half to show, half veil the deep intent." —*Pope.*

c Sir S. Baker.

the day of grace rejected

a He. xi. 27

"Has a servant, an agent, or an officer, deeply offended his superior, he will say to him, 'Take care never to see my face again; for on the day you do that, evil shall come upon you.' 'Begone, and in future never look in this face,' pointing to his own." —*Roberts.*

b J. G. Roberts.

phenomenon, that in a few minutes we were in actual pitchy darkness. At first there was no wind, and the peculiar calm gave an oppressive character to the event. We were in 'a darkness that might be felt.' Suddenly the wind arrived, but not with the violence that I had expected. There were two persons with me,—Michael Latfalla, my agent, and Monsieur Lombrosio. So intense was the darkness, that we tried to distinguish our hands placed close before our eyes; not even an outline could be seen. This lasted for upwards of twenty minutes: it then rapidly passed away, and the sun shone as before; but we had felt the darkness that Moses had inflicted upon the Egyptians."*c*

24—29. (24) **only .. stayed**, he is anxious to have a pledge for their return. (25) **give .. offerings**, *i.e.* allow us to take our own for that purpose. (26) **there .. behind**, not only we but all belonging to us shall go. (27) **Lord .. heart**, that He might introduce the last plague, a typical miracle. (28) **get**, *etc*. Pharaoh exasperated, is frantic with disappointment and rage: desperate madness, impotent malice. (29) **thou .. well**,*a* it shall be as thou hast said. **I .. more**, I appeal finally from Pharaoh to God.

Contrasted characters.—I. In this world often the worst of men come in contact with the best. It was so here.—1. Pharaoh was an idolater, Moses a true worshipper of the true God; 2. Pharaoh was the greatest of tyrants, Moses, the meekest of men; 3. Pharaoh was a signal monument of God's displeasure, Moses, an object of God's highest favour. II. It is possible that the worst may thus come in contact with the best without being at all benefited. The intercourse which Pharaoh had with Moses had a tendency to confer upon him inestimable blessings. Think of—1. The noble example which Moses set before him; 2. The important truths which he taught him. III. When such a case occurs, the parting between the two is deeply affecting. Pharaoh and Moses parted—1. When there might have been no necessity for it; 2. To meet with two very different ends: Red Sea—Pisgah; 3. Never to meet one another again.*b*

B.C. 1491.

the tenth plague

destruction of the firstborn

a Le. xxvi. 21.
b Ex. xii. 35.
c Am. iv. 10.
d Ex. xii. 30.
For *Mill,* see *Topics* ii. 22.

"The mill used by the Israelites, and prob. by the Egyptians, consisted of two circular stones, one fixed in the ground, the

CHAPTER THE ELEVENTH.

1—6. (1) **one .. Egypt**,*a* and more terrible than all the preceding (*note,* God may always have some judgment or punishment in store greater than any we have experienced). **he .. altogether**, as glad to be rid of you as hitherto he has been anxious to retain. (2) **borrow**,*b* *see* iii. 22. (3) **man .. great**, in power, estimation. (4) **midnight**, the time an additional element of terror in this last plague. (5) **firstborn .. die**, pride, hope, joy of every fam. **from .. maidservant**, no respect of persons. **that .. mill**, a hand-mill turned, sometimes by one, sometimes by two women. **and .. beasts**,*c* worship of beasts universal in Egypt. (6) **great .. more**,*d* a loud, deep, universal wailing.

The destruction of the Egyptian firstborn.—In considering the last plague, we must notice—I. The prediction of the judgment to be executed. It differs from every previous denunciation in that it was purely maledictory, and was not accompanied by any expostulation. II. The spoiling of the Egyptians by Israel

(vv. 35, 36). The spoil belonged to Israel. 1. By God's command; 2. By right of conquest: no warfare, except of words; but still a conquest; 3. By right of compensation. III. The difference put between Israel and Egypt. IV. The infliction of this terrible calamity. It was marked by many awful circumstances. 1. It was adapted to produce terror; 2. It left no opening for repentance; 3. It was the last and greatest.*

Borrowing.—Dr. Boothroyd, instead of borrow, translates "ask." Dr. A. Clarke says, "request, demand, require." The Israelites wished to go three days' journey into the wilderness, that they might hold a feast unto the Lord. When the Orientals go to their sacred festivals, they always put on their best jewels. Not to appear before the gods in such a way, they consider would be disgraceful to themselves and displeasing to the deities. A person whose clothes or jewels are indifferent will borrow of his richer neighbours; and nothing is more common than to see poor people standing before the temples, or engaged in sacred ceremonies, well adorned with jewels. The almost pauper bride or bridegroom at a marriage may often be seen decked with gems of the most costly kind, which have been borrowed for the occasion. It fully accords, therefore, with the idea of what is due at a sacred or social feast, to be thus adorned in their best attire. Under these circumstances, it would be perfectly easy to borrow of the Egyptians their jewels, as they themselves, in their festivals, would doubtless wear the same things. It is also recorded, the Lord gave them "favour in the sight of the Egyptians." It does not appear to have been fully known to the Hebrews, that they were going finally to leave Egypt: they might expect to return; and it is almost certain that, if their oppressors had known they were not to return, they would not have lent them their jewels.

7—10. (7) **dog..tongue**, prov. expr.=profound tranquillity; or, nothing shall harm. **difference**,*a lit.* wonderfully distinguisheth. (8) **thy..me**, the tyrants shall become suppliants, **all..thee**,*b lit.* who are at thy feet. **in..anger**,*c* a meek man moved to indignation by falsehood, cruelty, insolence. (9) **the..Moses**, *etc.*,*d* that thus instructed he might not be disappointed. (10) **Moses..Pharaoh**, *etc.*,*e* ref. to the whole preceding narrative.

The difference God puts between His people and others.—" The Lord doth put a difference" between His people and others. I. He has done so from the beginning. Go back to the antediluvian age, to the patriarchal times. Consult the history before us. Search the records of all succeeding ages. II. He does so at this present hour. He does so in—1. The dispensations of His providence; 2. The communications of His grace. III. He will do so to all eternity. Questions: 1. Do you believe this truth? 2. Do you live under its influence?

Obstinacy conquered.—It is said that Robert Raikes, the founder of Sunday-schools, one day visited a family in which was a bad-tempered child, who made her mother very unhappy by her obstinacy and sulkiness. Every effort for her improvement was fruitless. Mr. Raikes talked seriously with her, and told her that her first step must be to kneel down and ask her mother's pardon. She resisted all entreaty, and he proposed to humble himself for her. Kneeling before the mother, he asked her forgiveness. The

B.C. 1491.

"other turned by a handle. The work of grinding was extremely laborious, and performed by women of the lowest rank."—*Spk. Comm.*

e G. Wellford, M.A.

"I will believe in the right of one man to govern a nation despotically when I find a man born into the world with boots and spurs, and a nation born with saddles on their backs."—*A. Sidney.*

"I know that nothing comes to pass but what God appoints; our fate is decreed, and things do not happen by chance, but every man's portion of joy and sorrow is predetermined."—*Seneca.*

a difference put between Israel and Egypt

a Ex. viii. 22.

b Gk., "whom thou leadest;" Chal., "who are with thee;" Vulg., "who are subject to thee;" Aben Ezra, "who are in thy power;" Jarchi, "who follow thy counsel and thy steps."

c "To be angry at nothing but sin is the way not to sin in anger."—*Henry.*

d Ro. ix. 17.
e Ro. ii. 5.
f C. Simeon, M.A.

"Anger is a noble infirmity, the generous failing of the just, the one degree that

stubborn girl, seeing Mr. Raikes on his knees on her account, burst into tears, fell upon her knees, and asked her mother's forgiveness for herself. From that hour she became an obedient and gentle child.

B.C. 1491.
riseth above zeal, asserting the prerogative of virtue."—*Tupper.*

B.C. 1491.

institution of the passover
a Ex. xiii. 4; De. xvi. 1.
b Esth. iii. 7.
c *Bush.*
d "The whole host of Israel was divided into twelve tribes; these tribes into families: and the families into houses; the last being composed of particular individuals. In one family, therefore, there might be several houses."—*Bush.*
e "Law, man's sole guardian ever since the time when the old Brazen Age, in sadness, saw love fly the world."—*Schiller.*
f *Treas. of Bibl. Know.*

the selected lamb and sprinkled blood
a Le. i. 3, 10; xxii. 19, 21; De. xvii. 1; 1 Pe. i. 19; Heb. ix. 14.
b Le. xxiii. 5; 2 Ch. xxx. 15; Nu. xxviii. 46, 50; Is. liii. 6.
c De. xvi. 6.
d He. xii. 24; Eph. i. 7; He. ix. 22; 1 Pe. i. 2; Re. xiii. 8.
e De. xvi. 3, 4; 1 Co. v. 8.
f Le. vii. 15; De. xvi. 4.
g C. Simeon, M.A.
"To make an empire durable, the magistrates

CHAPTER THE TWELFTH.

1—4. (1) **spake**, or, had spoken. (2) **month**, Abib,[a] afterwards called Nisan.[b] **beginning**, the head. **first ..you**, first in order, highest in estimation, "the chief and most excellent month in the year."[c] (3) **lamb**, Heb. *seh* = lamb or kid. **house ..fathers**,[d] *lit.* a house of fathers. (4) **if ..lamb**, i.e. not enough to consume it. **every ..eating**, "this quantity, the Jewish writers say, was to be equal to the size of an olive."[e]

The passover (on the whole chapter).—In examining the typical character of the passover, we shall consider—I. What is said of the lamb itself. It was to be without blemish and without spot, and a male of the first year. II. The use and value of its blood. There was nothing in the manner of applying this blood that would impart any virtue to it. The virtue was in the blood itself. III. The use and value of its flesh. IV. The hope of the blood-besprinkled worshippers.

National value of Jewish feasts.—Apart from the religious aspect of these various festivals, and the occasions they provided for solemn worship, they were of national value as binding the tribes together, bringing them into fellowship, knitting the several communities into one body, having each a share in and a tie to that place which the Lord had chosen to put His name there. Jerusalem with its temple was not merely the political capital, but the religious home of the nation. And so Jeroboam felt when he devised his festivals to keep his subjects from resorting to the city of David (1 Kings xii. 26—33).[f]

5—10. (5) **lamb ..blemish**,[a] entire, whole, healthy. (6) **ye ..up**,[b] as select, dedicated. **whole ..kill**, i.e. each house shall kill its lamb. **evening**,[c] *lit.* between the two evenings. (7) **upper ..post**,[d] i.e. lintel. (8) **and ..it**,[e] their last taste of bitterness in Egypt: a vivid memorial of all their previous suffering. (9) **eat ..raw**, they were not to be in a hurry; but prepare it with calmness. **sodden**, past part. of *seethe*, to boil. **purtenance**, intestines: to be cooked whole, not a bone to be broken. **nothing ..morning**,[f] to prevent superstitious abuse. **that ..fire**, of parts not eatable.

The passover (on vv. 3—11).—From the words of our text we shall be led to notice—I. The ordinance itself. This was—1. Commemorative; 2. Typical. Enumerate particulars. II. The manner of its celebration. It was celebrated—1. With humble penitence; 2. With unfeigned sincerity; 3. With active zeal.[g]

History of sacrifice.—All nations have offered sacrifice to some beings whom they have deified. There is no region where the pilgrim's foot can travel, where you will not find offering, some sanguinary, some libidinous, some foolish, but all to propitiate the anger, or secure the protection, of some fancied object of worship. There comes a cry groaning out of the great heart of humanity, "What is the acceptable sacrifice?" Strange divinations and stre&ning altars ; cakes for the queen of heaven, and prostrations before the brazen image ; children for the insatiate Moloch passing through the scorching fire,—these are the responses from classical and pagan times. African Fetichism, Hindoo immolations, and Burman cruelties, and the atrocities of savage cannibalism,—these are the hollow answers from the uninstructed consciences of heathens. Cold morality, and rubrical exactitude, and sacramental efficacy, and ascetical self-denial,— these are the polite and conventional theories of modern formalism.[h]

B.C. 1491.

must obey the laws, and the people the magistrates." — *Solon.*
"The Law is what we must do; the Gospel what God will give."—*Luther.*
[h] *W. M. Punshon.*

11—13. (11) **thus** .. **it**, *etc.*,[a] as fully prepared for a journey. **ye** .. **haste**, as eagerly impatient to leave Egypt. **passover**,[b] Heb. *pesah*=a leap, transition. (12) **against** .. **judgment.**[c] **I** .. **Lord**, the one God of the whole earth. (13) **blood** .. **token**, "a sacramental pledge of mercy."[d]

The paschal lamb.—I. The paschal lamb was a type of Christ. 1. Not a bone broken ; 2. Perfect ; 3. Nothing passed to corruption. II. Its sacrifice typified the sacrifice of Christ. 1. It was a sacrifice ; 2. Offered in the holy place ; 3. Blood sprinkled on the altar. III. The entireness of the offering shadowed a perfect Saviour. 1. Roasted *whole* ; 2. *Roasted;* none of the substance lost.[e]

Idolatry in ancient Britain.—British Christians ought to recollect that their ancestors were once blind idolaters, serving them that by nature are no gods. Dr. Plaifere, in a sermon preached before the University of Cambridge, in 1573, remarks, that, before the preaching of the Gospel of Christ, no church here existed, but the temple of an idol ; no priesthood but that of paganism ; no God but the sun, the moon, or some hideous image. To the cruel rites of the Druidical worship, succeeded the abominations of the Roman idolatry. In Scotland stood the temple of Mars ; in Cornwall, the temple of Mercury ; in Bangor, the temple of Minerva ; at Malden, the temple of Victoria ; in Bath, the temple of Apollo ; at Leicester, the temple of Janus ; at York, where St. Peter's now stands, the temple of Bellona ; in London, on the site of St. Paul's Cathedral, the temple of Diana ; and at Westminster, where the Abbey rears its venerable pile, a temple of Apollo.[f]

how it was to be eaten
[a] Lu. xii. 35; 1 Pe. ii. 11.
[b] Is. xix. 1.
[c] Nu. xxxiii. 4.
[d] *Spk. Comm.*
[e] *Dr. Fowler.*

"Idolatry is one of the most unconquerable of all the corrupt propensities of the human soul. Miracles under the new dispensation had scarcely ceased, the apostolic fathers were scarcely cold in their graves, before idolatrous forms were again superinduced upon the pure spirituality of the Holy Gospel."—*J. B. Walker.*
[f] *Dr. Smith.*

14—20. (14) **memorial,** a commemorative ordinance. **keep** .. **Lord**, ye shall festivally keep it a feast. **by** .. **ever,**[a] *lit.* a statute of eternity. (15) **seven days,** *i.e.* fr. even. of 14th of Nisan to end of 21st. **leaven,**[b] that wh. produces fermentation or putrefaction : corruption. (16) **convocation,** solemn religious assembly. (17) **in** .. **day,** *lit.* in the strength or bone of this day. **armies,** not a confused rabble, but an organised host. **therefore** .. **ever,**[c] the perpetual memorial of a great deliverance. (18—20) Repetitions to emphasize the command and prevent mistakes.

The paschal feast.—I. The paschal feast recalled the bondage —1. Of Egypt and of sin : the bitter herbs ; 2. Leaven, the symbol of corruption, was left out of the bread. A lesson to us to flee temptation. II. The circumstances of the feast typified the Christian life. 1. Girded, expected to travel ; 2. Shod, ready for rough ways ; 3. Staff in hand, help and protection ; 4. In haste, waiting for orders ; 5. Haste, no excuse for neglect of duty.

the passover an ordinance for ever
[a] 2 Ki. xxiii. 21; Lu. xxii. 19.
[b] 1 Co. v. 7.
[c] Ex. xiii. 3, 8.
[d] *Dr. Fowler.*

"A multitude of laws in a country is like a great number of physicians, a sign of weakness and malady." — *Voltaire.*

266 EXODUS. [Cap. xii. 21–28.

B.C. 1491.

"As diseases must necessarily be known before their remedies, so passions come into being before the laws which prescribe limits to them."—*Liry.*
v. 14. *H. Grove*, i. 33.

the purpose of the sprinkled blood

a *Dr. Royle.*
b *Burckhardt.*
c Ho. xi. 28; Is. xxvi. 20.
d Ezek. ix. 6; Re. vii. 3; ix. 4; 2 Sa. xxiv. 16.
e Josh. v. 10.
f *Dr. Thomas.*

"The influence of costume is incalculable; dress a boy as a man, and he will at once change his own conception of himself."— *Bayle St. John.*

"If gratitude is due from children to their earthly parents, how much more is the gratitude of the great family of man due to our Father in heaven."—*H. Ballou.*

g Topics.

the passover to be explained to the children

a Ex. iv. 31.

"In the humblest condition, a power goes forth from a devout and disinterested spirit, calling forth silently moral and religious senti-

III. It also typifies the social life. 1. Feasted in companies; 2. This teaches the unity of families and Christians. Family-worship, etc.*d*

The exclusion of leaven.—The exclusion of leaven for seven or eight days might, as Harmer observes, be attended with some inconveniences in Great Britain, but none at all in Palestine. The usual leaven in the East is dough kept till it becomes sour, and which is kept from one day to another for the purpose of preserving leaven in readiness. Thus, if there should be no leaven in all the country for any length of time, as much as might be required could easily be produced in twenty-four hours. Sour dough, however, is not exclusively used for leaven in the East, the lees of wine being in some parts employed as yeast.

21—25. (21) **Moses**, being commanded proceeds now to obey. **families**, *see* vv. 3, 4. **and .. passover,** *i.e.* the lamb, whose blood should furnish the sign. (22) **hyssop,** prob. the caper plant*a* (*capperis spinosa*), called by Arabs *azuf*. The *aszef* of frequent occurrence in Sinai.*b* **none .. morning,***c* safety only under the protection of the sign. (23) **destroyer,***d* a personal agent, destroying angel. (24) **observe,** *etc., see* vv. 14, 17. (25) **when,***e* *etc.*, amid the blessings of the present, ye shall never forget this great deliverance.

The destroying angel.—Let us consider how the method of the Israelites' deliverance on this occasion illustrates the method of man's spiritual deliverance.—I. It involved a sacrifice of human life. A lamb was taken for every house. The young creature, the embodiment of innocence, was sacrificed for their deliverance. So the self-sacrificing love of Christ is our salvation. II. It transcended human invention. What man could have thought of such a means of deliverance as this? III. It proved completely efficient. Whoever tried it was saved. IV. It required for its application practical trust in God. V. It formed a memorable era in the history of the Jews. From the birth of Christ we date our history.*f*

Hyssop.—Stanley says, "The *lasaf* or *azaf*, the caper-plant, the bright green creeper which climbs out of the fissures of the rocks in the Sinaitic valleys, has been identified, on grounds of great probability, with the hyssop, or *ezob* of Scripture, and thus explains whence came the green branches used even in the desert, for sprinkling water over the tents of the Israelites" (Nu. xix. 6–18). Ritter, Forskal, Richardson, and others, also name the *aszef*. In every respect this plant answers to the requirements of Scripture.*g*

26—28. (26) **children,** *etc.*, the ordinance so kept as to excite their attention. (27) **say,** *etc.*, the fathers to be ready with an explanation. **people .. worshipped,***a* in token of faith and reverence. (28) **the .. away,** from tribal and other assemblies in wh. the directions had been given. **did .. they,** minute obedience in preparing for and keeping the passover.

The passover.—Of Divine institution (Ex. xii. 1, 2). Began 14th of 1st mo. at even. (2, 16, 18; Le. xxiii. 5; Nu. ix. 3): lasted seven days (Ex. xii. 15; Le. xxiii. 6). Called: Passover (Nu. ix. 5; Jo. ii. 23); Jews' P. (13, xi. 55); Lord's P. (Ex. xii. 11, 27); feast of unleavened bread (Mk. xiv. 1; Lu. xxii. 1); days of unleavened bread (Ac. xii. 3; xx. 6). Paschal lamb eaten 1st day (Ex. xii. 6, 8), and unleavened bread (15; De. xvi. 3). Laws relating to leaven (Ex. xii. 15—20; xiii. 7: De. xvi. 4). Convocations on first and last days (Ex. xii. 16: Nu. xxviii. 18, 25). Sacrifices during (19—24; Le. xxiii. 8); after Sabbath in, first-fruit of barley harvest offered (10—14). Commemorative of: Passing over firstborn (Ex. xii. 12, 13); deliverance fr. Egypt (17, 42, xiii. 9; De. xvi. 3). Perpetual observance (Ex. xii. 14; xiii. 10); children taught its nature (Ex. xii. 26, 27; xiii. 8; De. vi. 20—25); purification needful (2 Ch. xxx. 15—19; Jo. xi. 55); unclean kept it the 2nd mo. (Nu. ix. 6—11; 2 Ch. xxx. 2, 3, 15); uncircumcised excluded (Ex. xii. 43, 45); punishment for neglect (Nu. ix. 13), or improper keeping of (2 Ch. xxx. 18, 20). Noted occasions: As the exodus (Ex. xii. 28, 50); in the wilderness (Nu. ix. 3—5); entering Canaan (Jos. v. 10, 11); reign of Hezekiah (2 Ch. xxx. 1), of Josiah (2 K. xxiii. 22; 2 Ch. xxxv. 1, 18). Moses kept through faith (He. xi. 28); Christ observed (Ma. xxvi. 17—20; Lu. xxii. 15; Jo. ii. 13, 23): room lent to strangers (Lu. xxii. 11, 12); Lord's Supper instituted at (Ma. xxvi. 26—28); a prisoner released at (Ma. xxvii. 15; Lu. xxiii. 16, 17); Sabbath in, a high day (Jo. xix. 14, 31).[b]

29, 30. (29) **midnight,**[a] when Egypt was sleeping in fancied safety. **Lord,** by the hand of the destroyer. **from .. cattle,**[b] *see* xi. 5. (30) **rose .. servants,** startled by the midnight cry. **and .. Egypt,**[c] of the dying in their agony, of survivors in their grief. **house,** or family.
The death of the firstborn.—Note—I. That when miracles are needed they are never wanting. The smiting was a miracle in— 1. The prediction; 2. The simultaneousness of the stroke: 3. Taking only Egyptians: 4. Taking only the firstborn. II. That when God smites us, He smites us where we feel. Pharaoh, humbled, sends for Moses whom he had refused to see again. In affliction men surrender. We should repent in fair weather. III. That God is no respecter of persons. He smites from the prince to the prisoner.[d]
The exodus.—The exodus of Israel was a sublime national fact. It is not mentioned on the monuments. References to any fact disparaging to Pharaoh or his people, it is necessary to observe here, were never inscribed on the monuments. This is a well-established practice. But in the pages of writers external to Egypt, and friendly to it, we find unmistakable references to the exode, only described according to distorted traditions. Manetho, who lived two hundred years before Christ, gives the following version of this event:—" The whole country of Egypt was afflicted with leprosy, which prevailed chiefly in one class. The king was ordered by the gods to clear the country of the lepers. He therefore set them to work in quarries, as slaves. They afterwards revolted and made a priest of Heliopolis, named Moses, their leader, and were expelled."[e]

31—36. (31) **he,** Pharaoh. **by night,** that same night: lest with the new day there should come new judgments. **said,** *etc.*, the humbled king is anxious to be rid of them. (32) **take .. gone,** Pharaoh surrenders at discretion. **and .. also, with** crushed spirit he craves a blessing through Moses. (33) **urgent, strong,** *i.e.* in their entreaties for Israel to depart. **for .. men,** they dreaded more than they had suffered. (34) **kneading-**

B.C. 1491.

ment, perhaps in a child, or some other friend, and teaching, without the aid of words, the loveliness and peace of sincere and single-hearted virtue." — *Channing.*
"With threats he forbade Moses to see his face again; and Moses sealed this rejection of the day of grace with the words, 'Thou hast spoken well, etc.'"— *Smith's Old Test. Hist.*
b *Topics.*

the destruction of the firstborn
a 1 Th. v. 3.
b Job xxxiv. 19, 20.
c Pr. xxi. 13; Jas. ii. 13.
d Dr. Fowler.

"Death, whether it regards ourselves or others, appears less terrible in war than at home. The cries of women and children, friends in anguish, a dark room, dim tapers, priests, and physicians, are what affect us the most on the deathbed. Behold us already more than half dead and buried." — *H. Home.*
e *Quiver.*

Israel borrows of the Egyptians

"Liberty must be a mighty thing; for by it God punishes and rewards

B.C. 1491.

nations." — *Ide. Stretchine.*
a Ps. cv. 37; Pr. xvi. 7; Ge. xv. 14.
b Bush.
c Dr. Fowler.
"Liberty is an old fact. It has had its heroes and its martyrs in almost every age. As I look back through the vista of centuries, I can see no end of the ranks of those who have toiled and suffered in its cause, and who wear upon their breasts its stars of the legion of honour." —*Chapin.*
"Liberty is to the collective body, what health is to every individual body. Without health no pleasure can be tasted by man, without liberty no happiness can be enjoyed by society."—*Bolingbroke.*
d *Harmer.*

the Exodus

from Rameses to Succoth

a Ex. i. 11; Ge. xlvii. 11; Nu. xxxiii. 3.
b See Payne Smith's *Hampton Lectures*, 1869, p. 88.
c Nu. xi. 4.
"O, give me liberty! for even were paradise my prison, still I should long to leap the crystal walls."—*Dryden.*
d *Niebuhr.*

time of the sojourning in Egypt

a Ge. xv. 13; Gal. iii. 17.
b Hab. ii. 3.
c De. xvi. 6.

troughs, prob. small wooden bowls. **bound.. shoulders,** *i.e.* they made a bag of the folds of their dress. (35) **borrowed,** *see* iii. 22. (36) **lent, gave,** granted their request. **and.. Egyptians,**ᵃ "they go out from the land of their oppressors, greatly increased, mighty, and formidable; laden with the spoils of their cruel oppressors, the well-earned reward of the labours of many years, and of much sorrow."ᵇ

The flight from Egypt.—Observe—I. God appeals to motives. The awful terror, wailing mingled with groaning. The bondage of Israel hurries them out. We must decide, God only gives the convictions. II. God's wrath is just. 1. Warnings had failed; 2. The Egyptians only reaped what they had sown; 3. We should hear while it is called to-day. When God speaks, delay is not safe. III. The favour of God's people is a blessing. Pharaoh asked their blessing. IV. God's movements are organised.—1. Six hundred thousand warriors; 2. Women and lads with the flocks and herds; 3. Everyone something to do. Each child may do something.ᶜ

Kneading-troughs.— These were probably of leather. The Arabs use small wooden bowls for kneading the unleavened cakes which they prepare for strangers in the very desert through which Israel journeyed; but they have also among their kitchen furniture a round leather coverlid, which they lay on the ground, and which serves them to eat from. It has rings round it, by which it is drawn together with a chain that has a hook to hang it up by, either to the side of the camel or in the house. This draws it together, and sometimes they carry in it the meal made into dough; in this manner they bring it full of bread; and when the repast is over, carry it away at once, with all that is left, in the same manner.ᵈ

37—39. (37) **Rameses,**ᵃ one of the treasure cities, **Succoth,** *lit.* tents or booths: ab. half way betw. Rameses and Etham. **six.. foot,** *i.e.* the males who could march, or, above the age of twelve or fourteen. **children,** total number of Israelites prob. ab. two millions.ᵇ (38) **mixed.. them,**ᶜ other sojourners anxious fr. various causes to leave Egypt at this time. **flocks.. cattle,** provision for their journey. (39) **dough.. leavened,** *see* v. 34.

Bread-baking.—"The Arabians of the desert use a heated plate of iron in preparing their cakes, which are often as thin as wafers. When they have no iron plate, they roll their dough into balls, and put it either among the live coals, or into a fire of camel's dung, where they cover it till it is penetrated by the heat. They then remove the ashes, and eat the bread while it is scarcely dry, and still hot. In the towns, the Arabians have ovens like ours; their bread is of barley-meal, and of the form and thickness of our pancakes; but they never give it enough of the fire."ᵈ

40—42. (40) **four.. years,** reckoned prob. fr. time of promise to Abraham.ᵃ (41) **even.. pass,**ᵇ the length of sojourn and time of departure definitely stated. (42) **night,**ᶜ one of the most memorable nights of Scripture.

Redemption celebrated.—I. The events to be celebrated.—1. Great was the deliverance of Israel from Egypt; 2. Greater is our deliverance from sin. II. The day on which they are to be celebrated. III. The manner of their celebration. We should— 1. Keep a feast unto the Lord; 2. Dedicate ourselves to Him as His peculiar people.*d*

The sojourn in Egypt.—This passage has been conceived to contradict Gen. xv. 13, where it is announced to Abraham that his seed should be a stranger in a land that was not theirs, and should serve them, and should be afflicted four hundred years. But the passages are perfectly consistent, the computation being made from two different epochs. In Genesis, the time is calculated from the promise made to Abraham of a son, or from the birth of Isaac; but in Exodus, it is computed from his departure from his native country, in obedience to the Divine command. The probability is that there is a defect in the present Hebrew text, in the passage at the head of this article: for the Samaritan Pentateuch, in all its copies, as well as the Alexandrine copy of the LXX., reads, "Now the sojourning of the children of Israel, and of their fathers in the land of Canaan, and in the land of Egypt, was four hundred and thirty years." *e*

43—47: (43) **stranger**, uncircumcised, unproselyted. (44) **when .. him**, and he by that rite has been received into the congregation of the people. (45) **foreigner**, sojourner, dweller, inhabitant. (46) **house**, or company; *see* v. 4. **neither .. thereof**,*a* note the typical significance. (47) **all**,*b* etc., without exception, through all generations.

Cooking in the East.—Thevenot says in his *Travels* that it is also common in Persia to roast sheep and lambs whole. This is done in an oven, which has an opening at the top; after it is well heated, the meat is hung up in it, and a dripping-pan put under to receive the fat; and in this manner it is well done on all sides. He mentions another way to roast a sheep, customary among the Armenians, and in which they likewise avoid fuel that yields smoke. After the animal is killed, and the skin is taken off, it is again wrapped in it, and laid in an oven on burning coals, and likewise covered with them; as it has in this manner fire on all sides, it is well done, and the skin prevents its burning.

48—51. (48) **then .. it,** his partaking of the passover conditional on his submitting to this rite. **he .. land**, having equal privileges, under the same laws. (49) **one law,** *etc.*, all the circumcised were to constitute one nation. (50) **thus,** ref. to all that Moses had commanded so far. (51) **the .. day,** *see* v. 41. **armies,** ranks: organised acc. to tribes and fams.*a*

Witnesses from the dead.—A truly interesting portion of the history of Egypt began with the birth of Moses, and ends with the passage through the Red Sea. The *tebah*, or ark, in which the infant Moses was laid and entrusted to the river, is frequently represented on the monuments as having been used for keeping birds or small animals. Belzoni copies from the tombs of the kings an ark of bulrushes, in which is an infant with a hawk's head—the hieroglyphic symbol of wisdom. The princess who rescued Moses was named Thuoris. She was a daughter of Pharaoh-Rameses, and wife of Siptha, a mere child, according to Egyptian law, who was joined ostensibly with her in the viceregency of Egypt. On her tomb are the suggestive inscriptions, "Priestess of Eve, and the wife of Adam." On an obelisk we

---

B.C. 1491.

d C. Simeon, M.A. "Liberty will not descend to a people; a people must raise themselves to liberty; it is a blessing that must be earned before it can be enjoyed. That nation cannot be free, where reform is a common hack, that is dismissed with a kick the moment it has brought the rider to his place."—*Colton.*

e Dr. Kennicott.

bye-laws of the passover feast

a Jo. xix. 33, 36.

b Nu. ix. 13; Is. liii. 6.

"The only rational liberty is that which is born of subjection, reared in fear of God and love of man, and made courageous in the defence of a trust, and the prosecution of a duty."—*Simms.*

a Nu. xi. 14; Is. lvi. 6, 7; Gal. iii. 28; Eph. iv. 4—6.

"Many politicians are in the habit of laying it down as a self-evident proposition, that no people ought to be free till they are fit to use their freedom. The maxim is worthy of the fool in the old story, who resolved not to go into the water till he had learned to swim."—*Macaulay.*

find her described as "royal wife," "lady of both countries," "the daughter of Pharaoh," this last designation being the Scriptural one. Moses, we are told, "refused to be called the son of Pharaoh's daughter."[b]

CHAPTER THE THIRTEENTH.

sanctification of all the firstborn

B.C. 1491.

1—4. (1) **Lord .. saying**, prob. these precepts were given in Succoth. (2) **firstborn**,[a] protected from the destroyer, they were esp. His. (3) **out .. bondage**, *lit.* house of servants. (4) **Abib**,[b] *lit.* an ear of corn.

Redemption of the firstborn.—The law of Moses declared the firstborn, if a boy, to be sacred to God, and required him to be redeemed from the priest. The modern Jews maintain, "if the firstborn of an Israelite be a son, the father is bound to redeem him, from the thirtieth day forward. If he redeem him before that time it is not accounted a redemption. If he omit it after that, he is guilty of neglecting an affirmative precept. On the thirty-first day the father sends for a priest and places his little son on a table, saying, 'My wife, who is an Israelitess, has brought me a firstborn, but the law assigns him to thee.' The priest asks, 'Dost thou therefore surrender him to me?' The father answers in the affirmative. The priest then inquires which he would rather have, his firstborn, or the five shekels required for his redemption. The father replies, he prefers his son, and charging the priest to accept the money, pronounces a form of benediction. The father then produces the value of five shekels, and the priest asks the mother if she had been delivered of any other child, or miscarried. If she answers no, the priest takes the money, lays it on the head of the child, and says, 'This son being a firstborn, the blessed God hath commanded us to redeem him, as it is said, "And those that are to be redeemed, from a month old thou shalt redeem them, according to thine estimation, for the money of five shekels, after the shekel of the sanctuary, which is twenty gerahs" (Numb. xviii. 16). Whilst thou wast in thy mother's womb thou wast in the power of thy Father who is in heaven, and in the power of thy parents; but now thou art in my power, for I am a priest. But thy father and mother are desirous to redeem thee, for thou art a sanctified firstborn, as it is written, "And the Lord spake unto Moses, saying, Sanctify unto Me all the firstborn; whatsoever openeth the womb among the children of Israel, both of man and of beast, it is Mine"' (Exod. xiii. 2). He then turns to the father, and says, 'I have received these five shekels from thee, for the redemption of this thy son; and, behold, he is therewith redeemed, according to the law of Moses and Israel.'" This ceremony is followed by feasting. When the father dies before the thirty-first day, the mother is not bound to redeem her son, but a piece of parchment or small plate of silver is suspended on the child's neck, with a Hebrew inscription, signifying a firstborn son not redeemed, or a son of a priest.[c]

a Ex. xxii. 29, 30; De. xv. 19; Le. xxvii. 26; Nu. iii. 13; Lu. ii. 23; 1 Co. xv. 20; Col. i. 15; He. xii. 20.

b De. xvi. 1. "From *abab*, to produce fruit, esp. early spring fruit; comp. *Aprilis*, fr. *aperio*, to open; and ἄνοιξις, the modern Greek wd. for the season of Spring, fr. ἀνοίγω, to open."—*Wordsworth.*

"Historians ought to be precise, truthful, and quite unprejudiced, and neither interest nor fear, hatred nor affection, should cause them to swerve from the path of truth, whose mother is history, the rival of time, the depositary of great actions, the witness of what is past, the example and instruction to the present, and monitor to the future."—*Cervantes.*

c Dr. Cox.

J. Saurin, Dis. Hist. ii. 91; and Disser. 399.

the purpose of the passover to be explained to the children

5—10. (5) **Lord .. land**,[a] *etc.*, *see* on iii. 8. **service**,[b] ordinance, memorial. (6, 7) **seven days**,[c] *etc.*, *see* xii. 15, 20. (8) **thou .. son**,[d] *see* xii. 26. (9) **sign .. eyes**,[e] prob. fig., taken by Heb. writers in a lit. sense, and hence phylacteries. **that ..**

mouth,' *i.e.* be familiar and often spoken of. (10) **keep .. season**, at the appointed time. **from .. year**, *lit.* fr. days onward to days.
Phylactery for the head.—The box of which the phylactery for the head is made has on the outside to the right the regular three-pronged letter *shin*, which is designed as an abbreviation of the Divine name *Shadai*, "the Almighty," whilst on the left side it has a four-pronged *shin*, the two constituting the sacred number seven. The leather case consists of four cells, in which are deposited four slips of vellum, whereon are written the four passages of Scripture, already mentioned, in the following order:—

4.	3.	2.	1.
De. xi. 13, 22.	De. vi. 4—9.	Ex. xiii. 11—16.	Ex. xiii. 2—10.

Each slip is rolled up, tied with white and well-washed hairs of a calf or cow's tail, and deposited in the respective compartments as indicated above. A flap connected with one side of the brim is then drawn over the open part, and sewed to the brim in such a manner as to form a loop on one side. Through this loop is passed a very long leather strap, which when tied together according to measure yields a band for the head.*g*

11—16. (11) **Lord .. land**, *see* v. 5. (12) **set apart,***a* *lit.* caused to pass over, *i.e.* transference of ownership. (13) **thou .. lamb**, wh. being given to the Lord, he retained his ownership of the ass. **thou .. neck**, thou shalt not be advantaged by what has once been devoted, unless thou dost redeem it. (14) **and .. son,***b* *etc.*, *see* xii. 26. (15) **when .. go**, *lit.* when Pharaoh hardened against sending us out. **but .. redeem**, for law of redemption, *see* Nu. xviii. 16. (16) **token**, *etc.*, *see* v. 9.

Redemption of the firstborn.—The ordinance here mentioned the Jews, to the latest generations, were bound to observe as—I. A memorial of God's mercy. Now the deliverance vouchsafed to us infinitely exceeds theirs. Everything therefore should serve to bring it to our remembrance. II. An acknowledgment of their duty. In this view God called upon the Jews, and He now calls upon us to—1. Consecrate ourselves to Him; 2. Serve Him with the best of all that we have. Conclusions—(1) Inquire into the nature and ends of God's ordinances; (2) Devote yourselves to the service of your God; (3) Endeavour to instruct others in the great work of redemption.*c*

The phylactery for the arm.—The phylactery for the arm consists of the same sized box as the one for the head. It has, however, no letter outside, and only one compartment inside. The four passages deposited in it are written on one slip of vellum in four columns, having seven lines each. The slip is rolled and tied, and closed up in the same manner as the others. The large leather strap which is passed through the loop is made into a noose for the arm to pass through. Before commencing his morning prayers the youth of thirteen puts on first the phylactery for the arm. Having put his left naked arm through the sling in such a manner that when it is bent it may touch the flesh and be near to the heart, to fulfil the precept, "Ye shall lay up these

---

B.C. 1491.

a Ex. vi. 8.
b Ex. xii. 25.
c 1 Co. v. 7; xii. 23.
d Ps. lxxviii. 2, 7.
e De. xi. 18; Pr. vi. 20, 21.
f Josh. i. 8; De. xxx. 14.

"The only vice that cannot be forgiven is hypocrisy. The repentance of a hypocrite is itself hypocrisy."—*Hazlitt*.

"The hypocrite and the Pharisee, like some beasts, are only valuable for their skin and their fine colours."—*Cudworth*.

g Dr. Ginsburg.

the sanctification of firstborn to be observed in Canaan

a Nu. viii. 17; De. xv. 19; Ezek. xliv. 30.
b De. vi. 20, 25.

"The reason of the injunction is evidently that the ass could not be offered in sacrifice, being an unclean animal; possibly the only unclean animal domesticated among the Israelites at the time of the Exodus."—*Spk. Com.*
c C. Simeon, *M.A.*

"Religion is as necessary to reason, as reason is to religion. The one cannot exist without the other. A reasoning being would lose his reason, in attempting to account for the great phenomena of nature, had he not a

272 EXODUS. [Cap. xiii. 17—22.

B.C. 1491.

Supreme Being to refer to; and well has it been said, that if there had been no God, mankind would have been obliged to imagine one."—Washington.

d Dr. Ginsburg.

My words in your heart" (De. xi. 18); he first twists the long strap three times close to the phylactery in the form of the letter *shin*, which stands for *Shadai*, " the Almighty," and pronounces the following benediction : " Blessed art Thou, O Lord our God, King of the universe, who hast sanctified us with Thy commandments, and enjoined us to put on phylacteries." He then twists the strap seven times around the arm, forming two *shins*, one with three prongs, and the other with four. He next puts on the head phylactery, placing it exactly in the centre between the eyes, so as to touch the spot where the hair begins to grow, in accordance with De. xi. 18, and pronounces the following benediction before he finally secures it : " Blessed art Thou, O Lord our God, King of the universe, who hast sanctified us with Thy commandments, and enjoined upon us the command about phylacteries."*d*

they journey from Succoth to Etham

a Ex. xiv. 11, 12; Nu. xiv. 3, 4; Jer. x. 23; Pr. xvi. 9; Ps. cvii. 7; 1 Co. x. 13.
b Nu. xxxiii. 1; De. xxxii. 10.
c Ge. l. 24, 25; Josh. xxiv. 32; Ac. vii. 15, 16.
d "The situation of Etham is placed by Mr. Stuart Poole at the present Seba Biar, or seven wells, where the cultivated land ceases, about three ms. fr. the W. sides of the ancient head of the gulf. It lies at the S. of the bitter lakes, through which the present Suez canal passes."—Alford.
e Ex. xiv. 19; Nu. ix. 15; Ne. ix. 12; Ps. lxxviii. 14; xcix. 7; Ac. vii. 39; Is. iv 5; 1 Co. x. 1, 2; Ps. cxix. 105.
f Ne. ix. 19; Ps. cxxi. 4.
g Dr. Fowler.
"The richest endowments of the mind are temperance, prudence, and fortitude. Prudence is a universal virtue, which enters into the composition of

17—22. (17) **Philistines,** conspicuously warlike in a war like age. **although..near,** they occupied S. of Palestine, hence the Israelites were led in a S.E. direction. **lest..war,**a for wh. long years of servitude had unfitted them. **and..Egypt,** more willing to be slaves than conquerors. (18) **Red Sea,**b Heb. *Yam-Suph*, Arab. *Bahr Souf*, *i.e.* the Weedy Sea. **harnessed,** marshalled in orderly array. (19) **took..him,**c prob. his mummy. (20) **Etham,**d (*boundary of the sea*, or *sanctuary of Tum*). (21) **Lord..them,** preternatural and safe guidance. **pillar..way,**e condescendingly adopting the cust. sign of leadership (*see below*). **night..light,** they were thus assured both of His presence and the way. **to..night,** this unusual ; but circumstances required a forced march. (22) **took..people,**f until all their wanderings were over.

The fire-pillar.—Consider this pillar of fire as—I. A guide to Israel. 1. Chose the line of march, and their encampment; 2. Was seen from afar by night and by day. II. A type of the guidance given to us by God. 1. Israel was not ready for Canaan ; 2. The people needed to acquire courage. For example, note—Pharaoh's approach; the sighing for flesh-pots; the fear at the reports of the spies. 3. The burdens were tempered to their strength; 4. They are not taken by the shortest road to Canaan ; nor are we to heaven always. III. A prophecy of prosperity (*see* Rev. vii. 15, 16). IV. A fit emblem of Christ.—1. It indicated the Divine presence ; 2. It was out of the field of art, and could not be made to debase God ; 3. It was self-poised ; 4. Though its base was immense as a cloud, yet it was high enough to be called a pillar ; 5. It was both a shelter and a sun ; 6. It was light to Israel and darkness to their enemies. V. The symbol of His presence.—1. It contained some of the Divine glory ; 2. It is called the angel of God (Ex. xiv. 19). God's name means His Divine nature ; angel of God, the angel of the Divine presence. This title carried forward to Christ (Mal. iii. 1). 3. The Shekinah ; 4. The *Oracle* of the chosen people ; 5. It watched over Israel. Learn—" I am the Way."*g*

Fire-signals.—Passages are quoted from classical writers which show that the Persians and Greeks used fire and smoke as signals in their marches. Curtius describes the practice of Alexander, who gave the signal for departure by a fire on a tall pole over his tent. and says, "*observetur ignis noctu fumus interdiu*," Vegetius and Frontinus mention it as a general custom, esp.

among the Arabians. The success of some important expeditions, as of Thrasybulus and Timoleon, was attributed by popular superstition to a Divine light guiding the leaders. To these well-known instances may be added two of peculiar interest, as bearing witness to a custom known to all the contemporaries of Moses. In an inscription of the ancient empire an Egyptian general is compared to "a flame streaming in advance of an army." (*See Chabas*, V. E. p. 54; the inscription is in the *Denkmaler* II. pl. 150, 2.) Thus, too, in a well-known papyrus (Anast. I) the commander of an expedition is called "A flame in the darkness at the head of his soldiers." By this sign, then, of the pillar of cloud, the Lord showed Himself as their leader and general.[h]

B.C. 1491.
all the rest; and where she is not, fortitude loses its name and nature."—*Voiture*.
"Prudence is a necessary ingredient in all the virtues, without which they degenerate into folly and excess."
J. Collier.

[h] *Spk. Comm.*

CHAPTER THE FOURTEENTH.

B.C. 1491.

1—4. (1, 2) **turn**, towards the S.W. **Pi-hahiroth**[a] (*the place where the sedge grows*), W. of the bitter lakes; perh. Ajrud.[b] **Migdol** (*tower*), prob. *Bir Sureis*, about two miles fr. Suez. **Baal-zephon** (*place of Typhon*, or *sacred to Typhon*, otherwise *lord of the north*, or *place of a watch-tower*), near Kolsum or Suez. (3) **entangled**, perplexed, wearied physically and mentally. He knew not of their guide. **the .. in**,[c] their retreat cut off, and the sea before them. (4) **honoured**, glorified. **that .. Lord**,[d] His enemies know Him by His judgments, His friends by His mercy.

Baal-worship.—The festival of Baal or Balder was celebrated on midsummer night in Scandinavia and far up into Norway, almost to the Loffoden Isles, until within the last fifty years. A wood-fire was made upon a hill or mountain, and the people of the neighbourhood gathered together in order, like Baal's prophets of old, to dance round it, shouting and singing. This midsummer's night fire has even retained in some parts the ancient name of Balder's bal, or Balder's fire. Leopold von Buch long ago suggested that this custom could not have originated in a country where at midsummer the sun is never lost sight of, and where, consequently, the smoke only, not the fire, is visible. A similar custom also prevailed until lately in some parts of our islands. Baal has given the name to many Scandinavian localities, as, for instance, the Baltic, the great and little Bolts, Belte turga, Baleshaugen, and Balestranden.[e]

Pi-bahiroth, Migdol, Baal-zepho.
[a] There are places which still bear the name *Ghuwebel-el-Boos, i.e.* the bed of reeds.
[b] *Niebuhr*, voyage, i. 175.
[c] Ps. lxxi. 11.
[d] Ex. ix. 16; Ro. ix. 17, 22, 23.
"A stubborn mind conduces as little to wisdom or even to knowledge, as a stubborn temper to happiness."—*Southey*.
[e] *Lubbock's Prehistoric Times.*
See *Bp. T. Cooper's Brief Expos.*

5—9. (5) **fled**, this sugg. by their change of route. **heart .. people**,[a] recovering fr. their terror, they were filled with rage. (6) **made .. chariot**, *lit*. he bound his chariot, *i.e.* yoked his horses to it. (7) **six .. chariots**,[b] each drawn by two horses, and carrying two men—a driver and a warrior. **captains .. them**, *lit*. captains over the whole of them. (8) **went .. hand**,[c] openly, boldly, powerfully; though the Egyptians said they fled. (9) **overtook**, came up with: they travelled swiftly in their chariots, impelled by rage.

The hour of peril.—I. The inexperienced recruits. II. The women, children, and flocks. III. The whole host hemmed in; mountains on the right, sea on the left and in front, Pharaoh behind. IV. The sight of their old masters armed for slaughter. So Satan sometimes encompasses us.[d]

the pursuit of the Israelites
[a] Ps. cv. 25.
[b] Ps. xx. 7; Ex. xv. 4.
[c] De. xxvi. 8.
[d] *Dr. Fowler.*
"The lust of dominion innovates so imperceptibly that we become complete despots before our war-

The army of Pharaoh.—To the student of Egyptian antiquities there is something of much interest in these two verses, which describe the forces of the Egyptians. Here the pursuing force is described as composed solely of chariots. This is entirely in conformity with the existing testimony of the monuments, which exhibit no kind of military force but war-chariots and infantry—no cavalry, properly so called, that is, warriors on horseback. But few horsemen are at all represented on the monuments, and these are not Egyptians, but foreigners. In a hot pursuit like this, the infantry could, from the nature of the case, take no part, and there being no mounted cavalry, the matter was left entirely to the chariot-warriors.*e*

10—12. (10) **afraid**, being unarmed. **cried**..**Lord,**a their only help. (11) **they**..**Moses,** bitterly taunting him. **because Egypt,** prob. sugg. by the numerous and vast cemeteries in Egypt. **die..wilderness?** where we must lie unburied. **wherefore..Egypt?**b perh. they thought from Moses' antecedents that he was after all playing into the hands of Pharaoh. (12) **better..wilderness,**c a craven-spirited people who preferred a shameful bondage to heroically dying while attempting to escape. The Hebrews were a brave people; and this shows the demoralising effect of long years of slavery.

Difficulty in duty.—Here is difficulty in duty—I. Deeply felt. Three facts may explain why duty in this life should be so invariably connected with difficulty. 1. Our temporary well-being here greatly depends upon the conduct of our contemporaries toward us; 2. The majority of our contemporaries are governed by corrupt principle; 3. The man, therefore, who carries out in his daily life the principles of duty, must more or less excite the anger of his contemporaries. II. Testing character. Look at the influence of this difficulty upon—1. The Israelites. Observe —(1) Their cowardice; (2) Their ingratitude; (3) Their apostasy; 2. Moses. III. Divinely overcome. Thus it is ever ultimately with all difficulty in duty—it is overcome. 1. The nature of moral progress shows this; 2. The promises of God's word insure it.*d*

The path of duty.—Old Humphrey has a good paper against wandering from the path of duty, suggested by a notice at the entrance of a park: "Take notice. In walking through these grounds, you are requested to keep the footpath." Bunyan has supplied the same theme for solemn warning, in the pilgrims straying into By-path-meadow.*e*

13, 14. (13) **stand still,**a *lit.* stand firm, be not dismayed. **and..Lord,** great and complete. **which..day,**b immediate and manifest. **whom..seen,** *lit.* as ye have seen them. (14) **Lord..you,**c and be more than all against you. **ye..peace,**d *lit.* ye shall be silent, confessing it is He who giveth us a victory.

Help from God.—I. When God is in a way of mercy and salvation to His people, He often brings them into great straits. 1. To humble them; 2. Because He delights in the exercise of faith; 3. That He may draw out their prayers; 4. To discover the wicked; 5. That adversaries may vent their malice; 6. That Christ's work may be more manifest. II. In these straits God's people are often mightily troubled. Because—1. The flesh is powerful; 2. There is guilt within; 3. We are prone to worldly

Cap. xiv. 15—18.]   EXODUS.   275

confidence. III. In the time of these straits it is our duty to stand still, and look for God's salvation.—1. For the quieting of our spirits; 2. To expect salvation from God. IV. The sight of salvation coming after straits is glorious to behold.*e*

The great salvation.—Of the various views we can take of this blessed work, this is the most suitable, to consider it as the most glorious deliverance that ever was or will be. Other remarkable deliverances of God's people are considered as shadows and figures of this: Moses, Joshua, David, and Zerubabel, were types of this great Joshua; according to His name, so is He, Jesus a Deliverer. The number of the persons delivered, shows the glory of this deliverance to be unparalleled; it was but one single nation that Moses delivered, though indeed it was a glorious deliverance, relieving sixty thousand at once, and a great deal more, but this was incomparably more extensive. The Apostle John calls the multitude of the redeemed, a multitude that no man could number (Rev. vii. 9), of all nations, kindreds, people, and tongues. The unparalleled glory of this deliverance appears not only in the number of the delivered, but also in the nature of the deliverance. It was not men's bodies only that it delivered, but immortal souls, more valuable than the world (Matt. xvi. 26). It was not from such a bondage as that of Egypt, but one as far beyond it as eternal misery is worse than temporal bodily toil: so that nothing can equal the wretchedness of the state from which they are delivered, but the blessedness of that to which they are brought.*f*

15—18. (15) **wherefore .. Me?***a* Moses prob. also in great anguish of mind. **go forward**, and yet the sea was before them. (16) **divide**, cleave, rend: the waters did not subside, but being torn asunder, were hurled to the right and left, leaving an open path. (17, 18) *see* v. 4.

Go forward.—In seeking to enforce this mandate especially upon young believers, it will be desirable to notice that it comes to those—I. Who have been delivered from bondage. II. Who are beset by foes and confronted with difficulties. III. Who are seeking a better country. Conclusion:—These words are not meant for all. The command for some of you is not "Go forward," but "Stop." For sinners to go forward is death and destruction.*b*

Making salvation sure.—Four travellers, not very well acquainted with the cross-road they were journeying, began to look out for a finger-post. Soon after this one of them cried out, " I think I can see one yonder, in the distance." "And I believe that I can see it too, about half-a-mile off," rejoined another. "And I am almost certain that I can see it," added the third, " it stands up higher than the hedges." "Well, well!" said the fourth, "you may be right or you may be wrong, but we had better make the best of our way to it, for while we keep at such a distance, whether it be a finger-post or not, it will be of little use to us." Now, I want you all to draw near to the Saviour of sinners, and not to be satisfied with "thinking," or " believing," or being "almost certain" that He is your Redeemer; I want you to see Him as your Saviour, as distinctly as you can see the sun in the skies, and to break out with all the conviction and fervency of Thomas the Apostle, "My Lord and my God!" John xx. 28.*e*

B.C. 1491.

remember that they ought not to raise expectations which it is not in their power to satisfy; and that it is more pleasing to see smoke brightening into flame than flame sinking into smoke."— *Johnson.*
e J. Burroughs.
"Faint not; the miles to heaven are but few and short."—*Rutherford*
"Fortune is the best school of courage when she is fraught with anger, in the same way as winds and tempests are the school of the sailor boy." — *Metastasio.*
f J. Maclaurin.

Moses commanded to divide the sea

a Is. lxv. 24; Ro. viii. .6.

b A. G. Maitland.

"It is difficulties which give birth to miracles. It is not every calamity that is a curse, and early adversity is often a blessing. Perhaps Madame de Maintenon would never have mounted a throne had not her cradle been rocked in a prison. Surmounted obstacles not only teach, but hearten us in our future struggles; for virtue must be learnt, though, unfortunately, some of the vices come as it were by inspiration." —*Rev. Dr.Sharpe.*

c G. Mogridge.

B.C. 1491.

the passage of the Red Sea
a Ex. xxiii. 20;
Nu. xx. 16; Is.
lxiii. 9.
b Jude 13.
c Col. i. 12.
d 2 Co. iv. 13.
e Ne. ix. 11; Ps.
lxxiv. 13, cvi. 9,
civ. 3, lxxI. 6;
Josh. iii. 16.
f 1 Co. x. 1, 2;
Hab. iii. 10.
g Dr. Fowler.

"The man who seeks freedom for anything but freedom's self is made to be a slave." — De Tocqueville.

"The cause of freedom is identified with the destinies of humanity, and in whatever part of the world it gains ground by-and-by, it will be a common gain to all those who desire it." — Kossuth.

"Know ye not who would be free themselves must strike the blow? by their right arms the conquest must be wrought?" — Byron.

"Long may it remain in this mixed world a question not easy of decision, which is the more beautiful evidence of the Almighty's goodness, the soft white hand formed for the ministration of sympathy and tenderness, or the rough hard hand which the heart softens, teaches, and guides in a moment." — Dickens.

the Egyptians

19—22. (19) **angel of God**,ᵃ *etc.*, how grt. the astonishment and the reassurance of the Israelites when they beheld this. (20) **between .. Israel**, to check the one and encourage the other. **cloud .. them**,ᵇ who, therefore, saw not the way to pursue. **light .. these**,ᶜ making the road of safety a shining pathway. **so .. night**,ᵈ another memorable night, during which Israel escaped. (21) **east wind**, to have caused an extremely low tide, as some say, the wind must have blown from the N. or N.-W. **divided**,ᵉ into two parts, not forced back by the wind in one part. (*Note* the word *back* in the text is in italics.) (22) **dry**, the wind dried it. **waters .. left**,ᶠ preternaturally kept in check.

The sea-path.—I. The deed of valour. 1. Moses walking down the gravelly beach into the sea; 2. Israel following. A lesson to us to come with boldness. II. The miraculous way. 1. Watery walls; nothing difficult; 2. The dry ground; 3. The way prepared for Israel by the Lord. We walk in new and unseen ways. III. The overthrow of the enemy. 1. His wrath; 2. His foolhardiness; forgetting the plagues. All sin is irrational; 3. His sudden destruction. Death surprises the impenitent. IV. The same instruments both defending and destroying. 1. The cloud; 2. The water; 3. The Gospel. V. What Israel found in the seapath. 1. Rebuke for their murmurings; 2. Filial fear; 3. Trust in God; 4. Trust in Moses; 5. Nationality; before, they were all slaves, then free men, now a nation. Learn—(1) All people must struggle and dare; (2) Our characters come from soulstruggles where self is abandoned, and trust is put in God; (3) Man's extremity is God's opportunity; (4) God will, out of every temptation, make a way of escape.ᵍ

The passage of the Red Sea.—To suppose, as many do, that the Israelites crossed the fords near the head-waters of the sea on the shoals laid bare by a strong north-east wind blowing down the bay at low tide, and that Pharaoh and his hosts were overwhelmed by the returning tide, is to degrade the miracle, to do violence to all the conditions of the narrative, and to annul the effect of this stupendous deliverance upon the nations which should be dismayed by the report of it. In what sense were the children of Israel "entangled in the land," with an open ford before them across the sea? or the waters "a wall unto them on the right hand and on the left, so that the waters stood upright as an heap, and the depths were congealed in the heart of the sea?" Whence the consternation and distress of the Israelites, or the dismay of the nations from afar, at the report of their deliverance? "The people shall hear, and be afraid: sorrow shall take hold on the inhabitants of Palestina. Then the dukes of Edom shall be amazed; the mighty men of Moab, trembling shall take hold upon them; all the inhabitants of Canaan shall melt away. Fear and dread shall fall upon them." And why? Because the Israelites went in safety over the fords at low water, as is customary to this day; but the Egyptians in pursuit were drowned by the returning tide! An English gentleman and author, who had committed himself publicly to the defence of this theory, on examination of the ground at the same time with us, abandoned the theory as utterly untenable and absurd.

23—25. (23) **pursued**, the cloud following Israel, leaving the open path. (24) **in .. watch**,ᵃ which began at two and ended about six. **looked .. troubled,** God's look always troubles the wicked. (25) **took .. wheels,** bound them, *i.e.* by the rocky, sandy bed of the sea. **so .. said,** overwhelmed with a sudden panic, and now in inextricable confusion.

The destruction of the Egyptians.—Consider this destruction of Pharaoh and his host as—I. A judgment. It was—1. Sudden in its execution. No warning given; 2. Terrible in its nature. Involving the destruction of a whole army, the picked men of the most powerful nation in the world; 3. Well merited by the subjects of it. Repeated warnings were conveyed in the plagues, yet all were now disregarded. II. A deliverance. Israel delivered from Pharaoh—1. Out of a perilous situation; 2. Notwithstanding their want of faith; 3. By a glorious miracle. III. A lesson to—1. The sinner. Beware lest your end be like Pharaoh's; heed the warnings given to you; 2. The Christian. Learn to know the greatness of your deliverance from the host of Satan.[b]

Napoleon at Suez.—My next object, as a mere matter of amusement, without reference to the important question of the scenes of the exodus, was to find out the exact spot where Napoleon was overtaken by the waves near Suez. Actuated by latent rationalism, and desirous to contradict the miracle, or at any rate to render it easy of belief to unbelievers, by proving that it was conformable to the ordinary laws of nature, he one day waited for the ebb of the tide, and made an attempt to follow what he supposed were the footsteps of Moses in passing the creek. In regard to his effort in this way, it has been remarked by the author of *Eothen* that he and his horsemen managed the matter in a manner more resembling the failure of the Egyptians than the success of the Israelites. The tide came up, regardless of him and his staff, and it was with great difficulty that any of them reached the land. Some of the people at Suez told me that Napoleon fell from his horse into the sea, and was only dragged out by the assistance of the natives on shore. Others said that he spurred his horse through the water, breast high, back to the beach in front of the English hotel, and that his faithful steed manifested more firmness and sagacity than its rider.[c]

26—31. (26) **the .. Moses,**[a] while the Egyptians were in this sorry plight. (27) **overthrew,**[b] shook them off. (28) **there .. them,**[c] a consideration of the circumstances will show that escape was impossible. (29) **walked,**[d] *etc.*, see v. 22. (30) **saw .. shore,** comp. with their last sight of Egyptians; see v. 10. (31) **great work,** *lit.* great hand.[e]

The sea a vast cemetery.—The sea is the largest of all cemeteries, and its slumberers sleep without monuments. All other graveyards in all other lands show some symbol of distinction between the great and small, the rich and poor; but in that ocean cemetery the king and the clown, the prince and the peasant, are alike distinguished. The same waves roll over all; the same requiem by the minstrelsy of the ocean is sung to their honour. Over their remains the same storm beats and the same sun shines; and there unmarked, the weak and the powerful, the plumed and the unhonoured, will sleep on until awakened by the same trump, when the sea shall give up its dead.[f]

B.C. 1491.

pursuing are troubled

a " At sunrise, a little bef. 6 a.m. in April."—*Spk. Comm.*

b *H. Barnard, B.A.*

"It is sometimes of God's mercy that men in the eager pursuit of worldly aggrandisement are baffled; for they are very like a train going down an inclined plane, — putting on the brake is not pleasant, but it keeps the car on the track."
—*Beecher.*

"How disappointment tracks the stepsof hope."
—*Miss Landon.*

c *Dr. Aiton.*

"We cannot think too oft there is a never, never sleeping Eye, which reads the heart, and registers our thoughts." —*Bacon.*

the sea returns and destroys Pharaoh and his host

a Ps. lxxvii. 16—19.

b De. xi. 4; Hs. xi. 29.

c Ex. i. 22; Ma. vii. 2.

d Ps. cvi. 8—10.

e "The power of the great hand." —*Chaldee.*

"Praise the sea, but keep on land."-*G. Herbert.*

f *Mantell.*

CHAPTER THE FIFTEENTH.

the song of Moses

B.C. 1491.

"The division of the song into three parts is distinctly marked — 1—5, 6—10, 11—18. Each begins with an ascription of praise to God; each increases in length and varied imagery unto the triumphant close." — *Spk. Comm.*

a Ps. lxii. 6—8; Is. xii. 2, xlv. 17, xxv. 1; Ps. lix. 17.

b Ps. cxxxii. 4, 5; 1 Ki. viii. 27; Is. lvii. 15; Jo. xiv. 22; Eph. ii. 22.

c Ps. xxiv. 8, lxxxiii. 18; Re. xix. 11.

d *W. W. Wythe.*

"What is so beneficial to the people as liberty, which we see not only to be greedily sought after by men, but also by beasts, and to be preferred to all things?" — *Cicero.*

"Is life so dear, or peace so sweet, as to be purchased at the price of chains or slavery? Forbid it, Almighty God! I know not what course others may take; but, as for me, give me liberty or give me death." — *Patrick Henry.*

1—3. (1) **triumphed gloriously**, *lit.* gloriously glorious, rider, or charioteer. (2) **the .. song**,ᵃ *lit.* my strength and my song is Jah, the subject of my song, the author of my salvation. **I .. habitation**,ᵇ *lit.* I will glorify Him. (3) **the .. war**,ᶜ mighty in battle, achiever of victories.

The living God.—I. Who was the God of our fathers? 1. A pure being: not the "chance" of the Atheist; 2. A conscious being: not the "mere law" of the Deist; 3. A personal being: not "the all" of the Pantheist; 4. A perfect being, as revealed in the Bible; 5. An emotional being, as manifest in Christ; 6. A communicative being, as imparted by the Holy Spirit. II. What is it to exalt Him? 1. Not by tall spires; 2. Not by a gorgeous ritual; but—3. To adore Him as the object of our worship; 4. To give Him the chief place in our affections.ᵈ

A national emancipation.—From slaves they had become free, from an oppressed tribe, an independent nation.ᵉ It is their deliverance from slavery. It is the earliest recorded instance of a great national emancipation. In later times religion has been so often and so exclusively associated with ideas of order, of obedience, of submission to authority, that it is well to be occasionally reminded that it has other aspects also. This, the first epoch of our religious history, is, in its original historical significance, the sanctification, the glorification of national independence and freedom. Whatever else was to succeed to it, this was the first stage of the progress of the chosen people. And when in the Christian Scriptures and in the Christian Church we find the passage of the Red Sea taken as the likeness of the moral deliverance from sin and death, when we read in the Apocalypse of the vision of those who stand victorious on the shores of "the glassy sea, mingled with fire, having the harps of God, and singing the song of Moses, the servant of God, and the song of the Lamb," these are so many sacred testimonies to the importance, to the sanctity of freedom, to the wrong and the misery of injustice, oppression, and tyranny. The word "redemption," which has now a sense far holier and higher, first entered into the circle of religious ideas at the time when God "redeemed His people from the house of bondage."

4, 5. (4) **cast**, hurled: term applied to throwing of darts. **his .. captains**, *lit.* the choice of his captains, *i.e.* the flower of Egyptian chivalry. (5) **sank .. stone**, clad in mail: their destruction was inevitable.

The flippancy of warfare.—Fifty thousand souls! In studying wars we acquire an almost flippant familiarity with great loss of life, and hardly recognise what it is. We have to think what a beautiful creature any man or woman is, for at least one period of his life, in the eyes of some other being; what a universe of hope is often contained in one unnoticed life; and that the meanest human being would be a large subject of study for the rest of mankind. We need, I say, to return to such homely considerations as the above, before we can fairly estimate the sufferings and loss to mankind which these little easy sentences

—"There perished ten thousand of the allies on this day." "By that ambuscade we cut off nineteen hundred of the enemy." "In this retreat, which was well executed, they did not lose more than five thousand men"—give indication of.*a*

6—10. (6) **right hand,**^a Divine omnipotence: figure for highest degree of power. **hath .. enemy,**^b utterly scattered and destroyed. (7) **wrath,** *lit.* burning: the fire of wrath. **which .. stubble,**^c sugg. the ease as well as the totality of the destruction. (8) **with .. nostrils,**^d prob. allusion to the E. wind. **floods .. heap,**^e most indubitably this was not an ebb of the water or a spring-tide. **depths .. sea,** like a wall of masonry. (9) **said,**^f *etc.*, their boastful vauntings contemptuously referred to. (10) **wind,** *see* xiv. 21. **lead,** helpless, motionless.
God the Deliverer of the Church.—Observe—I. When the enemies of the Church are in the highest fury and resolution, and the Church itself in the greatest extremity and dejection, then is the fittest time for God to work her deliverance fully and perfectly.—1. There are four seasons on the part of the enemy God takes hold of:—(1) Flourishing prosperity; (2) Swelling pride; (3) Eager malice; (4) Confident security. 2. In the same manner, God hath some regard to the Church's straits. It is His usual method to let the Church be in great distress before He commands deliverance. He does this—(1) To exalt His own power; (2) To make to the Church's advantage. II. God is the Author of all the Church's deliverances, whosoever are the instruments. He delivers it—1. Suddenly; 2. Magnificently; 3. Severely; 4. Universally; 5. Totally, irrecoverably; 6. Justly; 7. Wisely.*g*

11, 12. (11) **among .. gods?**^a *lit.* among the mighties: among the potentates. **glorious in holiness,**^b *lit.* glorified in the holy ones, *i.e.* amongst saints and angels. **fearful in praises,** terrible in praiseworthy manifestations of Himself. **wonders?**^c things wonderful, prodigies. (12) **the .. them,** fig. meaning, they have utterly passed fr. sight.
Holiness the supreme end of life.—God's holiness—I. Inspires us with peace of heart. II. Is a strong support to all our endeavours to attain moral and spiritual perfection. III. Lies at the very root of the redemptive work of our Lord Jesus Christ. It is just because God is so holy that He set His heart upon redeeming us from the power of sin. Reconciliation to Him, therefore, cannot be obtained, without our acceptance, among other things, of this, His great end in relation to us.*d*

13—15. (13) **Thy mercy,** not their worthiness. **redeemed,** bought out of bondage. **Thy .. habitation,**^a the dwelling Thou hast chosen for them. (14) **people,**^b of surrounding lands. **the .. Palestina,** *i.e.* the Philistines: in Heb. *pelasheth* = the country of the Philistines. (15) **dukes,** *see* Ge. xxxvi. 15. 16. **mighty .. Moab,**^c renowned for strength and stature. **Canaan .. away,**^d they disappeared "little by little."
Knowledge of salvation.—When the *Royal Charter* was lost, one of the few saved passengers was asked how he had escaped when so many perished? He did not know; he could not tell; all he could say in the matter was that he remembered how the irresistible waters swept him off from where he stood; he was plunged into the deep, and then suddenly found himself cast upon the shore. He was saved though he could not tell how.

B.C. 1491.
a Arthur Helps.

a Ps. cxviii. 15, 16.
Second division of the song; the details more fully given.

b Re. xviii. 21.

c Is. xlvii. 14; Mal. iv. 1; Ma. iii. 12.

d Ex. xiv. 21; Job iv. 9.

e Hab. iii. 10.

f Is. xvii. 13, 14.

"That is a most wretched fortune which is without an enemy."—*P. Syrus.*

v. 7. *Dr. A. Grant,* ii. 139.

g S. Charnock.

a 1 Ki. viii. 23; Ps. lxxxix. 6—8; lxxxvi. 8; Jer. x. 6; 2 Sa. vii. 22; Ps. lxxvii. 14.

b Is. lvii. 17; Lev. xix. 2; Ps. ii. 11; Is. vi. 5; Hab. i. 13; Ps. cxlv. 17.

c Ps. cxxx. 4; Re. xv. 3, 4; Is. vi. 3.

d R. W. Dale, M.A.

a Ps. lxxiii. 24; lxxviii. 54; cxxxv. 21.

b Josh. ii. 9, 10; Ps. xlviii. 6.

c Nu. xxiii. 3; Hab. iii. 7.

d Josh. v. 1.

v. 13. *M. Anderson,* 131.

v. 16. *Dr. J. Gill,* i. 315.

B.C. 1491.

c J. Bate.

This is not the case with the Gospel salvation. He who is saved from his sins, saved from hell, and saved into heaven at last, possesses the knowledge of how he was saved in every instance and in every degree. He knows that it is by the unmerited mercy of God, through the infinite merit of the Saviour's blood. He believed and was saved.*c*

a Is. xliii. 1, 3.
b Ti. ii. 14.
c Ps. lxxx. 8, xl. 2.
d Ps. lxxxvii. 1, 2.
e Ps. cxlvi. 10; vii. 27.
f Pr. xxi. 31.

16—19. (16) **still .. stone**, petrified with wonder and fear, **till .. over,**a *i.e.* over the wilderness, and reached Canaan. **purchased,**b acquired for Thyself from amongst others. (17) **Thou .. in,** finishing what Thou hast commenced. **plant,**c firmly establish. **in .. inheritance,** *see* v. 13. **which .. in,** Canaan the chosen place of the Lord's, as well as His people's, earthly habitation. **sanctuary,**d holy place, ref. to Temple. (18) **reign .. ever,**e allusion to His universal and eternal dominion. (19) **for,** *etc.,*f wh. event is the subject of our song, the ground of our confidence, the source of our joy.

"If you wish to behold God, you may see Him in every object around; search in your breast, and you will find Him there. And if you do not yet perceive where He dwells, confute me, if you can, and say where He is not."—*Metastasio.*

g Mrs. Hemans.

The sound of the sea.—

Thou art sounding on, thou mighty sea,
  For ever and the same!
The ancient rocks yet ring to thee,
  Whose thunders nought can tame.

Oh! many a glorious voice is gone
  From the rich bowers of earth,
And hush'd is many a lovely one
  Of mournfulness or mirth.

But thou art swelling on, thou Deep,
  Through many an olden clime,
Tho billowy anthem, ne'er to sleep
  Until the close of time.*g*

Miriam with a timbrel leads the women's dance
a Nu. xii. 2.
b Top. ii. 122.
c Ps. cxlix. 3; 2 Sa. vi. 5; Ps. cl. 4.
d Mic. vi. 4; Ez. iii. 11; 1 Sa. xviii. 7.
e Ge. xxv. 18.

"The hand drum (Span. *Adujfa,* or *Doeff,* and *Duff,* tambourine; Septuagint, τυμπανον), consists of a hoop of wood or metal, of about one hand breadth, and covered over with leather; it is still a very favourite instrument in the East on festive and sacred occasions (Je. xxxi. 27; Job xxi. 12;

20—22. (20) **Miriam,** of whom we have heard nothing since we found her watching her infant brother. **prophetess,** so called bec. subject of special Divine teaching.*a* **timbrel,**b Heb. *toph* ; a kind of tambourine. **dances,**c quick, moving steps ordered by the measure of the music. (21) **answered,**d they sang alternate stanzas in companies : prob. the men and the women thus responded to each other. (22) *Shur,*e *see* Ge. xvi. 7, prob. the whole district betw. Egypt and Palestine. **they .. water,** fr. *Ayoun Musa* and *Hawara,* the first spot where water is found on the root, is 33 geog. ms.

*Eastern dances.—*Lady M. W. Montague, speaking of the Eastern dances, says, "Their manner is certainly the same that Diana is said to have danced on the banks of Eurotas. The great lady still leads the dance, and is followed by a troop of young girls, who imitate her steps, and if she sings, make up the chorus. The tunes are extremely gay and lively, yet with something in them wonderfully soft. Their steps are varied according to the pleasure of her that leads the dance, but always in exact time, and infinitely more agreeable than any of our dances." (*Letters,* vol. ii. p. 45.) This gives us a different apprehension of the meaning of these words than we should otherwise form. "Miriam the prophetess, the sister of Aaron, took a timbrel in her hand, and all the women went out after her, with timbrels and dances." She led the dance, and they imitated her steps, which were not conducted by a set well-known form, but extemporaneous. Probably David did not dance alone before the Lord when the ark was removed, but led the dance in the same authoritative kind of way. (2 Sam. vi. 14. Judges xi. 34. 1 Sam. xviii. 6.)*f*

23—27. (23) **Marah**ᵃ (*bitterness*). prob. now '*Ain Howarah*,ᵇ where there is still a salt and bitter fountain. (24) **people** .. **Moses,** they praised God for all that went right, and grumbled at Moses for all that went wrong. **saying,** *etc.*, their song of joy exchanged for a murmuring wail. (25) **tree** .. **sweet,**ᶜ there are bushes of the shrub Ghûrkûd about, but no tree can now cure the bitterness. **statute** .. **them,**ᵈ " the healing of the water was a symbol of deliverance from physical and spiritual evils."ᵉ (26) **diseases,**ᶠ afflictions, judgments, **for** .. **thee,**ᵍ *lit.* I am Jehovah thy healer. (27) **Elim** (*trees*, perh. *palmtrees*), prob. the *Wady Ghurundel,* or else *Wady Useit*.ʰ **wells, springs. and** .. **trees,** wh. gave them a grateful shade. **they** .. **waters,** a pleasant rest after a weary march.

The waters of Marah sweetened.—Notice—I. Their trial. This was indeed severe ; but their murmuring was wrong. II. Their deliverance. God declared by this—1. That He is never at a loss for means whereby to effect His purposes ; 2. That He will put honour upon humble and believing prayer. III. God's design in each. He sought to bring them to a sense of—1. Their duty ; 2. Their sinfulness. Learn—(1) To mark the effects of trials and deliverances on our own minds ; (2) To distrust our religious feelings ; (3) To place an entire and uniform dependence on God.ⁱ

The wilderness of Shur.—The Hebrew word Shur means a wall, and when the eastern shore of the Red Sea was examined at the spot where or whereabouts the passage of the Israelites must have taken place, a long slip of desert plain was found fringing the sea-shore, and beyond it a steep barrier or wall of limestone, 1,000 feet in height, stretching parallel to the coast, and forming a most prominent feature in the landscape. No doubt the wilderness derived its name from this long escarpment of limestone rock, and although the name Shur had disappeared, they found the physical features of the district bearing out the Bible nomenclature.ᵏ *A waterless desert.*—Now, for just three days' journey southward along the coast the desert plain is practically speaking waterless, there being only a few wretched brackish springs, about one in every hundred square miles, of which the water is unfit for use.ˡ

B.C. 1491.
Is. v. 12)."—*Kalisch.*
f Burder.
the waters of Marah and the camp at Elim
a Ex. xvii. 3.
b Burckhardt.
c Ps. l. 15; Ex. xvi. 4.
d Jud. ii. 22; Ps. lxvi. 10; lxxxi. 7.
e Spk. Comm.
f De. vii. 12, 15.
g Ps. xli. 3, 4; ciii. 3; cxlvii. 3; 2 Ch. xxx. 20; Pr. iv. 22.
h Stanley Sin. and Pal., pp. 37, 68.
"Wellsted observes that when he tasted the water, and muttered the word, 'Marah,' his Bedouin said, 'You speak the word of truth; they are indeed Marah.'" — *Spk. Comm.*
i C. Simeon, M.A.
"It is a great happiness to get off, without injury and heartburning, from one who has had the ill-luck to be served by you. It is a very onerous business, this of being served, and the debtor naturally wishes to give you a slap."—*R. W. Emerson.*
k Bibl. Treas.
l Capt. Palmer.

CHAPTER THE SIXTEENTH.

1—3. (1) **unto** .. **sin,** the desert-plain *el-Kâa,* wh. begins at *el-Murkhah* and extends to nearly the S. end of Sinaitic Peninsula. (2) **murmured,**ᵃ for want of food, now first felt after six weeks fr. the Exodus. (3) **flesh-pots,** or meat-dishes. **when** .. **full,** though slaves well fed : God designed something better than the supply of mere bodily need. **kill** .. **hunger,**ᵇ yet God provided food for both body and soul.

Constant complaints.—Some people are always "out of sorts." The weather is always just what they don't want. I met one of these men a while ago, a farmer, who raised all manner of crops. It was a wet day, and I said, "Mr. Nayling, this rain will be fine

B.C. 1491.
from Elim to the wilderness of sin
a Ps. cvi. 25; 1 Co. x. 10.
b Lam. iv. 9; Nu. xi. 4, 5.
"O mourner! say not that thou art a target for all the arrows of the Almighty; take not to thyself the pre-

EXODUS. [Cap. xvi. 4-15.

b.c. 1491.

eminence of woe: for thy fellows have trodden the valley too, and upon them are the scars of the thorns and briers of the dreary pathway."—Spurgeon.
c *Dr. Todd.*

the manna and quails promised

a 1 Sa. viii. 7; Lu. x. 16; Ro. xiii. 2.

"It is calculated that not less than one million of the children of Israel died in the wilderness by God's judgment for their murmurings in forty years."—*Bowes.*

b *T. Brooks.*

murmuring of the people and mercy of God

a 1 Ki. viii. 10, 11.

"A people never fairly begins to prosper till necessity is treading on its heels. The growing want of room is one of the sources of civilisation. Population is power, but it must be a population that, in growing, is made daily apprehensive of the morrow."—*Simms.*

r. 11, 12. *G. Austin,* 17.

b *Guizot.*

manna.
a Nu. xi. 31; Ps.

for your grass-crop."—"Yes, perhaps; but it is bad for the corn, and will keep it back. I don't believe we shall have a crop." A few days after this, when the sun was shining hot, I said, "Fine sun for your corn, sir."—"Yes, pretty fair; but it's awful for the rye. Rye wants cold weather." Again: on a cold morning, I met my neighbour, and said, "This must be capital for your rye. Mr. Nayling."—"Yes; but it is the very worst weather for the corn and grass. They want heat to bring them forward."c

4—8. (4) said .. **Moses,** apparently without waiting for a direct appeal. **I .. you,** *i.e.* I am about to rain, *etc.* **a .. day,** *lit.* the matter of a day in his day. **that .. them,** whether they will trust Me. (5) **sixth day,** day bef. the sabbath. **twice .. daily,** provision for the sabbath. (6) **even .. know,** by the sign that should then be given. (7) **glory .. Lord,** the peculiar brightness of the cloud a sign of God's special presence and favour. **what .. us?** what have *we* done? what can *we* do? (8) **your .. Lord,**a whose servants and instruments we are.

Murmuring a mother sin.—As the river Nile bringeth forth many crocodiles, and the scorpion many serpents, at one birth: so murmuring is a sin that breeds and brings forth many sins at once. It is like the monstrous hydra,—cut off one head, and many will rise up in its room. It is the mother of harlots, the mother of all abominations, a sin that breeds many other sins; viz., disobedience, contempt, ingratitude, impatience, distrust, rebellion, cursing, carnality: yea, it charges God with folly: yea, with blasphemy. The language of a murmuring soul is this— "Surely God might have done this sooner, and that wiser, and the other thing better."b

9—12. (9) **come .. Lord,** *i.e.* before the luminous cloud. (10) **glory .. cloud,**a it kindleth into an unwonted brightness. (11) **and .. Moses,** in the presence of the people, that they might see clearly the source of his authority. (12) **even,** *lit.* between the two evenings. **flesh .. bread,** *see* v. 13.

The complainer.—The man who is fond of complaining, likes to remain amidst the objects of his vexation: it is at the moment that he declares them insupportable, that he will most strongly revolt against every means which could be proposed for his deliverance. Indecision is in his character, and the misfortune of having to decide would be to him the greatest of all; for a choice always supposes a preference for some advantage, or an inconvenience to be shunned; and this man would not wish it to be supposed, or to suppose himself, that there is a single circumstance in his life in which he is able to follow his inclinations, or meet with an advantage: that there is even one in which he is not obliged to have the greatest possible inconvenience. He therefore increases misfortune. he wishes for mishaps; the fatal influence of his destiny is his favourite topic. A power against which no act can set him free, which compels him to suffer, without being able to protect himself, and permits him to complain without the fear of obtaining justice,—this is what suits him. he asks nothing better than to sigh over his position, and to remain in it.b

13—15. (13) **quails,**a Heb. *slav,* the common quail b (*Coturnix dactylisonans*); Arab. *selwa*. **came .. camp,** see Nu. xi. 31. (14) **a .. thing,**c minute, atom-like. (15) **manna,**d Heb. *man-*

hu = what is this? for .. **was**, hence the name it went by was significant of their ignorance: it was a mystery, like Christ its antitype the Bread of Life.*e*
Jesus the living bread that came down from heaven.—The old manna—I. Sustained the body. So Christ sustains the spirit. II. Was supplied in the wilderness of Sinai. So Christ is present in the world-wilderness of sin. III. Had to be renewed daily. So our spiritual food must be constantly fresh. IV. Prefigured the broken body in the sacrament of the Lord's Supper. V. Came from heaven. So did Jesus. VI. Was to be gathered in the morning. A lesson to seek Christ early. VII. When neglected, was lost. So with Christ.*f*

Characteristics of the quail.—Resembles partridge, but smaller, ab. 7½ in. long; found in Asia, Africa, and S. Europe; migratory, immense flocks cross the Mediterranean in autumn, and return in spring; 100,000 have been caught in a day on W. coast of S. Italy within an area of four or five miles; body heavy for expanse of w:.g. hence do not fly high, and need to rest often. In crossing the M. Sea they alight on some of the islands, hence those islands were called Ortigia from ορτυξ = a quail. "From those circumstances," observes Bewick, "it appears highly prob. that the quails of Ex. and Num. were driven into the wilderness on their way north by a S.-W. wind sweeping over Ethiopia and Egypt towards shores of Red Sea." The words "two cubits high upon the face of the earth" mean that they were beaten not only from their course by the "wind from the Lord," but downward to within ab. 3 ft. off the earth's surface, and were therefore thus faint with struggling against the wind—easily caught. "Nothing is easier than to take these birds when they have recently arrived, exhausted by their aërial pilgrimage" (*K.P.H.P.* ii. 409). Dr. Bonar, describing the Wady Mukatteb (in desert of Sinai) says, "Flocks of pigeon-looking birds, which we were told were quails, occasionally met us." Hasselquist says, "I have met with it in the wilderness of Palestine, nr. the Dead S. and Jordan, and in the deserts of Arabia Petræa." The pugnacity of the male bird originated the ancient proverb, "as quarrelsome as quails in a cage."*g*

16—21. (16) **gather .. eating**, enough for use, but not for waste. **omer,***a* perh. = to six half-pints, or cotylæ.*b* (17) **and .. less**, and after the gathering distributed an omer each. (18) **omer .. lack,***c* some think they see a miracle here. (19) **let .. morning**, but trust in Him for to-morrow, who has provided to-day. (20) **some .. morning**, through lack of faith. **and .. stank,***d* miraculous.*e* to teach that mercies abused may become curses. (21) **they .. morning,***f* time appointed: cool of the day. **when .. melted**, *i.e.* that wh. was left ungathered melted.

The manna.—I. The want it was intended to supply. The Israelites required bread. II. The manner in which it was given. It was fresh every morning. III. The regulations concerning it. When the sun rose, it melted. If any was kept till the next morning, it "bred worms, and stank." All gathered alike of it. IV. The lessons to be learnt from it. 1. Dependence on God; 2. Appreciation of His goodness.*g*

Gum, or manna, of the tamarisk.—There is a kind of tree or shrub—a species of tamarisk found in this and other regions—

B.C. 1491.

lxxviii. 27, 28, cv. 40.

b Old Fr. *quaille;* It. *quaglia;* Du. *quackel;* Low Lat. *quaquila;* fr. the sound the bird makes.

c Ps. lxxviii. 23—25.

d De. viii. 3.

e Jo. vi. 55—58; Ps. cxxxvi. 25; Re. ii. 17.

f Dr. Fowler.

"One meal a day is enough for a lion, and it ought to suffice for a man."—*Dr. G. Fordyce.*

"Food, improperly taken, not only produces original diseases, but affords those that are already engendered both matter and sustenance; so that, let the father of disease be what it may, intemperance is certainly its mother."—*Burton.*

g Topics.

quantity to be gathered daily per head

a Ex. xvi 36.

b Josephus.

c 2 Co. viii. 13—15.

Lack, *to want;* Dut. *lack, laecke,* want; defect; akin to lax and slack.

d Jas. v. 2, 3.

e "No such tendency to rapid decomposition is recorded of common manna."—*Spk. Comm.*

f Ma. vi. 31—34

284   EXODUS.   [Cap. xvi. 22—26.

B.C. 1491.

g A. M. Heathcote. "At the working man's house hunger looks in, but dares not enter; nor will the bailiff or the constable enter; for industry pays debts as despair increaseth them."—*Franklin.*

"Industry is not only the instrument of improvement, but the foundation of pleasure. He who is a stranger to it may possess, but cannot enjoy; for it is labour only which gives relish to pleasure. It is the appointed vehicle of every good to man. It is the indispensable condition of possessing a sound mind in a sound body."—*Blair.*

h *Kitto.*

none to be gathered on the Sabbath

a Ga. ii. 3; Ex. xxxi. 15; xx. 8; xxxv. 3.

b Ex. xx. 9, 10.

"The green oasis, the little grassy meadow in the wilderness, where, after the week-day's journey, the pilgrim halts for refreshment and repose."—*Dr. Reade.*

"The Sunday is the core of our civilisation, dedicated to thought and reverence. It invites to the noblest solitude and to the noblest society."—*Emerson.*

c *Beecher.*

d Sir R. Peel.

which yields at certain times and in small quantities a kind of gum, to which the name of manna has been given, in the belief that it really was, or that it resembled, the manna by which the Israelites were fed. If any human infatuation could surprise a thoughtful and observant mind—and especially if any folly of those, who deem themselves wiser than their Bible, could astonish —it might excite strong wonder to see grave and reverend men set forth the strange proposition, that two or three millions of people were fed from day to day, during forty years, with this very substance. A very small quantity—and that only at a particular time of the year, which is not the time when the manna first fell—is now afforded by all the trees of the Sinai peninsula; and it would be safe to say, that if all the trees of this kind, then or now growing in the world, had been assembled in this part of Arabia Petræa, and had covered it wholly, they would not have yielded a tithe of the quantity of gum required for the subsistence of so vast a multitude. Indeed, it remains to be proved, that it would be at all salutary or nutritive as an article of constant and substantial food. To us this explanation, which attempts to attenuate or extinguish the miracle, by supposing this natural product to have been at all times and in all places sufficient; to have fallen regularly around the camp, in all its removals, and to have been regularly intermitted on the seventh day, is much harder of belief than the simple and naked miracle —much harder than it would be to believe that hot rolls fell every morning from the skies upon the camp of Israel. A miracle we can understand, however difficult of comprehension; but that which attempts to elucidate a miracle on natural grounds must make no demands upon our faith, must be full and satisfactory, must be consistent and coherent in all its parts.*h*

22—26. (22) **bread**, the manna not a condiment or confection, but substantial food. (23) **to-morrow .. Lord**,*a* the institution of the Sabbath wh. already existed may have been neglected, it is now revived and was afterwards established by law. **bake .. seethe**, wh. shows that manna could be ground and treated as meal. (24) **and .. therein**, God honoured the Sabbath by miraculous preservation of freshness. (25) **to day .. field**, another Divine mark of the Sabbath. (26) **six .. it**,*b* fr. day to day : daily bread.

The Sabbath.—A world without a Sabbath would be like a man without a smile; like a summer without flowers; like a homestead without a garden.*c* I never knew a man to escape failures in either mind or body, who worked seven days in a week.*d* Ceasing from work on the Sabbath is a true economy of time and strength. In the long run men do more in six days who rest on the Sabbath than those who work from week's end to week's end, ignoring the Lord's day. This has been demonstrated by experiment. In 1832, the House of Commons appointed a committee to investigate the comparative effects of working seven days and six days. One of the witnesses, J. R. Farre, M.D., of London, an acute and experienced physician, said—" I consider that, in the bountiful provision of Providence for the preservation of human life, the sabbatical appointment is not simply a precept partaking of the nature of a political institution, but is to be numbered amongst the natural duties, if the preservation of life be admitted to be a duty, and the premature destruction of it a suicidal act."*e*

27—31. (27) **went .. gather,**[a] regardless of the Sabbath. and .. **none,** and had to fast that day. (28) **how long .. laws?**[b] what time and what evidence do you require? (29) **Lord .. Sabbath,** the Sabbath made for man: a gift, a privilege, a blessing, as well as an ordinance. **therefore .. days,** that you may rightly observe and fully enjoy the Sabbath. **abide .. place,** *i.e.* within the camp. (30) **so,** *etc.*, from toil and travel. (31) **called .. manna,** which was not a name defining its nature, but a question confessing their ignorance of its nature. **like .. seed,** Heb. *gad* = coriander[c] (*coriandrum sativum*); an annual, two feet high (nat. ord. *umbelliferæ*) **white,**[d] greyish-white.

The giving of the manna.—It is to be observed that we have all the conditions and characteristics of Divine interpositions. I. The condition of a recognised necessity; for all writers agree that under any conceivable purposes the preservation of the Israelites would otherwise have been impossible. II. The condition of a harmony with a Divine purpose, the preservation of a peculiar people on which the whole scheme of providential government and the salvation of mankind depended. III. We have the usual characteristics of harmony between the natural and the supernatural transaction. God fed His people not with the food which belonged to other regions, but with such as appertained to the district. The local colouring is unmistakable. We may not attempt to give an explanation how the change was effected: to such a question we have but to answer that we know nothing. One thing certain is, that if Moses wrote this narrative, it is impossible that he could be deceived, and equally impossible that he could have deceived contemporaries and eye-witnesses. As for ourselves, we must be content to bear the reproach that we are satisfied with a reference to the almightiness of Jehovah, in which alone faith finds any explanation of the mystery of the universe.[e]

32—36. (32) **that .. bread,** *etc.*, evidence of past mercy miraculously preserved. (33) **pot,**[a] urn. casket. vase. (34) **testimony,**[b] the Law, *i.e.* the ark in which the Law was deposited. (35) **did .. years,** the supply never failed, though they may not have fed exclusively on manna. **until `.. Canaan,**[c] no further need of manna in a land flowing with milk and honey. (36) **omer .. ephah,** both wds. Egyptian; precise quantities not known.

Physical providence.—Consider—I. That God's physical providence recognises the personal wants of each individual: manna fell for each, babe and man—not one overlooked. II. That the enjoyment of God's physical providence depends on trustful labour. III. That an avaricious accumulation of the blessings of physical providence will disappoint the possessor. IV. That the seeking of the blessings of physical providence should never interfere with religious institutions. To prevent labour on the Sabbath, a double portion came on the sixth day. This suggests that religion—1. Does not require us to neglect the body; 2. Has special claims.[d]

The manna of the tamarisk.—Tamarisk, Heb. *eshel*, trans.

B.C. 1491.

e The Hive.

the rule of the Sabbath violated

a 2 Ki. xvii. 14; Ps. lxxviii. 10, 11, 22, 23.

b Ps. cvi. 10, 14.

c Gk. κοριαννον, fr. κορις, a bug; the seeds, when fresh, have a bug-like smell; when dry, this smell passes off, and it has an aromatic odour, and a sweetish taste. Used medicinally as a carminative. "We found it abundant in the valley of the Jordan."—*Tristram.*

d Nu. xi. 7, 8.

"He that remembers not to keep the Christian Sabbath at the beginning of the week will be in danger of forgetting before the end of the week that he is a Christian."—*Sir E. Turner.*

e Spk. Comm.

the pot of manna to be laid up

a He. ix. 4.

b Ex. xxv. 16—21; De. x. 5; Nu. xvii. 4, 10.

c Josh. v. 12; Rev. vii. 16.

d Dr. Thomas.

"O what a blessing is Sunday, interposed between the waves of worldly business like the divine path of the Israelites through Jordan! There is nothing in which I would advise you to be

B.C. 1491.

more strictly conscientious than in keeping the Sabbath-day holy. I can truly declare that to me the Sabbath has been invaluable." — Wilberforce.

"Perpetual memory of the Maker's rest."— *Mant.*

"A world without a Sabbath would be like a man without a smile, like a summer without flowers, and like a homestead without a garden. It is the joyous day of the whole week."—*Beecher.*

e Topics.

"grove" in Gen. xxi. 33, and "tree" in 1 Sam. xxii. 6, is considered by Royle = to Arabic *asul* or *athul*, which = the large Eastern tamarisk tree (*Tamarix orientalis*). It thrives in arid sandy situations. A friend of the writer often saw it in the wadys of the Sinaitic peninsula. It is one of two plants connected with the Rationalistic theory that manna was simply an exudation of some shrub. One of these is the *Alhagi*, camel's thorn, or Judæan manna (*M. hebraica*), from the leaves of which in summer the so-called manna—a kind of honey-dew—exudes. The other is the T. Josephus first gave currency to this supposition (*An.* iii. 16). "This fable foundation has had a great superstructure reared on it by writers who hold that there are no mysteries in God's ways with man, and no true miracles recorded in the history of those ways." The exudation of the T. is sugar, and does not contain mannite. "The monks of St. Katharine, on Sinai, gather the manna of the T. and sell it at a high price to Europeans as the veritable food on which Israel fed for forty years in the wilderness." Dr. Bonar gives twelve reasons to show that this could not be *the* manna. "If Israel had lived on the manna of the T., two miracles would have been necessary; one to render the T. ab. 10,000 times more productive than they are (and this all the year through), and then another to keep the Israelites in bodily health while living on that *one* article." T. manna is a medicine, not food.*e*

CHAPTER THE SEVENTEENTH.

B.C. 1491.

Rephidim
a Robinson, Bib. Res. i. 121.
b Stanley, Sin. and Pal., p. 40. See Kitto, D. Bib. Read.
c Nu. xx. 3.
d Ps. lxxviii. 18, 19, 40—42; xcv. 8, 9.
e Ex. xiv. 11, 12; xv. 24; xvi. 2, 3; Nu. xiv. 2, 3; xxi. 5.

"It is a folly for an eminent man to think of escaping censure, and a weakness to be affected with it. All the illustrious persons of antiquity, and, indeed, of every age in the world, have passed through this fiery persecution. There is no defence against reproach but obscurity; it is a kind of concomi-

1—3. (1) **Rephidim**, (refreshments, rests), locality not identified; perh. *Wady es-Sheikh*,*a* or *Wady Feiran*.*b* there .. drink, a dry and thirsty land. (2) did .. **Moses**,*c* words of complaint and reproach. wherefore .. **Lord?** by doubting His care, and chiding His servants. (3) kill,*d* *i.e.* make or suffer to die.*e*

Rephidim.—The two great events described in Scripture as having taken place at or near Rephidim are—1st, a miraculous production of water from the rock in Horeb : 2nd, a fierce battle with the powerful tribe of the Amalekites, who at that time inhabited the peninsula. About two miles below Paran, on the side towards Egypt from which the Israelites would have approached, there is a spot never noticed by former travellers, which is connected by Bedawin tradition with the miracle of water in Rephidim. It is called Hesy-al-Khattatin, the "concealed spring of the writer," the name writer being often applied by the Bedawin to Moses as the writer of the book of God's law. Here, say they, he struck the rock in obedience to Divine command, so that the water gushed forth to the thirsty tribes. No moisture is now seen about the surface, but there is water they tell you beneath the soil; hence its name. In the next place there is every reason to suppose that Paran is just the spot which the Amalekites would have been sure to defend against an invading force. It contains a beautiful oasis well worth fighting for, and the place is capable of being easily defended against large numbers by a comparatively small force. Besides, as early at least as the seventh century the traditions of the country pointed to this neighbourhood as the site of Rephidim. One of the

Cap. xvii. 4–13.] EXODUS. 287

early geographers. Antoninus Martyr, speaks of having seen a monastic chapel or oratory built upon the spot on which Moses stood during the battle of Rephidim, and on the summit of a hill 600 feet high, Jebel Tahimeh, which overlooks the whole of Feiran—in fact, the whole of that space which would have formed the scene of the contest; the expedition had discovered the ruins of just such a chapel or oratory as Antoninus Martyr describes. At the base of this hill is a low mound, regarded by the early monks with peculiar veneration, which may very well answer to that on which, after the battle of Rephidim, Moses erected the altar of Jehovah-nissi, as described in the 17th of Exodus.*f*

4—7. (4) **they** .. **Me**,*a* the impatience of the people tending towards rage. (5) **take** .. **Israel**, as witnesses. **rod** .. **river**,*b* past wonders to inspire present confidence. (6) **rock**,*c* which tradition points out to this day.*d* (7) **Massah** (*temptation*). **Meribah**, (*strife*).

The rock-fountain.—In great distress, appeal to God. Moses in distress and fear called on God; disciples on the stormy sea. Peter sinking. Note the miracles of the rod on water. On—I. The Nile. II. The fountains. III. The Red Sea. IV. The rock. The rocks obey God, even when men murmur.*e*

Water the purest drink.—Water is the fittest drink for all persons, of all ages and temperaments: of all the productions of nature or art, it comes nearest to that universal remedy so much searched after by mankind, but never discovered. By its fluidity and mildness, it promotes a free and equable circulation of the blood and humours through all the vessels of the body, upon which the due performance of every animal function depends; and hence water-drinkers are not only the most active and nimble, but also the most cheerful and sprightly of all people. In sanguine complexions, water, by diluting the blood, renders the circulation easy and uniform. In the choleric, the coolness of the water restrains the quick motion and intense heat of the humours. It attenuates the glutinous viscidity of the juices of the phlegmatic, and the gross earthiness which prevails in the melancholic temperaments. And as to the different ages, water is good for children, to make their tenacious milky diet thin and easy to digest; for youth and middle age, to sweeten and dissolve any scorbutic acrimony or sharpness that may be in the humours, by which means pains and obstructions are prevented; and for old people, to moisten and mollify their rigid fibres, and to promote a less difficult circulation through their hard and shrivelled vessels.*f*

8—13. (8) **Amalek**,*a* see Ge. xxxvi. 12, 16: a nomad people, dwelling in tents, rich in flocks and herds. (9) **Joshua**,*b* (whose *help is Jehovah*, or *Jehovah the salvation*) now forty-five years of age; orig. name Oshea, called Jesus in N. T.*c* **choose** .. **Amalek**, men to do their part, not neglecting the use of means. **to-morrow** .. **hand**, while using the means he trusted in God. (10) **Hur**, (*cavern*) acc. to Jews husband of Miriam,*d* or her son by Caleb.*e* **went** .. **hill**, to watch the fight and intercede for Israel. (11) **when**,*f* etc., the battle won by prayer not by prowess. (12) **heavy**, weary. **they** .. **thereon**, sympathy with, and help for a man of prayer. **Aaron** .. **side**, strengthening influ-

---

B.C. 1491.

tant to greatness, as satires and invectives were an essential part of a Roman triumph."—*Addison.* "The usual fortune of complaint is to excite contempt more than pity." *Johnson.*
f Capt. Palmer.

the rock is smitten and yields water

a 1 Sa. xxx. 6; Jo. viii. 59.

b Ex. vii. 20.

c "This stone made more impression upon me than any natural object claiming to attest a miracle ever did."—*Dr. Durbin, Obs. on the East*, i. 140. See also *Dr. Hollin, Trav. in the East*, i. 417.

d Nu. xx. 10, 11; Ps. cxiv. 7, 8; Is. xli. 17, 18; xliii. 20; lv. 1; Ps. cv. 41; 1 Co. x. 4; Jo. iv. 14; vii. 37—39; Re. xxii. 17.

e Nu. xx. 13; Ps. lxxxi. 7; He. iii. 8; Ps. xcv. 8.

f Dr. Fowler.

v. 6. W. A. Gunn, 87; *A. Roberts, M.A.*, 323.

Amalek defeated

a Nu. xxiv. 20; xxv. 17—19; a Sa. xv. 2.

b Nu. ii. 18 16.

c Ac. vii. 45; He. iv. 8.

d Josephus.

e Jarchi Ch. Ib. 19.

EXODUS. [Cap. xvii. 14—16.

B.C. 1491.

f Jas. v. 16; Ps. lvi. 9; He. vii. 25; il. 10.

g Spurgeon.
"War makes a better soldier than the most earnest considerations of duty,—familiarity with danger enabling him to estimate the danger. He sees how much is the risk, and is not affected with imagination; knows practically Marshal Saxe's rule; that every soldier killed costs the enemy his weight in lead."—*Emerson.*

h The Hive.

Jehovah-nissi

a 1 Sa. xv. 3, 7, xxx. 1, 17; Pr. x. 7; Ps. lxxxiii. 4, 7; Re. xvii. 4.
b Ps. xx. 5, lx. 4.
c Nu. xxiv. 20; De. xxv. 19.
d W. Jay.
"The course of none has been along so beaten a road that they remember not fondly some resting places in their journeys, some turns of their path in which lovely prospects broke in upon them, some soft plats of green refreshing to their weary feet. Confiding love, generous friendship, disinterested humanity, require no recondite learning, no high imagination, to enable an honest heart to appreciate and feel them."—*Talfourd.*
"It is usually the case that those

ence of prayerful sympathies. **hands .. sun,** a fiercely contested battle lasting a whole day. (13) **with .. sword,** an express. sig. not so much the weapon used as *great slaughter.*

The war of truth.—We have to notice—I. The great warfare, which we think is typical by the contest between the children of Israel and Amalek. Note, that this war—1. Is not with men, but with Satan and with error; 2. Is a most righteous war; 3. Is of the greatest importance; 4. Is waged against very powerful foes; 5. Is to be of perpetual duration. II. The appointed means to be used in this warfare.—1. Hard blows, and hard fighting against sin; 2. Hard and earnest prayer. Both must be used; one is no good without the other. III. Some considerations to stir you up to the war.—1. It is an hereditary war; 2. There is a great prospect of ultimate victory.*g*

A place of rest.—God led Israel to Rephidim—"a place of rest." Israel turned it into a place of murmuring. God in compassion turned it into a place of mercy; and then, being a just God as well as a merciful, permitted it to become a place of conflict. On the field of Waterloo there stands, to mark the place of victory, a huge mound surmounted with the Belgic lion, and here and there may be seen monuments where heroes such as Picton and Ponsonby fell. The victorious Israelites erected not a monument, but an altar. So let us in our successes ascribe the glory to God, "who giveth us the victory."*h*

14—16. (14) **memorial,** past victories not to be forgotten. **and .. Joshua,** for his future encouragement and guidance. **for .. heaven,***a* a warning to those who obstruct the progress of God's people. (15) **altar,** acknowledging the source of victory with a sacrifice of thanksgiving. **Jehovah nissi,***b* (*Jehovah my banner*). (16) **because .. generation,***c* and under this banner God's people shall advance from victory to victory till all their enemies be destroyed.

Amalek destroyed.—This is the first time any mention is made of writing. Simple and familiar as the art now appears, it is difficult, if not impossible, to account for it without Divine origin. How much do we owe to it as Christians? What is the "Scripture" but the *writing?*—I. It is probable that from this time Moses began to keep a journal of striking and useful occurrences. Great men have frequently done the same for intellectual, and good men for religious purposes. II. Whatever may be said of the particular mode, the thing itself is of importance. If we are to be affected with transactions and feelings, they must be in some way secured and retained. III. A reason is assigned for the recording and rehearsing of this transaction in a dreadful menace. The threatening was executed partially by Saul: but fully by David. IV. The Scriptures cannot be broken. Whatever improbabilities appear—whatever difficulties stand in the way—whatever delays intervene—God's counsels of old are faithfulness and truth; not a jot of His Word shall fail.*d*

Early history of writing.—Various doubts have sometimes been thrown out as to the existence of writings at this period. Waiving the evidence of the Mosaic records, we may remark that hieroglyphical inscriptions upon stone were known in Egypt at least as early as the fourth dynasty, or B.C. 2450; that inscribed bricks were common in Babylonia about two centuries later, and that writing upon papyruses, both in the hieroglyphic and the hieratic characters, was familiar to the Egyptians under the eighteenth and nineteenth dynasties, which is exactly the time to which the Mosaic records would belong. It seems certain that Moses, if educated by a daughter of one of the Ramesséde kings, would be well acquainted with the Egyptian method of writing with ink upon the papyrus; while it is also probable that Abraham, who emigrated not earlier than the nineteenth century before our era, from the great Chaldean capital, Ur, would have brought with him and transmitted to his descendants the alphabetic system with which the Chaldeans of his day were acquainted. There is thus every reason to suppose that writing was familiar to the Jews when they quitted Egypt; and the mention of it as a common practice in the books of Moses is in perfect accordance with what we know of the condition of the world at the time from other sources.*

B.C. cir. 1491.

who have sharp and ready wits possess weak memories, while that which is acquired with labour and perseverance is always retained longest, for every hard-gained acquisition of knowledge is a sort of annealing upon the mind."
—*Plutarch.*

e *Rawlinson.*

CHAPTER THE EIGHTEENTH.

B.C. 1491.

1—6. (1) **Jethro**, *see* ii. 18, and iii. 1. **heard .. Egypt**, the report of such astounding events must have rapidly circulated. (2) **Zipporah**, *see* ii. 21, and iv. 25. **after .. back**, incompatibility of temper. Moses the meekest of men saw that her presence would hinder his work. (3) **Gershom**,*a* *see* ii. 22. (4) **Eliezer**, (*God is help*). (5) **came .. wilderness**, a valley near Horeb opening into *Er Rahah* is still called by the Arabs *Wady Shueib*, i.e. the valley of Hobab. **where .. God**, *see* iii. 12. (6) **said**, *etc.*, this the substance of the message that preceded the meeting.

Family reunions (vv. 1—12).—I notice in the account of the reunion of the family of Moses, three directions bearing on our family reunions, as to—I. The salutations at meeting. 1. There is courteousness. This general principle will exclude—(1) Excessive familiarity ; (2) Rudeness ; (3) Pride. 2. There are kindly inquiries ; 3. There is a hearty welcome. II. The subjects of conversation. They should be—1. On public affairs ; 2. On social matters ; 3. With recognition of God ; 4. Fit for mutual response. III. The mode of festivity. We learn—1. That such festivity may not be confined to the family; 2. That it may be preceded by an act of worship ; 3. That it should be with consciousness of the Divine presence. This will make us—(1) Happy; (2) Temperate; (3) Regardful of the soul's progress.*b*

A well-regulated family.—To see a well-regulated family acting as if they were one body informed by one soul; to see those who are embarked together in one bottom, whose interests are inseparably united, and, therefore, whose hearts ought to be so too, acting in concert, adopting each other's cares, and making them their own, uniting their friendly beams, and jointly promoting the common happiness, is a beautiful scene, and amiable even in the sight of that Being who maketh men to be of one mind in a house. To have those who will receive us with an open-hearted cheerfulness, to whom we can discharge the fulness of the soul, to whom we can unburden our cares; and by unburdening we lessen them (for sorrow, like a stream, grows weaker by being divided into several channels); to have those with whom we can share our joys (and joy, like light, by communicating grows greater, and burns brighter): this is a happi-

Jethro, etc., come out to meet Moses

a Ac. vii. 29.

"Nothing is more deeply punished than the neglect of the affinities by which alone society should be formed, and the insane levity of choosing associates by others' eyes."—*Emerson.*

"A frequent intercourse and intimate connection between two persons make them so like, that not only their dispositions are moulded like each other, but their very face and tone of voice contract a certain analogy."—*Lavater.*

b D. G. Watt, M.A.

"What an argument in favour of social connections is the observation that by communicating our grief we have less, and by communicating our pleasures we have more."—*Greville.*

B.C. 1491.

e Seed.

Moses rehearses the story of the Exodus

a Ps. cv. 2; cxlv. 10, 11.

b Ro. xii. 15.

c Ge. xiv. 20; 2 Sa. xviii. 28; Lu. i. 68.

d Ex. v. 2; xiv. 8; Ps. xcv. 3; Dan. iv. 37.

e 1 Co. x 31

f J. Foster.

"If thy friends be of better quality than thyself, thou mayest be sure of two things; the first, that they will be more careful to keep thy counsel, because they have more to lose than thou hast; the second, they will esteem thee for thyself, and not for that which thou dost possess."—*Sir W. Raleigh.*

g W. Irving.

Moses in the seat of justice

a Nu. xxvii. 5.

b De. xvii. 18; 1 Co. vi. 1.

c M. Henry.

"It is expedient to have an acquaintance with those who have looked into the world; who know men, understand business, and can give you good h-

ness, which a forlorn individual must be in a great measure a stranger to, who stands single in life, without any support to lean upon.*c*

7—12. (7) **welfare,** peace, *i.e.* material and spiritual prosperity. (8) **all .. sake,**" Moses meekly retires into the background: God is the worker. **travail, toil, trial, affliction. and .. them,** fr. Amalek. etc. (9) **rejoiced,***b* with religious joy as well as natural affection. (10) **and .. said,** *etc.,**e* joining Moses in ascribing all praise to God. (11) **Lord .. gods,***d* *see* xv. 11. (12) **Jethro .. God,** Jethro a priest. **eat .. God,***e* the rites of hospitality sanctified by the presence of religious thought.

The meeting of friends (v. 7).—We may notice several kinds of feeling which prevail in the meeting, after a considerable absence, of genuine friends. I. Kind affection. What a difference between meeting an estimable friend, and an entire stranger. II. Inquisitiveness. The mutual inquiries respecting welfare, are made in a very different spirit from unmeaning complaisance. III. Reflective comparison. Not invidious, but instructive. IV. Gratitude to God, in pious minds at least. V. Faithful admonition. They must be a most rare and singular example of friends, if nothing should be mutually seen for admonition. VI. Serious anticipation. Each meeting should admonish them that their life is shortened, sometimes much shortened, since they met before.*f*

The family gathering.—The family meeting was warm and affectionate; as the evening was far advanced, the squire would not permit us to change our travelling dresses, but ushered us at once to the company, which was assembled in a large old-fashioned hall. It was composed of different branches of a numerous family connection, where there were the usual proportion of old uncles and aunts, comfortable married dames, superannuated spinsters, blooming country cousins, half-fledged striplings, and bright-eyed boarding-school hoydens. They were variously occupied; some at a round game of cards; others conversing around the fireplace: at one end of the hall was a group of the young folks, some nearly grown up, others of a more tender and budding age, fully engrossed by a merry game: and a profusion of wooden horses, penny trumpets, and tattered dolls, about the floor, showed traces of a troop of little fairy beings, who, having frolicked through a happy day, had been carried off to slumber through a peaceful night.*g*

13—16. (13) **sat .. people,** entering upon his public functions. **and .. evening,** many causes: sugg. of strife, etc. (14) **why .. alone,** he saw the evils that might come of absolute government. (15) **to .. God,***a* *lit.* to seek God, *i.e.* to know His mind and will. (16) **matter,***b* word, controversy, **statutes .. laws,** as yet unwritten: prob. ref. to principles of equity.

Moses, the judge (v. 13).—Consider how Moses discharged his duties as judge. He acted with—I. Great consideration. II. Great condescension to the people who stood by him. He was easy of access to all. III. Great constancy. He sticks to his duty.—1. Although Jethro was present as a visitor, which might give reason for a holiday; 2. Though he was advanced to great honour; 3. Though the people had but recently been provoking him (xvii. 4); 4. Though he was an old man.*c*

Another Brutus.—In the reign of Henry VIII., Fitz-Stephen, merchant, mayor of Galway, sent his only son, as commander of a ship, to Spain, for a cargo of wine. The son kept the money for the purchase of the cargo; and the Spanish merchant, who supplied the wine, sent his nephew to receive the debt. To conceal his fraud, young Fitz-Stephen conceived the plan of murdering the Spaniard; a project in which he brought the crew to combine. The Spaniard was seized in bed, thrown overboard, and the ship arrived in port. Some time after, one of the sailors was taken ill, and, being at the point of death, confessed the horrid deed in which he had participated. The father, though struck with horror, shook off the parent, and said, "Justice should take its course." And, as mayor, he caused his son to be committed, with the rest of the crew, and the father, like Brutus, sat in judgment on his son, and with his own lips pronounced the sentence which left him childless![d]

17—20. (17) **the .. good**, neither for thee nor for others. (18) **thou .. away**,[a] suffer from physical, mental exhaustion. **and .. thee**, who will become dissatisfied with the verdict of one person, or the delays occasioned by one judge trying all cases. (19) **voice .. counsel**, note the mental, moral, and religious character of Jethro. **be .. God**,[b] be the people's advocate in the presence of God. (20) **thou .. them**,[c] *etc.*, and God's interpreter of His will to the people.

Ministerial counsel (v. 19).—If you examine the words of our text, you may see that three subjects are plainly suggested for our consideration:—I. The nature of the counsel, which it is our bounden duty to give. II. The duty which you are expected to discharge: "Hearken now unto my voice." This includes—1. Deep attention; 2. Discreet judgment; 3. Reverential feelings; 4. Heartfelt eagerness after information; 5. A meek and teachable disposition; 6. Faith; 7. Prayer. III. The blessed effect which shall surely follow: "God shall then be with you."[d]

Good government.—It is essential to the goodness of a governor or king to guard the rights, secure the peace, and promote the prosperity of his subjects. No one can be called a good governor who does not exercise his supremacy and authority in framing and executing laws for the protection and safety of his subjects. It is as essential to the character of a good ruler to punish vice as to reward virtue; to avenge the wrongs of his subjects, as to secure their interests; yea, the former is essential to the latter, since it is only the fear of punishment that restrains wicked men from violence. Should a ruler suffer crimes to go unpunished, the laws, however good and righteous in themselves, would presently lose their authority, and government fall into contempt. Laws have no force any further than they are carried into execution; and authority loses its respect whenever it ceases to be exercised. Whenever the supreme magistrate neglects the execution of the laws, he loses the confidence of the people, and his regard to the public welfare becomes suspected. No one can confide in his public spirit when he suffers the disturbers of the peace to go unpunished; for ideas of true regard to public good as necessarily connect punishments with crimes as rewards with virtue.[e]

21—24. (21) **able men**,[a] *lit.* men of force, *i.e.* of character. **such .. God**,[b] fear of the Lord a legislator's and judge's first

---

Jethro's advice

the reason of it

[a] Nu. xi. 14; De. i. 9, 12.

[b] Ex. iv. 16, xx. 19; De. v. 5.

[c] De. iv. 1; Ps. cxliii. 8.

[d] B. H. Blacker, M.A.

"He that gives good advice builds with one hand; he that gives good counsel and example builds with the other; but he that gives good admonition and bad example builds with one hand and pulls down with the other."—*Bacon.*

"Advice is seldom welcome. Those who need it most like it least."

[e] *West.*

v. 17. J. Foster. Lect. ii. 208.

the nature of it

B.C. cir. 1491.

telligence and good advice when they are wanted." — *Bp. Horne.*

"Associate with men of good judgment; for judgment is found in conversation. And we make another man's judgment ours by frequenting his company."—*Fuller.*

[d] *Cheever.*

B.C. 1491.

a 2 Ch. xix. 5—10.
b Ge. xlii. 18.
c De. xvi. 19; Is. xxviii. 15; Pr. xxviii. 16; Nu. v. 15; Ma. x. 28; 2 Sa. xxiii. 3.
d Ac. vi. 3.
e Nu. xi. 16, 17.
f S. Ward, B.D.

"Government is only a necessary evil, like other go-carts and crutches. Our need of it shows exactly how far we are still children. All governing overmuch kills the self-help and energy of the governed."—W. Phillips.

"When Tarquin the Proud was asked what was the best mode of governing a conquered city, he replied only by beating down with his staff all the tallest poppies in his garden."—Livy.

"The principal foundations of all states are good laws and good arms."—Machiavelli.

g Ben Jonson.

parting of Moses and Jethro

a De. L 13, 14.
b Nu x. 29, 30.
c Dr. Caird.

"Power exercised with violence has seldom been of long duration, but temper and moderation generally produce

requisite. **truth,** both acting and speaking the truth boldly, kindly, and impartially. **covetousness,**c judges should not take bribes. **and .. them,** i.e. Israel. **rulers .. tens,** prob. involving superior as well as inferior courts. (22) **judge .. seasons,**d that justice may not be delayed. **that .. matter,** involving vital or important issues. **they,** i.e. the rulers. **so .. thyself,** and better for others since weighty matters would have the greater consideration. (23) **endure,**e lit. stand, i.e. continue in office and in strength. **people .. peace,** having obtained a speedy and equitable adjustment of difficulties. (24) **so .. voice,** etc., he who had been educated in all the learning of Egypt, who had dauntlessly confronted and confounded the mightiest king, meekly practises the advice of Jethro the shepherd-priest.

Jethro's justice of peace (vv. 21—23).—Here is the archetype, or first draught of magistracy known. Let us open this rich cabinet, and draw out the several jewels in it.—I. It gives order for care and circumspection in the choice: "Provide." II. It directs this choice by four essential characters of magistrates.—1. Men of ability; 2. Fearing God; 3. Men of truth; 4. Hating covetousness. III. It applies these four to magistrates of all degrees in an exact distribution of them, by way of gradation, descending step by step, from the highest to the lowest: "And place such over them to be rulers"—1. Of thousands; 2. Of hundreds; 3. Of fifties; 4. Of tens. IV. It prescribes to the magistrates, thus qualified and chosen, their offices, viz., to judge the people in the smaller causes, and be industrious therein. V. It propounds the blessed fruit and emolument that will ensue thereon—1. To Moses himself; 2. To the people.f

The difficulties of government.—
        Each petty hand
Can steer a ship becalm'd; but he that will
Govern and carry her to her ends must know
His tides, his currents, how to shift his sails;
What she will bear in foul, what in fair weather;
Where her springs are, her leaks, and how to stop them;
What strands, what shelves, what rocks do threaten her;
The forces, and the natures of all winds.
Gusts, storms, and tempests; when her keel ploughs hell,
And deck knocks heaven, then to manage her
Becomes the name and office of a pilot.g

25—27. (25, 26) **and .. people,** etc.,a see vv. 21, 22. (27) **depart,** sent away with customary formalities. **he .. land,**b Midian, where afterwards Moses met with his son, or brother Hobab.

The co-operation of the laity in the government and work of the Church (v. 25).—I. By the co-operation of Christian laymen in the practical work of the Church, the clergy are enabled to give more time and thought to the work of public instruction. II. The labours of a layman for the spiritual good of others are sometimes more influential than those of the clergyman, as being gratuitous and unprofessional. III. The combination of lay with clerical agency constitutes an admirable means for carrying the influence of the Church and of religion into the affairs of ordinary life.c

Partings.—
Farewell! There is a spell within the word;
Methinks I never heard it sound so mournful;
Oh, thou subdued, oft scarce articulate sound,
How powerful thou art, how strong to move
The hidden strings that guide us puppet mortals!
Password of memory—of bygone day—
Thou everlasting epitaph—is there
A land in which thou hast no dwelling place?
Wherein may be nor pageantry nor pride,
Nor altars, save the pure one of the heart,
Nor tombs, except for sorrow; and no tears?
There is a world, O God, where human lips
May say, Farewell! no more.[d]

B.C. 1491.

permanence in all things."— *Seneca.*

"Farewell! God knows when we shall meet again. I have a faint, cold fear thrills through my veins, that almost freezes up the heat of life." —*Shakespeare.*

[d] *Stadden.*

CHAPTER THE NINETEENTH.

B.C. 1491.

1—6. (1) **month**, moon. **the .. Sinai**, wilderness of Sinai, district at the S. end of peninsula formed by Gulfs of Suez and Akaba, in the midst of wh. is a group of mountains called Horeb, of wh. one is Sinai. (2) **Rephidim**, *see* xvii. 1, 8. **pitched**, in the plain of Er-Râhah.[a] (3) **mountain**, three mts., Serbal. Jebel-Musah, Ras-es-Sufsâfeh.[b] (4) **on .. wings**,[c] *i.e. as* on. *etc.*, speed, safety. (5) **if .. obey .. keep**,[d] *etc.*, Divine love and favour conditionated. **then .. treasure**,[e] obtained with effort, purchased at great cost, guarded with unslumbering vigilance. **for .. Mine**,[f] to give to whom I will. (6) **a .. priests**,[g] a royal priesthood. **and .. nation**, comprising holy people, laws, institutions.

Deliverance of Israel (v. 4). — "On eagles' wings." The qualities of the eagle admirably depict—I. The power with which God had delivered Israel. The eagle the most powerful bird of prey of ancient times. II. The astonishing quickness of this deliverance. The eagle most rapid in flight. III. The majesty which God had displayed in His intervention. The eagle soars the highest, and is the most majestic in its aërial courses. IV. The tender care of God towards Israel. The eagle is one of the most tender of birds to its young.[h]

Mount Sinai.—No fewer than five mountains in different parts of the peninsula had been identified or at least suggested by various writers as the true Sinai, and although the claims of three out of the five were so slight as to have attracted but little notice, the other two, viz., Jebel Musa (the Mountain of Moses), situated at about the centre of the peninsula, and Jebel Serbal, some twenty miles further west (Jebel being the Arabic for mountain), had divided between them, though with a preponderance in favour of the former, the support of the great majority of travellers and authorities of eminence in our own and past times. A spacious plain, El Rahah, confronts a precipitous cliff 2,000 feet in height, which forms the north-western extremity or front of that great mountain block called Jebel Musa, which Bedawin and monastic tradition alike point to as the mountain of the law. The appearance of this locality is extremely impressive and grand, so majestic indeed that its natural scenery at once rivets the attention, apart altogether from the sacred asso-

Mount Sinai

Moses goes up the mount

[a] *Stanley, Sin. and Pal.* p. 42; *Headley's Sacr. Mts.* p. 37—40.

[b] "There can be scarcely any doubt that the last is the Mt. of the Lord; every requirement of the sacred narrative is supplied, and every incident ill. by the features of the surrounding district."—*Kitto.*

[c] De. xxxii. 11; 12; Is. lxiii. 9; Ma. xxiii. 37.

[d] De. v. 2; xxix. 9.

[e] Ps. cxxxv. 4; De. vii. 6; Ti. ii. 14.

[f] Ps. xxiv. 1; l. 12.

[g] I.c. xx. 24—26; Is. lxii. 12; 1 Co. iii. 17; 1 Pe. ii. 5, 9; Re. i. 6; v. 9, 10; xx. 6.

"The exact meaning of this expression, as it was understood by all the ancient translators, and as it is explained in the New Tes-

B.C. 1491.

tament, is that Israel collectively is a royal and priestly race; a dynasty of priests, each true member uniting in himself the attributes of a king and priest."
—*Spk. Comm.*

h L. Gaussen.

"Earth has scarcely an acre that does not remind us of actions that have long preceded our own, and its clustering tombstones loom up like reefs of the eternal shore, to show us where so many human barks have struck and gone down."—*Chapin.*

i Capt. Palmer.

he lays the message before the people, and their reply before God

a De. v. 27; xxvi. 17.
b Ex. xxiv. 15, 16; Ps. xviii. 11, 12; Ma. xvi. 5.

"The minister should preach as if he felt that although the congregation own the church, and have bought the pews, they have not bought him. His soul is worth no more than any other man's, but it is all he has, and he cannot be expected to sell it for a salary. The terms are by no means equal. If a parishioner does not like the preaching, he can go elsewhere and get another pew, but the preacher cannot get

ciations. No one who examines it with special reference to the Bible account of the proclamation of the law can fail to be struck with its entire accordance with the details of the narrative. The plain derives its name Rahah from its level character; it is flat as the palm (rahah) of the open hand. It has been stated that this plain is not large enough to have held the vast hosts of the Israelites, but we have surveyed it, and our answer is that it is large enough not only to have held them as spectators, but if needs be to encamp them all. However, we are not necessarily confined to El Rahah in considering the site for the encampment. They may have and probably did spread into the wide lateral valleys which extend right and left from the base of the cliff, and have encamped before or in the presence of the Ras Sufsafeh, though the plain would have been the obvious place of assembly to witness any spectacle on the summit of the mountain. There are fully 400 acres of the plain proper exactly facing the mount and sloping down to it with just such a gentle inclination as would best enable a large number of people to see at once. The area of four hundred acres would accommodate with case about two millions of spectators at the ample allowance of a square yard each, and besides this there is a considerable further open space extending north-westward from the watershed or crest of the plain, but still in sight of the mount—the very spot it may be to which the trembling Israelites "removed and stood afar off" when they feared to come nigh unto the cloud and the thick darkness, when they said unto Moses, "Speak thou with us, and we will hear; but let not God speak with us, lest we die." *i*

7—9. (7) came .. people, that by the elders he might reach the rest. laid .. faces, for them steadfastly to consider. (8) all .. together, unanimous acceptance of covenant. all .. do,*a* a promise more easily made than kept. (9) I .. cloud,*b* dark to be visible, not so bright as to "blind with excess of light." Moses .. Lord, not so much for the Lord's information as for the people's instruction.

The prophet's message and the people's reply (vv. 7, 8).—I. The message: "All the words of the Lord." 1. Not his own words, but the Lord's. Hence he would feel his responsibility, exercise his memory, and faithfully discharge his trust (He. iii. 2); 2. No alteration of the message; "all the words." Without exception, addition, or perversion. II. The answer: "all that the Lord hath spoken we will do." 1. A promise; 2. A unanimous promise; 3. A promise laid before the Lord. Learn—(1) Preachers to publish the Lord's words boldly, exclusively, plainly; (2) Hearers to remember that their reply rests not with the preacher, but with the Master who sends the message. Preachers are responsible for the message, not for its reception.

Plain preaching.—A good minister had long preached to the same congregation without much apparent good result. It was a source of deep grief of soul to the pastor, who longed to see sinners converted. While studying on the matter one Saturday morning, after he had finished writing his sermon, the thought occurred to him : "Perhaps I shoot too high ; I will go down and see if Betty can understand it." Betty was a pious servant-girl. He went to the kitchen, and called Betty to come and hear his sermon. She hesitated. He insisted. She came. He read a few sentences, and asked her, "Do you understand that?"—"No." He

repeated the idea in simpler language, and asked if she saw it!—
"I see it a little, minister." He again simplified. She saw it
more clearly, and showed deep interest; but said to him. "Plain
it a little more." And once more he simplified. Then she exclaimed with ecstasy, "Now I see it : now I understand it!" He
returned to his study, and re-wrote his sermon in that simple style
that Betty could understand. On Sabbath morning he went to
church fearing and trembling, lest his people would be disgusted
with his sermon, but fully resolved to try the experiment. He
preached it. All was attention as never before. Many eyes were
filled with tears, and sinners began to cry out, "What must I
do?" He changed his style of language thenceforth, and the
Lord blessed his labours abundantly.*c*

10—15. (10) **sanctify,**^a not only bodily but spiritual preparation. **let .. clothes,**^b as an outward sign of inward purification. (11) **ready,** in heart and mind, to hear, remember, and
obey. (Should not our worship be preceded by preparation?)
(12) **bounds .. about,** limits beyond wh. they should not pass,
whosoever .. death,^c vividly to teach the holiness of God.
(13) **shot through,** transfixed with dart. **they .. mount,** *i.e.*
those to whom the privilege belonged. (14) **Moses,** having
received these instructions. **sanctified .. clothes,** *see* v. 10.
(15) **ready .. day,** *etc.*,^d their minds to be wholly absorbed by
the work of preparation.

Stoning to death.—" To be stoned to death was a most grievous
and terrible infliction. When the offender came within four
cubits of the place of execution. he was stripped naked, only
leaving a covering before, and his hands being bound, he was
led up to the fatal place, which was an eminence twice a man's
height. The first executioners of the sentence were the witnesses,
who generally pulled off their clothes for the purpose: one of
them threw him down with great violence upon his loins; if he
rolled upon his breast. he was turned upon his loins again, and if
he died by the fall there was an end; but if not, the other witness took a great stone, and dashed upon his breast, as he lay
upon his back; and then, if he was not despatched, all the people
that stood by threw stones at him till he died."*e*

16—20. (16) **thunders,**^a voices. **trembled,**^b at what they
heard and saw. (17) **stood .. mount,**^c *see* v. 12. (18) **mount
.. smoke,**^d which surrounded it in dense folds. **the .. greatly,**^e
terrors of the scene heightened by the earthquake. (19) **when
.. louder,** the preconcerted signal, v. 13. (20) **Lord .. mount,**
in fire. **and .. up,** when God had called him, not before.

The voice of God (v. 19).—Observe—I. God so heralds His
revelations as to leave no room for doubt. Look at—1. The
testimony of nature at Sinai ; 2. The witnesses for Jesus—
angels and a star ; 3. The miracles of Jesus. II. This voice
spoke fifty days after the passover, and was commemorated by
the apostolic Pentecost. A voice and a tongue—the voice of
God and a tongue of fire—were the armament of the Church. By
our testimony we conquer. III. God trains us by the Law for
the Gospel. First tutelage, then freedom ; the letter, then the
spirit ; Moses, then Christ ; the natural, then the spiritual. The
law our schoolmaster to lead us to Christ. IV. God's voice indicates some marked movement. 1. At the bush, deliverance ; 2.

B.C. 1491.

another soul."—*Chapin.*

"Grant that I may never rack a Scripture simile beyond the true intent thereof, lest, in stead of sucking milk, I squeeze blood out of it."—*Fuller.*

c Beecher.

the people to come before God
a Le. xix. 2; Josh. iii. 5; vii. 13; He. xii. 28, 29.
b Ge. xxxv. 2; He. x. 22.
c He. xii. 20, 21 ; Ro. iii. 20.
d Joel ii. 16; 1 Co. vii. 5.
"Dr. Stanley speaks of the low line of alluvial mounds at the foot of the cliff of Ras Safsafeh as exactly answering to the bounds which were to keep the people off from touching the mount; but the bounds here spoken of were to be set up by Moses."—*Spk. Comm.*
e Lewis's Origines Hebrææ.

God descends on Sinai
a Re. iv. 5, viii. 5, xi. 19.
b He. xii. 21.
Nether, beneath, lower; A.-S. *nithera,* comp. of *nither,* below.
c De. iv. 11; xxxiii. 2.
d "Those dense clouds fr. wh. the thunder broke forth had the appearance of smoke."—*Rosenmuller.*
e Ps. lxviii. 7, 8; Jud. v. 5; He. xii. 26; Ps. cxliv. 5.

B.C. 1491.

f Dr. Fowler. "The whole district is called Horeb in Scripture, which uniformly preserves the distinction between Sinai and Horeb, by using '*on* Sinai,' and '*in* Horeb.' The preposition *upon* is frequently used in reference to Sinai, but not once in reference to Horeb,—a clear indication that *Sinai* was the *mountain*, and *Horeb* the region." *Bonar.*
g Dr. Stewart.

warning against heedlessness repeated

a Ex. iii. 5; 1 Sa. vi. 19.

b So say the Jewish interpreters; see *Kalisch.*

c 2 Sa. vi. 7.

"Turks carefully collect every scrap of paper that comes in their way, because the name of God may be written thereon."—*Richter.*

"He who calls in the aid of an equal understanding doubles his own; and he who profits by a superior understanding raises his powers to a level with the height of the superior understanding he unites with."—*Burke.*

d Spurgeon.

B.C. 1491.

the moral law

first commandment

On Sinai, the Law; 3. At Christ's baptism, the entrance on public ministry; 4. At the Transfiguration, the type of coming glory. Learn—"Hear ye Him" in—(1) His Word; (2) His Church; (3) His Spirit.*f*

Thunder-storm at Mount Sinai.—Every ball, as it burst, with the roar of a cannon, seemed to awaken a series of distinct echoes on every side; . . . they swept like a whirlwind among the higher mountains, becoming faint as some mighty peak intervened, and bursting with undiminished volume through some yawning cleft, till the very ground trembled with the concussion. . . . It seemed as if the mountains of the whole peninsula were answering one another in a chorus of the deepest bass. Ever and anon a flash of lightning dispelled the pitchy darkness, and lit up the mount as if it had been day; then, after the interval of a few seconds, came the peal of thunder, bursting like a shell, to scatter its echoes to the four quarters of the heavens, and overpowering for a moment the loud howlings of the wind.*g*

21—25. (21) **charge**, warn. **lest . . gaze,**^a in their curiosity forgetting the command. *see* v. 12. (22) **priests**, prob. those (perh. the firstborn)*b* who discharged priestly functions before the office itself was definitely established. **sanctify . . them,***c* they were not to be officially presumptuous. (23) **said,** *etc.,* perh. deeming a descent for this purpose needless. (24) **away . . down**, God more thoughtfully merciful than man in that He repeats warnings to save His people. (25) **spake,** the warning, *see* vv. 12, 21.

Reverential coming before God (vv. 21, 22).—A duty—I. Marked by preparation (v. 15). II. Universally binding: priests as well as people (v. 22). III. To be spiritually discharged. Not in a spirit of idle curiosity (v. 21). IV. Fraught with danger to the careless (v. 21). Learn the great difference between worship under the Law and the Gospel. That marked by fear; this by love. Draw nigh with reverence, boldness, yet with godly fear (He. xii. 18—24).

Warnings.—A very skilful bowman went to the mountains in search of game. All the beasts of the forest fled at his approach. The lion alone challenged him to combat. The bowman immediately let fly an arrow, and said to the lion, "I send thee my messenger, that from him thou mayst learn what I myself shall be when I assail thee." The lion thus wounded rushed away in great fear, and on a fox exhorting him to be of good courage, and not to run away at the first attack, said: "You counsel me in vain, for if he sends so fearful a messenger, how shall I abide the attack of the man himself?" If the warning admonitions of God's ministers fill the conscience with terror, what must it be to face the Lord Himself? If one bolt of judgment bring a man into a cold sweat, what will it be to stand before an angry God in the last great day?*d*

CHAPTER THE TWENTIETH.

1—3. (1) **God . . words,***a* God, not Moses, the Author of the Law. (2) **I . . God,** *etc.,b* He reminds them of what He had done as an incentive to attention and grateful obedience. (3)

no . . gods,[c] as objects of love, trust, worship. **before Me,**[d] in preference to Me. in the place of Me, *lit.* before My face.

The Law given from Mount Sinai suited to the circumstances of man, and of universal adaptation (vv. 1—17).—I. Some preliminary remarks. 1. Man is a being possessed of a religious capacity ; 2. Man is a moral agent ; 3. It is possible for the reason, the understanding, and the moral sense of man to be brought to such a state, that he can have a right to have an opinion both upon morals and religion. II. The Law itself (*read* vv. 3—17). There are two parts of this law—that relating to—1. Religion. Here are four things—(1) The object of worship ; (2) A mode of worship ; (3) The inculcation of habitual reverence with respect to sacred things ; (4) An appointed season for the cultivation and perfection of the religious capacity ; 2. Morals. Here is—(1) Filial " honour ; " (2) Respect for life ; (3) Reverence for purity ; (4) Respect for property ; (5) Respect for reputation ; (6) Respect and regard to the source of all virtue—thine own heart. III. A few observations, tending to show that this law, as we have it here, is suited to the circumstances of man, and of universal adaptation. It is suited to humanity—1. In that it meets the essential capacities and elements of human nature ; 2. In its accidents ; that is, not only in its principles, but also in the mode in which these principles are to be carried out ; 3. In spite of some of the accidental and peculiar topics which are here and there introduced into it ; 4. If we consider what the world would be were this law universally obeyed ; and what if it were universally disobeyed. IV. The preceding point being made out, then I think the presumptions are in favour of this law having been given by God. 1. The history of man and the tendencies of human nature show that, if the original state of man had been barbarism, he never would have risen out of it by his own efforts, and never would have discovered such principles as are here put forth ; 2. In the most refined ages of ancient times, no moral system equal or even approaching in rationality, purity, and simplicity to this was ever taught either by philosopher, statesman, or priest ; 3. Even in our own times our philosophers, they who have rejected revelation and have given us moral systems, have taught principles subversive of these—Bolingbroke, Blount, Hume ; 4. This law unquestionably was given about the time it was said to be. We find that it must have been given by Moses. From whom did he obtain it ? 5 We now have the *fact*—" God spake all these words." V. Practical remarks. 1. Reflect on the internal evidence of the superhuman character of the Bible ; 2. Notice that infidelity is always associated with impurity and blasphemy ; 3. Meditate deeply how you stand in relation to the Law ; 4. Accept, in addition to the law of judgment, the Gospel of mercy.[e]

I am the Lord thy God.—A friend calling on the Rev. Ebenezer Erskine, during his last illness, said to him, " Sir, you have given us many good advices; pray, what are you now doing with your own soul ? " " I am doing with it," said he, " what I did forty years ago : I am resting on that word. ' I am the Lord thy God ; ' and on this I mean to die." To another he said, " The covenant is my charter, and if it had not been for that blessed word, ' I am the Lord thy God,' my hope and strength had perished from the Lord." The night on which he died, his

B.C. 1491.

a De. v. 25.
b Hos. xiii. 4.
c Jer. xxxv. 15; xxv. 6; De. vi. 4; 2 Ki. xvii. 35; xix. 17, 18.
d 1 Co. viii. 5, 6; Eph. iv. 6; Jas. iv. 4.
e *T. Binney.*

" It would be truly a fine thing if men suffered themselves to be guided by reason, that they should acquiesce in the true remonstrances addressed to them by the writings of the learned and the advice of friends. But the greater part are so disposed that the words which enter by one ear do incontinently go out of the other, and begin again by following the custom: The best teacher one can have is necessity." —*Francois la None.*
"There is the same love in the Law as in the Gospel, the difference is only in expression; as when I warn one against venturing into the roaring flood, and when, on his leaping madly in, I follow to save him. In the Law, love warns; in the cross, it redeems. Both are, as I undertake to show, the true mirror of Him who thus defines His own character—'God is love.'"—*Guthrie.*
"In civil jurisprudence it too often happens that there is so much law, there is no room for justice; and that

B.C. 1491.

the claimant expires of wrong in the midst of righteousmariners die of thirst in the midst of water."—*Colton*.

f Whitecross.

eldest daughter was reading in the room where he was, to whom he said, "What book is that you are reading, my dear?" "It is one of your sermons, sir." "What one is it?" "It is the sermon on that text, 'I am the Lord thy God.'" "O woman," said he, "that is the best sermon I ever preached." And it was, most probably, the best to his soul. A little afterwards, with his finger and thumb, he shut his own eyes, and laying his hand below his cheek, breathed out his soul into the hands of his living Redeemer. Happy the man that is in such a state! Happy the man whose God is the Lord!

the second commandment

a De. iv. 16, 18; xxvii. 15; Ps. xcvii. 7; Nu. xxxiii. 52

b Ex. xxiii. 24; Josh. xxiii. 7.

c Ex. xxxiv. 14; De. iv. 24; Is. xlviii. 11; Josh. xxiv. 19.

d Jer. ii. 9; Nu. xiv. 18, 33; Job xxi. 19; Le. xx. 5; xxvi. 39—42; 1 Ki. xxi. 20; Is. xiv. 20, 21; lxv. 6, 7.

e De. vii. 9; Ps. lxxxix. 34; Jo. xiv. 21; Ro. xi. 28; Mic. vii. 18 —20.

f M. Henry.

"God, who guides below and rules above; the great Disposer, and the mighty King; than He none greater, next Him none, that can be, is, or was; supreme He singly fills the throne."—*Horace.*

g R. W. Dale, M.A.

4—6. (4) **graven**, carved. **image**,[a] likeness, representation. **of .. heaven**, as heavenly bodies, etc. **or .. earth**, as men or animals. **or .. water**, fishes, reptiles, etc. (5) **thou .. them**,[b] nor even worship Jehovah Himself by means of them. **jealous**,[c] regarding with sensitiveness all entrenchments upon His honour. **visiting**, *etc.*,[d] this by the outworking of natural law. (6) **mercy**, *etc.*[e] God more abundant in mercy than in wrath.

The second commandment.— I. A prohibition. We must not—1. Worship even the true God by images; 2. Bow down to any image; we must not worship any even occasionally, much less regularly. II. Reasons enforcing this prohibition. 1. God's jealousy in the matter of worship; 2. The punishment of idolaters; 3. The favour to be shown by God to His faithful worshippers.[f]

Enduring nature of righteousness.—The sanction of this commandment suggests that the righteousness of men endures longer than their sin. "The third and fourth generation" may suffer the penalty of great crimes; but thousands of generations cannot wholly exhaust the reward of fidelity to God, and obedience to His commandments. The evil which comes from man's wickedness endures for a time, but perishes at last; the good that comes from man's well-doing is all but indestructible. The martyrs of the early ages of the Church still sustain our courage when we are tempted to be false to conscience and to God; the power of their persecutors to resist the faith of Christ has been broken for ever. The treachery of kings and the profligacy of nobles in the evil times of our own history cannot imperil our freedom or corrupt our national morality; but the sanctity, and the learning, and the zeal of Hooker, and Jeremy Taylor, and Howe, and Baxter, and Owen, are still among the strong defences of our religious life, and John Milton rekindles the fire of patriotism and of a noble passion for liberty in every new generation. It is the virtue of the remote past which is alive with us in the present; its vice has passed away. It is the wisdom which remains, the folly is forgotten.[g]

the third commandment

a De. v. 11; Ps. xv. 1—5; Ex. xxiii. 1; Le. xix. 12, xxiv. 16; Ma. v. 33—37.

"Profaneness is a brutal vice. He who indulges in

7. **take**, use, repeat, employ. **in vain**,[a] (1) lightly, frivolously; (2) false oaths; (3) general profanity.

Wrong using of the sacred Name.—This is seen—I. In profane swearing, which betrays—1. Absence of right thought towards God—the Almighty Creator, the bountiful Provider, the gracious Redeemer. Men would not so speak of earthly parents, friends, etc. 2. Absence of right feeling towards men—(1) It shocks the intelligence of the thoughtful worldling; (2) It grieves the heart of the true Christian. II. In light conversation, as in godless speaking of the book, the day, the works, etc., on which God's

Name is stamped. This—1. Shows irreverence towards the highest, holiest, and best Being. 2. Begets the habit of jesting about, or trifling with, all holy things. Learn—(1) He who thus uses the name of God is guilty of daring, presumptuous sin. (2) Let Christians exert their utmost influence to check the growth of irreverence in speech.

Punishment of impiety.—It was near the close of one of those storms that deposit such a volume of snow upon the earth, that a middle-aged man, in one of the southern counties of Vermont, seated himself at a large fire in a log-house. He was crossing the Green Mountains from the western to the eastern side; he had stopped at the only dwelling of man, in a distance of more than twenty miles, being the width of the parallel ranges of gloomy mountains; he was determined to reach his dwelling on the eastern side that day. In reply to a kind invitation to tarry in the house, and not dare the horrors of the increasing storm, he declared that he would go, and that the Almighty was not able to prevent him. His words were heard above the howling of the tempest. He travelled from the mountain valley where he had rested, over one ridge, and one more intervened between him and his family. The labour of walking in the snow must have been great, as its depth became near the stature of a man: yet he kept on, and arrived within a few yards of the last summit, from whence he could have looked down upon his dwelling. But he never reached it. He was found dead near a large tree, partly supported by its trunk; his body bent forward, and his ghastly intent features told the stubbornness of his purpose to overpass that little eminence. The Almighty had prevented him,—the currents of his life's blood were frozen. For more than thirty years that tree stood by the solitary road, scarred to the branches with names, letters, and hieroglyphics of death, to warn the traveller that he trod over a spot of fearful interest.[b]

8—11. (8) **remember,** with gratitude, reverence, and with suitable practice. **the .. day,**[a] *i.e.*, the day of rest (fr. toil, etc.) **to .. holy,**[b] *i.e.*, to sanctify or set it apart. (9) **six .. labour,**[c] and not any less number each week. **do .. work,** thy proper, lawful work. (10) **but .. day,**[d] of each week. **thou .. work,** save works of necessity and mercy. **thou .. son,** *etc.*, do not employ others on what is unlawful for thyself. **stranger,** proselyte. **that .. gates,** neighbours should share in our privileges. (11) **six days,** *etc.*, see Ge. ii. 2, 3.

The manner of keeping the Sabbath.—Let us consider how we are to keep holy the Sabbath-day: and notice—I. The negative duties implied in this act. 1. We are forbidden to do any work on the Sabbath; 2. We should not make it a day of pleasure; 3. It is not to be made a day of mere sloth. II. The positive duties. Portions of the day should be devoted to—1. Public religious worship; 2. Special private devotion; 3. Religious reading; 4. The Sabbath-school; 5. Family religion.[e]

Keeping the Sabbath.—One morning a gentleman was going to church. He was a happy, cheerful Christian, who had a very great respect for the Sabbath. He was a singular man, and would sometimes do and say what children are apt to call very "*funny* things." As he was going along he met a stranger driving a heavily-loaded waggon through the town. When this gentleman got right opposite to the waggoner, he stopped, turned

B.C. 1491.

"It is no gentleman. I care not what his stamp may be in society. I care not what clothes he wears; or what culture he boasts. Despite all his refinement, the light and habitual taking of God's name betrays a coarse nature and a brutal will."— *Chapin.*

"Swearing is properly a superfluity of naughtiness, and can only be considered as a sort of peppercorn rent, in acknowledgment of the Devil's right of superiority."— *R. Hall.*

"Let us consider the reason of the case. For nothing is law that is not reason."— *Sir Jno. Powell.*
[b] *Bibl. Treas.*

the fourth commandment

[a] Ex. xiii. 13, 14; i e. xix. 3, 30.
[b] De. v. 12; Is. lviii. 13.
[c] Ex. xxiii. 12, xxxi. 15; Le. xxiii. 3; Ex. xxxiv. 21, xvi. 26; Lu. xiii. 14.
[d] Ezek. xx. 12; Ex. xxxi. 13; Ne. xiii. 16—19.
[e] *H. Winslow.*

"Of one hundred men admitted to the Massachusetts State Prison in one year, eighty-nine had lived in habitual violation of the Sabbath and neglect of public worship."

B C. 1491.

"Sunday, that day so tedious to the trifler of earth, so full of beautiful repose, of calmness and strength for the earnest and heavenly-minded."—*Maria M'Intosh.*

round, and, lifting up both hands as if in horror, he exclaimed, as he gazed under the waggon, "There, there—you are *going* over it! You *have gone* right over it!" The driver was frightened. He drew up his reins in an instant; cried, "Whoa! whoa!" and brought his horses to a stand. Then he looked down under the wheels, expecting to see the mangled remains of some innocent child, or at least some poor dog or pig that had been ground to a jelly. But he saw nothing. So, after gazing all about, he looked up to the gentleman who had so strangely arrested his attention, and anxiously asked, "Pray, sir, *what* have I gone over?" "Over the *fourth commandment*," was the quick reply. "'*Remember* the Sabbath-day, to keep it holy.'"

the fifth commandment

a De. v. 16; Ma. xv. 14; Mk. vii. 10.

b Eph. vi. 2.

c W. Layng, M.A.

"The voice of parents is the voice of gods, for to their children they are heaven's lieutenants."—*Shakespeare.*

"I do not like punishments. You will never torture a child into duty; but a sensible child will dread the frown of a judicious mother more than all the rods, dark rooms, and scolding schoolmistresses in the universe."—*H. K. White.*

v. 12. Dr. J. Lightfoot. Wks. vii. 391.

12. honour,^{a} respect, esteem, obey. **that .. long,**^{b} filial obedience not only secures the Divine blessing directly, but tends to lengthen life—(1) By saving youth from perils; (2) and manhood fr. that violation of law to which a spirit of disobedience tends.

Obedience to parents.—I. This commandment is an express and positive injunction of Almighty God to the active exercise of a specified duty, with the promise of a particular blessing attached to it, as a reward. It is "the first commandment with promise." II. When, after the delivery of the law on Mount Sinai, the commandments were engraved on two tables of stone, this was placed first upon the second, thereby being introduced to the special notice of mankind. III. Of the importance of the injunction, we have further ample evidence in the attention bestowed on it by inspired writers. IV. Our Lord Himself has recommended it to all, by the sanction of His own most holy example.^{c}

An apt reply.—An old schoolmaster said one day to a clergyman, who came to examine his school, "I believe the children know the catechism word for word." "But do they understand it? That is the question," said the clergyman. The schoolmaster only bowed respectfully, and the examination began. A little boy had repeated the fifth commandment. "Honour thy father and thy mother," and he was desired to explain it. Instead of trying to do so, the little boy, with his face covered with blushes, said almost in a whisper, "Yesterday I showed some strange gentleman over the mountain. The sharp stones cut my feet, and the gentleman saw they were bleeding, and gave me some money to buy me shoes. I gave it to my mother, for she had no shoes either, and I thought I could go barefoot better than she could."

the sixth commandment

a Ge. ix. 6; Jo. viii. 14; Ma. xv. 19; Ge. iv. 8—12; 2 Sa. xii. 9; Ma. v. 21, 22; 1 Jo. iii. 13; Ro. xiii. 9; 1 Pe. iv. 15.

"From the earliest dawn of policy to this day, the invention of men has been sharpening

13. kill,^{a} take life violently or unjustly in the sense usually called murder (the Heb. *ratzah* diff. fr. *harag.* inasmuch as the latter properly means legal killing).

Murder.—Sad that human capacities for atrocious wickedness should render needful such a law. See the wrong that murder involves. I. In respect to the murdered. 1. The shortening of a human life—its unfulfilled duties, unenjoyed pleasures, unattained perfection: 2. The hurrying of a human soul into the presence of its Maker—perh. impenitent, unprepared, to be lost for ever. II. In respect to society. 1. Forcing upon it the work of making provision for punishment, and the machinery of justice, and executing the law; 2. Moral injury; through increase of anxiety concerning unsafeness of life; 3. The loss of

two of its members, the murdered and murderer; 4. The effect upon immediate survivors—shame on some, profound grief on others. III. In respect to the murderer. He brings—1. The guilt of Cain upon his soul; 2. The imprecations of society upon his name; 3. Disgrace upon his posterity; 4. Fearful peril to his eternal state. Learn—(1) To guard against incitements to passion—excessive use of intoxicating drinks, etc.; (2) To watch against murderous thoughts (see marg. refs.).
The evil of murder.—The real evil of murder (apart from its theftuous character—it is the robbing a man of his most precious possession, his life) lies in the principles and feelings from which it springs, and in its recklessness as to the consequences, especially the future and everlasting consequences of the act. It augurs a profound, malignant, and cold-blooded hatred of its victim: it shows the true spirit of the devil, who was a " murderer " as well as a " liar " from the beginning. " He that hateth his brother is a murderer;" and the converse is true: "the murderer intensely, fiendishly hates his brother." It is the antithesis to the Christian spirit of love and principle of forgiveness. The idea of murder reduces man, whose glory it should be to " look before and after," to the recklessness of a wild beast. Regarding not the consequences to his victim's family, friends, position in society, or to his immortal soul, he seeks only to flesh his fury in his blood, and often does deliberately what the wild beast does in haste and hunger. It *is* an awful thing to send a man unprepared into eternity. And hence Shakespeare is, as always, true to human nature, when, in *Hamlet*, he makes the ghost dwell so much on the fact that he was killed—

" With all his sins broad blown,
Unhouselled, unanointed, unanneled."[b]

14. adultery,[a] not only in the strict and exclusive sense, but in that of all unlawful intercourse.

The great sin.—This commandment forbids every form of sensuality in act or thought. I. The most fearful denunciations of Scripture are against sensuality. II. Nature protests against it. III. It breaks down the moral principalities. IV. It does violence to the virtues. V. It ruins others: it involves other persons in guilt. VI. It leads to every other sin. VII. It frustrates the great end of human life. Conclusion—1. Beware of beginnings; 2. Give this passion no allowance in your thoughts; 3. Be watchful against the least temptation; 4. Avoid bad associates; 5. Avoid every incentive to vice in dress, in fashion; 6. Attend to the words of wisdom; 7. Give your hearts to Christ.[b]

A clergyman challenged.—Anthony William Boehm, a German, born at Oestdorf, in the county of Pyemont, was a very worthy and learned clergyman: he preached at the court chapel in St. James's Palace from 1705 till 1722, and was highly esteemed by Queen Anne. The celebrated Dr. Watts was his intimate friend, and he was as much esteemed by the English nation as by his own countrymen. He once preached from Exod. xx. 14, " Thou shalt not commit adultery;" and a chevalier, who was one of his hearers, felt himself so much offended and insulted, that he challenged him to fight a duel, because he thought his sermon was designed to offend him. Boehm accepted the challenge, and appeared dressed in his robes; but, instead of a pistol, he had the

B.C. 1491.

and improving the mystery of murder, from the first rude essay of clubs and stones to the present perfection of gunnery, cannoneering, bombarding, mining."—*Lurke.*

" Man perfected by society is the best of all animals; he is the most terrible of all when he lives without law and without justice. If he finds himself an individual who cannot live in society, or who pretends he has need of only his own resources, do not consider him as a member of humanity; he is a savage beast or a god."—*Aristotle.*

b *Gilfillan.*

the seventh commandment

a 2 Sa. xii. 10; Ma. v. 28; Pr. xxii. 14, xxxi. 3; Jer. v. 7—9; Eph. v. 3—7; Col. iii. 5; 1 Thess. iv. 5—7; 2 Pe. ii. 9—14; Ro. xxi. 8.

b *W. Warren.*

" The freedom of some is the freedom of the herd of swine that ran violently down a steep place into the sea and were drowned." — *W. Jay.*

" Human brutes, like other beasts, find snares and poison in the provisions of life, and are allured by their appetites to their destruction." — *Swift.*

B.C. 1491.

"It is impossible to live pleasurably without living prudently and honourably and justly, or to live prudently and honourably and justly without living pleasurably."—*Epicurus*.

THE EIGHTH COMMANDMENT

a Le. xix. 11, 13;
De. v. 19; Ex.
xxii. 1—4; Pr.
xxii. 22, 23;
xxviii. 8, 24;
Josh. vii. 24, 25;
Pr. xxix. 24, xxx.
8, 9; 1 Co. vi. 10;
1 Toess. iv. 6;
Eph. iv. 28.

b *Dr. Poole.*

"Virtuosi have been long remarked to have little conscience in their favourite pursuits. A man will steal a rarity who would cut off his hands rather than take the money. It is worth. Yet, in fact, the crime is the same."—*H. Walpole.*

"Suspicion always haunts the guilty mind: the thief still fears each bush an officer."—*Shakespeare.*

"What is dishonestly got vanishes in profligacy."—*Cicero.*

c *J. Smith, African Missy.*

"Dishonesty is a forsaking of permanent for temporary advantages."—*Boree.*

Bible in his hand, and spoke to him in the following manner:—"I am sorry you were so much offended when I preached against that destructive vice; at the time I did not even think of you: here I appear with the sword of the Spirit, and if your conscience condemns you, I beseech you, for your own salvation, to repent of your sins, and lead a new life. If you will, then, fire at me immediately, for I would willingly lose my life, if that might be the means of saving your soul." The chevalier was so struck with this language, that he embraced him, and asked for his friendship.

15. steal," by force or craft deprive another of his property: man-stealing the worst form of dishonesty.

The eighth commandment considered in reference to motives and desires.—We will—I. Strongly insist on the controlling influence of motives and desires. II. Lay down as a positive truth that stealing rests not with the mere act—that its guilt is not limited to its notoriety or extent, but is chargeable where, and in a way, little suspected. Instance, the man of business, the man of slander, the self-plunderer. III. Show that this commandment may be broken in respect even to God Himself. Is not the "withholding part of the price" of our obligations to God, be that part small or great, a robbery? IV. Consider how very far short we may be in theory or practice of the true spirit and meaning of this precept.ᵇ

A Caffre horse-stealer.—A fine, tall, athletic young man, a Caffre, addicted to all the debasing and demoralising customs of his nation, one night resolved to go into the colony for the purpose of stealing a horse, which is a common practice with them. He immediately left his home, came into the colony, and watched for an opportunity of accomplishing his purpose, which soon presented itself. He found two horses grazing in a sheltered situation near a bush, and he instantly seized one of them, and made off with it as fast as he could. Elated with his success, and rejoicing in the prospect of securing his prize without being detected, he proceeded homewards, when all at once the thought struck him. "Thou shalt not steal." He could go no farther; he immediately drew up the horse, and said to himself, "What is this? I have frequently heard these words before in the church; but I never felt as I do now. This must be the word of God." He dismounted, and held the bridle in his hand, hesitating whether to go forward with the horse, or to return back with it, and restore it to its owner. In this position he continued for upwards of an hour. At last he resolved to take the horse back again, which he accordingly did, and returned home a true penitent, determined to serve God. When he reached his dwelling, he could not rest; sleep had departed from him; the arrows of conviction stuck fast in his conscience, and he could not shake them off. The next day he took an ox out of his kraal (or cattle place), and went to the nearest village to sell it, in order that he might buy European clothing with the money, and attend the house of God like a Christian. When he returned with his clothes, he went to the minister's house, told him all that had taken place, and requested to be admitted on trial as a church member. The minister, cheered with his statement, gladly received him; and, after keeping him on trial the appointed time, and finding him consistent in his conduct, a short time ago baptised him; and he is now a full member of the Christian Church, and adorning his Christian profession.^c

16. thou . . neighbour,^a either (1) by bearing testimony in a court of justice, or (2) giving currency to false reports in common conversation.

Bearing false witness.—This is done—I. When one commits perjury in a court of justice. The crime of which consists in—1. The injury done to the case prejudiced; 2. The depreciation of the value of judicial swearing; 3. The shaking of public confidence in judicial proceedings. II. When one testifies falsely to character. By which—1. Employers are deceived; 2. The worthy are prevented obtaining an honest livelihood; 3. The unworthy are helped to situations for which they are incompetent or morally disqualified. III. When one aids in the circulation of slander.

The Omniscient witness.—There is a little machine, called an "odometer," made something like a clock, which can be fastened on a carriage, and in some way connected with the motion of the wheels. It is so arranged, that it marks off correctly the number of miles that the carriage runs. A stable-keeper once had one upon a carriage that he kept for letting; and by this means he could tell just how many miles any one went who hired it of him. Two young men once hired it to go to a town some ten miles distant. Instead of simply going and returning, as they promised to do, they rode to another town some five miles farther; making the distance they passed over some thirty miles. When they returned, the owner of the establishment, without being noticed by the young men, glanced upon the face of the measuring instrument, and discovered how many miles they had travelled. "Where have you been?" he then asked them. "Where we were going," was the answer. "Have you not been farther than that?" "Oh, no!" they answered. "How many miles have you been in all?" "Twenty." He touched the spring, the cover opened; and there on the face of the instrument the thirty miles were found recorded. The young men were astonished at this unerring testimony of an unseen witness that they had carried with them all the way. The steps of all are measured; and the witnesses are ready against all sin.^b

17. covet,^a earnestly desire, long after; hence beware of vain passing wishes, since such may prompt strong and irrepressible desires.

Covetousness.—"Thou shalt not covet," because it is—I. Unsatisfying. II. Disgraceful. III. Injurious. IV. Sinful.^b *The danger and folly of covetousness.*—Consider—I. The sin itself. Although apparently a small sin, it is—1. Against God's commandments; 2. Degrading to the mind; 3. Full of folly. II. The danger arising from indulgence in it. It is the prelude to other and more heinous crimes. We *wish* for a thing; and then endeavour, by unlawful means, to obtain it.^c

Avarice punished.—Some time ago, the Duke of Buccleugh, in one of his walks, purchased a cow from a person in the neighbourhood of Dalkeith, and left orders to send it to his palace the following morning. According to agreement, the cow was sent, and the Duke, who happened to be in dishabille, and walking in the avenue, espied a little fellow ineffectually attempting to drive

---

B.C. 1491.

the ninth commandment

a Ex. xxiii. 1; De. v. 20, xix. 16 —19; Ps. xv. 1—4, cl. 5.

"It is not the many oaths that make the truth, but the plain single vow, that is vowed true."— *Shakespeare.*

"There is nobody so weak of invention that cannot make some little stories to vilify his enemy." —*Addison.*

"Any one who is much talked of must be much maligned. This seems to be a harsh conclusion, but when you consider how much more given men are to depreciate than to appreciate, you will acknowledge that there is some truth in the saying."—*A. Helps.*

b Sunday Teach. Treas.

the tenth commandment

a De. v. 21; Ma. v. 28; Pr. vi. 27 —29; Hab. ii. 9; Ro. vii. 7; He. xiii. 5; Lu. xii. 15; Ac. xx. 33; Eph. v. 3, 5.

b Dr. Newton.

c R. H. Wilton.

"He deservedly loses his own property who covets that of another."— *Phæ-drus.*

"Suppose a more

B.C. 1491.

complete assemblage of sublunary enjoyments, and a more perfect system of earthly felicity than ever the sun beheld, the mind of man would instantly devour it, and, as if it was still empty and unsatisfied, would require something more." — *Leighton*.

"Covetousness teaches men to be cruel and crafty, industrious and evil, full of care and malice; and after all this, it is for no good to itself, for it dares not spend those heaps of treasure which it has snatched." — *J. Taylor*.

"Of covetousness we may truly say that it makes both the Alpha and Omega in the devil's alphabet, and that it is the first vice in corrupt nature which moves, and the last which dies." — *South*.

the people are filled with awe

a He. xii. 18 *ff*.
b De. v. 25—27; 1 Ti. ii. 5.
c Is. xii. 10.
d De. viii. 2; xiii. 3; xxviii. 57; Is. viii. 1.
e Pr. iii. 7; xvi. 6; Nc. v. 15; Ma. x. 28.
f De. v. 5.
g C. Simeon, M.A.

"We always believe that God is like ourselves; the indulgent affirm Him in-

the animal to its destination. The boy, not knowing the Duke, bawled out to him. "*Flimun*, come here, an' gin's a han' wi' this beast." The Duke saw the mistake, and determined to have a joke with the little fellow. Pretending, therefore, not to understand him, the Duke walked on slowly, the boy still craving his assistance. At last he cried, in a tone of apparent distress— " Come here, mun, an' help us, an' as sure as onything. I'll give you half I get!" This last salutation had the desired effect. The Duke went and lent a helping hand. "And now," said the Duke, as they trudged along, "how much do you think you will get for this job?" "Oh, dinna ken," said the boy; "but I'm *sure o' something*, for the folks at the house are good to a' bodies." As they approached the house, the Duke darted from the boy, and entered by a different way. He called a servant, and put a sovereign into his hand, saying. " Give that to the boy who has brought the cow." The Duke returned to the avenue, and was rejoined by the boy. "Well, and how much did you get?" said the Duke. "A shilling," said the boy; "and there's the half o' it t' ye." "But you surely got more than a shilling," said the Duke. "No," said the boy, with the utmost earnestness, "as sure as death that's a' I got; an' d' ye not think it's a plenty?" " I do not," said the Duke; "there must be some mistake; and, as I am acquainted with the Duke, if you return, I think I can get you more." The boy consented, and they went back. The Duke rang the bell, and ordered all the servants to be assembled. " Now," said the Duke to the boy, "point me out the person that gave you the shilling." "It was that chap there with the apron," said the boy, pointing to the butler. The delinquent confessed, fell on his knees, and attempted an apology; but the Duke, interrupting him, indignantly ordered him to give the boy the sovereign, and quit his service instantly. "You have lost," said the Duke, "your money, your situation, and your character, by your covetousness; learn, henceforth, that honesty is the best policy." The boy by this time recognised his assistant in the person of the Duke; and the Duke was so delighted with the sterling worth and honesty of the boy, that he ordered him to be sent to school, kept there, and provided for at his own expense.

18—21. (18) **saw,** *etc., see* xix. 16. **they .. off,**[a] moved by fear and awe, and the warning. (19) **speak .. hear,** they could endure the familiar sound of a human voice. **but .. die,**[b] God mercifully speaks to us by His Son. (20) **fear not,**[c] seasonable encouragement from lips of authority. **prove,**[d] test, try. **fear .. faces,** stimulated by this spectacle of His majesty and power. **that .. not,**[e] fear of God a preventive of guilt. (21) **and .. off,** tremblingly obedient. **Moses .. near,**[f] also obedient to the Divine command.

The giving of the law (v. 18).—Consider why God published His law in this manner. He did so—I. To impress the people with a fear of His majesty. II. To show them the nature of that dispensation. III. To make them feel their need of a Mediator. Infer—1. How thankful we should be for the Christian covenant; 2. How careful we should be not to revert to the Jewish; 3. How studiously we should cultivate the fear of God.[g]

Fear and confidence.—St. Ambrose says that a Christian wife was on a journey with her heathen husband, when a terrific thunder-storm arose, which overwhelmed the man with terror.

His wife asked the cause. He replied, "Are not you afraid?" She answered, "No, not at all : for I know that it is the voice of my heavenly Father; and shall a child be afraid of a father's voice?" The husband saw that his wife had what he had not; and this led him to the adoption of Christianity.

22—26. (22) **talked .. heaven**, giving you laws from heaven for lives on earth; to make life on earth a preparation for life in heaven. (23) **silver .. gold**, the value of the material cannot make an idol of the soul's adoration. (24) **an .. earth**, (1) Such an altar suited to the need of a wandering people; (2) Prevented them having pride in the work of their hands. **burnt-offerings**, to effect reconciliation. **peace-offerings**, thanksgiving. (25) **if .. stone**,*a* stone in some places as easily obtainable as earth in others. **thou .. stone**, *i.e.* carved, with ornamental devices to elate the pride or divert the attention of the worshipper. (26) **neither**, *etc.*, "as the garments of the priests were long and flowing, their ascending a flight of steps might indecorously expose their persons."*b*

The Gospel in Exodus.—From these words (v. 24) we learn—I. That God demands from His creature man reverent and intell.gent worship. II. That such worship, to be acceptable to God, must always be associated with Divinely-appointed sacrifice. III. That such worship and sacrifice obtain for man the best blessings of heaven.*c*

Robes of holiness.—When the saintly John Chrysostom came to his dying day, he asked the brethren to bring him some clean white robes. Throwing aside his soiled garments, he arrayed himself in white, and so awaited his coming Lord. He closed his remarkably pure life, exclaiming, "Glory be to God for all things that happen!"

CHAPTER THE TWENTY-FIRST.

B.C. 1491.

1—6. (1) **judgments**,*a* decisions of the civil law. (2) **if .. servant**,—(1) he being in debt,*b* or (2) having committed theft.*c* **six .. serve**,*d* in point of fact it was his labour for the time being, and not the man himself that was purchased. **seventh .. nothing**,*e* however short the time before that seventh year when his bondage commenced. (3) **if .. married**, *etc.*, very diff. this fr. recent slave-laws. (4) **if .. wife**, she being a bondwoman her master's claim not lost by this gift. **he .. himself**, neither suffering wrong himself nor inflicting wrong on his wife, since both understood the conditions bef. they were married. (5) **if .. say**, it was for the servant and not for the master to decide. **I .. children**,*f* his fetters were those of love and self-imposed. **I .. free**, his continued bondage should be his own voluntary act. (6) **then .. judges**,*g* who shall be assured by the servant himself that he acts of his own free will. **bore .. awl**,*h* a common mark of slavery in the old times.*i*

Hebrew slavery.—It was altogether different from modern slavery in—I. The circumstances under which it was entered, which were threefold.—1. Crime (see xxii. 3); 2. Debt, or poverty; 3. Conquest by war. II. The time during which it lasted. Not for life, but till the next Sabbatical year. III. The condition on which it was left or renewed. Provisions made for voluntary action of the bondman.

B.C. 1491.

dulgent; the stern, terrible." —*Joubert.*

rules respecting worship

a De. xxvii. 5; Josh. viii. 30, 31; 1 Co. i. 17.
b Bush.
c F. W. Brown.

"Everything holy is before what is unholy; guilt presupposes innocence, not the reverse; angels, but not fallen ones, were created. Hence man does not properly rise to the highest, but first sinks gradually down from it, and then afterwards rises again; a child can never be considered too innocent and good." —*Richter.*

laws relating to civil matters

slaves

a Ex. xxiv. 3, 4; De. iv. 14; vi. 1.
b Le. xxv. 39.
c Ex. xxii. 3.
d De. xv. 12; Jer. xxxiv. 14; 1 Co vi. 20.
e Ro. vi. 17, 18; Gal. v. 1.
f De. xv. 16, 17.
g De. xvi. 18; Ps. xv. 4.
h Ps. xl. 6.
i *Xenophon, Anab.* III. i. 31; *Plautus, Pœnul.* V. ii. 21; *Juvenal*, I. 104; *Plut. Cicero*, C. 26.

Aul, old spell. = awl. A.-S. *æl, al, awel*, or *awul*; Ger. *ahle*. It is

B.C. 1491.

aute in the A. V. of 1611.
"Let thy servants be such as thou mayest command, and entertain none about thee but yeomen to whom thou givest wages; for those that will serve thee without thy hire will cost thee treble as much as they that know thy fare." — *Sir W. Ra'eigh.*
"We must truly serve those whom we appear to command; we must bear with their imperfections, correct them with gentleness and patience, and lead them in the way to heaven." — *Fénelon.*
k Geyer.

a No. v. 5.
b Mal. ii. 14, 15; De. xxi. 14.
c Ex. xxii. 17.
d 1 Co. vii. 3, 5.
e Nu. xix. 8.

"If idleness be the root of all evil, then matrimony is good for something, for it sets many a poor woman to work." — *Vanbrugh.*

"He that hath wife and children hath given hostages to fortune; for they are impediments to great enterprises, either of virtue or mischief. Certainly wife and children are a kind of disciple of humanity." — *Bacon.*
f Harmer.

murder and man- slaughter

Slavery the cause of national decay. — When we read Gibbon's eloquent and magnificent description of the Roman empire under the mild sceptre of the Antonines; an empire comprehending the entire civilised world of that day; full of flourishing cities, guarded at its frontiers by those unconquered legions, out of whose camps new cities sprang up; intersected in every direction by great and almost indestructible military roads, whilst its commercial navy united all the coasts of the Mediterranean, and, from the Red Sea, visited India; internally connected by a regular coast in the service of the government; covered with the monuments which, even in their ruins, continue to excite the amazement of posterity, and with schools for science and art, not only in Rome and Italy, but in Spain, Gaul, Greece, Africa, and Asia Minor; whose teachers were paid by the state, and encouraged, rewarded, and valued to such a degree that Marcus Aurelius seems rather to have wished to be a scholastic philosopher than an emperor;—when this picture rises up in our imagination, and we bear in mind the wonderful development of the Roman law, and of all forms, judicial and administrative, it is difficult to conceive that we contemplate a merely protracted decline; material prosperity, which is nevertheless partial and fallacious; mechanism with only external moving power: an artificial formation without life; and a general unhealthiness of mind which the upper classes sustain with stoic indifference, whilst the masses sink deeper and deeper in degradation. Yet so it was, and why? The majority in the ancient world were slaves.[k]

7—11. (7) **sell** .. **maidservant,**[a] *i.e.* sell her services, compelled by poverty. **she** .. **do,** but on better terms. (8) **if** .. **master,**[b] *lit.* if she be evil in the eyes of her master, *i.e.* wanting in personal attractions, etc. **who** .. **himself,** the service being prob. entered on that condition. **redeemed** (1), by her father or kindred; or (2) by entering the service of another. (9) **if** .. **son,** *etc.*[c] *i.e.* shall treat her as a free person, giving her dowry, etc. (10) **if** .. **wife,** in addition to this bondwoman. **her** .. **diminish,**[d] *i.e.* she shall not in any sense suffer thereby. (11) **three,** *see* v. 10. **then** .. **money,**[e] *i.e.* without compensation given to either her husband or his father.

Duties to wives in the East. — Though flesh meat is not wont to be eaten by these nations so frequently as with us in the West, or in such quantities, yet people of rank, who often have it in their repasts, are fond of it, and even those in lower life, when it can be procured. Our translation, then, does not express the spirit of the Mosaic precept, relating to the superinducing a second wife in the lifetime of the first. Exod. xxi. 10. "Her food, her raiment, and her duty of marriage, shall he not diminish;" in the original it is, *her flesh, her raiment,* &c., meaning that he should not only afford her a sufficient quantity of food as before, but of the same quality. The feeding her with bread, with herbs, with milk, etc., in quantities not only sufficient to maintain life, but as much as numbers of poor people contented themselves with, would not do, if he took away the flesh, and others of the more agreeable articles of food he had before been wont to allow her.[f]

12—14. (12) **he** .. **man,** deliberately. **shall** .. **death,**[a] punishment for wilful murder. (13) **if** .. **wait,**[b] premeditating assassination. **but**..**hand**, accidentally as we should say : case of manslaughter. **then**..**thee**, the place divinely-appointed alone safe. **whither**..**flee**,[c] until the case shall have been judicially investigated. (14) **presumptuously**,[d] proudly. **with a high hand. to..guile**, craftily killing him. **thou**..**altar**,[e] **to wh. he may have fled** for protection. **that**..**die**, his intention to kill being clearly established.

The doom of the murderer.—
Think, timely think, on the last dreadful day,
How you will tremble there, to stand exposed
The foremost in the rank of guilty ghosts,
That must be doom'd for murder ! think on murder !
That troop is placed apart from common crimes :
The damn'd themselves start wide, and shun that band
As far more black, and more forlorn than they.
'Tis terrible, it shakes, it staggers me ;
I know this truth. but I repell'd the thought.
Sure there is none but fears a future state ;
And when the most obdurate swear they do not,
Their trembling hearts belie their boasting tongues.[f]

15—17. [In addition to murder the three following crimes were punishable with death.] (15) **that..mother**,[a] though he might not kill. **shall..death**, how heinous, therefore, is the crime of the parricide. (16) **he..man**,[b] kidnapping (ill. by state of things on Zanzibar coast, and among islands of Polynesia). **and..him**, making a gain by a vile traffic : the slave-dealer. **if..hand**, having stolen or bought him : the slave-holder. **he..death**, slavery classed with murder. (17) **he..mother**,[c] reproaching, disparaging : violation of filial duty and respect.

Respect for parents.—George Washington, when quite young, was about to go to sea as a midshipman. Everything was in readiness. His trunk had been taken on board the boat ; and he went to bid his mother farewell, when he saw tears filling her eyes. Seeing her distress, he turned to the servant, and said, "Go and tell them to fetch my trunk back. I will not go away to break my mother's heart." His mother, struck with his decision, said to him, " George, God has promised to bless the children that honour their parents ; and I believe He will bless you."

18—21. (18) **if..together**, in a quarrel. **and..bed**, having received a severe personal injury. (19) **walk..staff**, be clearly recovering. **he..quit**, free of the charge and the punishment of murder or manslaughter. **he..time**, shall pay what if in health he would have earned. **and..healed**, defray the charges for medical attendance. (20) **if..rod**,[a] chastising for a fault. **he..hand**, being brutally ill-treated. **he..punished**, punishment prob. determined by the judges. (21) **if..two**, not beaten to death ; no intention to kill. **for..money**, the loss of wh. would be itself a punishment.

Treatment of servants.—Though the Israelitish master had the power of life and death, it has been alleged by some writers that he seldom abused it; for his interest obliged him to preserve his slave, who made a part of his riches. This is the reason of the law, That he should not be punished who had smitten a servant, if he continued alive a day or two after. He is his money, says

---

B.C. 1491.

[a] Ge. ix. 5, 6 ; Le. xxiv. 17; Nu. xxxv. 30, 31 ; Ma. xxvi. 52.
[b] Nu. xxxv. 22—25.
[c] De. xix. 3 ; Nu. xxxv. 10, 11 ; Josh. xx. 2 ; 1 Sa. xxiv. 4, 9, 10, 17, 18 ; Ma. x. 29, 30.
[d] Nu. xv. 30 ; xxxv. 20.
[e] De. xix. 11, 12 ; 1 Ki. ii. 28—31; He. x. 26.

" Our acts make or mar us.—we are the children of our own deeds."- V. Hugo.
[f] Dryden.

kidnapping
[a] 1 Ti. i. 9.
[b] De. xxiv. 7 ; Ge. xxxvii. 28.
[c] Le. xx. 9 ; Pr. xx. 20 ; Ma. xv. 4 ; Mk. vii. 10.

" I think it must somewhere be written that the virtues of mothers shall, occasionally, be visited on their children, as well as the sins of fathers."-Dickens.

accidental injuries and compensation
[a] Le. xxv. 45, 46 ; Eph. vi. 9.

" It is proper for everyone to consider, in the case of all men, that he who has not been a servant cannot become a praiseworthy master ; and it is meet that we should plume ourselves rather on acting the part of a servant

b.c. 1491.

properly than that of the master, first, towards the laws (for in this way we are servants of the gods), and next, towards our elders."—*Plato.*
b *Paxton.*

lex talionis
a Ex. xxi. 30.
b Le. xxiv. 20; De. xix. 21; Ma. v. 38.
c "This doth not mean, that if I put out another man's eye, therefore I must lose my own (for what is he better for that?), though this be commonly received; but it means, I shall give him what satisfaction an eye shall be judged to be worth."—*Selden.*
d *Cruickshank.*
e *Milton.*

criminal carelessness

vicious ox
a Ge. ix. 5; Nu. xxxv. 31.
Gore A.-S., *gar*, a spear.
Wont, pa. p. of Old E. *won, wone*, to dwell; A.-S., *weunian*, Ger. *wohnen*, to dwell; Ice., *vani*, custom.
b Ma. xxv. 15; Zech. xi. 12; Phil. ii. 7.

"A little neglect may breed great mischief; for want of a nail the shoe was lost; for want of a shoe the horse was lost; and for want of a horse the rider was lost; being

the lawgiver, to show that the loss of his property was deemed a sufficient punishment: and it may be presumed, in this case, that the master only intended his correction. But if the slave died under the strokes, it was to be supposed the master had a real design to kill him, for which the law commanded him to be punished. But considerations of interest are too feeble a barrier to resist the impulse of passions, inflamed by the consciousness and exercise of absolute power over a fellow-mortal. The wise and benevolent restraints imposed upon a master of slaves, by the law of Moses, clearly prove that he very often abused his power, or was in extreme danger of doing so; for laws are not made for the good, but for the evil-doer.*b*

22—27. (22) **and .. child,** the wife of one interfering to part them. **so .. her,** miscarriage, premature birth. **yet .. follow,** no fatal result to the woman. **according .. him,** he shall state the amount of compensation. **he .. determine,**a they shall assess the damages. (23) **if .. follow,** *etc.,* punishment shall follow as for man-slaying, or in proportion to the mischief done. (24, 25) **eye .. eye,**b *lex talionis:* or, law of like for like, prob. not so much retribution as compensation.c (26, 27) **he .. eye's sake .. tooth's sake,** i.e. he shall suffer punishment for his cruelty by the loss of his property.

Slave-rights.—We have heard a slave argue for his emancipation on the score of the accidental loss of an eye, in his master's service, from the recoil of a branch of a tree, and appeal to a traditionary law which entitles him to this compensation.d

God gave us only over beast, fish, fowl,
 Dominion absolute; that right we hold
By His donation: but man over man
He made not lord; such title to Himself
Reserving, human left from human free.*e*

28—32. (28) **ox,** domestic animal: responsibility of owner. **gore,** pierce, *i.e.* with the horn. **then .. stoned,** to induce carefulness in training and guarding of animals. **his .. eaten,** for the greater punishment of the owner. **but .. quit,** free from fine and punishment. (29) **wont,** accustomed, habituated. **and .. owner,** so that he knows the habit of his beast. **he .. in,** being reckless of consequences. **but .. woman,** wh. prudence might have prevented. **ox .. stoned,** to prevent further injuries. **owner .. death,** as an accomplice in the crime. (30) **if .. money,**a capital punishment being commuted for a fine, through lack of distinct evidence of carelessness. (31) **son .. daughter,** children under age. **according .. him,** *i.e.* acc. to the principle of this law shall he be dealt with. (32) **give .. silver,**b as a penalty for carelessness and a compensation to their owner.

Negligence.—Neglect is enough to ruin a man. A man who is in business need not commit forgery or robbery to ruin himself; he has only to neglect his business, and his ruin is certain. A man who is lying on a bed of sickness need not cut his throat to destroy himself; he has only to neglect the means of restoration, and he will be ruined. A man floating in a skiff above Niagara need not move an oar, or make an effort, to destroy himself: he has only to neglect using the oar at the proper time, and he will certainly be carried over the cataract. Most of the calamities of life are caused by simple neglect. Let no one infer that, because he is not a drunkard or an adulterer or a murderer, therefore he will be saved. Such an inference would be as irrational as it would be for a man to infer that, because he is not a murderer, his farm will produce a harvest ; or that, because he is not an adulterer, therefore his merchandise will take care of itself.*

33—36. (33) **pit .. it,** being carelessly left open. (34) **give .. them,** the value of the living animal. **and .. his,** to whom the pit belonged. (35) **then .. ox,**ª whose owner shall lose half the value. **dead .. divide,** *i.e.* the value of the hide, the flesh not being eaten. (36) **he .. ox,** to the owner of the ox killed. **and .. own,** *i.e.* a hide in the place of a living animal : a fine for carelessness.

Carelessness (vv. 33, 34).—Evils are wrought by want of thought, as well as by want of heart. I. Sin of him who leaves the pit open : a selfish and heedless disregard of the rights and personal safety of others. Apply this not only to pits literally (as open traps, doors, etc.), but to professions and callings which are as pits. The gin-palace keeper should be compelled to write up—" An open pit here." Keepers of brothels should be forced to have for their sign, " The way to the pit." II. Folly of him who, knowing there are such pits in the world, walks into them with his eyes open. He is to be blamed, while the man who falls down a trap-door, in a dark passage, may be pitied. Learn :— There is a great, uncovered, bottomless pit, in the pathway of every traveller.

Use your intellects.—In connection with this camp-illumination, I received another first "impression," and a very useful lesson. The distance from the hotel was about two miles. I walked forward alone. The road was wide and well-frequented, but the over-shadowing trees and the absence of the moon rendered it very dark. Not wishing to be run over by the numerous vehicles driving to the camp, I took the footpath by the side, equally well-defined and well-frequented. I could not suspect any danger or any need of caution in so public a thoroughfare. But suddenly I trod on nothing, and was falling forward into space. Happily, I was soon arrested, and found myself in a deep, narrow trench. There was a rock which my forehead had brushed, and which might have brought my tour in America to a sudden termination. I was thankful to find no limb broken, though my right wrist gave me considerable pain. I scrambled up, and discovered that a trench was being made for laying down pipes, and though cut along the public path, the workmen had gone away without taking any precaution whatever to prevent passengers falling in. Within a few yards, I came to a sentry on duty, and told him of my mishap. "Umph !" " But should not a lamp be put there, or a railing ? " " Umph ! " " But others may tumble too, and may possibly be killed ! " " Umph ! " I felt I had discharged my duty, and went forward to the camp, where I was amused by the innocent frolics of the youths, and their lamps and bonfires. Next morning I found my wrist swollen, and I had to carry my arm in a sling for a week. At breakfast I mentioned the circumstance to an American, who inquired what ailed me. His remark was peculiar—" Oh, you Britishers, you've no intellects ! " " Indeed," said I ; " pray, sir, what do you mean ? " " Why, in your country there would

B.C. 1491.

overtaken and slain by an enemy, all for want of care about a horse-shoe nail."—*Franklin.*
c *Barnes.*

uncovered pit, etc.
a Le. xvii. 1—6.

" Every man has something to do which he neglects, every man has faults to conquer which he delays to combat."—*Johnson.*

" Let us do our duty in our shop or our kitchen, the market, the street, the office, the school, the home, just as faithfully as if we stood in the front rank of some great battle, and we knew that victory for mankind depended on our bravery, strength and skill. When we do that the humblest of us will be serving in that great army which achieves the welfare of the world." — *Theo. Parker.*

" Aristotle has said that man is by nature a social animal, and, he might have added, a selfish one too. Heroism, self-denial, and magnanimity in all instances, where they do not spring from a principle of religion, are but splendid altars on which we sacrifice one kind of self-love to another." — *Colton.*

" Confidence in one's self is the chief nurse of magnanimity,

have been a lamp and a rail." "Just so," I answered, "and that, I think, is a proof that we *have* intellects." "You don't see what I mean: you don't *use* your intellects. Why, if such a thing were to happen in your country, I guess you'd bring an action against the man who left the road like that. You'll get no damages in this country, I'll tell you. In your country, if a man asks me to go down a mine with him, I go at once without question. But if asked to do so here, I first look at the basket, and the rope, and the engine, and see that all's right before I trust my life to him. In your country they take care of you without your having to take care of yourself. In this country you must use your intellect, sir ! Take my advice—use your intellect !"*b*

B.C. 1491.
which confidence, notwithstanding, doth not leave the care of necessary furniture for it; and therefore, of all the Grecians, Homer doth ever make Achilles the best armed."
—*Sir P. Sydney.*
b N. Hall, LL.B.

CHAPTER THE TWENTY-SECOND.

B.C. 1491.

theft, housebreaking
a 2 Sa. xii. 6 ; Lu. xix. 8.
b Pr. vi. 30, 31.

"The first step towards greatness is to be honest, says the proverb; but the proverb fails to state the case strong enough. Honesty is not only 'the first step towards greatness'—it is greatness itself."
—*Bovee.*

c Montaigne.

1—4. (1) **five** .. **sheep,**^a greater restitution for an ox, bec. of its greater value; used in ploughing, etc. (2) **thief** .. **up,** *lit.,* digging through, burglary. **be** .. **die,** justifiable homicide. (3) **sun** .. **him,** daylight; the burglar visible, his intention perceived. **there** .. **him,** under such conditions killing would be murder. **for** .. **restitution,** the burglar recognised might be punished. **then** .. **theft,** *i.e.,* he might have been sold. (4) **theft, thing stolen. alive, if** *dead,* see v. 1. **he** .. **double,**^b punishment for his intended crime.

An exceptional mode of making restitution.—I have taken notice of several in my time, who, convinced by their consciences of unjustly detaining the goods of another, have endeavoured to make amends by their will, and after their decease : but they had as well do nothing as delude themselves both in taking so much time in so pressing an affair, and also in going about to repair an injury with so little demonstration of resentment and concern. They owe over and above something of their own ; and by how much their payment is more strict and incommodious to themselves, by so much is their restitution more perfect, just, and meritorious ; for a penitency requires penance.*c*

trespass
"That which is won ill will never wear well, for there is a curse attends it, which will waste it; and the same corrupt dispositions which incline men to the sinful ways of getting will incline them to the like sinful ways of spending."—*M. Henry.*
a Harmer.

5, 6. (5) **cause** .. **eaten,** case of trespass. **shall** .. **beast, etc.,** case of fraud or carelessness. **restitution,** compensation. (6) **kindleth** .. **restitution,** punishment for carelessness.

Cattle in vineyards.—Chandler observes (*Travels in Asia Minor*) that the tame cattle were very fond of vine leaves, and were permitted to eat them in the autumn. "We remarked," he says, "about Smyrna, the leaves were decayed, or stripped by the camels and herds of goats, which are admitted to browse after the vintage." If these animals are so fond of vine leaves, it is no wonder that Moses, by an express law, forbad *a man's causing another man's vineyard to be eaten by putting in his beast.* The turning any of them in before the fruit was gathered, must have occasioned much mischief ; and even after it must have been an injury, as it would have been eating up another's feed.*a*

things put in trust
a De. xxv. ; 2 Ch. xix. 10.

7—13. (7) **thief** .. **double,** the custodian being absolved fr. blame. (8) **master** .. **house,** in such case open to suspicion. **whether** .. **goods,** the depositary being put upon his oath. (9) **whom** .. **neighbour,**^a (10) he who, professing to have lost, shall have unjustly accused another of finding and retaining,

Cap. xxii. 14—21.] EXODUS. 311

shall make compensation for the unjust accusation ; (2) he who had found and retained a missing article shall compensate its owner. (10) **man** .. **it**, there being no witness. (11) **oath**,[b] *etc.*, see v. 8. (12) **if** .. **him**, the thief being found. **he** .. **thereof**,[c] fr. the fine imposed on the thief. (13) **let** .. **witness**, proof, evidence. **he** .. **torn**, having been reasonably vigilant.

Tardy restitution.—As a gentleman in London entered his house, he found a well-dressed female sitting on the stairs, who asked pardon for the liberty she had taken, saying, that, hearing the alarm of a mad dog, she had taken refuge in his house. On hearing her story, he gave her some refreshment ; and she left, thanking him for his civility. In the evening, his lady missed her gold watch ; and it was concluded the female was the thief. Fifteen years afterwards, the watch was returned, with a note from this woman, saying the Gospel had changed her heart, and she desired to return the watch to its rightful owner.

b.c. 1491.

b 1 Ki. ii. 43 ; He. vi. 16.

c Ge. xxxi. 39.

"I have known a vast quantity of nonsense talked about bad men not looking you in the face. Don't trust that conventional idea. Dishonesty will stare honesty out of countenance any day in the week if there is anything to be got by it."—*Dickens*

14, 15. (14) **owner** .. **it**,[a] the borrower is the responsible keeper. (15) **owner** .. **it**, and therefore its custodian. **hired** .. **hire**, *i.e.*, for a price agreed upon.

The honest cabman.—One day, while he was Chancellor, Lord Eldon took a hackney coach to convey him from Downing-street, where he had been attending a Cabinet, to his own residence. Having a pressing appointment, he alighted hastily from the vehicle, leaving papers containing important Government secrets behind him. Some hours after, the driver discovered the packages, and took them to Hamilton-place, unopened, when his lordship desired to see the coachman, and, after a short interview, told him to call again. The man called again, and was then informed that he was no longer a servant, but the owner of a hackney coach, which his lordship had in the meantime given directions to be purchased, and presented to him, together with three horses, as a reward for his honour and promptitude.

things borrowed

a 2 Ki. vi. 5.

"It should seem that indolence itself would incline a person to be honest, as it requires infinitely greater pains and contrivance to be a knave."—*Shenstone.*
"Rich honesty dwells like a miser in a poor house, as your pearl in your foul oyster."—*Shakespeare.*

16, 17. (16) **entice**, by persuading blandishments ; false promises : case of seduction. **endow** .. **wife**,[a] marriage as a reparation for the wrong. (17) **father** .. **refuse**, wh. even in such cases he might, for various reasons. **according** .. **virgins**,[b] and suited to her station in life.

Temptations to incontinence.—In his solitary life, St. Benedict underwent many temptations : and he relates that, on one occasion, the recollection of a beautiful woman whom he had seen at Rome took such possession of his imagination as almost to overpower his virtue : so that he was on the point of rushing from his solitude to seek that face and form which haunted his morbid fancy, and disturbed his dreams. He believed that this assault upon his constancy could only come from the enemy of mankind. In a crisis of these distracted desires, he rushed from his cave, and flung himself into a thicket of briars and nettles, in which he rolled himself until the blood flowed. Thereupon the fiends left him : and he was never assailed by the same temptation.[c]

seduction

a De. xxii. 29.

b Ge. xxxiv. 12.

"The pleasantest part of a man's life is generally that which passes in courtship, provided his passion be sincere, and the party beloved kind with discretion. Love, desire, hope, all the pleasing emotions of the soul, rise in the pursuit."—*Addison.*
c *Mrs. Jameson.*

18—21. (18) **witch**,[a] one who invoked the aid of supernatural powers other than Divine (esp. for evil purposes), and thereby rebelled against God. (19) **whosoever**,[b] *etc.*, a crime of almost inconceivable magnitude, to wh. the Canaanites were addicted. (20) **he** .. **god**,[c] paying Divine homage to an idol.

witchcraft, etc.

a Le. xix. 20, 31, xx. 27; De. xviii. 10, 11 ; 1 Sa.

B.C. 1491.

xxviii. 3, 9; Gal.
v. 19, 20; Re.
xxii. 15.

b Le. xviii. 20 –
23, xx. 15.

c De. xiii. 1–15;
1 Co. xvi. 22.

d Ex. xxiii. 9;
Le. xix. 33, xxv.
35; De. x. 19;
Jer. vii. 6, 7;
Zech. vii. 10;
Mal. iii. 5.

"Superstition, that horrid incubus which dwelt in darkness, shunning the light, with all its racks, and poison chalices, and foul sleeping-draughts, is passing away without return. Religion cannot pass away. The burning of a little straw may hide the stars of the sky; but the stars are there, and will reappear."—Carlyle.

"Look how the world's poor people are amazed at apparitions, signs, and prodigies."—Shakespeare.

e Haydn.

f Sir W. Scott.

widows and orphans

a De. x. 18,
xxiv. 17, 18,
xxvii. 19; Is. i.
17, 23, x. 2; Ezek.
xxii. 7; Ps. xciv.
6 10; Jas. i. 27.

b Job xxxiv. 28;
Ps. xviii. 6, cxlv.
19; Jas. v. 4; Lu.
xviii. 7.

c Job xx. 23; Ps.
lxix. 24, cix. 9;
Lam. v. 3.

save .. only, the sole object of true worship. he .. destroyed, Heb. *yohoram*, anathematised. (21) **vex,**d **afflict,** distress. for .. Egypt, the past should teach compassion.

Civility to strangers (v. 21).—I. Whence it should arise. From—1. Proper human feelings; 2. A desire to make those who are away from home feel at home; 3. The consideration of what we may be, if not of what we have been (as case of Israel in Egypt). II. Opportunities for its exercise—1. Kindness to servants—stranger within thy gates; 2. Kindness to strange visitors to God's house; 3. Kindness to travellers, showing them the best way to their destination; 4. Children to be kind to strange scholars; 5. Kindness to new neighbours.

Witchcraft.—The punishment of witchcraft was commanded in the Jewish law, B.C. 1491,—" Thou shalt not suffer a witch to live." Saul, after banishing or condemning witchcraft, incurred the wrath of God by consulting the witch of Endor, 1056 B.C. But it must be recollected that God was then the real King of Israel, and manifested His will to His people visibly. Bp. Hutchinson's important historical *Essay on Witchcraft* was published in 1718. The Church of Rome subjected persons suspected of the crime to the most cruel torments. Pope Innocent VIII. issued a superstitious bull against witchcraft in 1484. In tens of thousands of cases the victims, often innocent, were burned alive, whilst others were drowned by the test applied; for if, on being thrown into a pond, they did not sink, they were presumed to be witches, and either killed on the spot, or reserved for burning at the stake.e Many learned men have affirmed that in this remarkable passage the Hebrew word *Chasaph* means nothing more than poisoner, although, like the word *veneficus*, by which it is rendered in the Latin version of the Septuagint, other learned men contend that it hath the meaning of a witch also, and may be understood as denoting a person who pretended to hurt his or her neighbours in life, limb, or goods, either by noxious potions, by charms, or similar mystical means. In this particular the witches of Scripture had probably some resemblance to those of ancient Europe, who, although their skill and power might be safely despised, as long as they confined themselves to their charms and spells, were very apt to eke out their capacity of mischief by the use of actual poison, so that the epithets of sorceress and poisoner were almost synonymous. This is known to have been the case in many of those darker iniquities, which bear as their characteristic something connected with hidden and prohibited arts.f

22—24. (22) **widow..child,**a taking advantage of their weak and friendless state. (23) **I..cry,**b in the place of the earthly husband and father. (24) **wives..fatherless,**c therefore treat widows and orphans as you would have others treat your survivors.

Adoption of orphans.—A sergeant and his wife in India, having no children, adopted first an orphan babe, then a little native child left uncared for. Afterwards, two orphans more were added to their family, making four in all. The regiment was ordered to march about two hundred miles. "What will you do now with your adopted family?" asked a lady of the sergeant's wife. "You will have to leave them behind."—"Leave my children!" said this noble-hearted woman. "No, never! They shall all go with us: we could not part with one of them."

25—27. (25) **My** .. **thee**, God cares for the poor. **usurer**, one who takes an exorbitant interest. **neither** .. **usury**," money for the *use* of the loan. (26) **take** .. **pledge**,[b] for loan of money or provisions. **thou** .. **shalt**, *etc.*, even though the loan be not repaid. (27) **wherein** .. **sleep?** to this day the poor often sleep wrapped simply in the clothes they wear by day. **that** .. **hear**,[c] *etc.*, I will avenge the poor.

Sleeping in day-clothes in Africa.—In all parts of Southern Africa, the skin cloak is the covering of males and females by day, and that in which they sleep by night : they have no other bed-clothes. The Hottentot cloak is composed of sheep skins, retaining the wool on the inside of it, in which he sleeps comfortably under a bush or tree wherever he goes. Deprive him of that covering, and he would find himself most uncomfortably placed. It would be a cruel act. The nations farther in the interior have cloaks made from hides of oxen or cows, which they have a method of rendering soft and pliable. and use exactly for the same purposes as the others, viz., for clothing and for sleeping in. The Israelites sleeping in the wilderness in this simple manner, would always be ready to remove when the trumpet intimated the moving of the pillar of fire ; like the dogs when they shook themselves. they might be said to be dressed and ready to march. The God who gave such a humane, considerate law to the Israelites might well be called a gracious God.[d]

28—31. (28) **gods**,[a] Heb. *elohim*, either (1) God ;[b] or (2) the deities of other nations ;[c] or (3) chief-rulers. **curse**,[d] vilify, speak evil of. (29) **first**,[e] thy fulness, *i.e.* fully ripe fruits. **liquors**, *lit.* tear, *i.e.* wine and oil wh. distil as tears. **firstborn** .. **Me**,[f] *see* xiii. 2. (30) **seven** .. **dam**,[g] this prob. for the mother's sake. (31) **neither** .. **field**,[h] even by their diet as well as higher things they were to be distinguished from all things.

The first ripe fruits (v. 29).—Notice—I. The signs of the ripe fruits fit for God and heaven. 1. Fulness ; 2. Colour ; 3. Fragrance : 4. Tenderness and softness. II. How they become such. 1. They must be planted in suitable soil ; 2. There must be spiritual cultivation ; 3. They must have heavenly sunshine : 4. There must be rain and dew. Conclusion—(1) The harvest is approaching'; (2) Are we becoming fit for the garner : (3) Learn the necessity of constant self-examination ; (4) Some fruits ripen very early.[i]

The temper of the mind shown by gratitude.—Gratitude is a temper of mind which denotes a desire of acknowledging the receipt of a benefit. The mind which does not so feel is not as it ought to be. When the Apostle Paul says of the heathen, "Neither were they thankful," he seems to stamp the sin of ingratitude as peculiarly odious. But, like every other grace which is required of us, virtuous gratitude depends, in part, on right views. A right view of benefits received, of the source from whence they flow, and of our own demerit, has a direct tendency to excite gratitude ; and while the mind is influenced by sovereign grace, this will be the pleasing effect. The devout Christian surveys the sovereign benevolence of the Creator in every person, in every object, in every quality, and in every event. Sovereign benevolence forces itself on every sense. and pervades his grateful heart. And then, when he extends his views to a future state,

---

B.C. 1491.

pledges, usury

[a] Le. xxv. 36, 37 ; De. xxiii. 19, 20 ; Ne. v. 7 ; Ps. xv. 5 ; Ezek. xviii. 8, 9.

Usury, a using, interest paid for use of money: Lat. *usura—utor, usus*, to use. See also D.M., N.T., i. 193.

[b] De. xxiv. 6, 12, 13, 17.

[c] Ex. xxxiv. 6 ; Ch. xxx. 9 ; Ps. lxxxvi. 15.

[d] *African Light.*

reverence, gratitude, holiness

[a] Ps. lxxxii. 6 ; Jo. x. 34 ; Ac. xxiii. 5.

[b] De Wette, Keil, *etc.*

[c] Josephus, Ant. iv. 8, 10.

[d] Jude 8 ; Eccl. x. 20 ; Ro. xiii. 4; Ti. iii. 1.

[e] Pr. iii. 9, 10 ; Ex. xxiii. 16, 19 ; Mal. iii. 10.

[f] Ex. xxxiv. 19.

[g] Le. xxii. 27 ; De. xv. 19.

[h] Ezek. xliv. 31 ; Le. xxii. 8 ; Ezek. iv. 14.

[i] Dr. Burns.

"Now, it was well said, whoever said it, ' That he who hath the loan of money has not repaid it, and he who has repaid has not the loan ; but he who has acknowledged a kindness has it still, and he who

B.C. 1491.

has a feeling of it has required it." – *Cicero*.

k Dr. E. Williams.

and contemplates the operations of grace—sovereign, distinguishing, efficacious grace—he is melted into reverential awe and grateful praise, and exclaims, "Why me, Lord!" Glory, everlasting glory to Him that sitteth on the throne, and to the Lamb of God that was slain, who hath redeemed us to God by His blood, and hath given us the earnest of His own inheritance.[k]

B.C. 1491.

CHAPTER THE TWENTY-THIRD.

false reports, evil fashions, compassionate weakness

a Ex. xx. 16; Le. xix. 16; Ex. xxiii. 7; Ps. ci. 5.

b Pr. xxiv. 28; x. 18; Ma. xxvi. 59 61; Ps. xxxv. 11; Ac. vi. 11, 13; Eph. iv. 25.

c Pr. i. 10, 15; iv. 14, 15; Ma. vii. 13; Job xxxi. 34; Ma. xxvii. 24 - 26; Mk. xv. 15; Ac. xxiv. 27.

d Spk. Comm.

e De. i. 17; Ps. lxxii. 2; Le. xix. 15.

"He that easily believes rumours has the principle within him to augment rumours. It is strange to see the ravenous appetite with which some devourers of character and happiness fix upon the sides of the innocent and unfortunate." – *Jane Porter*.

f Dr. J. R. Beard.

1—3. (1) **not .. report,**[a] rather not take it up, repeat, or circulate it. **put .. witness,**[b] not take part in plots, conspiracies, etc. (2) **thou .. evil,** *etc.*[c] *lit.*, thou shalt not follow the many to do evil; neither shalt thou bear witness in a cause so as to incline after the many to pervert justice,[d] *i.e.*, do not pursue a wrong thing bec. many others do. (3) **countenance .. cause,**[e] *i.e.*, simply bec. he is poor.

Following the multitude (v. 2).—I. Explain the nature of the text. 1. It is assumed that the multitude do evil; 2. It is implied that we are in danger of copying their example. II. Urge reasons to induce to its observation. The multitude is a guide, that is—1. Unlawful and unconstituted; 2. Bad; 3. Dishonourable; 4. Unprofitable; 5. Dangerous. III. Impart advice for the direction of those who wish to escape the ensnaring wiles of the multitude. 1. Get your minds deeply impressed with the awfulness of your situation; 2. Seek the regenerating grace of God; 3. Guard against the seductive influence of the multitude; 4. Follow the happy few who strive to do good.

Ancient oaths.—Other beings beside God are sometimes added to the form of an oath. Elijah said to Elisha, "As the Lord liveth, and as thy soul liveth." The party addressed is frequently sworn by, especially if a prince: "As thy soul liveth, my lord, I am the woman," etc. (1 Sa. i. 26; xvii. 55). The Hebrews, as well as the Egyptians, swore also by the head or the life of an absent as well as a present prince: "By the life of Pharaoh" (Ge. xlii. 15). Hanway says that the most sacred oath among the Persians is, "by the king's head." Aben Ezra asserts that in his time (A.D. 1170) this oath was common in Egypt under the caliphs. Death was the penalty of perjury. The oath-taker swore sometimes by his own head (Matt. v. 36), or by some precious part of his body, as the eyes; sometimes, but only in the case of the latter Jews, by the earth, the heaven, and the sun, as well as by angels; by the Temple (Matt. xxiii. 16), and even by parts of the Temple. They also swore by Jerusalem, as the holy city (Matt. v. 35).[f]

treatment of enemies, justice to the poor, love of truth

a Trapp.

b Pr. xxiv. 17, 18; xxv. 21, 22; Ma. v. 43–45.

c Ro. xii. 19–21; 1 Th. v. 15.

d De. xxvii. 19; Is. x. 1, 2; Eccl.

4—7. (4) **meet .. astray,** "how much more his soul."[a] **surely .. again,**[b] thus do good to an enemy. (5) **wouldest .. him,** as the first motion of a resentful spirit. **thou .. him,**[c] conquering thyself. (6) **wrest,** pervert. **judgment,** award, favourable decision. **thy .. cause,**[d] comp. with v. 3, i.e., do not favour him if wrong, nor be adverse if right. (7) **keep .. matter,** do not countenance it by word or deed. **innocent .. not,**[e] however powerful their oppressors.

The example of Euclid.—Euclid, a disciple of Socrates, having offended his brother, the brother cried out in a rage, "Let me die, if I am not revenged on you one time or other": to whom Euclid replied, "And let me die, if I do not soften you by my kindnesses, and make you love me as well as ever." What a reproof to unforgiving professors of Christianity. *Aristides in judgment.*—Aristides being judge between two private persons, one of them declared that his adversary had greatly injured Aristides. "Relate rather, good friend," said he, interrupting him, "what wrong he hath done to thee, for it is thy cause, not mine, that I now sit judge of."

8—13. (8) **gift**,*a* as a bribe. **the .. wise,** to that wh. is just and true. **perverteth .. righteous**,*b* so bringing courts of justice into contempt. (9) **also,** *etc.*,*c* see xxii. 21. (10) **six .. land**,*d* *etc.*, fr. yr. to yr. (11) **seventh .. still,** first mention of Sabbatical yr. **that .. eat,***e* whence it seems that the poor might then cultivate the land as their own. (12) **six days,***f* *etc.*, *see* xx. 8, 9. (13) **all .. you,** each one of these Divine precepts. **circumspect,***g* self-restrained. **mention .. gods,** *etc.*, either in blessing or cursing, that unnamed they may be forgotten.

The Sabbath and how to keep it (v. 12).—I. The object of the seventh day Sabbath is rest. This is shown by—1. The name by which the day is called ; 2. The reason assigned by Moses for its appointment ; 3. The commandments by which it has been confirmed ; 4. The Divine prohibitions by which it is defended ; 5. The inclusion of cattle in the commandments concerning it ; 6. The punishments which, in Scripture, are threatened and visited on work on that day ; 7. The connection of the idea of rest with it throughout the Bible ; 8. The definition which Christ gives of its object. II. The intended effect of Sabbath rest is refreshment. Therefore, the day must not be spent—1. In sleep ; 2. In listless thought ; 3. In entire solitude, or the opposite ; 4. Unreligiously.*h*

Types of the Sabbath.—Stations on the line of your journey are not your journey's end ; but each one brings you nearer. A haven is not *home ;* but it is a place of quiet and rest where the rough waves are stayed. A garden is a piece of common land, and yet it has ceased to be common land : it is an effort to regain paradise. A bud is not a flower : but it is the promise of a flower. Such are the Lord's Days. The world's week tempts you to sell your soul to the flesh and the world. "The Lord's Day" calls you to remembrance, and begs you rather to sacrifice earth to heaven and time to eternity than heaven to earth and eternity to time. The six days not only chain you as captives of the earth, but do their best to keep the prison doors shut, that you may forget *the way out.* "The Lord's Day" sets before you an open door. Samson has carried the gates away. "The Lord's Day" summons you to the threshold of your house of bondage to look forth into immortality,—*your immortality.* The true Lord's Day is the eternal life : but a type of it is given to you on earth, that you may be refreshed in the body with the anticipation of the great freedom wherewith the Lord will make you free.*i*

14—19. (14) **feast,***a* religious festival. (15) **feast .. bread,***b* *etc.*, *see* xii. 15 ff. (16) **and .. harvest,** or feast of weeks observed 50 days after waving the sheaf of firstfruits, hence called *Pentecost* = the *fiftieth.* **and .. ingathering,***c* on 15th day of 7th month. (17) **males .. Lord,** in humble acknowledgment

B.C. 1491.

v. 8 ; Am. v. 12 ; Mal. iii. 5.

c De. xxvii. 25 ; Pr. xvii. 15 ; Ps. xciv. 21—23 ; Ma. xxvii. 4.

bribes, strangers, sabbatical year, sabbath, careful obedience

a 2 Ch. xix. 7 ; De. xvi. 19 ; 1 Sa. viii. 3 ; xii. 3.

b Pr. xv. 27 ; xxvii. 8, 23 ; xxix. 4 ; Ezek. xxii. 12 ; Am. v. 12 ; Ac. xxiv. 26.

c De. x. 19 ; xxvii. 19.

d Le. xxv. 3, 4.

e De. xv. 1, 9

f De. v. 13 ; La. xiii. 13, 14.

g De. iv. 9 ; Josh. xxii. 5 ; Ps.xxxix. 1 ; Eph. v. 1 ; 1 Ti. iv. 16.

h S. Martin.

"Judges and senates have been bought for gold."—*Pope.*

"Petitions, not sweetened with gold, are but unsavoury and oft refused ; or, if received, are pocketed, not read." — *Massinger.*

"And sell the mighty space of our large honours for so much trash as may be grasped thus ?"- *Shakespeare.*

i J. Pulsford.

the three yearly feasts

a Ex. xxxiv. 23 ; Le. xxiii. 4 ; De. xvi. 16.

b Le. xxiii. 5, 6 ; De. xvi. 8, 16.

B.C 1491.

c Ex. xxxiv. 22;
Le. xxiii. 10; De.
xvi. 13.
d Ex. xxxiv. 23;
Le. ii. 11; De.
xvi. 14.
e Bush.
"When in our days Religion is made a political engine, she exposes herself to having her sacred character forgotten. The most tolerant become intolerant towards her. Believers who believe something else besides what she teaches, retaliate by attacking her in the very sanctuary itself."—*Beranger.*
"He who possesses religion finds a providence not more truly in the history of the world than in his own family history; the rainbow, which hangs a glistening circle in the heights of heaven, is also formed by the same sun in the dewdrop of a lowly flower."—*Richter.*
f *Burder.*

promised guidance, preservation, conquest, etc.

a Ge. xlviii. 15, 16; Ex. xxxiii. 14; xiv. 19, 20; Is. lxiii. 9; Ac. vii. 38; 1 Co. x. 9.

b De. xviii. 19.

c Nu. xiv. 11; He. iii. 10, 16; Ps. lxxviii. 40, 56, 57; Eph. iv. 30.

d Nu. xiv. 35; 1 Jo. v. 16.

e Is. ix. 6; Jer. xxiii. 6.

f Josh. xxiv. 8—11.

of Him as their great Master and King. (18) **thou .. bread,** *etc.,* ref. to mode of keeping the Passover, *see* xii. 8. (19) **first-fruits .. God,** in acknowledgment of Him as the great Landowner. **kid .. milk,** *i.e.* "during the period necessary for its own nutrition and the case of its dam," *see* xxii. 30.

All the males before the Lord.—To those that may wonder how Jerusalem could receive such multitudes, as were obliged by the Jewish law to attend there three times a year, and as we know did sometimes actually appear in it, I would recite the account that Pitts gives of Mecca, the sacred city of the Mohammedans, and the number he found collected together there, for the celebration of their religious solemnities, in the close of the 17th century. This city, he tells us, he thought he might safely say, had not one thousand families in it of constant inhabitants, and the buildings very mean and ordinary. That four caravans arrive there every year, with great numbers of people in each, and, the Mohammedans say, there meet not fewer than seventy thousand souls at these solemnities; and that though he could not think the number quite so large, yet that it is very great. How such numbers of people, with their beasts, could be lodged and entertained in such a little town as Mecca, is a question he thus answers. "As for house-room, the inhabitants do straiten themselves very much, in order at this time to make their market. As for such as come last, after the town is filled, they pitch their tents without the town, and there abide until they remove towards home. As for provision, they all bring sufficient with them, except it be of flesh, which they may have at Mecca; but all other provisions, as butter, honey, oil, olives. rice, biscuit, etc., they bring with them, as much as will last through the wilderness, forward and backward, as well as the time they stay at Mecca; and so for their camels they bring store of provender, etc., with them." The number of Jews that assembled at Jerusalem at their passover was much greater; but had not Jerusalem been a much larger city than Mecca is, as in truth it was, yet the present Mohammedan practice of abiding under tents, and carrying their provisions and bedding with them, will easily explain how they might be accommodated.*f*

20—25. (20) **send .. thee,**^a visible presence of Jehovah. **keep . way,** Divine protection. **bring .. place,** Divine guidance, prepared place for a prepared people. (21) **beware .. Him,** fear Him. **obey,**^b proof of fear. **provoke .. not,**^c by disobedience. **he .. transgressions,**^d wilful sins after repeated warnings. **for .. Him,**^e the name of a jealous God of truth. (22) **if . speak,** and be universally obedient. **then,** *etc.,* I will be practically thy friend and helper. (23) **bring .. Amorites,**^f *etc.,* i.e. under the land now occupied by these nations. **and .. off,** as I have said: when their iniquity is full. (24) **not .. gods,**^g adopt their religion. **nor .. them,** submit to their rule. **nor .. works,**^h imitate their customs. (25) **bless .. water,**ⁱ make the simplest fare more nourishing than choicest dainties. **take .. thee,**^k health a special Divine blessing.

The Saviour's guidance (vv. 20, 21).—Let us consider—I. The gracious purpose of God as revealed in the text: "I send an angel before thee," *etc.* 1. The nature of that Divine messenger: it was Christ; 2. The object of His guidance: "to keep thee in the way, and to bring thee into the place which I have prepared." II. The caution given, in connection with the promise: "beware of Him," *etc*. They were—1. To look up to Him with awe ; 2. To live holy lives, lest they provoked Him ; 3. To obey Him in everything. Thus was their path to be blessed.*[i]*

Motive in obedience.—Nothing can be love to God which does not shape itself into obedience. We remember the anecdote of the Roman commander who forbade an engagement with the enemy, and the first transgressor against whose prohibition was his son. He accepted the challenge of the leader of the other host, met, slew, spoiled him : and then, in triumphant feeling, carried the spoils to his father's tent. But the Roman father refused to recognise the instinct which prompted this, as deserving of the name of love. Disobedience contradicted it, and deserved death.*[m]*

26—33. (26) **number .. fulfil,**[a] promise of long life, including freedom from accident and sickness. (27) **send .. thee,**[b] their march to be preceded by a panic, arising from reports of their numbers, strength, and prowess. **backs,** *lit.* necks, *i.e.* they shall be easily subdued. (28) **hornets,**[c] perhaps used figuratively for discouragements.[d] (29) **drive .. year,** as they perh. would wish. **lest,** *etc.*, giving reasons for that wh. not understood might discourage them. (30) **little .. thee,**[e] for above reasons, and discipline of patience and perseverance. (31) **unto .. Philistines,** *i.e.* the Mediterranean. **desert,** the Arabian. **river,**[f] the Euphrates. (32) **thou shalt,** *etc.,*[g] *see* v. 24. (33) **lest .. Me,**[h] corrupting power of evil.

Progressive sanctification (v. 30).—The words of the text may be considered as relating to the progress of the Church now. We here have—I. A gracious promise, on God's part, to those who are now His true Israel, and who look for a better possession than the earthly Canaan. II. An admirable criterion by which to discover the sincerity of our profession ; and our progress in it. III. A warning that the work of sanctification must be gradual. God does not give us a rapid victory over our sins.—1. In order to keep us humble ; 2. To incite us to prayer, watchfulness, and exertion ; 3. To increase our desires after that land where peace and purity reign for ever. IV. A guarantee of future victory, though it may be progressive.[i]

The hornet.—The hornet is abundant in the Holy Land ; the species are larger than ours : instances are on record in profane history, where hornets have multiplied to such a degree as to become a pest to the inhabitants. But it is probable here—considering that nothing is related of any such material allies of Israel, and that in ref. Josh., where the hornet is stated to have been sent, and to have driven out Sihon and Og, we know that they were otherwise overcome—that the word is metaphorically used of a panic, and means, as Augustine interprets it, "sharp stings of fear, by which flying rumours stung them so that they fled."[k] Roberts notes that the sting of the H. of the E. is more poisonous than in Europe, and the insect is larger ; and that he has heard of several who died from a single sting—a woman stung by a H. in the cheek died the next day ; the people often curse each other by saying, "May all around thee be stung by the H." The god Siva is said to have destroyed many giants by hornets.

B.C. 1491.

g Ex. xx. 5; xxxiv. 13.

h I.e. xviii. 3.

i De. vii. 12, 13; xxviii. 5, 8; 1 Ti. iv. 8; Ma. vi. 33.

k Ex. xv. 26; De. vii. 15; 1 Sa. xii. 24.

l W. H. Perkins.

m F. W. Robertson.

promise of blessing and inheritance in Canaan

a Jo. v. 26; Ge. xxv. 8; xxxv. 29; Job xlii. 17; 1 Ch. xxiii. 1; Ps. lv. 23.

b Ge. xxxv. 5; De. ii. 25; xi. 25; Josh. ii. 9, 11.

c Josh xxiv. 12.

d Topics, i. 70.

e Josh xxi. 44.

Jud. i. 4; xi. 21; 2 Sa. viii. 3.

f 1 Ki. iv. 21, 24; Ge. xv. 18; De. xi. 24; Ps. lxxii. 8.

g Ex. xxxiv. 12; Ps. cvi. 34—38; 2 Co. vi. 14, 15.

h Josh. xxiii. 13; Jud. ii. 3.

i P. Maitland, B.A.

k Dr. Tristram.

"Nature knows no pause in progress and development, and attaches her curse on all inaction."—*Goethe.*

Hornet: fr. A.S. *Hyrnet, horn.*

Avoid the pugnacious, poisonous, quarrelsome character of the hornet; such are proverbially called "waspish;" a number of them called a "hornet's nest."

CHAPTER THE TWENTY-FOURTH

B.C. 1491.

Moses, Aaron, etc., called to the mount

the altar and the pillars

a Ex. xxviii. 1; Lc. x. 1, 2.

"Let the day have a blessed baptism by giving your first waking thoughts into the bosom of God. The first hour of the morning is the rudder of the day."—*Beecher.*

"Sweet is the breath of morn, her rising sweet with charm of earliest birds."—*Milton.*

b *Vaughan.*

the altar, etc., sprinkled with blood

a Ex. xii. 23.

b Josh. xxiv. 24.

c He. ix. 18–20.

d He. xiii. 20; 1 Pe. i. 2.

e Dr. Spencer.

"Obedience is our universal duty and destiny, wherein whoso will not bend must break. Too early and too thoroughly we cannot be trained to know that 'would,' in this world of ours, is a mere zero to 'should,' and for most part, as the smallest of fractions, even to 'shall.'"—*Carlyle.*

"Obedience, as it regards the

1—5. (1) **Nadab**[a] (*spontaneous, liberal*), eldest son of Aaron. Abihu, *see* vi. 23. (2) **but .. nigh,** *see* xix. 12. (3) **all .. do,** *see* xix. 8. (4) **rose .. morning,** a good day cannot begin too soon, nor an evil day too late. **altar,** sign of a present God. **and .. pillars,** sig. that the twelve tribes were there before God. (5) **he .. men,** having strength and skill for the work.

Early rising and prayer.—

  Serve God before the world ; let Him not go
  Until thou hast a blessing : then resign
  The whole unto him, and remember who
  Prevailed by wrestling ere the sun did shine :
  Pour oil upon the stones, weep for thy sin,
  Then journey on, and have an eye to heaven.
  Mornings are mysteries ; the first world's youth,
  Man's resurrection, and the future's bud.
  Shroud in their births, the crown of life, light, truth,
  Is styled their star—the stone and hidden food,
  Three blessings wait upon them, one of which
  Should move—they make us holy, happy, rich.

  When the world's up, and every swarm abroad,
  Keep well thy temper : mix not with each clay ;
  Despatch necessities : life hath a load
  Which must be carried on, and safely may :
  Yet keep those cares without thee ; let the heart
  Be God's alone, and choose the better part.[b]

6—8. (6) **half basons,** *see* v. 8. **half .. altar,**[a] a sign of God's faithfulness to His people. (7) **book .. people,** that they might clearly understand the law under which they would live. **all .. do,**[b] *see* v. 3. (8) **and .. blood,**[c] that in the basons, v. 6. **and .. people,**[d] in token of their pledged fidelity to the covenant : prob. it was sprinkled on the pillars representing the tribes. **behold,** *etc.,* and wh. you promise to accept and obey.

*The Lord's Supper a covenant.—*We will show—I. That the covenant which God made with the Israelites was essentially the same as that which He makes with us. This appears from—1. The nature of the case : 2. The language of the Scriptures. The covenant of the Israelites embraced the same spirituality, and the same Saviour—its violators are presented as monitory examples to us—it contained the same promises—it urged fidelity by the same sanctions—and differed only in the circumstances under which it was made. II. What were these circumstances under which it was made? Recount the history from their delivery from Egypt. III. Its nature. IV. Its voluntary pledge. God compels no man to covenant with Him. The act must be voluntary. V. Its extensive obligation : "all that the Lord hath said will we do." VI. The bloody seal. A seal on the part of—1. God : a seal of forgiveness—grace—redemption—and heaven ; 2. The sinner : a seal of trust in Christ's righteousness—reliance on His grace—obedience to His laws—and of entire surrender of all to Him.[e]

*Willing obedience.—*A musician is not recommended for playing long, but for playing well; it is obeying God willingly is accepted; the Lord hates that which is forced, it is rather paying a tax than an offering. Cain served God grudgingly; he brought his sacrifice, not his heart. To obey God's commandments unwillingly is like the devils who came out of the man possessed, at Christ's command, but with reluctancy, and against their will. Good duties must not be pressed nor beaten out of us, as the waters came out of the rock when Moses smote it with his rod; but must freely drop from us, as myrrh from the tree, or honey from the comb. If a willing mind be wanting, there wants that flower which should perform our obedience, and make it a sweet-smelling savour to God.*f*

9–11. (9) **went,** *etc.*, *see* v. 1. (10) **saw .. Israel,**[a] the glorious Shekinah more distinct and glorious than ever. **and .. feet,** *etc.*,[b] "the pure blue of the heaven above them lent its influence to help the inner sense to realise the vision wh. no mortal eye could behold."[c] (11) **nobles,** chiefs, grandees. **He .. hand,** to smite them. **also .. God,** fr. afar off on the plain. **and .. drink,** securely, joyously, in Jehovah's presence.

A sight of God a feast to the soul (v. 11).—Notice—I. Their vision. The circumstances of this vision are particular, and deserve attentive consideration—1. The persons to whom it was vouchsafed; 2. The time at which they were thus favoured; 3. The manner in which God revealed Himself. Note, that such a vision is now vouchsafed to us under the Gospel. II. Their feast. They feasted on their sacrifice in the Divine presence. This was like their vision, of a typical nature.[d] *On the mountain.*—Note that—I. God encourages social communion. Moses and the seventy saw God's glory. II. God especially honours individual communion. Moses dwelt in the all-consuming glory. III. Exalted spiritual state is compatible with natural and temporal relations and duties. The seventy looked upon the glory, and ate and drank. IV. Communion with God ennobles. Before they ascended they were "elders;" after, "nobles."[d]

The elders.—Among this people the elders exercised great authority, and were held in high respect (Josh. xxiii. 2; xxiv. 1; Job xii. 12), as their experience made them the natural counsellors and judges of the nation. At a later period the word became a regular title, conferred on those who by their wealth or wisdom had placed themselves at the head of a tribe, or taken a lead in public affairs. They are found among the Hebrews in Egypt, in the desert, and at every epoch of the national history. Sometimes the elders of all Israel are mentioned (Josh. vii. 6; 1 Sam. iv. 3; 2 Sam. iii. 17; 2 Chron. x. 6); sometimes those of a tribe or of the cities (Deut. xix. 12; xxi. 20; Judges viii. 14; 1 Sam. xi. 3; 1 Kings xxi. 8). In certain expiatory rites they represented the city or the whole nation (Deut. xxi. 2; Lev. iv. 15; ix. 1). They were the municipal authorities, and frequently formed a court for trying crimes (Deut. xxi. 19; xxii. 15; xxv. 7). They also assisted the chief with their counsels, with whom we often find them in direct union; whom also they sometimes compelled to yield to their will. Moses at the time of a dangerous revolt, availed himself of their services by selecting a body of seventy to aid in supporting his authority (Numb. xi. 16). Joshua, after a defeat, fell down before the ark with the elders of Israel (Josh. vii. 6). They required Samuel to resign his office

B.C. 1491.

social relations, the laws of society, and the laws of nature and of nature's God, should commence at the cradle and end only at the tomb."—*H. Ballou.*

f T. Watson.

the glorious vision of the Holy One

a Ex. xxxiii. 20, 23; Jo. i. 18; 1 Jo. iv. 12; 1 Ti. vi. 16; Ex. iii. 6; 1 Ki. xxii. 19; Is. vi. 1, 5.

b Ezek. i. 26, x. 1.; Re. iv. 3; Ma. xvii. 2.

c Spk. Comm.

d C. Simeon, M.A.

"I ask no truer image of my heavenly Father than I find reflected in my own heart—all loving, all forgiving."—*H. Ballou.*

e Dr. Fowler.

"I know by myself how incomprehensible God is, seeing I cannot comprehend the parts of my own being."—*Bernard.*

"It is one of my favourite thoughts, that God manifests Himself to men in all the wise, good, humble, generous, great, and magnanimous men."—*Lavater.*

B.C. 1491.

f Pierotti.

Moses enters the cloud and remains on the mount forty days

a Ex. xxxi. 18; De. v. 22.
b Ex. xviii. 25, 26.
c Ex. xix. 9, 16.
d Ma. xvii. 5; Ex. iii. 2.
e Ex. xix. 18; He. xii. 18, 29.
f Ex. xxxiv. 28; De. ix. 9; 1 Ki. xix. 8; Ma. iv. 2.

g J. Houtson.

"There is no God but God, the living, the self-subsisting."— *Koran*.

h Paxton Hood.

Moses commanded to exhort the people to contribute to the tabernacle

a 1 Ch. xxix. 9, 14; Pr. xi. 25; Ro. xii. 8; 2 Co. viii. 12, ix. 7.
b "The public service of Jehovah was to be instituted by free-will offerings, and not by an enforced taxation."-*Spk.Comm.*
c Ex. fr. shellfish called *murex*.
d Ex. fr. shellfish called *purpura*.
e Lit. worm of the red, *i.e.* the *coccus ilicis* of Linnæus, found on the *ilex aquifolia*.
f "The hair of

and appoint a king (1 Sam. viii. 4), and at a later period conferred the royal power on David (2 Sam. v. 3); and many other examples of a similar kind might be cited, if it were necessary, to show what was the nature of the position which they occupied.*f*

12—18. (12) **tables.. written,**^{*a*} prob. the ten commandments. **that.. them,** to all Israel. (13) **minister, servant,** attendant. (14) **tarry.. you,** a hint that his absence *might* be protracted. **let.. them,**^{*b*} as representing me for the time being. (15) **went.. mount,**^{*c*} alone. Joshua left. see v. 2. **and.. mount,** into wh. at the end of six days Moses entered. (16) **seventh.. cloud,**^{*d*} the voice of God specially addresses man on the Sabbath day. (17) **sight,** appearance. **devouring,**^{*e*} intensely brilliant. **Moses.. nights,**^{*f*} during wh. time he fasted.

Forty days and nights (v. 18).—These were "forty days and forty nights" of—I. Communion with God. 1. Enjoyment of His presence; 2. Benefit derived from His influence. II. Total seclusion from the world. From—1. Its sins; 2. Its sorrows; 3. Its sufferings. III. Miraculous support. We learn elsewhere (De. ix. 9.) that Moses fasted during this period. IV. Foretaste of future blessedness. Moses, on Horeb, was at the gates of heaven.^{*g*}

The custom of the place.—" Is it possible that any man can fast forty days?" the Rabbi Meir was asked; and he replied, "When thou takest up thy abode in any particular city, thou must live according to its customs. Moses ascended to heaven, where they neither eat nor drink; therefore he became assimilated to them. We are accustomed to eat and drink, and when angels descend to us they eat and drink also." " Truly," says Mr. Grosart, " it was a heavenly, not an earthly life, in the case equally of Moses, Elijah, and the Lord."^{*h*}

CHAPTER THE TWENTY-FIFTH.

1—9. (1) **and.. Moses,** while he was in the Mt. (2) **offering,** a lifting, an elevation: things offered to God are *lifted. up* from lower to higher uses. **willingly,**^{*a*} a willing giver makes a willing receiver. **heart.. offering,**^{*b*} and from no others. (3) **brass,** copper, or perh. bronze. (4) **blue.. scarlet,** *i.e.* violet-purple,^{*c*} red-purple,^{*d*} crimson.^{*e*} **fine linen,** Heb. *shesh, i.e.* fabric made fr. plant of that name. **goat's hair,**^{*f*} finer than wool of sheep. (5) **rams'.. red,** red morocco, **badgers',** Heb. *tchashin*. The Heb. *tachash* not unlike the Arab. *tuchash*, name given to seals, etc., found in the Red Sea,^{*g*} or to sharks and dog-fish:^{*h*} it certainly was not the badger. **shittim,**^{*i*} the *acacia seyal*. (6) **oil,** olive.^{*k*} **spices,** incenses, perfumes. (7) **onyx,** *see* Ge. ii. 12. **ephod,** *etc., see* Ex. xxviii. 4, ff. (8) **sanctuary,**^{*l*} holy place. (9) **pattern,** model, likeness. **tabernacle,** building. **even.. it,**^{*m*} acc. to the Divine plan, not acc. to human ingenuity.

The command to build the tabernacle.—Consider the direction of the text as—I. Given to the Jews. Notice—1. The general direction; 2. The particular limitation of it. II. Applicable to us. The tabernacle typified, not only the Lord Jesus, but us also:

"the Church of God is His house." To us, therefore, this direction may fitly be addressed."

Rams' skins dyed red.—Salim led me through an entire street of shoe-shops this morning. Is the red leather which the shoemakers use the rams' skins dyed red, which formed one of the three covers of the tabernacle? No doubt, and there is a definiteness in the name rams' skins which is worth noticing. From time out of mind, the southern part of Syria and Palestine has been supplied with mutton from the great plains and deserts on the north, east, and south; and the shepherds do not ordinarily bring the females to market. The vast flocks which annually come from Armenia and Northern Syria are nearly all males. The leather, therefore, is literally rams' skins dyed red. It is pleasant to meet such perfect accuracy in the most incidental allusions and minute details of the Mosaic record.*o*

10—16. (10) **ark**, box, coffer. **shittim**, the acacia is hard, close-grained, "wood that will not rot."*a* **two**, *etc.*,*b* size of ark: length 4 ft. 4½ in., breadth and height 2 ft. 7¼ in.*c* (11) **overlay . . gold**, prob. thin plates, though the art of gilding was then known. **crown**, moulding. (12) **corners**, bases, or feet: the ark when carried would therefore be elevated above the heads of the bearers. (13) **staves**, for bearing-rods. (14) **ark . . them**, on the shoulders of the bearers. (15) **they . . it**,*d* perh. to prevent the ark fr. being touched. (16) **testimony**,*e* stone tables of ten commandments.

The ark, a type of Christ.—I. The ark was an assurance of God's presence among His people: Christ, the assurance of God's presence among us. II. Where it was, there it was lawful to sacrifice, and nowhere else: our acceptance by God is through Christ. III. In it was the pot of manna: in Christ is the nourishment for our souls. IV. It had a crown of gold about it: here is signified Christ's regal power. V. It kept in it the two tables of the law: Christ keeps the law perfectly for us. VI. When it was set in Dagon's temple, the idol fell down before it: so when Christ enters the temple of idolatry, sin will fall before Him. VII. Where it was, there was God's glory: where Christ, there is God's glory also.*f*

Shittim-wood.—Concerning the shitta-tree, mentioned by the prophet Isaiah with the cedar and the myrtle, different opinions are entertained by commentators. The name is derived from the Hebrew verb *shata*, to decline or turn to and fro, having for the plural *shittim*. It is remarkable for being the wood of which the sacred vessels of the tabernacle were made. The Seventy interpreters generally render it by the term ἀσηπια, incorruptible. Theodotion, and after him the Vulgate, translate it by Spina. a thorn. The shittim-wood, says Jerome, resembles the white thorn in its colour and leaves, but not in its size; for the tree is so large, that it affords very long planks. Hasselquist also says it grows in Upper Egypt, to the size of a large tree. The wood is hard, tough, smooth, without knots, and extremely beautiful. This kind of wood grows only in the deserts of Arabia; but in no other part of the Roman empire. In another place he remarks, it is of an admirable beauty, solidity, strength, and smoothness. It is thought he means the black acacia, the only tree found in the deserts of Arabia. This plant is so hard and solid, as to become almost incorruptible. Its wood has the colour of the

VOL. I. L

B.C. 1491.

the eastern goats, particularly of the Angola species, is of the most delicate and silky softness; and wrought into the kind of cloth known by the name of *camlets.*"
—*Bush.*
g Tristram.
h Fürst.
i Is. xli. 19.
k Ex. xxvii. 26.
l He. iii. 5, 6.
m 1 Ch. xxviii. 19.
n C. Simeon, M.A.
o Dr. Thomson.

the ark of the covenant
a LXX.
b Ex. xxxvii. 1, 2.
c So *Alford*, who takes the measure of the sacred cubit—21-in., while the *Spk. Comm.* prefers the ordinary cubit of 18-in.
d 1 Ki. viii. 8.
e De. x. 1, 2, 5, xxxi. 36; 1 Ki. viii. 9; 2 Ch. v. 10.
f B. Keach.

"The works of a person that builds begin immediately to decay, while those of him who plants begins directly to improve. In this, planting promises a more lasting pleasure than building, which, were it to remain in equal perfection, would at best begin to moulder and want repairs in imagination. Now, trees have a circumstance that suits our taste, and that is annual variety."
—*Shenstone.*

"If it be the characteristic of a worldly man that he desecrates what is holy, it should

B.C. 1491

be of the Christian to consecrate what is secular, and to recognise a present and presiding divinity in all things." — *Chalmers.*

g *Purton.*

r. 10. *D. S. Deyling. Obs.* i. 76; *Dr. J. Spencer, De legibus Heb.* ii.

the mercy-seat

a He. ix. 5; 1 Pe. i. 12.
b Le. xvi. 22; Ex. xxix. 42, 43.
c Ps. lxxx. 1; 2 Ki. xix. 15; He. iv. 16.
d *Anon.*

"We may imitate the Deity in all His attributes, but mercy is the only one in which we can pretend to equal Him. We cannot, indeed, give like God, but surely we may forgive like Him." — *Sterne.*

"Between the humble and contrite heart and the majesty of heaven there are no barriers. The only password is prayer." — *H. Ballou.*

"When we pray for any virtue, we should cultivate the virtue as well as pray for it. The form of your prayers should be the rule of your life; every petition to God is a precept to man. Look not, therefore, upon your prayers as a short method of duty and salvation only, but as a perpetual monition of duty —

lotus tree; and so large, that it furnishes plank twelve cubits long. It is very thorny, and even its bark is covered with very sharp thorns; and hence it perhaps had the Hebrew name *shitta*, from making animals decline or turn aside by the sharpness of its spines. The interpretation now given, seems to be confirmed by the following remark of Dr. Shaw: "The acacia being by much the largest and the most common tree of these deserts, we have some reason to conjecture, that the shittim-wood, of which the several utensils of the tabernacle were made, was the wood of the acacia. This tree abounds with flowers of a globular figure, and of an excellent smell; which is another proof of its being the shitta tree of the Scriptures, which, in the prophecies of Isaiah, is joined with the myrtle and other sweet-smelling plants.*g*

17—22. (17) **mercy-seat,** Heb. *kapporeth,* covering. (18) **cherubims,** Heb. *kerubim,* prob. resembling human figures with wings. **beaten .. them,** of solid gold: formed by repeated blows of hammer. (19) **and make,** *etc.,* not large, but in size proportioned to size of ark. (20) **stretch .. high,** emblematical of readiness to obey the Divine will. **covering,**a overshadowing. **faces .. another,** emblem of union, sympathy, fellowship. **toward,** *etc.,* emblem of devout inquiry: consideration. (21) **ark .. thee,** *see* v. 16. (22) **there .. thee,**b to communicate My will: impart My blessing. **from .. cherubims,**c in a bright cloud: the shekinah.

The mercy-seat.—I. The design of this appointment. It was intended to—1. Furnish a meeting-place for God and man; 2. Encourage communion with God; 3. Impart instruction. II. Its peculiarities. 1. It was all of Divine appointment; 2. Its true name is the Propitiatory; 3. Its position is very significant. III. The superior privileges it typified. 1. Free access to God through Christ; 2. The assurance of pardoned sin; 3. Supplies of grace and strength for all we need; 4. Relief from all our trials.d

Arks.—Sacred chests, bearing much the resemblance in principle to this ark, have been found in different ancient and modern nations; and expositors have entered into many wearying disquisitions whether this ark, or the ark of Noah, or else some primitive model (the existence of wh. is inferred fr. xxxiii. 7, 10), sugg. the first idea; while Spencer and others think, as they do in the case of the tabernacle, that the Hebrew ark was itself copied fr. the heathen. We incline to suppose that the others were either copies of the Mosaic ark, or else that the idea was sufficiently simple and natural to occur among people who had no inter-communication or common source of knowledge. Without discussing any of these questions, we may state a few of the more striking instances of coincidence. The Egyptians, on some occasions, carried in solemn processions a sacred chest, containing their secret things and the mysteries of their religion. The Trojans also had their sacred chest; and the *palladium* of the Greeks and Romans was something not very unlike. It is further remarkable, that as the Hebrew tabernacle and temple had a Holy of Holies, in wh. the ark was deposited, so had the heathen, in the inmost part of their temples, an *adytum* or *penetrale,* which none but the priests might enter. Something very similar may also be traced among barbarous and savage nations. Thus, Tacitus, speaking of the nations of Northern Germany, of whom our own Saxon ancestors were a branch, says that they gen. worshipped Herthum, or the Mother Earth (*Terram matrem*); believing her to interpose in the affairs of men, and to visit nations; and that to her, within a grove in a certain island, was consecrated a vehicle covered with a vestment, and which none but the priests were allowed to touch.*e*

23—30. (23) **table**, of wh. a carved representation on the arch of Titus. **two**, *etc.*, hence it was 3 ft. 6 in. long, 1 ft. 9 in. broad, 2 ft. 7½ in. high. (24) **overlay**, gild or plate. **crown**, ornamental moulding. (25) **border**, frame, prob. to connect and strengthen the legs. (26) **corners**, extremities. (27) **over border**, *i.e.* on the ends of the legs where the frame was united to them. (28) **table .. them**, raised above the shoulders of the bearers. (29) **dishes**, bowls. **spoons**, or cups. **bowls**,*a* chalices. (30) **shewbread**,*b* *lit.* bread of faces, or bread of presence, so called prob. fr. being always set bef. the face and presence of God.

The table of shewbread (v. 30).—Introduction :—This table of shewbread may remind us of the bread on *our* tables. There is a sense in which a table with bread (food) upon it, is a table of shewbread. Shewbread means bread of faces; *i.e.* it is before the face of the Lord. Our bread being before Him, He takes note of—I. The way by wh. it was obtained. Whether by—1. Oppression, fraud, or any species of dishonesty: 2. Honest toil: 3. A parent's loving care. II. The spirit in wh. it is partaken of. Whether of—1. Murmuring about quantity or quality; 2. Thankfulness to the Giver of our daily bread: Jesus gave thanks: 3. Pious remembrance of Him who is the Bread of Life. III. The manner in which it is distributed. 1. Do we distribute of our abundance ungrudgingly? God saw the number and size of the crumbs that fell from the rich man's table; 2. Do we heedlessly waste it? "Wilful waste," etc.; 3. Do we greedily clamour for more? Learn:—Jesus is the Bread of Life. Our relation to Him is before the Lord. God notices our treatment of Jesus.

The table of shewbread.—In the first apartment of the tabernacle also, on the N. side, was a table, made of acacia-wood, two cubits long, one broad, and one-and-a-half high, and covered over with laminæ of gold. The top of the leaf of this table was encircled with a border or rim of gold. The frame of the table, immediately below the leaf, was encircled with a piece of wood of about four inches in breadth, around the edge of wh. there was a rim, or border, the same as around the leaf. A little lower down, but at equal distances from the top of the table, there were four rings of gold fastened to the legs of it, through wh. staves, covered with gold, were placed for the purpose of carrying it. The rings here mentioned were not found in the table of shewbread wh. was afterwards made for the temple, nor indeed in any of the sacred furniture where they had previously been, except in the ark of the covenant. Twelve unleavened loaves were placed upon this table, which were sprinkled over with frankincense, and, it is stated in the Alexandrine version (Le. xxiv. 7), with salt likewise. They were placed in two piles, one above another, were changed every Sabbath-day by the priests, and were called *the bread of the face*, because it was exhibited before the face or throne of Jehovah, *the bread arranged in order*, and *the perpetual bread*.*e*

B.C. 1491.

"by what we require of God we see what He requires of us."— *J. Taylor.*
e Kitto.

the table of shewbread

a Nu. iv. 7.

b Le. xxiv. 5, 6; Ps. xxiii. 5; 1 Co. x. 31.

"I thank my heavenly Father for every manifestation of human love; I thank Him for all experiences, be they sweet or bitter, which help me to forgive all things, and to enfold the whole world with a blessing."— *Mrs. L. M. Child.*

"Cicero calls gratitude the mother of virtues, reckons it the most capital of all duties; and uses the words 'grateful' and 'good' as synonymous terms inseparably united in the same character." —*John Bate.*

"As flowers carry dewdrops, trembling on the edges of the petals, and ready to fall at the first waft of wind or brush of bird, so the heart should carry its headed words of thanksgiving, and* at the first breath of heavenly flavour let down the shower, perfumed with the heart's gratitude."—*Beecher.*

c. 30. *D. S. Deyling.* Obs. ii. 157.

c Jahn.

B.C. 1491.

the golden candlestick

a 1 Ki. v. 49; He. ix. 2; Ro. i. 12. iv. 5; Pr. vi. 23; 2 Pe. i. 19.

b Heb. *shakēd*, fr. *shakad*, to make haste, hence, to be vigilant, to watch.

"Children always turn toward the light. O that grown-up people in this world may become like little children."—*Hare*.

"And as the eye is the best composer, so light is the first of painters. There is no object so foul that intense light will not make beautiful. And the stimulus it affords to the sense, and a sort of infinitude which it hath like space and time, make all matter gay."—*Emerson*.

c B. Keach.

"The light in the world comes principally from two sources—the sun and the student's lamp."—*Bovee*.

vv. 31, 32. J. Henley, M.A. A Ser. (1730).

d Bibl. Treas.

the seven lamps, tongs, etc.

a Nu. viii. 4; Ac. vii. 44; He. viii. 5.

"I once asked a distinguished artist what place he gave to labour in art. 'Labour,' he, in effect, said, 'is the beginning, the middle, and

---

31—36. (31) **candlestick,**[a] Heb. *menorath*, a lamp-bearer, to support oil-lamps. **shaft,** *etc.,* this candlestick also represented on the arch of Titus. **branches, arms. bowls,** calyx or cup. **knops,** prob. the branches were prob. ornamented with these. **flowers,** floral-work. (32) **three,** *etc.,* it was symmetrically formed, prob. about 3 ft. high and 2 ft. wide. (33) **almonds,**[b] like the almond-flower. (34) **candlestick,** here prob. the stem or shaft is meant. (35) **according .. candlestick,** *i.e.* each pair of branches was divided fr. the next pair by a small spherical ornament. (36) **all .. gold,** gold pure, solid, hammered.

The candlestick a type of Christ.—I. It was the only thing that held the light wh. enlightened the sanctuary: from Christ all the light of grace comes for the benefit of His Church. II. It had seven lamps (v. 37), to signify that perfection of light that is in Christ. III. It was placed in the sanctuary: so is Christ as a glorious light placed in His Church. IV. It had an upright stem, which bore the many branches issuing from it. V. The branches were adorned with bowls, knobs, flowers, etc. So are Christ's ministers adorned with many graces. VI. Aaron dressed those lamps and renewed their oil daily: so our High Priest is the only enlightener of His faithful ministers. VII. The candlestick had snuffers and snuff-dishes of pure gold; wh. might figure forth the good and godly discipline of the Church whereby evil persons who hinder its glory, are taken away.[c]

The golden candlestick.—The golden candlestick was placed in the first apartment of the tabernacle, on the south side. It stood on a base, from which the principal stem arose perpendicularly. On both sides of it there projected upwards, in such a way as to describe a curved line, three branches. They arose from the main stem, at equal distances from each other, and to the same height with it. The height in the whole, according to the Jewish rabbins, was five feet; and the breadth, or the distance between the exterior branches, three and a half. The main stem, together with the branches, was adorned with knops, flowers, and other ornaments of gold. The seven extremities of the main stem and branches were employed as so many separate lamps, all of which were kept burning in the night, but three only in the day (Ex. xxx. 8; Le. xxiv. 4). The priest, in the morning, put the lamps in order with his golden snuffers, and carried away the filth that might have gathered upon them, in golden vessels made for that purpose. The weight of the whole candlestick was a talent, or one hundred and twenty-five pounds.[d]

37—40. (37) **seven,** *i.e.* one for each branch and one for the stem. **that .. it,** *i.e.* in front of it, throwing the light forward. (38) **tongs,** or snuffers, for trimming the wick. **snuff-dishes,** to receive the burnt wick. (39) **talent,** weight and value, variously estimated: perh. 94 pounds in weight, and from £4,000 to £6,000 in value. (40) **look,**[e] *etc.,* no human additions or alterations permitted.

Something about everything in the Bible.—A number of local wits were once passing a merry hour in the house of a mutual friend, when the conversation turning on the Bible, one remarked that he could see nothing in it. A minister, who happened to be present, said, there was so much in the book that he doubted if they could name anything which was not either named, alluded to, or suggested by some adapted text. And he added that as he would not take advantage of his professional relation to the book, they might test this by questioning a poor man who was a servant in the family of their host, and whose knowledge of Scripture was very considerable. Presently the footman entered the room, and one of the company said abruptly to him, pointing, at the same time, to the snuffers on the table. "John, is there anything in the Bible about snuffers?" "Yes," replied John; "it is written in the book of Exodus, 'The tongs thereof, and the snuff-dishes thereof, shall be of pure gold,' and a little farther on it is said, 'He made his seven lamps, and his snuffers, and his snuff-dishes, of pure gold.'" The minister, who afterwards told the story, said that the scorner was completely snuffed out.

B.C. 1491.

the end of art. Turning then to another — 'And you,' I inquired; 'what do you consider as the great force in art?' 'Love,' he replied. In their two answers I found but one truth."—*Bovee.*

CHAPTER THE TWENTY-SIXTH.

1–6. (1) **tabernacle,** the habitation proper, as distinguished from tabernacle of v. 7. **curtains,**[a] or breadths. of wh. five formed a curtain; hence there were two curtains joined by taches. **fine .. linen,** woven with extreme fineness and strength. **with .. them,** *i.e.* they were skilfully embroidered with cherubim. (2) **length,** 49 ft. **breadth,** 7 ft., but as five breadths made a curtain, the total width would be 35 ft. (3) **five .. coupled,** *i.e.* five breadths formed one curtain. (4) **loops,** or tapes, to fasten the breadths together. (5) **fifty,** *i.e.* a foot apart. (6) **taches,** prob. an oblong button, or frog,[b] fastened to the loop on one curtain, was passed through the loop on the other.

The tabernacle of God.—God manifested His presence among them thus, in a tabernacle—I. In compliance with their state while in the wilderness. He suits the tokens of His favour to His people's wants and necessities. II. To represent the state of His Church in this world: it is a tabernacle state. "no abiding city" below. We shall never be fixed till we come to heaven.[c]

The plan of the tabernacle.—The portable temple of the Israelites had, indeed, in its whole arrangement, a resemblance with the temples of other nations of antiquity. As they had spacious forecourts, so had the tabernacle an oblong quadrangular forecourt, two hundred feet long, and one hundred broad, which was formed by the hangings or curtains which hung on pillars. The tabernacle itself was divided into two parts, the holy and the most holy; in the latter was the ark of the covenant, with the symbols of the Divine qualities, the cherubims; and no human being dared to enter this especially sanctified place, except the high priest, once a year (on the feast of reconciliation). Thus, also, in many Grecian temples, the back part was not to be entered by anybody. (Lackemacher's *Antiq. Græcor. Sacr.*) This part, where, in the heathen temples, the statue of the deity was placed, was generally towards the west, and the entrance towards the east. (Spencer *De Leg. Hebræor. Ritual.*) In the same manner the entrance of the tabernacle was towards the east, and, consequently, the most holy place to the west. In the most holy, a solemn darkness reigned, as in most of the ancient temples. A richly-worked curtain divided the most holy from the holy, and thus, in the Egyptian temples,

the tabernacle

the inner curtain

a Ex. xxxvi. 8.

b Frog, an ornamental cloak-button swelled in the middle.

Tache, a catch, a loop, a button; Fr. *attacher*; Ital. *attaccare.*

c *M. Henry.*

"Since I have known God in a saving manner, painting, poetry, and music have had charms unknown to me before. I have received what I suppose is a taste for them, or religion has refined my mind and made it susceptible of impressions from the sublime and beautiful. O, how religion secures the heightened enjoyment of those pleasures which keep so many from God by their becoming a source of pride." — *H. Martyn.*

"The learned understand the reason of the art, the unlearned feel the pleasure."-*Quintilian.*

B.C. 1491. *d Rosenmuller.*	the back part, where the sacred animal, to which the temple was dedicated, was kept, was divided from the front part by a curtain embroidered with gold.*d*
the outer curtain *a* Ex. xxxvi. 14. *b* Tab. in v. 1 refs. to the interior; here the wd. tab. refs. more to the exterior. See *Kalisch*.	**7—14.** (7) **make .. hair,***a* a kind of camlet. **tabernacle,***b* tent. **curtains**, breadths. (8) **length .. cubits**, 52 ft. 6 in. **breadth .. cubits**, 7 ft. **and .. curtains,** *i.e.* breadths. (9) **double .. curtain,** *i.e.* equally divided, leaving one half to overlap the curtain of five breadths in front and the other half to overlap the same curtain at the back, *see* v. 12. (10) **fifty .. edge,** rather more than a foot apart. (11) **fifty .. brass,** *etc.*, *see* v. 6. (12) **remnant,** *i.e.* the half breadth (or curtain), *see* v. 9. (13) **and a cubit,** *etc.*, the tabernacle cloth, *see* vv. 1, 2, was 40 cubits by 28; this tent-cloth was 44 cubits by 30; hence, whence spread over the former, it reached at the back and front two cubits (the half-breadth of vv. 9, 12) lower than the other. **hang .. side,** here on each side it fell one cubit farther than the other. (14) **rams' skins,** *see* xxv. 5.
"The refining influence is the study of art, which is the science of beauty; and I find that every man values every scrap of knowledge in art, every observation of his own in it, every hint he has caught from another. For the laws of beauty are the beauty of beauty, and give the mind the same or a higher joy than the sight of it gives the senses. The study of art is of high value to the growth of the intellect."—*Emerson.* *c Topics* ii. 49.	*The art of weaving.*—Anc. art lost in antiquity. [Acc. to Gk. tradition, the idea gathered fr. web of spider. Minerva changed Arachne into spider, because surpassed her in weaving and spinning (hence the spider class called Arachnida).] W. more anc. than spinning; at first matting, simple interlacings of shreds of bark, lacustrine plants, vegetable stalks (straw, rushes). At length fibres were used (flax, hemp, cotton, silk); presently wool (first mentioned by Homer), and hair. Wool, dyed, brought in costly vase; spindles or distaffs of precious material; spinning, etc., by ladies of quality. Hence the present of Queen of Egypt to consort of Menelaus, on their return from Troy:— "Alcandria, consort of his high command, A golden distaff gave to Helen's hand: And that rich vase, with living sculpture wrought, Which, heap'd with wool, the beauteous Phyle brought; The silken fleece, empurpled for the loom, Rivall'd the hyacinth in vernal bloom." (*Odyssey*, iv.) Formerly all women in a fam. spun, esp. the unmarried daus. of a house. Hence spinster, a woman who spins = an unmarried female. Anc. same in principle and similar in form to modern hand-loom.*c*
the boards, etc. *a* Mr. Tristram states that there are acacia trees near England which would furnish boards four feet wide. *b* "In the sides of the boards shall be made two mortises, whereby one board may be joined to another board."—*Vulgate.* "Art neither belongs to religion nor to ethics;"	**15—18.** (15) **boards,** planks. (16) **cubits .. board,** hence the side of the tab. was 17 ft. 6 in. high. **cubit .. breadth,** perh. the boards were joined.*a* (17) **tenons,** Heb., *yadoth.* hands. These prob. projected fr. the side of each board, and fitted into cavities in the next board.*b* (18) **twenty .. southward,** the length of the tabernacle would therefore be 52 ft. 6 in. *The shittim tree (Acacia Seyal).*—A notorious sceptic has put forth the objections that there could be no timber found in Sinai in sufficient quantity, and that the acacia does not grow to sufficient size to supply such planks. To the second objection I can only refer to numerous trees which I have measured in the neighbourhood of the Dead Sea, and in wadys in the south country of Judah. To the first, that there is every evidence of the former abundance of the tree. The use of timber for smelting in Sinai has been already referred to. Rambling on foot among the mountains of Sinai, the Rev. F. W. Holland has found many old mines the workings of which may yet be seen, of

which history gives no hint. Great heaps of slag and scoria abound everywhere, marking the ancient smelting-works. Perhaps the Hebrew bondmen toiled at them before the Exodus. There must have been timber then, for fuel could never be brought there from a distance. The seyal, the tree which now sparsely occurs, grew in forests to provide for such consumption, and when the supply of shittim-wood was exhausted, the mines were abandoned. All wore another aspect when timber covered the sides of the hills. Streams washed the dry ravines, which still bear the marks of their former presence; rain would be attracted by the foliage, and herbage would carpet the soil. Nor would this perish at once with the denudation of the wood. Its extinction would be the work of time, as the streams gradually failed, and the sun converted the turf to dust. At the time of the Exodus, then, we have every reason to believe that the state of the Peninsula of Sinai was very different from what it is now. Doubtless those granite peaks made it still "a great and terrible wilderness," but its valleys and plains might afford no inconsiderable sustenance for cattle.*c*

19—25. (19) **sockets**, bases: a metal base would serve the purpose of preventing decay. (20) **north .. twenty,** *see* v. 18. (21) **forty,** *etc., see* v. 19. (22) **six boards,** hence the width of the tabernacle was 15 ft. 9 in. (23) **two .. corners,** prob. more like pillars than planks. (24) **they .. corners,**a and their thickness would thus increase the length of the end to about ten cubits. (25) **they .. boards,** *i.e.* the six (v. 22), and the two corners (v. 23).

Silver as referred to in the Bible.—Described as white and shining (Ps. lxviii. 13, 14); fusible (Ez. xxii. 20, 22); malleable (Je. x. 9). Manufacture: Found in earth (Job xxviii. 1); in impure state (Pr. xxv. 4); purified by fire (Pr. xvii. 3; Zec. xiii. 9); when purified, called refined (1 Ch. xxix. 4); choice (Pr. viii. 19); working in, a trade (Ac. xix. 24). Uses: Money from earliest times (Ge. xxiii. 15, 16, xxxvii. 28; 1 K. xvi. 24); presents (1 K. x. 25; 2 K. v. 5, 23); made into cups (Ge. xliv. 2); dishes and bowls (Nu. vii. 13, 84, 85); plates (Je. x. 9); chains (Is. xl. 19); wires (inferred from Ecc. xii. 6); sockets for tabernacle (Ex. xxvi. 19, 25, 32, xxvi. 24, 26, 30, 36); ornaments and hooks, for same (Ex. xxvii. 17, xxxviii. 19); candlesticks (1 Ch. xxviii. 15); tables (1 Ch. xxviii. 16); couches (Est. i. 6); vessels (2 Sam. viii. 10; Ezr. vi. 5); idols (Ps. cxv. 4; Is. ii. 20, xxx. 22); personal ornaments (Ex. iii. 22). Historical: Patriarchs, rich in (Gen. xiii. 2, xxiv. 35); commerce of Tarshish in (Jer. x. 9; Ez. xxvii. 12); abundant in the reign of Solomon (1 K. x. 21, 22, 27; 2 Ch. ix. 20, 21, 27); given for tabernacle (Ex. xxv. 3, xxxv. 24); for temple (1 Ch. xxviii. 14, xxix. 2, 6—9); taken in war often consecrated to God (Jos. vi. 19; 2 Sam. viii. xi.; 1 K. xv. 15); also purified by fire (Nu. xxxi. 22, 23; tribute paid in (2 Ch. xvii. 11; Ne. v. 15). Value: comparative (Is. lx. 17); wisdom worth more (Job xxviii. 15; Pr. iii. 14).*b*

26—30. (26) **bars .. boards,** one sufficiently long to reach from end to end of the tabernacle, the four others being less than half the length of the longer, the whole being put in three rows. (27, 28) **five,** *etc., see* v. 26. (29) **overlay .. gold,** the plates very thin, otherwise the bars very heavy. (30) **fashion,**a

---

b.c. 1491.

but, like these, it brings us nearer to the Infinite, one of the forms of which it manifests to us. God is the source of all beauty, as of all truth, of all religion, of all morality. The most exalted object, therefore, of art is to reveal in its own manner the sentiment of the Infinite."
— V. *Cousin.*

c *Dr. Tristram.*

the sockets and couplings

a Eph. iv. 15, 16.

"Many persons feel art, some understand it; but few both feel and understand it."—*Hillard.*

"Art is the effort of man to express the ideas which nature suggests to him of a power above nature, whether that power be within the recesses of his own being or in the Great First Cause of which nature, like himself, is but the effect."— *Lytton.*

"Art must anchor in nature, or it is the sport of every breath of folly." —*Hazlitt.*

b *Topics.*

the bars, etc.
a Ac. vii. 44; He. viii. 5; Eph. ii. 19—22.

"Moral beauty is the basis of all

B.C. 1491.

true beauty. This foundation is somewhat covered and veiled in nature. Art brings it out, and gives it more transparent forms. It is here that art, when it knows well its power and resources, engages in a struggle with nature in which it may have the advantage." — *Victor Cousin.*
b *Topics.*

the vail
a 2 Co. iii. 14, 18; He. ix. 3, 6—8, x. 1; Ma. xxv. 51; 2 Ti. i. 10; He. x. 19, 20, ix. 24, vi. 19.

"Colour is, in brief terms, the type of love. Hence it is especially connected with the blossoming of the earth; and, again, with its fruits; also, with the spring and fall of the leaf, and with the morning and evening of the day, in order to show the waiting of love about the birth and death of man." — *Ruskin.*
b *Keach.*

"The human heart yearns for the beautiful in all ranks of life. The beautiful things that God makes are His gift to all alike. I know there are many of the poor who have fine feeling and a keen sense of the beautiful, which rusts out and dies because they are too hard pressed to procure it any gratification." — *Mrs. Stowe.*
c *Mrs. Jameson.*

etc., another warning not to depart from the Divinely-given pattern.

Properties, etc., of gold.—Symb. Au., atomic weight, 99·6. Occurs crystallised, or in plates, or ramifications, or nodules (nuggets). Malleability: can be beaten into thinness of one two-hundredth of an in.; one grn. will thus cover 56 sq. inches. Ductility: one grn. will yield 500 ft. of wire. Tenacity; a wire one-eighteenth of in. thick will support 500 lb. May, by intense heat (oxyhydrogen), be dispersed in purple vapours. Fuses at 2016°. Our coinage, 11 pts. gold, one of copper, to harden it. Combined with mercury, forms amalgam, used in gilding. Value: standard gold = £3 17s. 6d. an oz. [Silver.] Symb. Ag., equiv. 108, sp. gr. 10·53. Found crystallised or in fibrous masses. Malleability: may be beaten out to one one-hundredth of an in.*b*

31, 32. (31) **vail,**a Heb. *paroketh*, a separation. **blue .. scarlet,** *see* xxv. 12. **fine .. work,** *etc.*, *see* v. 1. (32) **upon .. silver,** the sockets belong to the pillars not to the hooks.

The vail of the Holiest (v. 31).—I. It was glorious, of embroidered work: this faith guild signified the body of Christ, filled with the fulness of God, or beautified with all the most excellent graces of the Spirit. II. It was replenished and wrought full of cherubim, noting thereby that serviceable and ready attendance of the angels on Christ's natural and mystical body. III. It was borne up by costly pillars, to show that the humanity of Christ, esp. in His sufferings, should be borne up by His Deity. IV. By the vail only, there was entry into the holiest place of all: so by the vail, *i.e.* the flesh of Christ, which was rent, as it were, upon the cross, a new and living way is made for us to the Father.*b*

Colours emblematical.—We find colours used in a symbolical or mystic sense; and until the ancient principles or traditions were wholly worn out of memory, or set aside by the later painters, certain colours were appropriate to certain subjects and personages, and could not arbitrarily be applied or misapplied. In the old specimens of stained glass, we find these significations scrupulously attended to. Thus, white, represented by the diamond or silver, was the emblem of light, religious purity, innocence, virginity, faith, joy, and life. Our Saviour wears white after His resurrection. In the judge, it indicates integrity; in the sick man, humility; in the woman, chastity. Red, the ruby, signified fire, Divine love, the Holy Spirit, heat, or the creative power, and royalty. White and red roses express love and innocence, or love and wisdom. In a bad sense, red signifies blood, war, hatred, and punishment. Blue, or the sapphire, expressed heaven, the firmament, truth, constancy, fidelity. Yellow, or gold, was the symbol of the sun, of the goodness of God, initiation or marriage, faith or faithfulness. In a bad sense, yellow signifies inconstancy, jealousy, deceit. Green, the emerald, is the colour of spring, of hope (particularly hope in immortality), and of victory, as the colour of the palm or laurel. Violet, or the amethyst, signified love and truth, or passion or suffering. Black expressed the earth,—darkness, mourning, wickedness, negation, death, and was appropriate to the prince of darkness. White and black together signify purity of life, and mourning or humiliation.*c*

33—37. (33) **taches,** *i.e.* of the tabernacle cloths, *see* v. 6. **holy .. holy,** the latter containing the ark. (34) **in .. place,**[a] so called bec. the place of Divine manifestation. (35) **table .. vail,**[b] in the holy place. **over against,** opposite to. (36) **hanging,** covering. curtain. **needlework,** embroidered, the designs on the other vail being inwoven. (37) **fire .. wood,** of wh. it is supposed the centre pillar would be taller than the others, supporting a ridge-piece; the others of shorter length supporting purlines, across wh. the cloth would fall, sloping down fr. the ridge to the planks on each side. Hence the front of the tabernacle would resemble the gable end of a house.[c]

Eastern embroidery.—We passed Lahar, close to a small valley, where we found several snug encampments of the Eclauts, at one of which we stopped to examine the tent of the chief of the *obah*, or family. It was composed of a wooden frame of circular laths, which were fixed on the ground, and then covered over with large felts, that were fastened down by a cord, ornamented with tassels of various colours. A curtain, curiously worked by the women, with coarse needlework of various colours, was suspended over the door. In the king of Persia's tents, magnificent *perdhas*, or hangings of needlework, are suspended, as well as on the doors of the great mosques in Turkey; and these circumstances combined, will, perhaps, illustrate Ex. xxvi. 36.[d]

D.C. 1491.

the most holy place
a Ex. xl. 21; Le. xvi. 1; He. ix. 5.
b He. ix. 2.
c See cut in *Spk. Comm.*

"It was a very proper answer to him who asked why any man should be delighted with beauty, that it was a question that none but a blind man could ask; since any beautiful object doth so much attract the sight of all men, that it is in no man's power not to be pleased with it." *Clarendon.*
d *Morier.*

CHAPTER THE TWENTY-SEVENTH.

1—4. (1) **altar,**[a] Heb. *misbëah*, for sacrifice. **five,** *etc.*, 8 ft. 9 in. long and broad, and 5 ft. 3 in. high. (2) **horns,**[b] projections or pinnacles, perh. horn-shaped. (3) **pans,** pots. **to .. ashes,** in wh. to carry them away; shovels, hoe-shaped scrapers. **basons,** for catching the blood. **fleshhooks,** for placing the victim on the altar. **firepans,** braziers in which fire was carried from one place to another. (4) **grate .. brass,** through which the ashes would fall.

Building-timber in the wilderness.—Mr. Palmer, the Professor of Arabic at Cambridge, who has recently explored the Wilderness of the Wanderings, or the Desert of Tih, and has recovered many of the ancient sites hitherto quite unknown, as Hazeroth, Hormah, and others, discovered some very interesting ruins at Contillet Geraiyah, a spot thirty miles south of Kadesh Barnea, and eighty miles south of Beersheba. "Digging into the ruins," he says, "we found some sun-dried bricks, and beams of wood with signs of mortises. bolts, etc., which proved to be a sort of framework covering a series of large amphoræ, or water-jars, four of which we uncovered. One of these we dug out and put together; it was marked on the shoulder with a Phœnician aleph. . . . The use of wood in the building was worth notice, as the pieces we found were of *seyal* or shittim-wood, and, excepting one on Wady Fahdi, there is not a single tree of the kind in the Tih at the present day. Indeed, the only tree we saw after leaving Sinai, besides the one just mentioned, was the *nebuk* or *sidr* (thorn-tree) beside the fort at Nakhl." We have thus a proof that in Hebrew times, far beyond the limits of South Judæa, the shittim was the ordinary timber of the country.[c]

the altar of burnt offering
a Ex. xxxviii. 1; Ezek. xliii. 14; Ho. xiii. 10.

b Ps. cxviii. 27; Le. iv. 7, xvi. 18; 1 Kl. i. 15; Ho. vi. 18.

"Order is a lovely nymph, the child of beauty and wisdom. Her attondants are comfort, neatness, and activity; her abode is the valley of happiness. She is always to be found when sought for, and never appears so lovely as when contrasted with her opponent, disorder."—*Johnson.*

c Dr. *Tristram.*

EXODUS. [Cap. xxvii. 5–15.

Margin notes (left column)

b.c. 1491.
the staves, etc.

a Trapp.

"Whatever may be the means, or whatever the more immediate end of any kind of art, all of it that is good agrees in this, that it is the expression of one soul talking to another, and is precious according to the greatness of the soul that utters it."—*Ruskin.*

b Dr. Kitto.

the court of the tabernacle

curtains for the length
a Ex. xxxviii. 9.
b Haydn.
"There is scarcely a single joy or sorrow, within the experience of our fellow-creatures, which we have not tasted; yet the belief in the good and beautiful has never forsaken us. It has been medicine to us in sickness, richness in poverty, and the best part of all that ever delighted us in health and success."—*Leigh Hunt.*

curtains for the breadth
"Order is the sanity of the mind, the health of the body, the peace of the city, the security of the state. As the beams to a house, as the bones to the microcosm of man, so is order to all things."—*Southey.*

Main text

5—8. (5) **compass .. beneath,** a ridge projecting round the interior of the altar. **net,** *see* v. 4. **even .. altar,** half-way betw. the top and the bottom. (6, 7) **staves,** "as ever ready to remove. Here we have no assured settlement."*a* (8) **hollow,** *etc.*, prob. plated with bronze, to resist action of fire. **as .. mount,** the pattern of each part as of the whole tabernacle minutely given.

The altar of burnt-offering.—This altar was a sort of square chest of shittim-wood overlaid with brass. It was five cubits long by five broad, and three in height (about three yards square and five feet high), and had a horn or projection at each corner. It was hollow within, and in the middle of its surface was a sunk grating of brass to support the fire, which was furnished with four rings, that it might be taken out and carried separately from the body of the altar. The ashes from the fire sunk through the grating, and were received in a pan that was placed under it. The altar had four rings or staples at the sides, into wh. poles of shittim-wood covered with brass were inserted when the altar was to be moved from place to place. This is the account which seems to agree best with the text, although some of the details have been differently understood by various expositors.*b*

9—11. (9) **court,***a* enclosed space within wh. the tabernacle stood. **hundred .. side,** *i.e.* 175 ft. (10) **sockets,** bases. **fillets,** connecting-rods. (11) **likewise,** *etc., see* vv. 9, 10.

Linen.—A fabric of very remote antiquity. Pharaoh arrayed Joseph in vestures of fine linen. It was first manufactured in England by Flemish weavers, under the protection of Henry III., 1253. Bef. this period woollen shirts were gen. worn. A company of linen-weavers established itself in London in 1368; and the art of staining linen became known in 1579. A colony of Scots in the reign of James I., and other Presbyterians who fled from persecution in that country in succeeding reigns, planted themselves in the N.E. part of Ireland, and there established the linen manufacture. It was liberally encouraged by the Lord-Deputy Wentworth in 1634, by Wm. III. in 1698 (to the discouragement of the woollen manufactures), and by succeeding governments. The hemp, flax, linen, thread, and yarn from Ireland, were permitted to be exported duty free, 1696. The Irish linen-board was established in 1711; the Linen Hall, Dublin, was opened, 1728; the board was abolished in 1828. A board of trustees to superintend the Scotch linen manufacture was established in 1727. Dunfermline in Fifeshire, Dundee, and Barnsley in Yorkshire, are the chief seats of our linen manufacture.*b*

12—15. (12, 13) **breadth .. cubits,** *i.e.* 87 ft. 6 in. (14, 15) **fifteen cubits,** or 26 ft. 3 in. each side of the gate wh. would therefore be 35 ft.

The importance of order.—The most important results may depend on the right place and position of things. Should earthquakes shake the ground, or even storms violently agitate the air, that pyramid stands insecure which, according to the poet—

"Like an inverted cone.
Wants the proper base to stand upon."

What a monster in nature, how hideous of aspect, and happily of brief existence, were that body which should have its organs and members so misplaced, that the hands occupied the place of the feet, and the heart palpitated in the cavity of the brain! And who, besides, does not know that the fruitfulness, the beauty, the very life of a tree depends not only on its having both roots and branches, but on these members being placed in their natural order? Let a tree be planted upside down—set the roots in the air, and the boughs in the earth, and I need not ask how much fruit it would yield, nor how many seasons the unhappy plant would survive such barbarous and blundering treatment.*a*

16, 17. (16) **hanging,** curtain. (17) **shall .. silver,** connected with silver bars. *Curious needlework.*—For nearly half a century, in old Savile House, on the N. side of Leicester Square, was exhibited the gallery of pictures in needlework which Miss Mary Linwood, of Leicester, executed through her long life. She worked her first picture when 13 yrs. old, and the last piece when 78; beyond wh. her life was extended 12 yrs. The collection ultimately consisted of sixty-four pictures, most of them of large or gallery size, and copied fr. paintings by great masters. The gem of the collection, *Salvator Mundi,* after Carlo Dolci, for wh. 3,000 guineas had been refused, was bequeathed by Miss Linwood to H.M. Queen Victoria. In the year after Miss Linwood's death, the pictures were sold by auction, by Christie and Manson; and the prices they fetched denoted a strange fall in the money-value of these curious works. *The Judgment on Cain,* wh. had occupied 10 yrs., brought but £64 1s.; *Jephtha's Rash Vow,* after Opie, 16 guineas; two pictures from Gainsborough, *The Shepherd Boy,* £17 6s. 6d., and *The Ass and Children,* £23 2s.; *The Farmer's Stable,* after Morland, brought £32 11s. A portrait of Miss Linwood, after a crayon picture of Russell, R.A., brought 18 guineas; and *A Woodman in a Storm,* by Gainsborough, £33 1s. 6d.; Barker's *Woodman* brought £29 8s.; *The Girl and Kitten,* by Sir Joshua Reynolds, £10 15s.; and *Lady Jane Grey,* by Northcote, £24 13s. In the Scripture Room, *The Nativity,* by Maratti, was sold for £21; *Dead Christ,* by Caracci, 14 guineas; but the *Madonna della Ledia,* after Raffaelle, was bought in at £38 17s. A few other pictures were reserved; and those sold did not realise more than £1000.*a*

18—21. (18) **length .. cubits,** *see* vv. 9—11. **breadth .. where,** *see* vv. 12—15. **height .. cubits,** *i.e.* 8 ft. 9 in. (19) **pins .. court,** tent-nails; spikes to which the boards, hangings, etc., were attached by cords. (20) **pure .. light,** oil obtained by bruising, hence "cold-drawn." **lamp,** candlestick. **to .. always,**a *i.e.* every night. (21) **tabernacle .. congregation,** tabernacle of appointment, place of stated meeting. **without .. vail,**b the holy place. **Aaron .. Lord,**c *i.e.* shall superintend the oil, the lamps, and the lighting.

Oil for the light.—I. The source whence the oil was obtained: the "olive." Thus is grace, free and full, obtained from Christ, the "Plant of renown." II. The qualification it was to possess: it was to be "pure." All the grace which comes from Christ is pure and unalloyed. III. The instruments of its dispensation: "the children of Israel." The children of God are now the recipients and dispensers of Christ's grace. IV. The uses to which it was put: it caused "the lamp to burn always." Grace

---

B.C. 1491.

"So work the honey-bees, creatures that by a rule in nature teach the act of order to a peopled kingdom."— *Shakespeare.*
a Dr. Guthrie.

the gate and pillars of the court

"In the art of design colour is to form what verse is to prose —a more harmonious and luminous vehicle of the thought."— *Mrs. Jameson.*

"The mother of useful arts is necessity; that of the fine arts is luxury. For father the former has intellect; the latter genius, which itself is a kind of luxury." *Schopenhauer.*

"That is the best part of beauty which a picture cannot express." *Bacon.*

a Book of Days.

beaten oil for the light
a 1 Jo. ii. 20; Ps. cxix. 105; Ma. v. 16.
b Ex. xxvi. 31, 32.
c Ac. xx. 27, 28.
d S. Thomas.
"The golden beams of truth and the silken cords of love, twisted together, will draw men on with a sweet violence whether they will or no."
—*Cudworth.*
"Truth is a torch, but a terrible one; therefore we all try to

causes the life of each Christian to shine with a brighter glow.*d*

Beaten oil.—By the expression oil-olive, this oil is distinguished from other kinds. The addition beaten, indicates that it is that oil obtained from olives pounded in a mortar, and not pressed from olives in the oil-mill. The oil obtained from pounded olives is, according to Columella's observation, much purer and better tasted, does not emit much smoke, and has no offensive smell.*e*

CHAPTER THE TWENTY-EIGHTH.

1—5. (1) **that .. office,**^a after the tent and the altar comes the priest to serve in the one and at the other. **Nadab,** *etc.,* see vi. 23. (2) **holy garments,**^b garments of holiness, *i.e.* set apart for special holy services. **glory,** honour, the office honourable. **beauty,** ornament, decoration. (3) **wise-hearted,**^c expert, ingenious, skilful. **to .. him,** *i.e.* to be a badge of his consecration. **minister .. office,** not a lord of the heritage, but a servant of God. (4) **breastplate,** *see* v. 15 *ff.* **ephod,**^d *see* v. 6 *ff.* **robe,** *see* v. 31 *ff.* **coat,** *see* v. 39. **mitre,** *see* v. 36 *ff.* (5) **take .. linen,** materials of which the priestly garments should be wrought.

Vestments.—Let us contemplate the spiritual teaching suggested by some of the high-priest's vestments. They all denote the excellencies, merits, and grace of Jesus.—I. The first vestment: it was made of fine linen, and enveloped the whole person. Being snow-white, it was emblematical of Christ's holiness. II. The second vestment: this was a kind of tunic worn upon the linen ephod, of a light azure hue, and reached only to the knees. It was adorned with—1. Pomegranates; denoting fruitfulness; 2. Golden bells; reminding us of the interceding voice of the beloved Lord. III. The third vestment: a robe of magnificence, shorter than the second. It was "of gold, of blue, of purple, of scarlet, and fine twined linen, with cunning work;" and was the robe of—1. Joy: worn on festival-days: 2. Authority: none but the high-priest wore it. Learn:—(1) How precious Christ's people are to Him : "I am glorified in them ;" and what glory is His! (2) How secure they are. The breastplate hung on the robe of authority ; even so are we kept by His power : (3) How honoured they are. Ever connected with Christ !*e*

Vocation of the artist.—Very sacred is the vocation of the artist, who has to do directly with the works of God, and interpret the teaching of creation to mankind. All honour to the man who treats it sacredly ; studies, as in God's presence, the thoughts of God which are expressed to him : and makes all things according to the pattern which he is ever ready to show to earnest and reverent genius on the mount.*f*

6—12. (6) **ephod,**^a Heb. *éphod.* fr. *aphad.* Gk. ἐπωμις (Vulg. *superhumerale*), shoulder-piece, to wh. the breastplate was attached. **cunning,** skilful. (7) **shoulder-pieces,** prob. badges of dignity, etc., like the modern epaulette. **joined,** *etc.,* prob. the ephod was formed of two principal pieces, one for the back, the other for the front, connected by shoulder-straps. (8) **curious,** ornamented. **gird'e,**^b band. **shall .. same,** material and kind of work. (9) **onyx,**^c *see* Ge. ii. 12. (10) **according ..**

---

b.c. 1491.

reach it with closed eyes, lest we should be scorched."— *Goethe.*

e Dr. Burder.

the high priest's vestments

a Nu. xviii. 7; He. v. 1, 4.

b Ex. xxix. 5, 6, 29; Le. viii. 30; Ps. cxxxii. 9, 16; Is. lxi. 10; Jo. i. 14; He. vii. 26.

c Ex. xxxi. 3, 6, xxxvi. 1; 1 Co. xii. 8—11; Jas. i. 17.

d Le. viii. 7, 8; 1 Sa. xxiii. 9—12.

e R. A. Griffin.

"There is no more potent antidote to low sensuality than the adoration of beauty. All the higher arts of design are essentially chaste, without respect of the object. They purify the thoughts, as tragedy, according to Aristotle, purifies the passions."—*Schlegel.*

"Beauty itself is but the sensible image of the Infinite."—*Bancroft.*

f J. B. Brown, B.A.

the ephod
a 1 Sa. ii. 18, xxii. 18, 2 Sa. vi. 14, 15.
b Re. i. 12, 13; Is. xi. 5; Eph. vi. 14.
c " Sardonyx "— *Josephus*; "Beryl" — LXX. and *Philo.*

[Cap. xxviii. 13—21.] EXODUS.

birth, in the order of age. (11) **engraver**, artificer, worker. **signet**, seal or ring. **ouches**,[d] settings, sockets. (12) **put .. shoulders**,[e] thus sig. that the priest bore the burden of Israel in the presence of the Lord. **memorial**,[f] remembrance: the priest remembered whose representative he was: the Lord remembered His covenant people.

Their names upon his shoulders.—Consider this duty, which Aaron was to perform, in—I. Its literal meaning. Aaron as the representative of the people, was to bear their names before the Lord upon his shoulders. Note: the shoulders, the strongest part of the body. II. Its symbolical character. It is typical of Christ's intercession for us. He—1. Supports us: 2. Intercedes with the Father for us: 3. Imparts to us a part of His own glory.[g]

The religiousness of art.—Never is Piety more unwise than when she casts beauty out of the church, and by this excommunication forces her fairest sister to become profane. It is the duty of religion not to eject, but to cherish and seek fellowship with every beautiful exhibition which delights, and every delicate art which embellishes human life. So, on the other hand, it is the duty of art not to waste its high capabilities in the imitation of what is trivial, and in the curious adornment of what has only a finite significance. The highest art is always the most religious; and the greatest artist is always a devout man. A scoffing Raphael or Michael Angelo is not conceivable.[h]

13—16. (13) **ouches**, see v. 11. (14) **wreathen**, twisted like cords. **and .. ouches**, fr. these chains the breastplate was suspended. (15) **breastplate**, *lit.* ornament. **judgment**, prob. in ref. to its use as an oracle. (16) **span**, about 9¼ in.

Qualities of the artist.—

He is a being of deep reflection—one
That studies nature with intensest eye;
Watching the works of air, earth, sea, and sun—
Their motion, altitude, their form, their dye—
Cause and effect. The elements which run,
Or stagnant are, he traces to their source,
With vivid study, till his pencil makes
A perfect likeness; or, by fancy's force,
A new creation in his heart he takes,
And matches nature's progress in his course
Towards glory. In the abstractions of the mind,
Harmony, passion, and identity,
His genius, like the summer sun, is shrined,
Till beauty and perfection he can see.[a]

17—21. (17) **sardius**,[a] or ruby, or perh. cornelian. **topaz**,[b] perh. the chrysolyte, greenish yellow. **carbuncle**, prob. the emerald.[c] (18) **emerald**, prob. the garnet.[d] **sapphire**, the well-known azure-coloured stone. **diamond**, Heb. *yahalom*, fr. *halam*, to smite upon, so called from its hardness.[e] (19) **ligure**,[f] perh. amber. **agate**, well known. **amethyst**,[g] Heb. *ahlamah*, purple of diff. shades. (20) **beryl**, doubtful; perh. a kind of topaz. **jasper**, prob. the brown Egyptian variety,[h] or the green jasper.[i] **inclosings**, settings. (21) **according .. names**,[k] both in number and order.

Four rows of stones (v. 17).—Observe—I. The shining of the

B.C. 1491.

d Use! in the sense of jewels by old writers, as Shakespeare, Spencer, etc.; old Eng. *nouche*; low Lat. *nusca, nochia*; old Ger. *nusche*.
e Acc. to Rabbins, on the right, Reuben, Simeon, Levi, Judah, Dan, Naphtali; on the left, Gad, Asher, Issachar, Zebulun, Joseph, Benjamin.—*Josephus*, with a view to their mothers, places them thus —on the right, Reuben, Levi, Issachar, Naphtali, Gad, Joseph; on the left, Simeon, Judah, Zebulun, Dan, Asher, Benjamin.
f 2 Ti. ii. 19; He. vii. 25; Is. ix. 6;
Eph. v. 27.
g Anon.
h Blackie.

the breastplate

"The misfortune in the state is that nobody can enjoy life in peace, but that everybody must govern; and in art, that nobody will enjoy what has been produced, but that everyone wants to reproduce on his own account." *Goethe*.

a *Wordsworth*.

the stones of the breastplate

a Gk. σάρδιον, *sardine*, perh. tr. Sardis or Sardinia, where first found.
b Gk. τοπάζιον, wh. Pliny says is fr. *Topazos*, an isle in the Red Sea.

B.C. 1491.

c Rosenmüller.

d When this stone is cut with a convex face, it is called a carbuncle.

e Gk. ἀδάμας, invincible; hence we say as hard as adamant. "A champion cased in adamant."— Wordsw'rth. "Ou adamant our wrongs we all engrave, but write our benefits upon the wave." —*King.*

f "An opal."— De Wette.

g Gk. ἀμέθυστος, not drunken; wine fr. an amethyst cup supposed by ancients to prevent intoxication.

h *Bush.*

i *Spk. Comm.*

k Is. xliii. 4; Mal. iii. 17.

l *Dr. Taylor.* Sardonyx is a precious stone; probably named from its likeness to both the sardius and the onyx. It is dark, variegated with bluish white, black, and red lying in circles, as if inlaid by art. It is only mentioned in Rev xxi. 20; appearing to be the fifth row of stones on which the heavenly city in John's vision seemed to rest.

vv. 15 21. *Dr. D. Featley Clair's Mystica 498.*

v. 18. See *Ainsworth's Annot. in loc.*

m *Bailey.*

the fastenings of the breastplate

stones: pointing to the purity of Christ and His Church. II. Their price: of great value and worth, signifying what a price Christ valued His Church at. III. Their place or situation: they are set in the pectoral, and Aaron must carry them on his heart, signifying that Christ hath as much care of His Church, as if it were enclosed in His heart,—lets out His blood to make room in His heart for them. IV. Their number: twelve, noting that with Christ is plentiful redemption. V. Their order: they stood in a comely quadrangle; Christ hath established a comely order in His Church, and we must keep our ranks. VI. The figure: the foursquare, signifying the stability and firmness of the Church; Satan and all deceivers shall not pick one stone out of Christ's pectoral. VII. Their use: that Aaron must bear them on his heart, signifying Christ's ardent affection to His, and constant intercession for them. VIII. The quantity: as all the names of Israel were gathered into a narrow compass, so Christ shall "gather together into one all the dispersed sons of God," and present them before God as the most beautiful and precious parts of the world.*l*

The value of jewels in their association.—

HELEN. Why, what could it be?
Jewels are baubles only; whether pearls
From the sea's lightless depths, or diamonds
Cull'd from the mountain's crown, or chrysolith,
Cat's eye or moonstone, or hot carbuncle,
That from the bed of Eden's sunniest stream
Extracted, lamped the ark, what time the roar
Of lions pining for their free sands, smote
The hungry darkness,—toys are they at best.
Jewels are not of all things in my sight
Most precious.
        FESTUS. Nor in mine. It is in the use
Of which they may be made their value lies;
In the pure thoughts of beauty they call up,
And qualities they emblem. So in that
Thou wearest there, thy cross:—to me it is
Suggestive of bright thoughts and hopes in Him
Whose one great sacrifice availeth all,
Living and dead, through all eternity.
Not to the wanderer over southern seas
Rises the constellation of the cross
More lovelily o'er sky and calm blue wave,
Than does to me that bright one on thy breast.
As diamonds are purest of all things,
And but embodied light which fire consumes
And renders back to air, that nought remains;
And as the cross is symbol of our creed,
So let that ornament signify to thee
The faith of Christ, all purity, all light,
Through fervency resolving into heaven.
Each hath his cross, fair lady, on his heart;
Never may thine be heavier or darker
Than that now on thy breast, so light and bright,
Rising and falling with its bosom-swell."*m*

22—25. (22) **chains .. gold,** see v. 14. (23) **rings ..**
rings, for the chains. (24) **chains .. breastplate, by wh.**

the breastplate was suspended. (25) **and the other**, *etc.*, minute directions: God's people have need to be taught little things.

Durability of gold.—For a foundation, men prefer rock to sand, because it is durable; and, to this property, gold itself owes much of its value. It does not melt like ice, nor rust like iron, nor burn like wood, nor crumble into dust like stone. On opening the grave of an old Etruscan king, they found him lying robed and crowned as his warriors had entombed him two thousand years before. An impressive spectacle! but one they had hardly seen, when it vanished from their sight. Touched by the fresh air admitted at the open door, body and robes dissolved in a moment, leaving nothing where they had lain but a thin layer of dust. Not so the golden fillet that bound his brows: of all that funeral pomp, it only remains unchanged. Not time, nor even fire itself, destroys this precious metal: the flames may cleanse, but they cannot consume it. They esteem themselves happy who have their coffers filled with it; but how much happier those who have obtained what the Spirit counsels men to buy,—" gold tried in the fire, that thou mayest be rich!"

26—29. (26) **rings** .. thereof, attached to the two lower corners. **inward**, behind and out of sight. (27) **two sides .. forepart .. coupling**, these were attached to the shoulder-pieces, just above their union with the girdle. (28) **breastplate .. ephod**, safe keeping, ill. the close connection betw. the Church and the great High Priest. (29) **Aaron .. heart**,*a* seat of affections, the priest to sympathise with the people.

Aaron's breastplate.—Consider—I. Its primary use. 1. Show what this breast-plate was; 2. Enlarge upon its particular use. II. Its typical intent. It was designed to represent what Christ —1. Is doing for us: He " appears in the presence of God " for us; 2. Will do in us.*b*

The breastplate.—This was a piece of rich cloth, set with twelve precious stones, one for each tribe of Israel. the size and beauty of which, according to Josephus, placed this ornament beyond the purchase of men. The cloth was of the same embroidered stuff as the outer robe or ephod, over which it was placed, and this stuff was doubled, the better to hold the precious stones with which it was set. When thus doubled it was a span (or nine inches) square. There was at each corner a ring of gold, to the two uppermost of which were attached wreathed chains of gold, by which the breastplate was fastened to the shoulder-pieces of the ephod; and the two under-rings were furnished with blue laces, to be fastened to rings in the embroidered girdle of the ephod.*c*

30—32. (30) **Urim**, lights. **Thummim**,*a* perfections. " These were prob. some well-known means for casting lots."*b* **and .. heart**, they were prob. kept in the bag formed by the doubling of the breastplate, *see vv.* 15, 16. (31) **robe .. ephod**, worn beneath, and seen above and below the ephod: without seam. (32) **hole .. thereof**, hence it was drawn on over the head. **woven work**, no cunning handiwork employed upon it: this robe woven throughout (ill. Christ's seamless coat: He, the great High Priest, had no breastplate, the names of His people being *in* His heart). **habergeon**,*e* coat of mail (chain-armour) covering head and shoulders, drawn on over the head,

---

B.C. 1491.

"Like other beautiful things in this world, its end (that of a shaft) is to be beautiful; and, in proportion to its beauty, it receives permission to be otherwise useless. We do not blame emeralds and rubies bec. we cannot make them into heads of hammers."—*Ruskin.*

"In days of yore nothing was holy but the beautiful."—*Schiller.*

the use and place of the breastplate

a Cant. viii. 6; Is. xl. 11, xlix. 16.

b C. Simeon, M.A.

"When I behold the passion for ornamentation and the corresponding power, I feel as if women had so far shown what they are had for rather than what they are good for."—*Julia W. Howe.*

"Ornaments were invented by modesty."—*Joubert.*

c Dr. Kitto.

Urim and Thummim: and robe of the ephod

a The manifestation and the truth: Aq., "Enlightenings and certainties;" *Sam.,* "Elucidations and perfections;" *Syr.,* "the lucid and the perfect;"

B.C. 1491.

Arab., "Illuminations and certainties:" *Lat. Vulg.,* "doctrine and verity;" *Luth.,* "light and right."

b *Spk. Comm.*

c French, *haubergeon,* dim. of old Fr. *haubers,* obs. E. *hauberk*—A.S. *healsbeorga*—*head's,* neck, *beorgan,* 'to defend.' "Clothid with the *habutioun* of rightwisnesse."— *Wycliffe.* "'And be ye apparelled or clothed,' saith Paul, 'with the *habergeon* or coatarmour of justice."—*Latimer.*

d B. Keach.

"Every true specimen of perfection, or even excellence, of whatever kind it may be, from the moral down to the physical, elevates every instance of an inferior degree of excellence that we meet with, and sheds over it a portion of its own perfection." —F. Lieber.

"Among the other excellences of man, this is one, that he can form an idea of perfection much beyond what he has experience of in himself; and is not limited in his conception of wisdom and virtue."— *Hume.*

e Dr. Kitto.

the hem of the robe

a Grows wild in the E., fruit size of orange flattened at the end

Aaron a type of Christ.—I. Aaron, a teacher, or the mountain of fortitude; so is Christ the true teacher of God's Word. II. Aaron was Moses's mouth to the people; so is Christ His Father's mouth to men, declaring His will and mind to them. III. Aaron was the blesser of the people (Lev. ix. 22); so is Christ the true blesser of His people (Acts iv. 27). IV. Aaron was the high priest of the Lord; Jesus Christ is the only true High Priest of the Church. V. Aaron died upon the mount; Christ was crucified on Mount Calvary.*d*

Urim and Thummim.—Much ingenious speculation has been brought to bear on the subject of the Urim and Thummim, through wh. the High Priest obtained responses fr. God. The questions on wh. the discussion has turned have been: Were the Urim and Thummim distinct from or identical with the precious stones of the breastplate? if distinct, what were they? and in what manner were they instrumental in obtaining answers from God to the questions of the High Priest? The word "Urim" means "lights," and the word Thummim "perfections," and might be very well applicable to the precious stones of the breastplate, if taken as epithets instead of names. The most judicious interpreters are generally disposed to concur in the statement of Josephus, that the Urim and Thummim were identical with the precious stones. It does, indeed, seem remarkable that, had they been something separate, they should not have been described in this minute statement; and we are inclined to think, that a careful examination of the different texts will leave little doubt as to their identity. In the description of the breastplate in Ch. xxxix. 8—21, the Urim and the Thummim are not mentioned, but the precious stones are; while in the description in Lev. viii. 8, the Urim and Thummim are mentioned, but not the stones, from whence it is obvious to infer that they were the same things. Even the text before us, as compared with the preceding verse, can only be well understood by supposing the Urim and Thummim to be the substance on which the names of the tribes were engraven. In the previous verse Aaron is directed to wear the *names upon his heart before the Lord continually;* and in the present text he is directed to wear the *Urim and Thummim upon his heart before the Lord continually.* This certainly seems a more reasonable and proper account than that of Gesenius and others, who imagine that the Urim and Thummim were small oracular images, like the teraphim, by which revelation and truth were personified, and which were placed in the inner cavity of the breastplate. Spencer and others, who had previously entertained a similar view, fancy that the ornament was derived from the Egyptians, whose chief priest, who was also their supreme civil judge, wore, suspended from a golden chain around his neck. We do not see much resemblance in this, except so far as any jewelled ornament worn about the neck may be said to resemble another. The jewel worn by the Egyptian judges was wholly judicial: whereas the Urim and Thummim were not only judicial but oracular and sacerdotal.*e*

33—35. (33) **hem,** bottom of the skirt. **make,** embroider. **pomegranates,**a *lit.* apples full of grain, emblem of fruitfulness. (34) **bell,** *etc.,*b ill. the *sound* of the Gospel and the *fruit* of preaching. (35) **sound..Lord,**c by wh. the people might know he was discharging the functions of his office, and be

[Cap. xxviii. 36.] EXODUS. 337

themselves incited to devotion. **that .. not**, by appearing before the Lord in an incomplete or unwarranted costume, *see* v. 43.

A chime of bells.—Consider the Gospel as having many voices like to bells, and note that these are—I. Golden bells. No one can estimate the value of the Gospel. It is the sweetest sound to sinners, the best consolation to mourners, and the mightiest hope for all. II. Bells of invitation. When the Jews heard the clash of those bells in the hem of the priest's robe, they knew it was an invitation to worship. III. Bells of warning. The Jews were warned by the bells to worship, lest God should be offended. The Gospel warns us to serve God. IV. Bells of joy. They announced to the Jews the possibility of pardon. The Gospel announces this now to us. V. Bells of triumph.*d*

The sacredness of bells in the East.—The bell seems to have been a sacred utensil of very ancient use in Asia. Golden bells formed a part of the ornaments of the pontifical robe of the Jewish high priest, with which he invested himself upon those grand and peculiar festivals when he entered into the sanctuary. That robe was very magnificent, it was ordained to be of sky-blue, and the border of it, at the bottom, was adorned with pomegranates and gold bells intermixed equally, and at equal distances. The use and intent of these bells is evident from these words: "And it shall be upon Aaron to minister, and his sound shall be heard when he goeth in unto the holy place before the Lord, and when he cometh out, that he die not." The sound of the numerous bells that covered the hem of his garment, gave notice to the assembled people that the most awful ceremony of their religion had commenced. When arrayed in this garb, he bore into the sanctuary the vessel of incense; it was the signal to prostrate themselves before the Deity, and to commence those fervent ejaculations which were to ascend with the column of that incense to the throne of heaven. "One indispensable ceremony in the Indian Pooja is the ringing of a small bell by the officiating brahmin. The women of the idol, or dancing girls of the pagoda, have little golden bells fastened to their feet, the soft harmonious tinkling of which vibrates in unison with the exquisite melody of their voices." (Maurice's *Indian Antiquities*.) "The ancient kings of Persia, who, in fact, united in their own persons the regal and sacerdotal office, were accustomed to have the fringes of their robes adorned with pomegranates and golden bells. The Arabian courtesans, like the Indian women, have little golden bells fastened round their legs, neck, and elbows, to the sound of which they dance before the king. The Arabian princesses wear golden rings on their fingers, to which little bells are suspended, as well as in the flowing tresses of their hair, that their superior rank may be known, and they themselves, in passing, receive the homage due to their exalted station."*e*

36. **plate, cincture, fillet**, prob. simply a small, florally-embossed plate. **holiness .. Lord,***a* *Heb., kodesh la-Jehovah,* holiness to Jehovah, sig. the holiness with which, by virtue of his calling, the priest was invested.

Aaron's mitre.—This was intended to foreshow—I. The holiness of our great High Priest. 1. It was necessary that He should be spotless Himself; 2. It seems to have been particularly ordained of God that Christ's innocence should be established by

b.c. 1491.

a like an apple, beautiful colour, choice flavour, brownish red when ripe, inside like the orange, but filled with many reddish seeds.

b "Shadowing out—(1) The prophetical office of Christ here, and His perpetual intercession in heaven: (2) The duty of ministers; which is, to live sermons, to be fruitful as well as painful teachers; not like him of whom it was said, that when he was out of the pulpit, it was pity he should ever go into it; and when he was in the pulpit, it was pity he should ever come out of it." —*Trapp.*

c Ps. ii. 11.

d Dr. Talmage.

"Music is the art of the prophets, the only art that can calm the agitations of the soul; it is one of the most magnificent and delightful presents God has given us."—*Luther.*

"How sour sweet music is, when time is broke and no proportion kept." — *Shakespeare.*

e Calmet.

the plate of the mitre

a Le. xxi. 1, 7, 8, x. 4; Ha. vii. 26; 1 Co. i. 30.

"Blessed is the memory of those who have kept

B.C. 1491.
themselves un-
spotted from the
world! yet more
blessed and more
dear the memory
of those who
have kept them-
selves unspotted
in the world."—
Mrs. Jameson.

b *C. Simeon, M.A.*

"Think not thy
love to God
merits God's love
to thee: His ac-
ceptance of thy
duty crowns His
own gifts in thee.
Man's love to
God is nothing
but a faint reflec-
tion of God's love
to man."—
Quarles.

c *Dr. Kitto.*

**the linen
coat, mitre,
and girdle**

Mitre, a head-
dress; Fr.; Lat.
mitra; Gk. *mi ra*,
head-dress, akin
to *mitos*, thread.

a *Trapp.*

b Le. i. 4; Jo. i.
29; He. ix. 28;
1 Pe. ii. 24; Jo.
xvii. 19; He. iv.
14—16.

c *Josephus.*

"In the time of
Josephus the
shape of the
mitre had be-
come somewhat
altered. It was
circular, was
covered with a
piece of fine
linen, and sat so
closely on the
upper part of the
head (for it did
not cover the
whole of the
head) that it
would not fall off
when the body
was bent down."
—*Jahn.*

every possible proof ; 3. Thus, a sure foundation was laid for all the hopes that are built upon Him. II. The need we have of an interest in it. We need an atonement. III. Its efficacy in our behalf. Through Christ's holiness we are accepted before God. This subject is well calculated—(1) To humble the self-righteous; (2) To encourage the desponding ; (3) To direct and animate the godly.*b*

Mitre.—This mitre was a turban of fine linen (v. 39), furnished in front with a plate of pure gold, on which were inscribed the words, "Holiness to the Lord," or "Holy to Jehovah," and which was attached to the turban by a blue lace. The word translated "plate," signifies a flower, and is rendered πέταλον, "petal," in the LXX., which seems to show that the plate was wrought with flowered work, or was itself in the form of a flower or petal. In Ch. xxxix. 6, this ornament is called *nezer*, from a verb signifying "to separate," and hence denoting a crown, as a mark of separation or distinction. The same word is applied to the diadem of kings. Indeed, such turbans of fine linen, with an encircling or front ornament of gold or precious stones, seem to have been the usual diadems of ancient kings. Thus we read, in Justin, that Alexander the Great took his diadem from his head to bind up the wounds of Lysimachus ; which shows clearly enough that it was of linen, probably with some distinguishing ornament on the same principle as this on the turban of the Hebrew pontiff.*c*

37—39. (37) **put .. lace**, a band or fillet, to wh. the plate (v. 36) was attached. **mitre**, turban, Heb., *tzanaph*, to roll round. (38) **bear**, *etc.*, "get the people's pardon ; this Christ did indeed for all His."*a* **that .. Lord**,*b* the people accepted in the person of the priest. (39) **coat .. linen**, a kind of tunic or cassock : prob. worn next the skin.*c* **girdle .. needlework**, embroidered : a piece of fine linen to confine the coat at the waist.

The iniquity of holy things (v. 38).—By these words we are reminded—I. That our best performances are not without sin. 1. Our prayers may be narrow, selfish, etc. ; 2. Our praises designed more to set forth the power of the voice than the goodness of God ; 3. Our worship may be wanting in sincerity, etc ; 4. Even if we are unconscious of sin, it may yet be present. II. That the sin of our holy things needs pardon : otherwise the very things that would be a means of blessing, become a curse. III. That forgiveness is granted through our great High Priest. "Holiness to the Lord," written on the mitre, by which God is supposed to be reminded, when He looks upon it, of the holiness of the great Mediator whom Aaron represented ; *see* Ps. lxxxiv. 9, and cxxxii. 9, 10.

A fable of art.—Minerva was the goddess of Wisdom, and presided over the arts. Arachne, a mortal maiden of renowned skill in weaving and embroidery, whose fingers made the wool into rolls, twisted it into threads, and wrought it into divers patterns, challenged the goddess to a trial of competition. Minerva, in the guise of an old woman, dissuaded her in vain. She then threw off her disguise, and the trial began. Each spread out the warp, hurled the shuttle, and struck the woof into its place. Minerva wrought in her web a scene representing the glory of the gods. Arachne, presumptuous, in hers pictured the errors and failings

[Cap. xxix. 1—3.] EXODUS. 339

of the gods. The goddess admired the maiden's work, but, stung by the insult, struck it from the loom, and changed the aspiring girl into a spider, to go on spinning and hanging herself for ever. Now science has wrested the thunderbolt from Jove, the trident from Neptune, and the distaff from Minerva.

40—43. (40) **bonnets,** caps. **glory .. beauty,**[b] *see* v. 2. (41) **thou .. them,** *etc.*,[c] neither the office nor its dress to be self-assumed. (42) **breeches,** drawers, *see* xx. 26. (43) **that .. die,**[d] by appearing before God in the discharge of priestly functions negligently attired.

The high priest's vestments.—Apart from their significance they may suggest some useful reflections on dress. We observe—I. That dress may be employed, as in this case, as the insignia of office, King's robe and crown,—Judge's robe, etc. II. That dress should be adapted to social stations; maids often more gairishly attired than mistresses. III. That dress may often be regarded as an index to character. Modesty, cleanliness, etc., without weak leanings to absurd extravagances of fashion, ought to be aimed at. IV. A few words on the soul's dress,—" Be clothed with humility."—" The robe of righteousness," etc.

The love of dress.—A man following the occupation of wood-cutting, wrought with exemplary zeal the six working-days, hoarding every cent not required to furnish him with the most frugal fare. As his "pile" increased, he invested it in gold ornaments, — watch-chain of massive links, shirt and sleeve buttons, shoe-buckles, then buttons for vest and coat, a hat-band of the precious metal, a heavy gold-headed cane; and, in short, wherever an ounce of it could be bestowed upon his person, in or out of taste, it was done. The glory of his life, his sole ambition, was to don this curious attire (which was deposited for safe keeping during the week in one of the banks) on Sunday morning, and then spend the day, the "observed of all observers," lounging about the office or bar-room of the St. Charles. He never drank, and rarely spoke. Mystery seemed to envelop him. No one knew whence he came, or the origin of his innocent whim. Old citizens assured you, that, year after year, his narrow savings were measured by the increase of his ornaments, until at length the value of the anomalous garments came to be estimated by thousands of dollars. By ten o'clock on Sunday night, the exhibition was closed. His one day of self-gratification enjoyed, his costly wardrobe was returned to the bank-vault, and he came back into the obscurity of a wood-chopper.[e]

Side notes:
B.C. 1491.
v. 39. J. *Alting*, *Op.* ii. 175.
vestments and consecration, etc., of priests
a Vulg. *tiaras*.
b Ex. xxxix. 27—29; Ezek. xliv. 17, 18; Ma. xxii. 12, 13; Eph. vi. 13.
c Le. viii. 12.
d Le. v. 17, xxii. 9.
In the Bible the body is said to be more than raiment. But many people read the Bible Hebrew-wise, backward; and thus the general conviction now is, that raiment is more than the body.
"Dress has a moral effect upon the conduct of mankind. Let any gentleman find himself with dirty boots, soiled neckcloth, and a general negligence of dress, he will, in all probability, find a corresponding disposition by negligence of address." — Sir J. *Barrington*.
e W. H. *Milburn*.

CHAPTER THE TWENTY-NINTH.

1—3. (1) **hallow,** sanctify, set apart. **one .. bullock,** *lit.* a youngling of the herd. **and .. blemish,**[a] perfect. (2) **tempered,**[b] mixed with. **wafers,** thin cakes, pancakes.[c] (3) **them .. basket,** *i.e.* the bread, etc.

The doctrine of sacrifice universal.—In addition to the fact that life is daily sacrificed for the sustentation of life, the belief of a higher sacrifice would also seem to be one of man's most unconquerable instincts. Search for him when we will, or where we will, in every age of the world, in every country under heaven,

Side notes:
consecration of priests
their hallowing
a Mal. 1. 13, 14.
b Le. vi. 20, 22.
c Ital. version has *fritella,* fritters.

[Cap. xxix. 4—14.

B.C. 1491.

"In Sophocles, Jocasta prays to the Lycian Apollo, and says 'that she came to his temple because it was the nearest.' This was but a sorry compliment to his godship. It is the same, however, that people generally pay to religion, who abide by the doctrines and faith they have been bred up in, merely to save themselves the trouble of seeking farther."— *Sterne.*

d T. Ragg.

sunk in ignorance and barbarism, or raised to the highest pitch of civilisation, that doctrine, more or less developed, still is his companion. He slays the victim as an offering to God; or he punishes himself, morally or physically, as an expiation of his sin. And whence the universal prevalence of such an idea? It is idle to speak of it as the result of superstition. Blindness and ignorance can lead to no such uniformity of result. If in some one dark nation of antiquity, or among some one of the races of mankind, such a notion as expiation had been discovered, it might with sufficient reason have been assigned to superstition as its originator. If a few of those nations or races had seemed strangely to agree in such a doctrine, it might have been accounted a remarkable fact, an illustration of the doctrine "of transmitted instincts;" and would among ethnologists have been considered a powerful evidence of their identity of origin. But the idea is as extensive as the species. Its universal prevalence is an irrefragable evidence of one out of two facts. It is either a proof that the doctrine was taught by the common progenitor of mankind, to whom it was in some way supernaturally communicated; or that it was an instinct implanted by the Author of our being, which, like all other instincts, must meet with its appropriate answer.*d*

their purification and anointing

a Le. viii. 6; Ti. iii. 5; He. x. 22.

b 1 Pe. iii. 21.

c Trapp.

d He. i. 9; 1 Jo. ii. 27.

e He. vii. 28.

f "The filling of the hands is nothing else than an initiation when one enters upon any business that he may be continued in it from that day forward." — *Rabbi Solomon.*

g Dr. Jenkyn.

4—9. (4) **wash .. water,***a* symbol of necessary spiritual cleanliness,*b* "a type of Christ's baptism."*c* (5, 6) *see* xxviii. 41. (7) **take .. head,***d* type of anointing of the Holy Spirit. (8) **thou .. sons,** the High Priest first, then the others in their order. (9) **consecrate,***e Heb.*, fill their hands,*f i.e.* with sacrifices.

The unction of holiness.—The spirit of holiness gives to the Church an aptness and a grace in all its movements and efforts for the conversion of the world. The influences of the Holy Spirit are, on that account, as well as for the sweet odour with which they perfume the Church, called "the unction of the Holy One." The Agonistes in the Grecian games anointed themselves with unguents in order to attain quickness, agility, and nimbleness of action : and this gave a grace and beauty to their various movements. Before they could attain this, the unguent must have pervaded their frame, and not glistened in superficial application. In like manner, before the Church can acquire a grace in doing good, and in acting "after the Spirit," the unction from the Holy One must penetrate all the muscles of its frame, and all the members of its body.*g*

the putting away of their sin

a Le. i. 4; Is. liii. 4, 6; 2 Co. v. 21. "My faith would lay her hand on that dear head of Thine."—*Watts.*

b Le. viii. 15.

c He. xiii. 11—13. "The due completion of the various ceremonies above de-

10—14. (10) **put .. head,***a* symbol for transference of sin to the victim. (11) **door,** *etc.*, that the priest might enter in as one to whom sin was not imputed. (12) **horns .. finger,***b see* xxvii. 2. **pour .. altar,** where there was a trench to receive it. (13) **caul,** perh. the gall-bladder, or pericardium. (14) **burn .. camp,***c* to show intense hatred of sin : Jesus suffered without the camp.

The necessity of holiness.—If a physician were called to see a patient who had a cancer on his breast, the only thing to be done would be to cut it out from the roots. The physician might give palliatives, so that the patient would have less pain; or he might make his patient believe it was no cancer, or forget that he had a cancer near his vitals : but, if the physician were to do this instead of removing the evil, he would be a wicked man, and the enemy of his patient. The man's case was such, that the only favour which could be conferred upon him would be to cut out the cancer. Now all agree that sin is the great evil of the soul of man. Nothing can make man more spiritually happy here, or fit him for happiness hereafter, than the removal of sin from his nature. Sin is the plague-spot on the soul, which destroys its peace, and threatens its destruction unless removed. It is therefore certain that if the love of God were manifested towards man, it would be in turning man from sin which produces misery, to holiness which produces happiness.*d*

B.C. 1491.

scribed was followed by the oblation of their sacrifices for Aaron and his sons: (1) A sin-offering; (2) A burnt-offering; (3) A peace-offering."—*Bush.*

d J. B. Walker.

15—18. (15) **shalt .. ram,** *i.e.* one of the two, v. 1. **and .. hands,** as acknowledging that they were sinners. **upon .. ram,** believing their sin to be transferred. (16) **blood,**a without shedding of which no remission. (17) **wash,** *etc.,* this signified that entire holiness, *see* 1 Thess. v. 23.*b* (18) **sweet savour,***c* *lit.* a savour of rest, *i.e.* an appeasing odour pacifying Divine displeasure.*d*

The righteousness of Christ.—Before you stands a bath, as it is called,—a large vessel full of acid liquor. At one end, immersed in the fluid, hangs a sheet of silver; while above, and passing from side to side, is extended a thread of metal ready to be connected with a powerful battery, which, when I saw the process, was concealed in a room below. A vessel of common metal, being produced, was hung on the wire, and plunged into the bath; in which, I may remark, the fluid was so clear, that you could see to the bottom. The wire on which it was suspended was then connected with the electric battery: and what happened? A very remarkable result. By means of the mighty though unseen agent that was thus brought into action, the particles of silver were taken from the sheet of it, and, passing invisibly through the translucent fluid, were transferred to the vessel that had been immersed in the bath. No sound accompanied the mysterious process, no violent action, no sign of motion; the eye saw nothing but the dull metal beginning to assume a brilliant appearance; and in time, through what looked more like magic than common art, this base metal shone in a coating of the purest silver. Such a change, but far greater and more thorough, is wrought on the soul through the unseen and almighty influence of the Holy Spirit, as soon as faith has established a connection between the Saviour and the sinner. Righteousness is withdrawn from the former, and transferred to the latter. In the words of an inspired apostle, the believer puts on Christ, to stand before God covered with those merits, and justified by that righteousness, which makes a sinner just. If this process of art suggested that resemblance, it presented under one aspect a mighty difference. Robbed of its precious metal, what was once a sheet of silver became in time a dull, attenuated, worthless thing. Its treasures were exhausted, Christ's never are; it could coat and cover a certain number, no more: but in Him there is righteousness for all the world, enough of mercy in the Father, of merit in the Son, and of grace in the Spirit, for every child of guilt.*e*

an offering made for them

a 1 Pe. i. 2.

b Trapp.

c Ge. viii. 21; Eph. v. 2.

d See *Bush.*

"Virtue is the nursing-mother of all human pleasures, who, in rendering them just, renders them also pure and permanent; in moderating them, keeps them in breath and appetite; in interdicting those which she herself refuses, whets our desires to those that she allows; and, like a kind and liberal mother, abundantly allows all that nature requires, even to satiety, if not to lassitude."—*Socrates.*

See *Saurin Dis. Hist.* ii. 329, and *Diss.* 518. *S. Mather, M.A.* 529.

e Dr. Guthrie.

19—24. (19) **shalt .. ram,**a *etc., see* v. 15. (20) **put .. ear,** dedication to God of the sense of hearing. **thumb .. hand,** executive power dedicated. **toe .. foot,** obedience: their way

their wave-offering

a Le. viii. 22.

[Cap. xxix. 25—28.

b He. ix. 12, 22;
1 Pe. ii. 5; Re. i.
5, 6.

c Gesenius, Rosenmuller. For *sheep*,
see *Topics* i. 20,
25, 59; ii. 39.

d "As acknowledging God's
omnipresence;
and that many
should come
from east, west,
north, and south,
to partake of the
merits and
benefits of
Christ, our true
Sacrifice." —
Trapp.

e *Anon.*

"A part of the
blood of the ram
of consecration
was sprinkled
upon the ears of
Aaron and his
sons, to remind
them always to
listen to the commands of God;
upon their hands,
to enjoin the duty
of activity and
zeal in the service of God; and
upon their feet,
to symbolise
their walking in
the ways of the
Law."—*Kalisch.*

f *Dr. Burder.*

**their heave-
offering**

a Nu. xviii. 11,
18; De. xviii. 3.

"The waving
consisted in turning the offering
to all the four
parts of the earth
and to heaven,
as a symbol that
it was destined
for the Lord of
heaven and
earth; but the
heaving was only
a movement of
the offering up

in life consecrated. (21) **blood .. garments,**[b] our robes made
white with the blood of the Lamb. (22) **fat .. rump,** perh. the
thick, fatty tail of Syrian sheep[c] (*ovis laticaudata*). **for consecration,** *i.e.* for consecrating the initiation of the priests into
their office. (23) **loaf,** *etc.*, see v. 2. (24) **wave offering,** *lit.*
thou shalt wave them a waving : the offering when made was
agitated, moved backwards and forwards, or up and down.[d]

Personal consecration.—I. That Christians are priests. As
such, they are Divinely chosen. They are the leaders of God's
worship, and repositories of saving knowledge; illustrious privileges are theirs. They fulfil the office of intercession for their
fellow-men; consecration is required in them. II. Some illustrations of the character of their consecration. Observe its
universality: blood on the extremes of the frame.—1. The ear :
all intellectual faculties ; 2. The thumb : all practical activities;
3. The toe : all personal movements.[e]

Broad-tailed Syrian sheep.—On the large tail of one species of
the eastern sheep, Russell (*Hist. of Aleppo,* p. 51), after observing
that they are in that country much more numerous than those
with smaller tails, adds, "This tail is very broad and large, terminating in a small appendix that turns back upon it. It is of a
substance between fat and marrow, and is not eaten separately,
but mixed with the lean meat in many of their dishes, and also
often used instead of butter. A common sheep of this sort, without the head, feet, skin, and entrails, weighs about twelve or
fourteen Aleppo rotoloes, of which the tail is usually three
rotoloes or upwards; but such as are of the largest breed, and
have been fattened, will sometimes weigh about thirty rotoloes,
and the tail of these ten. These very large sheep, being about
Aleppo kept up in yards, are in no danger of injuring their tails ;
but in some other places, where they feed in the fields, the
shepherds are obliged to fix a piece of thin board to the under
part of their tail, to prevent its being torn by bushes and thistles,
as it is not covered underneath with thick wool like the upper
part. Some have small wheels to facilitate the dragging of this
board after them." A rotoloe of Aleppo is five pounds. With
this agrees the account given by the Abbé Mariti (*Travels through
Cyprus*). "The mutton is juicy and tender. The tails of some
of the sheep, which are remarkably fine, weigh upwards of fifty
pounds." This shows us the reason why, in the Levitical sacrifices,
the tail was always ordered to be consumed by fire.[f]

25—28. (25) **burnt-offering,** not a whole burnt-offering,
but strictly a peace-offering. (26) **wave,** *etc.,* see v. 24. (27)
heave-offering,[a] perh. moved up and down, while the wave-
offering was moved to and fro. (28) **even .. Lord,** so should
we *heave* up our hearts to God in gratitude for His mercies.

Guilty offerings.—Many of the mosques at Cairo are doubtless
monuments of sincere piety; but not a few have certainly
originated in ways far from creditable to their founders. I
passed by one, a handsome building, respecting which I was told
the following anecdote :—The founder, on the first occasion of
opening his mosque for the ceremonials of the Friday prayers,
invited the chief 'Ulama to attend the service ; and each of
these congratulated him before the congregation, by reciting
some tradition of the Prophet, or by some other words of an apposite nature, excepting one. This man the founder addressed,

asking wherefore he was silent. " Hast thou nothing to say," he
asked, " befitting this occasion ?" The man, thus invited, readily
answered, " Yes. If thou hast built this mosque with money
lawfully acquired, and with a good intention, know that God
hath built for thee a mansion in paradise, and great will be thy
felicity. But if thou raised this temple by means of wealth
unlawfully obtained, by money exacted from the poor by oppression and tyranny, know that there is prepared for thee a place
in hell, and evil will be the transit thither." The latter was
the case; and within a few hours after he had thus spoken, the
only one among the company of 'Ulama who had dared to utter
the language of truth on this occasion—to do which, indeed,
required no little courage—suddenly died, a victim, as well
known, of poison.b

B.C. 1491.

and down." —
Kalisch.

"Among the Jews the wave-offering was waved horizon-tally to the four points, and the heave - offering heaved up and down, to signify that He was Lord of Heaven and earth."—*Bowes.*

b *Mrs. Poole.*

29, 30. (29) **garments .. him,**a symbol of succession in
office : the robe of Christ's righteousness inherited by His people.
(30) **seven days,** perfect consecration : seven the perfect
number.

days of preparation for duty

a Nu. xx. 26, 28.

The parish priest.—
A parish priest was of the pilgrim train ;
An awful, reverend, and religious man.
His eyes diffused a venerable grace,
And charity itself was in his face.
Rich was his soul, though his attire was poor
(As God hath cloth'd His own ambassador) ;
For such, on earth, his bless'd Redeemer bore.
With eloquence innate his tongue was arm'd :
Though harsh the precept, yet the people charm'd ;
For, letting down the golden chain from high,
He drew his audience upward to the sky :
And oft with holy hymns he charm'd their ears
(A music more melodious than the spheres) :
For David left him, when he went to rest.
His lyre ; and after him he sung the best.b

"Beauty com-monly produces love, but cleanli-ness preserves it. Age itself is not unamiable while it is preserved clean and unsul-lied; like a piece of metal con-stantly kept smooth and bright, we look on it with more pleasure than on a new vessel can-kered with rust."
—*Addison.*

b *Chaucer.*

31—37. (31) **seethe,** boil, prepare as food. (32) **eat .. ram,**
i.e. the remainder of the ram so prepared. (33) **eat .. made,**a
so there must be perfect union with Christ, the Lamb of God, the
great atoning sacrifice. **stranger,** prob. the term is here limited
to one not of Aaron's family. (34) **burn .. fire,** gratitude to be
prompt and complete : the thank-offering not kept till the morrow.
(35) **things,** office, garments, ceremonies, etc. (36) **atonement,** expiations, propitiations, reconciliations : these for the
priests and the altar. (37) **whatsoever .. holy,**b priest,
victim, etc.
*Meaning of atonement.—*The word atonement occurs but once
in the English translation of the New Testament, Ro. v. 11 ; but
the Greek word, of which in that case it is a translation,
καταλλαγη, and the verb of the same origin and meaning,
καταλλάσσω (" to change, exchange, to reconcile "), occur together
ten times in the New Testament, viz. Ro. v. 10, twice ; ver. 11 ;
xi. 15 ; 1 Co. vii. 11 ; 2 Co. v. 18, twice ; ver. 19, twice ; and ver.
20. In every case the verb is translated " to reconcile ;" and,
except in Ro. v. 11, the noun is rendered " reconciliation ;" the
mode of this reconciliation being clearly indicated, Ro. v. 10, viz.,
" by the death of His Son," Throughout the Old Testament the

the sin-offering for atonement

a Le. x. 14.
b Ex. xxx. 26, 29; He. x. 11.

" We are saved from nothing if we are not saved from sin. Little sins are pioneers of hell. The backslider bo-gins with what he foolishly con-siders trifling with little sins. There are no little sins. There was a time when all the evil that has existed in the world was com-prehended in one sinful thought of our first parent,

EXODUS. [Cap. xxix. 38—44.

b.c. 1491.

and all the now evil is the numerous and horrid progeny of one little sin.—*Howell.*

"He that hath slight thoughts of sin never had great thoughts of God."—Dr. Owen.
e Dr. Hodge.

the daily sin-offering
a Nu. xxviii. 3; 2 Ch. xiii. 10, 11; Jo. i 29; 1 Pe. i. 18, 19; He. vii. 24—27.

b Ps. lv. 17.

c 2 Ki. xvi. 15; Dan. ix. 21.

"The Ædiles among the Romans had their doors always standing open, that all who had petitions might have free access to them. The door of heaven is always open for the prayers of God's people."—T. Watson.

"Prayer is intended to increase the devotion of the individual, but if the individual himself prays he requires no formula; he pours himself forth much more naturally in self-chosen and connected thoughts before God, and scarcely requires words at all."—W. Von Humboldt.
d R. T. S.

the tabernacle sanctified

a Ex. xxv. 22; Le. xvi. 2; Nu. xxviii. 6.

b Ex. xl. 34; 2 Ch. v. 14; vii. 1; Hag. ii. 7—9; Mal. iii. 1.

word atonement is constantly used to signify the reconciliation of God by means of bloody sacrifices, to men alienated from Him by the guilt of sin. The priest made atonement for the transgressors of the law, by sacrifices, and it was forgiven them. Le. iv. 20; v. 6; vi. 7; xii. 8; xiv. 18; Nu. xv. 25. On the great "day of atonement," the high priest made atonement, first for his own sins, by the sacrifice of a bullock; and for the sins of all the people, by the sacrifice of a goat; and then the sins thus atoned for were confessed and laid upon the head of the live goat, and carried away by him into oblivion. Le. xvi. 6—22.*e*

38—41: (38) **now**, the priests being consecrated and initiated, and atonement made for them. **this .. altar**, for the whole people. **two .. continually,**_a_ daily remembrance and acknowledgment of sin. (39) **one .. morning**, acknowledging the possibility of sinning. **other .. even**,*b* acknowledgment of sin. (40) **tenth deal**, *i.e.* an omer or tenth part of ephah. **hin**, an Egyptian word: the hin = one-sixth of ephah. The fourth of hin = therefore about a pint and a half. **beaten oil**, *see* xxvii. 20. (41) **even**,*c lit.* between the two evenings: so the Lamb of God was offered. **shalt .. morning**, *see* v. 40. **sweet savour**, *see* v. 18.

The atonement the gist of the Gospel.—The late Thomas, Earl of Kinnoul, a short time before his death, in a long and serious conversation with the Rev. Dr. Kemp, of Edinburgh, thus expressed himself:—" I have always considered the atonement the character of the Gospel: as a system of religion, strip it of that doctrine, and you reduce it to a scheme of morality, excellent, indeed, and such as the world never saw; but, to man, in the present state of his faculties, absolutely impracticable. "The atonement of Christ, and the truths immediately connected with that fundamental principle, provide a remedy for all the wants and weaknesses of our nature. Those who strive to remove those precious doctrines from the Word of God do an irreparable injury to the grand and beautiful system of religion which it contains, as well as to the comforts and hopes of man. For my own part, I am now an old man, and have experienced the infirmities of advanced years. Of late, in the course of a severe and dangerous illness, I have been repeatedly brought to the gates of death. My time in this world cannot now be long, but with truth I can declare that, in the midst of all my past afflictions, my heart was supported and comforted by a firm reliance upon the merits and atonement of my Saviour; and now, in the prospect of entering upon an eternal world, this is the only foundation of my confidence and hope." Resting on the sure foundation God has laid in Zion, this venerable nobleman was released from a "body of sin and death," to be "for ever with the Lord," Dec. 27, 1787.*d*

42—44. (42) **door**,*a etc.*, entrance of tent. (43) **tabernacle**,*b* not so much the tabernacle as the space between it and the altar. (44) **sanctify**, consecrate, make holy: Israel to be a holy nation.

Influence of the atonement.—Kazainak was a robber chieftain, inhabiting the mountains of Greenland. He came to a hut where a missionary was translating the Gospel of John. He wanted to know what he was doing; and when the missionary told him how the marks he was making were words, and how a book could speak, he wished to hear what it said. The missionary read the story of Christ's sufferings; when the chief immediately asked, "What has this man done? has he robbed anybody? has he murdered anybody?" "No," was the reply: "he has robbed no one, murdered no one: he has done nothing wrong."—"Then why does he suffer? why does he die?"—"Listen!" said the missionary. "This man has done no wrong; but Kazainak has done wrong. This man has not robbed anyone; but Kazainak has many. This man has murdered no one; but Kazainak has murdered his brother, Kazainak has murdered his child. This man suffered that Kaizainak might not suffer; died, that Kaizainak might not die."—"Tell me that again," said the astonished chieftain; and the hard-hearted murderer was brought to the foot of the cross.

45, 46. (45) **dwell .. Israel,**[a] a holy God among a consecrated people. **will .. God,**[b] object of worship; source of blessing; sure protection; unerring guide, etc. (46) **know,** by the fruits of My presence, the manifestations of My glory, the communications of My will. **that .. Egypt,** I will be to them in the future the mighty deliverer that I have been in the past. **that .. them,**[c] this knowledge resulting in obedience and reverence shall render possible for Me and pleasant to them My dwelling among them.

God's presence among His people.—Take this text as illustrating the following propositions:—I. That God *does* condescend to dwell amongst His people. II. That, in order to possess this presence among us, He must be acknowledged as our Lord and God: "will be their God." Note the positiveness of the expression. "That I may dwell among them." See the condition on which this depends. III. That if God's presence is really merited by us, and bestowed upon us, great and unthought-of blessings will be the result.[d]

The Divine presence.—"I shall never forget," said a young minister, "the last words of my dear mother as I started from home to engage in business for myself. It was midnight. The family had remained up to make the last evening at home as pleasant as possible for the boy who was to go from them. The time for parting arrived. My mother came to me, and putting her arms around my neck, gave me a sweet kiss, and said in tones so full of sweetness, 'My dear boy, live near to God.' I shall never forget the sadness of that parting, the paleness of that dear face, the tenderness of that farewell embrace, but I remember them all, through the depth and force of that parting sentence, 'My dear boy, live near to God.'"

B.C. 1491.

"Let us accept different forms of religion among men, as we accept different languages, wherein there is still but one human nature expressed. Every genius has most power in his own language, and every heart in its own religion."—*Richter.*

the promise of Divine presence

[a] Zech. ii. 10; Jo. xiv. 17, 23; 2 Co. vi. 16.
[b] Re. xxi. 3.
[c] Jo. i. 14.

"The name of the Deity is spelt with four letters in a majority of languages. In Lat. *Deus;* Fr. *Dieu;* Gk. *Theos* (θεός); Ger. *Gott;* Scandin. *Odin;* Swed. *Codd;* Heb. *Aden;* Syr. *Adad;* Pers. *Syra;* Tartar. *Idgy;* Span. *Dias;* E. Ind. *Eysi* or *Zeni;* Turk. *Addi;* Egypt. *Amun* or *Zent;* Japan. *Zain;* Peruvian, *Lian;* Wallachian, *Zene;* Etrurian, *Chur;* Irish, *Deih;* Arab. *Alla.*"
[d] *A. G. Mitchell.*

"Nothing can be hostile to religion which is agreeable to justice."
—*Gladstone.*

CHAPTER THE THIRTIETH.

1—5. (1) **altar .. upon,**[a] *lit.* an incense-altar of incense, or, an altar perfumatory of perfume. (2) **cubit,** *etc.*, 1 ft. 9 in. long and broad, and 3 ft. 6 in. high. (3) **overlay,** gild or plate. **crown,** moulding. (4) **two .. rings,** one on each side. **corners,** *marg.* ribs, prob. in the centre of the side under the moulding. (5) **staves .. gold,** *see* xxv. 28.

The altar of incense (v. 1).—Introduction:—Rites and ceremonies of the old dispensations symbolical of things higher and

the altar of incense

its pattern, etc.

[a] Ps. cxli. 2; He. vii. 25; Re. viii. 3.

better under the new. Reminders of truths, etc. This altar of incense may remind us of many things concerning prayer. I. Its size: not very large, the smallest altar. A good prayer need not be long. God knows what we have need of. Like the Lord's Prayer, it may include much. II. Its design: symmetrical. Prayers should not be one-sided, but well-proportioned. Not all about one thing, or too many things. There was a simple beauty about the altar. Foursquare, crown of gold. III. Its material: choice, the best wood and metal. In prayer there may be the word of human infirmity and need; but there must be the fine gold of truth, etc. IV. Its place: in the Holy Place, in front of the vail that concealed the most holy. There should be prayer bef. entering God's house, as well as inside the house. V. Its use: to burn incense, offering to God of holy desire, thanksgiving, praise. Note—1. This incense, carefully compounded of the most precious ingredients. Not to be used for ordinary purposes. Prayer is holy to the Lord; 2. The lamp was lighted opposite when the incense was kindled. Prayer needs Divine illumination: should bear the light as being without hypocrisy; 3. The incense was burnt morning and evening. Our days should begin and end with prayer.

The fable of Midas: gold.—Bacchus once offered Midas his choice of gifts. "He asked that whatever he might touch should be changed into gold. Bacchus consented, though sorry that he had not made a better choice. Midas went his way, rejoicing in his newly-acquired power, which he hastened to put to the test. He could scarce believe his eyes, when he found a twig of an oak, which he had plucked, become gold in his hand. He took up a stone; it changed to gold. He touched a sod: it did the same. He took an apple from a tree; you would have thought he had robbed the garden of the Hesperides. His joy knew no bounds; and, when he got home, he ordered the servants to set a splendid repast on the table. Then he found, to his dismay, that, whether he touched bread, it hardened in his hand, or put a morsel to his lips, it defied his teeth. He took a glass of wine; but it flowed down his throat like melted gold." In consternation, fearing starvation, he held up his arms, shining with gold, to Bacchus, and besought him to take back his gift. Bacchus said, "Go to the River Pactolus, trace the stream to its fountain-head, there plunge your head and body in, and wash away your fault and its punishment." Hence Midas learned to hate wealth and splendour.

its place and use

6—10. (6) **before**,[a] *i.e.* outside, opposite the ark, and between the candlestick and the shewbread. (7) **burn .. morning**, emblem of prayer, thanksgiving. **he .. lamps**,[b] light of truth needful to teach us to pray aright. (8) **perpetual .. generations**,[c] repeated mercies call for constant praise. (9) **strange .. incense**,[d] *i.e.* of humanly-devised ingredients: our prayers must be of God's dictating. (10) **atonement**,[e] etc., *i.e.* on the great day of atonement.

The altar of incense.—Consider this as—I. 'A typical institution. Notice here—1. Its daily use; 2. Its annual expiation. II. An emblematic rite. In this view, it marks—1. The privilege of Christians; 2. The ground of their acceptance. Application: —(1) How highly we are privileged under the Christian dispensation; (2) What a holy people we should be unto the Lord.[f]

B.C. 1191.

"Each time thou wishest to decide upon performing some enterprise, raise the eyes to heaven, pray God to bless thy project, if thou canst make that prayer, accomplish thy work."—*L. Schefer.*

"Leave not off praying to God; for either praying will make thee leave off sinning, or continuing in sin will make thee desist from praying."—*Fuller.*

"O, when the heart is full, when bitter thoughts come crowding quickly up for utterance, and the poor common words of courtesy are such a very mockery, how much the bursting heart may pour itself in prayer."—*Willis.*

"Prayer is the wing wherewith the soul flies to heaven, and meditation the eye wherewith we see God."—*Ambrose.*

a He. ix. 24.
b Lu. i. 9.
c Ex. xxvii. 20, 21.
d Le. x. 1, 2.
e Le. x. 1, 28.
f C. Simeon, M.A.

"Perfect prayers without a spot or blemish, though not one word be spoken, and no phrases known to mankind be tampered with.

[Cap. xxx. 11–16.] EXODUS. 347

No one prays for me.—A young lawyer, who scoffed at religion, was made the subject of special prayer and effort by a pious young man. Not long after he was found at the prayer-meeting, but even the pastor hesitated to speak to him, supposing he had come merely for amusement. The young man continued faithful to his friend, and soon rejoiced in seeing him a humble believer in Jesus. The lawyer was riding with another companion of his own, not long after. "Out of the abundance of the heart the mouth speaketh;" so the conversation quite naturally turned to the subject of personal salvation. The new convert spoke freely, and told of the faithfulness of his kind friend K——, but for whom he might have been left to perish. "I had friends once who prayed for me," said the other, thoughtfully. "but I have been so careless they have all given me up. I don't suppose there is one person on earth who prays for me now." "You are mistaken," said the other. "K—— prays for you, very earnestly." "Is it possible?" said the youth, pausing in great astonishment. It was like a lightning flash to his soul—and not long after he, too, was rejoicing in Jesus. Are we offering such "effectual, fervent prayer," for any soul? Should the Christian ever suffer himself to be without the burden of some immortal spirit upon his heart? Such prayer does avail much. God's Word declares it, and the experience of ten thousand souls verifies the declaration. Whom will you take this week of all your impenitent acquaintances, as a subject of earnest prayer and labour?—*D. C.*

11–16. (11) **Lord .. Moses**, concerning the contributions of the people. (12) **sum**, census. **ransom,**[a] a gift acknowledging that he was ransomed. **that .. them**, inflicted for lack of faith, as manifested by withholding of the ransom. (13) **passeth**, they passed before the tellers, who counted them one by one. **half a shekel**, present value about 1s. 3½d. **shekel .. sanctuary**, *i.e.* shekel of full weight. **gerahs**, gerah,[b] *lit.* bean, prob. of the carob tree. **half .. Lord**, God no respecter of persons: rich and poor equal in His sight: the small sum not a measure of the blessing, but an acknowledgment of it. (14) **twenty .. above,**[c] the others exempted not bec. they had not been ransomed, but bec. they were without means. (15) **rich .. more,**[d] fr. a proud estimate of personal worth. **poor .. less**, on the plea of poverty or little value. (16) **take .. money**, so the ransom was called. **service**, use, purchase of material, etc.

The atonement money.—Let us notice—I. The tax levied. Being "a ransom, and an atonement for their souls," it evidently had a spiritual import; and, from the same being levied upon all, we observe—1. That the souls of men are of equal value in the sight of God; 2. That all equally need reconciliation with God; 3. That all must seek it on the same terms. II. Its use and application. It was intended—1. To obtain acceptance for the offerers; 2. To convey instruction to the rising generation; 3. To give honour unto God.[e]

The cost of redemption.—Yonder ermine, flung so carelessly over the proud beauty's shoulder, cost terrible battles with polar ice and hurricane. All choicest things are reckoned the dearest. So is it, too, in heaven's inventories. The universe of God has never witnessed aught to be reckoned in comparison with the redemption of a guilty world. That mighty ransom no such contemptible things as silver and gold could procure. Only by

---

B.C. 1491.

"always pluck the heart out of the earth and move it softly, like a censer, to and fro beneath the face of heaven."—*J. Weiss.*

"Premeditation of thought and brevity of expression are the great ingredients of that reverence that is required to a pious and acceptable prayer."—*South.*

"No man can hinder our private addresses to God; every man can build a chapel in his breast, himself the priest, his heart the sacrifice, and the earth he treads on the altar."—*J. Taylor.*

atonement money

[a] Ex. xxxviii. 25; 1 Ti. ii. 6; 1 Pe. i. 18, 19.

[b] "Used as the name of a small weight, as our word *grain* came into use from a grain of wheat."—*Spk. Comm.*

[c] Ex. xxxviii. 26; Ne. x. 32; Ma. xvii. 24.

[d] Job xxxiv. 19; Pr. xxii. 2; Eph. vi. 9; Jas. ii. 1.

[e] C. Simeon, M.A.

"Man is by nature weak he is born in and to a state of dependence. He therefore naturally seeks and looks about for help; and where he observes the greatest power, it is there that he applies and prays for protection."—*H. Brooke.*

348　　　　　　　　　　　EXODUS.　　　　　　　[Cap. xxx. 17—28.

B.C. 1491.

f T. L. Cuyler.

the brazen laver

a Ex. xxxviii. 8.

b Ps. xxvi. 6; Is. lii. 11; Jo. xiii. 8 —10; Jas. iv. 8; He. x. 12.

"Who has a breast so pure but some uncleanly apprehensions keep lets and law-days, and in session sit with meditations lawful?"—*Shakespeare*.

c B. Keach.

"Religion is universal; theology is exclusive—religion is humanitarian; theology is sectarian—religion unites mankind; theology divides it—religion is love broad and all-comprising as God's love; theology preaches love and practises bigotry. Religion looks to the moral worth of man; theology to his creed and denomination. Religion is light and love, and virtue, and peace, unadulterated and immaculate; but theology is the apple of discord, which disunites and estranges one from another."—*Dr. M. Lilienthal*.

d Spurgeon.

the holy anointing oil

its ingredients

a See Top. i. 110.
b Ibid.

one price could the Church of God be redeemed from hell, and that the precious blood of the Lamb,—the Lamb without blemish or spot,—the Lamb slain from the foundation of the world./

17—21. (17, 18) **laver**,*a* Heb., *kiyor*, large vessel or cauldron. **brass**, bronze. **wash**, symbolising the need of inward cleansing. (19) **wash .. hands .. feet**,*b* sym. the need of purity of action and life. (20) **that .. not**, through a thoughtless forgetfulness of their sin, or an unbelieving disregard of the Divine law. (21) **even to him**, *etc.*, successive generations guilty, and needing cleansing.

The brazen laver (vv. 18—25).—I. The brazen laver served for the priesthood to wash in before they ministered before God; typifying that inward washing by Christ's blood is necessary to us all before we can be accepted in God's sight. II. After the priests had washed and arranged themselves, they entered into the holy place: so, after the godly are washed by Christ's blood, and adorned with His righteousness, they become fit members of the true Gospel Church. III. They shall wash themselves, saith the Lord, lest they die (v. 21); to show that all persons must be purged by faith in Christ's blood, or die eternally. IV. He that toucheth, or washeth in, the laver, it being anointed, shall be holy, saith the Lord; signifying that all they who, by faith, touch Christ, shall be spiritually sanctified.*c*

Holy water.—Holy water, indeed! a vile mixture, neither fit for man nor beast. You see this liquid virtue at the doors of all the churches ready for the brows of the faithful, but what is far more curious, you observe it in little pots placed for use in the cemeteries: and that the passer-by may give the dead a showery benediction, there are little sprinkling brushes in the pots with which to scatter the precious mixture. A mother's tears over her dead babe are far more in place than such foolery. Holy water! bah! See how the rain pours down from yonder black cloud which has passed over the rugged crags of Pilatus; that sort of holy water is infinitely more likely to moisten the clay of the defunct, and bring plenteous blessing to the living, than all the hogsheads of aqueous fluid that priests ever mumbled over. Holy water, indeed! If there be such a thing, it trickles from the eye of penitence, bedews the cheek of gratitude, and falls upon the page of holy Scripture when the Word is applied with power. Standing where, when the rain is over, one can see the fair Lake of Lucerne brimming with crystal, and the clouds among the Alpine peaks all charged with moisture, rendered golden by the sun's clear shining, one feels indignant at the idea that the little driblets of nastiness in yonder pots and shells should be venerated, and all nature's reservoirs accounted common or unclean. It needs no small measure of prudence to restrain a man from tumbling pots and pans and holy liquids headlong to the ground. Human folly, how far wilt thou not go when priests lead thee by the nose!*d*

22—28. (22, 23) **myrrh**,*a* gum of a thorny tree (*balsamodendron myrrha*) growing in Arabia, etc., *see* Gen. xxxvii. 25. **cinnamon**,*b* the inner bark of a tree of the laurel kind (*cinnamomum zeylanicum*) growing in Ceylon, etc. **two .. shekels**, about 7 lb. 10 oz. **calamus**, Heb., *kaneh*. prob. the lemon-grass, a fragrant beard-grass (*andropogon aromaticus*; also called *cala-

[Cap. xxx. 29—38.] EXODUS. 349

*mus odoratus*ᵉ) growing in India and Arabia. (24) **cassia,**ᵈ Heb., *kiddāh*, the barkᵉ of an Indian tree (*cinnamomum cassia*). **hin,** *see* xxix. 40. (25) **art,** skill. **apothecary,** *lit.* a seasoner, having knowledge of method and quantity. (26—28) **anoint,**ᶠ *etc.*, consecrating the whole as one united and perfect whole to the service of God.
The anointing oil.—I. The universal need there is of the Holy Spirit's influence. 1. There was nothing under the Law so holy, but that it needed this Divine unction : 2. Nor is there anything under the Gospel which does not need it. II. His sufficiency for all to whom that influence is applied. This appears—1. From the preciousness of the ointment which was used ; 2. From the virtue infused into everything anointed with it. Application— (1) Seek the Holy Spirit for your own souls : (2) Guard against everything that may reflect dishonour upon Him.ᶠ
Sweet cinnamon.—A species of laurel, which grows in Ceylon and other parts of India. The leaves, when young, are red at the top. The fruit is about the size of a damson, and when ripe is of a black colour. The shrub grows from about twenty to thirty feet in height, and is spread into numerous branches. Neither the leaves nor flowers give forth any smell ; and it is not till the season for gathering the spice arrives, that a walk through the cinnamon gardens would yield delight in respect of fragrance. But when the Cingalese are engaged in their annual employment of peeling the twigs, the beauty of the gardens and the fragrance of the spice is delightful. The bark is stripped off with great rapidity by means of a sharp iron instrument, and then laid in the sun to dry, when it curls into the shape in which we see the cinnamon sticks, as sold in our shops.ʰ

29—33. (29) **whatsoever . . holy,** *see* xxix. 37. (30) **minister . . office,**ᵃ being specially set apart for that work. (31) **this . . generations,** the perpetual use significant of perpetual consecration. (32) **man's . . poured,** *i.e.* men not in the priesthood. **neither,** *etc.*, to be employed for private purposes. **holy . . you,** specially in regard to nature and use. (33) **stranger,** *see* xxix. 33.
Diffusing holiness.—Holiness is the only means by which holiness can be diffused. It is like salt, its usefulness to others must begin with itself. The man who fails to persuade himself to be holy is sure to be unsuccessful with others. It is the wise man that can impart wisdom to others, it is the good man that can diffuse goodness, and it is only the holy man that can diffuse holiness. Every man can bring forth to others only out of the treasures deposited first in his own heart. He who undertakes to restore mankind to clear-sightedness must be of clear and accurate vision himself, for he who has a beam in his own eye is not likely to remove either beam or mote from the eye of the world. The physician, who is to restore health to others, must not himself be fretting with the leprosy.ᵇ

34—38. (34) **stack,** *lit.* a drop ; prob. the gum of the storax-tree (*styrax officinalis*), found in Syria, etc. **onycha,** prob. the crustaceous covering of the shells of certain species of shell-fishᵃ (*trochus* and *conus*), somewhat resembling the human nail, hence the Heb. *shecheleth* may mean shell or scale. **galbanum,** the gum of a shrub, prob. *bubon galbanum*, or *galbanum officinale*, of

B.C. 1491.

c The root, the stem, and the leaves, when bruised, are very fragrant, and an aromatic oil is distilled from them.
d See *Top.* i. 110; Ps. xlv. 8.
e "It bears a strong resemblance to cinnamon, but is more pungent and of coarser texture. It was prob. in anc. times, as it is at present, by far less costly than cinnamon; and it may have been on this account that it was used in double quantity."—*Spk. Comm.*
f Cant. i. 3; He. i. 9; 1 Jo. ii. 20; Is. lxi. 1, 3; 2 Co. i. 21, 22; Le. viii. 10.
g C. Simeon, M.A.
h Bibl. Treas.

its use

a Le. viii. 12, 30.

"Man, being not only a religious but also a social being, requires for the promotion of his rational happiness religious institutions which, while they give a proper direction to devotion, at the same time make a wise and profitable improvement of his social feelings."—*H. Ballou.*

b Dr. Jenkyn.

the materials of the incense

a "It is found in the waters of India and Arabia, and is frequently

n.c. 1191.
used as an ingredient for incense; for although It is, in itself, by no means of fragrant smell, it enhances it if it is intermixed with other perfumes."—*Kalisch.*

b Ma. ix. 49.

"In the reformed churches the use of incense was abandoned at the same time with other practices which have been laid aside by them as without 'warrant of Scripture.'"—*Chambers' Ency.*

c *Chambers' Ency.*

Bezaleel
a Ezek. xxxvi. 1.

b Is. liv. 16; Jas. i. 17; Ac. ii. 4; 1 Co. xii. 11.

"Genius is supposed to be a power of producing excellences which are out of the reach of the rules of art — a power which no precepts can teach and which no industry can acquire."—*Sir J. Reynolds.*

' Genius is not a single power, but a combination of great powers. It reasons, but it is not reasoning; it judges, but it is not judgment; it imagines, but it is not imagination; it feels deeply and fiercely, but it is not passion. It

Don; *opoidia galbanifera* of Lindley, growing in Arabia, etc. **frankincense**, Heb. *lebonah*, gum of *boswellia serrata*, found in India, where it is called *salai*. (35) **confection**, compound, art, *etc., see* v. 25. **tempered**, salted, mixed, hence prob. the all, of our Lord.b (36) **beat..congregation**, as if for special Divine inspection. (37, 38) **perfume**, this like the oil, v. 32, specially made for an exclusive use.

Incense.—Heb. *miktar, kitter,* and *kitturoth.* A perfume, the odour of which is evolved by burning, and the use of which, in public worship, prevailed in most of the ancient religions. The incense at present in use consists of some resinous base, such as gum olibanum, mingled with odoriferous gums, balsams, etc. There is no regular formula for it, almost every maker having his own peculiar recipe. The ingredients are usually olibanum, benzoin, styrax, and powdered cascarilla bark. These materials well mingled are so placed in the censer or thurible as to be sprinkled by falling on a hot plate, which immediately volatilises them, and diffuses their odour through the edifice. Among the Jews the burning of incense was exclusively employed as an act or worship, and, indeed, would appear to have been in itself regarded in the light of a sacred offering. The same would also appear for the religion of Egypt; but the Persian sculptures exhibit the burning of incense as one of the marks of honour offered to royalty.c

CHAPTER THE THIRTY-FIRST.

1—5. (1. 2) **Bezaleel,**a (*in the shadow of God*); he appears to have been the general superintendent of the whole work, while he had special skill in working in metals, and in carving in wood and stone. (3) **filled,**b *etc.*, special gifts bestowed for a special work : all human skill, art, science, invention from God. (4) **devise..works,** *lit.* to think thoughts, ponder devices, devise works of skill. (5) **work..workmanship,** required in the construction of the tabernacle and its vessels.

Spiritual gifts (v. 3).—I. Prize them inestimably. II. Covet them earnestly. III. Seek for them diligently. IV. Ponder them frequently. V. Wait for them patiently. VI. Expect them hopefully. VII. Receive them joyfully. VIII. Enjoy them thankfully. IX. Improve them carefully. X. Retain them watchfully. XI. Plead for them manfully. XII. Hold them dependently. XIII. Grasp them eternally.

Art and prayer.—Fra Giovanni da Fiecoli, known as Beato Angelico, never commenced any work—whether an elaborate fresco or an illumination for a missal—without praying ; and he always, we are assured, carried out the first impression, "believing it to be an inspiration ;" he never retouched or altered anything left as finished. Mr. Ruskin affirms that when once we begin at all to understand the handling of any great executor, such as that of the three great Venetian painters, of Correggio, or Turner, the awe of it is something greater than can be felt from the most stupendous natural scenery. "For the creation of such a system as a high human intelligence, endowed with its ineffably perfect instruments of eye and hand, is a far more appalling manifestation of infinite power, than the making either of seas or mountains." In his *Modern Painters*, the Professor, with deliberate emphasis, applies the word "inspired" to Turner: "Be it irreverent or not," he says, "this word I must always use; and the rest of what work I have before me is simply to prove the truth of it with respect to" the great artist just named.[c]

6—11. (6) **Aholiab**, (*tent of his father*) whose special department was to engrave and embroider. **Ahisamach**, (*brother of support*) many fathers would have remained unknown had it not been for the fame of their sons. **wisehearted**, *see* xxviii. 3. **make .. thee**, acc. to the Divine pattern. (7—11) *see* above.
The Holy of Holies.—The Holy of Holies taught God's holiness—I. By the materials.—1. Acacia, or shittim-wood, most durable and light; shadowing forth the permanence of Divine requirements that were not grievous; 2. Gold, the symbol of Divine glory, teaching inner purity, unostentatious charity, and great glory. II. By the furniture. Ark of the covenant, mercy over law. III. By the regulations concerning it. Entered only once a year.[a] *The tabernacle*.—The tabernacle—I. Was of vast moment: it was the mystical embodiment of the Church. II. Was the parable of God in creation.—1. Darkness in His pavilion; 2. He has made a tabernacle for the sun (Ps. xix. 4); 3. The heavens were spread out like curtains. III. Secured the unity of God. IV. Meant meeting God: it was God's home amongst men. V. Makes room for Christ in our thoughts.—1. Our Sacrifice; 2. Our High Priest; 3. Our Mercy-seat; 4. Our Way.[b]
Inspiration of art and genius.—Consult the acutest poets and speakers—the suggestion occurs in a sermon by Dr. South—" and they will confess that their quickest and most admired conceptions were such as darted into their minds like sudden flashes of lightning, they knew not how or when;" and not by any certain consequence or dependence of one thought upon another, as in matters of reasoning. The reader of James Watt's narrative of his great discovery is struck by the fact, that the principle itself seemed to "flash" upon him at a particular time and place, with a spontaneity which has been called remarkable as a natural phenomenon, and which in other ages, says one of his biographers, would have been ascribed to supernatural agency. The system of anatomy which has made so memorable the name of Oken is, in Sir Humphry Davy's phrase, the consequence of a "flash of anticipation" which glanced through the naturalist's mind when he picked up, in a chance walk, the skull of a deer, bleached by the weather, and exclaimed, "It is a vertebral column."[c]

12—14. (12, 13) **verily .. keep**,[a] *see* xx. 8. **sign .. generations**, true sabbath-keeping, a sign by wh. the true Israel is known. **know .. you**, fr. the experience of Sabbath mercies, and observance of Sabbath service. (14) **for .. therein**,[b] *see* xx. 9—11. **soul .. people**, a threat afterwards executed.[c]
A poor man's argument for the Sabbath.—" I now beg permission," says a missionary, "to relate the simple argument of a pious poor man with a Sabbath-breaker. I had it from the poor old man a few weeks since, in the course of a conversation with him, which very much interested me; he is a member of our church at Mattishall. In reasoning with the Sabbath-breaker, he said, 'Suppose now, I had been at work hard all the week, and earned seven shillings; suppose now I met a man, and gave six

B.C. 1491.

is neither because it is all."-*Whipple*.

c F. Jacox, B.A.

Aholiab
"Art needs solitude, or misery, or passion. Lukewarm zephyrs wither it. It is a rockflower flourishing by stormy blasts and in stony soil."— *A. Dumas.*
"The highest art is always the most religious; and the greatest artist is always a devout man. A scoffing Raphael or Michael Angelo is not conceivable." — *Blackie.*
a Dr. Fowler.
b Ibid.
"The summit charms us, the steps to it do not; with the heights before our eyes, we like to linger in the plain. It is only a part of art that can be taught; but the artist needs the whole. He who is only half instructed speaks much and is always wrong; who knows it wholly is content with acting and speaks seldom or late."—*Goethe.*
c F. Jacox, B.A.

the law of the Sabbath
a Le. xix. 30; Ezek. xx. 10, 12; xxxvii. 28.

b De. v. 12; Ex. xxxv. 2; Is. lviii. 13, 14; Jer. xvii. 21, 22.

c Nu. xv. 32—35.

"If there be any person in a country enlightened with the

EXODUS. [Cap. xxxix. 15–18.

B.C. 1491.

"Gospel, who would banish the blessing of the Sabbath from the world, he must be a stranger to all the feelings of humanity as well as to all the principles of religion and piety."—*Jones.*

shillings out of the seven, what should you say to that?' 'Why, I should say that you were very kind, and that the man ought to be thankful.' 'Well, suppose he was to knock me down, and rob me of the other shilling; what then?' 'Why, then he would deserve hanging.' 'Well, now, this is your case; thou art the man: God has freely given you six days to work in, and earn your bread, and the seventh He has kept to Himself, and commands us to keep it holy; but you, not satisfied with the six days God has given, rob Him of the seventh; what then do you deserve?' The man was silenced."—*Thoughtful regard for the Sabbath.*—It is said of the pious and learned Mr. Gouge, that as he forbore providing suppers on the evening before the Sabbath, that servants might not be kept up too late, so he would never suffer any person to tarry at home to dress any meat on the Lord's day for any friends, whether they were mean or great, few or many.

a Ge ii. 1, 2.
"On the sides of an English coalmine, limestone is in constant process of formation. When the miners are at work, the dust of the coal colours the formation black; when they rest, it is white. For each Sabbath, the Sabbath has a white line; hence it is called 'the Sunday Stone.' There is also a record of the Sundays of all people."
"Life and blessing will attend the man who observes the Sabbath. The Sabbath of rest is a continual lesson to him to turn his eye from all created objects, and look to that heavenly rest into which God is entered, and which is promised to man."—*J. Milner.*
b Whitecross.

15—17. (15) **six ..done,** *etc., see* xx. 9. (16) **wherefore,** bec. God commands it and man needs it. (17) **sign,** *see* v. 13. **for .. days,**ᵃ *see* xx. 11. **refreshed,** *lit.* took breath, anthropomorphic expression.

Providence enforcing the law of the Sabbath.—An old man lived on the Jura mountain in Switzerland, where the winter is very long, and the summer very short, and where it is of great consequence to preserve their hay, and put it up in good order; because, if they run out, their cattle must starve, as the snow lies so long and so deep, they cannot go to their neighbours to get any, even if they had sufficient to spare. This man had the love of Jesus and the fear of God in his heart, and kept the Lord's-day as the Lord commands His people to keep it. Once Lord's-day, when the hay was just in the finest order for putting up, his sons came to him, and proposed to him to go and put up the hay: but he said, "Not so, my sons; this is the Lord's-day." However, his sons were tempted by the value of the hay, and the fineness of the weather, to prepare themselves for work; but the moment they put their forks into it, a storm broke over their heads, and the rain poured upon them in torrents—one of the most violent storms they ever had—and the hay was completely destroyed. The old man addressed his sons: "Thou shalt do no work on the Sabbath-day. Six days shalt thou labour, and do all thy work; but the seventh day is the Sabbath of the Lord thy God; in it thou shalt not do any work, thou, nor thy son, nor thy daughter, thy man-servant, nor thy maid-servant, nor thy cattle, nor thy stranger that is within thy gates. My sons," continued the old man, "you have done a work to save your hay, and the rain has destroyed it. Learn from this to respect the commandments of the Lord." His sons never forgot this lesson; and they never again did common work on the Lord's-day.ᵇ

the two tables of testimony in the handwriting of God
a Ex. xxiv. 12; Jo. i. 17; Jer. xxxi. 53.
"Laws were made to restrain

18. **when .. him,** concerning the preceding civil and ecclesiastical matters. **testimony,** so called bec. they testified God's will, and the people by receiving them testified their willingness to obey. **stone,**ᵃ a durable material sym. the durability of the law. **written .. God,** *i.e.* God not Moses the author of the moral law.

Revelation above human nature.—It is an historical fact which has not been sufficiently noticed, that human nature is always

Cap. xxxii. 1—6.] EXODUS. 353

below revelation. This fact indicates the Divine origin of revelation. Great discoveries are usually the product of preceding ages of thought. One mind develops the idea; but it is the fruitage of the age ripened in that mind. A pearl is found; but the location had been indicated by previous researches. But revealed religion is something different from this. It is separate from and superior to the thought of the age. It calls the wisdom of the world foolishness, and introduces a new stand-point, and starting-point, around which it gathers what was valuable in the old, and destroys the remainder. Hence it will always be found true that a struggle is necessary to bring up the human mind, and keep it up to the level of revealed religion, and that revealed religion produces the struggle. The human mind naturally falls below it; hence frequent struggles are necessary to restore it from its relapses. Even those who profess to be the friends of the dispensation retrograde so soon as its power is in anywise abated; and new applications of the same power have to be made to rescue them, and bring them up again nearer to the requirements of their dispensation.*b*

CHAPTER THE THIRTY-SECOND.

1—6. (1) **when .. delayed,**a *lit.* that Moses caused shame. **gathered,** tumultuously. **Aaron,** chief authority in absence of Moses. **up .. us,** they clamoured for a visible god. **for .. Moses,** spoken contemptuously. **man .. Egypt,** yet they are forced to admit the deliverance effected by him. **we .. him,** nor did they seem to care. (2) **break .. earrings,**b perh. he thought he should evade their request by demanding what they were unwilling to give. (3) **all,** *i.e.* the great majority. (4) **and .. tool,** finished it. **after .. calf,**c wh. appears to have been cast in a mould. **which .. Egypt,** the form of the idol seem: to identify it with Egyptian idolatry.d (5) **when .. it,** *i.e.* saw how the people regarded it. **said .. Lord,** breaking His law, yet professing to serve Him. (6) **sat .. drink,** feast on the remainder of the sacrifices. **rose .. play,**e singing, dancing, merry-making.

The impatient multitude (vv. 1, 2).—What was the matter with this giddy multitude? They were weary of waiting for— I. The promised land. They thought themselves detained too long at Mt. Sinai. We must first wait for God's laws before we catch at His promises. II. The return of Moses. Observe—1. How slightingly they speak of him: 2. How suspiciously they speak of his delay. III. A Divine institution of religious worship among them.f

The golden calf.—It has been questioned whether the reading c. "graving tool" is correct, since it is said that the calf was made in a furnace. But the tool, possibly either a file or a chisel, was employed to give a finishing touch to anything cast in a mould. Most of the large idols of antiquity had a wooden centre, the metal being, by way of preparation, cast into a flat sheet which the goldsmith hammered and spread out. This was evidently the nature of Aaron's calf, by the account given of its destruction. First of all it was burnt, and the interior being thus converted into charcoal, the coating was beaten or crushed to pieces.

VOL. I. M

B.C. 1491.

and punish the wicked: the wise and good do not need them as a guide, but only as a shield against rapine and oppression; they can live civilly and orderly, though there were no law in the world."—*Feltham.*
"Law is a rule of action, and in its most extensive sense it is applicable to all actions, whether of matter or mind."—*R. Watson.*
b *J. B. Walker.*

the golden calf

a Ex. xxiv. 13; Ac. vii. 39, 40; Ma. xxiv. 48—51; 2 Pe. iii. 3, 4.

b Ex. xii. 35.

c Ex. xx. 23; Ps. cvi. 19, 20.

d Josh. xxiv. 14; Ezek. xx. 8, xxiii. 3, 8.

e 1 Co. x. 7.

"The many-headed multitude, whom inconstancy only doth by accident guide to well-doing! Who can set confidence there, where company takes away shame, and each may lay the fault upon his fellow?"—*Sir P. Sidney.*

f *M. Henry.*

"It has been very truly said that the mob has many heads, but no brains."—*Rivarol.*

[Cap. xxxii. 7—14.

B.C. 1491.

Moses sent down to the camp
a De. ix. 12.
b Ex. xix. 8.
c Ne. ix. 16, 17; Is. xlviii. 4; Ac. vii. 51.
d Jer. xiv. 11, xv. 1; Jas. v. 16.
e "God is fain to bespeak His own freedom; as if Moses' devotion were stronger than God's indignation. Great is the power of prayer; able, after a sort, to transfuse a dead palsy into the hand of Omnipotence."—*Trapp.*
f Ma. iii. 9.

Moses intercedes for the people
a De. ix. 18, 26—29; Ps. cvi. 23.
b De. xxxii. 26,27.
c Ps. lxxix. 8—10.
d Ge. xxii. 15—17; Ho. vi. 13, 14; De. ix. 27.
e Ps. cvi. 45; Jer. xviii. 8, xxvi. 13; Joel ii. 13; Jo. iv. 2.
f M. Henry. "No attribute so well befits the exalted seat supreme, and power's disposing hand, as clemency. Each crime must from its quality be judged; and pity there should interpose, where malice is not the aggressor."—*Sir W'm Jones.*
"Let us pity the wicked man; for it is very sad to seek happiness where it does not exist. Let our compassion express itself in efforts to bring

7—10. (7) **go .. down**, quickly.*a* (8) **turned .. them**, so soon after their solemn promise.*b* (9) **stiff-necked**,*c* proud, resisting the yoke. (10) **now .. alone**,*d* do not interpose prayer.*e* **that .. them**, sugg. of God's intense anger. **and .. nation**,*f* transferring the fulfilment of the covenant to Moses.

Punishment to be prevented rather than cured.—Lord Coke, in his epilogue to his *Third Institute*, which treats of the Crown law, after observing that frequent punishment does not prevent crime, says—" What a lamentable case it is that so many Christian men and women should be strangled on that cursed tree, the gallows, insomuch as if in a large field a man might see together all the Christians that but in one year, throughout England, come to that untimely and ignominious end, if there were any spark of grace or charity in him, it would make his heart to bleed for pity and compassion." His lordship then proceeds to show that the method of preventing crime is—1. By training up youth in the principles of religion and habits of industry; 2. In the execution of good laws; 3. In the granting pardon very rarely, and upon good reasons. He then concludes —" that the consideration of this prevention were worthy of the wisdom of Parliament; and in the meantime expert and wise men to make preparation for the same *ut benedicat eis dominus.* Blessed shall he be that layeth the first stone of the building; more blessed that proceeds in it; most of all that finisheth it, to the glory of God and the honour of our king and nation."

11—14. (11) **why**, *etc.*,*a* not so much inquiring as earnestly seeking to dissuade. **which**, *etc.*, he refers to what had been done as an argument for continuance. (12) **Egyptians**,*b* *etc.*, why should Thy enemies have strengthened their false conceptions of Thy character? **repent .. people**,*c* *i.e.* spare them fr. punishment. (13) **remember**,*d* *etc.*, Moses pleads the covenant. (14) **Lord .. people**,*e* *i.e.* He was propitiated or reconciled by the intervention of a Mediator.

Moses' intercession (vv. 11—13).—Observe—I. His prayer: "Turn from Thy fierce wrath." II. His pleas. He urges—1. God's interest in them, and the great things He had already done for them; 2. The concern of God's glory; 3. The promises to the patriarchs. God's promises our pleas in prayer.*f*

The doctrine of mediation.—How vain, then, are the objections of the infidel against the doctrine of mediation, whose actions are observable everywhere around us, as well as forming one of the very foundations of the Christian revelation. The principle follows us into the minutest details of private life. What is he, who, in the hour of danger, interposes with his strong arm for the protection of the weak, or, with his maturer wisdom, for the rescue of the thoughtless and inexperienced, but a mediator between them and peril? What is she, who, with noiseless step, paces the sick room where the once stalwart man is laid prostrate with weakness, watching his eyes to catch their language, that the lips may be saved the necessity of speaking; anticipating his every want and desire, smoothing his pillow so softly that his aching head is eased, and his heart is reconciled to affliction by the thought of the loving attention it awakens—what is she but a mediator between him and the fell disease with which he is grappling? What is that mother, who, with simple and eloquent words, and tears more eloquent, pleads with a sterner father for the hopeless boy whose early sins have nearly caused his expulsion from under the parent roof—what but a mediator between him and the unknown evils that impended? What is she, who, by uncomplaining sighs and tears, and far more by patient, and therefore eloquent and silent, endurance, has weaned a degraded and besotted husband from the poison cup of intoxication or the maddening influence of the gaming-house to a love of his own hearth and home, and the society of those who are bone of his bone, and flesh of his flesh — what is she but a mediator between him and ruin?*g*

B.C. 1491.

him gently back to sacred principle, and if he persist, let us pity him the more for a blindness so fatal to himself."—*De Charnaye.*
g Ragg.

15—18. (15) **testimony,**^a see xxv. 16. (16) **writing** .. God, see xxxi. 18. (17) **Joshua**, who had patiently waited for Moses on the outside of the cloud, see xxiv. 13, 15. **there** .. **camp**, so his warlike nature interpreted it. (18) **not** .. **mastery**, shout of victory. **neither** .. **overcome**, the cry of distress. **noise** .. **sing**, sound of revelry.

Foolish haste of the mob.—A singular instance of a mob cheating themselves by their own headlong impetuosity is to be found in the life of Woodward, the comedian. On one occasion when he was in Dublin, and lodged opposite the Parliament House, a mob who were making the members swear to oppose an unpopular bill, called to his family to throw them a Bible out of the window. Mr. Woodward was frightened, for they had no such book in the house, but he threw out a volume of Shakespeare, telling the mob they were welcome to it. They gave him three cheers, swore the members upon this book, and afterwards returned it without discovering its contents.

Moses and Joshua hear the people
a De. ix. 15.

"The strongest minds are often those of whom the noisy world hears least."— *Wordsworth.*
"I will not choose what many men desire, because I will not jump with common spirits, and rank me with the barbarous multitude."—*Shakespeare.*

19—21. (19) **Moses** .. **hot,**^a and yet M. was the meekest of men. **cast** .. **hands,** *etc.*, prob. feeling that the people were unworthy of such a code of law. (20) **burnt** .. **fire,**^b some think it was a wooden calf overlaid with plates of gold. **made** .. **it,**^c he had cast it into the water that flowed from the rock. (21) **said** .. **Aaron**, whom he had left in charge. **what** .. **thee**, naturally supposing they had used strong coercion. **that** .. **them**, by permitting them to do this evil thing.

Moses' indignation against the worshippers of the golden calf.—Consider—I. The grounds of his indignation. The worshipping of the golden calf was a sin of most extraordinary enormity. II. His expressions of it. 1. He broke before their eyes the tablets of the Law, which God had committed to him; 2. He ground the calf to powder, and constrained the people to swallow it with their drink. Learn—(1) The danger of sanctioning the evils around us; (2) In what way we should be affected with them.^d

Curious gloss on the golden calf.—There was a French Bible, printed at Paris in 1538, by Anthony Bonnemere, wherein is related "that the ashes of the golden calf which Moses caused to be burnt and mixed with the water that was drunk by the Israelites stuck to the beards of such as had fallen down before it, by which they appeared with gilt beards, as a peculiar mark to distinguish those which had worshipped the calf." This idle story is actually interwoven with the thirty-second chapter of Exodus. And Bonnemere says in his preface this French Bible was printed in 1495 at the request of his most Christian Majesty Charles VIII., and declares further that the French translator

Moses breaks the tables of the Law
a Jer. xxxi. 32; Mk. iii. 5.
b De. ix. 21.
c Pr. xiv. 14; Ps. cix. 18.

"The powder mixed with their drink signified to them that the curse they had thereby brought upon themselves would mingle itself with all their enjoyments, and embitter them; that it would enter into their bowels like water, and like oil into their bones."—*Henry.*
"A mob is a society of bodies voluntarily bereaving themselves of reason, and traversing its work. The mob is man voluntarily descending to the

B.C. 1491.

nature of the beast. Its fit hour of activity is night. Its actions are insane, like its whole constitution." — *Emerson.*
d C. Simeon, M.A.

Aaron's excuse
a Ex. xvii. 4; Do. ix. 20; Ro. iii. 10.

b M. Henry.

"It is an easy and vulgar thing to please the mob, and not a very arduous task to astonish them; but essentially to benefit and to improve them is a work fraught with difficulty, and teeming with danger." —*Colton.*

"An excuse is worse and more terrible than a lie; for it is a lie guarded." - *Pope.*

"It is no disgrace not to be able to do everything; but to undertake or pretend to do what you are not made for, is not only shameful, but extremely troublesome and vexatious." - *Plutarch.*

"There are certain people fated to be fools; they not only commit follies by choice, but are even constrained to do so by fortune." —*La Rochefoucauld.*
c Montaigne.

the Levites slay the rebels
a Ge. iii. 10, 11; 2 Ch. xxviii. 19.
b Nu. xxv. 5.

"I know not how to tell thee! Shame rises in

" has added nothing but the genuine truths, according to the express terms of the Latin Bible, nor omitted anything but what was improper to be translated!" So that we are to look upon this fiction of the gilded beards as matter of fact; and another of the same stamp, inserted in the chapter above mentioned— viz., that "upon Aaron's refusing to make gods for the Israelites, they spat upon him with so much fury and violence that they quite suffocated him."

22—24. (22) let .. hot, language of respect, fear, conscious guilt. thou .. people," *etc.*, he shifts the blame to the people. (23) make .. us, it was for Aaron to command rather than to obey. (24) **whosoever .. off**, see v. 2. **cast .. fire**, and afterwards into a mould. **and .. calf**, so he glosses over his part in the manufacture of a god.

Aaron's excuse.—I. He deprecates the anger of Moses only, whereas he should have deprecated God's anger in the first place. II. He attempts to lay all the fault upon the people. Sin is a brat that nobody is willing to own. III. He casts a reflection upon Moses for staying on the mount so long. IV. He extenuates and conceals his own share in the sin: " I cast it into the fire, and there came out this calf."*b*

Anger not always to be repressed.—A slave who was a lewd and vicious man, but yet whose cares were somewhat fedde with philosophicall documents, having for some faults by him committed, by the commandment of Plutarche his master, beene stripped naked, whilst another servant of his whipped him, grombled in the beginning that he was whipped without reason, and had done nothing; but in the end, mainly crying out, he fell to rayling and wronging his master, vpbraiding him, that he was not a true philosopher, as he vanted himselfe to be, and how he had often heard him say that it was an vnseemly thing in a man to be angrie. And that he had made a booke of it: and now all plonged in rage, and engulfed in choller to cause him so cruelly to be beaten, was cleane contrarie to his owne writing. To whom Plutarche, with an vnaltered and mildesettled countenance, said thus vnto him—" What, thou raskall! whereby dost thou judge I am now angrie? Doth my countenance, doth my voice, doth my colour, or doth my speech give thee any testimonie that I am either mooved or chollerike? Me seemeth, mine eyes are not staringly-wilde, nor my face troubled, nor my voice frightfull or distempered. Doe I waxe redde? Doe I foame at the mouth? Dooth any word escape me I may repent hereafter? Doe I startle and quake? Doe I rage and ruffle with anger? For, to tell thee true, these are the right signes of choler and tokens of anger." Then turning to the party that whipped him, " Continue still thy worke," quoth he, " whilst this fellow and I dispute of the matter."*c*

25—29. (25) **naked**,*a* unruly, licentious, or as some think deprived of Divine protection. **Aaron .. enemies**, through sin as helpless as unarmed men. (26) **gate**, principal entrance. **place of judgment. who .. side?** *i.e.* those who truly repent of this sin; or were not accomplices. **let .. me**, range themselves around me. **all .. him**, not the whole of the Levites, but all who gathered to him were Levites. (27) **put .. aside**, *etc.*,*b* those slain were prob. in open spaces, the rest in their tents bewailing

[Cap. xxxii. 30—35.] EXODUS.

their guilt,*c* (28) **fell .. men**, being unarmed and helpless, *see* v. 25. (29) **even .. brother**,*d* jealous regard for God's law superior to natural instincts and affections. **that .. day**, when he sees you regard God more than man.

The two sides (v. 26).—I. There are but two sides that can possibly be taken. Each one is either a believer or an unbeliever. II. Every one, if faithful to himself, may ascertain on which side he is. III. There are good and sufficient reasons why all should be on the Lord's side. It is the side—1. That is right: 2. Of real and permanent enjoyment; 3. That must ultimately prevail.*e*

30—32. (30) **ye .. sin**,*a* of those who remained some had shared in it, while none had tried to prevent it. atonement, reconciliation, as Mediator, Intercessor. (31) **have .. gold,***b* in our day how many worship gold. (32) **if not**, *etc.*,*c* he would rather die than witness the destruction of his people.

Moses intercedes for Israel (vv. 31—33).—Notice—I. The sin of Israel. This was a dreadful compound of ingratitude, folly, and impiety. Its greatness will be easily imagined from the indignation which both God and Moses expressed against it. II. The intercession of Moses. 1. He reminds God of His relation to them; 2. He reminds Him also of His promise to their fathers; 3. He expresses his concern respecting God's honour among the heathen; 4. He humbly confesses the greatness of their sin; 5. He wishes to be punished in their stead. III. The reply of God. He remits their punishment.*d*

An example of intercession.—Said a servant to President Bacchus, "The physician said, sir, that you cannot live to exceed half an hour." "Is it so? Then take me out of my bed, and place me upon my knees; let me spend that time in calling upon God for the salvation of the world." It was done. He died upon his knees, praying for the salvation of sinners.

33—35. (33) **him .. book**,*a* only *him*, not the whole people. (34) **lead .. thee**,*b* the people shall be spared, and Moses' name not blotted out. **angel**,*c* *see* xxiii. 20. **nevertheless**,*d* *etc.*, "He chastised the individuals but did not take His blessing fr. the nation."*e* (35) **plagued**,*f* prob. ref. to future scourges and calamities suffered during their wanderings.

God's answer to Moses (vv. 33, 34).—Note that—I. God's administration is based on justice. II. Sin may be followed by endless results. Notice the sin of Adam—of Jeroboam. III. Pardon of gross sins is hypothetical, restraining alike from rashness and despair. IV. Prevailing prayer is offered from the altar of sacrifice.*g*

The Book of Life.—In the public registers, all that were born of a particular tribe were entered in the lists of their respective families under that tribe. This was the book of life; and when any of these died, his name might be considered as blotted out of the list. "In China, the names of the persons who have been tried on criminal processes are written in two distinct books, which are called the Book of Life and the Book of Death; those who have been acquitted, or who have not been capitally convicted, are written in the former; those who have been found guilty, in the latter. These two books are presented to the emperor by his ministers, who, as sovereign, has a right to erase

B.C. 1491.

"my face, and interrupts the story of my tongue."— *Otway.*

c See *Bush.*

d Nu. xxv. 11—13; De. xiii. 6—9; Ma. x. 37.

e Dr. *Magie.*

Moses' intercession

a 1 Sa. xii. 20—23; Ps. xxv. 11.

b De. ix. 18; Ex. xx. 23.

c De. ix. 12-14; Lu. x. 20; Phil. iv. 3; Rev. iii. 5, xx. 12, 15, xxii. 19; Jo. x. 27, 28; Da. xii. 1.

d C. Simeon, M.A.

vv. 30—35. Dr. R. Gordon, i. 457.

God pardons the people

a Ezek. xviii. 4.

b Ex. xxxiii. 14—17.

c Nu. xx. 16.

d Jer. v. 9; Ro. ii. 5, 6.

e Spk. Comm.

f Jer. ii. 19.

g Dr. Fowler.

"The book here spoken of is the book of life. It was even then the custom of every city in a literary community to keep a list of the burgesses. The Israelites were familiar with the custom of keeping a register of families (Ge. v. 1). Hence Moses

b.c. 1191.

uses a familiar figure in speaking of God's book (Ps. lxix. 29; Da. xii. 1).

any name from either; to place the living among the dead, that he may die; or the dead, that is, the person condemned to death, among the living, that he may be preserved. Thus he blots out of the Book of Life, or the Book of Death, according to his sovereign pleasure, on the representation of his ministers, or the intercession of friends."

CHAPTER THE THIRTY-THIRD.

the promise renewed
a Josh. xxiv. 1, 11.
b Ex. xxiii. 21, xxxiv. 9; Hab. i 13.
"Such declarations rather express what God justly might do, what it would become Him to do, and what He would do were it not for some intervening consideration, than His irreversible purpose; and always imply a reserved exception, in case the party offending were truly penitent."—*Scott*.
c *Chambers' Ency.*

the tabernacle pitched outside the camp
a Ex. xxvii. 21, xxix. 42.
b C. Simeon, M.A.
"The slightest sorrow for sin is sufficient, if it produce amendment; and the greatest is insufficient if it do not."—*Colton*.
"What is past is past. There is a future left to all men who have the virtue to repent and the energy to a-one."—*Lytton*.
"Repentance without amendment is like continually pumping without mending the leak."—*Dilwyn*.

1—3. (1) said, prob. during first sojourn on top of mount. saying, see Ge. xvii. 8; xxviii. 13. (2) drive out,ᵃ etc., see Ge. xv. 18, 21. (3) land .. honey, see iii. 8. will .. thee,ᵇ etc., this a merciful threat: the sins of a people might involve them in fruits of vengeance from a present God.

Honey.—From the remotest times, honey has been employed as an article of food; and to the ancients, who were unacquainted with sugar, it was of more importance than it now is. "A land flowing with milk and honey" offered the highest conceivable advantages to the Eastern mind. Taken in moderate quantity, honey is nutritive and laxative, but dyspeptic persons often find that it aggravates their symptoms. Its therapeutic action is prob. not very great, but it is employed with advantage to flavour and give a demulcent character to various drinks or mixtures prescribed for allaying cough; and in the form of *oxymel*, which is usually prepared by mixing honey, acetic acid, and water, it is frequently added to gargles, or mixed with barley-water, so as to form an agreeable, cooling drink in febrile and inflammatory affections, or given as an expectorant in coughs and colds.ᶜ

4—7. (4) heard .. tidings, the worst news a man or a people can hear is the threatened withdrawal of God. mourned, those who grieve not for sin will grieve for sin's punishment. (5) that .. thee, when I see thee obedient and truly penitent. (6) stripped .. Horeb, the scene of their sin the place of their repentance. (7) pitched .. camp, sign of Divine anger and alienation. sought .. camp,ᵃ hence the fact of Divine alienation was vividly impressed.

Repentance of the Israelites.—I. God is not able to exercise mercy towards an impenitent transgressor. He cannot do this, because it would—1. Be inconsistent with His own perfections; 2. Be ineffectual for the happiness of the persons themselves; 3. Introduce disorder into the whole universe. II. Where humiliation is manifested, mercy may be expected. This appears from—1. The very mode in which repentance is here enjoined; 2. The experience of penitents in all ages. Application:—(1) Consider what obstructions you have laid in the way of your own happiness; (2) Endeavour instantly to remove them.ᵇ

The delight of repentance.—"Which is the most delightful emotion?" said an instructor of the deaf and dumb to his pupils, after teaching them the names of our various feelings. The pupils turned to their slates: one wrote "joy," another, "hope;" another, "gratitude;" another, "love." One turned back with a countenance full of peace; and the teacher was surprised to find on her slate the word "repentance." He turned to her, and asked why it was the most delightful emotion. "Oh!" said she in the expressive language of looks and gestures, "it is so delightful to be humbled before God!"

B.C. 1491.

8—11. (8) **all .. up,** *etc.*, personal respect and reverence mingled with religious faith, fear, hope. (9) **Moses .. descended**,[a] a sign to the people that their intercessor was not rejected. (10) **people,** *etc.*, each praying for himself while Moses pleaded for all. (11) **face .. friend**,[b] *i.e.* familiarly, plainly. **departed .. tabernacle,** perh. this rendering is defective.[c]

Moses enters the tabernacle
[a] Ex. xxv. 22; Ps. xcix. 7.
[b] Nu. xii. 8; De. xxxiv. 10.
[c] It might read, "he turned again into the camp, (he) and his servant Joshua, the son of Nun, a young man; but He (i.e. the Lord, as appearing in the cloud) departed not out of the tabernacle." Thus Pode, Patrick, Scott, etc.

Moses and God (v. 11).—See in these words a picture of—I. Man's privilege: to speak with God. Moses spake with God— 1. Not as an enemy; 2. Not as a mere stranger; 3. But as a friend, face to face. Prayer the medium by which we may speak to God. II. God's favour. God condescended to speak to Moses not as a king speaks to a subject; but as a man to his friend. Our prayers He will—1. Hear; 2. Answer; 3. Answer for our best good. Learn—(1) Be grateful for the privilege of prayer; (2) Show your gratitude by using it aright.[d]

"Sorrow is Mt. Sinai. If one will go up and talk with God, face to face."—Beecher.

"There never was a great man unless through Divine inspiration."—Cicero.
[d] J. S. Lindsay.
[e] Sir R. K. Porter.

Eastern tents.—"The pasha's tent, pitched near Cairo, was a very lovely tent, and reckoned to be worth ten thousand crowns; it was very spacious, and encompassed round with walls of waxed cloth. In the middle was his pavilion of green waxed cloth, lined within with flowered tapestry, all of one sort; within the precincts behind, and on the sides of his pavilion, were chambers and offices for his women; round the pale of his tent, within a pistol shot, were above two hundred tents, pitched in such a manner that the doors of them all looked towards the pasha's tent; and it is ever so, that they may have their eyes always on their master's lodging, and be in readiness to assist him if he be attacked."[e]

12—17. (12) **thou .. me**,[a] anxious to know who the angel is. (13) **shew .. way,**[b] not only road to Canaan, but plans, purposes. **consider .. people**,[c] however unworthy and sinful, still *Thine.* (14) **presence**,[d] face. **rest**,[e] safety, also promised land. (15) **If,** *etc.*, God's presence the only guarantee for safety, success, happiness. (16) **wherein .. us?**[f] Divine presence the only proof of Divine favour: not wealth nor power. **separated .. earth,** the presence and worship of the true God the distinguishing characteristic of Israel. (17) **will .. spoken**,[g] having spoken well, the prayer answered to the full. **for .. sight,** desiring not wisdom, wealth, or power, but the presence of God.

Moses again intercedes
[a] Ex. xxxii. 34; Jo. x. 14, 15; 2 Ti. ii. 19.
[b] Ps. lxxxvii. 11, ciii. 7.
[c] De. ix. 26; Joel ii. 17.
[d] Ex. xiii. 21; xl. 34.
[e] Josh. xxi. 44.
[f] Nu. xiv. 14; De. iv. 7; 2 Sa. vii. 23; 1 Ki. viii. 53.
[g] Ge. xix. 21; Jas. v. 16.
[h] J. S. Knox, M.A.

Jehovah the Guide and the Rest of His people (v. 14).—Consider —I. The fact that, as mankind are divided into two classes— the believer and the unbeliever—so, too, the sense of God's presence will affect these persons differently, according to the classes to which they belong. II. The nature of the rest promised in the text. It was not a torpid rest that was promised; but a rest of active love.[h] *God with His people* (v. 14).—I. The journey. 1. From bondage; 2. In a wilderness; 3. Among enemies; 4. Going home. II. The company. 1. Divine; 2. Visible; 3. Continual; 4. Cheering. III. The rest. 1. Tranquil; 2. Perfect; 3. Godlike; 4. Eternal.[i]

"God governs the world, and we have only to do our duty wisely, and leave the issue to Him."—John Jay.
[i] W. W. Wythe.

The Divine Presence.—Captain Richardson, of the Sailors' Home, was recently speaking of a pious sailor, one of their

B.C. 1491.

"When we have broken our god of tradition, and ceased from our god of rhetoric, then may God fire the heart with His presence."—*Emerson.*

vv. 15, 16. *Dr. E. Payson,* ii. 517.

he prays to see the Divine glory

a Ex. xxiv. 16, 17; 2 Co. iv. 6; 1 Jo. iii. 2.

b Ex. xxxiv. 6, 7.

c Ro. ix. 15, 16.

d 1 Ti. vi. 16; De. v. 22; Ge. xxxii. 30; Is. vi. 5; Jud. xiii. 22.

e 1 Co. xiii. 12; 1 Jo. iii. 2; He. i. 3.

f *W. G. Maxwell.*

"Amid so much war, and contest, and variety of opinion, you will find one consenting conviction in every land, that there is one God, the King and Father of all."—*Maximus Tyrius.*

g *H. W. Beecher.*

God promises to partially reveal Himself

a Is. ii. 21; Ps. xci. 1–4.

b Jo. i. 18.

"Space is the statue of God."—*Joubert.*

"One of the most ancient hieroglyphic representations of God was the figure of an eye upon a sceptre, to denote that God

---

boarders, who spends much time in trying to do good to his brother seamen, in their boarding-houses and other places. One morning he noticed him coming out of his room, and going forth into the streets. Shortly after he returned to his chamber, and after remaining there some time, he again came down to go out. Captain Richardson having observed something peculiar in his manner, inquired after the reason of his movements. He replied, "After I got out, I found Jesus was not with me. I could not go without Jesus; so I went back to my closet to find Him. Now He is with me, and I can go." How simple and beautiful the lesson! How important the truth contained in the Christian philosophy of this humble sailor! "Without Me ye can do nothing."

18—20. (18) **shew .. glory,**^a answered prayer prompts larger requests: manifest Thyself to me. (19) **goodness,**^b this goodness is the glory of God. **gracious .. mercy,**^c God's will is final: God will be gracious and merciful to the humble, obedient, and penitent mind. (20) **canst .. face,**^d fully, completely: this from physical and moral imperfections of man. **there .. live,**^e the unveiled glory of the Infinite more than the finite could endure.

God not to be seen (v. 20).—Consider—I. In what God is invisible to us. He is invisible with regard to—1. His essential nature: "God is a Spirit;" 2. His almighty power. We see but slight manifestations of it; we cannot understand the whole. *That* is too great for our small minds. II. In what we may see Him. He is to be seen in the works of—1. Creation; 2. Redemption. Learn: (1) The power of God; (2) The impotence of man.^f

Human inability to comprehend God.—Partly arising from discussions, and partly from the remaining thorns and nettles with which sectarianism oftentimes whips us, there is a great deal of unnecessary sensitiveness on the part of many persons at calling Christ God. It is a sensitiveness that is not reasonable. No man can analyse or synthesise the Divine Being. No man can put together the elements of being, one and another, saying, "So much makes a man, so much more makes an angel, and now a God begins, and at length such elements make a full and complete Divinity." Have you an interior knowledge of what are the constituent elements of God? You are a man, therefore it is impossible for you to understand God fully."^g

21—23. (21) **thou .. rock,** only on the Rock, Christ, can we see the glory of the goodness of God. (22) **cleft .. rock,**^a "Rock of ages, cleft for me," etc. **while .. by,** prob. the cloud illuminated to its full extent passed by the place where Moses stood. **thou .. parts,** the skirts of the cloud, the fringe of the streaming radiance. **but .. seen,**^b by mortal man, a merciful regard for human weakness.

The invisibility of God.—Krummacher says, that an idolatrous tribe chose a Jew named Abiah to rule over them, who was greatly grieved at the idolatry of his subjects, and angry because they would not reform. The Lord said to him, "Thinkest thou I cannot destroy their idols? and yet I suffer the sun to shine upon them. Go thou, and do likewise." Abiah suffered them, and had a successful reign. When he came to die, he told the people that his son would be their king; that he had never seen his face, but should know his government by the fruits thereof. The people promised obedience, kept the promise, and prospered greatly, though they had never seen their king. Wise commands came from the palace. Like the beams of the sun, the kind influence of the invisible monarch spread over the nation, reaching every child of want. Then they all marvelled and said, "We see him not; how can he see us?" Then the people longed to see and bless him, as they did their idols. They made images of him. At last they came together before the palace-gates, and implored, "Oh, let our lord the king suffer us to see his face." Then the king came forth in simple raiment, and the people rejoiced and wondered, and said, "We know thy face;" for he had often walked among them unknown. Then the king said, "Now you see that I am a man like you. Think ye that this mortal flesh has reigned over you? Not so: that which has guided you ye cannot see; neither can I. Can ye see wisdom, kindness, and justice? Now ye see me, but ye do not see them. Judge ye what is my earthly form. Can the visible create the invisible? That which is in me, also, is not mine, but His who made me your king." After this the people returned to their homes, blessing their king. They broke in pieces their pictures, images, and idols, and believed in Him who is invisible.

B.C. 1491. sees and rules all things. The Egyptian hieroglyphic was a winged globe and a serpent coming out of it; the globe to signify God's eternity, the wings His active power, and the serpent His wisdom. The *Thracian* emblem was a sun with three beams; one shining upon a sea of ice, and melting it; another upon a rock, and melting it; and a third upon a dead man, and putting life into him."—*Bowes.*

CHAPTER THE THIRTY-FOURTH.

1—3. (1) **two .. first,**ª which were the work of God exclusively. **write .. tables,** God does not forget His law. (2) **ready .. morning,** see xxiv. 4. (3) **man .. thee,** *etc. see* xix. 11—13, 20—24.

Be ready in the morning (v. 2).—We may take this narrative as typical of the approach of a soul to God. Moses was—I. To go alone: "no man shall come with thee." God's communications to the soul are personal. II. To go "in the morning." 1. When his mind was most vigorous; we should not leave our praying until our body is too weary to enjoy or rightly perform the exercise; 2. When the works of God appeared most glorious. III. To go up the mount: "in the top of the mount." 1. Perhaps it was a steep and difficult ascent; but he who would have communion with God must "go up:" self-sacrifice and exertion are consequent upon seeking Him; 2. We know it was a solitary place: retirement is another necessity to devotion; 3. He was to ascend to the very top of the mountain. He was to have no commerce with man while he had communion with God. IV. To prepare: "Be ready." We need preparation before we enter the presence of God.ᵇ

The only God.—One day when Mr. Richards, missionary in India, was conversing with the natives, a fakeer came up, and put into his hand a small stone about the size of a sixpence, with the impression of two human likenesses sculptured on the surface; he also proffered a few grains of rice, and said, "This is Mahadeo!" Mr. Richards said, "Do you know the meaning of Mahadeo?" The fakeer replied, "No." Mr. R. proceeded, "Mahadeo means the great God, He who is God of gods, and besides whom there can be no other. Now, this great God is a

Moses commanded to prepare two tables of stone

a De. x. 1, 2; Ex. xxxii. 16; 2 Co. iii. 3.

"The God of merely traditional believers is the great Absentee of the universe."—*W. R. Alger.*

b *R. A. Griffin.*

"Let your sleep be necessary and healthful, not idle and expensive of time, beyond the needs and conveniences of nature; and sometimes be curious to see the preparation which the sun makes when he is coming forth from his chambers of the east."—*J. Taylor.*

"Spill not the morning (the quintessence of

B.C. 1491

the day) in recreation, for sleep itself is a recreation. Add not, therefore, sauce to sauces."— *Fuller.*

spirit: no one can see a spirit, who is intangible. Whence, then, this visible impression on a senseless, hard, immovable stone? To whom will ye liken God? or what likeness will ye compare unto Him? God is the high and lofty One that inhabiteth eternity, whose name is Holy. He hath said, 'I am Jehovah; there is no God besides Me.'" The poor fakeer was serious, respectful, and attentive; continually exclaiming, "Your words are true."

God passes before Moses

a Ex. xxxiii. 19.

b 2 Ch. xxx. 9; Ne. ix. 17; Ps. lxxxvi. 15, ciii. 8, cxii. 4, cxvi. 5; Joel ii. 13.

c Ro. ii. 4

d De. v. 10.

"Even the most enlightened nations put the thunder into the right hand of their Jupiter; they placed the eagle at his feet; they represented him as ruining the world by terror: but it was reserved for revelation to emblazon the Divine character in the full circle of His perfections. The name of the God of the Jews, who is also the God of the Christians, is 'The Lord God, merciful and gracious, long-suffering, and abundant in goodness and truth.'"--*Waugh.*

e Pres. Davies.

f T. F. Laurence.

a Dr. Fowler.

4—7. (4) took .. stone, to receive the Divine writing. (5) name,*a* character, perfections. *see* xxxiii. 19. (6) merciful,*b* pitiful, compassionate. gracious, treating with unmerited favour. long-suffering, holding back anger. abundant .. truth,*c* *i.e.*, in manifestations and gifts of, etc. (7) keeping, treasuring, preserving. thousands, mercy inexhaustible. visiting,*d* etc., *see* xx. 5, 6.

The name of God proclaimed by Himself (vv. 5—7).—The text teaches us—I. That God is self-existent and independent. II. That His existence is necessary. It is impossible for Him not to be. III. That He is eternal; He always was, is now, and ever will be. IV. That He is unchangeable, ever the same.*e* *God revealed* (vv. 5—7).—We learn from the text that God is a Being— I. Full of mercy and condescension. II. Patient in the endurance of man's iniquity. III. Who is the very essence of all truth and virtue. IV. Forgiving towards real penitents. V. Strictly just in His judgments. VI. Terrible in His wrath against the wicked.*f* *The Name* (vv. 5—7).—A name is a definition. God here describes Himself. Our duty to worship the God of the Bible. Accept all His revealed attributes. An idol made by the thought as offensive to God as one made by the hands. Our God is omnipotent. Mercy is His nature. I. Tenderness. II. Patience. III. Goodness. IV. Truth. His justice is still maintained—I. In His nature. II. In His action. Justified in Christ, we find mercy. Rejecting Christ, we are not cleared.*g*

A word to hinderers.—A pious man was sorely tried with the enmity of his wife against himself and his religion. She told Mr. Griffin that she often opposed him on account of his religion, which she could not bear, though it made him one of the best of husbands. From curiosity, and by his persuasion, she came to hear Mr. Griffin. "In addressing myself to the people," says Mr. G., "I said: 'There may be some here who are not only careless about their own salvation, but hindrances to others, preventing them either by force or temptation.' (I had no knowledge of such a person as Mrs. J—— in the world.) 'O sinner, if you are determined to go to hell, go by yourself; leave your child, brother, or partner, to go to heaven, if you will not.' This sentence sank into her heart like the stone into Goliath's forehead, and brought her to the feet of Christ. By her future behaviour she gave satisfactory evidence of her conversion to God. One soul seemed to govern herself and her husband. Their dwelling was no longer the abode of contention, but that of united prayer and love."

Moses asks for the presence of God

a Ps xxxiii. 12, xcv. 14; De. xxxii. 9; Jer. x.

8, 9. (8) haste, eagerness of religious feeling, desire, etc. bowed, *etc., see* iv. 31. (9) if, *etc., see* xxxiii. 13, 17. inheritance,*a* possession, a property to be cultivated.

The paternal character of God.—You cannot bring yourself into the posture and the feelings of a child, as you are commanded to do, if you are all the time praying to a governor, to a lawgiver, or to a judge. If you go before a judge you go before him in some relation of law; if you go before a lawgiver, you go before him as a subject; if you go before a governor or ruler, you go in your citizen's character, and in a civil relation. If you are going to God as a child, you must find a God that shall answer to a Father. There must be that which shall draw the child. And hence, Christians should accustom themselves to think of God as paternal, and not as governmental. It makes a great deal of difference whether you are in the habit of thinking of God as a Governor, or whether you are in the habit of thinking of Him as a Father. It makes a great deal of difference whether you draw your rules for measuring sin, and the desert of sin, from a government administered over a state, or from a government administered over a household,—from a government administered by a father, or from a government administered by a ruler.*b*

10—17. (10) **covenant**, mutual agreement. **marvels**, wonders, miracles. **people . . art**,*a* *i.e.* Israel. **with thee**, as My instrument. (11) **drive out**, *etc.*, *see* iii. 8. (12) **take heed**,*b* *etc.*, *see* xxiii. 32, 33. (13) **but ye**,*c* *etc.*, *see* xxiii. 24. (14) **jealous**,*d* *see* xx. 5. (15) **lest**, *etc.*, *see* vv. 10, 12, and ref. **one . . thee**,*e* invitations and inducements to sin are never wanting. (16) **take . . gods**,*f* *etc.*, influence of ungodly wives (Ahab—*Jezebel*; Solomon—*Egyptian princess*). (17) **thou . . gods**, *see* xx. 4.

Jehovah a jealous God (v. 14).—Let us contemplate—I. The character of God, as here described. 1. Jealousy *does* exist in the bosom of Jehovah; 2. Nor is this unworthy of His character. II. Our duty, as arising from it. We must not allow— 1. Any alienation of our affections from Him; 2. Any abatement in our attention to Him; 3. Any unnecessary intercourse with things which have a tendency to draw us from Him.*g*

The jealousy of God.—On one occasion, when the Assembly of Divines was convened at Westminster, a long-studied discourse was made in favour of Erastianism, to which none present seemed readily to give any reply. Mr. George Gillespie being urged by his brethren, the Scottish Commissioner repeated the substance of the whole discourse, and refuted it, to the admiration of all persons who were present. And what struck them most was, that though it was common for the members to take notes of what was spoken in the Assembly as helpful to their memory, and Mr. Gillespie appeared to be so employed during the delivery of that speech to which he afterwards made a reply, yet the persons who sat next him declared, that upon looking into his note-book, they found nothing of that speech written, but in different places, "Lord, send light—Lord, give assistance—Lord, defend Thine own cause."

18—20. (18) **feast . . bread**,*a* *see* xii. 15, 20. (19) **all**,*b* *etc.*, *see* xiii. 2, 12; xxii. 29. (20) **but**, *etc.*, *see* xiii. 13. **more . . empty**, each worshipper to bring an offering: we are all empty of goodness: may the Lord fill our hearts with His grace!

The over-ruling Providence of God.—Many persons live, and feel, and act as if God had nothing to do with the government of the world. They seem to shut Him out altogether. He comes to

---

B.C. 1491.

16; Zech. ii. 12.

"As the human mind is finite, and conceives by defining the limits of its thought, and as God is known to us to be infinite, it is evident that the human mind can never be capable of conceiving God adequately as He is, or of defining His being."—*Hodge.*

b H. W. Beecher.

God renews the covenant

a 2 Sa. vii. 23; Ps. cxlvii. 20; De. x. 21; Ps. lxv. 5.

b Josh. xxiii. 12, 13; Ps. cvi. 36.

c De. xii. 3.

d Jas. iv. 4.

e Pr. i. 10, xvi. 29; Jas. i. 14.
f Nu. xxv. 1, 2; Ezra ix. 2; 2 Co. vi. 14—16.

g C. Simeon, M.A.

Simonides, the philosopher, being requested to describe God, asked a week to think of it; and after that a month, and then a year; then, being still unable, he declined the task, declaring that the more he thought of so great a Being, the less he was able to describe Him.

the feast of unleavened bread

a Ex. xiii. 4—7, xxiii. 15.

b Lu. ii. 23.

"In many pieces, and in some

B.C. 1491.

ancient Bibles, Moses is described with horns. The same description we find on a silver medal; that is, upon one side Moses horned, and on the reverse the commandment against sculptured Images. Which is conceived to be a coynage of some Jews in derision of Christians, who first began that pourtrait."
—*Brown.*

c Sankey.

the Sabbath, the feast of weeks, etc.

a Ex. xxiii. 12, xxxv. 2; De. v. 12, 13.

b Le. xxiii. 15; De. xvi. 10, 13.

c De. xvi. 16.

d Ps. lxxviii. 55, lxxx. 8.

e Pr. xvi. 7.

f De. xxvi. 2, 10; Pr. iii. 9, 10.

g C. Simeon, M.A.

"The sun shines by his own nature, the air only by participation of light from the sun. So whatever good the creatures have, is by derivation from Jehovah, the fountain of being. Take away the light of the sun, the air ceaseth to shine, and so it is here."
—*Dr. Arrowsmith.*

Moses fasted forty days and nights
a Ex. xxxi. 18, xxxii. 16.

His own in the daily blessings of His providence and grace : but His own receive Him not. I do not mean that they deny the general superintendence of His providence over the greater affairs of the world, as, for instance, the succession of the seasons, the rise and fall of empires and kingdoms; but I mean that they forget that God overrules all the little concerns of every individual of His creatures; that every worm that creeps upon the ground, and every flower that blooms on earth, does so by His special interference, that every hair of our heads is numbered, and not a sparrow falleth to the ground without His special permission. These are the points which the Christian ever bears in mind, but which others, if they do not deny, at least forget: these are the points in which he acknowledges God. He knows that every pulse that beats within his veins, and, above all, every pulse of spiritual life of which he is sensible, beats at His command; so that there is not a single event of all his life, whether as regards his body or his soul, in which a Christian does not in this way acknowledge God. Every mercy and every comfort which he enjoys, he traces up to this source; and to see the hand of Omnipotence and Love in all these things is his delight and his privilege.*c*

21—26. (21) **six days,***a* *etc., see* xx. 9—11. **earing,** *see* Ge. xlv. 6. (22) **observe .. weeks,***b* or harvest. *see* xxiii. 16. (23) **thrice .. year,***c* *etc., see* xxiii. 14, 17. (24) **for .. out,***d* *etc., see* xxiii. 27—30. **borders,** limits of country, *see* xxiii. 31. **neither .. land,***e* suggestion of perfect safety; thy strength so great that such desires shall be useless. (25) **neither .. morning,** *see* xii. 10. (26) **firstfruits,***f* *etc., see* xxiii. 19.

The three yearly feasts at Jerusalem (vv. 23, 24).—We will—I. Draw your attention to the institution recorded in the text. Consider—1. Of what nature this appointment was: partly political, and partly religious; 2. What care God took to guard against the objections to which it was liable. II. Suggest some observations founded upon it. 1. The service of God is of paramount obligation; 2. They who serve the Lord shall be saved by Him.*g*

Earing.—"Earing" is an old English word for ploughing, and the Hebrew word so translated in the command before us is rendered ploughing in other passages—*e.g.* Ps. cxxix. 3. In several passages—such as Ge. xlv. 6; De. xxi. 4; 1 Sa. viii. 12; and Is. xxx. 24—the distinction between earing and harvest, which occurs in the text at the head of this article, is also observable. The Latin translators, Junius and Tremellius, for our words, "earing time," employ an expression which describes ploughing or tilling time only. Wiclif, in Lu. xvii. 7, has, "But who of you hath a servant earing." The Vulgate has "ploughing" or "tilling." Indeed, the old word ear, employed in such a sense, is derived from the Latin *arare*, to plough: as arable land, or, as an old translator of *Tacitus on the Manners and Customs of the Germans* has it, "earable land," signifies land that is under tillage.

27, 28. (27) **write .. words,** prob. preceding as well as following precepts. **tenor,** substance, meaning. (28) **forty .. nights,** *see* xxiv. 18. **neither .. water,** being miraculously sustained. **he .. wrote,***a* the Lord wrote, *see* v. 1.

Origin of alphabetical writing.—It is extremely probable that. previous to the giving of the Ten Commandments, Moses was only acquainted with the hieroglyphic mode of writing, which he must have learned in Egypt; but partly in order to discountenance image-worship, and partly with a view to give facility to the transmission of the truths of Divine revelation, God furnished him, on this occasion, with an important specimen of alphabetical Scripture, and taught him how to compose in it the other laws and ordinances which He revealed to him. At all events, it is certain, we possess no accounts from antiquity which go to show that letters were invented prior to the time of the Jewish legislator; while the concurrent testimony of ancient writers, referring their introduction to some period near to that in which he flourished, corroborates the opinion so naturally suggested by the sacred narrative, that they were of Divine origin.[b]

29—32. (29) **Moses .. shone,**[a] *etc.*, intercourse with God makes the whole character and life luminous with holiness. (30) **saw .. shone,** holiness imparted is holiness visible. **they .. him,** afraid of this human reflection of Divine holiness; how much more had they been afraid of that glory which Moses saw. (31) **Moses .. them,** telling them what he had seen and heard in the holy mount. (32) **afterward .. nigh,** summoned to a solemn convocation.

Moses and Stephen; the Old Testament and the New (v. 30; also *see* Ac. vi. 15).—Compare these men, not in their own lives, but in the periods to which they belong in God's revelation. We may compare—I. That view of God which is reflected from the face of each of them. II. The effect of the view on the immediate witnesses. III. The crisis of life in which each of these transfigurations occurred. IV. The effects on the surrounding spectators. V. The permanence of the transfigurations in the subjects of them.[b]

33—35. (33) **put .. face,**[a] "Moses had more glory by his vail than by his face."[b] (34) **he .. out,** the Source of glory could behold its reflection. (35) **and .. again,**[c] whence it appears that the radiance was not a passing gleam, but continued some time.

The vail of Moses (v. 33).—Notice the veiling of Moses' face as—I. A kind expedient. His face shone with a dazzling and overpowering splendour. To facilitate their access to him, he wears the vail. II. An instructive emblem. It represented—1. The darkness of that dispensation; 2. The blindness of the human mind; 3. The benefit to be expected from the promised Messiah.[d]

The influence of holiness.—There is an energy of moral suasion in a good man's life, passing the highest efforts of the orator's genius. The seen but silent beauty of holiness speaks more eloquently of God and duty than the tongues of men and angels. Let parents remember this. The best inheritance a parent can bequeath to a child is a virtuous example, a legacy of hallowed remembrances and associations. The beauty of holiness beaming through the life of a loved relative or friend is more effectual to strengthen such as do stand in virtue's ways, and raise up those that are bowed down, than precept, command, entreaty, or warn-

---

B.C. 1491.

"Moderation, which consists in an indifference about little things, and in a prudent and well-proportioned zeal about things of importance, can proceed from nothing but true knowledge, which has its foundation in self-acquaintance." — *Lord Chatham.*
b *Dr. Henderson.*

Moses descends from Sinai: his face shines
a 2 Co. iii. 7, 9, 11—17.
b *J. Ker.*

"Of Sertorius it is said that he performed his promises by words only; and of the Emperor Pertinax, that he was rather kind-spoken than beneficial to any. Not so the Almighty."—*Trapp.*

Moses places a vail over his face
a Nu. xii. 3; Mk. iv. 33; 1 Co. ii. 1—3, ix. 22.
b *Bp. Hall.*
c 2 Co. iii. 18.
d *C. Simeon, M.A.*

"His face was radiant, and dispersing beams like many horns or cones about his head; which is also consonant unto the original signification, and yet observed in the pieces of our Saviour, and the Virgin Mary, who are commonly drawn with scintillations, or radiant halos,

B.C. 1491.

about their head; which, after the French expression, are called the Glory."—*T. Brown.*

c *Dr. Chalmers.*

ing. Christianity itself, I believe, owes by far the greater part of its moral power, not to the precepts or parables of Christ, but to His own character. The beauty of that holiness which is enshrined in the four brief biographies of the Man of Nazareth has done more and will do more to regenerate the world and bring in everlasting righteousness, than all the other agencies put together. It has done more to spread His religion in the world, than all that has ever been preached or written on the evidences of Christianity.*c*

CHAPTER THE THIRTY-FIFTH.

Moses rehearses the law, etc.

the Sabbath

a Le. xxiii. 3.
b Nu. xv. 32, 35; Lu. xiii. 14, 15.
c Ex. xvi. 23.

"Sunday is the golden clasp that binds together the volume of the week."— *Longfellow.*

"However it may seem to lie, and in one respect really may lie, within the power of the will to shorten or lengthen the usual period of labour, I am thoroughly convinced that the six days are the really true, fit, and adequate measure of time for work, whether as regards the physical strength of man or his perseverance in a uniform occupation."—*Humboldt.*

"The division of the year into months is very old, and almost universal; but the period of seven days—by far the most permanent division of time, and the most ancient monument of astronomical knowledge—was used by the Brah-

1—3. (1) **gathered**, *etc.*, *see* xxxiv. 32. (2) **six days,**a *see* xx. 9, 10. **whosoever .. death,**b violation of the Sabbath a capital crime. (3) **kindle .. day,**c the Sabbath to be observed even at the cost of self-denial.

The unkindled fire (v. 3).—In the old time it was a law that each night, at a prescribed hour, a bell should be rung, on hearing which the people were to put out their fires (the curfew-bell, fr. *couvre-feu*, cover the fire). This a law not about putting fires out each day, but against lighting a fire on one particular day. Why this law? I. To show that on the Sabbath, especially, men should attend to the interests of the soul rather than the comforts of the body. II. To remove frivolous excuses for non-attendance on religious worship. III. To guard the time of females or servants from unrighteous invasion; and teach men that women had religious rights and duties equally with themselves. IV. To inculcate, in all, the duty of self-sacrifice in matters relating to the soul and God.

The Sabbath-day.—For not only did this mode of computing time thus universally prevail, but the seventh day was deemed sacred, and a certain mysterious power was supposed to attach to the number seven, as though it were an expression of a natural law. Tertullian, in his *Apology*, intimates that the Persians observed the Sunday with religious solemnities. His words are: —" If we, like them, celebrate Sunday as a festival and day of rejoicing, it is for a reason vastly different from that of worshipping the sun." Lucian tells us that children at school were exempted from their studies on the seventh days. Clemens Alexandrinus says: " The Greeks, as well as the Hebrews, observe the seventh day as holy." Josephus declares that no city of Greeks or barbarians could be found which did not acknowledge a seventh day's rest from labour. Philo asserts it to be a festival not peculiar to any one people or country, but common to the whole world; and that it may be named the general and public festival, and that of the nativity of the world. Porphyry relates that the Phœnicians consecrated one day in seven as sacred: and Theophilus of Antioch, writing of the seventh day, calls it the day which all mankind celebrate. Notices of its sanctity are also found in the writings of the ancient poets. Tibullus, giving an account of the excuses he assigned for his unwillingness to leave Rome, says.—

" Urged still to go, a thousand shifts I made,—
Birds now, now festivals, my voyage stayed."

So his words stand in the poetical translation of Grainger; but

Cap. xxxv. 4—9.] EXODUS. 367

when given in literal prose, they are, "Either I laid it on the birds," meaning that the auguries were not encouraging, "or else that bad omens detained me on the sacred day of Saturn." Two allusions may be given from Homer. In one verse he says, "Then came the seventh day, that is sacred." And in another, he says, "It was the seventh day, wherein all things were made perfect." Hesiod styles this day, "The illustrious light of the sun." Linus says of it, "The seventh day, wherein all things were finished;" and in another place, "The seventh day among the best things, the seventh is the nativity of all things. The seventh is among the chiefest, and is the perfect day." And the true theory of the time of creation is preserved in two hexameter verses, ascribed to Callimachus, of which the following is a literal translation:—"In seven all things were perfected in the starry heavens, which appear in their orbs in the revolving years."

4—9. this .. thing, *etc., see* xxv. 1—7.

Willinghood (v. 5).—I. Describe the willing offerer. He is one who gives—1. As much as he can; 2. Of the best he has; 3. Cheerfully, as to the Lord. II. Offer some reasons for willingness in the service of God. 1. The Lord loves a cheerful giver; 2. The value of what is given is enhanced by the manner of the bestowment; 3. The willingness of one stirs the liberality of others; 4. Good works are often delayed, fatally, by the slowness of giving; 5. We are not our own, and all we have is God's; 6. God gave "this unspeakable gift" willingly.

The uses of obedience.—A farm-servant, one day having nothing to do, was desired by his master to take his horse and cart, and help a man to remove rubbish from his house in a neighbouring village, to which the servant objected, on the ground of his having engaged to work only on the farm. "Oh, I see how it is," said his master; "you see there is no work here for the day, and you object to working elsewhere, that you may enjoy the sweet repose of sloth at home. But I shall find work for you. Go, take the wheelbarrow, and remove that heap of stones to the other side of the corn-yard, and tell me when you are done, that I may find more work for you." On finishing that job, he told his master, who then commanded him to wheel the stones back to the place from whence he had taken them. And on appearing again, after executing the second appointment, he was instructed to place the stones as first commanded, when, with humble tone, he said, "Oh, master, why are you making me to work in this way, for no good purpose?" To this was answered, "I have the best of ends in view by these appointments. I intended them, in the first place, for solving the question, whether you or I shall be master. Secondly, I intended them for leading you to see whether you would gain most by following your own foolish passions, or by complying with my reasonable appointments. Thirdly, I adopted this plan for showing you that it is better to work for little or no advantage than to go idle at the hazard of forming habits of sloth. And, lastly, I have acted on this odd plan for making the stronger impression on your mind, that you may not offend again, to your own injury more than to mine. If these ends are accomplished, neither my commands nor your service this day will be in vain." To this the servant bowed, with expressions of humble and grateful submission, and ever after studied to please by a becoming deportment.

B.C. 1491.

mins in India, with the same denomination employed ny uz and was alike found in the calendars of the Jews, Egyptians, Arabs, and Assyrians. It has survived the fall of empires, and has existed, among all successive generations."—*Mrs. Somerville.*

he exhorts Israel to offer material for the tabernacle

"The secret of giving affectionately is great and rare; it requires address to do it well; otherwise we lose instead of deriving benefit from it. This man gives lavishly in a way that obliges no one; the manner of giving is worth more than the gift. Another loses intentionally at a game, thus disguising his present; another forgets a jewel, which would have been refused as a gift. A generous booby seems to be giving alms to his mistress when he is making a present."—*Corneille.*

"We are as answerable for what we give as for what we receive; nay, the misplacing of a benefit is worse than the not receiving of it; for the one is another person's fault, but the other our own."—*Seneca.*

"When you give, give with joy and smiling."—*Joubert.*

EXODUS. [Cap. xxxv. 10—29.

B.C. 1491.

the wise-hearted are to do the work

a Ex. xxxvi. 1, 2;
1 Po. iv. 10.
b Le. xxiv. 5, 6.

"Genius may at times want the spur, but it stands as often in need of the curb."—*Longinus.*

"The effusions of genius are entitled to admiration rather than applause, as they are chiefly the effect of natural endowment, and sometimes appear to be almost involuntary."— *W. B. Clulow.*

the contributions of the people

"Posthumous charities are the very essence of selfishness, when bequeathed by those who, when alive, would part with nothing."— *Colton.*

"He was one of those men, moreover, who possess almost every gift except the gift of the power to use them."— *C. Kingsley.*

"Gifts are as gold that adorns the temple; grace is like the temple that sanctifies the gold."— *Burkitt.*

"That which is given with pride and ostentation is rather an ambition than a bounty."—*Seneca.*

a Dr. Fowler.

the labour of the women.

10—19. (10) **wise-hearted,**[a] *see* xxxi. 6. (11) **tabernacle,** *etc., see* xxvi. (12) **ark,** *see* xxv. 10. (13) **table,**[b] *etc., see* xxv. 23 ff. (14) **candlestick,** *see* xxv. 31. **oil,** *see* xxvii. 20. (15) **incense altar,** *see* xxx. (16) **altar** .. **offering,** *see* xxvii. 1, ff. (17) **court,** *etc.,* Ex. xxvii. 9. (18) **pins,** *see* xxvii. 19. (19) **garments,** *see* xxviii. 2, ff.

Wise-hearted work (v. 10).—The work of the wise-hearted : i.e. of those to whom God has given heavenly wisdom, will be—I. Promptly executed. II. Cheerfully undertaken. III. Perseveringly performed. IV. Graciously accepted.

The arch of Titus.—Amongst the existing memorials of ancient Rome there is one on which the Christian traveller cannot choose but gaze with an absorbing interest. It is the triumphal arch of Titus, reared to commemorate the capture of Jerusalem by that famous general, and representing, in its bas-reliefs, the golden candlestick, the table of shew-bread, and other sacred articles which formed part of the spoils of the Temple. These trophies were borne conspicuously in the triumphal procession with which Titus and his conquering army were honoured on their return to Rome. The sculptures on the arch represent this procession, the figure of the candlestick being the most prominent of the sacred symbols.

20—24. (20) **departed** .. **Moses,** to fulfil his command. (21) **stirred,** lifted. **willing,** *see* xxv. 2. (22) **brought** .. **gold,** all kinds of precious things : nothing too good for the service of God : **bracelets** = brooches, earrings, signet-rings, tablets, ornaments, as lockets. (23, 24) **with** .. **found,** *etc.,* they gave acc. to their possessions.

Willing workers (vv. 20—22).—I. The service of God must be as hearty as the service of Satan has been. They gave their earrings for the golden calf, now they give them to God. Saul passed from a persecutor to an apostle. Let grace succeed sin. II. The spirit in which an offering is made fixes its value. The widow's mite : Ananias and Sapphira. Not burnt offerings, but obedience. III. God invites, but does not compel. 1. The human will is incapable of compulsion ; 2. Every sin is in spite of God ; 3. The sense of guilt involves choice. IV. Everyone is to do what little he can. 1. Each brought what he had ; 2. Each man built over against his own house ; 3. All the littles make the whole. V. Christ's kingdom rests on the affections. 1. Its motive is love ; 2. Its object is the perfection of love. Learn—The Lord loveth a cheerful giver.[a]

The beauty of hands.—Two charming women were discussing one day what it is constitutes beauty in the hand. They differed in opinion as much as the shape of the beautiful member whose merits they were discussing. A gentleman friend presented himself, and by common consent the question was referred to him. It was a delicate matter. He thought of Paris and the three goddesses. Glancing from one to the other of the beautiful white hands presented for his examination, he replied at last, "I will give it up. The question is too hard for me. But ask the poor, and they will tell you the most beautiful hand in the world is the hand that gives."

25—29. (25) **women** .. **hands,** skilful at that particular work. (26) **wisdom,** skill, ingenuity, persevering toil. (27, 28) rulers, *etc.*, their gifts proportioned to their position and wealth. (29) **brought .. Lord,**[a] willinghood enhanced the value of each contribution.

Women's work for God (v. 25).—Consider—I. The work they did—1. Adapted to their sex; 2. Exercised their ingenuity; 3. Disciplined their patience; 4. Filled their hands and their hearts. II. The motives by which they were influenced. 1. Gratitude: their children saved from death; themselves thrust out from cruel bondage and toil; 2. Consideration of the benefits to be derived from the offices of religion. Every home would be blessed by the tent they helped to make. III. The whole as a lesson for women. 1. It prescribes their duty: to discharge religious service within the limits of womanly life. The *men* carved, etc., *they* span; 2. It suggests their privileges: to them as well as to men belongs the honour of working for God.

The art of giving.—A woman who was known to be very poor, came to a missionary meeting in Wakefield, and offered to subscribe a penny a week to the mission fund. "Surely," said one, "you are too poor to afford this?" She replied, "I spin so many hanks of yarn a week for my living, and I'll spin one hank more, and that will be a penny a week for the society."[b]

30—35. *See* xxxi. 2—6.

Men for the time.—I. There have been times in the world's history when special work needed to be done. III. this from the history of nations and of the Church. II. At such times the Lord of Providence has raised up special men to do the work needed. Columbus discovers a continent, to be presently a place of refuge for the persecuted. Gutenberg invents printing, and diffuses the Word of Life. Luther starts the Reformation, and an age of light succeeds the dark ages. Cromwell arises at a time when the liberties of England were threatened. Wesley is summoned to quicken a dead and formal religiousness. III. Learn not only to read the signs, and mourn over the necessities of the times: but also to trust in God, in whose hands are the hearts of all men, and the issues of life.

Ancient master artisans.—Taking the metals the Bible in its first chapters shows that man first conquered metals there in Asia, and on that spot to-day he can work more wonders with those metals than we can. One of the surprises that the European artists received when the English plundered the summer palace of the King of China, was the curiously wrought metal vessels of every kind, far exceeding all the boasted skill of the workmen of Europe. English surgeons going to India are advised to have their instruments gilded, because English steel cannot bear the atmosphere. Yet the Damascus blades of the Crusades were not gilded, and they are as perfect as they were eight centuries ago. There was one at the London Exhibition, the point of which could be made to touch the hilt, and could be put into a scabbard like a corkscrew, and bent every way without breaking. If a London chronometer maker wants the best steel to use in his chronometer, he does not send to Sheffield, the centre of all science, but to the Punjaub, the empire of the five rivers, where there is no science at all. The first needle ever made in Europe was made in the time of Henry VIII., and made by a negro; and when he died, the art died with him. Some of the first travellers in Africa stated that they found a tribe in the interior

---

B.C. 1491.

and the gifts of the rulers

[a] 1 Ch. xxix. 9, 14.

"True generosity is a duty as indispensably necessary as those imposed upon us by the law. It is a rule impressed upon us by reason, which should be the sovereign law of a rational being."
—*Goldsmith.*

[b] *Spurgeon.*

Bezaleel and Aholiab chosen for the work

"The whole difference between a man of genius and other men, it has been said a thousand times, and most truly, is that the first remains in great part a child, seeing with the large eyes of children, in perpetual wonder, not conscious of much knowledge,—conscious, rather, of infinite ignorance, and yet infinite power; a fountain of eternal admiration, delight, and creative force within him meeting the ocean of visible and governable things around him."—*Ruskin.*

"There is nothing so remote from vanity as true genius. It is almost as natural for those who are endowed with the highest powers of the

who gave them better razors than they had. Scott, in *Tales of the Crusaders,* describes a meeting between Richard Cœur de Lion and Saladin. Saladin asks Richard to show him the wonderful strength for which he is famous, and the Norman monarch responds by severing a bar of iron which lies on the floor of his tent. Saladin says, "I cannot do that;" but he takes an eider down pillow from the sofa, and, drawing his keen blade across it, it falls in two pieces. Richard says, "This is the black art; it is magic; it is the devil; you cannot cut that which has no resistance;" and Saladin, to show him that such is not the case, takes from his shoulders a scarf which is so light that it almost floats in the air, and, tossing it up, severs it before it can descend. George Thompson states that he saw a man in Calcutta throw a handful of floss silk into the air, and a Hindoo sever it into pieces with his sabre. We can produce nothing like this.*

CHAPTER THE THIRTY-SIXTH.

1—7. (1) **Bezaleel,**ª always named first, seems to have been the prime director. (2) **Moses,** who received the contributions, distributed them and explained the plan. (3) they .. morning, continuing to bring from day to day. (4) **came .. made,** wh. they were employed in making. (5) **people .. enough,** such the liberality of a people when acting under a Divine impulse. (6) let .. sanctuary, the first and last time such a proclamation was made. so .. bringing, now they have to be *constrained* to give. (7) **for .. sufficient,** *etc.,* there are always means for accomplishing great works when hearts are willing.

The offerings for the tabernacle (vv. 5—7).—It will be proper to notice—I. The object of the people's zeal. II. The operation. Note—1. Their liberality; 2. Their diligence. III. The effect: abundance of gifts: indeed, more than enough. Improvement:—(1) Let the cause of God be dear unto our souls; (2) Let us cordially and universally co-operate for its advancement.*ᵇ*

Giving heartily.—Andrew Fuller, when on a begging tour for the cause of missions, called on a wealthy nobleman to whom he was unknown, but who had heard much of Fuller's talents and piety. After he had stated to him the object of his visit, his lordship observed that he thought he should make him no donation. Dr. Fuller was preparing to return, when the nobleman remarked that there was *one man* to whom, if he could see him, he thought he would give something for the mission, and that man was Andrew Fuller. Mr. Fuller immediately replied, "My name, sir, is Andrew Fuller." On this, the nobleman, with some hesitation, gave him a guinea. Observing the indifference of the donor, Mr. Fuller looked him in the face with much gravity, and said, "Does this donation, sir, come from *your heart*? If it does not, I wish not to receive it." The nobleman was melted and overcome with this honest frankness, and, taking from his purse ten guineas more, said, "These, sir, these come from *my heart.*"

8—13. *See* xxvi. 1—6.

The beautiful to be wedded to the good in all work for God.—The old Spartans asked their gods to grant them the beautiful with the good. I. When God made a house for man, He made the world not only useful but beautiful—illuminated it with the lamps of heaven, threaded it with silver streams, embroidered it with rainbow-tinted flowers, perfumed it with incense from ten thousand painted chalices, and appointed it a band of feathered choristers in every grove. II. When God gave man a commission to build a house for Him, He modelled the plan upon His own principle by uniting the beautiful with the good. This, that it might be pleasant to the eye, as well as good for use; that it might be worthy of Him who was to be worshipped. III. If God willed thus in the case of a wandering people, whose resources were small; how much more in our case! All the treasures of our coffers, all our intelligence, are not too great to raise a temple for Him whom the heavens cannot contain. IV. If God was pleased to dwell in such a house, how beautiful and good should be that heart in which it is hoped that God will dwell: "with that man will I dwell," etc.

B.C. 1491.

should dimly perceive the beauty that is ever around us, 'a perpetual benediction.' Nature, that great missionary of the Most High, preaches to us for ever in all tones of love and writes truth in all colours, on manuscripts illuminated with stars and flowers."—*Mrs. L. M. Child.*

14—19. *See* xxvi. 7—14.

Right things in right places.—By the distribution of gold, silver, brass, goats' hair, rams' skins, and badgers' skins, etc., in the tabernacle, we are reminded of the fitness of things and the Divine order—right things in right places. I. We see this in the order of nature. II. We mark it in the distribution of offices and gifts in the Church. III. We are reminded of the application of this order to our own lives; 1. Not to employ our highest powers upon trivial matters; 2. Not to appoint our best men to small offices; 3. Not to give the best of each day, or of our life, to unworthy pursuits. Let the gold, silver, brass, be rightly bestowed and distributed.

A covering of badgers' skins.—Ruppel, an African traveller, is of opinion that the material referred to in the text is the skin of a species of *Dugong*, an animal of the whale order. It "is the only animal yet known that grazes at the bottom of the sea, usually in shallow inlets, which it is enabled to accomplish by its power of suspending itself steadily in the water, and by having its jaws bent down at an angle in such a manner as to bring the mouth into nearly a vertical direction, so that it can feed upon the sea-weeds much in the same manner as a cow does upon the herbage."ᵃ

they make the covering

"Work, according to my feeling, is as much of a necessity to man as eating and sleeping. Even those who do nothing which to a sensible man can be called work, still imagine that they are doing something. The world possesses not a man who is an idler in his own eyes." —*Humboldt.*

ᵃ *Kirby's Bridgewater Treatise.*

20—23. *See* xxvi. 15—18.

Common material made useful by the highest art.—Note how this applies in the familiar manufactures, and illustrate by facts in the life of man. I. Wood, a common material, applied by art to honourable uses: men—common men—adapted by Providence and grace to useful service (give examples). II. Wood, fashioned by art, had to be hacked, sawn, chiselled, planed, and polished before rendered fit for service: men have to undergo pruning and planing to qualify them for place and duty. III. Wood, common material, as much thought of by the Divine architect and His inspired servants, as rare gems and precious metals: men, however humble, are not overlooked by God, not to be undervalued by men.

Work honourable.—Nor can I honour too highly the faithful and industrious mechanic, the faithful man who fills up his chink in the great economy by patiently using his hammer or his wheel: for he does something. If he only sews a welt, or planes a knot, he helps to build up the solid pyramid of this

they make the boards

"Work is of a religious nature, — work is of a brave nature, which it is the aim of all religion to be. 'All work of man is as the swimmer's.' A waste ocean threatens to devour him; if he front it not bravely, it will keep its word. By incessant wise defiance of it, lusty rebuke and buffet of it, behold how it loyally supports

B.C. 1491.

him.—bears him as its conqueror along. 'It is so,' says Goethe, 'with all things that man undertakes in this world.'"—*Carlyle.*

a Dr. Chapin.

they make the silver sockets

"Beauty is an all-pervading presence. It unfolds to the numberless flowers of the spring; it waves in the branches of the trees and the green blades of grass; it haunts the depths of the earth and the sea, and gleams out in the hues of the shell and the precious stone. And not only these minute objects, but the ocean, the mountains, the clouds, the heavens, the stars, the rising and setting sun, all overflow with beauty."—*Channing.*

they make the coupling bars

"I know that there is one God in heaven, the Father of all humanity, and heaven is therefore one. I know that there is one sun in the sky, which gives light to all the world. As there is unity in God, and unity in the light, so is there unity in the principles of freedom. Wherever it is broken, wherever a shadow is cast upon the bright

world's welfare; while there are those who, exhibiting but little use while living, might, if embalmed, serve the same purpose as those forms of ape and ibis *inside* the Egyptian caverns,—serve to illustrate the shapes and idolatries of human conceit. At any rate, there is no doubt of the essential nobility of that man who pours into life the honest vigour of his toil over those who compose the feathery foam of fashion that sweeps along Broadway; who consider the insignia of honour to consist in wealth and indolence; and who, ignoring the family history, paint coats of arms to cover up the leather aprons of their grandfathers.*

24—30. *See* xxvi. 19—25.

Wooden planks and silver sockets.—This reminds us how, in the ways of God, the useful is adorned, strengthened, and preserved by the ornamental and precious. This may be true of—I. A man. He may be lowly, poor, etc., yet God takes care of him, provides him with protection. II. A life. It may be spent among the lowly. Its memory, like a silver socket, may save it from decay. III. An action. A lowly deed, perhaps; but enriched by the adornment of the Spirit. Grace gilds the cup in which the cold water is passed to the thirsty. IV. A prayer. Of homely material, yet the silver socket of faith fixes it secure in the promise and favour of God.

Examples of giving to God.—When Mr. Dee Stafford's property (Boston, U.S.) was worth £9,000, he resolved it should never be any more. Though he had given largely for years before, he then resolved that all his income should be devoted to benevolent objects. This was literally and faithfully carried out. During the remainder of his life he gave over £14,000 to benevolent objects. His memoir shows also the way to give. It was not done indiscriminately, but as the result of personal examination, giving his time and his earnest Christian labour and sympathy, as well as his money. He was a very busy man, and a very happy man, because his hands were more and more full of work for Christ, till he died at the age of sixty-three. He gave his sons £2,000 each, and the rest of his property he left to his wife, to be used according to her discretion in works of benevolence.

31—34. *See* xxvi. 26—29.

Union is strength.—The coupling bars by which the boards of the tabernacle were held together may well remind us of some of the advantages of union. I. By it weak things become strong. II. Plain things beautiful. III. Useless things of the highest service. IV. Detached things a compact whole. (Ill. each point and apply to individual and Church life.)

Past and present.—The tomb of Moses is unknown; but the traveller slakes his thirst at the well of Jacob. The gorgeous palace of the wisest and wealthiest of monarchs, with cedar, and the gold, and ivory, and even the great temple of Jerusalem, hallowed by the visible glory of the Deity Himself, are gone; but Solomon's reservoirs are as perfect as ever. Of the ancient architecture of the Holy City not one stone is left upon another, but the pool of Bethesda commands the pilgrim's reverence at the present day. The columns of Persepolis are mouldering into dust, but its cistern and aqueducts remain to challenge our admiration. The golden house of Nero is a mass of ruins, but the Aqua-Claudia still pours into Rome its limpid stream. The

Temple of the Sun at Tadmor, in the wilderness, has fallen; but its fountain still sparkles in its rays. It may be that London will share the fate of Babylon, and nothing be left to mark it save mounds of crumbling brickwork. The Thames will continue to flow as it does now. And if any work of art should rise over the deep ocean, time, we may well believe that it will neither be a palace nor a temple, but some vast aqueduct or reservoir; and if any name should flash through the mist of antiquity it would probably be that of the man who, in his day, sought the happiness of his fellow-men, rather than glory, and linked his memory to some great work of national utility or benevolence. This is the true glory, which outlives all others, and shines with undying lustre from generation to generation, imparting to works some of its own immortality, and in some degree rescuing them from the ruin which overtakes the ordinary monument of historical tradition or mere magnificence.

35—38. (35, 36) *see* xxvi. 31, 32. (37) see xxvi. 37. (38) **chapters,** capitals, heads of the pillars. **fillets,** connecting-rods.

The vail in the tabernacle.—I. Its similitudes.—1. Like nature between man and God: 2. Like forms and ceremonies between the worshippers and objects of worship; 3. Like parabolic teaching between carnal thought and Divine truth. II. Its beauty. Gorgeous colours, quaint devices, skilful making, hanging, etc. III. Its use—1. Important: to conceal the ark, etc., and yet by devices, etc., to reveal. To stimulate inquiry, and yet to check unhallowed curiosity; 2. Temporal: the vail is abolished; so nature, forms, parables, etc., will pass away: and we shall see face to face, know as we are known, be led into all truth.

The Bayeux Tapestry.—I had the satisfaction of inspecting that famous piece of furniture which, with great exactness, though in barbarous needlework, represents the history of Harold, King of England, and of William, Duke of Normandy, from the embassy of the former to Duke William, at the command of Edward the Confessor, to his overthrow and death, at the battle fought near Hastings. The ground of this piece of work is a white linen cloth, or canvas. The figures of men, horses, etc. are in their proper colours, worked in the manner of the samplers, in worsted, and of a style not unlike what we see upon the China and Japan ware: those of the men particularly, being without the least symmetry or proportion. There is a small border which runs at the top and the bottom of the tapestry, with several figures of men, beasts, flowers, and even fables, which have nothing to do with the history, but are mere ornaments. At the end of every particular scene there is a tree, by way of distinction; and over several of the principal figures there are inscriptions, but many of them obliterated. It is annually hung up on St. John's Day, and goes round the nave of the church, where it continues eight days; and at all other times it is carefully kept locked up in a strong wainscot press, in a chapel on the south side of the cathedral, dedicated to Thomas à Becket. By tradition it is called "Duke William's toilet," and is said to be the work of Matilda, his queen, and the ladies of her court, after he had obtained the crown of England.[a]

B.C. 1491.

rays of the sun of liberty, there is always danger to free principles everywhere in the world."—*Kossuth.*

"Union does everything when it is perfect; it satisfies desires, it simplifies needs it foresees the wishes of the imagination; it is an aisle always open, and becomes a constant fortune."—*De Sénancour.*

they make the vail

"The enemy of art is the enemy of nature. Art is nothing but the highest sagacity and exertion of human nature; —and what nature will he honour who honours not the human?'—*Larater.*

"Excellence in art is to be attained only by active effort, and not by passive impressions: by the manly overcoming of difficulties by patient struggle against adverse circumstances, by the thrifty use of moderate opportunities. The great artists were not rocked and dandled into eminence, but they attained to it by that course of labour and discipline which no man need go to Rome, or Paris, or London, to enter upon."—*Hillard.*

[a] Dr. Ducarel.

CHAPTER THE THIRTY-SEVENTH.

B.C. 1491.

they make the ark

"It is to labour, and to labour only, that man owes everything possessed of exchangeable value. Labour is the talisman that has raised him from the condition of the savage; that has changed the desert and the forest into cultivated fields; that has covered the earth with cities, and the ocean with ships; that has given us plenty, comfort, and elegance, instead of want, misery, and barbarism."--*M'Culloch.*

a Dr. Kitto.

they make the mercy seat

"There are no principles but those of religion to be depended on in cases of real distress; and these are able to encounter the worst emergencies, and to bear us up under all the changes and chances to which our life is subject."--*Sterne.*
"The guardian angel of life sometimes flies so high that man cannot see him; but he always is looking down upon us, and will soon hover

1—5. *see* xxv. 10—14.

Precious things for holy uses.—The ark was simply a chest or coffer to contain certain sacred articles. I. It was made of durable material, to teach that the contents were to be carefully preserved. II. It was skilfully and artistically wrought, to teach that the intelligence and strength of men were to be employed in the guarding of the law, etc., of God. III. It was constructed for easy transport, to teach that man should make provision for the accompaniment of religion and its services through the journey of life.

Sacred chests.—Perhaps the most curious analogy (to the ark) is that discovered by Captain Cook at the island of Huaheine, in the South Sea. In Hawkesworth's account it is described as "a kind of chest, or ark, the lid of which was nicely sewed on, and thatched very neatly with palm-nut leaves. It was fixed upon two poles, and supported upon little arches of wood, very neatly covered: the use of the poles seemed to be to remove it from place to place in the manner of our sedan-chair. In one end of it was a square hole, in the middle of which was a ring touching the sides, and leaving the angles open, so as to form a round hole within, a square one without. The first time Mr. (afterwards Sir Joseph) Banks saw this coffer, the aperture at the end was stopped with a piece of cloth, which, lest he should give offence, he left untouched. Probably there was then something within; but now the cloth was taken away, and, on looking into it, it was found empty. The general resemblance between this repository and the ark of the Lord among the Jews is remarkable; but it is still more remarkable that, upon inquiring of the boy what it was called, he said *Ewharre no Etau*, the "house of God;" he could, however, give no account of its signification or use.a

6—9. *See* xxv. 17—20.

The cherubic symbol.—Teaches—I. That the place of a true worshipper should be near the mercy seat. II. That the aspect of the true worshipper should be towards the mercy seat. III. That the spirit of the true worshipper should be God-ward. (The cherubs were at *each end* of the mercy seat: their *faces* towards it, and their wings *spread out on high*.)

Place of worship.—It was formerly, and for hundreds of years, only in one place where God would be worshipped. Salvation was then confined to the Jews: and where the ark of the covenant, and the high priest, and the altar, and all the symbols of salvation were, there, and there only, would God be worshipped. Thither "the tribes of the Lord went up;" and, when banished from that place, they worshipped "*towards it.*" So Solomon prayed at the dedication of the Temple. So Daniel, in captivity in Babylon, threw open his window, "and prayed towards Jerusalem." "I will worship toward Thy holy temple." There the great God actually dwelt in the Holy of Holies; and only there would He be worshipped. But our Lord teaches the woman of Samaria that this whole system of local worship was passing away. "The hour was coming," nay, "was come," when the mountain of Samaria would be as holy as Mount Zion, the steppes

[Cap. xxxvii. 10—24.] EXODUS. 375

of Russia and the prairies of America as sacred as the land of Canaan; when neither in one place more than in another would God be worshipped, but anywhere and everywhere. "Where two or three are gathered together in My name, there am I in the midst." That is My church, My temple, My holy mountain, in the midst of the hearts of My praying people. "To all that in every place call upon the name of Jesus Christ our Lord."a

B.C. 1491.

nearer to us."— Richter.

a Dean Close.

10—16. *See* xxv. 23—29.

Working to order.—It is often difficult to get an order well executed. He who gives the order should know what he wants. He who executes it should not assume that he knows better than his employer. In the making of the tabernacle we have an example of working to order. I. Who gave the order? God, who also gave full directions. II. Who executed the order? Bezaleel, etc. Men divinely inspired for the work. III. How was their work done? 1. With fidelity to the plan; 2. With docility; they asked no questions, made no suggestions; 3. With dispatch, as to time.

The dignity of labour.—An American President, when asked what was his coat of arms, replied, "A pair of shirt-sleeves." Lord Tenterden was proud to point out to his son the shop in which his father had shaved for a penny. A French doctor once taunted Flechier, Bishop of Nismes, who had been a tallow-chandler in his youth, with the meanness of his origin; to which he replied, "If you had been born in the same condition that I was, you would still have been but a maker of candles."

they make the table for the shew bread

"It is not work that kills men; it is worry. Work is healthy; you can hardly put more upon a man than he can bear. Worry is rust upon the blade. It is not the revolution that destroys the machinery, but the friction. Fear secretes acids; but love and trust are sweet juices." —*H. W. Beecher.*

17—24. *See* xxv. 31—39.

The beautiful light-holder.—For the purpose of suspending the lamps, a more simple form and more common materials would have served the purpose. The candlestick was to be not only of pure gold, but richly ornamented. It illustrates—I. The light-giving Word: the Bible. Its truths "more precious than gold; yea, than much fine gold." Its beauty equal to its preciousness. It is richly adorned with flowers of poetry, biography, etc. II. Light-giving men: ministers and teachers who hold forth the word of life, and light—for "the entrance of Thy Word giveth light"—should be adorned with the true beauty of zeal, faith, love, etc.

Candles in the Church.—In the *Formula* of Marculphus, edited by Jerome Bignon, he tells us, with respect to lights, that the use of them was of great antiquity in the Church; that the primitive Christians made use of them in the assemblies which they held before day out of necessity, and that afterwards they were retained even in daylight, as tokens of joy, and in honour of the Deity. Lactantius says, speaking of the absurdities of the wax lights in Roman churches. "They light up candles to God, as if He lived in the dark; and do they not deserve to pass for madmen who offer lamps and candles to the Author and Giver of light?" It is really astounding to our ideas that wax candles as long as sergeants' pikes should be held as necessary in the worship of God. That it is so held, and that by a large class of Christians, every one must allow, for they may have ocular demonstration of the singular fact. The show is, however, extremely imposing. 35,750 pounds of wax lights were burned every year, for 900 masses said in the Castle of Wittenburg! Melanchthon speaks

they make the candlestick

"Art does not imitate nature, but it founds itself on the study of nature,—takes from nature the selections which best accord with its own intention, and then bestows on them that which nature does not possess, viz., the mind and the soul of man."—*Lytton.*

"All men are in some degree impressed by the face of the world; some men even to delight. This love of beauty is taste. Others have the same love in such excess that,not content with admiring, they seek to embody it in new forms. The creation of beauty is art."—*Emerson.*

EXODUS. [Cap. xxxviii. 1–16.

B.C. 1491.

they make the incense altar

"Never believe to be right those who, having but a piece of metal in their chests, would persuade you that to be cold is to be wise. Warmth is the vivifying influence of the universe, and the heart is the source of noble deeds."—*Kossuth*.

"There are many people the brilliancy of whose minds only depends upon the heart. When they open that, it is hardly possible for it not to throw out some fire."—*Desmahis*.

of a Jesuit who said that "he would not extinguish one taper, though it were to convert all the Huguenots."

25—29. (25—28) *see* xxx. 1–5. (29) **anointing oil**, *see* xxx. 23—25. **incense,** *see* xxx. 34—37.

The preparation of the heart for prayer.—The incense-altar to be of a given form, and size, and material, and no other, may teach—I. That the praying heart should be equally balanced, having its sides of affection, sympathy, faith, earnestness, lying towards all quarters of truth. II. That the praying heart should be pure in thought, desire, etc., and be framed by the direction of the Spirit of God. III. That the praying heart should accompany the believer in all his wanderings, etc.

Ancient incense-chariot.—An incense-chariot has been found in a tomb at Cervetri, in Etruria, and unquestionably belongs to a very remote date of the archaic period. It was used in the ritual services of the ancients, and seems to have been destined for burning incense. The perfume was, no doubt, placed in the concave part, and the fact of the whole being mounted upon four wheels proves that it was intended to be moved about, which, in religious services, may have been a great convenience. The borders are adorned by a row of flower-shaped ornaments, the graceful forms of which will be appreciated in the side-view of it. It must be confessed, indeed, that this monument, which is marked by the stamp of an antiquity so remote, displays within the limits of its archaic character much elegance, conveying the idea of a highly refined taste, suitable to a person of dignified position, as the priest or king may be supposed to have been, to whom the article belonged.

CHAPTER THE THIRTY-EIGHTH.

they make the altar of burnt offering

"Religion is the fear of God, and its demonstration good works; and faith is the root of both: 'For without faith we cannot please God;' nor can we fear what we do not believe."—*Wm. Penn*.

a Dr. Kitto.

1—7. *See* xxvii. 1–8.

The altar of burnt-offering.—It is thought that both this altar and the larger one made by Solomon, by which it was superseded, had the lower part of the hollow filled up, either with earth or stones, in compliance with the injunction in xx. 24, 25. Josephus says, that the altar used in his time at the Temple was of unhewn stone, and that no iron tool had been employed in its construction. None of the altars which the Scripture assigns to either the tabernacle or Temple were of this construction, but that erected at Mt. Ebal by Joshua was so (Josh. viii. 31), and apparently others which were set up in different parts of the land of promise. It seems to us that the commands in chap. xx. about altars applies as a general instruction respecting those which the Israelites might wish to erect in the provinces or elsewhere, and which were not in constant use, without excluding for the chief place of worship such particular variations as its peculiar circumstances, and the frequent sacrifices which were offered there, rendered necessary.*a*

they make the brazen laver, and the court

Sceptics ridicule the statement that looking-glasses were used

8—15. (8) **laver,** *see* xxx. 18. **looking-glasses,** bronze mirrors, Heb., *maroth*. fr. *raah*, to see, den. reflectors or mirrors of any kind, (9—15) *see* xxvii. 9—15.

The bronze mirrors and the brazen laver (v. 8).—When Carthage was besieged, the women gave their long hair to make the strings of bows and catapults; here was vanity sacrificing at the shrine

Cap. xxxviii. 16—23.] EXODUS. 377

of patriotism. The warriors of Carthage would think the hair looked better in the bow than on the head. Here the women give up their mirrors to provide a laver—the instruments by which the perfections of their own face or form were studied, to provide the means for the perfection of the priest. I. Vanity sacrificing at the shrine of humility. II. The instruments of pride become a visible confession of uncleanness. III. The women of Israel looked lovelier in the sight of God than they had to themselves in their own mirrors. IV. The mirror reflected physical and transient beauty; the laver revealed moral and abiding grace.

16—20. *See* xxvii. 15—19.

The uses of little things.—Only the pins, *i.e.* the tent-pegs, of the tabernacle; yet I. Having an important use. By them the whole structure fastened. II. Teaching important truths; 1. The character made up of little graces: 2. The life made up of little actions; 3. Time made up of small moments. III. As carefully made and preserved as the rest. Take care of little things; the great will then take care of themselves.

Influence of small things.—In walking across Alpine glaciers, travellers often come upon narrow and apparently insignificant fissures, that seem to be merely superficial cracks; while the guides know that, if one but sounds them, they shall be found sinking down, fathom after fathom, to the very bottom; and sometimes, though small to the eye externally, they are cavernous, and at the bottom torrents rush and roar in silence; for so far down are they, and so ice-covered, that their angriest noises are smothered. It is just so in human life. The depths of the heart often have the smallest openings out to the surface. The least important things have the most power in this world of expressing themselves. The most wonderful interior histories sink down in life, unuttered and unrecorded. Griefs, longings, loves, and fears, flow hidden and voiceless as if the heart were a glacier.[a]

21—23. (21) **sum,**[a] reckoning, inventory. (22, 23) see xxxi. 2, 6.

Co-partnerships in labour (vv. 22, 23).—I. A great building firm: Bezaleel and Aholiab. 1. Bezaleel, *i.e.* under the protection of God. Happy for the toilers of earth when they labour under the Divine care: 2. Aholiab, *i.e.* the tent of his father. His name may suggest the happiness of those who bring honour to their father's house; or of those who provide a home for their father. II. A union of great talents for a great work. The administrative talent of the one, the skill and taste of the other. One grasps the whole, the other works it out in all the details.

Good works.—Good works may exist without saving principles, and therefore cannot contain in themselves the principles of salvation; but saving principles never did, never can, exist without good works. Men often talk against faith, and make strange monsters, in their imagination, of those who profess to abide by the words of the Apostle interpreted literally, and yet in their ordinary feelings they themselves judge and act by a similar principle. For what is love without kind offices whenever they are possible? (and they are always possible, if not by actions, commonly so called, yet by kind words, by kind looks, and where

---

B.C 1491.

in such early times (Ex. xxxiii. 5), glass not having been discovered. But Moses says they were of "brass." Brazen mirrors, or reflectors, for the same purpose as the mirrors we now make from glass, *were* used by the Egyptians and Israelites in those times.

they make the hangings for the court

"The just temper of the human mind in this matter may, nevertheless, be told shortly. Greatness can only be rightly estimated when minuteness is justly reverenced. Greatness is the aggregation of minuteness; nor can its sublimity be felt truthfully by any mind unaccustomed to the affectionate watching of what is least."—*Ruskin.*

a H. W. Beecher.

the sum of the tabernacle

the chief workmen

a He. viii. 2, ix. 12.

"Clay and rock are given us, not brick and squared stone. God gives us no raiment; He gives us flax and sheep. If we would have coats on our backs we must take them off our flocks and spin them and weave them. If we would have anything of benefit, we must earn it, and earning it, must be-

EXODUS. [Cap. xxxix. 1–14.

B.C. 1491.

come shrewd, inventive, ingenious, active, enterprising."—Beecher.

b Coleridge.

the gold, the silver, and the brass

"Accustom yourself to master and overcome things of difficulty; for if you observe, the left hand for want of practice is insignificant, and not adapted to general business; yet it holds the bridle better than the right, from constant use."—Pliny.

"What is difficulty? Only a word indicating the degree of strength requisite for accomplishing particular objects; a mere notice of the necessity for exertion; a bugbear to children and fools; only a mere stimulus to men."— S. Warren.

these are out of our power, by kind thoughts and fervent prayers!) yet what noble mind would not be offended, if he were supposed to value the serviceable offices equally with the love that produced them; or if he were thought to value the love for the sake of the services, and not the services for the sake of the love?*b*

24—31. (24) **gold**, reckoning 3,000 shekels to the talent of 125 pounds, and this at £4 per ounce, the gold would be worth about £175,000. (25) **silver**, about 40,000, *i.e.* at 5*s.* per ounce. (26) **bekah**, *lit.* a half. **six .. men**, *see* xii. 37. (27, 28) **chapters**, *etc., see* xxxvi. 38. (29) **brass**, *i.e.* bronze, value uncertain. (30, 31) **sockets**, *see* xxvi. 37, also xxvii. 10, 17.

The cost of a great undertaking.—The cost of the tabernacle reminds us—I. That however great the cost, it may be defrayed by the many. II. That however small each contribution, it helps to make up the great whole. A child's handful of goat's hair not to be despised. III. That nothing is impossible to diligent minds, industrious hands, and earnest hearts.

Cost of churches built by Sir Chris. Wren:—

	£	s.	d.		£	s.	d.
St. Paul's	736,752	2	3½	St. Michael, Queenhithe	4,351	3	8
Allhallows the Great	5,641	9	0	,, Wood-street	2,554	2	11
,, Bread-street	3,348	7	2	,, Crooked-lane	4,641	5	11
,, Lombard-street	8,058	15	6	,, Cornhill	4,686	5	11
St. Alban's, Wood-street	3,165	0	8	St. Martin, Ludgate	5,378	18	8
St. Anne and Agnes	2,448	0	10	St. Matthew, Friday-street	2,301	8	2
St. Andrew's, Wardrobe	7,060	16	11	St. Margaret Pattens	4,986	10	4
,, Holborn	9,000	0	0	,, Lothbury	5,310	8	1
St. Antholin's	5,685	5	10¾	St. Mary, Abchurch	4,922	2	4¼
St. Austin's	3,145	3	10	,, Magdalen	4,291	12	9½
St. Benet, Grailchurch	3,583	9	5¼	,, Somerset	6,579	18	1¼
,, Paul's Wharf	3,328	18	10	,, -at-hill	3,980	12	3
,, Fink	4,129	16	10	,, Aldermanbury	5,237	3	6
St. Bride's	11,430	5	11	,, -le-Bow	8,071	18	1
St. Bartholomew's	5,077	1	1	,, -le-Steeple	7,388	8	7¾
Christ Church	11,778	9	6	St. Magnus, Loudon Bridge	9,579	10	10
St. Clement, Eastcheap	4,365	3	4½	St. Mildred, Bread-street	3,705	13	6½
,, Danes	8,786	17	0	,, Poultry	4,654	0	7¾
St. Dionis, Back Church	5,737	10	8	St. Nicholas Cole Abbey	5,042	6	11
St. Edmund the King	5,207	11	0	St. Olav, Jewry	5,580	4	10
St. George, Botolph-lane	4,509	4	10	St. Peter's, Cornhill	5,647	8	2
St. James, Garlic-hill	5,357	12	10	St. Swithin, Cannon-street	4,687	4	6
,, Westminster	8,500	0	0	St. Stephen, Walbrook	7,652	13	8
St. Lawrence, Jewry	11,872	1	9	,, Coleman-street	4,020	16	6
St. Michael, Basinghall	2,822	17	1	St. Vedast, Foster-lane	1,853	15	6
,, Royal	7,455	7	9				

CHAPTER THE THIRTY-NINTH.

the cloths of service and the ephod are made

1—5. (1, 2) **cloths**, *see* xxxi. 10. **garments**, *etc., see* xxviii. 4, 6. (3) **beat .. plates**, the malleability of gold long known. **wires**, wh. appear to have been *cut* into threads and not *drawn*, as now. (4, 5) *See* xxviii. 7, 8.

"Gold, like the sun, which melts wax and hardens clay, expands great souls and contracts bad hearts."— Rivarol.

The curious girdle (v. 5).—I. Its use. 1. To give strength to the wearer; 2. To provide a fastening for the breastplate. One part of the dress not complete without the other. II. Its suggestiveness. It may remind us of—1. Strength (1 Sa. xxii. 4; Ps. xviii. 39; lxv. 6): 2. Gladness (Ps. xxx. 11): 3. Sorrow (Lam. ii. 10); 4. Service (Jo. xiii. 4, 5); 5. Truth (Eph. vi. 14). All these—strength, gladness, etc., may remind us of the material and devices of the Christian's girdle.

they make the breastplate

6—14. (6, 7) *See* xxviii. 9—12. (8—14) *See* xxviii. 15—21. *The jewelled breastplate.*—Precious stones always counted

[Cap. xxxix. 15—26.] EXODUS. 379

among the earth's most precious things: these of the breastplate were—I. Various: ill. diff. qualities and characteristics of the tribes. II. Costly: the gifts of the rulers, Ex. xxxv. 27; prob. the rulers of each tribe presented the stone for their tribe. III. Durable: a lasting memorial. Names engraven would not be obliterated. IV. United in one breastplate: twelve tribes, one nation; many individuals, one people. V. Worn near the heart: significance of this as applied to our Great High Priest.

The breastplate.—The meaning of the Heb. word, *choshen* rendered *breastplate*, appears to be simply *ornament*. The names given to it in nearly all versions must therefore be regarded as glosses. The LXX., Philo, Josephus, and the son of Sirach (Ecclus. xlv. 10) call it λογεῖον, or λόγιον, and the Vulgate *rationale*, in ref. to its use as an oracle in making known the judgments of the Lord. It was from this use that it was designated the *Choshen of Judgment*. Symmachus renders the word as a receptacle, or bag (δόχιον), from what appears to have been its form. The names given to it by most modern translators (like our own *breastplate*) relate merely to its place in the dress. It was to be made of a piece of cunning work (the work of the skilled weaver, see xxxv. 35), the same in texture and materials as the ephod. This piece was a cubit (two spans) in length, and half a cubit (a span) in width, and it was to be folded together so as to form a square of half a cubit. Whether it was doubled with no other purpose than to give it stability (*Rosenmüller, Knobel, Kalisch*), or in order to form what was used as a bag (*Gesenius, Bähr, Fürst*), has been questioned; but the latter appears to be by far the more likely alternative. On the mode in which it was attached to the ephod, see v. 22, ff.[a]

15—21. See xxviii. 22—28.
The binding of the breastplate (v. 21).—I. How it was bound.— 1. With wreaths of gold; 2. By command of God; 3. Above and below. II. Where it was bound. 1. Over the breast; 2. To shoulderpieces and girdle. III. Why it was bound. That it might not be loosed. Significance of this How, Where, and Why.

The ephod.—This appears to have been a sort of close robe or vest reaching from the shoulders to the loins. It was made of a rich cloth of fine linen, embroidered with blue, purple, scarlet, and gold. The inferior priests also wore ephods, but they were of plain linen. It does not appear that even these were worn at first by the common priests. But we afterwards read of common priests wearing ephods; and indeed Samuel, who was only a Levite, wore one; and David, who was not even a Levite, did the same when he danced before the ark. On one occasion Saul consulted the Lord by Urim, and consequently used the ephod of the high priest (1 Sa. xxviii. 6); and on another occasion David did the same (1 Sa. xxx. 7). It is thought by some, however, that Saul and David did not themselves use the ephod, but directed the priest to use it, and this seems the most probable interpretation. It is, however, an opinion entertained by some, that the kings had a right to wear the ephod, and to consult the Lord by Urim and Thummim without the intervention of the priest.[a]

22—26. See xxviii. 31—34.
Woven throughout.—I. Simplicity of the robe of the ephod.

B.C. 1491.

"I cannot but take notice of the wonderful love of God to mankind, who, in order to encourage obedience to His laws, has annexed a present as well as a future reward to a good life; and has so interwoven our duty and happiness together, that while we are discharging our obligations to the one we are, at the same time, making the best provision for the other."—*Melmoth*.

"I do not want the walls of separation between different orders of Christians to be destroyed, but only lowered, that we may shake hands a little easier over them."—*Rowland Hill*.
a Spk. Comm.

they make the fastenings of the breastplate

"As the smallest birds of the earth are not taken without the will of our heavenly Father, so nothing good or evil happens to God's children without His provident will."—*Cawdray.*

a Dr. Kitto.

they make the robe of the ephod

EXODUS. [Cap. xxxix. 27-31.

B.C. 1491.

"Lord Bacon had music often played in the room adjoining his study. Milton listened to his organ for his solemn inspirations; and music was ever necessary to Warburton. The symphonies which awoke in the poet sublime emotions might have composed the inventive mind of the great critic in the visions of his theoretical mysteries."—*Disraeli.*

"Without the definiteness of sculpture and painting, music is, for that reason, far more suggestive. Like Milton's Eve, an outline, an impulse, is furnished, and the imagination does the rest."—*Tuckerman.*

On this no human handiwork, or embroidery of man's device. II. Typical character. Robe of our High Priest, a seamless coat woven throughout, Jo. xix. 23, and "that it should not rend;" so Christ's coat was not divided, Ma. xxvii. 35; cf. Ps. xxii. 18.— *Bells and pomegranates* (v. 26).—I. Let us listen to the bells. The sweetest music in the camp not Miriam's timbrel but the priest's bells, an harmonious prelude to—1. Priestly benedictions; 2. Priestly expositions of law; 3. Priestly exhortations to holiness. II. Let us taste the pomegranates. They were emblems of—1. Fruitfulness; 2. Refreshment; 3. Healthfulness; 4. Cheerfulness.

Bells of the ancients.—Bells were known in the earliest ages of wh. we have any certain record. But the bells of the ancients were very small in comparison with those of modern times, since, according to Polydore Virgil, the invention of such as are hung in the towers or steeples of Christian churches did not occur till the latter end of the fourth or beginning of the fifth century; when they were introduced by Paulinus, Bishop of Nola. The Jews certainly employed bells, since they are spoken of in the Scriptures; and the mention of them by Thucydides, Diod. Siculus, Suidas, Aristophanes, and other ancient writers, proves that they were used in Greece; while Plautus, Ovid, Tibullus, Statius, and others, speak of bells as in use among the Romans. But these bells of the ancients were all made for the hand: or were of a size to be affixed to other musical instruments, like those which were occasionally appended to the drum. Whether, when detached from other instruments, they were used on other occasions, or only in particular ceremonies, or as signals, is not known; nor have we any clue by which to guess whether they were turned in concordance with any scale, or whether they were unisons to each other, or not formed to any particular pitch, but merely used as sonorous auxiliaries to other instruments, without any regard to their agreement of tone, either with one another, or with the instruments they accompanied.

they make the linen coats, the mitre, and the girdle

a Re. xix. 8; Is. lxi. 10.

b Is. xi. 5.

c Dr. Kitto.

27—29. (27) **coats,** *etc.,*ª *see* xxviii. 40. (28) **mitre,** *see* xxviii. 4, 39. (29) **girdle,**ᵇ *see* xxviii. 39. **breeches,** *see* xxviii. 42.

Linen breeches.—More properly, "drawers." The ancient Jews, like the modern Arabs, and some other Orientals, did not generally wear drawers or trousers. Maimonides says that the drawers worn by the priests reached from above the navel to the knee, and had no opening before or behind, but were drawn up around the body by strings, like a purse. This resembles the linen drawers worn by the Turks and Persians at the present day, except that they reach rather below the knee. They are very wide altogether, and when drawn on are fastened very tight around the body by means of a string or girdle, which runs through a hem in the upper border.ᶜ

they make the golden plate for the mitre

"A well-cultivated mind is, so to speak, made up of all the

30, 31. *See* xxviii. 36, 37.

Consecrated thought.—The head the chamber of the brain; the brain, the seat of thought. The golden plate, with its inscription, fastened to the head, significant of consecrated intelligence. I. World full of the works of human intelligence. II. That such works may tend to good ends, the mind must be consecrated to God. III. Such consecration of mind will result in conscien-

[Cap. xxxix. 32-43.] EXODUS. 381

B.C. 1491.

tions study, holy labour, a pure literature; and those, in the welfare and progress of peoples, and the honour and glory of the all-wise God.

The noble employment of art.—Never were the arts more nobly employed than by our forefathers, when they raised those beautiful piles, our cathedrals, our churches, our universities, and our abbeys, to the honour of that religion which God had given to man. It is lamentable to think how these majestic edifices fell before the blind zeal, the ill-directed means (however desirable the end) of the Reformation. A second havoc among ecclesiastical edifices, and scarcely less destructive than the first, arose from the fury of the fanatic and the miserable sectaries of the time of Charles the First.*a*

"minds of preceding ages; it is only one single mind which has been educated during all this time."—*Fontenelle.*

"The very might of the human intellect reveals its limits."—*Mde. Swetchine.*

a Mrs. Bray.

32—37. (32) **thus**, *etc.*, acc. to the plan and in the manner prescribed. (33—37) *See* xxxv. 11—14.

Completed labour (v. 32).—I. The work was completed acc. to plan. II. It was completed in a short time. III. It was completed with great joy. The joy of—1. Knowing that each had done something, and that something his best; 2. Anticipation. IV. The completed work may remind us of the words of Him who said, "I have finished the work Thou gavest Me to do." V. As the house in the wilderness was finished down to the last pin: so the Church in the world, of which it was a type, shall be perfected down to the last and meanest member.

The Jewish tabernacle.—1. It was a school of object-lessons, designed to teach the ignorant and sensual Israelites the truths of the invisible and eternal kingdom of God. It was a small model of heavenly realities—a pattern of sight in the heavens (Heb. ix. 23). It was, in the realm of religious truth, something like the planetarium used in a recitation room in teaching astronomy. 2. The principal lessons it taught were—(1) The holiness of God; (2) the sinfulness of man; (3) The distance between God and man; (4) The fact that God will abide with man; (5) The Divine plan for bringing God and man into union.

the work is finished as commanded

"Venerable to me is the hard hand,—crooked, coarse,—wherein, notwithstanding, lies a cunning virtue indefeasibly royal, as of the sceptre of this planet. Venerable, too is the rugged face, all weather-tanned, besoiled with its rude intelligence; for it is the face of a man living manlike."—*Carlyle.*

38—43. (38—40) *See* xxxv. 15—18. (41) **cloths**, *etc., see* xxxix. 1, 2. (42) **Lord** .. **Moses** .. **work**, hence Moses faithfully repeated the command. (43) **Moses** .. **work**, careful inspection of plan, size, material. **and** .. **them**,*a* invoked the Divine blessing.

The inspection of the work.—I. The examination. 1. By whom conducted: Moses; 2. How pursued,—nothing omitted, all that they had done, pins, and cords, and all. II. The verdict. It was acc. to plan, the Divine plan. III. The blessing. 1. God afterwards blessed the work; 2. Moses now blessed the workers. IV. So, at last, will *all* our work be inspected. If we are blessed it will be through Him who has done all things well.

Christian work.—The builder builds for a century: we for eternity. The painter paints for a generation: we for ever. The statuary cuts out the marble that soon perishes; let us try to cut out the likeness of Christ to endure for ever and ever. A hundred thousand men were employed in Egypt to construct a pyramidal tomb for a dead king; let us feel that we are engaged in a far nobler work in constructing temples for the living God. In my humble judgment, the poorest parish-school in our land,

Moses inspects the work

a Nu. vi. 22—26.

"Thou wilt never be better pleased than when thou hast much to do of such things as thou knowest thyself able to go through with; for business by its motion addeth heat, and a delightful vigour to the spirits; while the unemployed, like standing waters, corrupt with their own idleness."—*Fuller.*

"Observe, without labour no-

B.C. 1491.

thing prospers."
—Sophocles.
b Dr. Cumming.

with no other ornament than the dewdrops of the morning to gild it, and the sunbeams to shine upon it, is a nobler spectacle than the loftiest European cathedral, with its spires glistening in the setting and rising suns of a thousand years.b

CHAPTER THE FORTIETH.

the tabernacle is ordered to be set up

1—8. (1, 2) first .. month, the work had occupied them about six months. thou .. congregation, thus was the first New Year's Day in the wilderness kept. (3) vail, see xxvi. 31. (4) table, see xxv. 23. candlestick, see xxv. 31. (5) altar .. incense, see xxx. 1. hanging, etc., see xxvi. 36. (6) altar .. offering, see xxvii. 1. (7) laver, see xxx. 17. (8) court, etc., see xxvii. 9, ff.

The tabernacle service commenced.—I. The work here assigned to Moses: to set up the tabernacle with everything belonging to it, and to commence the service of it. II. The corresponding work that is now called for at our hands. We are called—1. To realise in our minds the things here shadowed forth; 2. To get them spiritually wrought within our own souls.a

"If we traverse the world, it is possible to find cities without walls, without letters, without kings, without wealth, without coin, without schools and theatres; but a city without a temple, or that practiseth not worship, prayer, and the like, no one ever saw."—Plutarch.

a C. Simeon, M.A.

The tabernacle.—The fact that the sanctuary was originally portable—a tent-temple—is an actual testimony to the truth of the Pentateuch narrative, that the original institution of the religion of Israel took place during the time of their wandering life. The Hebrew literally is the "tent of assembling;" that is, as we may interpret it, the place where God and His people come together, and also the symbol of the kingdom of God under the old covenant. The relation was essentially a spiritual one. The holy of holies was God's special dwelling-place. There were sub-divisions in the part of the building accessible to the Israelites, owing to the circumstance that the nation required a mediation of priests as their representatives. The "holy place" was therefore only the ideal dwelling-place of the people, entered by them through their mediators; the fore-court, their actual dwelling-place. But it is evident that God receives His people as guests in the tabernacle; the two parties to the covenant do not abide there with equal rights.

the tabernacle is ordered to be anointed

9—11. See xxx. 26—28.

The solemn consecration.—I. Before the anointing. The altar, etc., mere human productions; evidences of human taste, and skill, and enterprise. II. After the anointing. The tabernacle, and contents, pass out of the hands of men into the exclusive service of God. It is now not only the tent of the congregation, but the House of the Lord.

"See, then, how powerful religion is; it commands the heart, it commands the vitals. Morality, — that comes with a pruning-knife, and cuts off all sproutings, all wild luxuriances; but religion lays the axe to the root of the tree. Morality looks that the skin of the apple

The anointing oil.—The use of oil in daily life may be described as threefold. In the first place, it was used for the anointing of the body, by which the skin was rendered soft and smooth; refreshed and invigorated. Orientals ascribed a virtue to it which penetrated even to the bones. Coincident with this was the use of oil in sickness, as a means of lulling pain and restoring health. The second use of oil in the preparation of food is to be looked at from the same point of view. Here also the object was, so to speak, to anoint the food, so as to make it soft and palatable. And thirdly, not less frequent and important was the use of oil for burning and giving light, surely also an anointing for the purpose of enlivening and invigorating. The thing to be anointed was the wick of the lamp. The wick would burn without oil, but only with a weak and miserable light, and very speedily it would become extinguished. All these modes of using oil are transferred to the symbolism of worship. The first we see at once is the anointing of the tabernacle, its vessels, and the priests themselves. The second is seen in the *minchah*, or meat-offering, not *meat* at all in our modern acceptation, but composed of wheat, commingled with oil (Lev. ii. 1—8). The third in correspondence is obviously the ever-burning sacred lamp of the Holy Place.[a]

12—16. (12) **bring,** *etc., see* xxix. 4. (13, 14) *See* xxviii. 41. (15) **their .. priesthood,**[a] *i.e.*, the common priests were anointed now once for all; but each successive high priest had his individual anointing. (16) **according .. he,** not subtracting from the Lord's commands, nor adding his own inventions.

The priestly office.—I. The priests of old were of Divine selection and appointment. II. They and the offerings they made are typical of the Great High Priest, and the sacrifice He made for sin. III. Only *one* High Priest then, only *One* now, He. vii. IV. All true believers are now a holy priesthood. 1 Peter ii. 5.

17—21. (17) **first .. month,** *i.e.* month Nisan: a year save 14 days after the Exodus. (18—21) *See* above.

New Year's Day in the wilderness.—I. It was inaugurated by solemn religious services. II. It marked a new epoch in the natural life. III. It influenced all their future. IV. It may supply us with an example of the thoughts, feelings, purposes, and services with which we should enter on each new year.

Beginning the new year.—Mr. Hardcastle, when dying, said, "My last act of faith I wish to be to take the blood of Jesus, as the high priest did when he entered behind the veil; and, when I have passed the veil, I would appear with it before the throne." So, in making the transit from one year to another, this is our most appropriate exercise. We see much sin in the retrospect; we see many a broken purpose, many a misspent hour, many a rash and unadvised word; we see much pride, and anger, and worldliness, and unbelief: we see a long track of inconsistency. There is nothing for us but the great Atonement. With that Atonement, let us, like believing Israel, end, and begin anew. Bearing its precious blood, let us pass within the veil of a solemn and eventful future. Let a visit to the Fountain be the last act of the closing year, and let a new year still find us there.[a]

22—33. (22, 23) **table,**[a] *see* xxv. 30. (24, 25) **candlestick,**[b] *see* xxv. 31. (26, 27) **golden altar,** *see* xxx. 1. (28) **hanging,** *see* xxvii. 16. (29) **altar,** *see* xxvii. 1. (30) **laver,** *see* xxx. 18. (31, 32) *see* xxx. 19, 20. (33) **so .. work,**[c] acc. to the pattern shown him in the Holy Mount.

So Moses finished the work (v. 33).—Better is the end of a thing than the beginning. The beginning six months before amid storm, tempest, etc.; the finishing on a bright New Year's Day. I. Explain the force of the words. Moses is said to have finished the work, because—1. He was the instrument in giving the plan: 2. He authorised the workmen and collected the material; 3. He inspected the work; 4. He blessed the people. II. Enforce the lessons—1. He who begins a great work should persevere to the end; 2. In the finishing of a great work there is reward for all toil and anxiety; 3. Happy is he who, at the finish, can feel he

---

B.C. 1491.

be fair; but religion searcheth to the very core."
—*N. Culverwell.*

a Kurtz.

the priests are ordered to be purified
a Nu. xxv. 13; Ps. cx. 4.
"Religion finds the love of happiness and the principles of duty separated in us; and its mission is to reunite them."—*Vinet.*

the tabernacle is set up as commanded
"Time is like a ship which never anchors; while I am on board, I had better do those things that may profit me at my landing, than practise such as shall cause my commitment when I come ashore."—*Feltham.*

a Dr. J. Hamilton.

so Moses finished the work
a Jo. vi. 56.
b Jo. i. 9; Ps. cxix. 105.
c Jo. xvii. 4; He. iii. 1—6; Jo. iv. 34.

"God is a worker. He has thickly strewn infinity with grandeur. God is love; He yet shall wipe away

Marginal notes (left column)

B.C. 1491.

Creation's tears, and all the world shall summer in His smile. Why work I not? The veriest mote that sports its one-day life within the sunny beam has its stern duties." — *A. Smith.*
d Dr. A.C. Thompson.

the Divine acceptance of the work
a Le. xvi. 2; Nu. ix. 15; 1 Ki. viii. 10, 11; Hag. ii. 7—9; Zech. ii. 5; Ro. xv. 8.

b 2 Ch. v. 13; Is. li. 10; He. ix. 24; Jo. 1 14; Col. ii. 9; Eph. ii. 21, 22.
c Nu. x. 11, 12.

d Nu. ix. 17, 22; Ps. xxxi. 15; Pr. iii. 5, 6.

e Ex. xiii. 21; Ne. ix. 19; Ps. lxxviii. 14; 1 Jo. i. 5; He. xii. 29.

"Be not sudden; take God's work together, and do not judge of it by parcels. It is, indeed, all wisdom and righteousness; but we shall best discern the beauty of it when we look on it in the frame when it shall be fully finished, and our eyes enlightened to take a clearer view of it than we can have here. What endless wondering will it then command!"— *Leighton.*

"God is goodness itself, and whatsoever is good is of Him."
— *Sir P. Sidney.*

f Dr. Fowler.
g Heber.

Main text

has done as God commanded, and not simply as his own heart has impelled.

The work done.—" I have finished the work which Thou gavest Me to do." Vinet repeated this, without being aware that his course was run, when he gave his last theological lecture upon these same words of our Lord. Anticipation overleaps Kedron, passes through Gethsemane, and, looking down upon Calvary, cries, " It is finished ! " So collected is our Lord in His own purpose, so at home amidst the certainties of the future, that without the slightest assumption he affirms, " I have finished the work which Thou gavest Me to do." Only eighteen hours more, and in literal act and moment is it to become true."*d*

34—38. (34) **cloud . . tent,** a sign to the people that their labour was accepted. **glory . . tabernacle,**a the consecration of the sanctuary. (35) **because . . thereon,**b the glory of the Lord more brightly revealed than even on the mount. (36) **when . . up,**c its movement indicated the Divine will. **children . . journeys,** following the cloud. (37) **they . . up,**d however short or long the time it rested, so long did they rest. (38) **cloud . . fire . . night,** the same cloud became luminous by night : manifestations of God adapted to circumstances and seasons. **sight . . Israel,** it was visible to all the camp. **throughout . . journeys,**e through the wilderness to the promised land, Israel was under the protection and guidance of God : then as now every true Israelite could say, " Nevertheless, I am continually with Thee : Thou hast holden me by my right hand. Thou shalt guide me with Thy counsel, and afterward receive me to glory."

The cloud of glory.—God enters every open door : the tabernacle was finished, then the cloud descended upon it. The Temple (1 Ki. viii. 10); Elijah and Baal (1 Ki. xviii. 38). When our hearts are opened, He comes in. The cloud of glory was a token of— I. Divine presence: God spake out of it. We have Christ, God manifest in the flesh. II. Divine protection.—1. Against enemies, at the passage of the sea ; 2. Against the sun in the wilderness (Ps. cv. 39; lxxxiv. 11). We have Christ as a shield. III. Divine guidance : it led them. We have Christ ; and the Bible. IV. Divine glory. Consider—1. His brightness in the tabernacle ; 2. His glory in the Temple ; 3. John's visions ; 4. Paul's vision of heaven (2 Cor. xii. 1—4). V. Christ's future dwelling among men. Conclusion—" Eye hath not seen, nor ear heard, neither have entered into the heart of man, the things which God hath prepared for them that love Him."*f*

The unsleeping eye.—

There is an Eye that never sleeps
    Beneath the wing of night ;
There is an Ear that never shuts
    When sink the beams of light.
There is an Arm that never tires
    When human strength gives way ;
There is a Love that never fails
    When earthly loves decay.
That Eye is fix'd on seraph throngs ;
That Ear is fill'd with angels' songs ;
That Arm upholds the worlds on high ;
That Love is throned beyond the sky.*g*

www.ingramcontent.com/pod-product-compliance
Lightning Source LLC
Chambersburg PA
CBHW030358230426
43664CB00007BB/643